Property of
Wayne Public Library
WAYNE, N.J. 07470

REFERENCE COLLECTION
Does Not Circulate

THE

SAGES AND HEROES

OF THE

AMERICAN REVOLUTION.

KENNIKAT AMERICAN BICENTENNIAL SERIES
Under the General Editorial Supervision of
Dr. Ralph Adams Brown
Professor of History, State University of New York

ENGRAVED BY T.B.WELCH FROM A PORTRAIT BY G.STUART.

G Washington

THE
SAGES AND HEROES

OF THE

AMERICAN REVOLUTION.

IN TWO PARTS

INCLUDING THE SIGNERS OF THE DECLARATION OF INDEPENDENCE.

TWO HUNDRED AND FORTY THREE OF THE SAGES AND HEROES ARE PRESENTED IN DUE FORM

AND MANY OTHERS ARE NAMED INCIDENTALLY.

BY L. CARROLL JUDSON

KENNIKAT PRESS
Port Washington, N. Y./London

THE SAGES AND HEROES OF THE AMERICAN REVOLUTION

First published in 1851
Reissued in 1970 by Kennikat Press
Library of Congress Catalog Card No: 74-120881
ISBN 0-8046-1274-9

Manufactured by Taylor Publishing Company   Dallas, Texas

KENNIKAT AMERICAN BICENTENNIAL SERIES

PREFACE.

This volume contains the condensed substance of more expensive works that have been published relative to the men and times of the American Revolution. The character and acts of the most prominent Sages and Heroes of that eventful era are delineated. A sufficient amount of documentary matter is inserted to enable the reader to fully understand the causes, progress and triumphant termination of that sanguinary struggle that resulted in FREEDOM to the new world and prepared an asylum for the oppressed. The French and Indian wars are prominently noticed. More Revolutionary names are rescued from oblivion in this book than in any other extant. I have introduced many practical remarks intended to rouse the reflective powers of the immortal mind and increase a patriotic love for our expanding Republic and glorious institutions. These remarks are designed to be living epistles animated with "thoughts that breathe and words that burn." There are many festering wounds on our body politic that need probing to the bottom—cancers that require the best treatment of the boldest operators in moral, religious and political surgery. The text is concise and not dressed in the dogmatical garb of *arbitrary* punctuation. In preparing the historical part I have consulted numerous documents and the most approved works in our libraries. Once for all I award a general credit. The relation of events is usually in my own plain laconic language. I believe this volume as free from errors as any of its illustrious predecessors. It has long been a cherished *desideratum* in my mind to place this *multum in parvo* within the reach of every working man in our land. I have exerted my best efforts to make it interesting and instructive by blending a perspective chart of human nature with the thrilling history of the times that tried the souls of the patriots of '76. It is my ardent desire that it may prove beneficial to readers and publisher.

L. CARROLL JUDSON,
of the Philadelphia Bar.

PHILADELPHIA, MARCH 4, 1851.

CONTENTS.

PART I.

Adams John	7	Heyward Thomas	168	Quincy Josiah	294
Adams Samuel	24	Hopkins Stephen	172	Read George	296
Arnold Benedict	32	Hopkinson Francis	179	Rodney Cæsar	300
Barney Joshua	39	Hooper William	182	Ross George	306
Bartlett Josiah	49	Huntington Samuel	186	Rush Benjamin	311
Braxton Carter	54	Irvine William	189	Rutledge Edward	316
Butler Zebulon	58	Jefferson Thomas	191	Sherman Roger	321
Carroll Charles	63	Kalb Baron de	205	Smith James	329
Chase Samuel	68	La Fayette G. M. de	208	Stark John	336
Clark Abraham	77	Lee Francis Lightfoot	219	Stockton Richard	343
Clymer George	80	Lee Richard Henry	223	Stone Thomas	348
Dickinson John	87	Lewis Francis	230	Taylor George	352
Ellery William	90	Livingston Philip	233	Thornton Matthew	355
Floyd William	96	Lynch Thomas Jr.	237	Varnum Joseph B.	359
Franklin Benjamin	101	McKean Thomas	240	Walton George	361
Gates Horatio	110	Marion Francis	246	Warren Joseph	366
Gerry Elbridge	114	Middleton Arthur	251	Washington George	368
Greene Nathaniel	121	Morris Lewis	255	Wayne Anthony	379
Gwinnett Button	129	Morris Robert	261	Whipple William Jr.	387
Hall Lyman	132	Morton John	267	Williams William	391
Hancock John	135	Nelson Thomas	270	Wilson James	394
Harrison Benjamin	141	Otis James	278	Witherspoon John	399
Hart John	148	Paca William	280	Wolcott Oliver	404
Henry Patrick	151	Paine Robert Treat	284	Wythe George	406
Hewes Joseph	161	Penn John	288	Yates Robert	410

PART II.

Allen Ethan	415	Blount Thomas	418	Brown Moses	420
Allen Ebenezer	416	Boudinot Elias	419	Brown Robert	420
Allen Moses	416	Bowdoin James	419	Bryan George	421
Alexander William	416	Bradford William	419	Burd Benjamin	421
Armstrong John	416	Broad Hezekiah	419	Burr Aaron	421
Barry John	416	Brooks Eleazer	419	Butler Richard	422
Beatty William	417	Brooks John	420	Butler Thomas	422
Biddle Nicholas	417	Brown Andrew	420	Cadwalader Thomas	423
Bland Theodoric	418	Brown John	420	Caswell Richard	423

CONTENTS.

Champe John	. . 423	Jasper William . . 442	Paine Thomas	. . 461
Chrystie James .	. 424	Jay John 443	Parsons Samuel H.	. 462
Clark George Rogers	424	Johnson Francis . . 443	Paulding John	. . 462
Clinton Charles .	. 424	Johnson Samuel . . 443	Peters Nathan	. . 462
Clinton George	. . 425	Johnson William . 443	Peters Richard	. . 463
Clinton James	. . 425	Jones John Paul . 444	Pettit Charles	. . 463
Comstock Adam .	. 425	Kennard Nathaniel . 445	Pickering Timothy	. 463
Coward Joseph .	. 426	King Rufus . . . 445	Pickens Andrew .	. 464
Croghan William	. 426	Kirkwood Robert . 445	Porter Andrew .	. 464
Cropper John	. . 426	Knowlton Thomas . 446	Preble Edward .	. 465
Cushing Thomas .	. 427	Knox Henry . . . 446	Prescott William .	. 466
Dale Richard . .	. 427	Kosciuszco Thaddeus 446	Prioleau Samuel .	. 466
Darke William .	. 427	Lacy John . . . 447	Pulaski Count .	. 466
Davie Richardson W.	427	Laurens Henry . . 448	Putnam Israel .	. 466
Davidson William	. 428	Laurens John . . 449	Putnam Rufus .	. 467
Dickinson Philemon.	428	Ledyard William . 449	Ramsay David .	. 468
Drayton Wm. Henry	429	Lee Arthur . . . 449	Randolph Edmund	. 468
Dyer Eliphalet .	. 429	Lee Charles . . . 450	Randolph Peyton	. 468
Elsworth Oliver .	. 430	Lee Henry . . . 450	Reed Joseph . .	. 468
Forrest Uriah .	. 430	Lee Ezra 451	Revere Paul . .	. 469
Gadsden Christopher	430	Lee Thomas Sim. . 451	Sargent Winthrop	. 469
Gansevoort Peter	. 431	Lincoln Benjamin . 451	Scammel Alexander	. 469
Gibson John . .	. 432	Lippitt Christopher . 452	St. Clair Arthur .	. 470
Gibson George	. . 432	Livingston Robert R. 452	Schaick Gosen Van	. 470
Greene Christopher .	433	Livingston William 453	Schuyler Philip .	. 470
Graeff George	. . 433	McClintock Nathaniel 453	Sedgewick Theodore	471
Griffin Cyrus . .	. 433	McKinstry John . . 453	Sergeant Jonathan D.	471
Gurney Francis .	. 434	McPherson William . 454	Smallwood William	472
Gwinn William .	. 434	Madison James . . 454	Steuben Francis Wm.	
Hale Nathan . .	. 434	Manly John . . . 454	Augustus Baron de	472
Hamilton Alexander	435	Marshall John . . 455	Strong Caleb . .	. 472
Hamilton Paul .	. 436	Mathews Thomas . 455	Sullivan John .	. 472
Hathaway Benoni	. 436	Mercer Hugh . . . 455	Sullivan James .	. 473
Hawkins Nathan	. 437	Meigs Return Jona'n	456	Stevens Edward .	. 473
Hawley Joseph .	. 437	Mifflin Thomas . . 457	Thomas John . .	. 473
Hayne Isaac . .	. 437	Miller Henry . . . 457	Thomas Thomas .	. 474
Heath William .	. 437	Monroe James . . 457	Truxton Thomas .	. 474
Heston Edward .	. 438	Montgomery Richard 458	Wadsworth Jeremiah	474
Holden Levi . .	. 438	Morgan Daniel . . 458	Ward Artemus .	. 475
Houston John .	. 438	Morgan John . . . 459	Ward Henry . .	. 475
Howard John Eager,	439	Morris Governeur . 459	Washington William	475
Humphrey David	. 439	Moultrie William . 459	Wheelock John .	. 476
Huntington Jedediah	439	Muhlenberg Peter . 460	Williams Otho H.	. 476
Irvine Andrew .	. 440	Nicholson James . . 460	Winder Levin .	. 476
Irwin Jared . .	. 440	Ogden Matthias . . 461	Wolcott Erastus .	. 476
Jackson Andrew .	. 440	Olney Jeremiah . 461	Wooster David .	. 476
Jackson James .	. 441	Orr John 461	Wyllis Samuel .	. 477
James John . .	. 441			

THE SAGES AND HEROES

OF THE

AMERICAN REVOLUTION.

PART I.

JOHN ADAMS.

The history of men should interest every reader. It is the mirror of mind—imparting lessons of thrilling interest, essential improvement, exquisite pleasure—substantial advantage. It is a matter of deep concern to the investigating student. Remoteness increases veneration. Human foibles are buried in the tomb. Faults are often eclipsed by towering virtues—find no place on the historic page and after generations gaze upon a picture of rare perfection, which, as time advances, assumes shades—richer and holier—until it commands the reverence of every beholder. The names of many of the ancients, whose crowning glory was virtue, over whose ashes centuries have rolled, are often referred to with as profound respect as if angel purity had given the impress of Divinity to their every action. A country—a nation may be lost in the whirlpool of revolution—the fame of good and great men is enduring as time. In the persons of the Sages and Heroes of the American Revolution, ancient and modern wisdom, patriotism and courage were combined. Let us join the admiring millions who are gazing on their bright picture and impartially trace the character of those who pledged their LIVES, FORTUNES AND SACRED HONORS in behalf of FREEDOM.

Among them, John Adams was conspicuous. He was a native of Quincy, Mass. born on the 19th of Oct. (O. S.) 1735. He was the fourth in descent from Henry Adams, who removed from Devonshire, Eng. with eight sons and located near Mount Wollaston.

During his childhood he was under the instruction of Mr. Marsh of Braintree and made rapid progress in his education. At the age of sixteen he entered Harvard college at Cambridge and graduated at the age of twenty-one with high honors.

At Worcester he commenced the study of law under Mr. Putnam, finished with Mr. Gridley, supporting himself by teaching a grammar class. Wisdom to discern the path of rigid virtue and uncompromising justice, with moral courage to *act*, marked his career from the dawn of manhood. He boldly grasped the past–present and future and made deductions truly prophetic. On the 12th of Oct. 1755, he wrote the following paragraph in a letter.

"Soon after the reformation, a few people came over into this new world for conscience sake. Perhaps this apparently trivial incident may transfer the great seat of empire into America. It looks likely to me, if we can remove the turbulent Gallics, our people, according to the exactest computation, will, in another century, become more numerous than England herself. Should this be the case, since we have, I may say, all the naval stores of the nation in our hands, it will be easy to obtain the mastery of the seas and then the united force of all Europe will not be able to subdue us. The only way to keep us from setting up for ourselves, is–*to disunite us*. Keep us in distinct colonies and then some men in each colony, desiring the monarchy of the whole, will destroy each other's influence and keep the country in equilibrio."

Mark two things referred to in this letter. He plainly saw that the navy is our right arm of defence and yet treated, by our government, with a parsimony that has long astonished the old world. "To DIS-UNITE US"–the only thing that can *ruin us* now that we *have* set up for ourselves. Lay this to heart ye demagogues who are sowing broadcast the seeds of disunion and no longer court a monarchy.

At the end of three years study Mr. Adams was admitted to the practice of law and commenced a successful professional career at Braintree. Constitutional law had become a subject of investigation. Disputes had commenced between the people and the officers of the crown who were employed in the custom-house and claimed the right to search *private* dwellings for the pretended purpose of discovering dutiable goods. This preliminary act of usurpation was frequently prompted by personal animosity without a shadow of evidence to raise even suspicion. The right of search was vigorously resisted. Writs of assistance were issued—the seeds of the revolution were sown. Mr. Gridley, the friend and admirer of Mr. Adams, defended the officers—not on constitutional ground but from the necessity of the case to protect the revenue, from which Mr. Adams strongly dissented. The question was argued before the Superior Court at Boston—Mr. Gridley for and Mr. Otis against the crown. Mr. Adams listened to both gentlemen with intense interest and has often been heard to say—" The oration of Mr. Otis against writs of assistance breathed into this nation the breath of life. American independence was then and there born."

The court *publicly* decided against the writs but *secretly* issued them. No richer fuel could have been used to increase the volume and force of the revolutionary fires already kindled. Mr. Adams was roused by the hypocrisy of the court and the audacity of the crown officers and at once took a bold stand in favor of justice. The Assembly interfered in behalf of the people and in 1762, prepared a bill to prevent the issue of these volcanic writs only upon specific information on oath—which was vetoed by the governor. The Assembly retaliated by reducing the salary of the judges.

In 1761 Mr. Adams rose to the rank of Barrister—in 1764 married the accomplished Abigail Smith, daughter of Rev. William Smith, who nobly participated with her husband in the thrilling scenes of their lives for fifty-four years. Judge of her patriotism from the following extract from one of her numerous and able letters.

" Heaven is our witness that we do not rejoice in the effusion of blood or the carnage of the human species—but, having been forced to draw the sword, we are determined never to sheathe it—*slaves to Britain*. Our cause, Sir, I trust, is the cause of truth and justice and will finally prevail, though the combined force of earth and hell should rise against it."

The Stamp Act kindled an enduring flame of indignation in the patriotic bosom of Mr. Adams. He at once became a champion for chartered rights and rational freedom. He published an essay on Canon and Feudal Law which proved him a fearless, able and vigorous writer. It penetrated the joints and marrow of royal power as *practised* and parliamentary legislation as *assumed*. He traced the Canon law to the Roman clergy—shrewdly planned, acutely managed and rigorously enforced to advance their own aggrandizement. He delineated the servile dogmas of the Feudal code, each manor being the miniature kingdom of a petty tyrant. He exposed the unholy and powerful confederacy of the two, aiming to spread the mantle of ignorance over mankind, drive virtue from the earth, producing the memorable era of the dark ages, shrouded in mental obscurity. He then ushered in the dawn of returning light, exhibited the gigantic struggles of the reformers–the bloody scenes of persecution and finally placed his readers upon the granite shores of New England, where, for a century, LIBERTY had shed its happy influence upon the sons and daughters of freemen, undisturbed by canons or feuds. " Tyranny has again commenced its desolating course–it *must be* arrested or we are *slaves.*" This is a mere syllabus of a pamphlet of over forty pages, strong in language, bold in sentiment and nervous in style.

Mr. Adams became associated with other prominent whigs, Samuel Adams, Quincy, Otis and many kindred spirits, whose influence produced the repeal of the Stamp Act and the removal of Mr. Grenville from the ministry. An apparent but delusive calm ensued on the part of the crown officers. At intervals, a cloven foot would be seen, festering wounds would be irritated and no balm was found to restore them to perfect soundness.

In 1766 Mr. Adams removed to Boston where his talents became so strongly developed that the king's governor thought him worth purchasing. He was offered the most lucrative office in the colony– Advocate General in the court of Admiralty. He spurned the bribe with the disdain that none but freemen can exhibit.

In 1769 he was on the committee that prepared instructions for the legislature, which were very obnoxious to the royal governor. He had outraged the people by quartering a mercenary army in the town– was unyielding in his purposes and hastened a tragedy that gave a fresh impetus to the embryo revolution.

On the 5th of March 1770, an affray occurred between the military and citizens, in which five of the latter were killed and others wounded. Mr. Adams thus describes the result.

" The people assembled, first at Faneuil Hall and adjourned to the old South Church, to the number, as was conjectured, of ten or twelve hundred men, among whom were the most virtuous, substantial, independent, disinterested and intelligent citizens. They formed themselves into a regular deliberative body–chose their moderator and secretary–entered into discussions, deliberations and debates–adopted resolutions and appointed committees. These public resolutions were conformable to the views of the great majority of the people–'*that the soldiers should be banished at all hazards.*' Jonathan Williams, a very pious, inoffensive and conscientious gentleman, was their moderator. A remonstrance to the governor, or governor and council, was ordained and a demand that the regular troops should be removed from the town. A committee was appointed to present this remonstrance, of which Samuel Adams was chairman. The soldiers were removed and transient peace restored."

Captain Preston was brought before the court charged with giving the order to fire upon the citizens. The regulars who committed the fatal act were also arraigned and tried. Each party charged the other with commencing the affray. Some inconsiderate citizens had thrown snow-balls at the King's troops who returned lead in payment. Mr. Adams was employed to defend the accused. A delicate task he performed, but so ingeniously did he manage the case that Captain Preston and all the soldiers but two were acquitted and the two were only convicted of manslaughter. When the trial closed Mr. Adams stood approved by the citizens, having performed his professional duty to his clients and at the same time vindicated the rights of the people.

The same year he was elected to the legislative body and boldly opposed the arbitrary measures of the British cabinet. He was one of the committee that prepared an address to the governor, the style of which induces me to think that it was penned by him. After clearly pointing out the violation of chartered rights the address concludes, "These and other grievances and cruelties, too many to be here enumerated and too melancholy to be *much longer borne* by this injured people, we have seen brought upon us by the devices of ministers of state. And we have, of late, seen and heard of *instructions* to governors which threaten to destroy all the remaining privileges of our charter. Should these struggles of the house prove unfortunate and ineffectual this Province will submit with pious resignation to the will of *Providence*–but it would be a kind of suicide, of which we have the utmost abhorrence, to be instrumental in our own servitude."

A blind obstinacy on the part of the ministers increased the opposition of the people, inducing a rapid accumulation of combustible materials, increasing the volcanic fires by their own strong exertions. Being alarmed at the boldness of the citizens, the governor ordered the legislature to convene at Cambridge contrary to the law which fixed the place of meeting–consequently, the members refused to do anything more than to adjourn to the proper place. A war of words and paper ensued, in which the patriots were victorious. Mr. Adams was one of the sharp-shooters and made great havoc among the officers of the crown. Mr. Brattle, the senior member of the council entered the field in defence of the ministry but was put *hors de combat* by our champion. The governor was compelled to direct the legislature to convene again at Boston. New causes of complaint were constantly accruing. The governor, judges and troops were paid by England instead of the colony–thus aiming to render the executive, judiciary and military, independent of the people, destroying all confidence in the servants of the crown. The tax on tea was another source of aggravation, striking more tender chords. Wo to the ruler who rouses the fair sex. He may more safely defy the fury of Mars and challenge the speed of Atalanta.

Tea became forbidden fruit–several vessel loads were sacrificed to Neptune–an oblation for the sins of the British cabinet–a jollification for the fish of Boston harbour. Royal authority increased in cruelty–patriots increased in boldness. The message of the governor to the legislature of 1773, maintained the supremacy of parliament. This was denied by the members and a reply written by Mr. Adams in answer to a second message from the governor, more strongly in favor of the crown. The pen of this functionary was paralyzed–his arguments proved fallacious–his mouth sealed upon this exciting subject. The reply of Mr. Adams was an exposition of British wrongs and American rights, so clearly presented that no sophistry could impugn–no logic confront. So highly was it appreciated by Dr. Franklin, that he had it republished in England–a luminary to patriots–confusion to tyrants.

On taking his seat in the legislature Mr. Adams was placed on the list of committees. So vindictive was governor Hutchinson that he erased his name–an act that recoiled with such force as to rapidly close his public career in the colony. He was succeeded by Governor Gage, who was more fully charged with ministerial fire–more successful in accelerating the millennium of Liberty. He placed his cross upon the name of John Adams–removed the legislature to Salem–enforced the Boston Port Bill and seemed to tax his ingenuity to enrage the people. On convening, the members of the legislature requested the governor to fix a day for a general fast which he peremptorily refused. As well might he have undertaken to extinguish a flaming fire with pitch, as to refuse this boon to the descendants of the Puritans. The people *en masse* venerated religion and would not yield to the violation of ancient custom.

The legislature then proceeded to project a general congress. Governor Gage sent his secretary with an order to *prorogue*–the door was locked against him–patriotic resolutions were passed and five delegates appointed to meet a national convention, one of whom was John Adams.

At the appointed time he repaired to Philadelphia–took his seat in that assemblage of sages, whose wisdom has been sung by the most brilliant poets, applauded by the most eloquent orators–admired by the most sagacious statesmen of the civilized world. On reading the proceedings of the first congress in 1774, Chatham remarked, " I have studied and admired the free states of antiquity, the master spirits of the world–but, for solidity of reasoning, force of sagacity and wisdom of conclusion, no body of men can stand above this congress."

Some supposed the ardent zeal of Mr. Adams might induce rashness. Not so–he was calm as a summer morning but firm as the granite shores of his birth-place. He was discreet, prudent–the last man to violate or submit to the violation of constitutional law. He kept his helm hard-up–knew when to luff–when to take the larboard tack–when to spread and when to take in sail. He was one of the few who believed the mother country would remain incorrigible–that petitions would be vain–addresses futile–remonstrances unavailing.

At the close of that congress Mr. Adams had a close conversation with Patrick Henry in which he expressed a full conviction, that resolves, declarations of rights, enumeration of wrongs, petitions, remonstrances, addresses, associations and non-importation agreements–however they might be accepted in America and however necessary to cement the union of the colonies, would be waste water in England. Mr. Henry believed they might make an impression among the *people* of England, but that they would be lost upon the government. Mr. Adams had just received a hasty letter from Major Hawley of Northampton, which concluded with these prophetic words, " *after all we must fight.*" Mr. Henry raised his hands and vehemently exclaimed, " I am of that man's mind." Richard Henry Lee held a contrary opinion–Washington was in doubt. The two former based their conclusions on the past and present from which they drew deductions for the future. They penetrated the arcanum of human nature, passed in review the multiform circumstances that were impelling the two nations to action–understood well that inflated power–backed by superior physical force–deluded by obstinacy and avarice, is callous to the refined feelings of humanity–deaf to wisdom–blind to justice. Lee, equally determined to vindicate *right* and oppose *wrong*, could not believe the ministry would dethrone reason and court ruin.

Washington, deep in reflection, an impartial and strong investigator-his soul overflowing with the milk of human kindness, did not arrive rapidly at conclusions on so momentous a subject. In weighing the causes of difference between the two countries—reason, justice and hope, on the one side—power, corruption and avarice on the other—at that time held his mind in equilibrio. He clearly perceived the right and fondly but faintly hoped England would see it too and govern herself accordingly. He was as prompt to act as the others when action became necessary.

Mr. Adams returned among his friends and stood approved by his constituents and his country. His pen was again brought into service, in answering a series of ingenious essays written by Mr. Sewell in favor of the supremacy of Parliament. Over the name of "Nonvanglus," Mr. Adams stripped the gay ornaments and gaudy apparel from the brazen image Mr. Sewell had presented to the public gaze. A meagre skeleton of visible deformity was all that remained. Attorney General Sewell trembled as he received the deep cuts from the falchion quill of this devoted patriot. So profound was his reasoning—so learned were his expositions—so clear and conclusive were his demonstrations—that his antagonist exclaimed, as he retired in a rage from the conflict, " He strives to hide his inconsistencies under a huge pile of learning."

The pile proved too "huge" for royal power and supplied the people with an abundance of light.

The supremacy of parliament was an unfortunate issue for ministers. It placed the patriots in a position to hurl their darts at *them* without refusing allegiance to the *king*. The British cabinet worked out its own destruction with regard to the American colonies—if not with fear and trembling it was with blindness and disgrace—impolicy and injustice—obstinacy and infatuation.

In May, 1775, Mr. Adams again took his seat in Congress with renewed responsibilities resting upon him. Revolution was rolling fearfully upon his bleeding country—hope of redress was expiring like the last flickerings of a taper—dark and portentous clouds were concentrating—the ministerial ermine was steeped in blood—the dying groans of his fellow-citizens and the lamentations of widows and orphans had fallen upon his ears and the prophetic conclusion arrived at by him and Henry but a few months previous, was forced upon the mind of every patriot, " *after all we must fight.*"

As a preliminary measure it was necessary to appoint a leader of the military forces to be raised. To fix upon the *best* man was of vital importance. Some thought the measure premature. Not so with the sons of New England. When the blood of their friends was wantonly shed upon the heights of Lexington they hung their siren harps upon the weeping willows that stood mournfully over the graves of their murdered brethren. In their view, war was inevitable. A commander-in-chief must be appointed. Several prominent persons were named in private conversations. John Adams, alone, had fixed his mind upon George Washington, in whom he saw the commingled qualities of philanthropist, philosopher, statesman, hero and Christian. All opposed his appointment at first but gradually yielded to the reasons urged by John Adams. Satisfied that the measure would be approved by a majority, he rose in Congress, and proposed that a commander of the American armies should be appointed. When his resolution passed, he described the requisite qualities of the man to fill this important station and remarked with great emphasis—*" such a man is within these walls."* But few knew to whom he referred, no one believing himself duly and truly prepared or properly vouched for as a military man. A pause—a painful suspense—then the name of Col. GEORGE WASHINGTON of Virginia was announced by Mr. Adams. No one could be more surprised than the nominee. No intimation of the intended honor had been made to him. The vote was taken the day following and was unanimous in his favor. So judicious was this selection that La Fayette remarked—" It was the consequence of Providential inspiration." Be it so—John Adams was the patriot who nominated him—thus placing at the head of the American armies just such a man as the crisis required—prudent, dignified, bold, sagacious, patient, persevering—universally esteemed by the friends of FREEDOM—admired by the most fervent friends of the crown.

In 1776, Mr. Adams again took his seat in the National Assembly. The period had arrived for decisive measures. Massachusetts had been disfranchised by Parliament. England had hired legions of soldiers from German princes to subdue rebels in America. The last note of peace had been sung by echo—every patriot became convinced that *resistance or slavery* were the two horns of the dilemma presented. INDEPENDENCE had been conceived but by a few. It was a startling proposition. At this juncture Mr. Adams marked out a bold course and had the moral courage to pursue it. On the 6th of May he offered a resolution, proposing that the colonies should organize a government independent of England. On the 10th of the same month it was modified and adopted, recommending such government by the colonies " as might be conducive to the happiness and safety of their constituents in particular and America in general." All admitted the justice of this measure but some opposed it on the ground of the physical imbecility of the colonies–already crowded with a hireling army and their shores lined with a powerful navy. Mr. Adams knew no middle course. He had succeeded in obtaining the adoption of the preface to his broad folio of an independent compact–he then proceeded to prepare the text. He had commenced the work of political regeneration. Each day new and genuine converts were made. The legislature of his own state encouraged him to strike for independence. North Carolina had openly started the ball–Virginia gave it a new impetus and on the 7th of June, Richard Henry Lee became the organ to present the proposition to Congress. A most animated discussion ensued. Then the powers of Mr. Adams were more fully developed. Mr. Jefferson said of him, in alluding to his debates on the Declaration of Independence– "John Adams was the pillar of its support on the floor of Congress–its ablest advocate and defender against the multifarious assaults it encountered. He was our Colossus on the floor–not graceful, not elegant, not always fluent in his public addresses–yet he came out with a power, both of thought and expression, that moved us from our seats."

The noblest powers of his soul were raised to the zenith of their strength, determined to accomplish the mighty work he had commenced. Although one of the committee to prepare the instrument of eternal separation, he confided the labor to his colleagues–spending his whole force upon the opponents of the measure. Manfully did he contend–gloriously did he triumph. He bore down upon his adversaries like a mountain torrent–a rushing avalanche–hurling the arrows of conviction with such precision and effect that a majority soon became converted to the measure.

The day for decision arrived. The 4th of July, 1776, dawned auspiciously upon the patriots. At the appointed hour they assembled. The past, the present, the impenetrable future, big with coming events– rushed upon their minds. Moments flew–the pulse quickened–the heart-throb increased–bosoms expanded–eyes brightened–patriotism rose in majesty sublime–the question was put–the Gordian knot was sundered–INDEPENDENCE was declared–the colonies were free–LIBerty was proclaimed—a nation was redeemed—regenerated—disenthralled and born in a day.

Early in the winter of 1776 Mr. Adams wrote a form of government for the colonies which was substantially the same as the present constitutions of the states. It was first submitted to Richard Henry Lee in a letter with these remarks.

"A constitution founded on these principles introduces knowledge among the people and inspires them with a conscious dignity becoming freemen. A general emulation takes place which causes good humor, sociability, good manners and good morals to be general. That elevation of sentiment, inspired by such a government, makes the common people brave and enterprising. That ambition which is inspired by it makes them sober, industrious and frugal. You will find among them some elegance, perhaps, but more solidity—a little pleasure but a great deal of business—some politeness but more civility. If you compare such a country with the regions of domination, whether monarchical or aristocratical, you will fancy yourself in Arcadia or Elysium."

Here is inscribed upon the tablet of truth the blessings derived from a government like our own in its principles—faithfully adhered to by every *true* patriot but trampled under foot by the demagogues of the present day and the aristocracy of all time.

Among all the great men of our country, no one has exhibited a more clear and minute conception of human nature and human government, than John Adams. He traced causes and effects through all their labyrinthian meanderings and deduced conclusions that seemed the result of inspiration. Many of his predictions of the future bear the impress of prophecy and show how deeply he investigated—how clearly he perceived.

On his return from Congress, Mr. Adams was elected to the legislature of Massachusetts under the new constitution. He was also appointed Chief Justice which he declined.

In 1777 he resumed his seat in Congress and performed an amount of labor, which, if imposed upon any ten *demagogue* legislators of the present day might induce suicide. He was an active member of ninety committees—chairman of twenty-five—chairman of the board of war and appeals, discharged all his duties promptly and was uniformly in his seat when any important measure was under discussion.

In December, 1777, he was appointed a commissioner to France. In February following he embarked on board the frigate Boston. During the voyage a British armed ship hove in sight—an action commenced—Mr. Adams seized a musket, gave the enemy a well-directed shot but was immediately deprived of this recreation by Capt. Tucker, who led him out of danger, pleasantly remarking—" I am commanded by the Continental Congress to carry you in safety to Europe and I will do it."

Before his arrival, Dr. Franklin and his colleague had succeeded in concluding a treaty of alliance with the French nation. After an absence of a little more than a year he returned and was elected to a convention of his native state, convened for the purpose of perfecting a constitution and the full organization of government. The original draft of the constitution of Massachusetts is from his pen. Before his term closed in this convention he was appointed by Congress—" A minister plenipotentiary for negotiating a treaty of peace and a treaty of commerce with Great Britain." In Oct. 1779, he embarked from Boston. The passage was boisterous, it being February before he arrived at Paris. Chagrin and pride prevented the British ministry from at once placing themselves on an equality with our own. The negotiation, on their part, commenced with equivocations. Mr. Adams could not be ensnared and was determined to submit to nothing wrong and left them to farther reflection.

On learning that Mr. Laurens, American commissioner to Holland, had been captured, Mr. Adams repaired to that kingdom. In August he received a commission from Congress to negotiate a loan—to conclude a treaty of amity and commerce and to accede to any treaty of neutral rights that might arise from regulations to be made by a congress of the European states then in contemplation. In a few months he was overwhelmed with important duties. Minister to Great Britain—to the States General of Holland—to all the European states for pledging the United States to the armed neutrality—with letters of credit to the Russian, Swedish and Danish envoys in Holland and a commissioner to negotiate a loan of ten millions of dollars for the support of the Home department and foreign embassies. All these duties he discharged with skill and approbation, a lasting monument of the gigantic powers of his mind. At every point he encountered intrigue which he uniformly discovered and crushed in embryo.

In July, 1781, he was directed to repair to Versailles to make a further attempt at negotiation with England. The terms offered did not fully recognize the rights of the United States as an independent nation. Peace was desirable and ardently urged by the Duke de Vergennes, who was the head and front of the French cabinet. Mr. Adams was anxious for peace—but only on just, dignified and honorable terms. The Duke, who had uniformly manifested a disposition to make the United States *feel* a dependence on France, dictated to Mr. Adams, placing him in the position of a subordinate agent. This was a *French* bull. Mr. Adams recognized no dictator but the Continental Congress and his own keen perception and penetrating judgment. This independence of the American minister enraged the Duke. He wrote to the minister of France in the United States to lay a formal complaint before Congress against the recusant for insubordination. This the minister did ingeniously but not successfully. As a matter of respect for their new and important ally, Congress partially modified the instructions of Mr. Adams but did not place him under the dictation of the Duke as requested. They knew the granite man too well to suppose he would ever compromise the dignity of his country. They had full confidence in his capacity to perceive right—in his moral courage to enforce it.

From all the evidence in the premises I am fully convinced that the motives of the French *Court* in aiding our country during the revolutionary struggle, were not based on patriotism but had ulterior objects in view. Not so with the noble La Fayette and others who came to the rescue.

Again Mr. Adams left ministers to arrive at a second sober thought and learn their true position. He then returned to Amsterdam.

Owing to sad reverses in the cause of freedom the French minister made such an impression in favour of the position of the French cabinet as an umpire between England and the United States, that congress added to the commission of Mr. Adams—Dr. Franklin, Jefferson, Jay, and Laurens—with the humiliating directions, " That they should govern themselves by the advice and opinion of the ministers of the King of France." The Duke de Vergennes was elated with triumph. He was virtually made sovereign minister of the United States. This act is the darkest spot upon the proud escutcheon of the Continental Congress—an act that I would gladly " expunge from the record." No full apology can be found. The tremendous revolutionary tornado that was then sweeping over our country, charged with the dismaying materials of terror, is a *partial* one and the true cause of this quailing error.

The exultation of the Duke was transient. Adams and Franklin were there, masters of ceremony. They dared to disobey instructions believing they had been improperly extorted by an intriguing and designing court. They at once took a bold stand and were promptly sustained by their colleagues and ultimately by congress, to which

Adams communicated the chicanery of the Duke and the duplicity, or rather the *toolicity* of the French minister in the United States. The result was glorious. An honourable peace was obtained–the dignity of our nation preserved. A provincial treaty was signed at Paris on the 30th of November, 1782 and a definitive treaty on the 3d day of September, 1783 and all without the advice or consent of the Duke de Vergennes, whose golden schemes of finesse proved abortive. He addressed a bitter letter of reproach to the American commissioners, expressing great astonishment at their presumption in daring to act independent of him, which was not answered.

Among the golden schemes of the court of France, two are worthy of particular note. 1. To secure to France and Spain the fisheries of the United States. 2. To secure the perpetual and uninterrupted navigation of the Mississippi. Very modest. Other propositions were made, equally absurd, all of which form an unanswerable excuse for our commissioners in disobeying instructions.

After the important commission of concluding peace with England was completed, Mr. Adams returned to Holland where he had negotiated a loan of eight millions of guilders in September, 1782, which was one of the means of terminating the war by enabling the United States to prosecute it with more vigor. It had a direct influence on England, inducing Lord Shelburne to make proposals of peace soon after this was known.

During the same year he was placed at the head of a commission empowered to negotiate commercial treaties with all foreign nations. He returned to Paris where he met Franklin and Jefferson who were associated with him–forming a trio of combined, versatile and exalted talent–never surpassed if ever equalled.

In 1785 Mr. Adams was appointed the first minister to Great Britain after the acknowledgment of the Independence of the United States. He was received with marked attention and courtesy so far as courtly etiquette was concerned but found the ministry morose and bitter towards the new Republic. They seemed disposed to treat the peace as a mere truce between the two nations. Mr. Adams performed the delicate duties of his station with great sagacity and wisdom–patiently removing subsisting difficulties. Nor did he forget the internal interests of his country at home. To win independence was *one* thing–to preserve it *another* and more important matter. The theories of a Republican form of government by Thurgot and others, had been freely circulated in the United States. These he deemed wild and visionary. This was proved by the transient existence of the first French Republic and has been more fully demonstrated recently in Europe and South America. More success might attend these experiments, even with imperfect skeletons of a free government were the people as well prepared to receive it as were the colonists at the time of the American Revolution. *Intelligence and primitive Christianity must pervade the mass.* The European pioneers came to this country with the bible in their hands and based our government upon its eternal principles, where it will securely rest until ignorance darkens intellect and the bible is banished. Let *all* read its plain truths, teaching, as they do, freedom in religion, freedom of conscience—pointing us to our high origin and final destiny—then our Republic cannot be destroyed by kingly influence, aristocratic corruption, ultra fanaticism, reckless demagogues, or heartless politicians. Troubles have arisen, now exist, may continue to occasionally break out—but they ever have been and I trust ever will be confined to a small portion of the great and accumulating mass—*the bone and sinew of our beloved country.*

To strip from these delusive theories of a free government their sophistry, Mr. Adams published a learned and able disquisition on Republican constitutions which became a polar star to his own country and operated powerfully in correcting error and allaying prejudices in England adverse to the United States. His "DEFENCE OF THE CONSTITUTION" placed him on a lofty literary eminence in view of the *literati* of Europe.

In 1788 he obtained permission to return home and in the autumn of that year was elected the first Vice President of the United States. He became the confidential counsellor of Washington on all important questions. He was re-elected in 1792 and in 1796 was elected President of that Republic for which he had freely periled life, fortune and honor.

At that time party spirit had commenced its reckless career which afforded an example set by Adams and Jefferson worthy of all praise and imitation. No bitterness of party spirit, no abuses from their partisans and party press, could sever the patriotic and moral ties of friendship that bound them together up to the time death removed them from the theatre of life. So high did party spirit rage that Mr. Jefferson thus rebuked a clique of politicians who were hurling slanders against Mr. Adams.

" Gentlemen, you do not know that man. There is not upon earth a more perfectly honest man than John Adams. Concealment is no part of his character. Of that he is utterly incapable. It is not in his nature to meditate anything he would not publish to the world. The measures of the general government are a fair subject for difference of opinion–but do not found your opinions on the notion that there is the smallest spice of dishonesty, moral or political, in the character of John Adams for I know him well and I repeat–that a man more perfectly honest never issued from the hands of the Creator." Demagogues–read the above just encomium upon his opponent by a candidate for an office–then search for a parallel case of magnanimity among modern politicians–if you find one, proclaim it to the people of our vast country that they may be convinced a true patriot is in our midst–a lump of genuine salt in the body politic.

Mr. Adams proceeded to the conscientious and independent discharge of his presidential duties, prompted by the best motives for the good and glory of the infant Republic. He was an open, frank old-school federalist. During his administration the ranks of the democratic party increased rapidly, which defeated his re-election. Much has been written and more said relative to the causes that produced his political overthrow. To my mind the solution is plain and brief. His cabinet was not of his own choice–he was too independent to bend to party intrigue–he opposed the humiliating demands of the then self-styled democratic France–he advocated the augmentation of the navy of the United States and recommended the law for the suppression of the venality of the press. In the two first points he was impolitic as the head of a party–in the two next he did what all now acknowledge to be right in principle. On the last, he took the wrong method to correct an evil that has caused unceasing trouble from that time to the present–an evil that will ever exist in a government like ours, because, in annihilating this, we should destroy an essential part of our political machinery–A FREE PRESS. The three last were the strong points seized upon by his opponents, which enabled them to achieve an easy victory. He retired with a good grace on the best of terms with his successful opponent and his own conscience. He supported the policy of Mr. Jefferson towards England and approved of the declaration of war in June 1812. He attributed the opposition of the eastern states to the impolicy of our government in neglecting the navy. He compared them to Achilles, who, in consequence of his being deprived of Briseis, withdrew from the Grecian confederacy. The increase of the navy was a long-nursed theory of his national policy. Had his views been carried out by our country, our nation would now have been mistress of the seas. As it is, we have scarcely armed vessels enough to protect the expanding commerce of our enterprising merchants–a fact that is often tauntingly referred to by Englishmen and has often crimsoned the cheeks of liberal-minded Americans. If all the money that has been expended within the last twenty years in worse than useless legislation and speech-making throughout these United States had been appropriated in building ships of war, our navy would now be larger than that of Great Britain. Add what has gone into the hands of peculators since the formation of our Republic–it would sustain that navy for thirty years. Some of our people have been occasionally a little *too* free.

Soon after his retirement from the presidential chair, Mr. Adams was solicited to become the governor of his native state, which he declined on account of his advanced age. In 1817 he was placed at the head of the list of presidential electors. In 1820 he was elected president of the convention that revised the constitution that he had written forty years previous. The compliment was duly appreciated by him but his infirmities did not permit him to preside. He imparted much counsel and rendered special aid in the revision. This was the last public act of this great man. Two years before this, the partner of his bosom had gone to her final rest–an affliction most keenly felt by him. She was a Christian–to know was to love her.

Surrounded by friends who delighted to honor him–his country prosperous and happy–enjoying the full fruition of divine grace which had produced the green foliage of piety through a long life–political animosities buried in oblivion–his now frail bark glided smoothly down the stream of time until the fiftieth anniversary of Independence dawned upon our beloved country. On the morning of the 4th of July 1826, an unexpected debility seized him but no one supposed he was standing on the last inch of his time. He was asked for a sentiment to be given for him at the celebration on that day. "INDEPENDENCE FOREVER," burst from his dying lips, which were the last words he ever uttered with a loud and animated voice. He expired about four in the afternoon without a groan, sigh, murmur or apparent pain, with a full assurance of a happy reception in that brighter world where sin and sorrow never interrupt the peaceful joys of the angelic throng.

On the same day and but a few hours previous, the immortal spirit of the illustrious Jefferson had left its tenement of clay, thrown off its mortal coil and returned to Him who gave it. Perhaps these kindred spirits met in mid air and ascended together to an ecstatic meeting with the friends they had loved and lost and whom they should gain, love and never lose.

This unparalleled coincidence in death produced a deep sensation in the United States and in Europe. The simultaneous departure of two of the noblest spirits that ever graced the theatre of human life—illuminating the world with freedom—whose acts had elicited the admiration of all civilized nations—whose mighty deeds will be a theme of praise through all time—was an incident that seemed designed by the great Jehovah to impress their precepts—their examples and their names upon the minds of the human family with all the force of Divinity.

Mr. Adams was a plain man, low in stature, not graceful in his movements—at times rather repulsive. In public he was austere but in the social circle, familiar, pleasing and instructive. He disliked formal ceremony and abhorred pedantry. He admired and exemplified strong common sense. He spoke his sentiments freely and could not have been transformed into a modern *technical* politician. His open frankness was proverbial. He called it one of his failings. When looking at Stuart's fine paintings, he fixed his eyes upon the portrait of Washington with compressed mouth—then upon his own, with open lips, and facetiously remarked—"Ah! that fellow never could keep his mouth shut." Such a man never can be a *popular* politician as the writer knows from experience.

The highest eulogy that can be pronounced upon John Adams is the history of his bright and useful career. For more than half a century he served our country ably and faithfully. He continued to impart salutary counsel until the curtain of death closed the scene.

In all the relations of private life he was too pure for the palsying touch of slander. The foulest of all pestiferous atmospheres—party spirit—could not, *dare* not approach his private character with its damning miasma or impute to his public action an iota of political dishonesty or impurity of motive. If any demagogue dares to contradict this position, let him hear the voice of Jefferson from the tomb—"AN HONESTER MAN THAN JOHN ADAMS NEVER ISSUED FROM THE HANDS OF THE CREATOR."

SAMUEL ADAMS.

MANY of the sages and heroes of the American Revolution were consistent and devoted Christians—some of them eminent ministers of the gospel of Christ. They all were evidently actuated by motives of purity, prompted by the demands of imperious duty based upon the inalienable rights of man. They had no innate love of military glory aiming only at conquest. Their pilgrim fathers fled from servile oppression—planted the standard of FREEDOM in the new world—spread civilization over our happy land and transmitted the rich behest to their children. With the principles of rational liberty each succeeding generation was made familiar. When tyranny reared its hydra head, the monster was readily recognized. The people were prepared to drive the invading foe from their shores.

Samuel Adams was one of the revolutionary sages who boldly espoused the cause of equal rights. He was born in Boston, Mass. on the 22d of Sept. 1722. His parents were highly respectable. His father was long a member of the Assembly of Massachusetts, from whom this son imbibed those liberal principles which he so fearlessly and successfully vindicated during his subsequent life. In childhood he exhibited a strong inquiring mind—talents of a high order. He was prepared for college by Mr. Lovell. His application to study was close—his progress rapid. His highest pleasure was found in his books. Being naturally sedate, his father placed him in Harvard College, believing him destined for the gospel ministry. In that institution he advanced rapidly in science and in favor. During his whole course he was reproved but once and that for sleeping too late. In conjunction with other studies he had thoroughly investigated theology. The affairs of state had also occupied his mind. When he graduated, he chose for his subject of discussion the following question. *"Is it lawful to resist the supreme magistrate if the commonwealth cannot otherwise be preserved?"*

His hearers were astonished at the masterly manner he advocated the affirmative of this bold proposition. With enrapturing eloquence and convincing logic, he painted in vivid colors the beauties of that liberty for which he so nobly contended during the Revolution. From that time he became a prominent politician—an advocate of equal rights—a stern opposer of British wrongs.

By rigid economy during his time in college he had saved a sum of money from that allowed him by his father to defray expenses. This first fruit of his pecuniary prudence he sacrificed upon the altar of Liberty. With it he published a pamphlet from his own pen entitled—"The Englishman's Rights." This was one of the entering wedges of the Revolution. It awakened a spirit of inquiry—kindled a flame of opposition to the increasing oppression of the crown. It did great credit to the head and heart of this devoted patriot then dawning into manhood.

Anxious that his son should embark in some business his father placed him in the counting-house of Thomas Cushing, an eminent merchant, that he might be prepared for commercial business. For this sphere nature had not designed him. Political knowledge, international law and the rights of man engrossed his mind. To this end he formed a club of kindred spirits for the purpose of political inquiry and discussion. They furnished political essays for the Independent Advertiser which were so severe in their strictures upon the conduct of the creatures of the crown, that the association obtained the name of "Whipping Post Club." The hirelings of the King treated these essays with derision—upon the people they exerted an influence that prepared them for the approaching crisis. Stamped with plain truth, sound reasoning, uncontroverted facts—they operated upon British power like the sea-worm upon a vessel—silently and slowly but with sure destruction. They contributed largely in perforating each plank of the proud ship of monarchy, then riding over the American colonies, until she sank to rise no more.

After remaining a suitable time with Mr. Cushing, his father furnished him with a liberal capital with which he commenced business. Owing to the pernicious credit system he lost all his stock in trade. By the death of his father he was left, at the age of twenty-five, to take charge of the paternal estate and family. In the discharge of that duty he proved himself competent to manage pecuniary matters. The estate was involved and under attachment—he relieved it entirely from debt. This done he again spent the most of his time in disseminating liberal principles. He was a keen sarcastic writer—analyzed every point at issue between our own and the mother country—exposed the British ministry in their corrupt and corrupting policy and roused the indignation of the populace against their oppressive measures. He was hailed as one of the boldest leaders of the whig party.

No man had examined more closely or understood better the relative situation of Great Britain and her American Colonies. He weighed every circumstance in the scale of reason—based his every action upon the sure foundation of immutable justice. He was not impetuous—appealed to the judgment of his hearers and readers—sought to allay—not to excite the passions of men. He was a friend of order—opposed to sudden bursts of popular fury—to every thing that could produce riotous and tumultuous proceedings. Religion, in its pristine purity, was ever his polar star.

Organized and systematic opposition against the unwarranted encroachments of the crown, emanating from the great majority of the sovereign people was his plan. Petitions, remonstrances—every thing consistent with the dignity of man to be resorted to before an appeal to arms. If this was rebellion it was in a very modified form.

When the offensive Stamp Act was proclaimed he exposed its odious features with unsurpassed severity and boldness. When the climax of oppression was capped by the imposition of taxes upon articles of daily consumption he believed forbearance no longer a virtue and openly advocated resistance as an imperious duty. He demonstrated fully that Great Britain had violated the constitution. Americans had vainly claimed protection under its banner–its sacred covering was rudely snatched from over them–they were left exposed to foreign officers who were drawing them closer and more effectually within the coils of tyranny. To be *slaves* or *freemen* was the question.

Being a member of the assembly and clerk of the house, Mr. Adams exercised an extensive and salutary influence. With great zeal he united prudence and discretion. From 1765, to the time he took his seat in congress he was a member of the state assembly. He had exerted the noblest powers of his mind to prepare the people for the approaching storm and had kindled a flame of patriotic fire that increased in volume as time rolled on. He was the first man who proposed the non-importation act–the committees of correspondence and the congress that assembled at Philadelphia in 1774. He corresponded with the eminent patriots of the middle and southern states and contributed largely in producing unity of sentiment and concert of action in the glorious cause of liberty throughout the colonies. Over his own constituents his influence was complete. At the sound of his voice the fury of a Boston mob would cease. He could lead it at pleasure with a single hair. The people knew well he would maintain what was clearly right and willingly submit to nothing clearly wrong.

When the affray occurred on the 5th of March, 1770, between the British soldiers and citizens, the influence of Samuel Adams prevented the further effusion of blood *after* the populace had become roused and were on the point of avenging the death of their friends who had just fallen. He obtained the immediate attention of the assembled enraged multitude–proposed the appointment of a committee to wait on the governor and request the immediate removal of the troops. His plan was approved–a committee appointed of which he was chairman. The governor at first refused to grant the request. The chairman met all his objections fearlessly–confuted them triumphantly and told him plainly that an immediate compliance with the wishes of the people would alone prevent disastrous consequences and that he would be held responsible for the further waste of human life. The governor finally yielded.

Mr. Adams was one day surprised by a message from Gov. Gage communicated through Col. Fenton, offering him what modern truckling politicians would call a great inducement to *change* and in case he refused, to inform him he would be arrested and sent beyond the seas there to be tried for high treason. To the last part of the message he listened with most attention and asked Col. Fenton if he would truly deliver his answer. Receiving an affirmative assurance Mr. Adams rose from his chair, assumed an air of withering contempt and said– " I trust I have long since made my peace with the KING OF KINGS. No personal consideration shall induce me to abandon the righteous cause of my country. Tell Gov. Gage it is the advice of Samuel Adams to him–*no longer to exasperate the feelings of an insulted people.*" This reply roused the ire of the royal governor and when he subsequently issued a proclamation offering a free pardon to those rebels who would return to what *he* termed their duty he excepted Samuel Adams and John Hancock–the highest compliment within his power to bestow on the two patriots. They received this mark of distinction as a special commission from the throne directing their future course– a royal diploma of liberty that left them as free as mountain air in their future action.

No bribe could seduce–no threat divert Mr. Adams from the path of duty. He placed his trust in the Rock of Ages–enjoyed the rich consolations of an approving conscience–the unlimited confidence of his friends, the approbation of every patriot. These were more dearly prized by him than all the dazzling honors of kings and potentates. He became an object of vengeance and was the immediate cause of the memorable battle at Lexington on the 19th of April 1775–the troops sent being in pursuit of him and John Hancock. Apprised of their mission Gen. Joseph Warren sent an express late in the evening to the two patriots warning them of approaching danger. In a few minutes after they had left, the British troops entered the house which they had just emerged from. In a few ominous hours the crimson curtain rose–the revolutionary tragedy commenced. The last maternal cord was severed–the great seal of the original compact was broken–the covenants of the two parties were cancelled in blood.

Mr. Adams remained in the neighborhood during the night. The next morning, as the sun rose without an intervening cloud, he remarked to a friend, " This is a glorious day for America." He viewed the sacrifice as an earnest of ultimate success and future blessings.

To rouse the people to action now became the sole business of this devoted friend of his bleeding country. The grand signal for action had been given—the tocsin of war had been sounded—the requiem of battle had been sung—its soul-stirring notes had been wafted far and wide on the wings of wind and were responded to by millions of patriotic hearts.

Mr. Adams mourned deeply the death of his friends, the martyrs of that tragical but auspicious day. He knew well that martyrs must be sacrificed and that the funeral knell of those who had just fallen would shake British colonial power to its very centre. He believed their blood would cry to Heaven for vengeance and incite the hardy sons of Columbia's soil to vigorous and triumphant action. The event added new strength to his propulsive powers and doubly nerved him to meet the fiery trials in reserve for him. As dangers increased he became more urgent for the people to maintain their rights. As the wrath of his enemies waxed hotter he was more highly appreciated by the people and was uniformly styled—*Samuel Adams the Patriot.* His fame and influence strengthened under persecution, his friends were animated by his counsels, his foes were astounded and chagrined at the boldness of his onward career. In the Assembly he effected the passage of a series of resolutions deemed treasonable by the royal governor.

In the Congress of 1776 he was among the first to advocate the Declaration of Independence—contending that it should have followed immediately after the battle of Lexington. In all his debates he was earnest and zealous but not rash—ardent and decisive but wise and judicious. When the Declaration of Rights was adopted he affixed his name to that important instrument without the least hesitation although he stood proscribed by the royal power.

During the darkest periods of the Revolution he was calm and cheerful and did much to reanimate the desponding. In 1777 when Congress was obliged to fly to Lancaster and a dismal gloom hung over the cause of the patriots like a mantle of darkness several of the members were in company with Mr. Adams lamenting the disasters of the American arms, concluding that the chances for success were desperate. Mr. Adams promptly replied—"If this be *our* language, they are so indeed. If *we* wear long faces they will become fashionable. Let us banish such feelings and show a spirit that will keep alive the confidence of the people. Better tidings will soon arrive.

Our cause is just and righteous. We shall never be abandoned by Heaven while we show ourselves worthy of its aid and protection." At that time there were but twenty-eight members in Congress. Mr. Adams said—" It was the *smallest* but *truest* Congress they ever had."

Soon after that dark period the surrender of Burgoyne was announced which proved a panacea for long faces and put a new aspect upon the cause of Liberty. Many recovered from a relapsed state—hearts beat more freely, courage revived from a typhoid stupor—the anchor of hope held the ship of state more firmly to her moorings.

The arrival of Lord Howe and Mr. Eden with what *they* termed the olive branch of peace from Lord North, added to the excitement. Mr. Adams was one of the committee to meet these high functionaries. On examining the terms proposed, the committee found that the proposed *olive branch* had been plucked from the Bohun Upas of an overbearing and corrupt ministry and promptly replied through Mr. Adams— " Congress will attend to no terms of peace that are inconsistent with the honor of an independent nation." This reply was as unexpected to the royal messengers as it was laconic and patriotic. The grand Rubicon had been passed—the galling chains had been thrown off—the Sodom of British power was doomed and nothing could induce the sages and heroes of '76 to look back or tarry on the plain of monarchy. Lord Howe and his colleague had permission to return—report progress of locomotion and walk again. Mr. Adams continued one of the strong pillars in the rising temple of liberty until the superstructure was completed—recognized and approved by the mother country and all Europe.

In 1787 he was a member of the convention of Massachusetts convened to act upon the Federal Constitution. He did not fully approve of some of its provisions but avoided opposition believing it to be the best policy to adopt it, subject to future amendments. He was most particularly opposed to the article rendering the states amenable to the national courts. He submitted sundry amendments that were adopted by the convention and submitted with the Constitution for the future consideration of Congress, some of which have since been adopted.

From 1789 to '94, Mr. Adams was lieutenant-governor of his native state and from that time to '97, was governor. He performed the executive duties with great ability and contributed largely in raising the commonwealth to a flourishing and dignified condition. He watched over all her interests with parental care—viewed her rising greatness with an honest pride. He had seen her sons writhing under the lash of oppression and their bones bleaching in the field. He now beheld the people independent, prosperous, virtuous and happy. He could now be gathered peacefully to his fathers when his time should arrive to depart. Age and infirmity compelled him to retire from the great theatre of public life where he had been so long conspicuous. His health continued to fail sensibly with each returning autumn. On the 3d of October 1803, his immortal spirit left its mansion of clay—soared aloft on the wings of faith to mansions of bliss beyond the skies. He died rejoicing in the merits of his immaculate Redeemer who had given him the victory. He had fought the good fight of faith as well as that of LIBERTY and felt a full assurance of receiving a crown of glory at the hands of King Immanuel.

Amidst all the turmoils of political and revolutionary strife Mr. Adams never neglected religious duty. When at home he was faithful to the family altar and uniformly attended public worship when practicable. He was a consistent every day Christian—free from bigotry and fanaticism—not subject to sudden expansions and contractions of mind—rather puritanical in his views yet charitable in his feelings and opposed to censuring any one for the sake of opinion. He adorned his profession by purity of conduct at all times.

Mr. Adams was of middle size, well formed, with a countenance full of intelligence indicating firmness of purpose and energy of action. As a public man and private citizen he was highly esteemed and richly earned a place in the front rank of the American patriots. He placed a low value upon wealth—died poor but not the less esteemed for his poverty which was *then* no crime. He placed a high value upon common school education and *properly* estimated the higher branches of science. General intelligence among the great mass he considered the strongest bulwark to preserve our independence.

As a writer Mr. Adams had few equals. His answer to Thomas Paine's writings against Christianity is probably superior to that of any other author. His few letters on government published in 1800, show a clear head, a good heart and a gigantic mind.

As an orator he was eloquent, chaste, logical—rising with the magnitude of his subject. He always spoke to the point—addressing the understanding—not the passions.

His manners were urbane, unaffected and plain—his mode of living frugal and temperate—his attachments strong—his whole life a golden chain of usefulness. Let his examples be imitated by all—then our UNION will be preserved from the iron grasp of ambitious partisans—the snares of designing demagogues—the whirlpool of blind fanaticism—the tornado of party spirit. Let these examples be discarded—our

Union will prove a mere rope of sand–the temple of our Liberty will crumble and moulder in the dust with Samuel Adams. O! think of this disorganizers and tremble!

BENEDICT ARNOLD.

Cause is treated with cold neglect by a large portion of the human family. All gaze at effect–but few trace it to its producing original. Especially is this true with men in forming opinions of the conduct of their fellow-men. Petty errors are construed into crimes–petty crimes into felonies. Often have I known this to be the case in sectarian churches where charity was loudly professed but sparingly practised. The causes that operated upon the erring brother may have been extenuating but are not examined. *Away* with him is the simultaneous cry. Kindness might have reclaimed and saved him. Too rarely are extenuating causes sought for–too partially are they credited when brought to light. But a limited number stop to analyze human nature–divest themselves of prejudice and become competent to pass an intelligent, impartial judgment upon the conduct of others. They do not inquire how formidable a force of temptation *they* could vanquish if attacked by the arch enemies of ethics and Christianity. They can never fully know their own strength in morals until they measure arms with the foe. In the balmy days of prosperity a man may act justly in all things and be the censor of others. Reverses may drive this same man into great error–perhaps crime. Keen adversity is a crucible from which but few emerge like gold seven times tried. Charity is the specific to ameliorate these evils but too cheap to obtain a wide circulation. Abstruse dogmas cost more labour and by many are more highly prized.

There are crimes so flagrant that no extenuating circumstances can form a legal excuse–crimes that blight like the sirocco–crimes so dark that they hide the noblest deeds–the most brilliant talents–the most towering genius–consigning the perpetrator to lasting disgrace–enduring infamy. Treason stands high on the black catalogue. But one traitor was found among the disciples of Christ–but one was found among the sages and heroes of the American Revolution. That traitor was Benedict Arnold, a Major General in the army of the illustrious Washington.

He was a native of New London, Connecticut. At the commencement of the struggle for liberty he resided at New Haven and was captain of a volunteer company. When the hoarse clarion of war was sounded on the heights of Lexington he was among the first to march his company to the American headquarters at Cambridge where he arrived in ten days after that painful event.

The Massachusetts authorities conferred upon him the commission of Colonel with directions to raise 400 men and make an attempt to capture Ticonderoga. He repaired to Castleton, Vermont, where he met Col. Allen. On the 10th of May, 1775, this fortress surrendered at discretion. On the 6th of September of that year he commenced his march for Canada through the dense forest with 1000 men from New England consisting of infantry, one company of artillery and three companies of riflemen. A portion of his troops were obliged to return for want of provision to sustain them all, through the wilderness. The balance endured the severest hardships on the march and arrived at Point Levi opposite Quebec at the end of six weeks. But from the fact that Arnold had sent a letter forward to a friend by an Indian who betrayed his trust by giving information of the approaching troops it is believed Quebec would have been easily captured. To prevent this all means of crossing the river had been removed and the fortifications put under rapid improvement. It was not until the night of the 14th of October that he led his little band of 700 men up the heights that had been surmounted by Wolfe and formed them near the memorable plains of Abraham. The city had become so well fortified that the summons to surrender was treated with contempt. To attack with so small a force would be a reckless waste of human life. In a few days he marched to Point aux Trembles twenty miles above Quebec to await the coming of Gen. Montgomery who arrived on the first day of December. A siege upon the city was immediately commenced which was successfully resisted. On the morning of the 31st of that month a simultaneous assault was made on two sides of the city in which Montgomery was killed and Arnold severely wounded in the leg. Officers and men behaved with great gallantry. No other assault was attempted–the blockade was continued to May 1776. On the 18th of June Arnold withdrew from Canada. He subsequently commanded the small fleet on Lake Champlain and exhibited great skill and bravery.

In August, 1777, he relieved Fort Schuyler, then besieged by Col. St. Leger with an army of near 1800 men. At the battle near Stillwater on the 19th September he fought like a tiger for four hours. After the British had been driven within their lines in the action of the 8th of October, Arnold pressed forward under a destructive fire and assaulted their works, forced their entrenchments and entered their lines with a handful of desperate followers and only retreated upon his horse being killed and himself severely wounded again in his unfortunate leg. For desperate bravery on the field of battle he had no superior. He seemed enchanted with danger and infatuated with military glory. But this was not his ruling passion. He was licentious, voluptuous, amorous and epicurean. The want of means to fully pamper these ruinous propensities, which had destroyed all sense of moral rectitude–solves the problem of his treason.

Being disqualified by his wounds for field service he was put in command of the garrison at Philadelphia. He made the house of Gov. Penn his headquarters which he furnished in princely style and commenced a course of extravagant living and equipage far beyond his salary. To raise funds he laid violent hands upon all property belonging to those who did not enter fully into the cause of the patriots. He oppressed, extorted, used public money and property for private purposes and made his public accounts more than duplicate. He rushed into unsuccessful trading speculations and made himself amenable to a series of grave charges and was summoned to appear before the commissioners of accounts who rejected more than half the amount of his charges against government. He appealed to Congress whose committee confirmed the report of the commissioners with the remark that Arnold had been allowed too much. So violent was his language and conduct towards his superiors that he was arraigned before a court-martial and sentenced to be reprimanded by Washington. This sentence was sanctioned by Congress and promptly executed. His mortification had now reached its zenith. He was bankrupt in means–his reputation wounded–his pride lacerated. He became surcharged with fell revenge–treason was the best panacea for that dark passion. He was quick to see that West Point would command the most money and inflict the deepest wound upon the cause of liberty. He suddenly professed deep repentance and applied to the New York delegation in Congress to obtain for him the command of that important post. Through Gen. Schuyler the same application was made to Washington who was anxious to have his services in the field but willing to comply with his wishes. Early in August, 1779, Arnold repaired to the camp of Washington and made the application in person without apparent anxiety, stating that his wounds disqualified him for field service. With full confidence in his fidelity he received the desired command.

It has been intimated by some writers that the plan of treason was suggested to Arnold by an English courtesan with whom he was intimate. It is true that he wrote to Col. Robinson of the British army upon the subject before he applied for the command. That letter opened to him a correspondence with Sir Henry Clinton who sanctioned the project and probably fixed the price of the base deed. On the conclusion of these preliminaries the traitor solicited the appointment he received. He repaired to the garrison at West Point and opened an ostensible mercantile correspondence with Major Andre the British agent to consummate the nefarious plot. The names assumed were Gustavus and Anderson. For convenience of escape the British sloop of war Vulture was moved up the river at a distance not to excite suspicion. An interview was arranged for the night of September 21, 1780. Andre was landed below the garrison under a pass for John Anderson. Arnold received him at the house of a Mr. Smith *within* the American lines in violation of his sacred promise not to do so to avoid the penalty of a spy–showing the reckless daring of the traitor. The sun rose upon them before their plans of operation were completed. Andre remained with Arnold during the day. When ready to leave in the evening it was found the Vulture had been compelled to move too far down the river for him to reach her with a boat. He exchanged his regimentals for a plain suit–received a pass from Arnold and proceeded by land for New York. On the 23d he had proceeded so far that he felt perfectly secure when one of a militia scout suddenly seized the reins of his bridle and brought him to a stand. Instead of producing his pass he asked the man where he belonged. He answered–" below." " So do I" was the response and declared himself an English officer on urgent business and wished not to be detained. At that moment two others of the scout came up when the spy discovered his true position. He offered a purse of gold and his gold watch to let him pass. To those patriot soldiers the offer was an insult. He then offered them any amount they would name in money or dry goods, with himself as a hostage until the amount should be received. Fortunately for the cause of freedom, British gold could not purchase these honest men in humble life. They had met the tempter and had moral courage to repel all his assaults. Their virtue paralyzed the treason of the only traitor in the American army. Let their names be handed down to posterity with profound veneration. John Paulding, David Williams and Isaac Vanwert secured Andre and foiled Arnold. Williams lived respected and died regretted in my native neighborhood. Often have I heard him relate the minute circumstances of that important capture. He claimed to be the one who first arrested the spy. These three men proceeded to examine their prisoner and found concealed in his boots an exact account of the garrison at West Point in detail in the handwriting of Arnold. They took him to Lieut. Col. Jameson who commanded the scouting parties. Anxious to save the traitor, he persisted in the character assumed and shrewdly asked that Arnold should be informed that Anderson was taken, who would explain and make every thing satisfactory. The ruse succeeded—an express was sent to the garrison which enabled Arnold to escape on board the Vulture on the 25th of September, a few hours only before Gen. Washington reached West Point. He proceeded to Sir Henry Clinton at New York where he received $50,000 and the commission of brigadier general in the British army—the price of his base treachery. Although the foul transaction was tolerated by the English government, all honorable men in England detested the traitor and his treason. This was frequently manifested after his location in that country at the close of the Revolution. Lord Lauderdale expressed his disgust on seeing Arnold seated on the right hand of the king and exclaimed—" His majesty is supported by a traitor." Lord Surry rose to speak in the House of Commons and on perceiving the traitor in the gallery sat down and exclaimed—" I will not speak while that man is in the House." In addition to the money paid and the disgrace of associating with this vile man—the British army lost one of its brightest ornaments in the death of Maj. Andre. Contrary to his sacred pledge Arnold made him a spy by taking him within the American lines. He was tried, convicted and hung. Washington would gladly have warded off the dreadful sentence could he have found any excuse for doing so. The law demanded the sacrifice—it was made from the necessity of the case.

The news of Arnold's treason created surprise and indignation among the people of his native country. At Philadelphia his effigy was made large as life and drawn through the streets at night in a cart with a figure of the devil at his side holding a lighted lantern to his face and the inscription in large capitals—TRAITOR ARNOLD. The cart was followed by a dense crowd with martial music playing the rogue's march. The principal being absent the representative was hung and then burnt. Arnold had become so hardened by a long indulgence in improper practices that he was apparently steeled against all reflection upon the past. Soon after he commenced his murderous career in the British service, Washington remarked of him in a private letter—" I am mistaken, if, *at this time* Arnold is undergoing a mental hell. He wants feeling. From some traits of his character which have lately come to my knowledge, he seems to have been so hackneyed in crime—so lost to all sense of honor and shame, that while his faculties still enable him to continue his sordid pursuits there will be no time for remorse." An ingenious, bold but unsuccessful attempt was made to abduct him from New York before the execution of the unfortunate Andre. He made a hair-breadth escape.

The baseness of Arnold's treason was increased in blackness by his subsequent conduct. He had the assurance to write to Washington the day he escaped on board the Vulture, stating that he was acting for the good of his country and requesting the commander-in-chief to protect his wife and pass her and his baggage to him. Mrs. Arnold was immediately forwarded to New York with her effects and those of her husband. Arnold professed to his new companions in arms to be radically changed to a staunch loyalist. The Declaration of Independence he declared a treasonable paper—its authors a company of ambitious rebels seeking power to enslave the people. He wrote a threatening letter to Washington relative to the execution of Andre and assured him of a fearful retaliation unless a reprieve was granted. He published an address to the people of America fully justifying his treasonable conduct. He then issued an artful tirade of insulting sophistry for the purpose of inducing others to plunge into the same quagmire of disgrace with himself—calling it a proclamation with the following caption. " To the officers and soldiers of the Continental army who have the real interests of their country at heart and who are determined no longer to be the tools and dupes of Congress or of France."

All his vile paper demonstrations deepened his infamy, increasing the boiling indignation of the American people without inducing a single one to desert the cause of his country. To do this was a part of the consideration of the Arnold purchase. Sir Henry Clinton was deceived by the traitor and egregiously mistaken in the stern integrity of the patriots. Finding his Proteus brigadier powerless over the minds of his former companions, Sir Henry deducted $100,000 from the $150,000 which was the stipulated price for West Point and the traitor and despatched him to Virginia to act upon the persons and property of the obstinate rebels. In January 1781 Arnold entered Chesapeake Bay with a protecting naval force and landed with about 1700 men. His cruelties, ravages and plunders along the unprotected coast could not be surpassed by a band of practised pirates. Revenge seemed to be the motive power of his action. During one of his predatory excursions he captured an American captain of whom he inquired what the Americans would do with him if he fell into their hands, to which the officer replied—"If my countrymen should catch you I believe they would first cut off that lame leg which was wounded in the cause of FREEDOM and bury it with the honors of war and afterwards hang the remainder of your body in gibbets."

After returning from Virginia he was sent on an expedition against New London where he first breathed the vital air. He landed his troops in two detachments—one on each side of the harbor. He led one against Fort Trumbull which could make but a feeble resistance. Fort Griswold made a spirited defence against the other division commanded by Lieut. Col. Eyre but was compelled to yield to an overwhelming force. When the Americans surrendered but seven men had been killed within the lines—after the surrender a murderous slaughter was commenced by the British and about 100 killed and wounded. On entering the fort an English officer inquired who commanded the garrison. Col. Ledyard presented his sword and answered—"*I* did—but *you* do now." His sword was taken by the officer and immediately plunged through his heart. In the attack the enemy had 48 killed and 145 wounded. Arnold commenced his favorite work of plunder—loaded and sent away 15 vessels mostly freighted with private property—fired the place and reduced 60 dwelling-houses and 84 stores to ashes and in his haste four of his own ships were burned. He completed this work of destruction and was absent from New York only eight days. Such expeditions afforded the richest aliment for the black heart of this traitor. He continued the scavenger of the British army to the close of the war and then removed to London where he died in 1801. To the lasting disgrace of the British government Arnold received a liberal pension to the time of his death which is continued to his descendants and is frequently complained of by the British press.

With the blackness of eternal disgrace resting upon his character this traitor has had apologists among American writers. They attribute his treason to a want of liberality on the part of our government. I have said the want of means to give full scope to his sordid passions was the cause. A want of liberality does not appear upon the record. He was allowed more than justice demanded—more than other officers under like circumstances. He was unsound at the core—void of moral rectitude—was proved dishonest before the commissioners of accounts—the committee of Congress and the court-martial. His name should *then* have been erased from the roll of officers regardless of consequences. That would have saved him from the treason he perpetrated–the accomplished Andre from the scaffold and thousands from the ravages subsequently committed by the reckless traitor. All apologies for Arnold are sophisms. His name is stamped with a lasting infamy that blots out the noble deeds that preceded his Lucifer-fall.

JOSHUA BARNEY.

The navy of a nation is justly termed the right arm of its strength. The life of a mariner is full of romance–often spiced with thrilling events–sometimes fraught with danger. The sons of the main are a hardy, noble, generous, bold class of men. None but those who have rode upon the green mountain waves of old ocean when lashed to a foaming fury by mighty wind, can fully appreciate the perilous service of a seaman.

The importance of increasing our navy is felt but by a few of our legislators and not urged by them. Americans are the favorite sons of Neptune. With shamefully limited means they have fought their way to the temple of fame. With a maritime force far inferior to the resources and magnitude of our prosperous and expansive country–far inferior to that of the enemy whom they met and conquered–they have snatched the laurels of victory from the mistress of the seas and placed them upon their own manly brows. Had our government been as forward in providing ships of war as our naval officers and noble tars have been in courting danger, shedding their blood and sacrificing life in defence of the star spangled banner–the combined forces of the old world would dread our power more than they now respect our flag. By an equal force our seamen cannot be conquered. History points to a long list of heroes–sons of America–who have carved their names as high on the temple of fame as Sidney and Nelson.

Among them is that of Joshua Barney–born in Baltimore, Maryland on the 6th day of July 1759. His father was a respectable farmer cultivating the soil now within the city limits. His son was sent to a common school until he was ten years of age and was then placed in a retail dry goods store at Alexandria. In 1771 he revealed to his parents his long nursed vision of a seaman's life. Reluctantly his father obtained for him a place on board a pilot boat commanded by an intimate friend. After a few months service he was apprenticed to Capt. Drisdall whose brig was bound to Ireland. After a long and rough passage the vessel reached the cove of Cork. From thence the Captain proceeded to Liverpool where he sold his cargo and brig.

Young Barney returned home by the way of Dublin. Soon after his arrival his father was killed by the accidental discharge of a pistol in the hands of a young son but seven years of age. Joshua subsequently made a voyage to Cadiz and Genoa. In 1775 he sailed to Italy. On arriving there the mate was discharged, the captain taken sick which put Barney in command of the ship. He was not then sixteen years of age.

In July of that year he joined an unsuccessful Spanish expedition against Algiers. In October 1776 he arrived in Chesapeake Bay where he was boarded by the officers of the British sloop of war King Fisher and plundered of all his letters and arms. He there first received intelligence of the battle of Bunker Hill. He was at length permitted to proceed to Baltimore where his vessel was laid up. He had been her captain eight months–had passed through many perils with courage and skill that would have done credit to a man ripe in years and experience. He had earned the fame of a skilful navigator and judicious commander. He was not long in choosing whom he should serve for the future. He was born a patriot. The fire of liberty illuminated his soul. Freedom pointed him to the service of his beloved country. He was appointed master's mate on the sloop of war Hornet under Capt. Stone. Com. Hopkins presented him with a flag which he mounted on a staff–obtained martial music–beat up for volunteers and in one day raised a full complement of men for the sloop. He was the first one who unfurled the star spangled banner in Maryland.

In November the Hornet and Wasp sailed for the Delaware to join Com. Hopkins. The British fleet was in Hampton Roads to intercept them but could not bag the game. On their arrival the fleet of the Commodore consisted of two small frigates, two brigs and four sloops. With this infant navy just bursting into life he sailed for the Bahama Island New Providence–took the fort without opposition–secured the military stores–treated the people and private property with due respect and returned safely to the Delaware with his booty. Soon after his return Barney was stationed on board the Wasp under Capt. Alexander who was ordered to conduct the ship beyond the capes that conveyed Benjamin Franklin to France. On its return the Wasp was closely pursued by two British ships carrying 72 guns and escaped by running into Wilmington creek. The next morning Com. Hazelwood went down from Philadelphia with several row gallies and boldly attacked the Englishmen which enabled the Wasp to come out and take part in the action. This little schooner stung the British brig

Tender so severely that she surrendered in a short time and was immediately taken to the Jersey shore. On his return to join the gallies amidst a dense fog, Capt. Alexander came in close contact with the fleet of the enemy. He met with a warm reception and returned the salutation promptly and effectually. After an exchange of the most impressive compliments he returned to the gallies. A brisk fire was kept up during the day which convinced the creatures of the crown that the infant navy was not to be trifled with. During the action young Barney went on board another vessel that was not fully manned. His bold and noble daring on that occasion elevated him in the esteem of his superiors and companions in arms. Robert Morris, then President of the Marine Committee, presented him with a lieutenant's commission and put him in command of the sloop of war Sachem. He was then but seventeen years of age. Shortly after receiving his commission Lieut. Barney participated with Capt. Robinson in a severe action of two hours which resulted in the capture of an English brig. A large sea turtle, designed as a present to Lord North, was one of the delicacies of the prize. It was presented to Robert Morris. In a few days after his return Lieut. Barney spread the canvas of his little craft in company with the Andrew Dorin with fourteen guns and the Lexington–all under the command of Capt. Barry and sailed for the West Indies. On their return they fell in with the British sloop of war Race Horse–tender to Admiral Parker's fleet, which he had sent out from Jamaica on purpose to capture these American "small craft." After a sanguinary action of two hours the English nag was cut in pieces, distanced and surrendered at discretion. Shortly after that brilliant victory the British sloop of war Snow was captured and Lieut. Barney placed on board as prize-master. He was overtaken by a gale that threatened to land all hands in Davy Jones' locker–was badly crippled and captured by the Perseus of twenty guns. During the passage young Barney was insulted by the purser of the Perseus and knocked him down the hatchway for which he was commended by the British captain. On their arrival at Charleston an exchange of prisoners took place which enabled Lieut. Barney to return to Philadelphia with fresh laurels on his youthful brow.

In the spring of 1777 he joined the squadron for the defence of the Delaware composed of the Delaware–32 guns–the Sachem, Andrew Dorin and several smaller vessels–all under the command of Com. Hazlewood. They were stationed near Fort Mifflin and bravely maintained their position until the next autumn when the little fleet and fort were compelled to yield to a superior force. Lieut. Barney was then ordered on board the frigate Virginia at Baltimore commanded by Capt. Nicholson. In an attempt to run her to sea at night the pilot brought up on the opposite shore where she and her crew fell an easy prey to the enemy. In August the ensuing year Lieut. Barney was exchanged–proceeded to Baltimore–took command of a small schooner with two guns and eight men and was again captured in an attempt to run out of Chesapeake Bay. He was soon exchanged and joined his old friend Capt. Robinson at Alexandria on board a vessel with 12 guns, 35 men and but a small supply of ammunition. On the third evening after leaving port they fell in with the British privateer Rosebud–fully manned and eager for action. A running fight was continued during the night. Daylight revealed a rapid opening and expansion of the Rosebud–she hauled off with 47 of her men killed and wounded. Capt. Robinson had none killed and but one man wounded. He then sailed to Bordeaux–mounted eighteen guns– shipped 70 men–took in a cargo of brandy and sailed for home. On his way he captured a valuable prize–placed it in charge of Lieut. Barney who arrived with it at Philadelphia in October 1779. He was received with great enthusiasm and applause. Lavished praises did not inflame his youthful mind. Vanity had no resting-place in his noble soul. Pomp and parade had no charms for him. He bore his prosperity with the calm dignity of a Socrates. He steered clear of the alluring quicksands of vice–the rocks of sinful pleasure on which many young men founder and are lost forever. His manly conduct gained the esteem of the great and good–his fame was based on substantial merit. Familiarity with scenes of blood and carnage– the rage of battle and the clash of arms did not enervate the exalted powers of his refined sympathies and softer passions. These were commingled with those of an accomplished daughter of Alderman Bedford of Philadelphia and were consolidated in one at the hymeneal altar before he left the city of brotherly love. After basking in the rays of the honey-moon for a few days he proceeded to Baltimore. On the way his money was stolen from the box of his carriage where he thought it more safe than in his pocket. He returned to Philadelphia–concealed his loss–went to sea in the Saratoga of 16 guns under Capt. Young.

Their first prize was a vessel carrying 12 guns. In a short time they came in contact with an English ship mounting 32 guns with 90 men accompanied by two brigs. Under the disguise of British colors Capt. Young ran alongside the ship. In a few brief moments the star spangled banner was floating in the breeze upon the three English vessels. Lieutenant Barney was put in charge of one of them. Becoming separated from the others he was captured by the seventy-four Intrepid commanded by Capt. Malloy and treated with great cruelty. On arriving at New York Lieut. Barney and 70 other prisoners were placed on board the ship of war Yarmouth by Admiral Rodney. They were confined under five decks in a dark filthy apartment but three feet between floors—twelve feet by twenty in area and ordered to England. They were 53 days performing the passage. Eleven of the prisoners died on the way—the survivors were scarcely able to walk. They were covered with vermin and when landed could not bear the light for some time. They were sent to Mill prison where they found nearly three hundred of their fellow-countrymen sharing the same tender mercies with themselves. Soon after this new accession of rebels preparations for escape were discovered. Lieut. Barney was suspected—loaded with heavy irons and thrown into a dungeon for thirty days. By the assistance of a soldier he made his escape from prison on the 18th of May 1781—was discovered and remanded. In a second attempt he succeeded—visited Bristol, London, Amsterdam, Rotterdam and the Hague. He reached Philadelphia in March 1782 amidst the heart-felt congratulations of his family and numerous friends. His sufferings had been aggravated and heart-rending. He had almost tasted death. The barbarous treatment of the American prisoners on board the English prison-ships is without a parallel. It has left a stigma on the Christian escutcheon of the British nation that time or angels' tears can never expunge—a foul blot, lasting as the pages of history. My strong language may be excused when I inform the reader that one out of eight of my patriot uncles was literally suffocated and starved to death on one of those ships in the port of New York. Were I to draw a full picture of the demoniac cruelties heaped upon the American prisoners in the loathsome dungeons of these floating Pandemoniums—a horror too painful to be borne would oppress the aching heart of the reader.

As a manifestation of the high value placed upon the services of young Barney, the State of Pensylvania presented him with a captaincy and placed him in command of the Hyder Ally of 16 guns with 110 men. In a few days he proceeded down the Delaware as a convoy. On the 8th of April 1782 he was anchored in Cape May road waiting for a more favorable wind. At 10 A. M. he discovered four vessels making all sail towards him. On nearing they proved to be a British frigate, ship, brig and sloop of war. About noon the frigate made for Cape Henlopen channel—the other vessels steering for Cape May. Capt. Barney weighed anchor and sailed up the bay to elude pursuit. At 1 P. M. the ship and brig came into the bay by Cape May channel—the frigate coming round under Cape Henlopen. The following account of the action is from a gentleman who was a volunteer on board the Hyder Ally.

"At one P. M. prepared for action—all hands to quarters. At three quarters past one the brig passed us after giving us two fires. We reserved our fire for the ship then fast coming up. We received very little damage from the brig which stood after our convoy. She mounted 16 guns and was formerly the Fair American privateer commanded by Capt. Decatur and equal to us in force. At 2 P. M. the ship ranged upon our starboard quarter and fired two guns at us. We were then at good pistol shot. We attempted to run her on board by laying her across the starboard bow—at the same time poured in our broad-side from great guns and small arms. Our fire was briskly kept up for twenty-six minutes when she struck her colors. Immediately sent our first lieutenaut on board and stood up the bay—the frigate being in chase under all sail and the brig ahead in pursuit of our convoy. We again prepared for action and stood for the brig. On perceiving this she tacked for the frigate and got aground. We were obliged to pass her as the frigate was gaining upon us. At 4 P. M. the frigate came to anchor in the bay—as we supposed for want of a pilot. We then spoke the prize for the first time and learned that she was his majesty's ship Gen. Monk—Capt. Rodgers—with 20 *nine*-pounders—136 men of whom 30 were killed and 53 wounded, including 15 out of 16 officers." The Hyder Ally had four killed and eleven wounded—mounted 12 *six* and 4 *nine*-pounders—a little more than half the weight of metal carried by the Gen. Monk—with a crew of 110 men and 5 volunteers who went on board as a matter of recreation. Capt. Barney proceeded to Philadelphia with his prize—treating his conquered foe with great kindness, soaring above retaliation for the recent base treatment he had received when a prisoner.

On his arrival at Philadelphia the welkin rang with plaudits of praise from the multitude who hailed him as one of the deliverers of their oppressed country. For his gallantry the legislature of Pennsylvania voted him a splendid sword which was presented to him by the governor with appropriate ceremonies. The General Monk was purchased by the U. S. government—fitted for a cruise and placed in command of Capt. Barney. He sailed for Paris in November of that year with despatches to Benjamin Franklin. His naval fame had preceded him in France and prepared the way for an enthusiastic reception at her proud metropolis. On his return he brought the loan that had been obtained by Franklin for the United States. That voyage closed his useful, adventurous, brilliant revolutionary career.

Subsequent to the revolution Capt. Barney purchased a tract of land in Kentucky for the purpose of a permanent residence. During 1786-7-8 he travelled through the West, the Carolinas and Georgia. He was a strong advocate of the Federal Constitution and freely expressed his views on all proper occasions. In 1789 he was in poor health and joined with another gentleman in the purchase of a brig. They sailed to Carthagena, South America and returned by the way of Havana. In 1792 he was at Cape Francois when the town was burned. Being on shore he was compelled to fight his way to his ship and brought off with him about sixty distressed women and children. On his return he was captured by an English privateer and all his crew taken from him except his carpenter, boatswain and cook. Three officers and eleven men were put in charge of the prize and ordered to New Providence. Capt. Barney was treated with cruelty because he refused to surrender the keys of his iron chest. Having secreted several loaded guns he and his three men retook the vessel, wounding two of the officers and compelling the Englishmen to work the ship into Baltimore. The little sleep Capt. Barney obtained up to the time his craft was moored at the monumental city was in his arm-chair on the quarter-deck. The next year he repeated his visit to Cape Francois and on his way home was captured by a British privateer—taken to Jamaica—his ship condemned and he confined in prison. It was acts like this that hastened the war of 1812. In 1794 Capt. Barney was again restored to his family. In company with James Monroe he visited the transient Republic of France in 1795 and was the bearer of the star spangled banner to the French convention. So delighted were the members with the veteran captain that they proffered him a command in their navy. The ensuing year he accepted the offer and arrived at Norfolk with two frigates where he was a long time blockaded by a British squadron. He offered to measure skill with an equal force which was prudently refused. In 1800 he surrendered his command without having had an action with the enemy. In 1805 he declined the offered command of the Navy Yard at Washington. In 1806-8 he was an unsuccessful candidate for Congress—the interests of party having become paramount to the substantial merit and righteous claims of a candidate who was not *politically available* although covered with scars and wounds received in the purchase of our liberty—endowed with sterling talents matured by cool reflection and long experience—with a pure and honorable reputation in all respects—deficient in one thing only—*a political gum-elastic conscience.*

In 1812 he removed to Elkridge with his family. On the declaration of war against Great Britain in June of that year he was immediately called into service. He was first commissioned to cruise in a privateer and succeeded in speedily capturing eighteen British vessels—several of a superior force to his. In 1813 he was invited to take command of the armed flotilla in Chesapeake Bay. On his arrival at Washington he was surprised to find a letter to the Secretary of the Navy from a merchant in Baltimore derogatory to his character. He at once called the writer to an account and settled the matter by the inverse rule of *false* honor by probing his breast with a blue pill which did not prove mortal. With the rank of Commodore, Barney took command of the flotilla in the spring of 1814. It consisted of twenty-six barges and nine hundred men. He first intended attacking the enemy at Tangier Island. On his way he met the British squadron off Patuxet and was compelled to run in there. During the summer he annoyed the enemy constantly—captured several of their smaller vessels and several times boldly attacked their frigates—materially injuring them—then retreating quickly into shoal water beyond their reach. On the first of July he was called to Washington to aid in devising the best plan of defence against the contemplated attack by the enemy. On the 3d he returned and moved the flotilla farther up the river. On the 16th of August the British fleet entered the Patuxet in full force. An express was despatched to the Secretary of the Navy apprising him of the movement. On the 21st Com. Barney landed most of his men—marched for Washington and joined Gen. Winder and Capt. Miller with his marines and five pieces of artillery. The marines were put under the command of the Commodore. On the 23d the troops were reviewed by the President and looked fine. On the 24th the enemy halted within three miles of the American camp. Skirmishing occurred between small advance parties. Com. Barney proceeded to the city and took station at the marine barracks determined to defend the bridge to the last extremity. Being advised of this the British changed their route by way of Bladensburg. The main body of the American troops met them there on the 25th about 11 A. M. At a late hour Com. Barney obtained permission from the President to join them. Within a mile of that town he found the Americans formed in irregular detached parties engaged in battle. His troops were nearly out of breath—having ran—not marched to the scene of action under the burning rays of an August sun. He had scarcely formed and brought his guns to bear when the militia broke in confusion and ran for dear life. The whole British army then advanced upon the Spartan band of Barney. He saw no hope of rallying the mushroom troops that were flying but determined not to be shot on the wing himself and fill a coward's grave. He reserved his fire until the enemy came within a few yards when a discharge of round and grape shot left the front ranks struggling in death. A second time the English veterans advanced—a second time their front ranks fell like grass before a scythe. The British then left the road and approached from another direction by fording the creek then very low. All the so-called American troops had left the Commodore and his brave phalanx. Still he stood his ground against an overwhelming force of the veterans of Waterloo. Although simultaneously charged on the right and left, he repulsed them several times with great slaughter. He had received a ball in his thigh which was bleeding profusely. At the same time his horse was killed under him. To add to his chagrin the mushroom militia had ran off with his ammunition wagon. On being nearly surrounded by the enemy and Capt. Miller severely wounded, he ordered those to retreat who were able to do so. He was carried a few yards by three of his officers and fell from loss of blood. Two of them he ordered to conduct the retreat of his gallant men. Gen. Ross and Admiral Cockburn were conducted to him and treated him kindly. They ordered him and Capt. Miller to be carried to a house in Bladensburg where their wounds were dressed and they made as comfortable as circumstances would permit. The British left 80 of their killed and wounded on the battle ground—who had fallen through the bravery of the bold sailors and marines who stood like men and fought like lions. The Americans had 60 killed and wounded 50 of whom were those who nobly defended the star spangled banner of the brave Barney and Miller, showing how early in the action the shrimp militia entered leg bail and distanced all pursuit—only ten being shot on the wing as they were courageously flying from the field of glory. Had they fought as did Barney and Miller with their ocean band they would have repelled the invading foe and saved the capital of our nation from desecration. The means for success were as formidable at Bladensburg as at Baltimore and New Orleans.

After having committed the most wanton waste at the shamefully deserted city of Washington Gen. Ross retreated on the 26th with a loss of over 1000 men. He could boast of having visited and devastated the capital of a great nation filled with defenceless females and children left to his mercy and generosity by most of their *gallant* husbands and fathers. The whole transaction as conducted by both armies does not reflect the *highest* honor on any concerned but the brave Commodore and his companions in arms.

The day after the battle Mrs. Barney, a son and the family physician repaired to Bladensburg to aid and comfort the Commodore. It was impossible to extract the ball from his thigh which remained through life. In a few days he was able to ride home in a carriage. On the 7th of October he was so far recovered as to visit the British fleet for the purpose of exchanging prisoners. For his gallantry on the battle ground of Bladensburg the state of Georgia voted him hearty thanks–the city of Washington presented him with a splendid sword. On the 15th of October he resumed the command of the flotilla–still suffering severely from the pressure of the ball. During the ensuing winter he prepared for a vigorous spring campaign. Peace put an end to further military operations. He sailed on a mission to Europe on the 25th of May 1815 and returned on the 19th of the ensuing October. So much did his wound disable him that he was compelled to send his despatches from Baltimore to Washington. He was conveyed to his family at Elkridge and subsequently removed to Baltimore.

In 1816 he visited his lands in Kentucky in company with his lady. They were received with marked attention on their whole route. So highly pleased were they with the noble bearing, open frankness and proverbial hospitality of the Kentuckians, that they resolved on removing there at the earliest time possible. In 1818 the arrangements were completed and the journey commenced. He started his men and effects in advance and met them at Brownsville on the Monongahela. Owing to low water he was detained for some time before reaching Pittsburgh. At that place he was detained from the same cause. When the water rose he went on board with his family in the evening for the purpose of an early start the next morning. During the night he was taken ill and was removed on shore. His disease increased–his wounded thigh became highly inflamed–death did its work. On the 1st day of December 1818 Com. Joshua Barney was numbered with the silent dead. He breathed his life calmly away and descended to the tomb in peace. He was buried by the sympathizing citizens of Pittsburgh with all the honors of sepulture in the graveyard of the first Presbyterian church where his remains reposed until 1849 when they were removed to the splendid Alleghany Cemetery three miles from Pittsburgh. After the funeral obsequies were over and the widow and her family had partially recovered from the shock of their sudden bereavement they proceeded to their place of destination and located upon their land in Kentucky. As a small compensation for the valuable services of her husband, Congress granted Mrs. Barney a pension for life.

But few men have lived whose web of life has been filled with as many exciting events and sudden changes as was that of Com. Barney. His was a life of industry and usefulness without reaching the lofty summit of fame on which many have perched whose substantial worth was inferior to his. He discharged every duty that devolved upon him with the strictest fidelity–with an eye single to the good and glory of his country–without parade, pomp or vain show. Such men should elicit the gratitude of our nation as much as those who have filled a higher rank but have not been more useful.

In all the relations of public and private life Com. Barney stood approved, admired and beloved. He lived respected and died regretted.

JOSIAH BARTLETT.

UNION–enchanting word–a harmonious euphony vibrates from its sound. It is the most mellow word in our language. It was the watchword in Heaven before this mighty globe was spoke into existence–its melody will be chanted there through the rolling ages of eternity. This magic word has rallied millions to deeds of noble daring both for good and evil. No language thrills through the soul of a patriot like the watchword of '76–"OUR UNION." Is this still the watchword of the great mass of the American people?–or is the unholy leaven of *Dissolution* working its fearful progress from demagogues and factionists? Shall our UNION be preserved to millions yet unborn? or will we follow in the awful wake of nations who once were but now are not? Will the bone and sinew of our dear America suffer patriotism to be basely strangled by party spirit and internal dissensions? These are questions big with importance and should be promptly answered by every friend of the UNION in a voice of patriotic thunder that shall carry terror into the heart of every fanatic and disorganizer in our land

For years too little attention has been given to the mental and moral qualifications of our legislators. *Available* to the party has been the watchword in most cases. Cliques nominate–electioneer and hoodwink the dear people so that the destinies of our nation are emphatically placed in the hands of a meagre minority and many of this minority men of just seven principles—two loaves and five fishes. People of the United States! awake to a sense of impending danger! Return no man to a legislative hall whose uniform conduct has not proved him to be a pure patriot and no one a second time who deals in billingsgate, legislates by force of arms or favors dissolution. Unless UNION is his watchword he cannot be trusted.

UNION was the glorious rallying word of the Sages and Heroes of the American Revolution among whom was Josiah Bartlett born at Amesbury, Mass. in November 1729. He was the son of Stephen Bartlett a man of sterling merit and liberal principles. Josiah received a good academic education which he completed at the early age of sixteen. He then commenced the study of medicine under Dr. Ordway and pursued it with great industry for five years. He then entered upon a successful practice at Kingston, New Hampshire, where he gained the confidence and esteem of the community. Two years after he commenced practice he was reduced very low by a fever and given up by his attending physicians. More consistent than some physicians he experimented upon *himself* and saved his life. He commenced taking small and frequent doses of cider—a free perspiration ensued—the fever left and he soon recovered. From that time he watched the indications and wants of nature more closely in his patients and often made judicious and successful deviations from the old beaten path of practice.

Dr. Bartlett was the first physician who boldly assumed the position that the *angina maligna tonsillaris* [canker] was *putrid* and not *inflammatory* and first gave Peruvian bark for this distressing disease. He also introduced the successful practice of using antiphlogistic remedies for *cynanche maligna* [sore throat] at that time terrific among children—four being sometimes buried in one grave from the same family. By the skill of this able physician this awful scourge was checked and stripped of its terrors. These improvements in his practice resulted from a close study and investigation of the laws of nature, ever in operation, which may be *aided* but never *controlled* by artificial means. Let doctors remember this fact and govern themselves accordingly.

Dr. Bartlett held several important offices under Gov. Wentworth both civil and military. Enjoying the confidence of the people he was elected to the New Hampshire Assembly where he became a prominent opposer of the infringements of the crown upon chartered rights. Republican blood only flowed in his veins. With an Argus eye he watched the movements of the British ministry and the royalists around him. In granting charters for towns the royal governors had uniformly reserved for the ostensible use of the Episcopal Church the cream of the location. This was one of the bones of contention between the people and the governors. Taxation for illegitimate purposes was the vertebra of the hated animal. In effecting their settlements the colonists had conquered the wilderness and the savage unaided by the mother country. They were unwilling to be robbed of their hard earnings by those who desired to roll in luxury at their expense. Resistance was natural—was right. Taxation and representation are inseparable principles that cannot be divorced. They were incorporated in the eternal code of Nature and like the Siamese twins must journey together where intelligence and social order predominate. Kingly power adopts the unholy aphorism that *might makes right*. Upon this sandy foundation the British ministers based their policy towards the American Colonies. *They* put the Revolutionary ball in motion—its rebounding force demolished the superstructure of their power over our hardy ancestors. At the commencement of their oppressions, so prompt was resistance that the king loosened the screws for a time. But under his old preceptor, Lord Bute, backed by Lord North, he was bound to court ruin and affiance it. Most effectually did he perform his plighted vows which were freely sanctioned by the patriots of America.

Gov. Wentworth thought to secure Dr. Bartlett by making him a member of the judiciary. But there was no gift within the power of monarchy that could seduce him from the path of liberty. As the crisis was urged on by the hirelings of the crown his opposition increased in an equal ratio. A circumstance occurred that made him at once conspicuous. The favorite measure of securing a majority in the Assembly at all hazards was resorted to by the Governor. He obtained the king's writ for three new members from towns that were then fully represented. This open violation of the known law of the land roused the indignation of the Doctor who carried with him others who had not before come out in favor of freedom. The three new members were expelled—opposition to the governor rose like a July thunder gust. He was obliged to take refuge from the popular fury on board the man-of-war Fowey. His Excellency proceeded to annul the power of all liberals under commission from him. By using this air-pump too freely he produced a vacuum that caused an irreparable collapse of his own power. The line of demarcation was drawn—the war cry was raised.

Dr. Bartlett was elected to the Congress of 1774 but on account of the recent destruction of his house by fire was unable to attend. In September 1775, he took his seat and was at once placed upon several important committees. About the same time he was made colonel of a regiment of provincial troops. In Congress his duties were arduous. That body met at nine in the morning and continued in session until four in the afternoon. After that hour most of the business of the committees was faithfully attended to. At this day of inglorious ease no one can fully appreciate and but few bestow a thought upon the immense labor, treasure and blood that our UNION cost. When we learn from the historic page the difficulties that surrounded the Continental Congress–a tremendous storm bursting over their heads–retreating before a relentless foe from place to place–their country bleeding at every pore–without resources–their army nearly annihilated–we are led to wonder and admire and ask why their well formed resolutions were not shaken when the yawning gulf of destruction seemed open to devour them. To my mind the solution is plain. A majority of the Sages and Heroes of that eventful period were truly pious and put their trust in Him who directs the destinies of nations. Their trust was well founded.

In 1776 Dr. Bartlett was again a member of Congress and took a decided stand in favor of severing the maternal cords of allegiance to the mother country and declare the child capable of self government. Many zealous patriots feared it was yet too weak. Much discussion occurred and a majority pledged themselves to take the nursling in charge. On the 4th of July 1776 the contract was signed which relieved mother Britain from further responsibility.

When the final question was taken the name of Josiah Bartlett was first called. With his eyes raised to Heaven he responded in a loud voice–*Yea* and *Amen!* Echo caught the words from his lips and carried them on wings of wind to the remotest bounds of a nation of freemen. They ran through the dense crowd of spectators hovering around the Hall of Independence who made the welkin ring with long and repeated responses–*Yea* and *Amen!!!*

Worn down by fatigue the health of the Doctor became impaired and prevented his further attendance in Congress for two years. During that time he was able to aid his state in organizing her new government and in raising troops for the northern army. He served in 1778 and took a final leave of the National Legislature that he might gather up the scattered fragments of his ruined fortune and aid his own state in her effort to advance the glorious cause of national freedom. He was appointed Chief Justice of the Common Pleas and muster master of the troops then enlisting. In 1782 he was made a justice of the Superior Court and in 1788 was appointed Chief Justice. His marked usefulness did not close with the war. The ushering in of peace made a false impression upon the great mass. Few understood the herculean task of rising from the paralysis of a seven years contest with a powerful foe—the formation of a government entirely different from the one which had stamped its customs upon the people. In my view the wisdom of the sages of the revolution was more severely taxed in perfecting our system of government than in driving the Britons from our shores. It often requires more wisdom to retain and enjoy, than to obtain an object.

In the new work of preparing the people for the rational enjoyment of the Independence they had achieved Dr. Bartlett took an active part. Numerous conflicting interests were to be reconciled—an enormous debt was to be paid—many abuses and corruptions were to be corrected—a concert of feeling and action to be produced—the art of self government to be acquired. Storm after storm arose that threatened to throw our nation back into primeval darkness. It required the combined sagacity and wisdom of the boldest sages to preserve the laurels of victory, the trophies of freedom and the chart of our liberty. Long and arduous were the labors that effected a confederated consolidation. During the time this subject was under consideration several of the states were shook to the very centre by internal commotion. That concert of feeling and action which had carried the people through the perils of the war was now lost in the whirlpool of self. UNION was no longer the rallying word with the mass. Fortunately for our country those who stood at the helm during the revolutionary storm were still at the post of duty. Reason slowly resumed her sway—wise counsels prevailed—order was restored—liberty was saved.

Dr. Bartlett was a member of the Convention of N. H. that adopted the Federal Constitution and gave it his zealous support. In 1789 he was elected to the U. S. Senate—the next year President of N. H. and in 1793 was elected the first governor of the state under the new order of things. He enjoyed the universal esteem of his constituents and discharged the duties of the numerous offices he filled with so much dignity, wisdom and prudence that envy and slander could find no crevice for an entering wedge.

Worn down with toil—old age ploughing deep furrows in his face for the last seed time—the confines of a brighter world just before him, he resigned his authority and closed his public career on the 29th of January 1794, covered with living honors and not a spot to tarnish the glory of his fair escutcheon. He then retired to private life full of hope—anticipating the domestic enjoyments always desirable to those who accept of public office for the sake of their country—not for the sake of the loaves and fishes. But these long desired enjoyments were of short duration. Disease fastened its relentless grasp upon him. On the 19th of May 1795, his happy spirit left its tenement of clay—ascended to Him who gave it—leaving a nation to mourn the loss of one of its brightest ornaments—one of its noblest patriots.

In his private character he fulfilled the duties of citizen, friend, husband, father and Christian. No man was more generally esteemed—no man more richly deserved it. In his whole life we have one of the fairest pictures drawn upon the easel of history. His public career was of that solid character that imparts substantial usefulness. Without dazzling, his course was right onward in the cause of universal philanthropy. He could look back upon a life well spent—he stood approved at the stern tribunal of conscience. He nobly fulfilled the design of his creation—discharged his duty to his country, his fellow men and his God. He left examples that stand as beacon lights to erring man to guide him safely through this vale of tears—to statesmen and patriots to induce them to put forth their noblest powers to preserve our UNION.

CARTER BRAXTON.

MEN who forget right and abuse power often undermine the foundation of their own citadel. In reaching after more authority and larger enjoyments improperly, they are often shorn of what they have. Thus it was with England when she imposed unwarranted taxes and restrictions upon the American Colonies. Previous to the causes that produced the Revolution the plan of an independent government was ideal and had entered the minds of but few. With these it was only a nursling in theory not practically anticipated. When the impolitic measures of the British ministry were first reduced to practice the Colonists stood upon the firm basis, the broad platform of their chartered rights clearly defined and well understood and believed their grievances must and would be redressed when respectful petitions should be laid before the king. These were repeatedly forwarded to him couched in allegiate and eloquent language to which he turned a deaf ear, thus forging the first link in the revolutionary chain. Parliament was vainly appealed to. Remonstrances formed the next link in this chain. These were treated with contumely. A formal demand to desist from oppression in bold but still respectful language—every word breathing allegiance to the king was the third link in this chain but all to no purpose. The ministerial horse leech cry—*give*-GIVE-GIVE—came rushing across the broad Atlantic from Albion's shore and pierced more deeply the wounded hearts of the imploring suppliants. Resolutions of non-importation formed the fourth link. These were answered by threats and menaces. Preparations to resist formed the fifth link. These resulted in an open and wanton attack upon American citizens on the heights of Lexington when the great seal of allegiance was dissolved in blood. The sixth link was the war cry which roused millions to resolve on liberty or death. The Declaration of Rights was the seventh and swivel link to the golden chain of Liberty forged by the patriots of '76 which formed an impassable barrier to the power of Great Britain over the colonies. The broad ring of the Federal Constitution perfected this mighty chain which has thus far held the ship of state safely to her moorings amidst the storms that have been raised by foreign foes and internal traitors.

Among those who aided in forging this golden chain of Liberty was Carter Braxton son of George Braxton a wealthy planter who resided on the north bank of the Mattapony river, where he owned a large tract of valuable land situated in the county of King and Queen in Virginia. At this delightful place Carter was born on the 10th of September 1736. His connections were numerous, wealthy and of the first respectability. Several of them were crown officers at various periods. Carter was raised amidst the splendor of opulence without the tender care of a mother to correct his childish foibles or the wise counsels of a father to guard him against the errors of youth. The former died when he was but seven days old—the latter when he was a small boy. He was liberally educated at the college of William and Mary. At the age of nineteen he married the beautiful and amiable Judith Robinson who was very wealthy. He entered into full possession of his large estate, which, united with that of his wife, constituted a princely fortune. She survived but a brief period leaving two daughters, the youngest but a few hours old.

Borne down by grief Mr. Braxton visited England where he remained nearly three years and added greatly to his previous stock of knowledge. He became familiar with the feelings and designs of that kingdom towards his native country. His rank and fortune gave him access to the nobility from whom he obtained much valuable information relative to the ministerial conclave then concocting plans to support royalty in Great Britain by forcing money from the hardy pioneers of America. Although his relatives and friends were many of them favorites of the King and everything around him was calculated to foster aristocracy and bind him to those in power, he became a bold opposer of British usurpations and a warm advocate of liberal principles and equal rights.

In 1760 he returned from Europe and was elected to the House of

Burgesses and became an active and prominent member. His knowledge of the intentions of the mother country to impose increasing burdens upon the Americans enabled him to fully understand every movement of the monarchical hirelings around him. In 1765 he was in the House of Burgesses and was a warm supporter of the bold resolutions offered by Patrick Henry relative to the Stamp Act. He was in the House in 1769 when the proceedings of the members excited the ire of Gov. Bottetourt so highly that he dissolved them without ceremony. They immediately repaired to a private room in Williamsburg and entered into a solemn agreement not to import any articles from the mother country until their chartered rights were restored. The same members were elected to the next session. Being aware of the kind of material he had to manage the shrewd Governor lulled them into a more quiet mood by the siren song of promises of redress. They had yet to learn that deceit is an important part of political machinery. Still cherishing hopes that their rights would be restored they waited in respectful but watchful silence. In the House there were seven standing committees—on courts of justice, public claims, elections, privileges, trade, grievances, proposition and on religion. Of the three last Mr. Braxton was uniformly a member.

In 1771 Governor Bottetourt died and was succeeded by Lord Dunmore. Being fresh from the fountain of high notions and ministerial corruption he dissolved the turbulent Assembly then in commission and issued his king's writ for a new election. Mr. Braxton was then sheriff of the county and could not serve in the House. Promises of redress were renewed with apparent sincerity. The people lived on hope until the 27th of May 1774, when the House of Burgesses again took a bold stand against oppression and were unceremoniously dissolved by the Governor. By this act he dissolved the original contract in view of the people—they became enraged and doffed their allegiance *instanter*. Immediately after the dissolution, eighty-nine of the members and many other bold patriots formed themselves into an association of resistance. From these live sparks the fire of freedom rose in curling flames.

In August of that year a convention met at Williamsburg to devise plans for future action of which Mr. Braxton was an efficient member. Seven delegates were elected to meet the Congress at Philadelphia and an agreement made to act in concert with the people of Boston in the common cause against the common enemy. Lord Dunmore had a new set of members elected to the House but being displeased with their proceedings prorogued them several times. On the night of the 7th of June 1775 the people in turn prorogued his lordship who took his final exit on board the armed ship Fowey never again to wield his iron rod of despotism over the freemen of America. He took up quarters on board this ship and occasionally issued his mandates which came to the people as talismanic messengers to invigorate their patriotism. In April following he caused the powder to be removed from the magazine under a pretence that it would be needed in another part of the province to repel an expected insurrection of the blacks. The enraged people assembled in large numbers with a determination to take this important item into their own keeping. Through the persuasion of Peyton Randolph they dispersed. Some being still discontented a Spartan band assembled headed by Patrick Henry and proceeded to Williamsburg determined to have the powder or its equivalent. An armed force was sent from the Fowey to sustain the governor's orders. This was like adding bitumen to a blazing fire. The fury of the patriots was about to be poured out upon the minions of the crown–blood was about to flow when Mr. Braxton and others interfered–the powder was paid for by a crown officer–Mr. Henry gave his receipt for the money and his young Spartans returned home.

For a time the government of Virginia was managed entirely by the Committee of Safety of which Mr. Braxton was an active member. On the 15th of December 1775, he was elected to the Continental Congress and entered upon his duties with great zeal. He advocated, voted for and signed the Declaration of Rights that formally dissolved the maternal ties that bound the pilgrim fathers in slavery. On his return from Congress the next year Mr. Braxton took his seat in the first legislature of his state convened under the new form of government. A formal vote of thanks to him and Thomas Jefferson for their faithful services in Congress was entered upon the records of that body on the 12th of October 1776. From that time to his death he was almost constantly a member of one or the other branch of the legislature and but four days previous to his decease had taken his seat in the Council.

He had lost a large portion of his princely fortune by the British and after the war closed was the child of adversity. For a time his friends assisted him in the prosecution of several speculative projects, all of which proved abortive, injuring them without benefiting him. He finally sunk under a ponderous weight of affliction which produced paralysis, a second attack of which closed his useful and eventful career at Richmond, Virginia, on the 10th of October 1797.

Under all these adverse and trying circumstances his reputation did not suffer. He was known to be an honest man and poverty *then* was not an unpardonable sin or even *prima facie* evidence of dishonesty. He lost none of his well-earned fame as an able and faithful public servant and worthy upright man. His private character was pure. He fulfilled all the relations of life with fidelity. He was one of the most polished gentlemen of the old school. His name is justly placed high upon the list of enduring fame. He was a faithful sentinel in the cause of freedom and contributed largely in consummating the Independence we now enjoy, the FREEDOM we inherit, the LIBERTY we are bound to cherish, protect, preserve and perpetuate with our lives, fortunes and sacred honors and transmit it to our children in all the beauty of pristine purity.

ZEBULON BUTLER.

WYOMING VALLEY is the Paradise of Pennsylvania. Captivating in its location–rich in its soil–irrigated by the crystal Susquehanna–bordered with magnificent scenery of romantic grandeur–enlivened by beautiful farm-houses and productive fields–crowned with the flourishing town of Wilkesbarre–ornamented by several small villages of tasteful neatness–refreshed by cooling springs and mountain streams filled with sportive trout–evergreen forests adjacent towering to the clouds and full of game–graduated hills on every side rich with minerals and reaching to the mountains–a healthful atmosphere rendered pure by the untiring operations of nature's laboratory–inhabited by intelligent, enterprising, hospitable people–it is one of the most beautiful and delightful valleys in our expansive country. Its early history renders it sacred to the philanthropist and is read with thrilling sensations of painful sympathy. It has engaged the pens of our best historians–our ablest poets. It has been painted with the finest touches of our boldest artists. When strangers pass the narrow confines of the majestic mountains on the south and are ushered into this grand amphitheatre of creative wisdom–they gaze with pleasing surprise and wonder at the weakness of the most vivid descriptions they have read, compared with the sublime reality of the enrapturing view before them

In this far-famed valley Zebulon Butler acted a conspicuous, brave and noble part. He was born at Lyme, Conn. in 1731. He received a good common school and religious education. The New Testament was then an approved school-book. He early planted himself on the firm basis of moral rectitude and primitive religious truth. Without these the laurels of the hero are less fragrant—the talents of the legislator less brilliant—the noblest attributes of man less perfect. By these remarks I do not mean Pharisaical religion, poisonous fanaticism nor blighting sectarianism. It is the honest, consistent, Golden Rule man I admire. Such a man was Zebulon Butler. He was one of the first patriots who opposed British tyranny and dared to be free. He entered early into the Provincial service and served the mother country through the French war. He commenced his military career an Ensign and soon rose to the rank of Captain. He participated in the memorable hardships of the campaign of 1758 on the frontiers of Canada—at Fort Edward, Lake George, Ticonderoga and Crown Point. In 1762 he was at the protracted siege of Havana. On his way he was on board one of the six vessels that were shipwrecked. All on board narrowly escaped a watery grave. They were on the beach nine days before they were relieved. On the 9th day of August the last of the fleet arrived before Havana. The defence was obstinate—the sufferings of the besiegers great.

Capt. Butler shared largely in the dangers of the attack—the glories of the victory. He sailed for his long absent home on the 21st of the ensuing October in the Royal Duke. He encountered many perils during the voyage. On the 7th of November the ship began to leak so rapidly that it was with difficulty that her crew were transferred to another vessel near by before she went to the bottom. He arrived at New York on the 21st of December and once more met the warm embrace of anxious relatives and friends. He had won enduring laurels—he stood high as a brave and skilful officer—an esteemed and valued citizen. He then left the army and enjoyed the peaceful pleasures of private life until the revolutionary storm began to concentrate its fearful elements. He was ready to brave its pitiless peltings. He had rendered arduous and valuable service to the mother country—he was well qualified to repel her ungrateful conduct and render efficient aid in the defence of his native soil. The goadings and insolence of British hirelings had deeply penetrated his patriotic soul and prepared him for bold and noble action. When the tocsin of war was sounded from the heights of Lexington he promptly tendered his services—was appointed a lieutenant-colonel in the Connecticut line and repaired to the post of honor and danger. He was actively engaged in the campaigns of 1777-8-9. During the last year he was commissioned colonel of the 2d Connecticut regiment. He was with Washington in New Jersey and greatly esteemed by him.

A short time previous to the revolution he was one of a company from his native place that had purchased Wyoming Valley from the Indians for a fair consideration. Many settlers had located there and cleared up much of the forest. Although fully remunerated for their lands pursuant to contract made with the Chiefs in grand council assembled—the red men were unwilling to leave a place so enchanting and congenial with their views of happiness. In that salubrious vale, fringed with hills and mountains on all sides, they fancied the Great Spirit had his dwelling-place and gave them audible audience as echo reverberated their stentorian yells from hill to mountain and back to the shores of the majestic Susquehanna. As the towering forest fell before the axe of the white man the Indians murmured and designed the extermination of the pale faces. In this they were encouraged by the British and black-hearted tories—most of the inhabitants having declared for liberty. Most of their effective force of near 200 men was in the American army. Soon after the departure of these troops the savages assumed a menacing attitude—manifesting a disposition to violate the terms of peace they had solemnly sanctioned when paid for their lands. Several stockade forts were erected—a company of rangers organized and placed under the command of Captain Hewitt. Every precaution was taken to guard against surprise—the movements of the red men were narrowly watched, their apparent designs closely observed. It soon became evident that they were preparing for a bloody sacrifice. An express was despatched to the board of war representing the approaching danger requesting the return of the troops who had recently joined the army—leaving their homes exposed to all the horrors of savage cruelty rendered more awful by the more blood-thirsty tories. The request was promptly granted but too late to ward off the fatal slaughter and carnage that took place when these brave men were within two days' march of their murdered wives, children and friends who slumbered in death deeply gashed with the tomahawk.

About the 1st of June 1778, a number of canoes were discovered descending the river just above the valley filled with Indian warriors. They attacked a party of the inhabitants who were at work on the bank of the Susquehanna—killing and making prisoners of ten. They were evidently concentrating their forces for the purpose of an attack upon the settlement. At that critical juncture Col. Butler arrived. A large body of the savages had assembled at the mouth of the Lackawanna at the head of the valley. The militia under the command of Col. Dennison assembled in the fort at Wilkesbarre on the 1st of July. They scoured the borders of the valley—discovered the bodies of those who had been massacred a few days before–killed two Indians and returned. Not supposing danger so near each man repaired to his own house for provisions. On the 3d most of the men able to bear arms assembled at the fort amounting to about 350. Some remained in the smaller forts with their families presuming on the delay of an attack. The command of the troops was given to Col. Butler. They were poorly armed and had but a small supply of ammunition. But few of them had ever been engaged in battle and were not familiar with military tactics. In a few moments after Col. Butler had assumed the command news was brought that the enemy had entered the upper end of the valley and were advancing rapidly. Fort Wintermote and another stockade fort was then in flames and their inmates weltering in blood and struggling in death. A council of war was held and an unfortunate resolve made to march out and attempt to arrest the savages in their career of desolation and carnage. The troops proceeded some distance from the fort and took an advantageous position on the bank of a creek where they supposed the enemy would pass on their way to the principal fort. There they remained for half a day without seeing the foe. Another council of war was held which resulted in adding to the error of leaving the fort that of attacking the enemy in their position contrary to the opinion of several officers who were as brave but more judicious than those who urged the fatal movement. The order to advance was given. They had not proceeded more than a mile when the advanced guard fired upon several Indians who were firing a house. The force of the enemy was concentrated at fort Wintermote amounting to near 1000 effective men commanded by Brandt, an Indian half-blood and Col. John Butler–not a relative of Col. Zebulon Butler as some writers have erroneously stated. Echo returned the demoniac yells of the savages from the surrounding hills–the forest resounded with the appalling war whoop. Another serious error was committed by the ill-fated Americans. Not until they were upon the battle-ground did they learn the superior force of the revengeful foe. As the little band approached they found the Indians and tories formed in a line–the right resting on a swamp commanded by Brandt–the left reaching to fort Wintermote headed by Col. John Butler. Col. Z. Butler led the right and Col. Dennison the left of the Americans to the attack. So determined was this Spartan band on victory that the left of the enemy gave way in a few minutes closely pursued by Col. Butler. In consequence of part of the Indians passing the swamp to gain his rear Col. Dennison ordered his men to fall back. Many supposing he had ordered a retreat the line became confused and broken. At that unfortunate juncture Brandt rushed upon it with such fury that it could not be rallied. At that critical moment Col. Butler rode towards the left and first learned the misfortune of Col. Dennison and saw his men retreating in disorder. He was then between two fires and near the advancing enemy. Before the troops on the right were apprised of the fate of the left they were nearly surrounded by the savages and compelled to retreat precipitately. The route was general–the slaughter horrible–the scene terrific. But about 50 survived among whom were Colonels Butler and Dennison who were more exposed than most of the others. The few who escaped from the dreadful carnage of that fatal day assembled at Forty Fort. So heart-rending was this defeat that the surviving inhabitants were willing to submit to any terms to save their lives. The enemy refused to treat with any officer of the continental army as unquestionably advised by the hyena tories. Nor would they give them or regular soldiers any quarter but insisted on their being delivered up to the Indians at discretion. Col. Butler at once left and proceeded to Gradenhutten on the Lehigh. On the 4th of July Col. Dennison entered into a capitulation with Col. John Butler and Brandt to surrender the Fort on condition the lives of the survivors should be preserved and not further molested in person or property. These conditions were solemnly agreed to by tory Butler and Brandt but most disgracefully violated. As the Indians marched in they commenced an indiscriminate plunder. Butler was appealed to and replied he could not control them–walked out and left them to finish their work in their own way. The man who could urge the savages on to murder could leave them to rob the helpless, regardless of his sacred pledge of honor.

Finding themselves still at the mercy of the Indians the inhabitants fled to the nearest settlement towards the Delaware about 50 miles distant through a dense wilderness and over rugged mountains. So rapidly did they fly on the wings of terror that numbers became exhausted from over fatigue and hunger and were carried on the last day by the stronger ones. After their departure the savage tories and red men laid waste the town of Wilkesbarre and most of the houses in the valley–plundering or destroying all the property they could find. They then drove the cattle and horses to Niagara. They had fully satiated their thirst for blood–desolation was completed–vengeance was gorged–nature mourned over the dismal scene.

From Gradenhutten Col. Butler communicated the sad intelligence of the bloody massacre to the Board of War and then proceeded to Stroudsburg, then in Northampton county, where he met the returning

Wyoming troops and a few of those who had escaped on the day of the unfortunate battle. In August he was ordered to return with such force as he could collect and take possession of Wyoming valley. On his arrival he found a few Indians who were collecting the cattle that the main body had left. They fled precipitately without their plunder. Col. Butler erected a new fort at Wilkesbarre and established a well regulated garrison which he commanded until the winter of 1780–keeping the tories and savages at bay–not risking a general action but killing them off in detail by scouting parties of sharp-shooters whenever they approached the settlement. The expedition of Gen. Sullivan in 1779 paralyzed the Indian power upon the Susquehanna and restored a good degree of confidence in the inhabitants.

In December 1780 Col. Butler was ordered to join the continental army and left Capt. Alexander Mitchell in command of the fort. After serving his country faithfully to the close of the war of Independence the Colonel returned to the vale of Wyoming to enjoy the fruits of his perilous toils and the gratitude of the inhabitants whom he had nobly aided and protected. He subsequently filled sundry civil offices with credit and fidelity. He lived to see his loved Wyoming bloom with the fruits of industry–its inhabitants peaceful, prosperous, happy. He was amply rewarded for the perils and hardships of the past by the full fruition of the enjoyments of the present. His happiness was as complete as it could be made this side of heaven. Dearly beloved by his immediate friends, esteemed by all who knew him–the waning years of Col. Butler were crowned with the most refined comforts of social and domestic life. He glided down the stream of time smoothly and calmly to the 28th of July 1795, when he threw off his mortal coil–resigned his quiescent spirit into the hands of its Creator–fell asleep in the arms of his Lord and Master deeply mourned and sincerely lamented. His career closed as brightly as it had been glorious and useful. He was an amiable companion, a virtuous citizen, a consistent Christian–a brave, noble, worthy, honest man.

A creditable monument has been erected on the battle ground in memory of those who fell on the memorable 3d of July 1778 in the far famed valley of Wyoming.

CHARLES CARROLL OF CARROLLTON.

The fond and faithful parents who have guided to manhood a family of sons whose every action is a source of pleasure and delight–who walk in wisdom's ways—who prove virtuous, generous, bold, brave and patriotic—whose lives shed new lustre on the world—whose achievements on the battle field or in the senate chamber stamp their names with enduring fame—enjoy a rich consolation, pure as the etherial sky—refreshing as evening zephyrs. More especially do their souls become enraptured with love if these sons deliver them from the iron grasp of a merciless tyrant—disenthrall them from the chains of slavery and make them free and independent.

All this was done for our country by her valiant sons who graced the memorable era of '76. Like a blazing meteor bursting from the clouds amidst the gloom of midnight darkness, they illuminated our nation with light—the world with glory—raised the star spangled banner and planted the tree of LIBERTY deep in the soil of FREEDOM. Noble sons of Columbia! Sages and heroes of the American Revolution! Your names will be held in grateful remembrance through the rolling ages of time. Millions yet unborn will chant your brilliant achievements, your triumphant victories, your unsurpassed wisdom, your godlike actions.

Among the sons of noble daring—champions of their injured country, was Charles Carroll of Carrollton, born at Annapolis on the 20th of September 1737. He was the son of Daniel Carroll who came from King's county Ireland and was named for his grandfather Charles Carroll. The elder Carrolls were highly charged with liberal principles and planted them deeply in the minds of their sons. Nor did the precious seed fall on barren ground. Obeying the precepts and imitating the examples of his patriotic sire, young Charles Carroll proved worthy of the high source from which he sprang. He was emphatically one of the same stamp.

At the early age of eight years his embryo talents shone so brightly that his father determined on giving them an opportunity to bud, blossom and expand amidst the literary bowers of Europe. He was first sent to a seminary in France. His untiring application to his studies and manly deportment at the different seminaries through which he passed, gained for him a finished education and the esteem of all his acquaintances. At the age of twenty he commenced the study of law in London, England, where he ripened into manhood and returned to his native State in 1764 with a rich fund of useful knowledge, prepared to act well his part through life.

The subject of oppression upon the Americans by the British ministry was freely discussed in England before he left and had prepared his mind for the exciting crisis that awaited the colonies. On his return he became an unflinching and able advocate for freedom. He possessed a clear head and discriminating mind. In action he was cool, deliberate, firm and decisive. His writing talent was of a high order. This was admirably developed in 1772. The governor had issued a proclamation derogatory to the constitutional rights of the people. In a series of essays published in the public papers, Mr. Carroll triumphantly vindicated the cause of his insulted constituents—conclusively answering and confuting the combined arguments of the governor and his cabinet in favor of the unwarranted pretensions of their master. So fully did these essays convince the people that the governor aimed at illegitimate power that they hung his proclamation upon a gallows and bid defiance to the minions of despotism. Before the writer was known the people instructed their representatives to record a vote of thanks to the author. When it was ascertained that Mr. Carroll was the champion who had bearded the British lion, they repaired to his house in great numbers and made the welkin ring with plaudits of thankful praise.

From that time he became a prominent leader of the liberal party—an espouser of equal rights—a stern opposer of ministerial wrongs. His benign influence radiated its genial rays upon the hearts and confirmed the wavering minds of many in the glorious cause of LIBERTY. In bold and glowing colors he portrayed the aggressions of the king, the corrupt designs of his ministers and the humiliating consequences of tame submission to their arbitrary demands. He was among the first to kindle the flame of resistance and light up the torch of Independence. He was among the first to sanction the Declaration of Rights—the last of the noble band of sages who signed it who lived to see 1832.

On the 18th of July 1776 he was a member of the Maryland Convention convened to elect delegates to the Continental Congress. He was selected for that important station—took his seat on the 2d of August and signed the Declaration of Independence. His talents and zeal were highly appreciated by the members of Congress. He had previously endeared himself to them by a voluntary mission to Canada, in conjunction with Franklin, Chase and Bishop Carroll. The object of their visit was to persuade the people of the Canadas to unite with the Colonies in throwing off the yoke of bondage imposed by the mother country. The Messrs. Carrolls were Roman Catholics, the prevailing religion of the Canadians. The other two gentlemen entertained universal charity for all good men irrespective of manufactured creeds. It was fondly hoped their mission would be crowned with success. The defeat of the American troops at Quebec and the death of Gen. Montgomery had thrown so much darkness over the future prospects of the American cause that they refused to enter the compact. The consequences of that course have been fearfully developed for years and the time is not far distant when the Canadas will be free from England to the mutual benefit of both countries.

On his return he was surprised to find that the Maryland delegates in Congress had been instructed by a vote of the Assembly to oppose the Declaration of Independence. His influence caused the rescinding of that vote and a reversal of the instructions. He felt a strong desire that his native state should do full service in the cause of freedom. To effect this he spent more time in her legislative hall than in Congress. In the formation of her constitution and laws he rendered efficient aid. From 1788 to 1791 he was a member of the U. S. Senate. From that year to 1801 he served in the senate of his own state. He then retired from the great theatre of public action in the rich enjoyment of the esteem of a nation of freemen. For thirty years he was spared to enjoy the cheering comforts of domestic felicity and survived all the others who had placed their names upon the Chart of our liberty.

In his retirement he delighted in beholding the onward march of this favored country, prospering under the care of an all-wise Providence–populated by a free and independent people–in rank second to no nation on earth–in enterprise traversing the globe–in genius eclipsing the old world–in talent equal to the best. Like a majestic oak that had long braved the raging tempest, he stood alone as a signer of our Magna Charta calmly awaiting the time when he should be riven and gathered to his fathers. Gradually the world lost its former charms. More and more his mind became fixed on anticipated scenes of future and purer bliss. He seemed to ascend the ladder of faith and reach out his hand for that crown of unfading glory prepared for him by his Lord and Master. In this beatific state his soul was summoned from its tottering, trembling, falling tenement of clay on the 14th of November 1832. Calm and resigned he entered Jordan's flood–angels escorted his immortal spirit to Immanuel's peaceful shores whilst his grateful country deeply mourned and strongly felt the loss of one of her noblest sons–society one of its brightest ornaments–his relatives one of their dearest kinsmen.

Charles Carroll was a man of consistency in everything. He was a devoted Christian in communion with the Roman Catholic Church but decidedly opposed to a want of charity and kind feeling. He deprecated a spirit of persecution by one sect of Christians towards another. He was one of the few who reasoned correctly and acted wisely upon this important subject. It is a fact known to but few at this late day that the Roman Catholics of Maryland were the first who placed religious toleration on a statute book in America. [See laws of Maryland 1647.] It is also a fact that the Protestants first introduced proscription there. After the restoration of Charles II. in 1761, they obtained an order from him prohibiting all Roman Catholics from holding any office, which was in violation of the charter granted to Lord Baltimore by Charles I. upon which the colony was based. Still more. The Protestants having become the bride of the state, continued to draw more tightly the cords of persecution by authority from William III. The Catholics were taxed to support the churches of their oppressors. By an act passed in 1704, the celebration of mass or the instruction of youth by a Catholic insured him transportation to England. In the land of the Puritans, the Baptist and Quaker sects were treated more rigorous, being persecuted even unto death and by those too who fled from the very persecution they practised the moment they obtained the power. So it ever has been–so it ever will be until mankind become fully and feelingly sensible that *sectarianism is not religion—is not a child of Heaven*–that charity is the crowning attribute of Deity–the brightest star in the Christian's diadem.

During the excitement in Maryland upon the unhallowed connection of church and state, the Carrolls used their best exertions to effect a reconciliation between the parties which was never fully done until the revolution compelled sectarianism to hide its hydra head by uniting all sects in the common cause against the common enemy and forever banishing its power from our land by the adoption of our Federal Constitution. Men are as prone to abuse power as the sparks are to fly upward.

In the life of Charles Carroll of Carrollton, we have examples rich with instruction for youth, manhood and old age–for the lawyer, the statesman, the patriot and the Christian. His career was guided by prudence and virtue. His every action was marked with frankness and honesty. He richly merited and freely received the esteem and veneration of a nation of Freemen. His private and public career were prompted and directed by a purity of motive that never fails to render a man useful in life–triumphant in death.

SAMUEL CHASE.

OSTRACISM was the title of a law once in full and practical force in the Republic of Athens. It required the banishment of any citizen when six thousand of the people voted for his expulsion—there being about twenty thousand voters—thus violating the fundamental principle of a republican government—*the majority must rule and be obeyed.* Ruin was the natural result.

Each voter wrote the name of the citizen that was to be banished on a shell called in Greek—*Ostrakon*. These were deposited as are ballots at our elections and were counted by persons appointed by law. To the ruin of Athens, envy, jealousy and intrigue caused the banishment of several of her most illustrious sages and heroes who loved their country more than they did political corruption. Among them was Aristides—a noble patriot, statesman and general. When the people were voting in his case he mingled with the crowd and met an illiterate peasant who did not know him, who asked him to write Aristides upon his shell. *What injury has Aristides done you?* The peasant quickly answered—*None at all but I am tired of hearing him called the just.* Without revealing himself the patriot wrote his own name upon the fatal shell and handed it back to the deluded voter. He bowed submissively to his sentence of banishment for ten years and invoked a blessing on his enemies as he departed.

A species of political persecution practically analogous to the law of ostracism commenced its career in our country as early as the American Revolution. Political cliques and venal presses have been the executioners. No one of the sages or heroes of that eventful period was so severely persecuted by party ostracism after the formation of our republic as Samuel Chase who was born in Somerset County, Maryland, on the 17th day of April, 1741. He was the son of Rev. Thomas Chase who came from England to that province and became pastor of St. Paul's Parish in Baltimore, then a new country village and destitute of good schools. At the age of two years Samuel was deprived of the tender care of his mother by her premature death. Under the instruction of his father he became an accomplished classical scholar. At the age of eighteen he commenced the study of law under the direction of John Hammond and John Hull of Annapolis. At the age of twenty he was admitted to the bar of the Mayor's Court and two years after to that of the County Court and the Court of Chancery. He located at Annapolis and filled up the rib vacuum by marrying the worthy and intelligent Ann Baldwin–a very sensible and fair business transaction.

Mr. Chase was not long in acquiring the reputation of a sound lawyer and able advocate. He was of a sanguine temperament–bold, fearless, undisguised, independent in mind, language and action but honest, patriotic, and pure in his motives–immovable in his purposes–qualities that dignify a man if prudently balanced and prepare him for just such times as the Revolution–qualities that often rouse the spirit of ostracism in those who aim to ruin those they cannot rule. These leading traits, constitutional with Samuel Chase, with the times and circumstances that influenced his judgment and governed his actions must be kept constantly in view to enable the reader to form a just estimate of his character which I will impartially and plainly portray.

On the flood tide of a prosperous business–celebrated for his legal acumen and forensic fame–in the full enjoyment of domestic felicity and social intercourse with friends–Mr. Chase glided smoothly along until his country began to writhe under kingly oppression. The Stamp Act, the first born of the scrofulous revenue system devised by the putrescent British ministry, met with a hostile reception at Annapolis. Mr. Chase and a band of kindred spirits under the cognomen of "Sons of Liberty," forcibly seized and destroyed the newly imported stamps and burned in effigy the stamp distributer. No further violence was then committed. The king's officers opened a newspaper battery against this "furious mob" directing their whole artillery against Mr. Chase complimenting him with the courtly names–" busy restless incendiary–ringleader of mobs foul mouthed inflaming son of discord and faction–a common disturber of the public tranquillity–a promoter of the lawless excesses of the multitude" and other similar emphatic appellations–conferring upon the young patriot a diploma of distinction little anticipated by them. His answers to these vituperations were manly, charged with strong and conclusive logic–keen and withering sarcasm. The attack brought him fairly into the political field. So delighted were the people with the manner he handled the hirelings of the crown that they elected him to the colonial assembly. There he took a conspicuous part and became the uncompromising opposer of all measures that were not within the pale of the constitution or were tinctured with oppression. So strongly was he in favor of liberal principles that he gave his whole influence and vote in favor of the repeal of the law that compelled the people to support the clergy by which the stipend of his father was reduced one-half. Pursuant to the law of primogeniture then in force this was voting money out of his own pocket. His bold and independent course made him a subject of persecution with the creatures of the crown and an object of pride and admiration with the people. His enemies found him a bramble full of the keenest thorns and were awfully scarified every time they approached him. His tongue, pen, logic, sarcasm—all were blighting as a sirocco wind.

After the repeal of the Stamp Act a calm in the public mind ensued but it was a calm of delusion such as precedes a tornado. The inquisitorial rack of the ministry was again put in motion—fresh impositions commenced—the fire of discontent was again blown to a blaze. The Bill closing the port of Boston with directions to the King's officers to seize and send to England for trial those who dared resist the royal authority—roused the indignation of colonies that had been rather passive. The Congress of 1774 was then devised of which Mr. Chase was a member. The deep solemnity, unparalleled wisdom and patient deliberations that marked the proceedings of that Congress—shed a lustre upon the cause of liberty then in embryo that forced applause from its most violent opposers. Had not the cabinet of Great Britain been blinded by sordid avarice, mad ambition and political delusion—had not the King been a mere automaton, scarcely a moving, walking, talking machine—the loyal and logical appeals from that august body of sages would have been treated with merited respect and quiet restored. The colonists asked for nothing but what was clearly right and asked in the most respectful and even suppliant manner. Ministers were left without excuse for their subsequent course. *Their* sacrilegious hands broke the great seal of the social compact—*their* agents sowed the seeds of rebellion—*their* cruelty kindled the flame that devoured them—*their* visionary policy severed the cords of maternal affection—*their* treachery spread the mantle of righteousness over the cause of the Revolution. We justly censure them for their corrupt designs but rejoice in the glorious result of their plans. Haman erected his own gallows. Grenville and North destroyed their own power.

In 1775 Mr. Chase was returned to Congress with instructions to pursue a conciliatory course contrary to his judgment but which he implicitly obeyed. He was active and persevering on committees and took a deep interest in every measure proposed in favor of freedom. He was returned to Congress the next year still trammelled with instructions which he truly predicted would soon be removed. In the spring of 1776 he was associated with Messrs. Franklin, Charles and Bishop Carroll on a mission to Canada to induce the people there to join in the struggle for liberty. They wanted courage to be free and still wear the yoke of bondage. On his return he was delighted to find the question of final separation from mother Britain under consideration and boldly advocated the measure. It was the very proposition to animate the soul of Samuel Chase. His instructions became burdensome as the discussion increased. They were removed just in time for him to record his vote in favor of that imperishable instrument that has immortalized the names of the signers and is the pride of every true American. The act of signing the Declaration of Rights gave him more joy than any public duty he had ever performed. A short time previous to the glorious 4th of July Mr. Chase discovered that a Judas was among them in the person of Rev. Dr. Zubly of Georgia who was clandestinely corresponding with the enemy. So bold and so suddenly did he expose the traitor on the floor of Congress that "the gentleman from Georgia" plead guilty and suddenly retired. His arrest was ordered but when the officer went to his cage the bird had flown and was never bagged. As an able statesman recently remarked, he was left in the very worst company—with himself. Mr. Chase was all industry in every position in which he was placed. In the discussions upon the Articles of Confederation he took a deep interest and active part. He considered their adoption indispensable in carrying on the good work of political regeneration. The basis of representation and the mode of voting were the two great points at issue that consumed the most time in argument.

In the fall of 1776 Messrs. Chase, Wilson, Clymer, Stockton and Smith were made a committee to take charge of the War Department—then the most important of either. Mr. Chase was upon the committee for suppressing internal enemies and became a terror to the tories and certain Quakers in and adjacent to Philadelphia who were circulating papers adverse to the American cause and were in communication with the enemy. A report, with documents proving the charge was submitted to Congress. Several leading members of the Society of Friends were confined—the seditious papers suppressed and a respectful neutrality induced on the part of that very respectable Society whose creed opposing war had led some of its members into an erroneous interference. The tories took shelter under the wings of the British army. The course pursued by Congress was then deemed harsh by some and will still appear so to a casual reader who is not familiar with the rules of war. Agreeably to the martial code of other nations—then the precedent guide for Congress—the punishment would have been much more severe. The mildness of the sentence was an antepast of a more enlarged liberty under the new form of government. By the religious tenets of the Friends it can never be sanctioned—by every friend of liberty the necessity of such a case is always regretted. Each social compact and individual in every government must be subject to the laws of the land—must submit to the ruling power that order may be maintained.

In 1778 the British Parliament devised a stratagem by which they hoped to create a division among the patriots. Printed papers were circulated among the people containing conciliatory and flattering propositions and announcing the appointment of commissioners to perfect these inglorious terms of peace. So ingeniously were these papers worded that it was deemed necessary to prepare an answer. This important task was imposed upon Mr. Chase. Most ably did he perform his duty. He unmasked the base hypocrisy of the scheme—exposed the delusive gull-trap to the consuming fire of sarcastic logic—poured upon it the burning lava of ridicule and raised the indignation and scorn of the people against it to ninety degrees above zero. So well was it received by Congress that a larger number than usual was ordered printed and a resolution passed recommending all the clergy to read it to their congregations after service on Sunday. Like all the other plans the British ministers devised to enslave the colonies—it recoiled upon their own heads with all the force of fearful reaction.

This brilliant display of talent closed the congressional labors of this devoted friend of liberty. He retired crowned with the rich honors of an able statesman, sage, patriot and honest man. He had stood firm at his post—a faithful public servant, a bold advocate for freedom, a safe counsellor in every emergency, a fearless champion when danger pressed, an ornament to his country, a terror to the enemies of liberty. As a working man he had no superior—as a debater he had few equals. Without the mellifluous elocution of a Cicero—free from pleonastic parade—he spoke forcibly, reasoned closely, demonstrated clearly, deduced conclusively. He sought to inform the judgment, enlighten the understanding and convince by sound argument. Until the close of the struggle for freedom he continued to render efficient service to the glorious cause and then resumed his profession in the full enjoyment of the confidence of his constituents and the consolation of an approving conscience.

Soon after the close of the Revolution Mr. Chase was employed by the state of Maryland to prosecute a claim for bank stock in England and obtained for it six hundred and fifty thousand dollars. His journal shows that he was a minute observer of men and things. His high legal attainments, scholastic and legislative reputation, gentlemanly deportment, thorough business habits—combined to make a favorable impression upon parliament, the English courts and barristers generally. He was absent less than a year and accomplished more business than some would have done in five. On his return he again took his place at the Bar.

In 1786 his worthy friend, Col. Howard, conveyed to him a square of ten lots in the city of Baltimore near the site of the public buildings, on condition of his locating there. He accepted the proposition and changed his residence to that city. This square is bounded by Eutaw, Lexington, Fayette and Paca streets. The mansion-house built by Mr. Chase is still owned by his descendants. In 1788 he was appointed Chief Justice of the new criminal court organized for the county of Baltimore. The same year he was a member of the Maryland Convention that ratified the Federal Constitution. In 1791 he was appointed Chief Justice of the General Court of Maryland. In 1796 he was appointed an Associate Judge of the Supreme Court of the United States by President Washington which dignified station he filled with great ability to the time of the illness which terminated his life. He was considered one of the ablest judges upon the bench. When he presided in the lower courts his decisions, when carried up to the higher legal tribunals, were seldom reversed. His expositions of law and charges to juries were plain, learned, luminous, logical, profound. His manner was forcible, impressive, commanding. With all this lustre clustering around him, encircled by the sacred halo of great and acknowledged services in the cause of Independence, still green and fresh in the memory of millions—Judge Chase was placed in the crucible of unrelenting ostracism prompted by political animosity created by the lofty independence of thought and expression constitutional with him and which prompted him to act a bold and conspicuous part when the vials of British wrath were poured out upon our bleeding country. As I shall attempt carrying him through his persecutions unscathed the critical attention of the reader is requested. He was a federalist—I am an old school democrat and go for the compromises and our UNION.

In January 1804, John Randolph obtained the passage of a resolution in the House of Representatives of the United States instituting an inquiry into the official conduct of Judge Chase. As a hypocritical salvo the name of Judge Peters was joined with his. No one was more competent and no one could be more persevering than was Mr. Randolph in his gigantic efforts to destroy Judge Chase. The committee to which the resolution was referred reported on the 6th day of the ensuing March, acquitting Judge Peters and recommending the impeachment of Judge Chase, the real object of political revenge. On the 26th of the same month articles of impeachment were reported based upon the following premises.

In 1800 Judge Chase presided on the bench of the U. S. Circuit Court at Philadelphia, assisted by Judge Peters of the District Court of Pennsylvania when and where John Fries was put upon his trial a second time for high treason against the Commonwealth of Pennsylvania, owing to some informality in his previous trial before Judges Iredel and Peters. Having been fully informed of the points of law at issue and of the proceedings at the first trial, Judge Chase had prepared an elaborate exposition of the law upon treason without referring to a single fact in the case. With the approval of Judge Peters he furnished a copy to the counsel for defendant, the District Attorney and reserved one for the jury after the trial should be completed. Messrs. Lewis and Dallas, counsel for the prisoner, affected to consider this a pre-judgment of the case and permitted Fries to be tried without the aid of counsel–unquestionably intending and successfully succeeding in creating a general sympathy that procured his pardon immediately after conviction. Fries subsequently called on Judge Chase and thanked him for his impartial and generous course upon the trial. The whole matter was then looked at in its true light–a *ruse* of ingenious counsel. No one attributed bad motives to the bench. The approval of honest clear-headed Judge Peters is conclusive proof that Judge Chase was judicially right–*prima facie* evidence that his motives were pure. He had written an opinion upon the *law*–not upon the *facts* of the case. This he had frankly furnished to the counsel–not to the jury before the trial. He was bound to explain the law to the grand jury before they should proceed to their business–to the traverse jury when he gave them their charge. This constituted the first charge in the articles of impeachment.

Shortly after the trial of Fries he presided at Richmond, Virginia, when and where one Callendar was tried under the Sedition Law for publishing a libel upon the President. During the trial Judge Chase refused the admission of certain testimony offered on the part of the prisoner which exasperated those who were opposed to the law in question. He honestly believed the law salutary as a check upon the venality of the press–others thought differently. Right or wrong–his oath of office bound him to act *under* the law so long as it remained in force. That his decision was legally correct must be presumed from the fact that under the great excitement then existing no writ of error was taken in the case. This formed the foundation of the second charge.

From Richmond he proceeded to New Castle, Delaware, where he presided, aided by Judge Bedford. In his charge to the grand jury he gave his views frankly upon the Sedition Law that they might fully understand what constituted a breach of its provisions, knowing that one or more cases of its violation would come before them. As an illustration he alluded to certain matter published in a high-toned party paper printed in that district that violated the provisions of this law. This gave great offence to the opposite party. The allusion to the paper was legal under any circumstances by way of explanation but may be considered uncourteous until we understand that it went immediately into the hands of the grand jury as testimony which made it in all respects a legitimate document to be alluded to by him. Ingenuity could not *then* nor with its prolific growth could it *now* construe the act into a pre-judgment of the case. The publication was before him—he alluded to *that* but to no individual. It was clearly a violation of the meaning and intent of the law—who published it was left for the jury to determine if they could. This constituted the ground of the third article of impeachment.

In delivering his charge to the grand jury in 1803, Judge Chase made sundry remarks upon the politics of the day reflecting upon certain acts of the democratic party. This was a surplusage of duty but not cause for impeachment. It resulted from his sanguine temperament, the great political excitement of that period—not from any impurity of motive. He believed laws had been passed for party purposes that were unconstitutional. If *he* was in error then, his position has often been verified since. Freedom of speech is a constitutional privilege—he used the same liberty practised by his opponents and which was not then trammelled by the obnoxious Sedition Law. It was not a proper time or place to read a political lecture but it does not follow that his designs were corrupt or his conduct criminal. The ermine of a judge is not beautified by being powdered with the farina of politics—his right to think and speak upon the subject none will question. If he speaks at an improper time and place it is an error—not a crime. He animadverted upon the change of the right of suffrage in the constitution of his own state to which he had strong objections. With him many of the devoted patriots of the revolution deemed the elective franchise unsafe with ignorant men who did not fully comprehend and appreciate their rights. The reasons for this opinion grow less as intelligence increases. In some of the states a property qualification is still necessary to entitle a man to vote and in others he must be a freeholder to entitle him to hold certain town offices. An anxiety to preserve the government pure unquestionably pervaded the bosom of Judge Chase.

In concluding his charge he spoke strongly against the changes that had been made in the judiciary system of the United States. He attributed them to party politics—deemed them personal in their object and not conducive to public good in their operations. As these related to his official duties they were legitimate points for remark. It was a matter of course that a man like him should comment freely and severely upon what he conceived a personal and public wrong. He never dined at the half-way house. In all that has been presented I can find nothing to impugn the honesty of his intentions or the purity of his motives.

Upon these premises six articles of impeachment were framed at first and at the next session of Congress two more were added—the natural increase of a year. On the 2d of January 1805 Judge Chase was arraigned before the Senate of the United States. A majority of the members were politically opposed to him but amongst them were men who loved justice more than party. The herculean powers of John Randolph were brought to bear upon him in the full plenipotence of their force. The trial continued until the first of March except a short recess. A portion of this time the Judge was confined by illness. He was ably and successfully defended by Messrs. Martin, Hopkinson, Harper and Key. Of five of the charges he was acquitted by a majority of the Senate. A constitutional number could not be obtained to convict him on the others—he stood approved, acquitted, triumphant over his enemies at the highest tribunal of his country—looking upon his collossal vanquished political foes, with mingled pity and contempt. He had never doubted the favorable result and properly regarded the prosecution as a political bagatelle.

From that period to the time of his last illness his peace was undisturbed. He continued to be an ornament to the judiciary, an honor to his country, the faithful friend of human rights and equal justice. On the 19th of June 1811, surrounded by his family and friends, he bade a last farewell to sublunary things and died peaceful and happy. A large number of relatives, an extensive circle of friends and a grateful nation mourned his loss.

In the character of this great and good man we find no corruption to condemn—many strong and brilliant traits to admire. As a revolutionary patriot he stood on a lofty eminence—as a statesman he rendered many and important services—as a lawyer he enjoyed a high reputation—as a judge he sustained an exalted position. All the charges against him have been faithfully spread before the reader. The result of their investigation caused his powerful enemies to weave for him a higher eulogium than language can express. I find no evidence of guile in his heart. He felt strongly—expressed his opinions freely and acted sincerely so far as we can judge from the record.

Against his private character slander and malice never directed an arrow. He was in all respects above suspicion. He was a kind husband, an affectionate father, a warm friend—an open, honorable, scarifying opponent. His sanguine temperament was calculated to gain strong friends and violent enemies. He handled his political opposers with great severity which accounts for the mighty effort made to ostracise him from the Bench. He possessed a noble and benevolent disposition—was a friend to the poor and needy, to education and to everything that enhanced the happiness of those around him and the human family. Under his benefaction the celebrated William Pinkey was educated and made a man. He often referred gratefully to his benefactor in after life. He was an active member of St. Paul's church and did much to promote practical piety, sound morals and social order. His force, vigor, decision of character and stern integrity were well calculated for the period in which he lived. If he sometimes offended by soaring above the non-committal system of technical politics, it resulted from the strong combination of conflicting circumstances that uniformly attend the period of a revolution, the formation of a new government and the asperity of high toned party feeling operating upon the sensitive feelings of an ardent, patriotic, honest, independent mind.

ABRAHAM CLARK.

A large proportion of the most substantial and useful men who have filled the measure of their country's glory and enrolled their names on the scroll of fame, were not ushered into public notice under the streamer of a collegiate diploma fluttering in the fickle wind of popularity. A clear head, strong common sense, an investigating and analyzing mind, with a judgment matured in the school of experience, are the grand requisites to prepare a man for sterling usefulness. Without these you vainly pour upon him the classic stream. It is like water poured upon the interminable sand—it invigorates for a moment, then sinks and leaves the surface dry and unproductive. If there is no substratum to retain the appliances of irrigation, the soil is not worth the labor. I do not undervalue high seminaries of learning and highly appreciate a liberal education. I only wish to correct the opposite extreme that is gaining rapidly among us, of placing too *high* a value upon them, making a classical course the grand requisite of prospective usefulness. I also wish to encourage those who have talent and only a good English education, to expand their wings of usefulness and imitate the examples of Franklin, Sherman, Abraham Clark and others who have graced the theatre of human action without the aid of a collegiate education. If they do not soar like eagles they may still be useful for there is more good to be achieved and more need of labor in low life than high. An humble bird saved Rome.

Abraham Clark was born at Elizabethtown, Essex county, New Jersey on the 15th of February 1726. He was the only son of Thomas Clark who held the office of Alderman, at that time a dignified station filled by men of merit. He was a farmer, a man of strong common sense and instilled into the mind of his son the enduring principles of moral rectitude that governed his actions through life. He received a good English education and was designed for the ennobling pursuit of agriculture. Of a slender frame and feeble constitution he was unable to endure hard labor but continued to superintend the improvement of the paternal domain left him by his father. He was an accomplished mathematician and was extensively employed in surveying and conveyancing. He was also an elementary lawyer and a safe gratuitous counsellor. He often saved his friends from the vexatious labyrinth of litigation by assuaging the angry elements of passion and leading them to the pure fountain of equal justice. He was called the poor man's counsellor and did much to allay disputes and promote harmony among his neighbors. He enjoyed the blessing pronounced on peace makers. His decisions were based on correct legal principles and impartial justice. He was often selected an arbitrator in different counties to settle disputed land titles. His knowledge and legal acquirements, united by an acute judgment, became so highly appreciated, that he was appointed by the Assembly to settle the claims to undivided commons. He filled the office of sheriff—was appointed clerk of the Legislature—doing credit to himself and dignifying every station he occupied. As he became known to the public his talents were more highly appreciated—not because they kindled to a blaze calculated to excite the huzzas of the multitude one day and possibly receive their execrations the next—but because they exemplified unwavering rectitude, strict justice, moral worth and disinterested patriotism.

When the vials of oppression were poured upon his native colony by the mother country Mr. Clark was among the first to contend for liberal principles and equal rights. Cool, reflective and deliberate—he had the confidence of his fellow citizens and exercised a wise and salutary influence over them. His actions flowed from the pure fountain of a good heart guided by a clear head and a mature judgment. He weighed impartially and felt most keenly British injustice towards the colonies. He was an active and bold leader in primary meetings firmly opposing the unreasonable claims of the crown. He was a prominent member of the Committee of Safety and did much to consolidate that phalanx of sages and heroes which stood firm and unbroken amidst the storms of wrath poured on them for seven years. He had a peculiar talent to rouse his fellow citizens to action on all proper occasions, always moving within the orbit of sound discretion.

In June 1776 he took his seat in the continental Congress where he fully sustained his previous high reputation for patriotism and good sense. To such men as him we owe the liberty we now enjoy. Revolution is too often the offspring of faction. When so, the successful actors, after annihilating the power assailed often plunge into tenfold corruption. Demagogues may rouse the angry passions of the multitude to a curling flame but it requires such men as Franklin, Sherman and Clark to ride upon the whirlwind, direct the tornado and rule the storm of passion. They could guide the liquid streams of mental fire and conduct them harmless in their course.

Although the American Revolution did not originate in fanaticism—the centrifugal zeal of many of its able advocates carried them beyond the orbit of prudence. Upon such men Mr. Clark exercised a happy influence. Although they may not be able to make a flowery speech of three hours or three days at the expense of thousands to our nation—yet it is to such men we must look for the perpetuity of our UNION. It is for them to steer the ship of State clear from the rocks and shoals of error and avoid the breakers of rashness, intrigue and corruption. They are the neutralizers of the inflammatory gases that fly from the fiery craniums of many of our legislators who are more classical than discreet—more in the forum than in the committe room—more anxious to advance their *party* than the good of their country.

Mr. Clark was warmly in favor of the Declaration of Independence. For this strong and important measure he had long been prepared from a strong conviction that no reasonable or honorable terms would be sanctioned by the ambitious and haughty ministry of Great Britain. He believed that abject slavery awaited the colonists unless the gordian knot of allegiance was cut at one bold stroke. On the 4th of July 1776, his affirmative vote and signature upon the chart of Liberty proved his sincerity and gained for him the approval of his conscience and the approbation of admiring millions.

He was continued in Congress for seven consecutive years, except spending one session in the state legislature. Owing to his naturally strong and highly cultivated mind, great industry and extensive fund of practical knowledge, he was one of the most useful members of the national legislature. From 1783 to 1788 he was a member of the legislature in his own state. So great was his influence that every act that excited public attention was attributed to him.

Mr. Clark was a strong advocate for the Convention that framed the Federal Constitution. He was appointed a member but extreme illness prevented his attendance. In 1788 he was again elected to Congress. At the next congressional election he was defeated for the first time. This reminds me of the law of Ostracism in the Republic of Athens under which many of its citizens were banished by the same demagogue party spirit that has banished many of our best men from the political arena. Mr. Clark was then appointed to the important station of commissioner to settle the state accounts with the general government. At the ensuing election the people, upon a sober second thought, again elected him to Congress of which he remained a member up to the time of his death. He died in June 1774 from the effects of *coup de soliel* [a stroke of the sun] in two hours from the time he was taken ill.

Mr. Clarke was truly pious, a pure patriot and an honest man. He was a faithful public sentinel, a kind and affectionate friend, an honorable and generous opponent. His death was deeply mourned by our nation and most keenly felt by his numerous personal friends. His fame is worthy of the highest encomiums—his example should be more closely imitated.

GEORGE CLYMER.

LEARNING makes the man, is an adage too old to be used as a quotation but which time or angels can never stamp with truth. Unless the *man* is made by the Creator of all good, learning cannot do it. The mental powers of man are as diversified as the soils of earth and as well deserve classification. Upon the minds of some we may pour a continued stream from the fountain of knowledge but like the desert of Sahara they are barren of fruit or flower. Upon other minds laborious efforts produce an improvement but never enrich them. Their upper crust is too light–their substratum too porous to retain the fructifying substances lavished upon them. Others yield a liberal harvest by good culture and become valuable by use. Like the alluvial prairies, others are adorned with fruits and flowers. They only require the introduction of seed to afford all the rich varieties of products that may be desired. Expose them to the genial rays of the sun of science–the germs of genius will immediately spring up–the embryo forms will bud and blossom like the rose.

The mental powers of George Clymer were composed of a deep and prolific mould capable of producing the richest fruits. Fortunately for our country it was not appropriated entirely to ornamental flowers and blooming shrubbery but to the substantial fruits that invigorate and support life. He was born in Philadelphia, Pa. in 1739. His father removed to that city from Bristol, England and died when George was but seven years old. William Coleman, his maternal uncle, took him into his family, treated him as a son and made him heir to most of his property. Being a literary man he gave his nephew every facility for the acquirement of a good education. He had an extensive library and rejoiced to see it explored by young George who manifested an early taste for reading and investigated critically every subject that came before him. He traced it through all its meanderings to its primeval source. This trait in his character rendered him vastly useful in the momentous concerns of his subsequent life. He dug deep and laid firmly the foundations of his education–the superstructure was on a firm basis.

From the seminary George went into the counting-house of his uncle and became thoroughly acquainted with the mercantile business in which he finally embarked. This calling was too precarious to suit his equipoised mind. He was opposed to sudden gains or losses– the one elated the mind too much–the other depressed it too low– destroying the divine equilibrium calculated to impart the greatest happiness to man and assimilate him to his Creator. He believed a virtuous equality in life more conducive to the prosperity of a nation than to have the majority of wealth wielded by a favored few. The former tended to republicanism–the latter to aristocracy. He was in favor of equal rights, a patriot of the Roman school, a philanthropist of the first water–opposed to all monopolies. His genius was of that original order, that, like some comets, visit our world only at long intervals. It traversed the circuit of human nature, metaphysics, philosophy, physiology, ethics and general science without an apparent effort—drawing from each conclusions peculiarly its own. He was a *virtuoso,* an amateur, a deep logician and an acute mathematician. A love of liberty was innate with him. His mind was richly stored with the history of other times and nations—he was well versed in the principles of law and government—he understood the chartered rights of his country and felt, most keenly, the increasing infringements upon them by the very power that was bound by the laws of nature, man and God to respect them. He was among the first to resist the oppressors of his country and proclaim to his fellow-citizens the principles of freedom. At the *tea meeting* held by the people of Philadelphia on the 16th of Oct. 1773, his powerful reasoning, deep sincerity, ardent zeal and enthusiastic patriotism—commanded the admiration of all who heard him. Free from pedantry and naturally retiring—his powers of mind were known only to his immediate friends. From that time his talents were claimed as public property. He was compelled to surrender possession without the formality of a *mandamus, quo warranto certiorari* or appeal.

When the final crisis arrived—when the shrill war-cry came rushing through the air from the heights of Lexington, Mr. Clymer took command of a company under Gen. Cadwalader and repaired to the tented field. He was a member of the Council of Safety and had served on most of the committees to prepare petitions, remonstrances and other measures of redress. On the 29th of July 1775 Congress called him from the camp to aid Michael Hillegas in managing the public treasury. He subscribed liberally to the loan raised for the public service and placed all the specie he could raise into the public chest and took in return ephemeral paper. His examples and influence caused many to rush to the rescue regardless of consequences. In July 1776 he was elected to Congress after the 4th and on taking his seat placed his name upon the Declaration of Independence. A part of the preceding delegation from Pennsylvania, finding the Declaration of Rights would be adopted, were seized with crown fits and nothing but absquatulating powders promised any relief to the spasmodic attack. As security for the payment of this medicine they put in leg bail and vanished. The people promptly filled their places with men who dared to be free.

In September of that year Messrs. Clymer and Stockton were sent by Congress to visit the northern army and confer with Gen. Washington upon future arrangements. In December of the same year Congress retired to Baltimore in consequence of the approach of the enemy, then devastating New Jersey. Mr. Clymer was one of the committee left to superintend the public interests and brave the perils that were rushing on like a tornado. He was re-elected to Congress and in April 1777 was again upon a visiting committee to the army to confer with Washington upon all subjects that required prompt attention which were neither few, small or far between. In the autumn of that year a fresh momentum was given to the patriotism of Mr. Clymer. He had removed his family and goods to Chester county. Immediately after the battle of Brandywine the tories led the British to his house who destroyed a large amount of his property. His family fled just in time to be saved the worse than savage tortures inflicted upon every prominent patriot's wife and mother they could seize. This sacrifice upon the altar of liberty strengthened him in the cause of freedom imparting fresh vigor to his exertions. Such conduct on the part of the British operated as a talisman in consolidating the colonies in one solid phalanx of unyielding opposition. Its eloquence soared above all words–it was action–action–action–demoniac action.

In December 1779 Mr. Clymer was one of a committee sent to Fort Pitt to induce the Indians to desist from hostilities. The mission consumed four months and was principally executed by him alone, narrowly escaping the tomahawk during his absence. It was found necessary to carry the war into the Indian settlements. During the year after his return he devoted his time in raising supplies for the army then in a very destitute condition. In 1780 he was again returned to Congress and served until November when he was associated with John Nixon in the organization of the Bank of North America which contributed largely in raising the prostrate credit of the government and yet stands upon a firm basis with fair prospects of surviving whilst our Republic continues. In May 1782 he was associated with Mr. Rutledge on a mission through the Southern States to induce them to meet more promptly the requisitions for supplies. During the entire period of the Revolution he devoted his whole time to the service of his country and discharged every duty faithfully. He stood high as an able and efficient co-worker in the vineyard of Liberty and when the harvest was past and the war ended, he retired from the field crowned with living honors enduring as the historic page.

When peace was proclaimed he removed to Princeton, N. J. for the purpose of resting from his toils and educating his children. The ensuing year he was persuaded to return to Philadelphia. He was immediately elected to the legislature and contributed largely in cutting from the old Constitution and laws of his native state the obnoxious branches of tyranny that still clustered around them. He stripped the penal code of its inquisitorial features and originated and successfully advocated the abolishment of death in all cases except for murder in the first degree. He was the father of the salutary penitentiary system now in full force at Cherry Hill near the city of Philadelphia-solitary confinement and labor. It may not be known to every reader that prisoners were formerly compelled to labor in chains, often in public places. The superiority of solitary confinement over all other modes of punishment has been fully demonstrated and is in a slow course of adoption throughout the confines of civilized humanity.

The mind of Mr. Clymer was prolific and happy in plans of usefulness and utility. To benefit his country and better the condition of mankind was his constant aim. To effect this he saw the necessity of reducing every department of government to system and order. American Independence was achieved—to preserve it by reconciling conflicting interests, green eyed jealousies, incongruous clamors and imaginary evils, was a herculean task only in embryo. He hailed with joy the convention to form the Federal Constitution and had the pleasure of being a member. The result of the labors of that body was charged with a deeper interest than the war-struggle for victory over the invading armies of England. It involved the fate of our infant Republic—then trembling on the verge of ruin. One more plunge and it would have been lost in the gulf of primeval chaos. The conflict was between members of the same family who had fought the enemy in one solid unbroken phalanx—now this band of brothers were separated by local interests and sectional jealousies. To bring the issue to a safe termination it required the deepest sagacity, the acutest wisdom, the most matured judgment, the profoundest legal learning, the most disinterested patriotism, the most exalted charity and the purest spirit of conciliation. Happily for our country and the cause of liberty these noble principles predominated—the glorious work was accomplished in which Mr. Clymer participated largely.

This noble patriot was elected to the first Congress that convened under the Federal Constitution. He was a stern republican in every thing. He was very properly opposed to tacking any titles to the name of any public man except that of the office which he held. Excellency, Honorable, &c., he considered to be what they really are—shadows of a shadow, too vain and imbecile for a freeman. He was wisely opposed to the right of instruction from his constituents because they must decide without hearing evidence or argument and were themselves uniformly directed by a few designing men actuated by motives based on prejudice or ignorance. He could not be made the passive tool of demagogue power or the automaton of party spirit. We greatly need many more of the same sort at the present time. In the organization of the general government he took a very active part. Every subject presented to Congress he analyzed with the acumen of a sage, philosopher and statesman. He was continued a member until 1790, when he made an effort to close his public career. But this he was not permitted to do. Under the Act of Congress passed in 1791, imposing a duty on distilled spirits Mr. Clymer was appointed to enforce its collection in his own state. In Pennsylvania this law produced the *whiskey rebellion* which required military force to restore order. No display of force could prevent Mr. Clymer from the performance of his duty. He appointed collectors in the different counties, advising the people to submit to the law whilst in force and pursue the constitutional remedy for its repeal if they believed it wrong. During the height of the excitement he mingled freely with the mobocracy when but few men would have been spared if clothed with the same office. When order was restored he resigned his situation. The last public service he consented to render was in conjunction with Colonels Pickens and Hasskins in negotiating a treaty with the Creek Indians which was consummated on the 29th of June 1796. He then retired to enjoy the fruits of his labors without any to disturb or make him afraid. He had periled his life, fortune and honor for his country—he had been her fearless advocate amidst the storms of revolution, civil discord and open rebellion—in his retirement he saw her peaceful, prosperous and happy with the illustrious Washington directing her destiny to fame and glory. The measure of his ardent desires was filled—he asked no more.

Although retired from the more prominent public arena, Mr. Clymer did not seek for inglorious ease—he remained active through life. He took a deep interest in every kind of improvement and to many extended his fostering care. He was a friend to the laboring classes and became familiar with the principles of agriculture and the mechanic trades. Among his private papers are many drawings of plans for bridges, canals, and various kinds of machinery and implements of husbandry with numerous recipes relative to the fine arts. Like Franklin he extended his researches to almost every subject within the grasp of man and extracted the essential oil from each. He always sought for solid substance that was of substantial use. He was opposed to pedantry, pomp and parade. He was what would now be called a plain blunt man. His bluntness was not of an offensive kind to common sense men. It consisted in laconic truth dressed in republican simplicity—a garb that was much admired *then* but is quite out of fashion *now*—a change of rather doubtful utility Although he originated many important measures in the national and state legislatures, he seldom spoke in the forum and was often unknown to the public when the author of wise and salutary propositions. He was ambitious only to do good and was not anxious that his name should be wafted on the breeze of popular applause or sounded in the high places of the earth. To be instrumental in benefitting the human family was the *ultimatum* of his soul.

When the importance of a subject induced Mr. Clymer to rise in debate he was listened to with profound attention. As a speaker his example is worthy of all imitation. Without any effort at refined eloquence he expressed in strong language what he strongly felt. He came directly to the point–adhered closely to it in a strain of keen, cutting, conclusive and laconic reasoning avoiding recrimination–was always brief, often casting into the shade in a few moments the labored and finely dressed speeches of his opponents that had cost them days, perhaps weeks to prepare and hours to deliver. He aimed his blows at the syllabus of their finely spun arguments and often demolished their ornamented superstructure at one bold stroke with the damask blade of sound logic drawn from the scabbard of plain common sense and wielded by the vigorous arm of lucid reason.

This useful man closed his earthly career at the residence of his son in Morrisville, Berks County, Pa., on the 23d of January 1813–most deeply mourned by those who knew him best. He was of the middle size, well formed, fair complexion, with a countenance attractive, intelligent, ingenuous, pleasing and expressive of a strong mind. In the private walks of life he was a model of human excellence. He was proverbial for punctuality in all things, if only to take a walk with a friend or present a promised toy to a child. In conversation he was agreeable and instructive–illuminating and enlivening the social circle with apothegms, aphorisms and pungent anecdotes–imparting pleasure and intelligence to all around him. In all this he was modest, chaste and discreet–avoiding any appearance of superiority, never making personal allusions even to his opponents. He spoke ill of no one and rebuked slander whenever he discovered it. His morals were of the purest order– his philanthropy of the loftiest kind. As a public servant, a private citizen, a kind husband, a faithful father, a warm friend, an honorable opponent and a noble patriot–George Clymer had no superior. He visited the widow and the fatherless in their distress and relieved them. He kept himself unspotted from the world and did all the good in his power. His were the fruits of primitive Christianity as taught by the Apostles. Let his examples be imitated by all–then our UNION is safe.

JOHN DICKINSON.

Frugality is an old fashioned virtue that is deeply covered with the alluvion of modern extravagance. With a large proportion of the community—economy is no longer a governing principle. More generally is this the case with public bodies and associations. When we look at the enormous and worse than useless expense of public buildings a large proportion of them are marked with an extravagance far from republican simplicity—large expenditures without enlarging comfort or convenience. Girard College is an example in point. A large portion of the money expended on that too splendid structure, was diverted from its legitimate channel—*the support and education of the poor orphan*. It is a tolerated—not an excusable error. So with many other public buildings erected with money drawn directly and indirectly from the hard earnings of the people. As inconsistent as it is—professing Christians have adopted this error with a vengeance—although the great Author of Christianity was born in a stable—cradled in a manger and preached his thrilling soul-cheering sermons in the open air. As churches are now conducted—how great the change—how alarming the contrast. The landmarks of primitive Christianity are buried by the alluvion of human inventions. Millions are expended in building extravagant edifices—furnishing them with velvet, damask or other cushions—the congregation involved in debt—the poor necessarily excluded—when half the amount contracted would have been sufficient and the other half should have been expended to alleviate the wants of the suffering poor and in sending the Gospel of Peace to the destitute. Extravagant professed followers of the lowly Jesus—think of this when you rise from reposing—perhaps *sleeping* on your gaudy church cushions. Think of the birth place of your Lord—of his life of poverty—his friendship to the poor—his constant efforts to do them good—of the habits and limited comforts of his disciples—and more—think how destitute you are of the very foundation of true religion—HUMILITY. How will you answer for these things at the searching tribunal of the great Jehovah? Even your funerals are marked with an extravagance that should be reduced to an amount that would leave a sum sufficient to make your poor neighbors comfortable for a long time. If you would honor the religion of the immaculate Redeemer—learn and practice frugality—enlarge your charity and adorn your conduct with consistency.

With the *true* patriots of the American Revolution frugality was proverbial. Independence Hall, built of plain brick and mortar, was deemed sufficiently splendid for the accommodation of the master spirits of that eventful era. A plain yard, with native forest trees for an ornament, was satisfactory. Now nothing but a marble structure, surrounded by extensive highly ornamented pleasure grounds, at an expense of MILLIONS, will answer for the legislators of this anti-republican era. The dear people are no longer consulted relative to the expenses of our government—to *pay* is their only privilege. Imported extravagance—imported customs—apish imitations of European usages—are fast driving republican simplicity from our once happy land. If the people tamely submit to these gross innovations they will ultimately reap the bitter fruits of their culpable neglect of duty.

Among the sages of the American Revolution, John Dickinson figured conspicuously. He was born in Maryland in 1732. After acquiring a good education he read law and had a lucrative practice in the city of Philadelphia. He was elected to the legislature at an early age and became a prominent member—an eloquent speaker and ready writer. He was a member of the General Congress in 1765 when he boldly exposed the unwarranted conduct of crown officers urged on by corrupt ministers. In 1767 he published a series of letters—boldly exposing the unconstitutional features of sundry acts of parliament. They contributed largely towards preparing the people for that resistance which resulted in FREEDOM.

Mr. Dickinson was a member of the important preliminary Congress of 1774 and wrote the lucid petition to the King that emanated from that body. He was the author of the declaration published by the Congress of 1775 which ably set forth the causes that impelled the down-trodden colonists to take up arms and resolve on victory or death. The second petition to the King was from his pen and adopted by Congress. All his writings were well suited to the occasions that induced them and were eminently calculated to advance the cause of the patriots. He was slow to believe England could not be brought to see and relinquish her suicidal course. He believed the Declaration of Independence premature and did not vote for it. He had great confidence in his own persuasive powers. His opposition to the Declaration of Rights caused his constituents to give him leave of absence. He subsequently sanctioned it and repented of his error. In 1779 he was again elected to Congress and became a zealous, active, useful member. The following extract from an address, adopted by Congress on the 26th of May 1779, is from his pen.

" Infatuated as your enemies have been from the beginning of this contest do you imagine they can flatter themselves with a hope of conquering you unless you are false to yourselves? When unprepared, undisciplined and unsupported—you opposed their fleets and armies in full conjoined force—then, if at any time, was conquest to be apprehended. Yet, what progress towards it have their violent and incessant efforts made? Judge from their own conduct. Having devoted you to bondage and after vainly wasting their blood and treasure in the dishonorable enterprise—they deigned at length to offer terms of accommodation with respectful addresses to that once despised body—the Congress—whose humble supplications, only for peace and safety, they had contemptuously rejected under pretence of its being an unconstitutional assembly. Nay more—desirous of seducing you into a deviation from the paths of rectitude from which they had so far and rashly wandered, they made most specious offers to tempt you into a violation of your faith given to your illustrious ally."

"Foiled again and stung with rage, embittered by envy—they had no alternative but to renounce the inglorious and ruinous controversy or to resume their former modes of prosecuting it. They chose the latter. Again the savages are stimulated to horrid massacres of women and children and domestics to the murder of their masters. Again our brave and unhappy brethren are doomed to miserable deaths in jails and prison-ships. To complete the sanguinary system—all the 'EXTREMITIES of war' are denounced against you by authority. * * Rouse yourselves, therefore, that this campaign may finish the great work you have so nobly carried on for several years past. What nation ever engaged in such a contest under such a complication of disadvantages so soon surmounted many of them and in so short a period of time had so certain a prospect of a speedy and happy conclusion. We will venture to pronounce that so remarkable an instance exists not in the annals of mankind. * * * Consider how much you have done and how comparatively little remains to be done to crown you with success. Persevere and you insure peace, FREEDOM, safety, glory, sovereignty and felicity to yourselves, your children and your children's children." * * *

"Fill up your battalions—be prepared in every part to repel the incursions of your enemies—place your several quotas in the constitutional treasury—lend money for public uses—sink the emissions of your several states—provide effectually for expediting the conveyance of supplies for your armies and fleets and for your allies—prevent the produce of your country from being monopolized—effectually superintend the behaviour of public officers (what a poser if the dear people should do this imperious duty now) diligently promote piety, virtue, brotherly love, learning, FRUGALITY and moderation and may you be approved before Almighty God—worthy of those blessings we devoutly wish you to enjoy."

Here is a bright specimen of the republican principles that governed the public officers and people of the Revolution. They are too simple for the present portentous era of imported extravagance and customs—too pure for the politicians of our time. They will be read with approving admiration—but few will put them in practice.

Mr. Dickinson filled the office of President of Pennsylvania and subsequently removed to the state of Delaware and there filled the same chair. His political writings were collected and published in 1810 making two volumes octavo. His famous "Farmer's Letters to the Inhabitants of the British Colonies" were so highly prized by the astute Franklin that he had them republished in London and sent a French translation to Paris. But few of the sages did as much with their pen as this patriot. He lived to enjoy the fruits of his labors to a good old age. He resided at Wilmington, Delaware, for a long time where he closed his earthly pilgrimage on the 15th of February 1808. He was a member of the Society of Friends. His private character was without reproach.

WILLIAM ELLERY.

CONTRACTS fairly entered into by parties competent to make and consummate them should be sacredly fulfilled in the minutest particulars. Individuals and social compacts from the common business firm up to the most exalted national engagements are bound by the laws of God, man and honor to keep inviolate their plighted faith. A deviation from the path of rectitude in this particular is uniformly attended with evil consequences and often with those most disastrous. The party that violates its obligations without a justifiable reason and especially if it attempts to advance its own interests regardless of, perhaps injurious to those of the other, comes to court with a bad cause. I have repeatedly remarked that the American Revolution resulted from a violation of colonial chartered rights by the mother country. To enter into a full exposition of the relations between the two high contracting parties would require more space than can be allowed in this work. Reference to some of the cardinal points in a single charter will give the reader a clue to them all. Some of a later date are rather more limited in privileges than that of Rhode Island to which I refer.

This charter secured religious freedom, personal liberty, personal rights in property—excluding the king from all interference with the local concerns of the colony and was virtually republican in its provisions. One of the early Acts of Parliament referring to Rhode Island contains the following language. "That no person within the said colony at any time hereafter shall be in any way molested, punished, disquieted or called in question for any difference of opinion in matters of religion that does not actually disturb the civil peace of said colony." The loyalty of the inhabitants up to the time oppressions commenced was unquestionable. The ancient records give full evidence of the fact. The addresses to the king begin thus. "The general Assembly judgeth it their duty to signify his majesty's gracious pleasure vouchsafed to us." Extract of a letter written to Sir Henry Vane in England. "We have long drunk of the cup of as great liberties as any people we can hear of under the whole heavens. We have not only been long free, together with all English, from the yokes of wolfish bishops and their popish ceremonies against whòse grievous oppressions God raised up your noble spirit in parliament but we have sitten down quiet and dry from the streams of blood spilt by war in our native country. We have not known what an excise means. We have almost forgotten what tythes are, yea or taxes either to church or common weal."

In addition to other declaratory acts of Parliament sanctioning and continuing chartered privileges generally in all the colonies, one was passed in March 1663, involving the very hinge upon which the question of the Revolution turned. Extract—"Be it further enacted—*That no taxes shall be imposed or required of the colonies but by the consent of the General Assembly*"—meaning the General Assembly of each colony separately and including the whole. This single sentence of that declaratory act, based upon a cardinal point in the British constitution and guarded by the sanctity of charter contracts that could not be annulled but by the mutual consent of the high contracting parties, solves the problem of the Revolution. Having lived in the full enjoyment of chartered privileges which had become matured by the age of more than a century, the colonists would have been unworthy the name of men had they tamely submitted to their annihilation. To the unfading honor of their names—*they did not submit.* A band of sages and heroes rose in all the majesty of man—met the invaders of their rights and drove them from Columbia's soil.

Among them was William Ellery, born at Newport Rhode Island on the 2d of December 1727. His ancestors were from Bristol, England. He was the son of William Ellery a graduate of Harvard College and an enterprising merchant. He filled many public stations and became one of the first men in the colony. Pleased with the docility of his son he became his instructor and prepared him for college. He entered Harvard and became a close and successful student. He was delighted with the classics and was enraptured with the history of the ancient republics. So great was his veneration for ancient authors that he continued his familiarity with them to the moment of his death. He was one of the most lucid classic philologists of that age. He graduated at twenty and commenced the study of law. In that ever expanding field of labor he was all industry and was admitted to the bar with brilliant prospects before him. Located in one of the most delightful towns on the Atlantic, surrounded by a large circle of friends who desired his success, blessed with superior talents improved by a refined education, esteemed by all who knew him—his situation was truly agreeable. He possessed an amiable disposition, a strong mind, a large share of wit and humor, polished manners and a vivid animation in conversation that dispelled ennui from every circle in which he moved. With these accomplishments he spread his sails to the public breeze.

He commenced a successful practice at the bar of Newport and realized the fond anticipations of his friends. He was highly honorable in his course and had the confidence of the citizens, the respect of his professional brethren and the esteem of the courts. To make more complete his standing and importance in community he entered into partnership with a most estimable lady until death should them part. The firm proved prosperous and happy. Up to the time British oppression commenced, his days passed peacefully and quietly along with an accumulating fortune flowing in. When the revolutionary storm loomed up from the horizon he became roused. A new impetus was given to his mental and physical powers. His townsmen were the first who had dared to beard the British lion. On the 17th of June 1769, in consequence of the oppressive conduct of her captain, the revenue sloop Liberty belonging to his Britannic majesty was forcibly seized by a number of citizens in disguise who cut away her masts, scuttled her, carried her boats to the upper part of the town and committed them to the flames under the towering branches of a newly planted LIBERTY TREE. This act was followed by another on the 9th of June 1772 in which blood was shed—that of seizing and burning the British schooner Gaspee. This was made a pretext for more severe measures by the hirelings of the crown who recommended to Parliament the disfranchisement of the colony. The revolutionary ball was in motion at Newport. In the midst of these turmoils Mr. Ellery was with the people and for freedom. He went for the preservation of rights that had become sacred and venerable by age and had the high sanction of the laws of man, of nature and of God. In 1774 he approved a suggestion made in a letter from Gen. Greene—*that the colonies should declare themselves independent.* This spirit took fast hold on the people of Rhode Island at the very inception of the Revolution.

In 1776 Mr. Ellery was elected to the Continental Congress. His constituents left him to act free as mountain air. He stood up to the post of duty boldly and became an active member. He was fully prepared to advocate and sanction the Declaration of Independence. An agreeable speaker, master of satire, sarcasm, logic and philosophy—he exercised a salutary and judicious influence. He was appointed on several important committees and rendered efficient service. Upon the marine committee he was the leading man. He was a strong advocate for the navy. Many of his constituents were bold mariners. He felt a just pride in referring to his fellow citizen—Commodore Ezek Hopkins, as the first commander of the little fleet of the infant republic. It was he who took New Providence by surprise—seized a large amount of war munitions amongst which were one hundred pieces of cannon—took the royal Governor, Lieutenant Governer and sundry others of his majesty's officers prisoners and gave an earnest of the future glory to be achieved by Yankee seamen.

When the time arrived for the final question upon the momentous instrument that was to be a warrant of death or the diploma of freedom, Mr. Ellery was at his post and fearlessly gave it his approving vote and sanctioning signature. With his usual vivacity he took his stand by the side of the Secretary, Charles Thomson, for the purpose of observing the apparent emotions of each member as he came up and signed the important document. He often referred to this circumstance in after life and said an undaunted resolution was observed on every countenance. He was continued a member of Congress until 1785—full evidence of the high estimation in which he was held by his constituents. In 1777 he was upon the committee that originated the plan of fitting out seven fire ships to annoy the British fleet and had the credit of suggesting and perfecting it.

When the enemy obtained possession of Newport their vengeance against this noble patriot was manifested by burning all his property within their reach. This did not move the equanimity of his mind only to make him more zealous in the glorious cause of liberty. In 1778 he strongly advocated a resolution making it death for any citizen-*alias* tory who should betray or aid in delivering into the hands of the enemy any of the adherents of the cause of freedom or give any intelligence that should lead to their capture. He spent nearly his whole time in Congress and toiled incessantly. In 1779 he was on the committee of foreign relations which had the settlement of some very unpleasant difficulties between the United States and the foreign commissioners. He was chairman of a committee to provide provisions for the inhabitants of Rhode Island who were destitute of the necessaries of life. From year to year he was arduously employed on most of the standing and many other important committees. Marine difficulties occurred between the general government and some of the states arising from a difference of opinion relative to the powers conferred by the Articles of Confederation. A committee was appointed to define those powers of which Mr. Ellery was the leading member. This committee determined that all disputed claims were subject to appeal from the Court of Admiralty to Congress where the facts and law were to be fully settled. On all occasions and in all situations he was diligent and punctual. When he discovered any long faces or forlorn countenances in Congress the artillery of his wit and humor was sure to pour a broadside upon them and often dispelled the lowering clouds that hung gloomily over the minds of members.

In 1782 he was an efficient member of the committee on public accounts the duties of which were large and perplexing. Speculation and peculation had rolled their dark waves over the public business of the nation—to do justice to all who presented claims was a problematical matter. In 1784 he was upon the committee to act upon the definitive treaty with Great Britain. He was upon the committee to define the power of the Treasury Board—the one upon Foreign Relations and the one upon the War Office. To crown his brilliant labors in Congress with resplendent glory, he advocated the resolution of Mr. King to abolish slavery in the United States. His whole force was brought to bear upon this subject in a strain of forensic eloquence and powerful logic that added fresh lustre to the substantial fame he had long enjoyed. *Then* the subject was legitimate for Congress—*now* it belongs to each state interested.

In 1785 Mr. Ellery retired from political life and repaired to his now peaceful home to replenish his ruined fortune and enjoy the blessings of the Independence he had so much aided in consummating. In the spring of 1786 Congress made him commissioner of the National

Loan Office for Rhode Island. Shortly after he was elected Chief Justice of the Supreme Court of his native state. On his accession to the Presidential chair, Washington appointed him Collector of Customs for Newport which station he ably filled until he took his tranquil departure to a brighter world. The evening of his life was as calm and mellow as an Italian sunset. Universally esteemed–he enjoyed a delightful intercourse with a large circle of friends. Honest, punctual and correct–he had the confidence of the commercial community in his official station. During the thirty years he was Collector of Customs, a loss of only two hundred dollars upon bond accrued to government and upon that bond he had taken five sureties. He spent much of his time in reading classic authors and in corresponding with eminent men. But three weeks before his death he wrote an essay upon Latin prosody and the faults of public speakers. His bible was a favorite companion from which he drew and drank the living waters of eternal life. Always cheerful, instructive and amusing–his company was a rich treat to all who enjoyed it. His writings combined a sprightliness and solidity rarely found.

His death was as remarkable as it was tranquil and glorious. It was that of a Christian and philosopher. On the morning of the 15th of February 1820 he rose in usual health and seated himself in the flag-bottom chair which he had used for fifty years and which was a relic rescued from the flames when the enemy fired his buildings. He commenced reading Tully's *Officiis* in his favorite Latin without the aid of glasses the print being no larger than that of a pocket bible. During the morning the family physician called in and seeing him very pale felt his wrist and found his pulse had ceased. He administered a little wine which gave a transient impetus to the purple current. The physician spoke encouragingly to whom Mr. Ellery replied–" It is idle to talk to me in this way. I am going off the stage of life and it is a a great blessing that I go free from sickness, pain and sorrow." Becoming extremely weak his daughter helped him on the bed where he sat upright and commenced reading *Cicero de Officiis* with the same composure as if in the full vigor of life. In a few moments his spirit left its tenement of clay without a motion, groan or sigh–his body still erect with the book under his chin as if asleep. William Ellery was dead–relations and friends wept–our nation mourned.

Thus usefully lived and happily died one of the brightest specimens of human excellence. His whole career presents a rare and rich picture upon which the imagination may feast with increasing delight and which cannot be rendered more beautiful or interesting by the finest touches of the pencil of fancy dipped in the most brilliant colors of romance. He was of the middle stature, well formed, with a large head, an intelligent and expressive countenance, moderate in his physical movements and with all his vivacity generally had a grave aspect. He was temperate, plain and uniform in his habits and dress and could seldom be induced to join in chase after the *ignis fatuus*–FASHION. For many years before his death his wardrobe was of an order belonging to a by-gone generation. His courtesy and hospitality were always conspicuous–the whole frame-work of his character was embellished with all the rich varieties of amiable and good qualities– uniting beauty with strength which ever gain esteem in life and tranquillity in death. Reader contemplate this bright picture until its impress is so deeply fixed upon your mind that nought but death can erase it.

WILLIAM FLOYD.

LEXICOGRAPHERS define ambition to be an earnest desire of power, honor, preferment, pride. Some who study party politics more than philosophy, physiology or ethics, call all the laudable desires of the heart AMBITION–aiming to strip the monster of its deformity that they may sail under false colors and play the pirate whenever an opportunity offers. The power that is gained by ambition is held by a slender tenure–often a mere rope of sand. Its hero may receive the homage of the multitude one day and be the victim of their fury the next. The summit of vain ambition is often the depth of misery. Based on a volcanic foundation it is in constant danger of an eruption. Inflated by a gaseous thirst for power, like a balloon with hydrogen, it is liable to an explosion from the very material that elevated it. Predicated on self–it spurns philanthropy, banishes charity, tramples on justice, despises patriotism, deals largely in the corrosive sublimate of falsehood, the elixir vitriol of revenge–the assafœtida of duplicity. Like a kite, it cannot rise in a calm and when up, is subject to fly from its fastenings and be rent by the cross currents ever in motion. The fulcrum of ignorance and the lever of party spirit form its magic power.

Some European writers have charged the patriots of the American Revolution with selfish ambition. They may be excused for this supposition from the fact that this is the motive power of *their* actions and they can understand no other. Very different was the fact. Private virtue, broad charity, genuine philanthropy, undisguised patriotism were marked characteristics of those who achieved our Liberty. They were actuated by pure and honest motives–not by wild ambition and political frenzy. Noisy partisans and intriguing demagogues were not the favorites of the people at that trying period. The man of genuine worth and modest merit was the one they delighted to honor and trust.

In the character of William Floyd these qualities were happily blended. He was born at Suffolk county, Long Island, State of New York on the 17th of December 1734. He was the son of Mr. Nicoll Floyd and the grandson of Richard Floyd who came from Wales in 1680 and settled at Setauket, Long Island. During his childhood William was remarkable for frankness, truth, docility and pleasing manners. He was an industrious student and acquired a liberal education. During the prosecution of his studies he devoted a short period almost daily to his gun in pursuit of game which gave him healthful exercise and a strong frame. His father died before William arrived at his majority leaving him an ample fortune. This he managed with prudence and economy. From his youth he had been the advocate of liberal principles. At manhood he became a prominent opposer to the innovations of the British ministers upon the chartered rights of Americans. As oppression increased his patriotic feelings were more frequently and freely expressed. He was an active and zealous member of the Congress of 1774. He had the unlimited confidence of his constituents–the esteem of all who knew him. His cool deliberation and calm deportment were well calculated to preserve an equilibrium among those of a more fiery temperament and rashness in action. That Congress was remarkable for clear and unanswerable argument, calm and astute discussion, wise and judicious plans–reasonable but firm purposes. The course pursued operated powerfully and favorably upon the minds of reflecting men whose influence it was important to secure.

Mr. Floyd had command of the militia of the county in which he lived. When the British attempted to land at Gardner's Bay he promptly assembled the yeoman troops and repelled the invading foe. In 1775 he was again at his post in Congress and became one of its very efficient members. He was a working man and almost constantly engaged on important committees. During his absence the enemy obtained possession of Long Island and compelled his family to flee to Connecticut for safety. His property was materially injured–his house converted into a military barrack and for seven years he was deprived of all resources from his farm. In 1776 he was a warm advocate of the Declaration and with great satisfaction placed his name upon that sacred instrument. In 1777 he was elected to the first Senate of the Empire State convened under the new order of things. He was a leading member and rendered important services in forming a code of republican laws.

In January 1779 he again took his seat in Congress and entered vigorously upon the work before him. In August of that year he resumed his seat in the New York Senate. Much important business was before the legislature, requiring experience, energy and unity of action. To raise the pecuniary credit of the state was of great importance. Mr. Floyd was at the head of a joint committee on this subject and reported a plan that proved him an able financier—a man of deep thought and investigation. It was based upon gradual, equal and just taxation. In October of that year he was one of three delegates appointed by his legislature to meet a convention of the Eastern States for the purpose of perfecting a system of furnishing supplies for the army without being compelled to suffer the enormous shaves of avaricious monopolists. On reading the account of the awful sufferings and privations of the army at certain periods of the Revolution and in view of the glory of the cause and the limited means of carrying on the unequal struggle, an honest man can scarcely believe men then existed who would speculate—yes more—*peculate* upon suffering humanity. So was the fact to an alarming extent—at least three millions a year. Avarice knows no mercy—seldom any honesty.

On his return from this convention he repaired to Congress. On the 3d of December he was elected one of the Board of Admiralty and on the 13th a member of the Treasury Board. By incessant application his health became impaired and in the ensuing April he obtained leave of absence. In June he took his seat in the New York Senate and was appointed upon a joint committee to act upon resolutions of Congress involving the important relations between the state and general government. He unsuccessfully opposed making bills of credit a legal tender but lived to see the law repealed. In September he was one of a committee of the senate to prepare a reply to the governor's message. To effect a proper organization of the general government was a desideratum with all the states. To this important subject the governor had specially referred. To confer upon Congress all necessary power clearly defined, was considered the only safe policy to insure future harmony and safety. This committee reported several resolutions upon this subject which were adopted and forwarded to Congress for consideration. They recommended the enactment of laws that should impose an equal responsibility on each of the states to bear its *pro rata* proportion of the war expenses in the way and manner prescribed by the general government.

In 1780 he again took his seat in Congress. An important and delicate duty devolved upon the New York and New Hampshire members under legislative acts–the subject of disputed territory comprising the present state of Vermont. The question was submitted to Congress, the members of each state advocating the claim for their constituents. In this matter Mr. Floyd rendered great service. During the same session he introduced a resolution for the cession of the western territories to the United States. On the 10th of August he nominated Robert L. Livingston to be Secretary of Foreign Affairs whose nomination was immediately confirmed. He was continued a member of Congress up to 1783 when he joined in the general soul-cheering peace and the freedom of his beloved country. He then retired and took possession of his once flourishing plantation amidst the sincere congratulations of his numerous friends, all animated by the resplendent glories of LIBERTY. That he might repair the ruin of his home he declined the urgent solicitations of his friends to return to Congress. He continued to serve in the senate of his native state up to 1788 when he was elected to the first Congress under the Federal Constitution. Worn out in the service of his country he retired from the public arena at the end of the term.

Owning a large tract of valuable wild land upon the banks of the Mohawk river he commenced gradual improvements upon it and in 1803 removed there. He was often urged to return to Congress but declined all legislative labors. With the exception of serving one year in the state senate and in the convention for the revision of the New York Constitution in 1801, he kept aloof from the turmoils of political life. He was four times a member of the Electoral College of his state for the election of President and Vice President. So ardent were his feelings in his old age that he travelled two hundred miles in the dreary month of December 1806 to give his vote for his old companion and friend–Thomas Jefferson.

He continued to improve his new home until he became surrounded by happy neighbors all basking in the clear sunshine of that freedom he had largely aided in acquiring. In all things he was systematic and practical–free from pomp and vanity–strong in his purposes and persevering in their accomplishment. He was blessed with a clear head, vigorous mind, good heart, sound judgment, great experience and a close knowledge of men and things. As a politician he was free from selfish ambition and went for his country–his whole country and the UNION for ever. He spoke but seldom in public assemblies and rarely entered into debate. Brighter would be the prospects of our UNION if we *now* had more men like William Floyd who would *talk* less and *work* more. Long and often electioneering speeches hang over our legislatures like an incubus and prevent the *few* who are well-disposed from doing the business of the people promptly.

General Floyd was of middle size, well-formed and commanding in his appearance. He was dignified in his deportment–affable in his manners. His physical powers were remarkable when in his prime. In all the relations of private life he was a model as worthy of imitation as that of his public career. He was warm in his friendship and rigidly honest. His morals were pure, his religion practical, his charity broad–his philanthropy co-extensive with the human family. For the last two years of his life his health was not good and on the 20th of August 1821 he was seized with general debility and on the 25th of that month, folded his arms quietly, closed his eyes peacefully and met the cold embrace of death with the fortitude of a sage, patriot and Christian.

Although Gen. Floyd did not possess the Ciceronean eloquence of a Lee or the Demosthenean powers of Adams and Henry, he was one of the most useful men of his day and generation. He marked out his path of duty from the reflections of his own mind and pursued it strictly and fearlessly. For more than fifty years he enjoyed the confidence of his fellow-citizens as a public man and but one year before his decease was made a member of the Electoral College. His example and his labors shed a lustre over his character as rich and enduring as those who were conspicuous in the forum. He was an important link in the golden chain of Liberty. He was a working man–working men were *then* properly appreciated. The congressional speakers of that day were also more highly appreciated than nine-tenths of them are now for the very good reason that they were laconic on all subjects. Long speeches were as uncommon as they are now frequent and useless. If we desire the prosperity of our country and the perpetuity of our UNION let us imitate the examples of the patriots whose actions we delight to rehearse and preserve in its pristine purity the rich boon of LIBERTY they have transmitted to us.

BENJAMIN FRANKLIN.

A man who is self-made and by his own exertions and untiring industry becomes a great man, often excels the mere student of the college in mental vigor as much as the hard fisted mechanic excels him physically.

The former, usually without the means and often without the advantages of paternal or maternal care, is compelled to become familiar with men and things, without a knowledge of which, the classics are a mere toy and the high branches of science only an ornament. With the never ending every day concerns of life where usefulness holds her dominion they have little to do. A man of letters who is unacquainted with the routine of business transactions is incapable of protecting his own interests–of course he cannot be useful to community until he goes through another and more important course of study. A great change is necessary in most of our colleges to make full men of students. Hence the blasted hopes of many a fond father who is led astray by the popular error–that colleges mould all their students into MEN. A large majority of the most useful citizens of our country, from its first settlement to the present time, never enjoyed a collegiate education. Especially was this the case with many of the sages and heroes of the Revolution whose memory we delight to honor and perpetuate.

Such was the case of Benjamin Franklin, born at Boston on 17th of January 1706–exactly ninety years before the writer. His father was among the Puritans who fled from persecution and sought repose in the wilds of Massachusetts. His parents were poor but honest and respectable. This may seem paradoxical to the aristocracy of the present day–but is unquestionably true. The time *was* when poverty was not a *crime* nor wealth a mask for corruption. Honesty and industry were *formerly* the brightest stars on the escutcheon of fame.

At an early age Benjamin Franklin exhibited a mind of superior cast and a strong desire for improvement. His pious parents advanced his education as far as their limited means would enable them being anxious to see this son prepared for the pulpit. At the age of ten years his father was compelled to take him from school to aid him in the chandler business. This did not arrest the onward course of his genius. Original in every trait of his character, eccentric in his manner, the child of bold experiment, he commenced the study of natural philosophy in the midst of candle wicks, tallow and soap. He first ascertained the precise quantity of sleep and food requisite to sustain nature and the kind of aliment most conducive to health. At that early age he adopted a system of temperance, frugality and economy, worthy the imitation of men. He accustomed himself to meet every disappointment without a murmur. He continued to improve his mind by reading during every hour he was not at labor. Nothing passed by him unnoticed. His expanding intellect drew philosophy from nature, things and men. He reasoned, analyzed, moralized and improved from everything he saw. Hence the vast and rapid expansion of his towering genius that ultimately commanded the awe of kings and the admiration of the world—comprehending the philosophy of mind, nature, science, art, government—all the relations of creation from the dust under his feet—the myriads of animalculæ in a drop of water, up to the bright seraphs in the skies and up to Nature's God.

A mind like his would not long be confined in a chandler shop. Open and honest at all times and under all circumstances, he apprised his father of his wish to change his occupation. He was bound to his brother to learn the art of printing. His industry enabled him to master his profession rapidly. All his leisure moments were employed in study, thus preparing himself for a useful and glorious career through future life—leaving a bright example worthy the imitation of every apprentice in our country.

So intently bent on the acquisition of knowledge—he often preferred his book to his meal and studied whole nights—defying the commands of Morpheus. He was paid a weekly sum for his board and adopting a simple vegetable diet was enabled to save money for the purchase of books. He selected them with reference to substantial usefulness. He studied with enthusiasm the Memorabilia of Xenophon and found a model in Socrates which he delighted in imitating.

About this time he was seized with the scribbling mania. Committing the usual error of youthful authors—he offered his first sacrifice to Calliope the goddess of heroic poetry. The production was applauded but his father turned his rhyming propensity into ridicule and encouraged him to write prose. Fearing the shafts of criticism, he had several articles published in the paper edited by his brother, in so clandestine a manner that the author was not suspected. Finding that they were admired, he says his vanity did not long keep the world ignorant of the writer.

Flattery from others caused him to assume an air of importance that soon resulted in an open rupture between him and his brother. For some time he endured a course of harsh treatment and at length resolved to free himself from the chains of bondage. He embraced the first opportunity for New York. Not being able to obtain business there he proceeded to Philadelphia on foot and alone. On his arrival he had but one dollar—was a stranger only seventeen years of age and knew not where to go. On entering Market street his eccentric appearance excited the gaze of the multitude as much as his gigantic talents subsequently did the gaze of the world. He had a roll of bread under each arm and proceeded to the margin of the Delaware river and partook of his bread and pure water. His pockets were enormously enlarged with the various articles of his wardrobe rendering him a fair representation of old Boniface.

There were then but two printing offices in Philadelphia. In one of these he obtained the situation of compositor. He now reduced his theories of economy to successful practice maintaining himself at a trifling expense—pursuing a correct and industrious career which gained for him the esteem of all his acquaintances. Among others, his talents attracted the attention of Sir William Keith, then Governor of the province, who invited him to his house and treated him with great kindness. The Governor was a man whose liberality in *promises* went beyond the dust in his purse. Anxious to see his young friend placed in more prosperous circumstances by his benefaction he proposed to set him up in business. He at once gave him letters to London. On his arrival there, Franklin found that no pecuniary arrangements had been made for him by his *tongue* benefactor. He was in a strange land, without money to pay his return passage. He took a new lesson in the school of experience in which he delighted to study. Disappointment did not deject him. He soon obtained employment and gained the confidence and esteem of his new acquaintances. At the end of eighteen months he embarked for Philadelphia. On his passage he digested a set of rules for future action substantially as follows. I resolve to be frugal—to speak truth at all times—never to raise expectations not to be realized—to be sincere, industrious, stable—to speak ill of no man—to cover rather than expose the faults of others and to do all the good I can to my fellow men.

Upon this foundation, formed of the unadulterated materials of *primitive* Christianity, he raised a superstructure, more beautiful and as enduring as the proudest memorials of Greece and Rome. When the whole human family shall adopt and fully exemplify these rules, we may hope to see millennial glory eclipse the meridian sun and cover the earth with one broad sheet of celestial light.

He arrived at Philadelphia on the 11th of October 1726 and became the clerk of the merchant who owned the goods brought over by the ship in which he took his passage. His proverbial industry made him as successful in the counting house as at the press–showing a rare versatility of talent. His future prospects in this new sphere of action brightened as time rolled on but were suddenly blasted by the death of his employer. He then returned to the types–worked a few months for his old patron where he found a partner with more money than skill and with him commenced a lucrative business. His industry and artistic talents were now put in full requisition. He manned his wheelbarrow in collecting material for business–put nature on short allowance and by punctuality and perseverance gained many valuable friends and money enough to purchase the interest of his partner who had become worthless and embarrassing to the firm.

Up to this time Franklin had been fortune's foot-ball. His life had been a complete checker board of changing vicissitudes, blasted hopes and keen disappointments. Amidst all the stormy trials that had tossed his youthful bark on the surges of misfortune–surrounded by the foaming breakers of vice in all its delusive and borrowed forms–he never became tarnished by corruption or the commission of a bad or mean action. The moral and religious principles deeply planted in his mind during childhood by parental instruction–were as lasting as life–a happy illustration of the faithfulness of parents towards their children. Fathers and mothers think of this and govern yourselves accordingly.

Having become liberated from his business partner, he felt the necessity and propriety of choosing one that would fill up the vacuum in his side and share with him the joys and sorrows flesh is heir to. In 1730, he entered into partnership for life with a widow lady whose maiden name was Read, for whom he had contracted an attachment previous to her first marriage. In him she found a kind husband–in her he found an agreeable and discreet companion.

Philanthropy predominated in the heart of Franklin. To better the condition of his fellow men gave him exquisite pleasure. The rules governing the "Junto" formed by him and now merged in the "Philosophical Society," exhibit a superior knowledge of human nature–illustrating clearly the duty of man to the creature and Creator. They breathe universal charity, kindness, benevolence and good will to all mankind. Among them is one for the suppression of intemperance–a prophetic prelude to the exertions of the present day in this noble cause. He had profited by the experience of the past which enabled him to steer clear of the rocks and quicksands of error on which many are ruined and lost. His bark had outrode many a storm–prosperity was his future lot. His new partner smiled upon him, his friends esteemed him, a life of usefulness was before him—in the pleasures of the present, past pains were lost.

In 1732 he commenced the publication of the "Poor Richard's Almanac" which he continued up to 1737, circulating 10,000 copies annually. Although under a humble title it was a work of great merit and usefulness—being replete with maxims and rules calculated for everyday use in the various relations of life—rules and maxims of the highest importance to be known and practised but not learned in high seminaries. So highly was it prized in Europe that it was translated into several languages. He also commenced the publication of a newspaper which was conducted with great ability—free from all personal abuse and scurrility—a messenger of truth and wholesome instruction. Would to God the same could be said of *all* the present public prints.

Franklin continued to pursue his studies—mastering the French, Italian, Spanish and Latin languages. By the "Junto" a small library was commenced which was the nucleus to the present large collection in the city of Philadelphia. He wrote and published a highly interesting pamphlet on the necessity of paper currency. He added to his literary fame by the production of essays on various subjects written in his peculiar style. He filled successfully the office of state printer, of clerk to the Assembly and of post-master in Philadelphia. He used unwearied exertions to perfect the municipal regulations of the city. He was the father and patron of the Philosophical Society, the Pennsylvania University and Hospital. All the enterprises in the city and province, of that time, were either originated by him or were advanced by his wisdom and counsel.

In 1741 he commenced the publication of a General Magazine filled with much useful matter but less acceptable than his former productions to many—probing, as it did, litigated points in theology. It was too universal in its charity to suit sectarians. Let these barriers be removed—then the gospel will have free course—run and be glorified.

The mechanic arts were also improved by him. He brought to their aid philosophy, chemistry and a combination of science, economy and the laws of nature. He improved chimneys—constructed a stove and proposed many useful and economical corrections in domestic concerns, from the cellar to the garret—from the plough to the mill. Science bowed to his master spirit, the arts hailed him as a patron, the lightning obeyed his magic rod and nature was proud of her favorite son.

In 1744 he was elected to the Assembly and continued a member for ten consecutive years. Although not a popular speaker, his clear conceptions of correct legislation and the duties of a statesman gave to him an influence over that body before unknown. In all his propositions he was listened to with profound attention.

During the period he was serving his province in the Assembly he explored the fields of experimental philosophy—explaining many of the mysterious phenomena of nature which spread his scientific fame to the remotest bounds of the civilized world. His discoveries in electricity were sufficient to have immortalized his name. He is the first man on record who imparted magnetism to steel—melted metals—killed animals and fired gunpowder by means of electricity. He was the first who reduced to practice the method of conducting the electric fluid from the clouds to the points of steel rods and by them harmless to the ground. All the elements—fluids, air, sea and land with their millions of various substances, passed in review before him.

In 1753 he was sent to Carlisle, Pennsylvania, to conclude a treaty with the Indians. In 1754 he was a delegate to the Congress of Commissioners which met at Albany to devise means of defence against the anticipated hostilities of the French and savages. He then submitted a plan that was unanimously approved by the Congress but was too republican for the creatures of the king.

On the decease of the Deputy Postmaster-General of America, Franklin was appointed to fill the vacancy and raised the department from embarrassment to a fruitful source of revenue to the crown.

Difficulties arose between the proprietaries and government of the province of Pennsylvania, which were referred to the mother country for adjustment. Dr. Franklin was sent by the province to guard its interests and embarked for England in June 1757. He executed the duties of his mission with his usual ability and address—the difficulties were settled and in 1762 he returned. He was then variously employed—regulating the Post-Office Department—making treaties with the Indians and devising means of defence on the frontiers.

New troubles arose between the proprietaries and assembly and in 1764 Dr. Franklin again sailed for England, with instructions to obtain the entire abolition of proprietary authority. On his arrival he was called upon to perform more important and perilous duties. The plan for taxing the colonies had been long agitated and was now matured by the British ministry. This project he had boldly opposed at the threshold and was now arraigned to answer numerous accusations brought against him by the enemies of liberty.

On the 3d of February 1766, he appeared before the House of Commons to undergo a public examination. He was found equal to the task–his enemies were astounded at his boldness, logic, dignity and skill, whilst his friends were filled with admiration at the able manner he confuted every accusation and defended the rights and interests of his native country. Amidst the attacks of artifice and insolence of power he stood unawed–unmoved–firm as a granite rock. He remained in England eleven years as the agent of the colonies, opposing the encroachments of the ministry upon the rights of Americans. During the whole time the combined efforts of flattery, malice and intrigue could not intimidate or ensnare him. He well understood the etiquette, corruptions and devices of diplomacy. He never bowed his knee to Baal or kissed the hand of a king.

The relations between the two countries had now arrived at a point so significant that Franklin returned to his long neglected home. His person was not safe in England–his services were needed in his now suffering country. He arrived in Philadelphia early in May 1775. He was received with great enthusiam and immediately elected to the Continental Congress. To this august body he added fresh lustre and dignity. In England he had exhausted every source of prospective reconciliation between the two nations. He feared the colonies were too weak to achieve their Independence but his course was right onward with his colleagues–resolved on LIBERTY OR DEATH.

The talents of Franklin were put in constant requisition. He was always selected to meet the agents of the crown who were at various times commissioned to offer terms of inglorious peace. He always proved himself the uncompromising advocate of Liberty–the shrewd and wary politician–the bold and zealous defender of the rights of his bleeding country–the unflinching friend of universal FREEDOM.

The disasters of the American army during the campaign of 1777, induced Congress to apply to France for aid. All eyes were turned on Franklin to execute this important mission. In October 1777 he embarked to perform this delicate embassy and succeeded in concluding a treaty of alliance with that nation on the 4th of February 1778, to the great joy of himself and his suffering countrymen. When the news of the alliance reached England, the ministry was much alarmed and despatched messengers to Paris to endeavor to induce Franklin to enter into a compromise with Great Britain. The terms rendered the effort too abortive to make him the bearer of even a message to Congress. To Mr. Hutton and others who came to him with the olive branch of peace, wreathed with scorpions, he replied–" I never think of your ministry and their abettors, but with the image strongly painted in my view of their hands red and dropping with the blood of my countrymen, friends and relations. No peace can be signed with those hands unless you drop all pretensions to govern us—meet us on equal terms and avoid all occasions of future discord."

He met all their intrigues at the threshold and convinced them that the hardy yoemanry of America could not be dragooned, flattered or driven from the bold position they had assumed. During the several interviews he had with these commissioners, Franklin was cautioned by Mr. Heartley to beware of his personal safety which had been repeatedly threatened. He thanked his friend and assured him he felt no alarm—that he had nearly finished a long life and that the short remainder was of no great value and ironically remarked—" Perhaps the best use such an old fellow can be put to is to make a martyr of him."

If it required all the skill and energy of a Franklin to *negotiate* a treaty of alliance with France, it required the combined skill of all Congress to preserve it. The French is the most effervescent nation known to history. A republican form of government is ever repugnant to kingly power. That the French officers and soldiers in the American army would drink freely at the fountain of liberal principles no one could doubt. That the thrones of Europe would be endangered on their return was truly predicted. By this very natural course of reasoning the British ministry exerted a powerful influence against the continuation of the alliance. Franklin and his colleagues anticipated all their dark intrigues—penetrated and frustrated them up to the time Great Britain was compelled to comply with the terms of an honorable peace and acknowledge the Independence of the United States of America by a definitive treaty of peace concluded at Paris on the 3d of September 1783.

Although anxious to be discharged from further public service it was not until 1785 that Franklin was permitted to return to his beloved country where he could breathe the pure air of republican FREEDOM—no longer polluted by kingly power. During his stay he concluded treaties of commerce between the United States and the Kings of Sweden and Prussia. On his departure from Europe every mark of respect was paid to him by Kings, courts, *literati* and by all classes of society whose adulation the loftiest ambition could desire. He was beloved by the millions—his departure was deeply regretted by all. His reputation was the personification of purity.

At the age of eighty years, borne down by disease, he returned to Philadelphia. He was hailed with enthusiastic joy, affection, esteem and veneration by all the friends of liberty—from the humblest citizen up to the illustrious Washington. He had been a pillar of fire to the American cause—a pillar of smoke to the enemies of human rights. As Thurgot truly observed—" He snatched the thunder bolt from Jove and the sceptre from

Kings." He stood–the Collossus of Liberty among the monarchs of Europe and wrung from them the homage due to a nation that dared to be FREE.

Notwithstanding his advanced age and his ardent desire for retirement, he was placed in the gubernatorial chair of Pennsylvania and in 1787 elected a delegate to the Convention that formed the Federal Constitution. Many of the bright traits of that important instrument received their finishing touch from his master hand. He was anxious to see his long nursed theory of a republican government reduced to as perfect system as its infancy would permit. He well knew, that for its manhood and old age additional provisions would be required. As necessary as this now is, so sacred has that instrument become that the mass would deem it sacrilege to disturb its long repose. It might be made to meet more fully the wants of an expanding country in some particulars but if once disturbed might be polluted by the apoplectic touch of party spirit and never recover from the shock. Caution is the parent of safety.

Early in 1790, Dr. Franklin was confined to his room by his infirmities but his mental powers remained in full vigor. Some of the strongest and most soul-stirring productions from his pen were written during his confinement. Early in April he began to fail more rapidly. He was fully sensible that he stood on the confines of eternity and that he should soon go to his final rest. On the 17th of April 1790, calm and resigned–cool and collected–peaceful and happy–he commended his spirit to Him who gave it–quitted this vale of tears with a full assurance of rising to a glorious immortality at the final resurrection and slumbered quietly and sweetly in the arms of death with a full assurance that his Lord and Master would rebind him in a new and more beautiful edition fully revised.

By his will he prohibited all pomp and parade at his funeral. He was anxious that the mournful obsequies of his burial should be marked with republican simplicity. He was laid in his grave on the 21st of April. It is in the northwest corner of Christ Church yard in the City of Philadelphia, where a plain marble slab–once even but now below the surface of the earth, shows where his ashes repose. By the side of his moulders the dust of his amiable wife.

His death was deeply lamented throughout the civilized world. Congress ordered mourning to be observed throughout the United States for thirty days. The event was solemnized in France and many eloquent eulogies pronounced. The national Assembly decreed that each of its members should wear a badge of mourning for three days. The sensation produced there by his death was similar to that evinced by our country on the death of La Fayette.

In the recapitulation of the life of this great and good man we are charmed with a versatile richness that has no parallel on the historic page. He filled every sphere in which he moved to the remotest lines of its orbit. No matter how bright the galaxy around him he was a luminary of the first magnitude. He entered upon the stage of action at a time when the world needed just such a man and continued upon it just long enough to complete all he had commenced. He was found equal to every work he undertook and always stopped at the golden point—when he had finished. He was emphatically the architect of his own fortune. No chartered college can claim him as a graduate—no patron rendered him gratuitous aid. Let the young men of our country imitate his examples that they may become useful—let our public men who have in charge our national destiny imitate them that they may be wise—let old men imitate them that they may be revered—let us *all* imitate them that we may do all the good we can to our fellow men in life and be happy in death.

HORATIO GATES.

War is a calamity to be deprecated at all times. Its history, from its sanguinary embryo to the present time, has but a few bright spots on which the philanthropist can gaze with admiring delight. The back-ground of most of these is so vividly shaded with crimson that the eye grows dim and the heart sickens on too close a scrutiny. We have many among us who preach loudly against war without delineating the innate materials in human nature that cause it. We have anti-war societies that have originated from motives pure as heaven but are planted on the abstract foundation of ills—futile as the baseless vision. Its evils may be portrayed in colors clear as the sunbeams of living light and enforced by all the arguments of human logic and Holy Writ without removing the smallest particle from the *cause* that produces this fearful calamity. This and the best remedy are not fully defined by the preamble, constitution or by-laws of any society within my knowledge and where partially explained are not always practically carried out by the members. *They* sometimes engage in a fierce personal war.

The cause exists in the nature of man influenced by the baser passions. Retaliation is among the first developments of the child. Self is a relentless tyrant. Revenge is as natural as our respiration. Anger, envy, jealousy, malice–all combine to perpetuate a disposition for war and lead men from the sublime destiny of immortal bliss.

The only remedy exists in the universal sway of that love inculcated by our immaculate Redeemer. It is under the melting influences of the religion of the Cross, stripped of all dogmatical illusions, that sullied human nature must be brightened–its tarnished lustre renovated– its pugnacious character changed and man prepared for peace and heaven. Let broad and universal charity pervade the whole human family–then a blow will·be struck against war that will resound through the wilderness of mind and cause it to bud and blossom as the rose.

The war of the American Revolution stands pre-eminent in point of justification. Among those who took a conspicuous part in its perils was Horatio Gates who was born in England in 1728. In early life he rose to the rank of major and was the aid of the British commander at the capture of Martinico in 1747. In 1748 he was stationed at Halifax where he continued for a considerable time. He was relieved from the monotony of a garrison in time of peace by the French war which resulted in the conquest of Canada. Under Braddock he was captain of infantry and fought by the side of the illustrious Washington and was saved by him in the judicious retreat of the survivors of that memorable day. He was severely wounded and for a long time unfit for duty. In 1763 he visited England with a high military reputation. He returned and located on a plantation in Virginia. He had the esteem and confidence of Washington and was warmly recommended by him to Congress as worthy of a conspicuous station in the Continental army. He was appointed Adjutant General with the rank of Brigadier in 1775. The ensuing year he was invested with the command of the troops destined to act against Ticonderoga and Crown Point. In the spring of 1777 he and Gen. Schuyler were appointed to the command of the northern army. For a short time he was superceded by Gen. Schuyler. Burgoyne was then advancing with his victorious army. The Americans were driven from Ticonderoga, Fort Ann and Skeensborough. From that point obstacles were thrown in his way by Sinclair, Schuyler, Stark and their companions in arms. Bridges were demolished, the navigation of Wood Creek obstructed–the roads filled with fallen trees–the cattle and other supplies removed which caused the British army a delay of twenty-five days before reaching Fort Edward on the Hudson. Gen. Burgoyne then supposed his embarrassments at an end. His reckoning was wrong. St. Leger failed in capturing Fort Schuyler–many of the Indians and Canadian militia took their back track–scanty supplies were obtained with great difficulty–his army was decreasing–the Americans were rallying–every day made his condition more perilous–his prospects more gloomy. Everything was prepared to insure his capture.

At this fortunate juncture for him, Gen. Gates superceded the indefatigable Schuyler and took the command on the 21st of August 1777. Anticipating aid from Sir Henry Clinton at New York, Burgoyne passed the Hudson and encamped at Saratoga. Gates advanced to Stillwater determined to oppose the further progress of the enemy. The British general resolved to open a passage with the sword and bayonet and on the 17th of September the armies were only four miles distant from each other. On the 19th a pretty general engagement occurred, which resulted in a drawn battle. Seeing no prospect of assistance from New York and the impossibility of then retreating with his cannon, Burgoyne resolved to fortify his position and act on the defensive. On the 8th of October the Americans made a vigorous attack and repulsed the British in every charge, occupying a part of their lines. Burgoyne hastened to his former camp at Saratoga in the night and meditated a retreat without artillery or baggage. He found every avenue securely guarded–the lion was caged–retreat he could not. Knowing that the British army had but a short supply of provisions, Gen. Gates well knew an attack upon his well fortified position or a surrender must speedily take place. He was well prepared for either. Finding it only a waste of human life to further engage the Americans in battle, Burgoyne surrendered on the 16th of October. Over 5000 prisoners, a park of fine artillery, 7000 muskets, a large amount of clothing, with all the camp equipage and military stores and the evacuation of all the frontier fortresses–constituted the spoils of this victory. What was of more vital importance–it imparted fresh lustre to the American arms and gave a vigorous impetus to the languishing career of Independence. It destroyed British power in the north–encouraged France to close the treaty of alliance and greatly deranged the equanimity of mother Britain. If impartially analyzed, it will be found the most important victory during the war of Independence and in closer alliance with that of Trenton than the final triumph over Cornwallis.

Although Gen. Gates had escaped the hard service of that campaign, he was the fortunate commander at its termination and was crowned with the laurels of a conquering hero in accordance with military usage and received the plaudits of his grateful countrymen—the thanks of Congress and a gold medal. As a further testimony of high esteem, he was placed at the head of the Board of War—a station next to that of commander-in-chief. He retired from that to his home in Virginia and for a time enjoyed domestic life. On the 15th of June 1780 he was put in command of the Southern army. The conquering troops of Cornwallis were sweeping over the Carolinas like a tornado—the few American soldiers were flying before them—towns were burning—everything seemed rapidly drawn towards the vortex of ruin. When Gen. Gates consented to go to the field an army of 15000 men, with complete supplies, was represented to him on paper, concentrating from the Carolinas and Virginia. When he arrived at head quarters he found about 1500 undisciplined troops, poorly armed, worse clad, with little food. Elated with his brilliant victory over the Northern army he was over anxious to meet the enemy and strike an effective blow. Contrary to the advice of those who better understood the country and the means of obtaining supplies on the march by taking a circuitous route—he selected a shorter road through a dismal district of pine thickets and swamps pregnant with disease and destitute of almost any kind of food except cattle occasionally found in the forest. Many of his men perished on the way—others were rendered unfit for duty by sickness. He ultimately reached Clermont from which Lord Rawdon had withdrawn and was joined by a few North Carolina militia and a small company under Capt. Potterfield. Troops continued to arrive from Virginia and other points until the army of Gen. Gates amounted to about 4000—mostly undisciplined militia unaccustomed to standing fire or steel. Rawdon and Cornwallis concentrated their troops at Camden amounting to less than 2000 men but all of the highest order of soldiers. Gen. Gates resolved on an attack. On the 16th of August the two armies met in mortal combat. The militia under Gen. Gates were quickly thrown into confusion—the regulars overwhelmed and the whole completely routed. This defeat of the Americans had no parallel during the war. Among those who did not trace effects to causes the fame of the Hero of Saratoga sank below zero. His error consisted in risking a battle with an army of British veterans opposed by the rawest kind of militia—not in any want of military skill in time of action. He was superceded on the 5th of the ensuing October—subjected to a court of inquiry—honorably acquitted and re-instated in 1782. The time had then passed for him to renovate his military laurels. The battles for Independence had been fought—the crowning victory won—LIBERTY achieved—FREEDOM secured.

Gen. Gates retired to his plantation in Virginia where he remained seven years when he liberated his slaves and removed to the vicinity of the city of New York where he lived respected until the 10th of April 1806, when he threw off his mortal coil and slumbered in death.

In person Gen. Gates was well formed—in his manners, polished and urbane—in disposition, mild and amiable—in his intercourse, just and honorable. In 1800 he served in the New York Legislature and enjoyed the confidence and esteem of all around him. He was an ardent patriot, a good citizen, a perfect gentleman, an honest man.

ELBRIDGE GERRY.

GAMBLING has become a fearful scourge in our expanding country. It is practised upon the humblest watercraft that floats upon our canals—the frail flatboat that descends our streams—the majestic steamboat that traces our mighty rivers. It lurks in the lowest groggeries that curse community—is tolerated in some of the most fashionable hotels. Its victims are found in all classes from the hod carrier in his bespattered rags up to the members of Congress in their ruffles. The gambling room is the enchanted ground of destruction. Once within its serpentine coils—a centripetal force rushes its votary to the vortex of ruin. Interested friends may kindly warn—the tender wife may entreat with all the eloquence of tears—children may cry and sob for bread—if within the fatal snare the infatuated mortal is seldom extricated in time. He combines the deafness of the adder with the desperation of a maniac. At the gambling table men and youth have been prepared to commit deeds registered on the black catalogue of crime. In blazing capitals RUIN is marked over the outer door of every gambling den. On the inner door is written in bold relievo— CASTLE OF DESPAIR. WRECKS OF FORTUNE AND DEMONS MADE HERE. One of the wicket gates that leads thousands into this labyrinth of misery consists in fashionable circles where games are played as an *innocent* amusement. It is there that many young men of talent, education and wealth, take the entered apprentice degree that leads them to the knight templars of destruction. Without any knowledge of a game but few would venture money at a gambling table. The gaming examples of men in high life have a baneful influence and practically sanction the high handed robberies of the finely dressed boa-constrictor black legs. The gambling hells tolerated and patronized in our cities are a disgrace to any nation bearing a Christian name and would be banished from a Pagan community with a Vicksburg vengeance. To the honor of the members of the Continental Congress they placed a veto upon this heaven provoking, soul destroying, reputation ruining, wealth devouring, nation demoralizing vice.

Among those who abhorred this practice was Elbridge Gerry, born at Marblehead, Massachusetts, on the 17th of July 1744. His father was an enterprising merchant and bestowed upon this son a classical education. He graduated at Harvard University in 1762 with a high scholastic reputation. Judging the tree by its fruit, the seed from which it sprang must have been of the purest kind and its vegetation not retarded by the absorbing and poisonous weeds of vice. Its incipient pruning must have been performed by a master hand to produce a specimen of so much symmetry of proportion, beauty of form and richness of foliage.

After having completed his collegiate studies Mr. Gerry entered the counting house of his father and ultimately became one of the most enterprising and wealthy merchants of his native town. In his kind of business he was amongst the first to feel the weight of the impolitic and unconstitutional revenue system. From the nature of his composition he was amongst the first to meet oppression at the threshold. A man of deep reflection and philosophical investigation–he examined closely the extent of American rights and British wrongs. He made himself acquainted with the principle and structure of government, international, civil, common, statute and municipal law, political economy, home and foreign policy. No one was better informed upon the natural, legal and practical relations between the mother country and the colonies. He was prepared to act advisedly and firmly. His extensive influence, decision of character, sound discretion and exalted patriotism–made him a master spirit to guide the public mind. He participated in all the movements in favor of liberty.

On the 26th of May 1773 he commenced his official career as a member of the Assembly of Massachusetts Bay then called the General Court. That body and the royal governor took a strong issue upon rights and wrongs. The unconstitutional acts of parliament were sanctioned by the latter and fearlessly censured by the former. A standing committee was appointed to scan the proceedings of ministers and parliament and to correspond with the other colonies relative to the important concerns of the nation. Mr. Gerry had been in that body but two days when he was made a member of this important committee. He became one of the principal actors on the tragic stage of the revolution, the drama of peace and formation of the Federal government. He walked shoulder to shoulder with Samuel Adams and John Hancock in the bold measures that roused the lion from his lair-the people to their duty. At the Boston tea party-in the opposition to the Port Bill-the impeachment of the crown judges-the controversy with Gov. Hutchinson-non-intercourse with Great Britain-Mr. Gerry stood firm as the granite shores of the Bay State. Nor did he waver when Gov. Gage took the helm with a military force to do his will and pleasure. When it was found that reason, appeal, remonstrance-all fell upon his adamantine soul like dew upon the desert of Sahara, the legitimate source of a righteous government was resorted to-THE PEOPLE-who nobly sustained their leaders in the hour of peril. Severe measures were adopted by parliament-the charter of Massachusetts was altered by *ex parte* legislation-illegal taxes were increased-the hirelings of the King became more insolent-the indignation of the people rose like a tornado-colonial blood flowed the war cry was raised-the clash of arms commenced-the fury of battle raged-the struggle was terrific-the lion was conquered-AMERICA WAS FREE.

In all the thrilling scenes that passed in Massachusetts before his election to Congress, Mr. Gerry took a leading part. He was an efficient member of the Committee of Safety and Supplies that were for a time virtually the government. In April 1775 he narrowly escaped the grasp of his foes. The night previous to the battle of Lexington Messrs. Gerry, Lee and Orne were at Cambridge through which the British passed on their way to the opening scene of hostilities. When opposite the house where these gentlemen were in bed a file of soldiers were suddenly detached and approached it rapidly. The patriots barely escaped by the back way in their linen. After the military had left they returned for their over clothes and immediately roused the people to resistance. The night previous to the death of his intimate friend, the brave Warren, Mr. Gerry lodged with him. The anxiety they felt for their country induced them to concert plans for future action rather than sleep. The lamented hero of Bunker Hill appears to have had a presentiment of his premature fate as indicated by the last words he uttered as they parted. "It is sweet to die for our country."

In July 1775 the government of Massachusetts adopted a new form of government. A legislature was organized and a judiciary established. Mr. Gerry was appointed Judge of the Court of Admiralty but declined that he might do more active service. On the 18th of January 1776 he was elected to the Continental Congress. Fearless, cautious, prudent-he was the kind of man to meet the momentous crisis of that eventful era. Standing on a lofty eminence of public reputation he was hailed as an able auxiliary in the cause of freedom. He had a place upon the most important committees and performed his duties strictly. To speculators and peculators that prowled around the public offices and army he was a terror during the war. He introduced into Congress many salutary guards against dishonest men who prey upon government like promethean vultures. With its age and experience our republic is now occasionally tapped at the jugular and gets a cut under the fifth rib–producing a laxity of the sinews of power.

When the Declaration of Independence was proposed in Congress the soul of Mr. Gerry was enraptured in its favor. He had long been prepared for the measure and gave it his ardent support. When the thrilling moment arrived for final action upon this important question he sanctioned it by his vote and signature and rejoiced in the fulfilment of prophecy–*A nation shall be born in a day*. He was continued in Congress and faithfully discharged his duties with unabated zeal. The committee rooms and the house were alike benefitted by his intelligence and extensive experience in general business. He rendered efficient aid in reducing to system every branch of the new government. He took a conspicuous part in the debates upon the Articles of Confederation and was listened to with great attention. He spoke well, reasoned closely–demonstrated clearly. He was truly republican and opposed to everything that did not bear the impress of sound sense, practical usefulness–equality of operation. For these reasons he opposed a resolution of thanks to his bosom friend, John Hancock, for his services as President of Congress. He said his friend Hancock had done no more than to ably perform his duty–all the members had done the same. It would be a singular entry upon the journal to record a vote of thanks to each. Etiquette prevailed over sound logic–the vote of thanks was passed–introducing a custom in the new government that has long since lost all efficacy by too frequent use on occasions of minor importance. Mr. Gerry was on the committee that devised the plan of operations for the Northern army that resulted in the capture of Burgoyne. He was upon the one to obtain supplies for the army and visited the camp of Washington in the winter of 1777. These multiform duties strictly discharged are stronger encomiums upon his talents, energy and patriotism than a volume of panegyric from the most accomplished writer.

It has afforded me great pleasure to be able to frequently refer to the religious and moral character of the members of the Continental Congress. The fact is illustrated in the history of the men and corroborated by the records of that body and responded to by the States. In 1778 a resolution was passed in Congress recommending them to adopt decisive measures against "theatrical entertainments, horse racing, gaming and such other diversions as are productive of idleness, dissipation and a general depravity of principles and manners." Another resolution strictly enjoined upon the officers of the army—"to see that the good and wholesome rules provided for the discountenancing of profaneness and vice and the preservation of morals among the soldiers are duly and punctually preserved." A third one was passed that would be a sweeper if revived at the present day. It arose from a disposition on the part of a few officers to disregard the one first cited and was a supplement to that. "Resolved—That any person holding an office under the United States who shall act, promote, encourage or attend such plays shall be deemed unworthy to hold such office and shall be accordingly dismissed."

Mr. Gerry supported and voted for all these resolutions and for those recommending days of fasting, humiliation and prayer. Sectarianism never polluted the members of the Continental Congress. Charity was the bright star in their diadem of fame. He was upon the grand committee of one from each State to examine foreign affairs and the conduct of foreign commissioners particularly that of Mr. Deane. This committee used the probe freely and recommended Congress to use the amputating knife upon every limb affected by the gangrene of political corruption. O! Jupiter! what a slaughter such an operation would make at the present time. On the 14th of October 1779 Mr. Gerry proposed the expedition against the Indians which was successfully executed by Gen. Sullivan. He proposed a resolution designed to guard against inducements to corrupt influence—"No candidates for public office shall vote in or otherwise influence their own election—that Congress will not appoint any member thereof during its time of sitting or within six months after he shall have been in Congress, to any office under the States for which he or any other for his benefit may receive any salary, fees or emolument." It was then lost but he revived and carried it in 1785. The principle has since been partly adopted under the Federal Constitution. As a member of the Committee of Finance he stood next to Robert Morris. In 1780 he retired from Congress after an arduous and faithful service of five years. In all situations and at all times he was energetic, zealous and active in the cause of liberty. When his duties called him to the army if there was any fighting on the tapis whilst he was in camp he always took an active part. In the battle of Chesnut Hill he shouldered a musket and entered the ranks. When Gen. Kniphausen engaged the American army at Springfield Mr. Gerry took his station by the side of Washington who invested him with a volunteer command during his stay.

The second year after his retirement he again took his seat in Congress. The business of the nation was then more perplexing than in the heat of the war. An empty treasury, a prostrate credit, an enormous debt presented a fearful aspect. To aid in bringing order out of chaos he was of great service. Committee labors were piled upon his shoulders as if he was an Atlas to carry the world or an Atalanta in the celerity of business. The local feelings and interests of the states had become effervescent. The half pay for life guaranteed to all officers who remained in the army during the war was satisfactory to but a few. This was settled by compounding the annuity for five years full pay. In 1784 he was on the important Committee of Foreign Relations—on the one to revise the Treasury Department. The same session he presented a resolution for the compensation of Baron Steuben who had rendered immense services by introducing a system of military tactics and discipline into the American army by which it was governed and which was strictly adhered to long after the Revolution. It was warmly supported by Mr. Jefferson and others but was lost, charity would suggest, in consequence of the embarrassed state of the finances. In 1785 Mr. Gerry closed his services in Congress and retired to Cambridge near Boston, with all the honors of a pure patriot crowned with the sincere gratitude of a nation of freemen.

Time soon developed to the sages of the Revolution that the Articles of Confederation that bound the colonies together when impending dangers and one common interest created a natural cement—were not sufficient to secure the liberty they had achieved. Local interests engendered jealousies, these produced dissatisfaction and this threatened to involve the government in anarchy. To remedy these evils Mr. Madison made a proposition that each state send delegates to a convention which convened in May 1781 at Philadelphia and framed the Federal Constitution in which Mr. Gerry took a very active part. He was amongst those who did not sanction or sign that instrument. For this act, dictated by his conscience, he was liberally abused by out door cynical partisans—not by the noble minded statesmen who differed with him in opinion—all honest in their views and patriotic in their motives. They soared above the acrimonious scurrility of venal party spirit. After the constitution was adopted no one adhered to it more strictly than Mr. Gerry—always holding sacred the great republican principle—

the majority must rule and be obeyed. He was a member of the first Congress under it and did much toward raising the beautiful superstructure now towering sublimely upon its broad basis. He served four years and again sought retirement. This was transient.

In 1797 the relations between our country and France had assumed a portentous aspect. President Adams determined on sending an able embassy to that government–to make a strong effort to conclude an amicable arrangement of difficulties before appealing to arms. Gen. Pinckney was then there. Mr. Gerry and Mr. Marshall, since Chief Justice of the United States, were appointed to join him, each empowered to act collectively or separately as a sound discretion should dictate. On their arrival the French Directory refused to recognize them. To prevent an immediate rupture–prudence and patriotism were necessary. After many fruitless attempts to enter upon a negotiation Messrs. Pinckney and Marshall were peremptorily ordered home and Mr. Gerry recognized as the official organ of the United States. By his discreet, firm and manly course he effected a settlement and prevented a war that seemed inevitable.

In 1805 he was a member of the electoral college. Although his state was decidedly federal he was elected governor in 1810 by the republican party by a large majority–conclusive evidence of his great popularity. He never entered into partisan feelings. In his first message he lucidly portrayed the danger of high toned party spirit. He felt and acted for his whole country. For many years he had anxiously desired to be excused from public duties but no excuse was accepted. In 1813 he was inaugurated Vice President of the United States. He discharged the duties of the office with great ability and dignity. His impartiality, correctness and candor gained for him the esteem of the elevated body over which he presided to the last day of his eventful and useful life–teaching by example his favorite precept–" It is the duty of every citizen though he may have but one day to live to devote that day to the service of his country." At the city of Washington a beautiful monument is erected to his memory with an inscription as follows.

THE TOMB OF
ELBRIDGE GERRY,
VICE PRESIDENT OF THE UNITED STATES,
WHO DIED SUDDENLY IN THIS CITY ON HIS WAY TO THE
CAPITOL, AS PRESIDENT OF THE SENATE,
NOVEMBER 23D, 1814,
AGED 70.

In the review of the life of Elbridge Gerry the pure patriot finds much to admire—the Christian nothing to condemn. Partisans may censure because he kept aloof from high toned party spirit—the maelstrom of nations that once were but now are not. His examples of devotedness to the good of his country, his untiring industry, his intelligence, his moral worth—are all worthy of imitation and shed a rich unfading lustre upon his character. He discharged all the duties of private life with the strictest fidelity. He was useful in every station where duty called, no perils retarded his onward course towards the goal of RIGHT. His purposes were deliberately formed and boldly executed. He was an honor to our country, the cause of freedom and enlightened, philanthropic and liberal legislation. He was a noble specimen of unalloyed patriotism—a patriotism that must be widely diffused among the increasing masses of our expanding country—then our UNION will be preserved—our land continue to be what it now is—THE LAND OF THE BRAVE—THE HOME OF THE FREE.

NATHANIEL GREENE.

THE history of the American Revolution will be read with intense interest through all time whether presented as a ponderous whole or in sections. Its most attractive form to the impatient and romantic reader is the delineation of noble and god like individual action. Numerous bold exploits were performed—hair-breadth escapes made by the private soldier that had an exciting ephemeral history worthy of record which is now buried with the meritorious actor and his immediate acquaintances. Some thrilling stories will have a more protracted existence in the annals of tradition but will ultimately lose their freshness, wither and die. Truthful living tradition belongs to the red man—not to us. In all nations—from the barbarous up to the refined civilized, the glory of the battle field has been awarded to the leaders who planned—not to the soldiers who executed. In our republican land of professed equality partial inroads upon this rule have been made. In our common militia and volunteer companies the soldier is often equal and sometimes superior to his commanding officer in point of talent and weight of character. This can rarely be the case among an oppressed people and still more rarely would the existing fact be admitted. During the revolution merit was clothed with its true dignity more than now. Many who stood upon this first legitimate stepping stone to office ascended from the ranks of the army to high commands—from the retired walks of life to the legislative halls and posts of honor in the various departments of government. The frame-work of the most liberal military system is adverse to the recognition of individual merit below the officer. The case must be very extraordinary to be officially announced. Hence large standing armies bind in the fetters of ignorance a vast amount of intellect that would be brought into mellow life and usefulness in a free enlightened republican government like our own.

Among the Heroes of the American Revolution whose merit brought him into notice was Nathaniel Greene, born at the town of Warwick, Rhode Island, in 1741. His parents were respectable members of the Society of Friends—of course opposed to the profession of arms. His father was an anchor manufacturer and gave his son a limited chance to obtain a common education. With this the mind of Nathaniel was not content. He pursued his studies every leisure hour and with his extra earnings purchased books. He mastered the Latin with but little aid from an instructor. The history of military chieftains he read with great delight. When he arrived at manhood he was a good mechanic and a bright scholar. For a time he followed the business of making anchors for vessels but was soon called to the more important work of aiding in the construction of the sheet anchor of FREEDOM. At an early age he was elected a member of the legislature where he became a conspicuous advocate of equal rights and boldly opposed the usurpations of mother Britain. His course obtained for him an expulsion from the Society of Friends and the esteem of every patriot. I respect the Quakers but not this paradox in their creed. They profess to love liberty—but few of them are willing to pay its price in coin—none of them can bear arms without excommunication.

On his return from the Assembly Nathaniel enrolled himself a private in a military corps that was suggested and formed by himself and chartered under the title of the *Kentish Guards*. It was placed under the command of Gen. Varnum. In 1775 the little patriotic state of Rhode Island raised three regiments—in all sixteen hundred rank and file—officered by the most distinguished military characters of the colony. No one could have been more surprised than young Greene on receiving the commission of Brigadier General. He was put in command of this small brigade and immediately marched them to head quarters at Cambridge, Mass. He applied himself closely to the study of military tactics and soon became an excellent disciplinarian—an able officer. For correctness of evolution, subordination and good order—his was a model brigade. His merits were quickly discovered by the acute Washington who often consulted him with confidence in cases of doubt and difficulty. This confidence he communicated to Congress. It arose from two strong points—Greene had superior talents and was a Christian. On the 26th of August 1776 Greene was commissioned a Major General of the regular army of the United States and put forth his noblest exertions to promote the interests of his bleeding country. At the battles of Trenton and Princeton he exhibited great skill and judicious conduct. At the battle of Germantown he commanded the left wing of the ar[my a]nd received the unqualified approbation of Washington for his coolness and bravery. In March 1778 he accepted the appointment of Quarter Master General retaining his rank and right to command in time of action according to the seniority of his commission. At the victorious battle of Monmouth he commanded the right wing of the army and led his troops to the onset with the terrific force of an avalanche.

In the siege of the British garrison at Newport, R. I. he served under Gen. Sullivan. When it was found necessary to retreat in consequence of the dispersion of the French fleet by a storm which prevented it from rendering the contemplated aid, the army was greatly indebted to the judgment and skill of Gen. Greene in extricating it from a perilous position.

The British power being measurably paralyzed in the north Lord Cornwallis turned his attention to the south where the defences were less—the plunder more. On the 26th of December 1779 he commenced his movement and landed thirty miles from Charleston, S. C. on the 11th of February ensuing. He then commenced the work of destruction and brutality with increased rigor. No respect was paid to private property, religious sanctity or defenceless females. After a spirited defence Charleston was compelled to surrender. The British carried dismay, victory and death in their whole course. Plunder, rapine and murder were the order of the day. *Booty* and *beauty* were the watch words of his most Christian majesty's officers and soldiers.

Under these heart rending circumstances Washington directed Gen. Greene to take command of the Southern army. In company with the brave Morgan he arrived at Charlotte on the 2d of December 1780. The so called army numbered 970 regulars—1013 militia, destitute of military stores, unpaid, nearly naked, poorly fed and no government supplies nearer than two hundred miles. Opposed was a powerful army rich in plunder, flushed with victory, liberally paid, abundantly fed, well clothed and amply supplied with military stores of every kind. The front view of the picture was dark and gloomy—on the back ground Greene and Morgan saw the rays of hope shedding their cheering beams on the spire of Liberty. Gen. Greene went to work for dear life. By his amiable deportment he gained the love and confidence of his soldiers—the esteem and respect of the inhabitants. From the surrounding country he gained short supplies and raised a few recruits. He despatched Gen. Morgan with a small force to the western part of the state which gave fresh courage to the patriots of that section. By a falling into the ranks the force of Morgan increased so much that Cornwallis ordered Col. Tarleton to disperse this band of rebels and put all to the sword who did not surrender at discretion. On the 17th of January 1781, Tarleton came up to this rough and ready party at the Cowpens. Although his force was inferior in numbers and two-thirds raw militia, Gen. Morgan determined to stand fire. Sure of an easy victory the proud Britons rushed on to action and were as much astonished to meet with an unbroken line streaming with fire as if they had been brought up all standing against an unperceived wire fence across the high way. Tarleton roared, foamed, raved and commanded his men to *charge*. Again the blazing streams of fire illuminated the lines of Morgan whose troops rushed upon the broken ranks of the enemy with the fury of a tornado. The struggle was short, the victory complete, the amazement of Tarleton paralyzing. Besides the killed, over five hundred of the enemy were taken prisoners and a convenient amount of the munitions of war fell into the hands of the victors. Supposing he had crushed the rebel power in the south Cornwallis was astounded at the result of this hasty recreative expedition. He immediately marched in pursuit of Morgan determined to rescue the prisoners and wipe out the disgrace Tarleton had brought upon the British arms. The hero of the Cowpens was too old a fox to be easily caught. He could do some things as well as others. He was as skilful in retreat as he was desperate in battle. He knew when, where and how to fight. He was courageous, not rash—bold, not imprudent and as watchful as an Argus. He effected a junction with Gen. Greene on the 7th of February. The chagrined Cornwallis advanced rapidly determined to annihilate the little American army at one fell swoop. Greene retreated into Virginia where he added to his numbers and supplies. So confident was the British general of overtaking him that he destroyed his heavy baggage to accelerate his movements. The patriots were not thus encumbered. Many of them had only their arms and remnants of tattered garments, being obliged to place tufts of moss on their shoulders to prevent the friction of the cartouch straps. To the pursuing enemy the Americans seemed an *ignis fatuus*—often to be seen but never reached. The chase was abandoned. In turn Greene annoyed Cornwallis by cutting off his supplies, capturing foraging parties and constantly watching all his movements. His situation became perilous, his numbers were constantly growing less by capture, desertion and disease. His supplies cost blood as well as treasure–the force of Greene was constantly augmenting–the tables were turned–he retreated to Hillsborough where he endeavored to raise new recruits by liberal offers of British gold. The yellow dust had lost its magic charm on Americans-patriotism was the more current coin.

Unwilling to be long separated from the noble lord, Green paid him a visit on the 15th of March. The interview took place at Guilford court house between one and two o'clock P. M. and continued nearly two hours. Owing to the militia that formed the front line flying at the sight of the red coats the Americans were obliged to give ground and make it a drawn battle–but the meeting was a sad one for Cornwallis. His loss was 532 killed, wounded and missing, among whom were several of his most distinguished officers. So crippled was the British army that a pecipitate retreat to Wilmington was ordered leaving those of the wounded who were not able to march. The loss of Gen. Greene was about 400 killed and wounded. Cornwallis claimed the victory–one not very auspicious to his military glory or royal master. Gen. Greene commenced offensive operations. He determined on attacking Lord Rawdon who was strongly fortified at Camden S. C. with 900 men. The American forces amounted to only 700 and encamped within a mile of the British lines cutting off all supplies from the enemy. Anticipating a reinforcement to the little army of Gen. Greene and being on short allowance his lordship made a sally on the 25th of April and boldly attacked the offending invaders. For some time victory perched upon the brow of Greene–his cavalry had taken over two hundred prisoners. One of his regiments made a move which compelled him to retreat with a loss of about 200 killed, wounded and prisoners. The loss of Lord Rawdon was 258. So flushed was the British general with this dear victory that he fled from Camden leaving his sick and wounded to the care of those who he knew would care for them. The back handed victories of Guilford and Camden so paralyzed the enemy that they soon abandoned a number of small fortifications–large quantities of military stores and concentrated a considerable force at the strong garrison of Ninety Six. On the 22d of May Greene commenced a siege upon that place but modestly retired to give place to three regiments of strangers fresh from England. Before doing this he made an unsuccessful assault at a cost of about 150 men. But for the reinforcements the garrison would have shortly surrendered.

During the ensuing two months nothing but skirmishing occurred. On the 9th of September the army of Gen. Greene had increased to 2000 men. The division of the British army under Col. Stewart was posted at Eutaw Springs. An immediate attack was made by the Americans in the following order. As he approached the enemy Gen. Greene formed his troops in two lines—the first composed of Carolina militia under Generals Marion, Pickens and Col. de Malmedy. The second was composed of regulars under Gen. Sumpter, Lieut. Col. Campbell and Col. Williams. Lieut. Col. Lee covered the right flank with his legion—Lieut. Henderson covered the left with the state troops. The cavalry under Col. Washington and the Delaware troops under Capt. Kirkwood were held in reserve. Scarcely was the line of battle completed when the British rapidly advanced. The Americans met the onset with the bravery of veterans but were compelled to give way. The battle raged with fearful fury. All depended on a sudden and desperate movement. Gen. Greene ordered the Virginia and Maryland regulars to advance with trailed arms—facing a shower of musket and grape shot. The order was instantly obeyed—they broke the lines of the British and drove them some distance to a thicket of trees and brick houses where they rallied and took a stand. The Americans took over 500 prisoners and remained on the field of battle. Under cover of night Col. Stewart retreated towards Charleston leaving 70 of his wounded and 1000 stand of arms. His total loss in men was near 1200—that of Greene 500 in killed and wounded. The English had the largest force in action. For this display of skill and bravery Congress presented Gen. Greene with a British standard and gold medal. What was dearer to him than all else—he received the high approbation of Washington and his country. From that time the torch of kingly power rapidly decreased until its last flickering light expired. For a time Charleston was occupied by the crown troops—offensive operations they dare not undertake only by small and transient *booty* and *beauty* squads.

It may seem mysterious to the young readers why soldiers fought so valiantly who were poorly paid, scantily fed and scarcely clothed. Hundreds of them were entirely naked at the Eutaw battle. Their loins were galled severely by their cartouch boxes. It was considered a great favor to obtain a folded rag to lay on the scarified part. Their food was often a scanty supply of rice or a few roasted potatoes. The officers suffered alike with the common soldiers. Gen. Greene was in the southern field seven consecutive months without taking off his clothes to retire for a night. *Love of liberty and love of their leading general and his brave officers* kept these soldiers together and rendered them desperate on the field of battle. This removes the mystery. If all could be made to realize the price of our Liberty, political asperity and party spirit would hide their polluting forms under the mantle of shame and retire to the peaceful shades of oblivion. Reader–never forget the blood, treasure and anguish your Liberty cost.

Finding that the wary Greene could not be conquered by force of arms British gold was once more put in requisition by the enemy. Several native foreigners had deserted to the English and were induced to form a plan to deliver up Gen. Greene and his principal officers. A sergeant and two domestics attached to the person of the General were bribed and in correspondence with the British. A time was fixed to deliver him and every officer of rank to the enemy. As usual a guardian angel was there. A female heard some unguarded expressions from the sergeant and promptly informed Gen. Greene. The troops were at once ordered on parade–the sergeant was arrested–confessed his guilt, was condemned and shot. When led to execution he warned all not to sully their glory or forego the advantages they would speedily realize from the successful termination of the war and if a thought of desertion was in their bosoms to banish it at once and for ever. He acknowledged the justice of his sentence–distributed his little all among his comrades–gave the signal and paid the penalty of his crime. Thus was a base and cowardly plot detected by angelic woman–the ringleader executed and the southern army saved from probable destruction. Not a single *native American* was concerned in this conspiracy.

Another circumstance occurred shortly after this that marred the happiness of Gen. Greene for a little time. The appointment of Col. Laurens to a command in their little army gave great umbrage to the officers generally who immediately tendered their resignation to the General. He affectionately recommended them to appeal to Congress for redress and not desert the noble cause of Liberty prematurely. They seemed determined in their course–he reluctantly received their commissions. On being separated from him their attachment was fully revealed to them. They found it impossible to leave their beloved General–again took their commissions and followed his advice. No officer could gain the affections of those under him more fully than did Gen. Greene. Kindness and even handed justice to all were amongst his marked characteristics. He shared the hardship and glory of the field with his soldiers. He did all in his power to supply their wants and alleviate their distress. By example and precept he taught his men to meet calamity with heroic fortitude, pointing to the goal of liberty as a final rest from the toils of war—to realms of bliss beyond the skies as the eternal rest of the virtuous and good.

Early in October the last lion was caged at Yorktown. There the struggle closed—there the victorious Cornwallis—the pride of mother Britain, was humbled, the shouts of victory and the clarion of freedom sounded and the sons of Columbia crowned with laurels of enduring fame. The battles of Gen. Greene were finished. He had served his country long and faithfully. He had surmounted the mighty barriers that opposed him—he had contributed largely in breaking the chains of slavery—Liberty had triumphed over despotism—his country was free, and was acknowledged independent by the power that had long sought to enslave it. Gentle peace shed fresh lustre on the care-worn countenances of the sages and heroes and diffused her refulgent rays from the shores of the broad Atlantic to the silver lakes of the far west.

On his way home Gen. Greene was hailed with grateful enthusiasm in every town through which he passed. On his arrival at Princeton Congress was in session there. As a testimony of respect for his valuable services that body presented him with two pieces of ordnance taken from the British army. The state of Georgia presented him with a valuable plantation near Savannah. The State of South Carolina conveyed to him a large tract of rich land which he sold to enable him to pay debts contracted to obtain supplies for his soldiers. In the autumn of 1785 he removed to his plantation in Georgia anticipating all the enjoyment of domestic felicity. This was of short duration. On the 12th of June 1786 he was attacked with inflammation upon his brain caused by a stroke of the sun and on the 19th of that month his spirit returned to the bosom of his God. Thus closed the brilliant career of one of the most distinguished sons of the Revolution. From his childhood to his grave he was the pride of his friends, a shining light to his country—a blessing to our nation. He was a prudent and brave general, an accomplished gentleman, a good citizen, an honest man, a consistent Christian. His character was pure as the crystal fountain—his fame enduring as the records of time. His examples are models for imitation, his history is full of instruction, his merits worthy of our highest admiration. His faults were completely eclipsed by the brilliancy of his superior worth.

BUTTON GWINNETT.

FALSE honor like false religion is worse than none. They both lead to destruction and are deprecated by all good men. The one is a relic of the barbarous ages—the other is older, having first been imposed on mother Eve amidst the amaranthine bowers of Eden. Inconsistency is an incubus that assumes numerous forms. In some shape it hangs over every nation and most individuals. It is human nature to err—but some errors are so plainly a violation of reason and common sense that it is passing strange sound men do not avoid them. Yet we often see those of high attainments rush into the whirlpool of inconsistency with a blind infatuation that the fine spun rules of the acutest sophistry cannot justify.

One of the fallacious and opprobrious inconsistencies that now disgraces our nation is duelling. Many in this country boast of our intellectual light and mourn over the ignorance of the poor untutored red man. In turn he can point us to a dark spot on our national character that never tarnished the name of a western or eastern Indian. This bohun upas thrives only in communities that claim civilization. In no country has it been tolerated with so much impunity as in our own. By our law it is murder. In no instance has this law been enforced. Widows may mourn, orphans languish, hearts bleed, our statesmen perish and the murderer still run at large and be treated by many with more deference than if his hands were not stained with blood. This foul stigma upon the American name should be washed out speedily and effectually. Let the combined powers of public opinion, legislative, judicial and executive action be brought to bear upon it with the force of a rushing avalanche. Flagrant crimes are suppressed only by strong measures.

Among the victims of this barbarous practice was Button Gwinnett, a man of splendid talents and a patriot of the American Revolution. He was born in England in 1732. His parents were respectable but not wealthy. Being a boy of promise they bestowed on him a good education. At his majority he commenced a successful mercantile career at Bristol in his native country. Surrounded by a large family he resolved on changing his location and came to Charleston S. C. in 1770, where he pursued merchandizing two years. He then sold out his store, purchased a plantation on St. Catharine Island, Georgia, to which he removed and became an enterprising agriculturist. He possessed an active mind and was a close observer of passing events. Having resided in England during the formation of the visionary and impolitic plan of taxing the colonies, he understood well the framework of the British cabinet. From the course he promptly pursued it is plain he was a Whig in England. The subject of raising revenue from the colonies of the new world had been fully and ably discussed in Great Britain. Many of her profound statesmen had portrayed, with all the truth of prophecy, the result of the blind unjust course of ministers towards the Americans. The most sagacious English statesman then in Parliament, Lord Chatham, exerted his noblest powers to bring the cabinet to a sense of common justice–the only path of safety. Mingling with intelligent men at Bristol, Mr. Gwinnett had become well informed upon the litigated points in controversy and was well acquainted with the relative feelings and situation of the two countries. When the question of liberty or slavery was placed before the people of his adopted land he declared in favor of freedom. Knowing the superior physical force of Great Britain and the weakness of the colonies, a successful resistance seemed to him problematical. His doubts upon the subject were removed by the enthusiasm of the patriots generally and especially by the lucid demonstrations of Lyman Hall, a bold and fearless advocate of equal rights with whom he became intimate. Convinced of the justice and possible success of the cause he at once became a champion in its favor. He had counted the cost, he had revolved in his mind the dangers that would accumulate around him and truly predicted his property would be destroyed by the devastating enemy–yet he nobly resolved to risk his life, fortune and honor in defence of chartered rights and constitutional franchises.

He enrolled his name among the leaders of the patriotic movements–became a member of several committees and conspicuous at public meetings. In her colonial capacity Georgia was the last to come to the rescue. Some of her noblest sons had become shining lights in the glorious cause. Patriotism was extending–oppression increasing, eyes opening, ears listening, minds working, hearts beating and those who were perching on the pivot of uncertainty were fast losing their balance. At length the cry of blood was heard from Lexington. The work was done. Georgia started from her lethargy like a lion roused from his lair and prepared for the conflict. Like green wood–she was slow to take fire but gave a permanent heat when ignited.

On the 2d of February 1776 Mr. Gwinnett was appointed to the Continental Congress and took his seat on the 20th of May ensuing. Although his constituents were determined to maintain their rights at all hazards most of them loked upon the plan of Independence as a project of visionary fancy—ideal, not to be hoped for or attempted. It gained strength by discussion and emerged from its embryo form. At this juncture a colleague of Mr. Gwinnett, the Rev. Mr. Zubly with a Judas heart, wrote a letter to the royal governor of Georgia, disclosing the contemplated measure, a copy of which was in some way obtained and placed in the hands of Mr. Chase who immediately denounced the traitor on the floor of Congress. The Iscariot at first attempted a denial by challenging the proof but finding that the betrayer had been betrayed he fled precipitately for Georgia in order to place himself under the protection of the governor who had just escaped from the enraged patriots on board a British armed vessel in Savannah harbor and had enough to do to protect himself without rendering aid or comfort to a traitor. He was followed by Mr. Houston one of his colleagues. Swift was the pursuit but swifter the flight. On the wings of guilt he flew too rapidly to be overtaken.

When the proposition came before Congress for a final separation from the mother country Mr. Gwinnett became a warm advocate for the measure. When the trying hour arrived, big with consequences, he gave his approving vote and affixed his name to the important document that stands acknowled by the civilized world the most lucid exposition of human rights upon the records of history—the Declaration of American Independence. In February 1777 he took a seat in the convention of his own state convened to form a constitution under the new government. He at once took a leading part and submitted the draft of a constitution which was slightly amended and immediately adopted. Shortly after this he was elevated to the Presidency of the Provincial Council, then the first office in the state—rising in a single year from private life to the pinnacle of power in Georgia. At this time an acrimonious jealousy existed between the civil and military authorities. At the head of the latter was Gen. McIntosh against whom Mr. Gwinnett had run the previous year for Brig. General and was unsuccessful. His elevation and influence annoyed the General. The civil power claimed the right to try military officers for offences that Gen. McIntosh contended came only under the jurisdiction of a court martial. Mr. Gwinnett had planned an expedition against East Florida and contemplated having the command. Gen. McIntosh conferred it upon a senior lieutenant-colonel. The expedition was a failure. The General publicly exulted over his hated enemy and gloried in the misfortune. Under the new constitution a governor was to be elected on the first Monday of the ensuing May. Mr. Gwinnett became a candidate. His competitor was a man far inferior to him in point of talents and acquirements but was elected.

Gen. McIntosh again publicly exulted in the disappointments that were overwhelming his antagonist. A challenge from Mr. Gwinnett ensued-they met on the blood stained field of false honor-fought at four paces-both were wounded, Mr. Gwinnett mortally and died on the 27th of May 1777, the very time he should have been in Congress-comment is needless-reflection is necessary.

Aside from this rash error the escutcheon of Mr. Gwinnett was without a blot. He was a splendid figure, commanding in appearance, six feet in height, open countenance, graceful in his manners and possessed of fine feeling. He was a kind husband, an affectionate father, a good citizen and an honest man.

LYMAN HALL.

DECISION gives weight to character when tempered with prudence and discretion. The individual who is uniformly perched on the pivot of uncertainty and fluttering in the wind of indetermination can never gain public confidence or exercise an extensive influence. To be truly beneficial decision must receive its momentum from the pure fountain of our own matured judgment and not depend upon others to point us to the path of duty. When the child becomes a man he should think and act as a man and draw freely from the resources of his own immortal mind. He may enjoy the reflective light of others but should depend upon the focus of his own, made more clear by reflectives. The man who pins his faith upon the sleeve of another and does not keep the lamp of his own understanding trimmed and burning, is a mere automaton in life and never fills the vacuum designed by his creation. When he makes his final exit from the stage of action he leaves no trace behind-no rich memento to tell that he once lived, moved and had a being upon the earth or bore the moral image of his God. The Sages and Heroes of the American Revolution left bright examples of self-moving action and decision of character.

Among those who were roused to exertion by the reflection of their own minds was Lyman Hall, born in Connecticut 1731. He graduated in Yale College at an early age, studied medicine, married a wife before he was twenty-one, removed to Dorchester, S. C. in 1752 and commenced the practice of medicine. After residing there a short time he joined a company of some forty families, mostly New Englanders and removed to Medway in the parish of St. John, Georgia. He became a successful practitioner and was esteemed for his prudence, discretion, clearness of perception, soundness of judgment—united with refinement of feeling, urbanity of manners, a calm and equable mind and great benevolence. He had only to be known to be appreciated. As years rolled peacefully along Dr. Hall became extensively acquainted and greatly beloved. He took great interest in the happiness of those around him and in the welfare of the people at large. He was a close observer of men and things—understood well the philosophy of human rights and the principles of the tenure by which the mother country held jurisdiction over the colonies. When the marked bounds of that jurisdiction were passed he was one of the first to meet the aggressors and point his countrymen to the innovations. As encroachments increased his patriotism grew warmer—enthusiastic zeal followed, tempered by the purest motives—guided by the soundest discretion. The indecision and temporizing spirit of Georgia, for a time, was painful to her truly patriotic sons who early espoused the cause of Liberty. It was extremely annoying to Dr. Hall but only tended to increase his exertions in the work of political regeneration. Over the people of his own district he exercised an unlimited—a judicious influence. He attended the patriotic meetings held at Savannah in 1774-5 and contributed much in promoting the glorious cause just bursting into life. His immediate constituents were with him in feeling and action. All the other colonies had united in defence of their common country determined to resist the common enemy. St. John being a frontier settlement and more exposed than any other in the province, he prudently laid the subject before his people and called upon them to choose whom they would serve. They promptly decided against domination of royalty and declared for Liberty. They at once separated from the other parishes—formed a distinct political community—applied for admission into the confederation of the other colonies—passed resolutions of non-intercourse with Savannah so long as it remained under kingly authority except to obtain the absolute necessaries of life and organized committees to carry these patriotic and decisive measures into effect. Placed on such an eminence they were welcomed into the general compact as men worthy of freedom. In March 1775 they elected Lyman Hall to the Continental Congress to represent the parish of St. John that stood like an isolated island of granite in the ocean regardless of the waves of fury that were foaming around it. This example had a powerful influence on the other parishes. From this lump of liberty-leaven the whole mass became rapidly impregnated—rose beautifully and was admirably baked in freedom's oven and soon fit for use. In July following Dr. Hall had the proud satisfaction of seeing Georgia fully represented by men honest and true—always excepting Judas Iscariot *alias* Zubly. To Dr. Hall may be justly attributed the first impetus given to the revolutionary ball in his district which was formed into a new county in 1777 and named LIBERTY.

On taking his seat in Congress Dr. Hall was hailed with enthusiasm as the nucleus of patriotism that would eventually draw to one common centre the people of his province. He was a valuable acquisition to the various committees on which he was placed and gained the esteem of all around him. On the floor he was listened to with profound attention. He reasoned closely and calmly, confining himself to the question under consideration without any effort to shine as an orator. His known patriotism, decision of character, purity of purpose and honesty of heart—gave him a salutary influence that was sensibly felt, fully acknowledged and judiciously exercised. In 1776 he again took his seat in Congress and became decidedly in favor of cutting loose from the mother country. He had induced his own district to present a miniature example that stood approved by every patriot. He felt the justice of the cause of Liberty. He believed Providence would direct a successful result. He was fully convinced the set time had come to free the colonies. With such feelings he hailed the birth day of our Independence as the grand jubilee of LIBERTY. He cheerfully joined in passing the mighty Rubicon—aided in preparing the sarcophagus of tyranny and signed the certificate of freedom with a joyful heart.

He was continued in Congress up to 1780 when he took his final leave of that body where he had rendered faithful and important service. In 1782 he returned to his own State and aided in rendering more perfect the organization of her government. The enemy had destroyed his property and wreaked a special vengeance on his district generally. His family had been compelled to fly to the North and depend on the bounty of others for support. In 1783 he was elected Governor of Georgia and contributed largely in perfecting the superstructure of her civil institutions and in placing her on the high road to peace and prosperity. This accomplished he retired from public life under the broad banner of an honest and well earned fame. He then settled in Burke County where he was again permitted to pursue the even tenor of his ways and enjoy the highest of all earthly pleasure—the domestic fireside with his own dear family. Calmly and quietly he glided down the stream of time until 1790 when he closed his eyes upon the transitory scenes of earth—entered the dark valley of death and disappeared from mortals to enjoy a blissful immortality. He was deeply mourned by his relatives and numerous acquaintances and by every patriot in our nation. His name is perpetuated in Georgia by a county being named after him as a tribute of respect for his valuable services.

Dr. Hall was among those who do good for the sake of goodness—not to be seen of men and applauded by the world. In person his appearance was prepossessing. He was full six feet in height with a graceful deportment and benignant countenance. His examples are worthy of imitation. Without the luminous talents that tower to the skies in a blaze of glory that dazzles every eye—he rendered himself substantially and widely useful. He was like a gentle stream that passes through a verdant field producing irrigation in its course without overflowing and tearing up its banks. Decision of character, prudence in action and discretion in all things marked his whole career. Not a stain tarnishes the bright lustre of his public fame or private character. He lived nobly and died peacefully. With such men our UNION is safe.

JOHN HANCOCK.

The thrilling history of American Independence is ever a subject of deep interest to the patriot and philanthropist. It has no parallel in the history of nations. Its causes, progress and successful termination combine to throw around it a sacred halo that fills the reader with wonder and admiration. The noble spirits who planned and achieved it command the profoundest respect over the civilized world. As time advances that respect is ripening into veneration. The names of the signers of the Declaration of Independence, like those of the twelve Apostles, are surrounded with a refulgent glory—unfading and enduring as the planetary system. Among them was John Hancock, born near Quincy, Mass., in 1737. His father was a clergyman of eminent piety, highly esteemed by his parishioners. He died when this son was an infant, leaving him under the guardian care of an uncle, who bestowed upon him all the attention and tenderness of a father. He graduated at Harvard College in 1754, with great credit to himself and satisfaction to his numerous friends.

His uncle was a wealthy and thorough merchant and placed his nephew in his counting house that he might add to his collegiate acquirements a more important acquisition—a knowledge of men and things. In 1760 he was sent to England–saw the mortal remains of George II. laid in the tomb and the crown placed upon the head of his successor. He continued in the employment of his uncle until 1761, who then died, leaving this nephew his entire estate, supposed to be the largest of any one in the province at that time.

John Hancock was long one of the Selectmen of Boston. In 1766 he was elected to the General Assembly. He there exhibited talents of a high order as a statesman, at once gaining the esteem and admiration of his colleagues. He also gained the particular attention of a certain clique, who determined to rule or ruin him. They placed him in the crucible of slander, from which he came like gold seven times tried–triumphant and unscathed.

In the Assembly he was uniformly chairman of the most important committees. He was also elected speaker but the Governor, jealous of his rising popularity and liberal principles, put his veto upon the election.

He was a man of deep thought, general intelligence and strong mind. He had thoroughly investigated the laws of God, of nature and of man. He well understood that men are endowed by their Creator with certain inherent privileges–that they are born equal and of right are and should be free. He drank largely at the refreshing fountain of liberal principles and was among the first to expose the blind and cruel policy of the British ministers. He contributed largely in rousing his fellow sufferers to a sense of impending danger.

Although deeply interested in commercial business and more exposed to the wrath of kingly power than any individual in the province–he boldly placed himself at the head of the association prohibiting the importation of goods from Great Britain. The other provinces caught the patriotic fire from these examples.and became prepared to act their part in the tragic scenes that resulted in the emancipation of the pilgrim fathers from monarchical domination.

As a mark of special attention to this uncompromising patriot, the first seizure that was made by the revenue officers under pretence of some trivial violation of the laws was one of his vessels. So great was the excitement produced by this impolitic transaction, that large numbers were speedily collected to rescue the property. It was placed under the guns of an armed ship ready to open a broadside upon any who should dare to reclaim the vessel. The populace rose like a thunder cloud–rushed to the onset–brought away the vessel–razed to the ground some of the buildings occupied by the custom house officers and committed to the flames the boat of the collector. For a time this fire was arrested by the strong arm of power but it was never extinguished–it was the fire of LIBERTY. It only required to be fanned by that ministerial oppression that ultimately blew it into curling flames.

To prevent the recurrence of a popular outbreak several regiments of British troops, with all their loathsome vices fresh upon them, were quartered upon the inhabitants. This was like pouring bituminous coal tar upon a lurid flame. The independent spirits of Boston were not to be *awed* into subjection. The consequences were tragical. On the evening of 5th of March 1770, a party of these soldiers fired upon and killed five and wounded others of the citizens who had collected to manifest their indignation against those they *hated* more than they *feared*. Had the town been placed in the terrific cradle of an earthquake and its foundations moved to the centre, the agitation could not have been greater. Had it been melting before the burning lava of a volcano the commotion could not have been increased. The tolling of bells–the groans of the dying and wounded–the shrieks of mothers, widows and orphans–the flight of soldiers–the rush of the inhabitants–the cry of revenge–popular fury rising into a tornado of vengeance–all combined to create a scene of consternation and horror at which imagination recoils, description quails, sympathy trembles, humanity bleeds. It is a commentary, eloquently strong, upon the gross impropriety of quartering soldiers upon citizens–of enforcing civil law by military force–of invading the sanctity of domestic peace and private enjoyment.

On the following day a meeting was called composed of the concentrated talent and virtue of Boston. Strong but discreet resolutions were passed. A committee was appointed to wait upon the governor to request him to remove the troops from the town, at the head of which were Samuel Adams and John Hancock. His excellency at first refused but finding that discretion was the better part of valor, at once ordered the soldiers to the castle. He also gave a pledge that the offenders should be arraigned and tried and thus restored transient tranquillity.

The solemn and imposing ceremony of interring those who were killed was then performed. Their bodies were deposited in the same grave. Tears of sorrow, sympathy, regret and indignation were mingled with the clods as they descended upon the butchered bodies of those victims of tyranny. For many years the sad event was commemorated with deep and mournful solemnity. A hymn was sung to their memory and the torch of Liberty re-illumed at their tomb.

At one of these celebrations during the progress of the Revolution John Hancock delivered the address. A few brief extracts will be read with interest.

"Security to the persons and property of the governed is so evidently the design of civil government that to attempt a logical demonstration of it would be like burning a taper at noonday to assist the sun in enlightening the world. It cannot be either virtuous or honorable to attempt to support institutions of which this is not the principal basis. Some boast of being friends to government. I also am a friend to government—to a righteous government, founded upon the principles of reason and justice—but I glory in avowing my eternal enmity to tyranny."

He then portrayed vividly the wrongs inflicted by the mother country and urged his fellow citizens to vindicate their injured rights. On speaking of the massacre his language shows the emotions of his heaving bosom—the feelings of his noble soul.

"I come reluctantly to the transactions of that dismal night, when, in quick succession we felt the extremes of grief, astonishment and rage—when Heaven, in anger, suffered hell to take the reins—when Satan, with his chosen band opened the sluices of New England's blood and sacrilegiously polluted her land with the bodies of her guiltless sons. Let this sad tale be told without a tear—let not the heaving bosom cease to burn with a manly indignation at the relation of it through the long tracts of future time—let every parent tell the story to his listening children till the tears of pity glistens in their eyes or boiling passion shakes their tender frames."

"Dark and designing knaves—murderous parricides! how dare you tread upon the earth which has drunk the blood of slaughtered innocence shed by your hands! How dare you breathe that air which wafted to the ear of Heaven the groans of those who fell a sacrifice to your accursed ambition!! But if the laboring earth doth not expand her jaws—if the air you breathe is not commissioned to be the minister of death—yet hear it and tremble! the eye of Heaven penetrates the darkest chambers of the soul and you, though screened from human observation, must be arraigned—must lift up your hands, red with the blood of those whose death you have procured, at the tremendous bar of God."

So bold had Mr. Hancock become that the adherents of the crown put every plan and artifice in operation that could be devised to injure him. His worst enemy, the governor, nominated him to the Council, knowing that his acceptance would turn the populace against him. The plan was just as feasible as to think of baking griddle cakes on the moon.

By a prompt refusal he put his enemies to shame and increased the confidence the patriots reposed in him. He was at this time Captain of the Governor's Guard and was immediately removed. His company was composed of the first citizens of Boston. As a testimony of respect to him the members promptly dissolved.

The dread crisis finally came. The war car was put in motion on the heights of Lexington. American blood was again shed by British soldiers. The people heard the dread clarion of Revolution–multitudes rushed to the conflict–the hireling troops fled in confusion–messengers of death met them on the whole route–retribution pressed on them at every corner–the trees and fences were illuminated with streams of fire from the rusty muskets of the native yoemanry and many of Briton's proud sons slumbered in their gore on that eventful day. The watchword was then fixed–LIBERTY OR DEATH.

On the reception of this news the governor issued his proclamation in the name of his most *Christian Majesty*, George the III. declaring the Province in a state of rebellion but *graciously* offering a pardon to all returning penitents–*excepting* John Hancock and Samuel Adams. A secret attempt was made to arrest them but was foiled by information sent by Gen. Warren. They were preserved to aid in the glorious cause they had boldly and nobly espoused and to become shining lights in the blue canopy of FREDDOM–bright examples of patriotism for future generations. Their proscription by the royal governor endeared them still more to the people and their personal friends. They asked no pardon–desired no royal favor.

In 1774 Mr. Hancock was unanimously elected President of the Massachussetts Provincial Congress and in 1775 he was called to preside over the Continental Congress. It was with great diffidence he accepted this high mark of esteem, many of its members possessing towering talents and were much his seniors in age. He discharged the duties of his station with fidelity, great ability and to the satisfaction of the members and the country. His was the only name affixed to the Declaration of Independence when first published and stands, in bold relievo, at the head of the list of that noble band of fearless patriots who bearded the British Lion in his den and drove him from Columbia's soil–whose names are enrolled on the historic sunbeams of unfading light, there to remain in living brightness to the remotest ages of time.

Impaired in health and worn down by fatigue, Mr. Hancock resigned his responsible station in Congress in October 1777, having presided over that body for two and a half years with a credit highly gratifying to his numerous friends and advantageous to the cause of human rights

Soon after his return he was elected to the convention of his native state to form a constitution for its government. His talents and experience were of great service in aiding to produce a truly republican instrument. In 1780 he was elected the first governor under the new constitution and continued to fill the gubernatorial chair five years when he resigned. At the expiration of two years he was again elected to that office and continued to fill that important station during the remainder of his life.

During his administration there were many difficulties to overcome—many evils to suppress. The devastation of the war had paralyzed every kind of business—reduced thousands from affluence to poverty—polluted the morals of society and left a heavy debt to be liquidated. Conflicting interests were to be reconciled—restless spirits subdued and visionary theories exploded. A faction of 12,000 men threatened to annihilate the new government. Riots were of frequent occurrence—the civil authority was disregarded and it became necessary to call out the military to enforce order. By the prudence, decision and wise conduct of the Governor and those acting under him, all difficulties were adjusted—the clamor of the people hushed—order restored and but few lives sacrificed at the shrine of treason.

By his firm and determined course the Governor incurred the displeasure of many prominent men for a time—but when reason resumed her station and prosperity alleviated the burdens that had been so strongly felt, their better judgment gained the ascendency, the sour feelings of party spirit lost their rancor—admiration and esteem for his sterling virtues and useful talents—the long and arduous services he had rendered his State and country—disarmed his enemies of their resentment and produced uniform love and respect. None but those who then lived can fully appreciate the Alpine barriers the patriots had to surmount to preserve the Independence they achieved and reduce to practice the long nursed vision of a Republican government. To recount them would require a volume. Let them slumber in the shades of oblivion.

Gov. Hancock was strongly in favor of the adoption of the Federal Constitution and left his sick bed in the last week of the session of the Assembly and did much by his advice and influence to induce his State to sanction that important instrument of confederation which has thus far withstood the assaults of demagogues—the thunder gusts of party spirit and held us in the bonds of Union, strength and power. Paralyzed be that arm that would cut the smallest fibre of the cord of our UNION. Silenced be that voice that would whisper the word *disso-*

lution even to a zephyr. If we are true to ourselves we are destined to become the greatest nation known to history. We are appointed by the sages and heroes of the Revolution executors in perpetual succession of the richest estate ever bequeathed to a nation—LIBERTY in its pristine purity. Let us see well to its preservation that when we meet the testators in the realms of bliss, we may find our account approved and passed in the high court of heaven.

John Hancock lived to see prosperity shed the benignant rays of happiness over the broad expanse of the infant republic. He saw her institutions, laws, trade, manufactures, commerce, agriculture—all based on the firm pillars of purchased freedom and eternal justice. His Pierian vision was reduced to a happy reality—he could then die peaceful and happy.

His ill health continued until the 8th of October 1793 when suddenly and unexpectedly his soul left earth and returned to Him who gave it to join the kindred spirits that had gone before and entered upon the untried realities of the eternal world.

Governor Hancock was a man of elegant person and accomplishments—amiable and pure in all the private relations of life—highly honorable in all his actions—a polished gentleman in his manners—fashionable in his dress and style of living—charitable and liberal—a friend to the poor—a visitor of the widow and orphan—diligent in business—open and frank in his disposition—a faithful companion—a consistent patriot—an HONEST MAN.

BENJAMIN HARRISON.

COOLNESS, united with sound discretion, deep penetration, wisdom to plan and energy to execute, is an important quality. In times of high excitement it is indispensably necessary in those who wield the destiny of a community. When the fires of passion, burning in the bosoms of an enraged multitude, unite in one cyclopean volume, the mental rod of cooling discretion is necessary to regulate, guide and direct it to a proper destination. If all were alike charged with boiling desperation in times when angry commotions disturb the public peace, the holiest cause would lose its efficacy and be overwhelmed by the murky waters of fell revenge. The cool deliberations of the first Continental Congress, writhing under the lash of oppression, shed upon it a lustre that attracted the admiration of a gazing world, the smiles of angels and the approval of Heaven. The mother country was left without an excuse or just reason for the continuation of her suicidal course. To the cool and discreet conduct of the Sages and Heroes of the American Revolution we may attribute the LIBERTY we now enjoy.

No one among them demonstrated more fully this quality combined with firmness of purpose and boldness of action than Benjamin Harrison a native of Berkley, Virginia, supposed to have been born about 1730, the precise time not being a matter of record. His family descended from a near relative of Gen. Harrison, a bold leader in the revolution of the English Commonwealth who was sacrificed on the scaffold for his liberal principles. This relative settled in Surrey, Virginia, about 1640. His descendants sustained the high reputation of their ancestors and filled many important stations in the colony. It is recorded of Benjamin Harrison, son of the ancestor that located in Surrey, that "he did justice, loved mercy and walked humbly with his God," leaving a memento of character that forms the crowning excellence of human attainments. Benjamin Harrison, the father of young Benjamin now under review, was killed by lightning with two of his daughters. At that time this son was prosecuting his studies at the college of William and Mary where he finished his education at an early age. Before he arrived at his majority he had the management of a large estate left him by his father. As good sense dictated and as in duty bound, he shortly after married Elizabeth, the accomplished daughter of Col. William Bassett and niece to Lady Washington. She possessed all the high requisites of a wife.

Before he arrived at the age then required by law, he was elected to the House of Burgesses and became a leading member. His talents were of the peculiar kind calculated to lead without an apparent desire to command. His magic wand was sound discretion coolly and firmly exercised, enlivened by a good humor and sprightliness that mellowed his otherwise stern qualities. Wielding a powerful influence, the creatures of the crown were particularly courteous to him just previous to the revolution and proposed to confer upon him the highest official dignity in the colony–except governor–who must be a *native* of the mother country. Mr. Harrison was too republican and far seeing to be caught in the silken web of ministerial intrigue or royal cunning. With all his wealth and influence he was a plain common sense man opposed to the pomp of courts and the flourish of high pretensions. He went for his country and the people. He scorned to be the hireling or slave of a king. As early as 1764 he was on the committee in the House of Burgesses that prepared an address to the crown, a memorial to the House of Lords and a remonstrance to the House of Commons of Great Britain predicated upon the Virginia Resolutions anticipating the odious Stamp Act. These documents as reported were then too hard metal in view of a majority in the House and were transmuted to soft solder by the process of political alchemy well understood by the creatures of the king. The time rolled on rapidly when hard metal was made the order of the day. As British oppression increased Virginia indignation kindled to a flame that illuminated the old Dominion to its utmost bounds. Mr. Harrison was a member of the convention that met at Williamsburg on the 1st of August 1774 and passed a series of strong resolutions in favor of equal rights—sanctioned the measures of opposition adopted by New England and appointed seven delegates to the general Congress, Mr. Harrison being one. The benefits resulting from the labors of that Congress may not now be apparent to many young readers as a deaf ear was turned to the dignified proceedings by the mother country. They were twofold. 1. The true position of the two countries was clearly defined and held up to the world leaving England without an excuse for her subsequent course. 2. A personal acquaintance and free interchange of views served to establish mutual confidence and produced a concert of action between the colonies.

On the 20th of March 1775 Mr. Harrison was a member of the convention that met at Richmond and passed the bold resolutions offered by Patrick Henry. Many had the royal film removed from their eyes at that time and came to the rescue. Anticipating the appointment of delegates to a second Congress, Lord Dunmore issued his proclamation forbidding the procedure affecting to treat the convention as a mere bagatelle. Royal proclamations had lost their original efficacy. The delegates were elected, among whom was Mr. Harrison. He repaired to his post which was then more imposing than the year preceeding. A crisis had arrived big with consequences. Amidst the flashes and roar of the gathering storm cool deliberation pervaded his bosom. Mr. Randolph, the President of the first Congress being absent, Mr. Hancock was elected to fill the vacancy. When his name was announced he seemed overcome with a modest diffidence and did not move. Mr. Harrison took him in his gigantic arms and placed him in the chair saying—" We will show mother Britain how little we care for her—by making a Massachusetts man our President whom she has excluded from pardon by public proclamation."

Action—noble and god-like action became the order of that eventful era. Each gale from the north brought tidings of fresh outrages and increasing aggressions on the part of mother Britain. Congress prepared for the worst although many of the members turned a willing ear to the siren song of peace. Mr. Harrison was one of the committee appointed to devise ways and means for defence and to organize the militia throughout the colonies that were represented. After laboring arduously for a month the plan of military operations was reported that carried the American Colonies through the war. Mr. Harrison was the military man of Congress. He had the unlimited confidence of Washington. In September of that year he was one of the committee of three to consult with the Commander-in-chief and with the authorities of the regenerated colonies relative to a preparation for vigorous action. On the 29th of November he was made chairman of the committee of five to take charge of the foreign correspondence. On the 2d of December he was sent to Maryland to aid in organizing a naval armament to repel the predatory warfare of Lord Dunmore along the shores of the Chesapeake. On the 17th of January 1776 he laid before Congress a plan for the recruiting service which was adopted. On the 21st of the same month he was placed upon the committee to organize the War Department. On the 23d he went to New York with Messrs. Lynch and Allen to aid Gen. Lee in devising plans and means of defence and for erecting fortifications upon the two confluent rivers. On his return he was placed on the committee for organizing the military departments of the middle and southern Colonies. On the 6th of March he was placed on the Marine Standing Committee—bestowing on him labor in proportion to his physical as well as mental powers. He was found equal to the task imposed.

On the 26th of March 1776 Congress published a full preface to the Declaration of Independence, setting forth the contempt with which the petitions, remonstrances and appeals for relief had been treated—portraying in lively colors the constitutional and chartered rights of the American people and the manner they were trampled under foot and steeped in blood by British hirelings. The same document authorised the colonies to fit out vessels of war to meet the mistress of the seas on her own element. Mr. Harrison was chairman of a committee to select and have fortified one or more ports for the protection of these vessels and such prizes as they might take. In May he was made chairman of the committee on the Canada expedition. After consulting Generals Washington, Gates and Mifflin, he laid a plan of operations before Congress which was adopted. On the 26th of the same month he was made chairman of a commiitee of fourteen to confer with the general officers of the army relative to the plan of operations for the ensuing campaign. When matured he laid it before Congress and during its consideration was chairman of the committee of the whole. With slight amendments the report was adopted. On the 15th of June he was made chairman of the Board of War and continued in that important station until he retired from Congress. In his discharge of its duties Judge Peters remarks of him—"He was chairman when I entered upon the duties assigned me in the War Department. This gave me an opportunity of observing his firmness, good sense and usefulness in deliberation and in critical situations and much use indeed was required of these qualities when everything around was lowering and terrific."

Mr. Harrison became very popular as chairman of the committee of the whole. If in the House he uniformly presided when important questions were under consideration. He was in the chair during the discussion of the Declaration of Independence. He presented the resolution that recommended the formal preparation of that sacred document and on the glorious 4th of July 1776 sealed his heart felt approval with his vote and signature. At the thrilling moment when the members were signing what many called their death warrant, as the slender Mr. Gerry finished his signature Mr. Harrison pleasantly remarked to him "when the hanging scene commences I shall have all the advantage over you. It will all be over with me in a minute but you will be kicking in the air half an hour after I am gone." During the protracted discussions upon the Articles of Confederation Mr. Harrison was uniformly in the chair. From August to the 5th of November he was engaged in the service of his own state in the formation of the new government when he again returned to his place. He was one of the committee to advise in the movements of the northern army. When the members of Congress were compelled to fly from Baltimore to Lancaster, where they remained but one day and from there to York, Pa. he remained firm at his post. The enemies of Liberty predicted a final dissolution but proved false prophets. They even reported that Mr. Harrison was about to desert the American cause. His coolness and deliberation were often made useful in softening down hasty and harsh propositions. When the question was agitated relative to punishing the Quakers he interfered in their behalf. In after life one of them often remarked of him—"He saved us from persecution. He had talents to perceive the right and firmness enough to pursue it however violently opposed."

At the close of 1777 Mr. Harrison resigned his seat in Congress and returned to the bosom of his family. No one member had performed more labor than him—no one was more highly esteemed and honored.

He was emphatically a working man—a colossus in the cause of liberty and human rights. He returned home to enjoy repose. This was of but short duration. He was immediately elected to the Virginia Legislature and made Speaker, which station he ably filled for five consecutive years. During that period the revolutionary storm spent its fury upon the Old Dominion. The traitor Arnold and the tyrant Cornwallis were tinging its streams and saturating its soil with the blood of its noble sons. Fire, sword, murder, rapine, ruin and destruction marked their savage course. Her legislature was driven from Richmond to Charlotteville—to Staunton—to the Warm Springs and found but a transient rest at either place. During these rapid removes Mr. Harrison remained cool, collected and firm and was prolific in the best measures to ward off impending dangers. He did much to rouse the people to action and dispel the terrors of their minds. He knew no "fugitive fear"—the assertion of another writer to the contrary notwithstanding and without any foundation in fact, for the purpose of raising his own hero above his proper level by climbing upon the shoulders of the towering reputation of Mr. Harrison. This fictitious capital will not answer even at this late day. Records speak for the dead in a voice that paralyzes the slanderer like the hand writing that shook the sturdy frame of Belshazzar.

In 1782 Mr. Harrison was elected Governor of Virginia and assumed a herculean task. The recent devastations of the British army aided by tories who remained on the soil, had thrown everything into one chaotic mass. He entered upon the discharge of his duties with an energy that showed no "fugitive fear" and became one of the most popular chief magistrates that ever filled the gubernatorial chair of the Old Dominion. He was re-elected twice and was then ineligible by the constitution and once more sought retirement, Without his knowledge or consent he was immediately after nominated for the legislature and for the first time defeated. This was effected by a cunning device of his opponent. When Governor he had ordered the militia to level the embankments at Yorktown which was the first and last unpopular act of his life. This was the political hobby-horse on which his opponent gained the race. Mr. Harrison removed into the adjoining county of Surry and was returned to the same Legislature with his successful competitor. To add to the chagrin of his opponents he was elected Speaker of the House. Before the year expired he was urged to return to his former residence. Old age and declining health induced him to permanently retire from public life.

In 1788 he was a member of the Convention of his State to which the Federal Constitution was submitted and was chairman of the first committee—that of privileges and elections. He opposed the document in some of its details as being too indefinite in defining the powers of the General and State Governments but approved it as a whole with certain amendments that were returned with it. So strong was the opposition to its adoption by nearly half of the delegates that this large minority held a private meeting in the night for the purpose of adopting plans of opposition that were calculated to produce the most fatal consequences. Fortunately this cool and deliberate patriarch of Liberty gained admittance and prevailed upon them to submit to the majority of nine and pursue the legal remedy for obtaining amendments after it became the law of the land. This noble and patriotic act formed the crowning glory of his public career.

In 1790 he was nominated for Governor but declined serving and used his utmost influence in favor of Mr. Randolph and induced his own son to vote against him who was a member of the House which elected the Chief Magistrate. Mr. Randolph was unpopular with some of the members who were confident of defeating him could they prevail upon Mr. Harrison to consent to be used as a party man. His Roman integrity and influence prevailed and Mr. Randolph was made Governor.

During the next year his health declined rapidly. Shortly after his unanimous election to the Legislature he was prostrated by a severe attack of the gout which terminated his long and useful life in April 1791, leaving a large family of children to mourn the loss of a kind father—his country to lament the exit of a favorite son and noble patriot. He was the father of the late President Harrison who survived just one month after his inauguration.

Mr. Harrison was a man of great muscular power—above the middle height, graceful but plain in his manners with an intelligent countenance indicating strength of mind and decision of character. During the latter part of his life he became quite corpulent in consequence of a quiet mind and good dinners. His private character was above reproach. His wit and humor made him a pleasant companion—his intelligence and good sense made him an instructive one. His cool head, good heart, sound judgment and agreeable temperament made him an important public servant just suited to the times in which he lived. Were all our legislators of the present day like him—fanaticism and ultraism could not flourish—our UNION would be safe.

JOHN HART.

No occupation is so well calculated to rivet upon the heart a love of country as that of agriculture. No profession is more honorable–but few are as conducive to health and above all others it insures peace, tranquillity and happiness. A calling independent in its nature–it is calculated to produce an innate love of Liberty. The farmer stands upon a lofty eminence and looks upon the bustle of mechanism, the din of commerce and the multiform perplexities of the various literary professions, with feelings of personal freedom unknown to them. He acknowledges the skill and indispensable necessity of the first–the enterprise and usefulness of the second–the wide spread benefits of the last–then turns his mind to the pristine quiet of his agrarian domain and covets not the fame that clusters around them all. His opportunities for intellectual improvement are superior to the two first and in many respects not inferior to the last. Constantly surrounded by the varied beauties of nature and the never ceasing harmonious operation of her laws–his mind is led to contemplate the wisdom of the great Architect of worlds. The philosophy of the universe is constantly presenting new phases to his enraptured view. Aloof from the commoving arena of public life but made acquainted with what is passing there through the medium of the magic press–he is able to form deliberate opinions upon the various topics that concern the good and glory of his country. In his retired domicil he is less exposed to that corrupt and corrupting party spirit that is raised by the whirlwind of selfish ambition and often rides on the tornado of faction. Before he is roused to a participation in violent commotions he hears much, reflects deeply, resolves nobly. When the oppression of rulers becomes so intolerable as to induce the yeomanry of a country to leave their ploughs and peaceful firesides and draw the avenging sword–let them beware and know the day of retribution is at hand.

Thus it was at the commencement of the American Revolution. When the implements of husbandry were exchanged for those of war and the farmers joined in the glorious cause of Liberty, the fate of England's power over the Colonies was hermetically sealed. The concentrated phalanx of commingling professions was irresistible as an avalanche in the full plenipotence of force.

Among the patriots of that eventful era who left their ploughs and rushed to the rescue was John Hart, born at Hopewell, Hunterdon County, N. J. about the year 1715. The precise time of his birth is not a matter of record–his acts in the cause of Liberty are. He was the son of Edward Hart, a brave and efficient officer who aided the mother country in the conquest of Canada and participated in the epic laurels that were gained by Wolfe on the heights of Abraham. He raised a volunteer corps under the cognomen of Jersey Blues–an appellation still the pride of Jerseymen. He fought valiantly and was recompensed with praise–not the gold of the mother country. John Hart was an extensive farmer, a man of strong mind improved by reading and reflection, ever ambitious to excel in his profession. In Deborah Scudder he found an amiable and faithful wife. In the affections and good conduct of a liberal number of sons and daughters he found an enjoyment which bachelors may affect to disdain but for which they often sigh. Eden's fair bowers were dreary until Heaven's first best gift to man was there.

Known as a man of sound judgment, clear perception, liberal views and pure motives, John Hart was called to aid in public business long before the Revolution. For twenty years he had served in various stations and was often a member of the legislature. He took a deep interest in the local improvements necessary in a new country. He was a warm advocate for education, was liberal in donations to seminaries of learning. He was a friend to social order and did much to produce an equilibrium in the scales of justice. In organizing the municipal government of his county he rendered essential service. He looked on public business as a duty to to be performed when required–not as a political hobby-horse to ride upon. The public men of that day said but little. They despatched business promptly with an eye single to the general good. Sinecures were unknown–office hunters few and far between. Industry, frugality and economy in public and private matters were marked characteristics of the pilgrim fathers. Golden days! when will ye return in the majesty of your innocence and banish from our land the enervating follies, the poisonous weeds, the impugning evils that augur the destruction of our far famed Republic.

Mr. Hart was quick to discern the encroachments of the British ministry upon the chartered and constitutional rights of the colonies and prompt to resist them. The passage of the Stamp Act on the 22d of March 1765 was followed by a commotion that indicated a slender tenure of kingly power in America. This odious Act was repealed on the 18th of March 1776. But the ministerial alchemists were madly bent on new experiments. The colonists had borne the yoke of artful and increasing restrictions upon their trade and industry for fifty years.

It was presumed their necks were hardened so as to bear a heavier burden. Deluded alchemists–they little understood the kind of metal put in their crucible. Direct taxation without representation was no part of the English constitution. This violation could not be tamely submitted to. The second edition of the revenue plan revised and stereotyped in 1767 by Charles Townshend, Chancellor of the Exchequer, imposing a duty on glass, paper, pasteboard, tea and painters' colors–kindled a flame in the Colonies that no earthly power could quench. Public meetings against the measure–resolutions of the deepest censure, remonstrances of the strongest character, arguments of the most conclusive logic were hurled back upon the ministry. Boston harbor was converted into a teapot and all the tea afloat used at one drawing. Non-importation agreements, committees of safety, preparations for defence, non-intercourse, bloodshed, war and Independence followed. In all these movements Mr. Hart concurred and firmly opposed the encroachments of the crown.

In 1774 he was elected to Congress and entered upon the high duties of his station with a deep sense of the responsibilities that rested upon that body at that particular time. Mild, deliberate, cautious, discreet and firm in his purposes–he became an important member in carrying out the measures then contemplated–reconciliation and a restoration of amity. On the 10th of May 1775 he again took his place in Congress. The cry of blood, shed on the 19th of the preceding April at Lexington, had infused a spirit among the members widely different from that which pervaded their minds at the previous meeting. It was then that the cool deliberation of such men as Mr. Hart was indispensable. The ardor and impetuosity of youth had passed away–propositions and arguments were placed in the balance of reason. Causes, effects, objects, ends, plans, means, consequences–all were put in the scales of justice and honestly weighed. In this manner every act was performed with clean hands, the cause of Liberty honored, prospered and crowned with triumphant success. At this time Mr. Hart was a member and Vice President of the Assembly of New Jersey and shortly after had the proud satisfaction of aiding in the funeral obsequies of the old government and joined in the festivities of forming a new one upon the broad platform of republicanism.

On the 14th of February 1776 he was again elected to the Continental Congress and when the Chart of Liberty was presented he carefully examined its bold physiognomy–pronounced its points, features, landmarks, delineations and entire combinations worthy of freemen gave it his vote, his nature and his benediction. At the close of the session he retired from public life and declined a re-election. As he anticipated, the British drove away his family, destroyed his property and after he returned hunted him from place to place and several times had him so nearly cornered that his escape seemed impossible. His exposure in eluding the pursuit of the relentless foe brought on illness that terminated his life in 1780. He was a worthy member of the Baptist church–a devoted Christian–an HONEST MAN.

PATRICK HENRY.

GENIUS is one of the indefinable attributes of man. We may think, see, talk and write upon this noble quality, rehearse its triumphant achievements, its magic wonders, its untiring efforts–but what *is* genius? that's the question–one that none but pedants will attempt to answer. The thing, the moving cause, the *modus operandi* can no more be comprehended and reduced to materiality than the spirit that animates our bodies. The man who can do this can analyze the tornado, put the thunder cloud in his breeches pocket and quaff lightning for a beverage. Metaphysicians, physiologists and craniologists may put on their robes of mystery, arm each eye with a microscope, each finger with the acutest phrenological sensibility, whet up all their mental powers to the finest keenness, strain their imagination to its utmost tension, tax speculation one hundred per cent. and then call to their aid the brightest specimens of this occult power–the combined force could not weave a web and label it GENIUS that would not be an insult to common sense. Genius is the essential oil of mental power. No frost can freeze it, no fog can mildew it, no heat can paralyze it, no potentate can crush it. In all countries and climes it springs up spontaneously but flourishes most luxuriantly and attains a more perfect symmetry and greater strength when nurtured by intelligence and freedom. So versatile is this concentrated essence of mental power that we can form no rule to pre-determine its personal locality, its time of development, its measure of strength or the extent of its orbit. Like a blazing meteor–it bursts suddenly upon us as in the darkness of night, illuminating the world and like the lightning thunder bolt–shivers every obstacle that stands in its way.

Thus it was with Patrick Henry born at Studley, Hanover County, Virginia, on the 29th of May 1736. His father was a highly reputable man of Scotch descent–his mother was the sister of Judge Winston who was justly celebrated as an eloquent speaker. During his childhood and youth Patrick was remarkable for indolence and a love of recreation. He arrived at manhood with a limited education and ignorant of all occupations. His mind was not cultivated, his native talents were not developed, his genius was not awakened until after he was a husband and a father. His friends vainly endeavored to put him on a course of application to business by setting him up in the mercantile line. Prefering his fishing rod and gun to measuring tape he soon failed. Finding himself bankrupt he concluded that the increasing troubles of his pilgrimage were too numerous to bear alone. He married the daughter of a respectable planter and became a tiller of the ground. Unacquainted with this new vocation he soon swamped in the quagmire of adversity. He then gibed, put his helm hard up and tacked to the mercantile business. Still he was unfortunate. Poverty claimed him as a favorite son and bestowed upon him special attention. An increasing family needed increased means of support. Creditors had the assurance to shower duns upon him and cruelly reduced him to misery and want. He then conceived the idea of studying law. For the first time he felt most keenly the waste of time in his childhood and youth. He saw many of his age who had ascended high on the ladder of fame whose native powers of mind he knew to be inferior to his. He bent his whole energies to study and in six weeks after he commenced was admitted to the Bar, more as a compliment to his respectable connexions and his destitute situation than from the knowledge he had obtained of the abstruse science of law during the brief period he had been engaged in its investigation. Folded in the coils of extreme want for the three ensuing years he made but slight advances in his profession. He obtained the necessaries of life by aiding his father-in-law at a *tavern* bar instead of being at the Bar of the court. He was still ardently attached to his gun. He often took his knapsack of provisions and remained in the woods several days and nights. On his return he would enter the court in his coarse and blood stained hunting dress–take up his causes –carry them through with astonishing adroitness and finally gained a popular reputation as an advocate.

In 1764 he was employed in a case of contested election tried at Richmond, which introduced him among the fashionable and gay whose dress and manners formed a great contrast with his. He made no preparation to meet his learned and polished adversaries. As he moved awkwardly among them, some, who were squinting at him and his coarse apparel, suppossed him *non compos mentis*. When the case was tried the audience and court were electrified by his torrent of native eloquence and lucid logic. Judges Tyler and Winston who were upon the bench declared they had never before witnessed so happy and powerful an effort in point of sublime rhetoric and conclusive argument. The towering genius of Patrick Henry then burst from embryo into blooming life. From that time his fame spread its expansive wings and soared far above those of gayer plumage but of less strength. A lucrative practice banished want, sunshine friends returned and flashed around him, he leaped upon the flood tide of prosperity. From his childhood he had been a close observer of human nature—the only germ of genius visible in his juvenile character. He had studiously cultivated this important attribute which was of great advantage to him through life. So familiar had he become with the propensities and operations of the mind that he comprehended all its intricacies, impulses and variations. This gave him a great advantage over many of his professional brethren who had studied Greek and Latin more but human nature less than this self-made man. He took a deep and comprehensive view of the causes that impel men to action and of the results produced by the multifarious influences that control them. He grasped the designs of creation, the duty of man to his fellow and his God, the laws of nature, reason and revelation and became a bold advocate for liberty of conscience, equal rights and universal freedom. From the expansive view he had taken of the rights of man, the different forms of government, the oppression of kings, the policy pursued by the mother country towards the American colonies, he was fully convinced that to be great and happy a nation must be free and independent. With the eye of a statesman he had viewed the increasing oppression of the crown. They had reached his noble soul and roused that soul to action. Patrick Henry first charged the revolutionary ball with patriotic fire in Virginia and gave it an impetus that gathered force as it rolled onward.

In 1765 he was elected to the Assembly and at once took a bold decisive stand against British oppression. He introduced resolutions against the Stamp Act that were so pointed and bold as to alarm many of the older members although they admitted the truth and justice of the sentiments expressed. They had not his genius to design or his moral courage to execute. To impart a share of these to them and allay the palpitations of their trembling hearts was the province of this young champion of freedom. In this he succeeded—his resolutions were passed. Each was drawn from the translucent fountain of eternal justice—based upon equity and law and within the orbit of Magna

Charta that had been the polar star of the English government ever since the 19th of June 1215. Read them and judge.

"Resolved—That the first adventurers and settlers of this his majesty's colony and dominion brought with them and transmitted to their posterity and all other his majesty's subjects since inhabiting in this his majesty's said colony—all the privileges, franchises and immunities that have at any time been held, enjoyed and possessed by the people of Great Britain.

"Resolved—That by two royal charters granted by King James I. the colonies aforesaid are declared entitled to all the privileges, liberties and immunities of denizens and natural born subjects to all intents and purposes as if they had been born and abiding within the realm of England.

"Resolved—That the taxation of the people by themselves or by persons chosen by themselves to represent them who can only know what taxes the people are able to bear and the easiest mode of raising them and are equally affected by such taxes themselves, is the distinguishing characteristic of British freedom and without which the ancient constitution cannot subsist.

"Resolved—That his majesty's liege people of this most ancient colony have uninterruptedly enjoyed the right of being thus governed by their own Assembly in the article of their taxes and internal police and that the same hath never been forfeited or in any other way given up but hath been constantly recognized by the king's people of Great Britain.

"Resolved therefore—That the General Assembly of this colony has the sole right and power to lay taxes and impositions upon the inhabitants of this colony and that any attempt to vest such power in any person or persons whosoever other than the General Assembly aforesaid has a manifest tendency to destroy British as well as American freedom."

The cringing sycophants of a corrupt and corrupting ministry could not—*dare* not deny the correctness of these resolutions. They were hailed by every patriot as the firm pillars of American liberty. They were based upon the well defined principles of the English constitution and confined within the limits of the ancient landmarks of that sacred instrument. They were enforced by the overwhelming eloquence and logic of Mr. Henry and seconded by the cool deep calculating Johnson, who sustained them by arguments and conclusions that carried conviction and conversion to the minds of many who were poising on the agonizing pivot of hesitation a few moments before. Some members opposed them who subsequently espoused the cause of equal rights with great vigor. This opposition brought out in fuller, richer foliage the genius of the mover. He stood among the great in all the sublimity of his towering intellect the acknowledged champion of that legislative hall which he had but recently entered. Astonishment and delight held his electrified audience captive as he painted the increasing infringements of the hirelings of the crown in bold and glowing colors. He presented in perspective the torrents of blood and seas of trouble through which the colonists had waded to plant themselves in the new world. With his paralyzing finger he pointed to the chains forged by tyranny already clanking upon every ear with a terrific sound. To be free or slaves was the momentous question. He was prepared and determined to unfold the banner of LIBERTY–drive from his native soil the task-masters of mother Britain or perish in the attempt. His opponents were astounded and found it impossible to stem the mighty current of popular feeling put in motion by the gigantic powers of this bold advocate of right. The resolutions passed amidst cries of *treason* from the tories–*Liberty or death* from the patriots. The seeds of freedom were deeply planted on that day and Old Virginia proved a congenial soil for their growth. From that time Patrick Henry was hailed as one of the great advocates of human rights and rational liberty. He stood on the loftiest pinnacle of fame, unmoved and unscathed by the fire of persecution calmly surveying the raging elements of the revolutionary storm in boiling commotion around him.

In August 1774 a Convention met at Williamsburg and passed a series of resolutions pledging support to the eastern Colonies in the common cause against the common enemy. Peyton Randolph, Richard Henry Lee, George Washington, Richard Bland, Benjamin Harrison, Edmund Pendleton and Patrick Henry were appointed delegates to the general Congress. On the 4th of September this august assembly of patriotic sages met in Carpenter's Hall at the city of Philadelphia. The object for which they had met was one of imposing and thrilling interest, big with events, absorbing in character and vast in importance. The eyes of gazing millions were turned upon them–the burning wrath of the king was flashing before them–the anathema of the ministers was pronounced against them. But they still resolved to go on. The hallowed cause of freedom impelled them to action. After an address to the God of Hosts imploring his guidance the proceedings opened by appointing Peyton Randolph of Virginia President. A deep and solemn silence ensued. Each member seemed to appeal to Heaven for aid and direction. At length Patrick Henry rose in all the majesty of his greatness. Echo lingered to catch a sound. Like a colossal statue there he stood and surveyed the master spirits around him–his countenance solemn as eternity. O, my God! what a moment of agonizing suspense! His lips opened–his stentorian voice broke the painful silence–respiration regained its freedom–the hall was illuminated with patriotic fire. With the eloquence of Demosthenes, the philosophy of Socrates, the justice of Aristides and the patriotism of Cincinnatus he took a bold, broad, impartial and comprehensive view of the past, present and future–held up to the light the relations between the mother country and the Colonies–unveiled the dark designs of the corrupt unprincipled ministry–exposed their unholy claims to wield an iron sceptre over America–demonstrated clearly that their ulterior object was the slavery of the people and extortion of money and painted a nation's rights and a nation's wrongs in flaming colors of lurid brightness. The dignity and calmness of his manner, the clearness of his logic, the force of his arguments, the power of his eloquence, the solemnity of his countenance and voice–combined to inspire an awe and deep toned feeling until then unknown to the astonished audience. His elevation of thought seemed supernatural and purified by divinity. He seemed commissioned by the great Jehovah to rouse his countrymen to a sense of impending danger. He sat down amidst repeated bursts of applause the acknowledged Demosthenes of the new world–the most powerful orator of America.

In March 1775 he was a member of the Virginia Convention that convened at Richmond, where he proposed resolutions to adopt immediate measures of defence sufficient to repel any invasion by the mother country. In these he was strongly opposed by several influential members who were still disposed to cringe to royal power. Reeking with wrongs and insolence as it was, *he* held that power in utter contempt. His dauntless soul soared above the trappings of a crown backed by bayonets and sought for rest only in the goal of freedom. The following extract from his speech on that thrilling occasion will best convey the tone of his emotions–deeply felt and strongly told. His overwhelming eloquence we can but faintly imagine.

"Mr. President–It is natural for man to indulge in the illusions of hope. We are apt to shut our eyes against a painful truth and listen to the songs of that siren till she transforms us into beasts. Is this the part of wise men engaged in a great and arduous struggle for liberty? Are we disposed to be of the number of those, who, having eyes see not and having ears hear not the things that so nearly concern their temporal salvation? For my part whatever anguish of spirit it may cost, I am willing to know the whole truth–to know the worst and provide for it. I have but one lamp to guide my feet and that is the lamp of experience. I know of no way of judging the future but by the past. I wish to know what there has been in the conduct of the British ministry for the last ten years to justify those hopes with which gentlemen are pleased to solace themselves and the House? Is it that insidious smile with which our petition has lately been received? Trust it not sir—it will prove a snare to your feet. Suffer not yourselves to be betrayed by a kiss. Ask yourselves how this gracious reception of your petition comports with those warlike preparations that cover our waters and darken our land. Are fleets and armies necessary to a work of love and reconciliation? Have we shown ourselves so unwilling to be reconciled that force must be called in to win back our love? Let us not deceive ourselves sir. These are the implements of war and subjugation—the last arguments to which kings resort. I ask gentlemen, sir, what means this mortal array if its purpose be not to force us to submission? Can gentlemen assign any other possible motive for it? Has Great Britain any enemy in this quarter of the world to call for all this accumulation of navies and armies? No sir—she has none. They are meant for *us*, they can be meant for no other. They are sent over to bind and rivet upon us those chains which the British ministry have been so long forging. And what have we to oppose to them? Shall we try argument? Sir, we have been trying that for the last ten years. Have we anything new to offer upon the subject? Nothing. We have held the subject up in every light of which it is capable but it has been all in vain. Shall we resort to entreaty and humble supplication? What terms shall we find that have not already been exhausted? Let us not, I beseech you sir, deceive ourselves longer. Sir, we have done everything that could be done to avert the storm that is coming on. We have petitioned—we have remonstrated, we have supplicated, we have prostrated ourselves before the throne and have implored its interposition to arrest the tyrannical hands of the ministry and Parliament. Our petitions have been slighted, our remonstrances have produced additional violence and insult, our supplications have been disregarded and we have been spurned with contempt from the foot of the throne.

"In vain after these things may we indulge the fond hope of peace and reconciliation. *There is no longer room for hope.* If we wish to be free—if we mean to preserve inviolate those inestimable privileges for which we have been so long contending—if we mean not basely to abandon the noble struggle in which we have been so long engaged and which we have pledged ourselves never to abandon until the glorious object of our contest shall be obtained—*we must fight!* I repeat it sir—*we must fight!!* An appeal to arms and the God of Hosts is all that is left us. It is vain sir, to extenuate the matter. Gentlemen may cry—*peace! peace!*—but there is no peace. The war is actually begun. The next gale that comes from the north will bring to our ears the clash of resounding arms. Our brethren are already in the field. What is it gentlemen wish? What would they have? Why stand we here idle? Is life so dear and peace so sweet as to be purchased at the price of chains and slavery? *Forbid it Almighty God!* I know not what course others may take but as for *me—give me Liberty or Death!!!"* See the resolutions to which he thus spoke in the life of Nelson.

The effect of this speech was electrical. It insulated nearly every heart with the liquid fire of patriotism. The cry *to arms—Liberty or death* resounded from every quarter, rang through every ear and was responded by every patriot. The resolutions were seconded by Richard Henry Lee and adopted without further opposition and a committee appointed to carry them into effect. From that time the Old Dominion was renewed, regenerated and free. Her noble sons rushed to the rescue and cheerfully poured out their blood and treasure in the cause of rational liberty. Soon after, the convention adjourned to August. About that time Lord Dunmore removed a quantity of powder from the magazine at Williamsburg on board the armed ship to which he had retreated. On learning this fact Mr. Henry collected a military force and demanded the restoration of the specific article or its equivalent in money. The needful was paid and no claret drawn. A royal proclamation was issued against these daring rebels which united the people more strongly in favor of their orator and soldiers whose conduct they sanctioned in several public meetings.

In August when the Convention met Mr. Henry was again elected to the Continental Congress and remained one of the boldest champions of right and justice. In June 1776 he was elected governor of his native state. He served faithfully for two years and although unanimously re-elected declined serving longer. In 1780 he was a member of the legislature of his state and manifested an unabating zeal in the cause he had nobly espoused and essentially advanced. In 1788 he was a member of the Virginia Convention convened to consider the Federal Constitution. To that instrument he was strongly opposed because he believed it consolidated the states into one government destroying the sovereignty of each. His eloquence on that occasion is believed to have reached its zenith for the first time. His closing speech surpassed all former efforts and operated so powerfully that only a small majority voted for the adoption of the Constitution. During his remarks an incident occurred that enabled him almost to paralyze his audience. After describing the magnitude of the measure on which hung the happiness or misery of the present generation and millions yet unborn–with a voice and countenance solemn as the tomb–his eyes raised upward, he appealed to the God of Heaven and to angels then hovering over them to witness the thrilling scene and invoked their aid in the mighty work before him. At that moment a sudden thunder storm commenced its fury and shook the very earth. Upon the roar of the tempest his stentorian voice continued to rise–he figuratively seized the artillery of the elements as by supernatural power–enveloped his opponents in a blaze of liquid lightning–hurled the crashing thunderbolts at their heads and seemed commissioned by the great Jehovah to execute a deed of vengeance. The scene was fearfully sublime–the effect tremendous. The purple current rushed back upon the aching heart–every countenance was pale, every eye was fixed, every muscle electrified, every vein contracted, every mind agonized–the sensation became insupportable–the members rushed from their seats in confusion and left the room without a formal adjournment.

Mr. Henry remained in the legislature of his state until 1791 when he retired from public life. He had toiled long, faithfully and successfully for his country and his state. He anxiously desired and sought that felicity and repose found only in the family circle. In 1795 his revered friend, President Washington, tendered him the important office of Secretary of State. With a deep feeling of gratitude he declined the proffered honor. In 1794 he was again elected governor of Virginia but was in too poor health to serve. In 1799 President Adams appointed him Envoy to France in conjunction with Messrs. Murray and Ellsworth. His rapidly declining health would not permit him to accept this last of his appointments. Disease was fast consummating the work of death and consuming the iron constitution and athletic form that had enabled him to perform his duty so nobly during the toils of the Revolution. He was sensible that the work of dissolution was nearly completed and looked to his final exit with calm submission and Christian fortitude. On the 6th of June 1799 he bowed to the only monarch that could conquer him–the death king. With a full assurance of a crown of unfading glory in Heaven he threw off the mortal coil and was numbered with the dead. His loss was deeply mourned by the American nation and most strongly felt by those who knew him best. The following affectionate tribute is from one who knew him well.

"Mourn, Virginia, mourn! your Henry is gone. Ye friends to liberty in every clime drop a tear. No more will his social feelings spread delight through his house. No more will his edifying example dictate to his numerous offsprings the sweetness of virtue and the majesty of patriotism. No more will his sage advice, guided by zeal for the common happiness, impart light and utility to his caressing neighbors. No more will he illuminate the public councils with sentiments drawn from the cabinet of his own mind ever directed to his country's good and clothed in eloquence sublime, delightful and commanding. Farewell–first rate patriot–farewell! As long as our rivers flow or mountains stand–so long will your excellence and worth be the theme of our homage and endearment and Virginia, bearing in mind her loss, will say to rising generations–IMITATE MY HENRY!"

In tracing the character of this great and good man his examples in public and private life are found worthy of imitation. As by magic he threw off the cumbrous mass that so long confined his mighty genius and at once became a gigantic and brilliant intellectual man. Nature had so moulded him that the ordinary concerns of life never roused him. Had not the momentous subject of freedom engaged the mind of this bold and noble patriot he might have closed his career with its strongest powers unspent and left his loftiest talents to expire beneath the surface of the quarry from which they sublimely rose in peerless majesty. It required occasions of deep and thrilling interest to bring his latent energies into action. The exciting causes of the revolution were exactly calculated to bring him out in all the grandeur of his native greatness. As an advocate, orator, patriot and statesman– he was the colossus of his time. As Grattan said of Pitt–there was something in Patrick Henry that could create, subvert or reform–an understanding, a spirit, an eloquence to summon mankind to society or break the bonds of slavery asunder and rule the wilderness of free minds with unbounded authority–something that could establish or overwhelm empires and strike a blow in the world that should resound through the universe. He maintained his opinions with great zeal but held himself open to conviction of error. When under discussion he opposed the Federal Constitution but subsequently approved its form and substance.

His private character was as pure as his public career was glorious. He was twice married and the father of fifteen children. As a husband, father, friend, citizen and neighbor he had no superior. The closing paragraph of his will is worthy of record, showing a profound veneration for religion. "I have now disposed of all my property to my family. There is one thing more I wish I could give them and that is the Christian religion. If they had this and I had not given them one shilling they would be rich and if they had not that and I had given them all the world they would be poor."

Coming from one of the clearest minds that ever investigated the truths of revelation this short paragraph speaks volumes in favour of that religion which is despised by some–neglected by millions and is the one thing needful to prepare us for a blissful immortality beyond the confines of the whirling planet on which we live, move and have a transient being. Ponder it well, dear reader and govern yourself accordingly.

JOSEPH HEWES.

CHARITY, like the patriotism of '76, is more admired than used–more preached than practised. It descended from heaven to soften the hearts of the human family–mellow the asperities of human nature. It is the substratum of philanthropy, the main pillar of earthly felicity, the brightest star in the Christian's diadem, the connecting link between man and his Creator, the golden chain that reaches from earth to mansions of enduring bliss. It spurns the scrofula of green-eyed jealousy, the canker of self-tormenting envy, the tortures of heart-burning malice, the typhoid of boiling revenge, the cholera of damning ingratitude. It tames the fierce passions of man, prepares him for that brighter world where this crowning attribute of Deity reigns triumphant. Could its benign influence reach the hearts of all mankind the partition walls of sectarianism would be lost in pure philanthropy, individual and universal happiness would be immeasurably advanced, many of the dark clouds of human misery would vanish before its heart cheering soul reviving rays like a morning fog before the rising sun. It is an impartial mirror set in the frame of love embossed with equity and justice. Let broad and universal charity pervade the family of man with its sunbeams of living light–then a blow will be struck for the KING of kings that will resound through the wilderness of mind and cause it to bud and blossom as the rose. Then the human race will be rapidly evangelized and made free in the fraternizing gospel of the WORD–a gospel untrammelled by the inventions and dogmas of men–a gospel crowned with all the glory of original simplicity and heavenly love.

These practical remarks are induced from a review of the life of Joseph Hewes whose father was one of the persecuted Quakers of New England and was compelled to fly from Connecticut in consequence of his religious tenets. A marked inconsistency has often been fearfully exemplified by those who have fled from religious persecution. The moment they obtained the reigns of power they have become the relentless persecutors of all who would not succumb to their authority and dogmatical dictation. In the biography of Charles Carroll the reader has one example. Under the administration of the Saybrook and Cambridge platforms a sterner policy was pursued towards the Quakers of New England than against the Roman Catholics of Maryland. Before these platforms were systematically dovetailed together the Baptist denomination was banished from the old settlements. Roger Williams came from Wales to Massachusetts in 1631 and preached the Baptist doctrine at Salem and Plymouth until 1636 when he and his flock were banished for their religious opinions. He and his adherents removed into the wilderness of Rhode Island and commenced the town of Providence. They formed the first church in New England where undisturbed freedom of conscience was enjoyed with a republican form of church government. The framework of the Cambridge platform was commenced by an ecclesiastical convention in 1646 and the superstructure completed in 1648. On this platform the municipal and legislative proceedings of Massachusetts were based for sixty years. In 1656 the legislature passed a law prohibiting any master of a vessel from bringing a Quaker into the Colony under a penalty of one hundred pounds. The next year a law was passed inflicting the most barbarous cruelties upon the members of this peace-loving sect—such as cutting off their ears, boring their tongues with a hot iron, unless they would desist from their mode of worship and doff their straight coats and ugly bonnets. In 1669 a law was passed banishing them on pain of death. Four of them who refused to go were executed. Some historians have had the effrontery to excuse this cruelty because the Quakers promulged their doctrines too boldly and thus provoked the Cambridge authorities. This sophistical apology is too far fetched. It shrinks from the mellow touch of charity and the fair scrutiny of justice. The cruelty admits of no palliation until we can convert the baser passions into virtues. By recurring to the bigotry and fanaticism of that period we can readily learn *why* such a course was pursued. This affords no healing balm for the mind of a true philanthropist. We can only regret the past and rejoice that charity and liberty have so far triumphed in our now free and happy country as to dispel religious darkness and restore man to a degree of reason that has paralyzed persecution unto blood for opinion's sake—the brightest luminary in the constellation of a free government.

To avoid the penalties imposed, Adam Hewes, the father of Joseph, fled from Connecticut with his wife Providence and located near Kingston, New Jersey, where they lived peacefully and died happily. When they crossed the Housatonic river in their flight they were so closely pursued by the Indians that Providence was severely wounded in the neck by a ball from one of their guns. Joseph Hewes was born at the new residence of his parents in 1730. After receiving a good education in the Princeton school he commenced a commercial apprenticeship in Philadelphia. On completing this he entered into a successful mercantile business. For several years he spent his time in New York and Philadelphia and engaged largely in the shipping business. He was of a cheerful turn, had a penetrating mind, a sound judgment, a good heart and was persevering in all his undertakings. He was fond of social intercourse, convivial parties and sometimes exhibited the light fantastic toe. He entered into the full fruition of rational enjoyment without abusing it.

In 1760 he located at Edenton, North Carolina. He was soon after elected to the Assembly of that province and became a substantial and useful member. He made no pretensions to public speaking, was a faithful working man, a correct voter and punctually in his place. When the revolutionary storm commenced he faced its fury without the umbrella of doubt or the overcoat of fear. He was among those who pledged their lives, fortunes and sacred honors in the cause of Independence. He was a member of the Congress of 1774 and one of the committee that reported the rights of the American Colonies—the manner they had been violated and the proposed means for obtaining redress. From this circumstance we may infer that Joseph Hewes was a man of cool deliberation, clearness of perception and understood well the principles of constitutional law and chartered rights. The report of this committee is a lucid and elaborate document. By referring to the Declaration of Independence the reader will have the features of the first part portraying the rights of the colonies. By reading the instructions from the primary convention of Pennsylvania in the biography of James Smith the second part will be seen pointing out the violations. The third part proposing the preliminary means for obtaining redress are fully set forth in the following extract. After relating the injuries of the mother country the report proceeds—

"Therefore we do, for ourselves and the inhabitants of the several colonies whom we represent, firmly agree and associate under the sacred ties of virtue, honor and love of our country as follows—

"*First.* That from and after the first day of December next we will not import into British America from Great Britain or Ireland, any goods, wares or merchandize whatsoever or from any other place any such goods, wares or merchandize as shall have been exported from Great Britain or Ireland—nor will we, after that day, import any East India tea from any part of the world nor any molasses, syrups, coffee or pimento from the British plantations or from Dominico nor wine from Madeira or the West Indies nor foreign indigo.

"*Second.* We will neither import nor purchase any slaves imported after the first day of December next, after which time we will wholly discontinue the slave trade and will neither be concerned in it ourselves nor will we hire our vessels nor sell our commodities or manufactures to those who are concerned in it."

"*Third.* As a non-consumption agreement, strictly adhered to, will be an effectual security for the observation of the non-importation, we as above solemnly agree and associate, that from this day we will not purchase or use any tea imported on account of the East India Company or any on which a duty has been or shall be paid and from the first day of March next we will not purchase or use any East India tea whatever—nor will we nor shall any person for or under us purchase or use any of these goods, wares or merchandize we have agreed not to import which we shall know or have cause to suspect were imported after the first day of December, except such as come under the rules and directions of the tenth article hereafter mentioned.

"*Fourth.* The earnest desire we have not to injure our fellow subjects in Great Britain, Ireland or the West Indies, induces us to suspend a non-importation until the 10th day of September 1775 at which time, if the said Acts and parts of Acts of the British Parliament therein mentioned [see them in the life of James Smith] are not repealed, we will not directly or indirectly export any merchandize or commodities whatsoever to Great Britain, Ireland or the West Indies except rice to Europe.

"*Fifth.* Such as are merchants and in the British and Irish trade will give orders as soon as possible to their factors, agents and correspondents in Great Britain and Ireland not to ship any goods to them on any pretence whatever as they cannot be received in America and if any merchants residing in Great Britain or Ireland shall directly or indirectly ship any goods, wares or merchandize for America in order to break the said non-importation agreement or in any manner contravene the same, on such unworthy conduct being well tested it ought to be made public and on the same being so done we will not from henceforth have any commercial connection with such merchants.

"*Sixth.* That such as are owners of vessels will give positive orders to their captains or masters not to receive on board their vessels any goods prohibited by the said non-importation agreement on pain of immediate dismission from service.

"*Seventh.* We will use our best endeavors to improve the breed of sheep and increase their number to the greatest extent and to that end we will kill them as seldom as may be, especially those of the most profitable kind nor will we export any to the West Indies or elsewhere and those of us who are or may become overstocked with or can conveniently spare any sheep will dispose of them to our neighbors, especially to the poorer sort, on moderate terms.

"*Eighth.* We will in our several stations encourage frugality, economy and industry and promote agriculture, arts and the manufactures of this country especially that of wool and will discountenance and discourage every species of extravagance and dissipation, especially all horse-racing and all kinds of gaming, cock-fighting, exhibitions of shows, plays and other expensive diversions and entertainments and on the death of any relation or friend, none of us or any of our family will go into any further mourning dress than a black crape or ribbon on the arm or hat for gentlemen and a black ribbon and necklace for ladies and that we will discontinue the giving of gloves and scarfs at funerals.

"*Ninth.* Such as are venders of goods and merchandize will not take the advantage of the scarcity of goods that may be occasioned by this association but will sell the same at the rate we have been respectively accustomed to do for twelve months last past and if any vender of goods or merchandize shall sell any such goods on higher terms or shall in any manner or by any device whatsoever depart from this agreement, no person ought nor will any of us deal with any such person or his or her factor or agent at any time hereafter for any commodity whatever.

"*Tenth.* In case any merchant, trader or other persons shall import any goods or merchandize after the first day of December and before the first day of February next, the same ought forthwith, at the election of the owners, to be either re-shipped or delivered up to the committee of the county or town wherein they shall be imported, to be stored at the risk of the importer until the non-importation agreement shall cease or be sold under the direction of the committee aforesaid—and in the last mentioned case the owner or owners of such goods shall be reimbursed out of the sales the first cost and charges, the profits, if any, to be applied towards relieving and employing such poor inhabitants of the town of Boston as are the immediate sufferers by the Boston Port Bill and a particular account of all goods so returned, stored or sold, to be inserted in the public paper and if any goods or merchandize shall be imported after the first day of February the same ought forthwith to be sent back again without breaking any of the packages thereof.

"*Eleventh.* That a committee be chosen in every county, city and town by those who are qualified to vote for representatives in the legislatures whose business it shall be attentively to observe the conduct of all persons touching the association and when it shall be made to appear to the satisfaction of a majority of any such committee that any person within the limits of their appointment has violated this association, that such majority do forthwith cause the truth of the case to be published in the Gazette to the end that all such foes to the rights of British America may be publicly known and universally condemned as the enemies of American liberty and henceforth we respectively will break off all dealings with him or her.

"*Twelfth.* That the committee of correspondence in the respective Colonies do frequently inspect the entries of the custom house and inform each other from time to time of the true state thereof and of every other material circumstance that may occur relative to the association.

"*Thirteenth.* That all manufactures of this country be sold at reasonable prices so that no undue advantage be taken of a future scarcity of goods.

"*Fourteenth.* And we do further agree and resolve that we will have no trade, commerce, dealings or intercourse whatsover with any colony or province in North America which shall not accede to or which shall hereafter violate this association but will hold them unworthy the rights of freemen and inimical to the rights of their country.

"And we do solemnly bind ourselves and our constituents under the ties aforesaid to adhere to this association until such parts of the several Acts of Parliament passed since the close of the [French] war as impose or continue duties on tea, wine, molasses, syrups, coffee, sugar, pimento, indigo, foreign paper, glass, painter's colors imported into America and extend the powers of the Admiralty Courts beyond their ancient limits, deprive the American subjects of trial by jury, authorize the judge's certificate to indemnify the prosecutor from damages that he might otherwise be liable to from a trial by his peers, require oppressive security from a claimant of ships or goods before he shall be allowed to defend his property are repealed. And we recommend it to the Provincial Conventions and to the committee in the respective Colonies to establish such further regulations as they may think proper for carrying into execution this association."

Upon this report all the subsequent proceedings of Congress were predicated. It is a reasonable conclusion that nothing but the most aggravated violations of their rights could induce such men as composed the first general Congress to enter into a solemn agreement like the one here recited. By every true patriot it was adhered to with the most scrupulous fidelity. The spirit of liberty was infused through the whole mass of patriots—men, women and children. The oppression had become intolerable.

After a session of about two months Congress adjourned to the ensuing May when Joseph Hewes again took his seat with the venerable sages of the nation. He was an important member of committees. He was continued at his post the next year and hailed with joy the proposition to cut the gordian knot that bound the Colonies to mother Britain. When the set time arrived to strike the final blow for liberty he sanctioned the procedure with his vote and signature. His industry, accurate knowledge of business, his systematic mode of performing every duty, gained for him the admiration and esteem of all the members, one of whom remarked of his duties upon the secret committee—" Mr. Hewes was remarkable for a devotedness to the business of this committee as even the most industrious merchant was to his counting house." He was upon several of the most important committees. Upon the one for fitting out a naval armament he stood in the front rank. He was virtually the first Secretary of the Navy. With scanty funds he speedily fitted out eight armed vessels. He was very active in raising supplies in his own state to strengthen the sinews of war and oil the wheels of the general government. In 1777 when the enemy threatened vengeance on his state he declined his seat in Congress and gave his services specially to her until 1779 when he resumed his place in the national legislature. He was then worn down with labor and in poor health. He attempted active duty but disease had prostrated his physical powers and sown the seeds of death. He continued to attend in the House when able until the 29th day of October when he left the Hall for the last time. On the 10th of November 1779 his immortal spirit left its earthy tabernacle and returned to Him who gave it. His premature death was deeply lamented and sincerely mourned. Congress passed the usual resolutions—the members and officers wore the badge of mourning for thirty days. His remains were buried in Christ Church yard, Philadelphia, followed by the members and officers of Congress, the General Assembly and Supreme Executive Council of Pennsylvania, the French minister, the military and a large concourse of other persons all anxious to pay their last respects to one whom they esteemed in life and whose memory they delighted to honor after death. The funeral ceremony was performed by Bishop White, then chaplain of Congress. His dust has ever since reposed in peace undisturbed by malice or slander. His name is recorded on the Magna Charta of our Liberty—his fame will live until the last vestige of American history shall be blotted from the world. Not a blemish rests upon his private character or public reputation. In all things he was an honest man.

The person of Joseph Hewes was elegant, his countenance open and intelligent, his manners pleasing and polished, his whole course honorable and just. He would have been a good man had there been no Heaven to gain or misery to shun. He practised virtue for its intrinsic worth not to gain the applause of men. It was not a cloak for him—it emanated from the inmost recesses of his pure heart. With such men to guide our ship of state our UNION is safe.

THOMAS HEYWARD.

MAN, to understand and correctly estimate the magnitude and design of his creation, must become familiar with the thousand springs of the undying spirit within him. The labyrinthian mazes of the immortal mind must be explored and traced from earth to native heaven. The depths of human nature must be sounded and its channels clearly marked.

Upon the axis of reason revolving thought performs its endless circuit with mathematical precision guided by the centripetal force of sound discretion—or it is projected from its legitimate orbit by the centrifugal power of random folly into the regions of senseless vacuity or visionary sophistry. Its ceaseless motion is as perpetual as the purple stream of our arteries—its momentum is inconceivable—its tenure—ETERNITY. It travels through space with more celerity than lightning—its earthly career can be arrested only by death.

To reflect, investigate, reason, analyze—is the province of our intellectual powers. To comprehend the grand and harmonious organic structure of nature—the wisdom of the great Architect of universal worlds—the relation man bears to his God and his fellow man—is to learn that human beings are endowed by their Creator with equal and inalienable rights and that they are in duty bound to maintain them.

Justice marks out the golden path, reason leads the way—patriotism impels to action. The man whose mind is cast in the mould of wisdom by the almighty hand of the great Jehovah—if he brings into proper exercise the combined powers of intellectual and physical force, can never be made a pliant slave. As his soul is expanded by the genial rays of intelligence he duly appreciates his native dignity, becomes enraptured with the blessings of LIBERTY—resolves to be free. If he is groaning under the oppressions of tyranny and wears the galling chains of servility—as light shines upon him he will be roused to a mighty effort to burst the ignominious thongs that bind him—assert his inherent rights—assume his proper sphere.

Thus acted the patriots of the American Revolution with whom Thomas Heyward was associated during that eventful period. He was the eldest son of Col. Daniel Heyward a wealthy and respectable planter and was born in the parish of St. Luke, S. C. in 1746. His opportunities for obtaining a liberal education were freely afforded by the father and faithfully improved by the son. He became ardently attached to the Greek and Roman classics and was enraptured with the history of their Republican Freedom with all its corruptions clustering around it. The principles of rational Liberty became deeply rooted in his mind at an early age. As manhood dawned upon him they were thoroughly matured.

On completing his collegiate education he commenced the study of law under Mr. Parsons. His proficiency in that intricate branch of science was rapid—substantial. He possessed an analyzing mind and never passed over a subject superficially. He was a close student—explored the vast fields of civil and common law with a zeal and rapidity as rare as it is necessary and commendable. When he became familiar with the principles laid down by Blackstone and understood fully the rights secured to persons and property by Magna Charta and the British Constitution and compared them with the iron rod of restriction held over the Colonies by the mother country—he was roused to a just indignation—more than *prima facie* evidence of a clear head and sound common sense.

After completing his course with Mr. Parsons he went to England and entered the Middle Temple where he became a finished lawyer—a polished gentleman. Although amply supplied with money he was not led astray by the fascinating allurements of pleasures that flatter to seduce—then ruin and destroy. To enrich his mind with science, legal lore and useful knowledge, was the *ultimatum* of his soul. He mingled with what was termed *refined* society in London which formed a striking contrast with the republican simplicity of the same grade in his own country. The fastidious hauteur of English etiquette was far from being congenial to his mind and did not accord with his ideas of social life. He there met claims of superiority over native Americans that he knew were based alone on vain pride or wilful ignorance. His feelings were often wounded by indignities cast upon his countrymen. This riveted his affections more strongly upon his native land. They served as fuel to replenish the glowing fire of patriotism already burning in his bosom. The pomp of royalty and the empty splendor of the court had no charms for him. The awful distance between the haughty monarch and the honest peasant—the towering throne and the worthy yeomanry, operated on his mind like a talisman and gave his soul a fresh impetus towards the goal of Liberty. The more he saw of practical monarchy, the more he became opposed to its iron sway. The more he saw of the action of ministers the more he was convinced the king was a mere automaton and did not exercise common volition. Officially he was a marble Colossus—impervious to all feeling—only to be gazed at. As a human being he was not to be consulted or troubled with complaints from his subjects but to act as directed by those whose tool he was.

After closing his course in the law temple he made the tour of Europe and returned to the warm embrace of his relatives and friends richly laden with legal attainments and experimental knowledge. He had become familiar with the theories of monarchical government and their practical demonstration. He understood well the policy of the mother country toward the American Colonies. He had seen her political artificers engaged at the forge of despotism preparing chains for his beloved countrymen. He had seen her coffers yawning to receive the ill gotten treasures wrested from his fellow citizens by the hireling tax gatherers. His own estate had been laid under contribution to swell the unholy fund. His neighbors were writhing under the lash of British oppression. To enlighten their minds, to make them fully understand their danger, their interests and their duty, became the business of this zealous patriot. Possessed of a bold and fearless mind directed by a clear head, an honest heart, a sound judgment and a rich store of useful intelligence—his exertions were crowned with auspicious success. His salutary influence was extensively felt—his sterling worth was duly appreciated.

Mr. Heyward was a member of the first Assembly of South Carolina that set British power at defiance. He was also a member of the council of safety. He discharged his duties with firmness, prudence and zeal. No fugitive fear disturbed his mind—no threatened vengeance moved his purposes. His eyes were fixed on the temple of freedom, his soul was insulated by the electric fluid of patriotism, he was resolved on liberty or death. His life, property and sacred honor were freely pledged in the glorious cause. He was elected to the Continental Congress in 1775 but declined serving because so young. A large delegation of his constituents subsequently waited upon him and persuaded him to take his seat in the Congress of 1776. He was a warm advocate for the adoption of the Declaration of Independence—the revered instrument that shed new lustre on the intellect of man. By his signature he confirmed the sincerity of his soul in all he had said in its favor. His conscience, his country and his God approved the act.

Under the new form of government he was appointed a Judge of the civil and criminal courts. In that capacity he was called to perform a painful but imperious duty. Several persons were arraigned before the court charged with treasonable correspondence with the enemy. They were tried, found guilty and condemned to be hung in sight of the British lines at Charleston. With feelings of deep sympathy and humanity but with the firmness of a Roman he performed his duty with great dignity and delicacy. He knew they had immortal souls and soared above the cold indifference—the keen invective that sometimes *have* but *never* should be resorted to.

Judge Heyward also participated in the perils of the field. He commanded a company of artillery at the battle of Beaufort and was severely wounded. At the attack upon Savannah he exhibited the bravery of a practised veteran. At the siege of Charleston he commanded a battalion and was one of the unfortunate prisoners who were incarcerated in the Spanish castle at St. Augustine, Florida. During his absence his property was destroyed by the enemy. To cap the climax of his severe afflictions, his amiable and accomplished wife had been laid in the tomb. She was the daughter of Mr. Matthews and married in 1773. The tidings of these heart rending occurrences did not reach him until he was exchanged and arrived at Philadelphia. With the calm and dignified fortitude of a Christian, philosopher and hero—he met the shafts of afflictive fate. He mourned deeply but submissively the premature exit of the wife of his youth, the companion of his bosom. His physical sufferings and loss of property he freely offered at the altar of liberty without a murmur.

He again resumed his duties upon the judicial bench and discharged them ably and faithfully up to 1798. He was an influential member of the convention that framed the constitution of his native state in 1790.

He married Miss E. Savage for his second wife. After the close of the trying and bloody scenes through which he had passed he sat down under his own vine and fig tree and enjoyed the rich fruits of that LIBERTY he had sacrificed so much to obtain. A peaceful quiet reigned in his bosom and around him. The British yoke had been thrown off–the Gallic chain had been broken–the increasing millions of his countrymen could look through the vista of the future with cheering hope and exquisite pleasure. In the enjoyments of the present–past pains were merged. He was happy.

Infirmity and old age admonished him that his mission on earth was fast drawing to a close. He retired from the public arena covered with epic and civic honors enduring as the pages of history. In the full fruition of a nation's gratitude and a nation's freedom his last years passed smoothly away. He went to his final rest in March 1809, leaving his tender wife to mourn the loss of a kind husband, his interesting children to feel deeply the loss of a tender father–his country to regret the exit of a devoted patriot, an able judge, an honest man. He was a noble philanthropist–an able judge–a discreet statesman–a pure citizen–a sterling patriot–a friend to our UNION.

STEPHEN HOPKINS.

MANY gravely contend that there should be at least two political parties to insure the safety of our Republic that one may watch and detect the corrupt designs of the other. If this position is sound we are pre-eminently safe for we have some half dozen distinct organizations besides remnants of old ones and guerrilla squads that plunder from each. The argument would have force if the people would fix political landmarks as distinctive as those of 1800–banish demagogue leaders–revive the patriotism of '76–be guided entirely by love of country, prudence, strict justice and the fear of God which is the beginning of all wisdom. As now constituted, for one to correct the faults of the other would be like Satan rebuking sin. There are good men under the banners of each party but they have neither brass or intrigue enough to become leaders. According to modern political tactics as *practised*, a successful party leader must unite an oily tongue with a gum elastic conscience, a grain of truth with a pound of falsehood, a spark of honesty with any quantity of deception circumstances may require and be ready to sacrifice honor, integrity and friends to carry out party plans–ever pressing toward the end with the force of a locomotive regardless of the means put in requisition. Merit is not sought for by demagogues. *Available* is the omnipotent word–the grand countersign–the magic passport to a nomination and *when* nominated the candidate *must* be voted for although destitute of capacity, moral virtue and every requisite of a statesman. The sad consequences are more fearfully demonstrated as time rolls onward. Dignity, decorum, common courtesy are often banished from our legislative halls. Crimination and recrimination usurp the place of sound logic–reason is dethroned, common decency outraged, the business of our country neglected, our national character disgraced–all because the people do not rise in their majesty and do their duty. We have an abundance of men in the back ground as pure as the patriots of '76. Let them be brought forward and put to work. The few of this kind who are in the public arena cannot long stem and never roll back the mighty torrent of political corruption now sweeping over this land of boasted freedom. To render our UNION safe our political leaders and public functionaries must be men who are influenced alone by an ardent desire to promote the general good of our whole country–aiming at holy ends to be accomplished by righteous means. Such were the sages of the American Revolution.

The patriarch Stephen Hopkins stood among them in all the dignity of an honest man. He was born at Scituate, Rhode Island, on the 7th of March 1707. He was the son of William Hopkins a thorough farmer whose father, Thomas Hopkins, was one of the pioneers of that province. The school advantages of Stephen were limited to the elementary branches of an English education, then very superficially taught. By the force of his own exertions he perfected this embryo basis and reared upon it a magnificent superstructure. He spent all his leisure hours in exploring the fields of science. At his majority he was a farmer in easy circumstances and devoted a portion of the day and his quiet evenings to the acquisition of useful knowledge. No profession not literary affords so much facility for mental improvement as that of agriculture. Independent tillers of the soil–if you are not intelligent the fault is your own. The time was when ignorance was winked at. That dark age has passed away. Now common sense and reason command all to drink at the scholastic fountain.

Mr. Hopkins acquired a thorough knowledge of mathematics at an early age and became an expert surveyor. At the age of nineteen he was placed in the ranks of men by marrying Sarah Scott whose paternal great grandfather was the first Quaker who settled in Providence. She died the mother of seven children. In 1755 he married the widow

Anna Smith a pious member of the Society of Friends. In 1731 he was appointed Town Clerk and Clerk of the Court and Proprietiers of the county. The next year he was elected to the General Assembly where he continued for six consecutive years. In 1735 he was elected to the Town Council and for six years was President of that body. In 1736 he was appointed a Justice of the Peace and a Judge of the Common Pleas Court. In 1739 he was elevated to the seat of Chief Justice of that branch of the judiciary. During the intervals of these public duties he spent much of his time in surveying. He regulated the streets of his native town and those of Providence and made a projected map of each. He was the Proprietary surveyor for the county of Providence and prepared a laborious index of returns of all land west of the seven mile line, which still continues to be a document of useful reference. Beauty and precision marked all his draughts and calculations.

In 1741 he was again elected to the assembly. The next year he removed to Providence where he was elected to the same body and became Speaker of the House. In 1744 he filled the same station and was appointed a Justice of the Peace for that town. In 1751 he was appointed Chief Justice of the Superior Court and for the fourteenth time elected to the assembly. In 1754 he was a delegate to the Colonial Congress held at Albany, N. Y. for the purpose of effecting a treaty with the Five Nations of Indians in order to gain their aid or neutrality in the French war. A system of union was then and there drawn up by the delegates similar to the Articles of Confederation that governed the Continental Congress which was vetoed by England.

In 1755 the Earl of Loudoun in command of the English forces made a requisition for troops upon several colonies and on Rhode Island for four hundred and fifty men to check the triumphant career of the French and Indians then devastating the frontier settlements. Mr. Hopkins rendered efficient aid in this service and had the pleasure of seeing the complement promptly made up. In 1756 he was elected Chief Magistrate of the colony and was found fully competent to perform the duties of the office. In 1757 the loss of Fort William Henry and the sad reverses of the English army made it necessary that the colonies should raise an efficient force for self-protection. A company of volunteers was raised in Providence composed of the first gentlemen of the town and Mr. Hopkins put in command over it. The timely arrival of troops from England deprived them of their anticipated epic laurels. The next year this useful man was again elected Chief Magistrate and served seven of the eleven following years.

In 1767 party spirit was rolling its mountain waves over Rhode Island so fearfully that it threatened the prostration of social order and civil law. Anxious for the welfare of the colony this patriotic Roman put forth his noblest efforts to check its bold career. In his message to the Assembly he expressed his deep solicitude for the restoration of harmony and proposed retiring at once from the public service if it would contribute in the slightest degree to heal the political breach. To prove his sincerity he shortly after left the public arena contrary to the wishes of his friends. His picture of that era so much resembles the political map of our country at the present time that an extract may be excused.

"When we draw aside the veil of words and professions—when we attend to what is *done* and what is *said*—we shall find that Liberty is a cant term of faction and freedom of speaking and acting, used only to serve the private interests of a party. What else can be the cause of our unhappy disputes? What other reason for the continual struggle for superiority and office? What other motive for the flood of calumny and reproach cast upon each other? Behold the leading men meeting in cabals [caucusses] and from thence dispersing themselves to the several quarters to delude the people. The people are called together in tippling houses, their business neglected, their morals corrupted, themselves deluded—some promised offices for which they are unfit and those with whom these arts will not prevail are tempted with the wages of unrighteousness and are offered a bribe to falsify their oath and betray their country. By these scandalous practices elections are carried and officers appointed. It makes little difference whether the officer who obtains his place in this manner is otherwise a good man—put in by a *party* he must do what *they* order without being permitted to examine the rectitude even of his *own* actions. The unhappy malady runs through the whole body politic. Men in authority are not revered and loose all power to do good. The courts of judicature catch the infection and the sacred balance of justice does not hang even. All complain of the present administration and hard times and wish they might grow better. But complaints are weak, wishes are idle, cries are vain—even *prayers* will be ineffectual if we do not universally amend."

This catalogue of evils is followed by a strain of paternal advice that should come home to the reader like a voice from the tomb.

"My countrymen permit me to remind you of the blood, the suffering, the hardships and labors of our ancestors in purchasing the Liberty and privileges we might peaceably enjoy. How can you answer it to fame, to honor, to honesty, to posterity if you do not possess these inestimable blessings with grateful hearts, with purity of morals and transmit them with safety to the next generation. Nothing is desired but that every man in community act up to the dignity of his own proper character. Let every freeman carefully consider the particular duty allotted to him as such by the constitution. Let him give his suffrage with candor for the person he sincerely thinks *best* qualified. Let him shun the man who would persuade him *how* to vote. Let him despise the man who offers him an office and spurn the sordid wretch who would give him a bribe. Let him think it his duty to give his vote according to his conscience and not depend on others to do his duty for him. * * * * Officers and magistrates I would humbly entreat to consider that your turn has come to serve the *commonwealth* and not yourselves. Your own discreet and exemplary behaviour is your best authority to do good. It is vain to command others to practice what we ourselves omit or to abstain from what they see us do. When moderation and example are insufficient to suppress vice, power ought to be used even to its utmost severity if necessary and above all–that in all cases and under all circumstances–*justice should be equally, impartially and expeditiously administered.*"

This plain lucid exposition of the duties of freemen merits the highest consideration of every private citizen and public officer. It is the inspired effusion of a clear head, a good heart and a noble soul. In language of sublime simplicity it exhibits laconically the only sure foundation of a republican government. It strikes at the very root of alarming evils that are now hanging over our beloved country like an incubus. It is plain truth plainly told and should be strongly felt and implicitly obeyed by all who desire the perpetuity of our glorious UNION.

In June 1769 Mr. Hopkins was called to aid in taking observations upon the transit of Venus over the disk of the sun. So highly were his services prized on that occasion that the pamphlet published on the subject was dedicated to him. This rare phenomenon occured in 1739–61–69 and will occur again in 1874 and 1996 if the planetary system continues its usual revolutions–of which no man knoweth–not even the angels in Heaven.

Previous to the American Revolution Governor Hopkins had incurred the displeasure of the British ministry by licensing vessels from his province to trade with the French and Spanish Colonies. In this he did not violate the constitution or any law of England. He continued to grant the privilege regardless of the authority illegally assumed by Great Britain to direct the local concerns of the Colony. He had long been convinced that the mother country cared more for the *fleece* than the *flock* she claimed in America which had been often left to contend alone against a merciless foe. With such convictions on his mind, a republican to the core and valuing liberty above life–he was prepared to resist the first scintillations of the unconstitutional claims made by corrupt and corrupting ministers. When the Stamp Act was passed his voice and pen were arrayed against it. He showed clearly that this and other Acts of parliament had no foundation in justice and were in violation of the British constitution.

In 1772 the mountain waves of local party spirit having subsided in Rhode Island and its effervescence calmed by the absorbing question of British oppression Mr Hopkins again took his seat in the Assembly and was continued for three years. In 1774 this patriarch statesman was elected to the Continental Congress and entered with a calm determined zeal upon the responsible duties of that august Convention. The same year he proposed and obtained the passage of a bill prohibiting the slave trade in his Colony which greatly incensed the crown officers. To show that he strongly felt what he earnestly advocated– he emancipated all his negroes–the descendants of whom still reside in Providence. He had incorporated their freedom in his will dated some time previous.

In 1775 he was appointed Chief Justice of his Colony–was a member of her Assembly and member of Congress. The ensuing year he was one of the immortalized band of patriots by whose exertions a nation was born in a day and who signed and delivered the certificate of legitimacy to their grateful constituency. The same year he was President of the board of commissioners of the New England States who convened at Providence to devise plans for the promotion of the glorious cause of freedom. The next year he presided over a similar board at Springfield, Mass. In 1778 he was a member of Congress for the last time. The next year he closed his long, useful and arduous public career in the Assembly of his native state and retired crowned with the rich foliage of unfading honors–the growth of near half a century. The pure escutcheon of his public fame and private worth was without a spot to obscure its brilliant lustre. As a municipal officer, judge on the bench, legislator, Chief Magistrate of the Colony and member of the Continental Congress–he discharged his duties faithfully, honestly and ably–with an eye single to the glory of his country.

As a public speaker Mr. Hopkins made no pretensions to elocution but was ever listened to with profound attention. His reasoning was strong–always to the point and his speeches short. His was a vigorous, clear, inquiring, analyzing mind, that surmounted every barrier with the same fortitude, energy and determined resolution that carried Bonaparte over the Alps, Roger Sherman to the pinnacle of fame,

Franklin to the summit of science. He was a laborious and extensive reader and a friend to education. He was the principal founder of the Providence library in 1750 and when it was destroyed by fire in 1760-contributed largely towards the purchase of a new supply of books. He was the father of the free school system still in successful operation in Rhode Island. He was a friend to unshackled religion-breathing charity for all whose deportment gave them the impress of divine grace-the only genuine touchstone of true piety. He admired most the creed of the Society of Friends who frequently held meetings at his house. All gospel ministers were made welcome to his hospitable mansion which many called the ministers tavern. He was plain in everything and deprecated pomp and vain show in others.

In addition to his multifarious public duties he was extensively engaged in agriculture, manufactures and commerce. He was a systematic and thorough business man-scrupulously honest, honorable and liberal. He never became wealthy but enjoyed a competence through life. He was repeatedly placed in the crucible of domestic affliction. Of the seven children by his first wife not one survived him. One son was murdered by the Indians, another died in Spain-the youngest, who was the fourth sea captain of the brothers, was presumed to have been lost at sea as his vessel was never heard from after leaving the port of Providence.

The eventful career of patriarch Hopkins was closed on the 13th of July 1785 after enduring the course of a lingering fever with the same calm fortitude that had marked his whole life. He had lived respected and esteemed-he died peaceful and happy. To the last moments of his life he retained full possession of his mental powers and approached the confines of eternity with a seraphic smile that augured heaven. He had long labored under physical infirmities of a nervous nature. For many years it had been difficult for him to write his name in consequence of an attack of paralysis. His ashes rest peacefully in the city of Providence in his native state. His death produced a mournful sensation over the whole country.

In the relations of husband, father, kinsman, friend, gentleman, citizen, benefactor, philanthropist, neighbor and Christian-this public sprited man and pure patriot was a model of human excellence. By the force of his own exertions he made himself one of the most useful men on record in our history. Let us all imitate his bright examples that we may do our duty in life, be triumphant in death and happy through the rolling ages of eternity.

FRANCIS HOPKINSON.

WIT and wisdom are seldom both prominently developed in the same person. Wit serves to amuse or exhilarate but rarely produces useful reflection or an improvement of mind. It is emphatically a plume and exposes the head it ornaments to many an arrow from the bow of revenge. Wit makes many conquests but no willing subjects. It produces many *bon mots* and but few wise sayings. It is an undefined and undefinable propensity—more to be admired than coveted—more ornamental than useful—more volatile than solid—a dangerous sharp edge tool—like a coquette, pleasing company for the time being but not desirable for a life companion.

Rare instances have occurred where the sage, statesman, philosopher and wit have been combined in the same person. Sheridan was such a man and in our own country Francis Hopkinson was the American Sheridan. He was the son of Thomas Hopkinson of Philadelphia, born in that city in 1737. His father was a man of superior attainments—his mother one of the best and most intelligent matrons of that age. His father died in 1751 and left the widowed mother with limited means to struggle with all the accumulating difficulties of raising and educating a large family of children.

Under her guidance and instruction young Francis improved rapidly in his education and exhibited a bright and promising intellect. To advance the interests of her children she confined herself to the absolute necessaries of life. Being devotedly pious, she took peculiar care in planting deeply in their tender minds the pure principles of virtue and cautiously guarding them against all the avenues of vice, the portals of which are ever open. She taught them the design of their creation—the duty they owed to God and their fellow men and that to be truly happy they must be truly good. With this foundation firmly laid, she placed this son in the University of Pennsylvania where he graduated at an early age and commenced the study of law under Benjamin Chew. He was a close student and made rapid advances in legal acquirements. He possessed a brilliant and flowing fancy, a lively imagination and captivating manners. Although ardently attached to the solid sciences he was fond of polite literature, poetry, music and painting. He excelled in humorous satire, keen as that of Swift and Sheridan. Fortunately these combined talents were brought into extensive usefulness.

In 1765 he visited London where he continued two years making the acquaintance of the leading men of that metropolis and learning the political aspect and designs of the ministers toward his native country. He added largely to the fund of knowledge before acquired and came home prepared to work.

Soon after his return he married the accomplished Ann Borden of Bordentown N. J. thus fulfilling an important part of the design of his creation. He also appreciated the value of the institution he had honored and the joys of connubial felicity. In rearing his children he took the system that had been so successfully adopted by his venerable mother whose instructions were fresh upon his memory. He could adopt no better plan or find a more perfect model to imitate. For a time the cares and pleasures of his family and his professional business engrossed his attention. A crisis soon arrived that arrested this translucent stream of happiness. The oppressions of the mother country had become alarming. Agitation had commenced among the people. The best services of every patriot were needed. His were promptly and efficiently rendered. It was for him to do much in opening the eyes of the great mass to a just sense of their violated rights. This he did by various publications written in a style so humorous and fascinating as to be generally read. He painted the injustice of the crown and the insults of its hireling officers in vivid colors. His Pretty Story–his Letters to James Rivington–his Epistle to Lord Howe–his two Letters by a Tory–his translation of a Letter written by a Foreigner–his Political Chatechism and the New Roof–were all productions of taste and merit. They were of vast importance in rousing the people to a vindication of their rights–the achievement of their Independence.

During the administration of Gov. Dickinson, political dissensions and party spirit rolled their mountain waves over Pennsyvlania threatening to destroy the fair fabric of her new government. The pen of Mr. Hopkinson was instrumental in restoring order. In an essay called–" A full and true Account of a violent Uproar which lately happened in a very Eminent Family"–he exposed the factious partisans to such keen and severe ridicule that they threw down the weapons of rebellion sooner than if a thousand bayonets had been pointed at their breasts.

He was among the first delegates elected to the Continental Congress and fearlessly recorded his name on the Declaration of Rights that has proved a consolation to the sons of FREEDOM–a Boanerges to the enemies of LIBERTY. Always cheerful and sprightly, he contributed much towards dispelling the gloom that often pervaded the minds of his colleagues amidst disaster and defeat. He knew their cause was righteous—he believed Heaven would crown it with ultimate success and triumphant victory. His personal sacrifices had been many—still he was ever cheerful and illuminated all around him with flashes of the most brilliant wit. At the commencement of the struggle he held a lucrative situation in the Loan Office under the crown and was a favorite of the king—but the king was not a favorite of his—he promptly severed the connection. With all his wit and humor he was firm as a herculus. With the fancy of a poet he united the soundness of a sage—with the wit of a humorist he united the sagacity of a politician.

He succeeded George Ross as Judge of the Admiralty Court and was subsequently Judge of the U. S. District Court in Philadelphia. He was highly esteemed for his judicial knowledge, impartial justice and correct decisions. He filled every station in which he was placed with credit and dignity. His frequent essays continued to do much towards correcting the morals of society by ridiculing its evils and abuses. Guided by a sound discretion, sarcasm and satire are the most powerful weapons wielded by man. Their smart upon the mind is like cantharides on the skin but often requires something more than a cabbage leaf and cerate to heal it. The wit of Mr. Hopkinson was of a noble cast flowing from a rich and chaste imagination—never violating the rules of propriety—always confined within the pale of modesty but keen as a finely finished rapier. He was an admirer of sound common sense and a zealous advocate of Common School education. He properly appreciated the bone and sinew of our country and knew well that the perpetuity of our Liberty depends more upon the general diffusion of *useful* knowledge fit for *every* day use in the ever varying business concerns of life than upon the high toned literature of colleges and universities. He admired the industrious mechanic—he esteemed the honest farmer. In the yoemanry of the soil and inmates of the shops he recognized the defenders of our country.

The useful career of Judge Hopkinson was closed prematurely by an apoplectic fit on the 9th of May 1791. He left a widow, two sons and three daughters to mourn his untimely end and their irreparable loss. He was amiable and urbane in his manners—open and generous in his feelings—noble and liberal in his views—charitable and benevolent in his purposes—an agreeable and pleasant companion—a kind and faithful husband—an affectionate and tender parent—a stern and inflexible patriot—a consistent and active citizen—a useful and honest man. He was like some rare flowers—while their beauty pleases their medicinal qualities are of great value. In the hands of such men our UNION can be preserved.

WILLIAM HOOPER.

An astute writer has beautifully observed—"If the sea was ink, the trees pens and the earth parchment, they would not be sufficient to write down all the praises due to God for Liberty." How few there are in our wide spread Republic who realize the truth of this sublime sentiment. How few among the directors of the destiny of our nation who make the law of God the beginning of wisdom. This apothegm is based upon reason, justice and sound philosophy. No sophistry can controvert it—no casuistry entangle it. To shun all wrong and practise all right is the great *desideratum* of earthly bliss. Vice is crowned with thorns and plumed with thistles. All the evil passions are a laboratory for the manufacture of the miseries of human life. The futile pleasures of earth—vanity, vain glory—the whole category may be richly clustered with blossoms but bear no nutritious fruit. We must look to the great Author of all good for substantial enjoyment. We must implicitly obey his laws to be truly wise. The greatest men who have ever graced the stage of action fully recognized the power and feared to offend the great Jehovah. The Sages and Heroes of the American Revolution were constantly under the influence of this salutary principle. This is inferred from their writings, examples and the proceedings of the Continental Congress. Days of humiliation and prayer were frequently fixed and recommended by legislative proclamation by the general government and by the states.

Among those of the sages who appear to have lived in the fear of God was William Hooper, born at Boston, Massachussetts, on the 17th of June 1742. He was the son of the Rev. William Hooper who came from Kelso, south of Scotland and was for many years pastor of Trinity Church in Boston. He was a man of high accomplishments, a finished scholar, a learned theologian, an eloquent preacher, a devoted Christian, a useful and beloved pastor. Being of a slender constitution William received the first rudiments of his education from his father. At the age of seven he entered the school of Mr. Lovell where he remained eight years. He then became a student of Harvard University. His talents were of a high order—his industry untiring. He was ever averse to fleeting pleasures and trifling amusements. During vacation he explored his father's library instead of indulging in a relaxation from study and mingling in the convivial circle. He had a great taste for the classics and belles lettres. He paid close attention to elocution and composition. He aimed at refinement in everything.

He graduated in 1760 and commenced the study of law under James Otis one of the most distinguished counsellors of that time. From the piety he had exhibited from his youth his father had hoped he would incline to the pulpit but freely yielded to his choice. He was a thorough law student and was admitted to the Bar richly laden with the elements of his profession. By several wealthy connections residing in Wilmington, North Carolina, he was induced to locate at that place where he soon obtained a lucrative business. To convince the people that he contemplated a permanent residence and a fulfilment of all the noble designs of his creation–he married Anna Clark, a lady of unusual accomplishments, strength of mind and high attainments. His legal fame rose rapidly upon a substantial basis. In 1768 he was employed to conduct several important public trials which he managed with so much skill and address as to place him in the first rank of able advocates. He was treated with marked attention by Governors Tryon and Martin and by Chief Justice Howard. His estimable character, superior talents and extensive influence were worth securing for their royal master. The ulterior object they had in view it required no Daniel to interpret. Mr. Hooper was one who had no price. He was not a man of principle according to his personal interest but a noble patriot of the first water. He had received his legal education in Boston where the designs of the British ministers had been probed for years. He had imbibed liberal views, was a friend to equal rights and had planted himself upon the firm basis of eternal justice from which flattery could not seduce or dangers drive him.

Previous to the Revolution he gave a sample of his moral and personal courage worthy of record. In 1766 a dangerous association was formed in North Carolina called *Regulators*–composed mostly of poor, ignorant, desperate men who were led by those of more intelligence but with baser hearts who promised them large rewards in the end. They had increased so rapidly that in 1770 they amounted to three thousand. They opposed the civil authorities–drove the judges from the bench, committed personal outrages and threatened to destroy all order, defying civil and military power. Mr. Hooper took a bold stand against them–advised a prompt attack by the military–his plan was approved–a severe battle ensued–the insurgents were dispersed and quiet restored. In 1773 he was elected to the Assembly of his province at the very time the creatures of the crown attempted to throw a ministerial coil around the people. In William Hooper they found a troublesome customer–a bold, fearless, eloquent, uncompromising opponent to their schemes of tyranny. In the legislative hall he met them with unanswerable arguments. By a series of essays he spread their designs before the people. He was no longer flattered by the crown officers but became a favorite with those he esteemed more highly—the people who returned him again to the Assembly. A question came before that body that tested the powers of Mr. Hooper. The statute creating the judiciary had expired. In framing a new one an attempt was made to model it so as to meet the designs of the British cabinet. So powerful was the influence of this friend of the people that he kept his opponents at bay and the province was a year without courts. He was then fully before his constituents the champion of equal rights. By the people he stood approved and admired.

On the 25th of August he was elected to the general Congress in which he rendered efficient services. He was one of the important committee that prepared a statement of the rights of the colonies, the manner these rights had been infringed and the most probable means of effecting their restoration. He was one of the committee that reported the statutes that affected the trade and manufactures of the colonies. Upon the report of these two committees the proceedings of that Congress were based which raises a fair presumption that the very best men were placed upon them. The next year he was returned to Congress and was chairman of a committee to prepare an address to the people of Jamaica relative to British oppression. It was written by him in a bold and vigorous style and proved conclusively that ministerial insolence was lost in ministerial barbarity—that resistance or slavery had become the issue.

On the 12th of June 1775 Mr. Hooper offered the following preamble and resolution which were passed by Congress, corroborating the intimation in the exordium to this article.

"It is at all times an indispensable duty devoutly to acknowledge the superintending providence of the great Governor of the world, especially in times of impending danger and public calamity—to reverence and adore His immutable justice as well as to implore his merciful interposition for our deliverance—therefore

Resolved—That it is recommended by Congress that the people of the American Colonies observe the 20th day of July next as a day of public humiliation, fasting and prayer."

The zeal and exertions of this ardent patriot in the glorious cause of freedom were constant and vigorous. He served industriously in committee rooms and was greatly esteemed as a forcible debater in the House. In the spring of 1776 he was a member of the conventions that convened at Hillsborough and Halifax in N. C. and was one of the leading and most eloquent speakers. He also prepared an address to the people of the British empire which was written with great nerve and energy. He then took his seat in Congress and boldly supported the Declaration of Independence. He had long been convinced of its necessity and rejoiced to find his views so warmly supported by the ablest men of that eventful era. When the thrilling moment arrived to take the final question his vote and signature sanctioned the bold measure.

In February 1777 he obtained leave of absence from Congress and returned to his family. When the news of the defeat of Washington at Germantown reached him he was surrounded by a circle of his friends who seemed dismayed at the intelligence. He rose calmly from his seat and earnestly remarked—" We have been disappointed but now that we have become the assailants there can be no doubt of the issue." Before his return from Congress his property at Wilmington had suffered from royal vengeance. His personal safety was then in jeopardy—he was compelled to flee to the interior to avoid the hemp. His family had removed several times. He and all the signers had made arrangements with the French minister to remove to one of the French West India islands in the event of the failure to maintain Independence. He did not return to Wilmington until it was evacuated by the enemy in 1781. During his absence his family remained exposed to the proverbial insults of his Christian majesty's officers and soldiers. He remained in the province for the purpose of rousing the people to action and was an efficient member of the new government. In 1782 he removed to Hillsborough for the purpose of resuscitating his long neglected private affairs and again took his place at the Bar. In 1786 he was appointed by Congress a member of the court organized to determine the controversy between New York and Massachusetts relative to disputed territory which was amicably settled by the parties.

Mr. Hooper continued to aid in the legislation of his adopted state and pursue his profession until 1787 when his health became impaired which compelled him to retire from public life and the bar and seek that repose in domestic enjoyment that had always been more congenial to his mind than public stations however lofty. In his retirement he carried with him the esteem of his fellow citizens and the gratitude of a nation of freemen. Not a blemish soiled the bright escutcheon of his public character or private reputation. He had served his country faithfully and sacrificed his fortune on the altar of liberty. With the strictest fidelity he had discharged the duties of husband, father, friend, citizen, lawyer, patriot, statesman. From the high eminence of conscious integrity he looked down upon a life well spent. With the eyes of faith he looked forward to a crown of unfading glory. In October 1790 he closed his eyes in death and returned to the bosom of that God whom to fear is the beginning of wisdom. Dear relatives, ardent friends and a grateful nation mourned his premature death. Mr. Hooper was of the middle height, slender and elegant in form, gentlemanly and engaging in his manners, with strangers rather reserved, with his friends frank and familiar, free from affectation, of a serious turn, at all times candid and sincere. His countenance beamed with intelligence and benignity, his powers of conversation were pleasing, instructive, chaste and classical. His habits were in strict accordance with the religion he exemplified. His disposition was benevolent, hospitable and kind. As a public speaker he was eloquent, logical, persuasive, sometimes sarcastic. As a whole he was among the best specimens of man as he comes from the clean hands of the Creator. Whilst we admire his virtues let us imitate his examples.

SAMUEL HUNTINGTON.

CONSISTENCY is the crowning glory of meritorious fame. It is a bright jewel in the escutcheon of a name. It sheds a radiating lustre over the actions of men. "Be consistent" was a Roman motto and once guided its sages, heroes and *literati* in the path of duty–the surest path of safety. Consistency dignifies the man and prepares him for noble and god-like deeds. It is based upon wisdom and discretion–the pilot and helm of the bark of life in navigating the ocean of time. Without it the breakers of chaos, the sand bars of folly–the rocks of disaster cannot be avoided. Without it the brightness of other talents and attainments of a high order are often eclipsed by the clouds of error and obscured by the breath of ridicule. With it–mediocrity shines and enables the plough-boy of the field–the mill-boy of the slashes–the apprentice of the shop to reach the pinnacle of enduring fame and leave the indiscreet classical scholar to sink into a useless gilded ornament in the world. Dr. Young has truly said–"With the talents of an angel a man may be a fool." Consistency is susceptible of cultivation and should be kindly and earnestly pressed upon youth by parents and teachers. It is of more importance than the entire contents of the magazine of classic lore combined with an eloquence that could move the world of mankind.

The sages of the American Revolution were remarkable for consistency. Many of them rose from the humble walks of life to eminence by the force of their own exertions guided by this darling attribute and became the most useful men of that eventful epoch.

Among this class Samuel Huntington held a respectable rank. He was born on the 2d of July 1732 at Windham, Connecticut. He was the son of Nathaniel Huntington a plain farmer, who gave this son only a common English education whilst three of the others graduated at Yale College, all of whom became ministers of the gospel, one of them attaining a fair eminence as a theological writer. Their pious mother led them to the pure fountain of gospel truth and had the pleasure of seeing the four walking hand in hand towards the goal of unfading joy. Samuel followed the plough until he was twenty-two years of age. He was remarkable for industry and sterling honesty. He was an extensive reader and a close observer of men and things. His native talent was strong, his judgment clear, his reflections deep. From his childhood to his grave consistency chastened every action. This was his strong forte and insured his success through life. It was a passport beyond the power of a college to give.

Samuel Huntington went from the plough to the study of law in his father's house, loaning books from Zedekiah Elderkin of the Norwich bar. With astonishing rapidity he mastered the elementary books—was admitted and opened an office in his native town. His reputation as an honest and consistent man was already on a firm basis. His fame as a safe counsellor and able advocate soon added another story to this superstructure. He did not aim at Ciceronean power or Demosthenean eloquence but closely imitated Solon and Socrates. His manner was plain but marked by a deep sincerity that seldom fails to impress the minds of a court and jury favorably—often foiling the most brilliant displays of forensic eloquence. With his other strong qualities he combined the motive power of business—PUNCTUALITY. Although he had gained a lucrative practice in his native town he removed to Norwich in 1760 where a wider field opened before him. Carrying out the principle of consistency, in 1762 he emerged from the lonely regions of celibacy with Martha, the accomplished daughter of Ebenezer Devotion and entered the delightful bowers of matrimony—thus giving him and her an importance in society unknown to single blessedness. Martha proved an amiable companion—blending the accomplishments of a lady, the industry of a housewife, the economy that enriches, the dignity of a matron—the piety of a Christian.

In 1764 Mr. Huntington was elected to the Assembly and made a very efficient member. In 1765 he was appointed king's attorney and performed the duties of that office until the pestiferous atmosphere of monarchical oppression drew him from under the dark mantle of a corrupt and impolitic ministry. In 1774 he was elevated to the bench of the Superior Court and the next year was a member of the Council of his state. When the all important subject of American rights and British wrongs came under discussion he threw the whole force of his influence in favor of the cause of equal rights. In October 1775 he took his seat in the Continental Congress and became a prominent and useful member. In January following he again took his seat in the Hall of Independence and fearlessly advocated the necessity of cutting the Gordian knot that held the Colonies to England. The solemnity of his manner, the strong force of his reasoning, the lucid demonstrations of his propositions and the unvarnished sincerity of his patriotism—were calculated to carry conviction to every heart and impart confidence to the wavering and timid. He was present at the birth of our nation on the 4th of July 1776 and aided in presenting the admired infant at the sacred font of LIBERTY and became a subscribing witness to the imposing ceremonies of that eventful day. He was continued in Congress until 1781 when ill health compelled him to retire for a season.

He was a man of great industry, honesty of purpose, profound research, clearness of perception and had acquired a large fund of practical knowledge. Human nature he had studied closely. He was well versed in general business, political economy, principles of government and rules of legislation which gave him a place upon important committees. He succeeded Mr. Jay as President of Congress and so ably discharged the duties of that responsible station that when compelled to retire from ill health a vote of thanks was placed upon the record. Hoping that he might be able to return the chair was not permanently filled for a long time. During a part of the *interim* of his absence from Congress he presided on the bench and was a short time in Council. In 1783 he returned to Congress and at the termination of the session declined a re-election. He had aided in finishing the mighty work of national freedom—the star spangled banner was floating in the breeze of Liberty—his country had triumphed over a merciless foe—her political regeneration had been consummated—America was disenthralled and he desired retirement from public life. This he was not permitted to enjoy. In 1784 he was appointed Chief Justice of his state—the ensuing year Lieutenant Governor and the next year was elected Governor of Connecticut, which office he held until the 5th of January 1796, when death took him from earth and its toils. He had lived the life of the righteous man—his last end was like his. He was a ripe shock full of corn—uniformly beloved in life—deeply mourned in death.

Mr. Huntington was a man of middle stature, dark complexion, keen eyes, countenance expressive, with a deportment calculated to make a favorable impression at first sight. In his life we find much to admire—nothing to condemn. His superior virtues and uniform consistency eclipsed the frailties of his nature. In the performance of all the duties of public and private life he was a model worthy of the closest imitation. From the plough in the field through his bright career to the presidential chair in Congress—to the chief magistracy of his own state—his every action was marked with consistency. His fame is based upon substantial merit—he rendered his name dear to every freeman. The history of his examples should exercise a salutary influence over the mind of every reader capable of appreciating the high importance of being consistent in all things and of perpetuating our UNION through all time.

WILLIAM IRVINE.

Mobocracy is a fearful spirit that is roused to action by a greater variety of elements than either of the unfortunate propensities of human nature. Based upon the boiling anger of those who put this ball in motion—reason is dethroned—reflection paralyzed—justice unheeded—mercy banished—the laws disregarded—power defied. It is the volcano of human society—the earthquake of social order—the whirlpool of brutality—the vortex of destruction. It is fanned by fell revenge—inflamed with burning fury—propelled by reckless impulse—delights in human gore—revels in demoniac confusion—rides on the tornado of faction—snuffs the whirlwind of discord and provokes the indignation of all peaceful citizens.

Occasions rarely occur to justify these sudden demonstrations of disorder and more rarely result in good. Deliberate action is usually the best to remedy evils that exist in fact—most certainly the best to cure those that are only imaginary. Thus reasoned the Sages and Heroes of the American Revolution and governed themselves accordingly. After petitions and entreaties for redress failed to remove the wrongs heaped upon them—a systematic and dignified mode of resistance was adopted—not mobocracy. They could then appeal to Heaven for the justice of their cause and elicited the admiration of gazing nations in the course they pursued.

Among those who put forth their noblest exertions to advance the interests of the cause of equal rights was William Irvine who was born near Enniskillen, Ireland, in 1742. His ancestors removed from the north of Scotland to the Emerald Isle. His grandfather was an officer in the corps of grenadiers that fought so desperately at the battle of the Boyne. The grandfather of General Wayne was a brave officer in the same service. The noble descendants of both were in the same corps in the glorious cause of American Independence.

After completing his school education Mr. Irvine became a student of the celebrated Dr. Cleghorn and proved to be an excellent surgeon and physician. On the completion of his studies he was appointed a surgeon on board a British man of war where he served for several years with great diligence and success. In 1763 he came to America and located at Carlisle, Pennsylvania. His eminent talents—professional acquirements and large experience, soon gained for him a liberal practice and proud reputation. Having no innate love for mother Britain, he was prepared to meet the fearful crisis of the American Revolution. There were numerous powerful influences in Pennsylvania adverse to war with England. There was a large number of the Society of Friends opposed to war under all circumstances, although quick to seize the benefits resulting from it. The Proprietary interests were very extensive and in favor of the crown. To rouse the people to resistance was a herculean task. In this work Mr. Irvine was active and successful. He was a member of the several preliminary conventions in the colony and became extensively influential in preparing the people for action.

In January 1776 he was commissioned to raise and command a regiment which duty he performed promptly. On the 10th of the following June he joined Gen. Thompson's brigade with his troops near the village of Trois Rivieres. A disastrous attack was immediately made upon the vanguard of the British army stationed at that place. Gen. Thompson, Col. Irvine and near two hundred subordinate officers and privates were taken prisoners and sent to Quebec. An exchange was not effected until April 1778. On his return Gen. Irvine was put in command of the second Pennsylvania brigade and continued in that position until 1781. He was then transferred to Pittsburgh and assigned to the important and delicate duty of guarding the north-western frontier. It was important because difficult to obtain supplies and was menaced with British and Indians. It was delicate because there existed strong animosities between the first inhabitants of that region and those from Western Virginia who claimed the territory occupied. Under these circumstances the appointment was a high compliment from the sagacious Washington. The happy results were a strong eulogy upon the wisdom of both. Gen. Irvine succeeded in reconciling the two contending factions–brought order out of confusion and restored harmony and good feeling among those who had long been at variance. This augmented his strength against the enemy and increased the confidence of the people in that entire section of country. He was continued in that command until the war closed and the star spangled banner waved triumphantly over the United States of America.

In 1786 Gen. Irvine was elected to Congress and proved an efficient and valuable member. He was active and useful in the board to settle the accounts between the states and the general government. He was a member of the Pennsylvania convention that sanctioned the Federal Constitution. In 1796 he was one of the commissioners who were despatched to visit the whiskey boys and endeavor to bring them back to reason, duty and safety. When it became necessary to order out a military force to quell the insurrection Gen. Irvine was put in command of the Pennsylvania troops.

A short time after he rendered this last service in the tented field he removed to Philadelphia. He there received the appointment of Intendant of military stores which office was subsequently long and ably filled by his son Callender. He was also President of the Society of Cincinnati. Peacefully and calmly Gen. Irvine glided down the stream of time until the summer of 1804 when he closed his active and useful career and took his departure for " that country from whose bourne no traveller returns." He had lived highly respected–his death was deeply mourned. His public and private reputation were untarnished–he performed all the duties of life nobly and fulfilled the great design of his creation.

THOMAS JEFFERSON.

Genuine moral courage is a sterling virtue–the motive power of the true dignity of man. It invigorates the mind like a refreshing dew falling gently on the flowers of spring. It is a heavenly spark–animating the immortal soul with the fire of purity that illuminates the path of rectitude. It is an attribute that opposes all wrong and propels its possessor right onward to the performance of all right. Based on virtue and equity, it spurns vice in all its borrowed and delusive forms. It courts no servile favors–fears no earthly scrutiny. No flattery can seduce it–no eclat allure–no bribe purchase–no tyrant awe–no misfortune bend–no intrigue corrupt–no adversity crush–no tortures can subdue it. On its breastplate is inscribed in bold relievo– *Fiat justitia–ruat cœlum.* [Let justice be done though the heavens fall.] Without it, fame is ephemeral–renown transient. It is the saline basis of a good name that gives enduring richness to its memory. It is a pillar of light to revolving thought–the polar star that points to duty, secures merit and leads to victory. It is the soul of reason–the essence of wisdom–the crowning glory of mental power. It was this that nerved the leaders of the American Revolution to noble and godlike action.

In the front rank of this band of patriots stood Thomas Jefferson, who was born at Shadwell, Albemarle County, Virginia, on the 24th of April 1743. His ancestors were among the early pioneers of the Old Dominion and highly respectable. They were Republicans to the core–in affluent circumstances and exercised an extensive and happy influence.

Thomas was the son of Peter Jefferson, a man much esteemed in public and private life. The liberal feelings imbibed from him by this son were conspicuous at an early age. From his childhood the mind of Thomas Jefferson assumed a high elevation–took a broad and expansive view of men and things.

He was educated at the college of William and Mary and was always found at the head of his class. Untiring industry in the exploration of the fields of science marked his collegiate career. He analyzed every subject he investigated, passing through the opening avenues of literature with astonishing celerity. His mind became enraptured with the history of classic Greece and republican Rome. Improving upon the suggestions of liberal principles found in the classics, he early matured his political creed and opposed every kind of government tinctured with the shadow of monarchy, hierarchy or aristocracy.

After completing his collegiate course he commenced the study of law under Chancellor Wythe, whose liberal views were calculated to mature and strengthen those already preponderating in the mind of Jefferson. With regard to the oppressions of the mother country–the justice and necessity of resistance by the Colonies, their kindred hearts beat in unison. By a thorough investigation of the principles of law and government, Jefferson became rapidly prepared to enter upon the great theatre of public life–the service of his injured country. Planting himself upon the broad basis of Magna Charta–encircling himself within the pale of the British Constitution–he demonstrated most clearly that the ministry of the crown had long been rapidly advancing beyond the bounds of their legitimate authority–exercising a tyranny over the Colonies not delegated to them by the constitution of the monarchy they represented. So luminous were his expositions of chartered rights on the one hand and accumulating wrongs on the other, that he became the nucleus of a band of patriots resolved on LIBERTY OR DEATH.

At the age of twenty-two he was elected to the legislature which enabled him to disseminate his liberal principles throughout the Colony. He proclaimed himself the unyielding advocate of equal rights and had engraved upon his watch seal–" Resistance to tyrants is obedience to God." By his eloquence and unanswerable arguments he kindled the flame of opposition in old Virginia which increased as tyranny advanced. In 1769 a resolution was passed by the legislature–*not to import a single article from Great Britain.* In the advocacy of this proposition by Mr. Jefferson, the adherents of the crown were astonished at the boldness and firmness with which he exposed and laid bare the venal corruption of the British cabinet. It gave a fresh impetus to the cause of Liberty just bursting into life.

With ample pecuniary means–with talents equal to the work he had undertaken, his soul illuminated with the fire of patriotism–his indignation roused against the hirelings of the king–his sympathies excited by the sufferings of his country–his moral courage raised to the zenith of its glory–Mr. Jefferson was amply armed for the conflict and became one of the master spirits of the Revolution–a gigantic champion of universal freedom–a pillar of fire, flashing terror and dismay into the ranks of the foe.

He wrote " A Summary View of the Rights of British America"–addressed it to the king respectfully but very plainly pointed to the true position of the two countries and the final result of the policy of ministers. The following is an extract. " Open your breast, sire, to liberal and expanded thought. It behooves you to think and act for your people. The great principles of right and wrong are legible to every reader. To perceive them needs not the aid of many counsellors. The whole art of government consists in the art of being honest." The art of being *honest* in matters of government is a knotty problem for some modern politicians to solve. Were they all *honest* a political millennium would illuminate our country–bring us back to primitive *tangible* landmarks and unmask multitudes of political wolves cunningly dressed in sheep's clothing.

So exasperated was Lord Dunmore on perusing this article from the pen of Jefferson that he threatened to arrest him for high treason. Finding most of the members of the legislature, then in session, quite as treasonable in their views he at once dissolved that body.

The following year the British ministry, in answer to petitions for redress of grievances, sent to the legislature of the Old Dominion a series of propositions that *they* termed conciliatory but which added insult to injury. Their fallacy was exposed by Mr. Jefferson in such a masterly strain of eloquent burning logic and sarcasm, that conviction was carried to a large majority of his colleagues. They were referred to a committee which reported an answer written by him and was very similar to the Declaration of Independence. This reply was immediately adopted. The ball of resistance was put in motion–the electric fluid of patriotism commenced its insulating powers in the north and south–extending from sire to son, from heart to heart, until the two streams of fire met in the centre–then rising in grandeur, formed the luminous arch of Freedom–its chord extending from Maine to Georgia–its versed sine resting on the city of Penn.

Under its zenith at Philadelphia, Mr. Jefferson took his seat in the Continental Congress on the 21st of June 1775. Although one of the youngest members of that venerated assembly of patriotic sages, he was hailed as one of its main pillars. Known as a man of superior intelligence, liberal sentiments, strict integrity, stern republicanism and unbending patriotism–his influence was strongly felt and judiciously exercised.

From the beginning he advocated a separation from the mother country and ably met every objection urged against it. In his view, oppression, not recognised by Magna Charta, had dissolved all allegiance to the crown–that the original contract had been cancelled on the heights of Lexington by American blood. Submission was no longer a virtue–the measure of wrongs had been overflowing for years–public sentiment demanded the sundering of the Gordian knot–a voice from Heaven proclaimed in tones of thunder–" *Let my people go.*"

The following year the Declaration of Independence was proposed. Mr. Jefferson was appointed chairman of the committee to prepare this momentous document. The work was assigned to him by his colleagues. He performed the task with a boldness of design and beauty of execution before unknown and yet unrivalled. The substantial result of his labor has long been before the world. Admiring nations have united in bestowing the highest encomiums upon this sacred instrument. As a masterpiece of composition–a lucid exposition of the rights of man–the principles of a free government–the sufferings of an oppressed people–the abuses of a corrupt ministry and the effects of monarchy upon the destinies of man–it stands unequalled. Pure in its origin–graphic in its delineations–benign in its influence and salutary in its results–it has become the chart of patriots over the civilized world. It is the *ne plus ultra* [nothing more beyond] of a gigantic mind raised to its loftiest elevation by the finest touches of creative Power–displaying its noblest efforts–brightest conceptions–holiest zeal–purest desires–happiest conclusions. It combines the attributes of justice–the flowers of eloquence–the force of logic–the soul of wisdom. It is the grand palladium of equal RIGHTS–the polar star of rational LIBERTY–the Magna Charta of universal FREEDOM and has crowned its author with laurels of enduring fame.

In the autumn of 1776 Mr. Jefferson was appointed a commissioner to the court of France in conjunction with Messrs. Franklin and Deane for the purpose of forming a treaty of alliance. Ill health of himself and family and an urgent necessity for his services in his native state, induced him to decline the proffered honor and resign his seat in Congress.

He was immediately elected to the first legislature of his state convened under the new Constitution. On taking his seat in that body his attention was at once directed to the demolition of the judicial code which had emanated from the British Parliament. The work of rearing a new superstructure was mostly performed by him. The first bill he introduced was aimed at the slave trade and prohibited the farther importation of negroes into Virginia. This is a triumphant refutation of the accusation often reiterated against Mr. Jefferson–*that he was an advocate of slavery*. To its *principles* he and a large majority of the South were always opposed and submitted to it *practically* by ENTAIL. It is a fact beyond dispute that he struck the first blow in the Colonies at the unhallowed trade of *importing* human beings for the purpose of consigning them to bondage. That this was the first great step towards a correction of the most cruel feature of this system, originated by philanthropic England, is equally true. To transfer those negroes, born in the United States, from one section of this country to another, bears no comparison in cruelty to the heart-rending barbarity of forcing the African from his native home–even should he fall into the hands of those *emancipators* who, instead of returning him to his native shores–*put him an "*APPRENTICE*" to hard labor on their own plantations.* Consistency thou art a jewel rather rare. Common humanity forbids the sudden emancipation of the slaves as proposed by emissary Thompson and his converts.

Mr. Jefferson next effected the passage of bills destroying entails–primogeniture–the church as established by England and various others–assimilating the entire system of jurisprudence in the state to its republican form of government. He reported one hundred and twenty-six bills, most of which were passed and constitute the present much admired statutory code of Virginia.

In 1779 Mr. Jefferson was called to the gubernatorial chair of his native state, then surrounded by perils. The British troops, led on by the proud Tarleton and the traitor Arnold, were spreading death and devastation over the Old Dominion and contemplated the capture of the governor. Terror seized the more timid patriots–the boldest were alarmed at the approach of the merciless foe. The energy of the governor was equal to the emergency. He rallied the bone and sinew of old Virginia, who " with hearts of oak and nerves of steel," checked the enemy in their bold career of indiscriminate slaughter. He imparted confidence and vigor to the desponding and roused them to bold and noble action. He dispersed the black cloud that hung over his bleeding state and inspired the friends of liberty with cheering hopes of ultimate success. So highly were his services appreciated during the eventful term of his administration that the legislature entered upon their records a unanimous vote of thanks to him for the able and efficient manner he had discharged his public duties–highly complimenting his talents, rectitude, moral courage and stern integrity.

In 1783 he again took his seat in Congress–one of the brightest luminaries in the galaxy of statesmen. The chaste and moving address to Washington when he surrendered his commission, was from the soul-stirring pen of Jefferson. He was chairman of the committee to form a territorial government for the extensive regions of the then far west. True to his long cherished desire to ultimately emancipate the negro, he introduced a clause prohibiting slavery in any of the territories or the states that should be formed from them after 1800.

In May, 1784 he was a minister plenipotentiary in conjunction with Dr. Franklin and John Adams, with power to negotiate treaties of commerce with several European nations. In July he embarked for France and arrived in Paris on the 6th of August. During his absence he visited several foreign courts but spent most of his time in France.

He commanded the highest respect and was made a welcome guest in the halls of literature, legislation and jurisprudence. Kings and courtiers treated him with profound deference and were convinced intelligence and talent were not exclusively confined to the old world.

He was in Paris when the French Revolution commenced and was often consulted by the leading members of the national convention relative to the best course to be pursued in order to establish their government upon the Republican basis. So far as was proper he gave his opinions freely in favor of rational Liberty.

He returned on the 23d of November 1789 and was received with great enthusiasm and kindness by his fellow citizens. Soon after his arrival he resigned his ministerial commission and became Secretary of State under President Washington. The appointment was a compliment to the matured judgment of the chief magistrate and proved a lasting benefit to our country. Familiar with every principle of government—comprehending the requisites necessary to perfect and perpetuate the new confederation—he proposed amendments to the constitution, which, with some suggested by John Adams and others, were adopted. He did much towards reducing the new order of things to harmonious system. Well versed in diplomacy, international law and the policy of European courts—he was prepared to plant the permanent land marks of foreign intercourse which stand as beacon lights to guide our nation safely in its onward career. A reciprocity of commerce and honorable peace with other governments—a rigid neutrality with belligerents—a careful avoidance of entangling alliances were some of his leading principles. To submit to nothing that was clearly *wrong*—to ask for nothing that was not clearly *right*—was a doctrine of Jefferson forcibly inculcated in his able correspondence with the French ministers during the brief period of their Republic. This motto has been handed down from sire to son and is firmly nailed to the flag staff of the star spangled banner.

To the domestic concerns of our country he devoted a laudable and laborious attention. He recommended the adoption of a uniform system of currency, weights, measures and many other things designed to advance the best interest of the infant Republic. He urged the importance of protecting our fisheries and of encouraging enterprise in all the branches of industry. He demonstrated the advantages of every species of commerce and the necessity of preventing others from monopolizing the sources that legitimately belonged to the United States. He exhibited a masterly exposition of existing facts, showing the increasing policy of European courts to restrict the intercourse of America that they might engross trade. He submitted to Congress an elaborate and able report relative to the privileges and restrictions of the commercial intercourse of this, with other countries, which showed great foresight, close observation and thorough investigation. It received great attention and was the foundation of a series of resolutions introduced by Mr. Madison, embracing the doctrines it contained—forming the great line of demarkation between the *old* school federal and democratic parties. It would require a skilful engineer to trace the original line *now* in consequence of the rapid growth of under brush.

Having served his country long and faithfully and contributed largely in placing her on the great highway of FREEDOM and prosperity, Mr. Jefferson retired from public life on the 31st of December 1793 enjoying for a season the more peaceful and substantial comforts of life at Monticello. He imparted comfort to all around him—treated his slaves in the kindest manner, reducing to practice the mode of treatment he always recommended to others. The education of his children—the cultivation and improvement of his land and the resumption of his scientific researches, gave to him an exhilarating consolation he had long desired and could never enjoy in the arena of public business and political turmoil. His manner of life at the time alluded to is happily described by the Duke de Liancourt who visited him during this brief time of repose.

" His conversation is of the most agreeable kind. He possesses a stock of information not inferior to any other man. In Europe he would hold a distinguished rank among men of letters and as such he has already appeared there. At present he is employed with activity and perseverance in the management of his farms and buildings and he orders, directs and pursues, in the minutest detail, every branch of business relating to them. I found him in the midst of harvest from which the scorching heat of the sun does not prevent his attendance. His negroes are nourished, clothed and treated as well as white servants could be. Every article is made on his farm—his negroes being cabinet makers, carpenters and masons The children he employs in a nail manufactory and the young and old negresses spin for the clothing of the rest. He animates them all by rewards and distinctions. In fine, his superior mind directs the management of his domestic concerns with the same ability, activity and regularity, which he evinced in the conduct of public affairs and which he is calculated to display in every situation of life."

During his recess from the toils of public life Mr. Jefferson was unanimously elected President of the American Philosophical Society with which he was highly gratified. It afforded him much pleasure to occupy the chair which had been ably filled by his revered friends—the illustrious Franklin and philosophic Rittenhouse.

After a repose of three years he was again called to the theatre of public action. President Washington had announced his determination to retire to the peaceful shades of Mount Vernon. The people had become divided in two political parties, each determined to nominate a candidate for the high and responsible office about to become vacant. The federalists nominated John Adams—the democrats Thomas Jefferson. The former was elected President—the latter Vice President of the United States. As the presiding officer of the Senate Mr. Jefferson discharged his duty with dignity and impartiality. Familiar with parliamentary rules, he was prepared to decide questions promptly and uniformly to the satisfaction of members.

At the next Presidential Election he was again opposed to Mr. Adams. The mountain waves of party spirit rolled over the United States like a sweeping torrent. Each party presented a bold front regardless of danger pressed on by a rear rushing to conflict. The two candidates were bosom friends. Honest political differences did not interrupt their private good feelings. Not a word fell from the lips of either disparaging to his opponent. They regretted the fever heat of their partisans during the canvass but could not allay it. The Democrats carried the election and returned an equal number of votes for Mr. Jefferson as President and Col. Burr as Vice President. This singular circumstance imposed the election of the Chief Magistrate upon the House of Representatives. To defeat the election of the great leader of the popular party, several of his opponents voted for Col. Burr. A very spirited contest ensued. Thirty-five ineffectual ballotings were made. The ambition of Burr for promotion induced him to omit doing at once what propriety dictated and that which would have rendered him popular and perhaps saved him from the vortex of disgrace into which he subsequently plunged—*the immediate withdrawal of his name.* This he was finally compelled to do and on the thirty-sixth ballot Mr. Jefferson was duly elected President by a majority of eight votes and Col. Burr Vice President.

I have long been convinced that the Federal Constitution should be amended with reference to the election of these two officers. The votes for each should be confined to each office independent of the other. *The election should never go to the House of Representatives,* especially as political honesty is constantly deteriorating. The history of all time shows clearly, that as a government grows older corruption increases until it finally dissolves the state. Let the President be elected for four years and until another shall be elected in his place and let this be done directly by the PEOPLE. Reckless party management would then be stripped of half its horrors. Better pay the expense of two elections than have one unworthy incumbent in the Presidential Chair. The following extract from the Inaugural Address of Mr. Jefferson should be committed by every man and boy in our country—the principles would then be better understood and perhaps more generally exemplified in practice.

"Equal and exact justice to all men of whatever state or persuasion—religious or political—peace, commerce and honest friendship with all nations—entangling alliances with none—the support of the state governments in all their rights as the most competent administrations for our domestic concerns and the surest bulwarks against anti-republican tendencies—the preservation of the general government in its whole constitutional vigor as the sheet anchor of our peace at home and safety abroad—a zealous care of the right of election by the people—a mild and safe corrective of abuses which are lopped by the sword of revolution when peaceable remedies are unprovided—absolute acquiescence in the decisions of the majority, the vital principle of Republics from which there is no appeal but to force—the vital principle and immediate parent of despotism—a well disciplined militia our best reliance in peace and for the first moments of war till regulars may relieve them—the supremacy of the civil over the military authority—economy in public expenses that labor may be lightly burthened—the honest payment of our debts and sacred preservation of the public faith—encouragement of agriculture and of commerce as its handmaid—the diffusion of information and arraignment of all abuses at the bar of public reason—freedom of religion, freedom of the press and freedom of the person under the protection of the *habeas corpus* and trial by juries impartially selected. These principles form the bright constellation which has gone before us and guided our steps through an age of revolution and reformation. The wisdom of our sages and blood of our heroes have been devoted to their attainment. They should be the creed of our political faith, the text of civic instruction, the touch stone by which to try the service of those we trust and should we wander from them in moments of error or alarm, let us hasten to retrace our steps and to regain the road which alone leads to peace, liberty and safety."

Here is a statesman's chart drawn by one of the ablest navigators that ever stood at the helm of government. His soundings were frequent—his observations were made with mathematical precision—he combined science and experience and traced his lines with boldness and truth. To follow its directions is to ensure safety. Its delineations are not designed for partisan use but for our whole country and the freemen of the world through all time.

Based upon these principles practically, the administration of Jefferson became popular, peaceful and prosperous. He understood the reasonable desires of the people and exerted his noblest powers to gratify them.

He knew that the art of governing harmoniously consisted in HONESTY and governed himself accordingly. He anticipated the future wants of the rising and expanding Republic and proposed in his annual and special messages to Congress wise and politic measures to meet them. So fully was his course approved that he was re-elected by a majority of one hundred and forty-eight. His second inaugural address reiterated the same magnanimous principles of his first, manifesting a deep and growing interest in the prosperity and welfare of our common country.

As he has been repeatedly charged with infidelity by those who descend so low as to desecrate the ashes of the illustrious dead and the charge repeated but a few days ago in a prominent print in the city of New York, I insert the following extract from his annual message, which sentiment is found in all his writings where the subject is alluded to. I have recently read two of his unpublished letters to a gentleman who is now a member of the New Jersey Senate, in which the same view is expressed.

"I shall need, too, the favor of that Being in whose hands we are, who led our forefathers, as Israel of old, from their native land and planted them in a country flowing with all the necessaries of life—who has covered our infancy with his Providence and our riper years with his wisdom and power." Washington and Adams said no more.

If all who profess the religion of the Cross discarded sectarianism and honored unsophisticated *practical* religion as much as did Thomas Jefferson, the prospect of christianizing the world would burst upon us with refulgent brightness. The partition walls of various creeds, claimed to be drawn from the same pure fountain, would be dissolved by heaven-born Charity and the superstructure of the Redeemer's kingdom would rise in majesty sublime.

Soon after Mr. Jefferson entered upon the duties of his second term, a portentous storm darkened the horizon of our country, charged with the lightning of discord. In consequence of being disappointed in riding into the presidency on the whirlwind of confusion he created at the time he was made Vice President and at the end of four years—dropped like a traitor as he was, Aaron Burr mounted upon the tornado of his wild ambition and attempted the formation of a new Republic in the Spanish Provinces on the Mississippi, aiming at an ultimate division, if not dissolution of the Union. He was arrested and tried for high treason but being a man of great foresight, consummate genius and deep cunning—no *overt* act could be proved against him within the technical meaning of the law and he was acquitted—yet the dark stigma is marked upon the splendor of his brilliant talents in traces so deep, that time nor angels' tears can ever remove it. Like a comet propelled by its own centrifugal force from its constitutional orbit, he fell to rise no more—our country was saved from his Cataline grasp by the Cicero of our nation.

About the same time France and Great Britain were at war—both of whom and more especially the latter—had repeatedly insulted the American flag under various but false pretences. Redress was promptly demanded and measures pursued to obtain it. Anxious to preserve peace but determined to vindicate our rights and dignity—Mr. Jefferson simultaneously prosecuted a negotiation and prepared for war. He well understood the importance of the importing and exporting trade to England. Among the means used to bring her to honorable terms, he recommended to Congress the embargo law which was passed on the 22d Dec. 1807. This measure was violently assailed by those opposed to his administration. As he anticipated, it had a salutary effect upon the British government and caused propositions to be made by England for an honorable adjustment of all differences.

Thus were the foreign relations of the United States situated when the second term of Mr. Jefferson closed. He then bid a final farewell to public life and consigned the destinies of his beloved country into other hands. He had been an efficient and faithful laborer in the vineyard of American Liberty nearly forty years. He left it richly covered with green foliage and fruit—in the full vigor of health—enclosed by the palisades of truth and honesty—adorned with the crowning glories of philanthropy and patriotism.

From that time he declined all public honors and remained in peaceful retirement to the day of his death—seldom leaving his sweet home—the beautiful Monticello. Unlike too many with ample means he did not lead a life of inglorious ease. The same innate activity that had marked his bright career from youth—the same nobleness of mind and energy of character that raised him to the loftiest pinnacle fame could rear, still prompted him to action. He reduced his time to a harmonious arrangement—his business to perfect system. He uniformly rose before the sun and held a supervision over all the concerns of his plantation. The various productions of his pen during the period of his retirement, show that he labored arduously in the fields of science and philosophy. For the promotion of literature and general intelligence, he opened an extensive correspondence with men of letters in this country and Europe. He considered the diffusion of knowledge among the great mass of the human family the greatest safeguard against tyranny and oppression–the purest source of earthly bliss–the surest passport to freedom and happiness.

Acting from this impulse, he submitted the plan of a University to the legislature of Virginia to be erected at Charlottesville, situated at the foot of the romantic mountain in front of his mansion. It was to be built with funds raised by donations from individuals in the state, himself to be a liberal contributor. The plan of the buildings and course of instruction were drawn by him and so much admired and approved by the members of the legislative body that an act was passed to carry into effect the design and Mr. Jefferson was appointed Rector. For the completion of this object he spent all necessary time and more money than strict justice called for. It became the doating object of his old age. His best efforts were exerted in its accomplishment, which were crowned with success and the University filled with students to whom he paid great attention. The course of instruction was designed to prepare youth for the general routine of business, public and private and was not strictly classical. The library was selected by him with great care, being composed entirely of solid useful books, treating on subjects important to every citizen in preparing him to discharge properly the duties he owes to his God, his family, his country and himself. A catalogue, written by Jefferson, is still there in a good state of preservation. He exercised a parental care over this institution until his physical powers failed.

Much of his time was devoted to visitors to whom he was hospitable and kind. Thousands of his own countrymen paid their grateful respects to him–Europeans of distinction thought their tour in this country incomplete until they took by the hand the patriot, sage, philosopher and philanthropist of Monticello. He was ever anxious to please, delight and instruct. He was familiar with every subject. His mind united the vigor of youth with the experience of age. The broad expanse of the universe–the stupendous works of nature–the Pierian fields of science–the deep recesses of philosophy and labyrinthian avenues of the intellect of man–seemed spread before him like the map of the world. He was an encyclopædia of the age he adorned–a lexicon of the times he enlightened–one of the brightest diadems in the crown of his country's glory.

With a calm and peaceful quietude Mr. Jefferson glided down the stream of time toward the ocean of eternity until he reached the eighty-fourth year of his age. Forty-four years had passed away since his amiable companion had been laid in the tomb. She was the daughter of Mr. Wayles, an eminent lawyer of Virginia. One of two interesting daughters was also resting in the grave. The charms of earth were receding from him–he felt sensibly that he stood on the confines of another and a better world. The physical powers and mechanical structure of his frame were fast decaying–the canker worm of disease was doing its final work–the angel of death hovered over him with a keen blade awaiting Jehovah's signal to cut the silver cord of life and set the prisoner free.

Early in the spring of 1826 his bodily infirmities increased. From the 26th of June to the time of his death he was confined to his bed. He then remarked to his attending physician–" My machine is worn out and can go no longer." His friends who attended him thought he would again recover but he was convinced that his voyage of life was about to close and that he would soon cast his anchor in the haven of rest. To those around him he said–" Do not imagine that I feel the smallest solicitude as to the result. I do not indeed *wish* to die but I do not *fear* to die." Do infidels die thus calm and resigned? Echo answers–Do infidels die thus?

On the second day of July his body became extremely weak but his mental powers remained as clear as a crystal fountain. He called his family and friends around him and with a cheerful countenance and calm dignity gave direction for his funeral obsequies. He requested that he might be interred at Monticello without pomp or show and that the inscription on his tomb should only refer to him as " The author of the Declaration of Independence–of the Statutes of Virginia securing religious Freedom and the Father of the University." He then conversed separately with each of his family. To his surviving daughter, Mrs. Randolph, he presented a small morocco case which he requested her not to open until after his death. It was found to contain a beautiful and affectionate poetic tribute to her virtues.

The next day, being told it was the 3d of July, he expressed a desire that he might be permitted to inhale the atmosphere of the fiftieth anniversary of our national freedom. His prayer was granted–the glorious 4th of July 1826 dawned upon him–he took an affectionate leave of those around him and then raising his eyes upward articulated distinctly, " *I resign myself to God and my child to my country*"–and expired as calmly as an infant sleeps in its mother's arms. Thus lived and thus died THOMAS JEFFERSON, universally esteemed in life–deeply mourned in death by a nation of freemen–sincerely lamented by every patriot in the civilized world.

In person he was slender and erect–six feet two inches in height–light and intelligent eyes–noble and open countenance–fair complexion–yellowish red hair and commanding in his whole appearance. In all the relations of public and private life he was the model of a great and good man. His whole career was calm and dignified. Under all circumstances his coolness, strong moral courage–deliberation and equanimity of mind, placed him on a lofty eminence and enabled him to preserve a perfect equilibrium amidst all the changing vicissitudes and multiform ills flesh is heir to. He kept his passions under complete control and cultivated richly the finer qualities of his nature. His charity, the brightest star in the Christian diadem, was as broad as the human family–his sympathies co-extensive with the afflictions of Adam's race. He was created for usefulness–nobly did he fulfil the design of his creation. If his were not the fruits of *practical* Christianity, the immaculate Redeemer and the Apostles did not truly describe them. You who basely charge THOMAS JEFFERSON with infidelity, remember–O! remember, that his last words were those uttered by many of the martyrs–" I RESIGN MYSELF TO GOD AND MY CHILD TO MY COUNTRY."

BARON DE KALB.

A LOVE for the land of our birth is natural–commendable. A continued oppression from those in power may drive us from that land–compel us to seek an asylum under a more congenial government–still the associations of our native spot are a source of frequent and pleasing thought never to be entirely eradicated from our minds.

No man should ever adopt a new country and government without a full determination to become a good and useful citizen and submit implicitly to the laws as they are until he shall find himself in a majority of the virtuous who rise in their majesty to change for the better. With this principle for a polar star–foreigners who seek a peaceful asylum in our country may become as staunch supporters of our national Constitution and UNION as native born patriots. If they cannot–they should retrace their steps quickly and return to the iron blessings of monarchy. We want none among us who do not love our country and her noble institutions. An open door–a hearty welcome awaits every foreign *patriot* that comes to this land of the brave and home of the free. We have an overplus of native demagogues, fanatics, ultraists, disunionists and bigots—without importing any from Europe.

During the American Revolution a number of illustrious and noble patriots of high standing came from the old world to aid in planting the tree of LIBERTY in the new. Among them was the brave Baron de Kalb, a native of Germany. Of his early history we have no record. He was a brigadier-general in the French army and had earned a high military reputation. He was a knight of the order of Military Merit and highly esteemed by his fellow officers. A philanthropist of high order—imbued with liberal principles—in favor of a Republican form of government—familiar with the oppressions of England in America—acquainted with the noble efforts of the oppressed to free themselves from tyranny—Baron de Kalb at once resolved to be the companion of the patriotic La Fayette. On his arrival he was commissioned a major-general in the Continental army and placed in command of the Maryland division. He readily gained the esteem and confidence of all who made his acquaintance. He was a man of strong common sense—great experience—a close observer of men and things—an admirable disciplinarian—a brave and prudent officer. With a robust frame and iron constitution—he was able to endure the proverbial fatigues and privations of the American army. He was remarkably abstemious—living mostly on bread and water. His industry and zeal in the glorious cause he had espoused were worthy of all praise. He was up early and late and spent all his leisure from official duty in writing in some retired place. Unfortunately his writings were lost and the subject matter was known to no one but himself.

The brilliant career of this noble patriot soldier was closed at the battle of Camden, S. C. He there commanded the right wing of the American army composed of regulars. The left wing was composed of militia who fled at the sight of the red coats advancing with fixed bayonets—as terrified as young horses at a locomotive. Not so with the right wing. Although contending against overwhelming numbers they stood their ground and fought like tigers. In his last desperate attempt to seize the laurels of victory—the Baron fell helpless with eleven wounds. In this prostrate condition a base attempt was made to pierce him with several bayonets which was prevented by one of his aids—Chevalier de Buysson—who threw himself over the fallen hero and received the bayonets in his own body—exclaiming " *Save the Baron de Kalb !*" The British officers interfered—saved him from instant death and made him their prisoner. He was kindly treated by his captors and survived but a short time. To an officer who expressed his sorrow for his sufferings he replied—"I thank you for your sympathy—I die the death I always prayed for—the death of a soldier fighting for the rights of man."

In his last moments he dictated a letter to Gen. Smallwood who succeeded him in command of his division. He expressed his ardent affection for his officers and men—lauded their bravery which had forced admiration from their enemies—urged them to persevere in the glorious cause of FREEDOM until triumphant victory should perch upon their manly brows. He then invoked a benediction on his beloved division—reached out his trembling hand to Col. de Buysson—resigned his soul to God and closed his eyes in death.

In that battle both armies suffered severely. Several others of the American officers were killed—among them Col. Potterfield who was a favorite of the whole army.

Baron de Kalb was a man of amiable disposition—modest and unassuming in his manners—frank and generous in his intercourse—strictly moral and temperate in his habits—was highly esteemed by all who knew him and died deeply lamented. He was buried at Camden. His memory is cherished by every friend of LIBERTY.

Some years after he had slumbered under the clods of the valley, Gen. Washington visited his grave. He contemplated it thoughtfully for a few moments and remarked—" So there lies the brave De Kalb—the generous stranger who came from a distant land to fight our battles and to water the tree of our LIBERTY with his blood. Would to God he had lived to share its fruits."

In 1780 Congress caused a monument to be erected to his memory in Annapolis, Maryland, with the following inscription,

Sacred to the memory of the
BARON DE KALB,
Knight of the royal order of Military Merit,
Brigadier of the armies of France,
and
MAJOR GENERAL
In the service of the United States of America.
Having served with honor and reputation
For three years,
He gave a last and glorious proof of his attachment to the liberties of mankind
And the cause of America,
In the action near Camden in the State of South Carolina

On the 16th of August 1780,
Where, leading on the troops of the
Maryland and Delaware lines
Against superior numbers
And animating them by his examples
To deeds of valor,
He was pierced with many wounds
And on the nineteenth following expired
In the 48th year of his age.
THE CONGRESS
Of the United States of America,
In gratitude to his zeal, services and merit,
Have erected this monument.

GILBERT MOTTIER DE LA FAYETTE.

PATRIOTISM is one of the noblest attributes of man. It is the soul of freedom—the fulcrum of liberty—the lever of independence. It soars sublimely above self—is prompted by honest motives—aims at glorious ends. It is the motive power of philanthropy and would gladly consolidate the human family in one harmonions universal brotherhood by the heavenly law of love which can fraternize the world. It is opposed to all oppression—abhors all tyrants—rejoices in the promulgation of liberal principles. Its desires to do good are diffusive as the sun light—it is not confined to country—nation or caste. No sectarianism can swerve it—no monarch suppress it—no obstacle paralyze it. The patriot may be crushed in person by illegitimate power—the principle—*never*. Chains and dungeons will kindle it to a brighter flame—persecution will increase its volume. The history of all time proves the truth of these assertions—they form a corollary firm as the perpetual hills—incontrovertible as the problems of Euclid. The man who is destitute of this noble attribute is a mere automaton. There is a vacuum in his soul which nature abhors and all despise—except kings, aristocrats and demagogues. Patriotism is the dread incubus that hangs over thrones. The true patriot delights to see all basking in the refulgent rays of rational liberty and is ever ready to peril life and fortune in the cause of equal rights whenever the people of any nation rise in their native dignity to reclaim them from oppressors.

Thus it was with Gilbert Mottier de La Fayette, born on the 6th of September 1757 at the castle Chavaniac in Auvergne. Soon after the birth of this son, his father fell at the battle of Minden. As childhood dawned upon young La Fayette he exhibited talents of unusual strength and vigor. Under the genial rays of science they rapidly burst from embryo–budded, blossomed and ripened into fruit of the most perfect kind. At the age of seven years he was placed in the college of Louis le Grand at Paris. His rapid progress in the elements of his education exceeded the fondest anticipations of his numerous friends. By his modesty, urbanity and innate goodness of heart he gained the esteem of all who knew him. He graduated at an early age and was made a page to the queen and soon rose to the rank of a commissioned officer–an honor then conferred upon none but those presumed to possess superior merit and talent. At the age of seventeen he married the Countess Anastatie de Noailles–one of the most beautiful and amiable ladies of France. With kindred spirits they united splendid fortunes sufficient to support them in princely style through a long life. They were in the enjoyment of all the pleasures earth could give–favorites at the gayest court in Europe–caressed and beloved by those they held most dear–an ornament to every circle in which they moved. Mutual esteem gave a rich zest to every enjoyment–their social felicity was complete. All things combined to rivet La Fayette to his happy–his enchanting home. Nothing but the loftiest patriotism–the purest philanthrophy could have induced him to burst these infatuating bands and peril his life, fortune and sacred honor in the cause of human rights in a foreign country.

Amidst the fascinating allurements that surrounded him, this noble youth paused, reflected and reasoned. Through the bright vista of the future Columbus saw the cheering vision of a new world. Through the same clear mirror La Fayette saw the sun of FREEDOM reflecting its refulgent rays over Columbia's prolific land. A band of patriots had sounded the clarion of LIBERTY. Echo had wafted it from Bunker's bloody mount to the ears of this young hero. The thought that there was a remnant left in the world who dared to assume their native dignity and strike for their just rights enraptured his soul. Contrary to the wishes of his friends and the King of the French, he resolved to fly to the aid of the oppressed Americans and participate in the unfading glory of planting the standard of FREEDOM in the western hemisphere. Nor did he split on the rock of resolves and re-resolves where many waste away their lives. He at once proposed to the American Commissioners, then in Paris, to enter the army of Washington. They informed him of the recent adverses of those who were struggling for Liberty. They could present no bright picture to induce him to hope for laurels or emolument. It was not necessary. Nobler motives incited him to action. He still resolved to go. Anxious as were Messrs. Franklin, Dean and Lee to secure his services, they had not the means to convey him to the scene of action. Obstacles of various kinds were vainly thrown across his path. Impelled to an onward course by the noble impulses of patriotism—no difficulties were too great for him to surmount—no hardships too severe for him to endure, no sacrifice of wealth too large for him to make. Embarrassments strengthened the resolution he had formed to enroll his name with the brave and the free, even should he perish in the attempt.

He immediately fitted out a vessel at his own expense—freighted it with munitions of war and clothing—received letters of high commendation from the American commissioners to the Congress of their bleeding country and embarked secretly for the land of the pilgrim fathers in the winter of 1777. He then looked forward with anxious sollcitude to that happy day when he should aid in unfurling the banner of freedom—in planting deep the tree of liberty in a soil congenial to its growth and take by the hand those bold and daring sages and heroes who had thrown the stars and stripes to the breeze in defiance of despotism—resolved on freedom or death. Nothing short of a deep, strong, inherent devotion to liberal principles could have induced La Fayette to leave his native country under the existing circumstances and peril everything in behalf of strangers. In vain we search history for a benevolence so broad and disinterested. Call it ambition if you please. Would to God the same laudable ambition reigned triumphant in the breast of every human being. We should then see tyrants trembling—thrones crumbling—crowns falling—fetters bursting and the grand jubilee of FREEDOM celebrated amidst the expiring groans of monarchy—the chaotic ruins of tyranny. Call it a thirst for glory. Would to God that all who have figured largely on the grand theatre of public action could have the same glory emblazoned on the escutcheon of their names. A purer, fairer sheet of biography would then meet the eyes of the present and generations to come.

On the 25th of April 1777 Lafayette and his companions landed in South Carolina near Charleston and were warmly welcomed by Gen. Moultrie, Major Huger and the little band of veterans around them. The destitute condition of the American soldiers excited the sympathy of the Marquis. He distributed clothing to those under Gen. Moultrie and a sword to each of his officers. From Charleston he hastened to Philadelphia and delivered his letters and despatches from the American Commissioners to Congress. He offered himself as a volunteer–desiring to enter the army with no remuneration except the proud satisfaction of unrolling his name with the brave heroes whose motto was–LIBERTY OR DEATH. His unassuming manners, patriotic sentiments, stern resolution, devotedness to the cause and dignified bearing–combined to inspire confidence in all who made his acquaintance. In July Congress passed a resolution accepting his services and commissioned him a Major-General in the Continental army. He immediately placed himself under the supervision of Washington and commenced a brilliant career that gained increased lustre during a long life of usefulness. Shortly after he entered the service he acted a conspicuous part in the battle of Brandywine where he was wounded and disabled for six weeks. In the battle of Germantown he proved himself a cool, brave and skilful officer. He soon gained the full confidence of Washington and was put in command of a choice corps of daring young men selected by himself and was entrusted with several expeditions which he conducted with great prudence and success and to the entire satisfaction of Washington and Congress. On all occasions he exhibited talents of the highest order. Discretion–the strong helm of human action, guided him in all his actions.

At that period the question of maintaining American Independence was truly problematical. Prospects darkened as time rolled on. The general gloom was an impetus to this young patriot that impelled him to more vigorous exertion. In the autumn of 1778 he returned to France and exerted his influence in favor of a treaty of alliance and greatly aided in consumating that *desideratum*. This imparted fresh courage to the American army–then writhing under privations and distress that truly tried the souls and bodies of men. Nothing short of an Almighty hand could have sustained the Sages and Heroes of the Revolution and nerved them to persevere in their noble undertaking until crowned with triumphant victory. La Fayette returned in the spring of 1780 and was followed by a French naval force in July which came to the rescue. A new impetus was thus given to the cause of human rights in America. La Fayette was put in command of the expedition against Lord Cornwallis in Virginia. He found his troops in a naked, forlorn condition and Congress without means to furnish them with the common comforts of an army. Upon his own credit he borrowed money from merchants in Baltimore–purchased a portion of the necessary supplies–appealed to the fair daughters of the monumental city who responded nobly to the call. Their eyes and needles brightened as they made up garments for the brave soldier boys–soon the Marquis saw his men comfortably clad, fully equipped—eager to drive the minions of tyranny from their blood stained soil.

La Fayette took the field with a force far inferior to that of Cornwallis who was the pride of his king and acknowledged no superior in the science of military tactics. In the wary and sagacious "boy" as La Fayette was termed by the veteran British General, Cornwallis found a leader too formidable to be treated with contempt—too cautious to be easily ensnared. He was constantly annoyed without being able to bring his antagonist to a general action. Chagrined and disgusted he retired to Yorktown and commenced formidable fortifications. As his army was now the bulwark of England in America, the combined forces of the United Colonies and France lost no time in concentrating in front of his entrenchments. A vigorous siege was commenced on the 29th of September 1781. The British General felt that an awful crisis had arrived. By a surrender—the Colonies were lost. A tremendous responsibility rested upon him. His resistance corresponded with these high considerations. His spirited defence was worthy of a better cause.

On the 14th of October it was found necessary to silence two redoubts that were pouring a destructive fire into the works of the besiegers. This was to be done with the bayonet. The young Marquis was selected to lead the assault. The order was no sooner received than obeyed. He led his men to the charge with the impetuosity of a tornado. Like a mighty avalanche, rushing from the mountain top with the fury of Mars —they bore down all opposition. Although the enemy were double in number—so sudden and irresistible was the onset that they were all killed or taken prisoners but six. Against such troops fighting for Liberty, Cornwallis found it useless to contend. The injured Colonists had risen in their might—a fearful retribution awaited him. The last ray of success was expiring in the socket of hope—his cruel military career was about to close in the new world. Keen and blighting anguish seized his tortured soul in view of outrages committed upon an oppressed people. The cries of murdered innocents rang through his ears—his courage lost its equilibrium and was supplanted by despair. On the 18th of October the proud hero of Britain surrendered his whole army to the illustrious WASHINGTON and the brave LA FAYETTE—the champions of liberal principles and human rights.

That signal victory closed the long, bloody, doubtful struggle. Several nations promptly acknowledged the Independence of the United States. The ensigns of royalty were banished from our shores—the star spangled banner waved triumphantly over the land of the brave and free. Washington and La Fayette mingled tears of gratitude and thankfulness for their preservation, success and final deliverance. They richly merited and freely received the plaudits of the American people and of admiring nations. A gazing world looked upon them with extatic delight as they stood on the loftiest pinnacle of fame in all the sublime majesty of republican simplicity. They were among the brightest of the dazzling luminaries of emancipation–the terror of tyrants–the hope of FREEMEN. The consummation of Liberty was then and there proclaimed to grateful and happy millions. Seraphs listened to the cheering news with thrilling joy–carried the glad tidings to the unerring chancery of the great Eternal where they received the sanction of Jehovah's high authority and were recorded on the unfading pages of the book of lasting renown in letters of gold by the Grand Scribe of Heaven. Echo caught the talismanic sound and wafted it to the remotest bounds of every nation on wings of mighty wind.

Having accomplished all in his power to establish the Independence of our country La Fayette prepared to return to the bosom of his anxious family in France. He had served more than six years and expended *one hundred and forty-seven thousand dollars* in the glorious cause he had nobly, ardently, successfully espoused. He asked no pecuniary emolument at the commencement of his services–he demanded no pay–presented no account at their termination. He had a richer reward, more precious than gold–more valuable than rubies–*the gratitude of the American nation* deeply felt and strongly expressed. He had the invaluable satisfaction of having contributed largely towards preparing a nursery for freemen–an asylum for the oppressed. His conduct stood approved at the dread tribunal of conscience.

> "The man who stands acquitted at that fearful bar
> Holds the first round prize the world has to give.
> 'Tis like Heaven's sunshine—PRICELESS."

At his departure he received the highest tokens of respect from Congress, the officers of the army and our nation at large. The richest blessings of a kind Providence were invoked for him. He was received with great enthusiasm on his arrival at home. He was hailed as a prominent hero of the new world–the tried friend of Liberty–the unyielding advocate of universal Freedom–the spotless patriot–the brave and skilful officer–the hope of the down-trodden and oppressed in the old world.

The success of the United States in shaking off the yoke of bondage had its influence on the nations of Europe as a natural consequence. That the people of France felt it *most* is not surprising. The French army had drank freely at the fountain of Liberty that had gushed out in the United States. The holy flame of freedom was burning in their bosoms and was soon communicated to their brethren at home. The insulating fire of patriotism ran through the mass and they too resolved to be free. Unfortunately for the cause of human rights they seized upon the abstract principles of Liberty without learning the art of self-government. They plucked the fruit before it was ripe–it disorganized their system producing a raging fever and wild delirium. So rapidly did the excitement rise that it was found necessary to convene the States General–an assembly that had slumbered 172 years–the dernier resort of that nation to suppress internal commotion. It consisted of deputies chosen by the nobility, clergy and common people. So terrific was the storm of passion that this august body trembled like a reed shaken by the wind. Anarchy mounted its desolating car–mad ambition rolled its mountain waves over reason and justice–malicious jealousy sought its victims in every avenue–Jacobinism reared its hydra head–the fountain of mercy was dried up–the bloody guillotine did its fearful work. Civil war raged in all the plenipotence of exterminating revenge–cruelty ceased only for the want of victims–the streets were deluged with the purple current. Such are the outlines of the first French Revolution. The picture is filled with darker shades.

Amidst this scene of dreadful carnage–this tornado of angry passions–La Fayette stood calm and undismayed. He commanded the military and had their confidence. At one bold stroke he might have cut off the cold hearted Robespierre–the cruel Mirabeau–the treacherous Duke of Orleans–the ambitious Paine–the bloody Nero–Murat. Under Washington and from his own innate goodness he had learned to soar above revenge and practice humanity. For some time he paralyzed the efforts of the various factions and succeeded in giving France a constitution approximating towards republicanism. But the typhoid of faction had become too firmly fixed on the body politic to be arrested in its sanguinary career by this panacea. It gathered new strength as it advanced. The awful whirlpool of boiling passion was fast drawing La Fayette to its vortex of destruction. The National Assembly yielded and became subservient to the Jacobins. Plans were suggested by which to rid themselves of the man they most dreaded. At this alarming crisis he exhibited moral and physical courage without a parallel. He repaired to the National Assembly and in language bold and strong portrayed the conduct of those whose wild ambition had brought upon France threatened ruin and impending destruction. His dignified manner, unanswerable logic, powerful eloquence, stern integrity, open frankness, anxious solicitude and noble boldness filled the delegates and leading Jacobins with awe and astonishment. They believed he had an armed force within call to protect him. When he had finished his address he immediately withdrew and resumed the command of the army then marching against the Austrian Netherlands. Learning that he had gone, the National Assembly became so courageous that they proscribed him and set a price upon his head. Finding the wild disorder of his country beyond his control and his life in jeopardy, he resolved to fly to the United States. With an aching heart he left, with seven companions. In their flight they fell into the hands of the Prussians and were delivered over to the Austrians. After enduring every indignity and insult La Fayette was thrown into a loathsome dungeon at Olmutz where a bed of rotten straw, a broken chair and an old table constituted all the furniture of his wretched apartment. There he suffered by privations and disease—neglected and alone until he was so reduced that the hair fell from his head and death seemed sure of an early victim. At the same time his estate was confiscated by the Jacobins and his amiable wife thrown into prison. To advocate him in France was a sure passport to the bloody guillotine.

England, the United States and several other governments looked upon the incarceration of La Fayette as a violation of the laws of nations, of common justice and humanity. Washington and many others made great exertions to obtain his release. The Emperor of Austria was inexorable. The staple of his mind was adamant—he delighted in human misery. He had caged the European Eagle of Liberty determined to immolate him slowly but surely on the altar of revenge and crush the embryo buds of liberal principles in the old world. A bold but unsuccessful attempt to rescue the prisoner was made by Col. Huger and Dr. Bollman of South Carolina. Its history is full of thrilling interest and does great credit to the heads and hearts of its persevering and ingenious authors.

The amiableness and dignity of Madame La Fayette forced respect from the bloodthirsty Jacobins who ultimately released her. Learning the forlorn condition of her husband her native tenderness rushed upon her noble soul like a mighty flood. She at once resolved to fly to him and share in all the vicissitudes that awaited him. With her two daughters she left France in disguise and arrived safe at Olmutz. Her application to see her husband could not be granted unless she consented never to leave the prison after entering it. With this inhuman decree she cheerfully complied. The most brilliant imagination can but faintly conceive—the strongest language can never portray to the life the thrilling—the melting scene that followed. The sunburnt cheeks of the soldiers who guarded the prison were flooded with the tears of sympathy and compassion. With the two pledges of their love Madame La Fayette passed the grating iron doors. The next moment she was clasped in the arms of the companion of her youth. *My loved husband*—was all she could utter. *My dear father*—burst from his angelic daughters as they clung around his emaciated form. *My dear wife—my lovely daughters*—passed his trembling lips in broken accents—a flood of tears from each told a tale of mingling woes and joys in the language of that mute eloquence which casts words into the shade. That scene can never be presented in full original force by the finest touches of the painter's pencil—the boldest stroke of the poet's pen—the loftiest flights of historic eloquence. At that meeting with his family the situation of La Fayette in prison was more enviable than that of a king of nations or a conquoror of worlds. The ministering angel—WOMAN—can convert a dungeon into a paradise and light up a smile in the deepest aspect of woe. Without her earth would be desolate—man miserable—a savage.

With Christian fortitude and heroic patience this affectionate family bore their privations and sufferings. Madame de Stael has well observed—" Antiquity offers nothing more admirable than the conduct of Gen. La Fayette, his wife and daughters in the prison of Olmutz."

Fresh exertions were made to obtain the release of these innocent sufferers. The question was agitated in the United States Congress and in the House of Commons in England. Nothing could move the obdurate heart of the tyrant who held them. They seemed doomed to waste away their lives in that loathsome dungeon. God had otherwise determined. The time was rolling on rapidly when they should be restored to liberty, their friends and their home. The conquering Bonaparte humbled the proud and cruel Emperor and compelled him to release these illustrious prisoners. In the treaty of Campo Formio in 1797 it was expressly stipulated that all the French prisoners at Olmutz should be immediately liberated. The Emperor of Austria attempted to impose restrictions on the future conduct of the Marquis. Amidst all his sufferings his dignity and liberal principles remained unimpaired. He spurned all conditions of a restrictive nature. His unconditional release occurred on the 25th of August 1797 when he and his family again inhaled the exhilarating atmosphere of Freedom. He had been in prison five years. His noble wife and affectionate daughters had shared with him the miseries of a damp dungeon twenty-two months. The release of these prisoners is one of the brightest stars in the diadem of Bonaparte.

When the French nation became more tranquil La Fayette and his family returned to the land of their birth. He located at La Grange and soon gained a salutary influence over those around him. He did all in his power to promote the interests of his country and the cause of human rights. Although he was truly grateful to Bonaparte for his release from a gloomy dungeon he believed he owed a duty to his nation paramount to all private considerations. He opposed all his measures that he considered dangerous to the prosperity and happiness of France. From the time of his return to that of his last illness, La Fayette took a conspicuous part in the civil and military departments of his country. With an Argus eye he watched her destinies through all her convulsing changes. The smiles of princes and the huzzas of the multitude could not flatter him—the miseries of a dungeon and frowns of tyrants could not depress him. Without those brilliant talents that dazzle and captivate every beholder, like his revered Washington he possessed an uncommon share of sound common sense, a clear head, a good heart, a discriminating judgment that gave him a more universal influence than any man then in Europe. His magic power over the enraged populace of Paris during the Three Days' Revolution of 1830 has no parallel when we consider the effervescent nature of the French people. In the short period of seventy-two hours he restored tranquillity—formed a new government and commenced a new era in the history of that impulsive nation. He could then have been crowned King of France. To him crowns were empty bubbles, expanding only to burst—airy phantoms, formed to allure for a time—then vanish in abdication, chaos or blood.

When he visited our country in 1824 his reception at every point was an earnest of the deep feeling of gratitude that pervaded the bosoms of our people. The presence of no man ever elicited more enthusiastic joy in any country. During his stay party spirit retired to its lair—all united in paying the profoundest respect to the benefactor of our nation—the companion of Washington—the noble philanthropist. In every crowd La Fayette sought his surviving companions in arms who had fought and bled by his side in the glorious cause of American Independence. When he met them the scene was always interesting—sometimes affecting. In some instances a simultaneous rush to each other at the moment of recognition and the eloquent tears that rolled down their veteran cheeks told what was passing in their kindred hearts more strongly than words can express. It affords me great pleasure to state—that the finances of our government were such at that time and the liberality of Congress in such a state of expansion that La Fayette was remunerated for his services and the large amount of money expended in obtaining our Independence--reversing the adage--*Republics are always ungrateful.* When he departed from our shores--bid a last farewell to his American friends and our country--he left a painful vacuum in the hearts of millions that was not speedily supplied. He was emphatically a man whom the people admired, loved, and delighted to honor. He arrived safely in France and continued to watch over her interests until the 18th of May 1834 when he took a violent cold in following on foot the remains of the patriot Dulong, to Pere le Chaise, or Garden of the Tombs. So violent was his illness that it baffled all medical skill and ended his eventful and useful life on the 21st of May 1834. He died in full faith of a blissful immortality in a better and brighter world He expired at his hotel in Paris.

The pageant of his funeral was of the most imposing character. He was a member of the Chamber of Deputies at the time of his decease. The marked attention and mingling tears of the members of that body--the deep lamentations of the French and American people--the demonstrations of grief by every civilized nation on receiving intelligence of his death--combined to show the high estimation in which he was held by the old and new world.

The grateful memory of La Fayette is held sacred by every friend of Liberty. His history has no parallel on the Eastern continent. His career was not tarnished with bold strides of misguided ambition or base attempts at self-aggrandizement. He was consistent to the last. Compared with his--all borrowed greatness is an empty show. Unblemished virtue marked his bright career--philanthropy his whole course--integrity his entire conduct--justice his every action. A calm resignation to the will of God under all circumstances and a confiding trust in His wisdom added a more brilliant lustre to all his noble and amiable qualities. Unborn millions will read his biography and sing the praises of this great and good man. He has left examples of human conduct worthy the contemplation and imitation of all who move in the private or public walks of life His influence did not terminate with his existence. Ages to come will be benefited by the rich fruits of his useful and monitory life. The sweet incense of FREEDOM will continue to ascend from his hallowed grave in cerulean perfumes with increasing fragrance until the old world shall be revolutionized, regenerated and FREE. Coming generations will gaze upon the bright picture of his history with enrapturing delight--the holy flame of patriotism and the pale torch of Liberty now glimmering in the old world will be replenished at the sacred tomb of LA FAYETTE.

FRANCIS LIGHTFOOT LEE.

The actions of men cannot be well understood without a thorough knowledge of human nature. We must trace the map of the immortal mind, learn the avenues of its circuit, follow it through the regions of revolving thought, become familiar with the passions that influence and control it–learn its natural desires, innate qualities, springs of action–its multifarious combinations. We must understand its native divinity, earthly frailty, malleability, expansions, contractions and its original propensities. In addition to all this knowledge, to judge correctly of the actions of an individual we must know the predominants and exponents of his mind–the impress it has received from education, the motives that impelled him to action, his propulsive and repulsive powers, the ultimatum of his designs and his ulterior objects. With all these guides we may still become involved in error unless we move within the orbit of impartiality, divest ourselves of all prejudice and have our judgments warmed by the genial influence of heaven-born charity. With all these lights we should never pass judgment of censure upon any person unless the good of community requires it or a court of justice demands it. Could this rule be strictly adhered to by individuals and the press–rays of millenial glory would burst upon the wilderness of mind and cause it to bud and blossom as the rose. A peaceful and quiescent rest would calm the angry feelings and boiling passions of men, daily lashed to a foaming fury by the unnecessary and often erroneous expressed opinions of others. On this point the Sages and Heroes of the American Revolution were examples worthy of imitation. Each one held most sacred the reputation of his co-workers. The few violations of this principle were frowned upon with an indignity that gave the recusants the Belshazzar trembles.

Among them no one was more tender of character than Francis Lightfoot Lee. He was the son of Thomas Lee–born in Westmoreland county, Virginia, on the 14th of October 1734. He was the brother of Richard Henry Lee whose eloquence rose higher but whose reflections were no deeper than those of Francis. In childhood he was admired for his docility and amiable deportment–in youth he was the pride of every circle in which he moved and when manhood dawned upon him he exhibited a dignity of mind and maturity of judgment that all delighted to honor.

He was educated by the Rev. Mr. Craig a Scotch clergyman of

high literary attainment and profound erudition. Under his tuition the germs of knowledge took deep root in the prolific mental soil of young Lee and produced plants of rapid and luxuriant growth. The Scotch *literati* are remarkable for deep investigation, thorough analyzation and lucid demonstration. I have never met one who was a pedant, a vain pretender or a superficial scholar. Under such an instructor the intellectual powers of Francis assumed a vigorous and healthful tone that placed him upon the substantial basis of useful knowledge and enduring fame. He was delighted with the solid sciences and spent less time in the bowers of Belles Lettres than his Ciceronean brother. The history of classic Greece and Republican Rome enraptured his mind with the love of liberty and liberal principles. He read closely, thought deeply and investigated thoroughly. He prosecuted his studies with untiring industry and became an excellent scholar without the advantages of European seminaries to which most of the sons of wealthy men were then sent to complete their education. Imitating the examples of his elder brothers who had received the highest polish of English gentilesse and French etiquette he became a polished gentleman in his manners. Raised in the midst of affluence, actuated by the purest ethics, free from a desire to participate in the follies of the world, living in the peaceful enjoyment of those refined pleasures that promote felicity without enervating the body or corrupting the heart, the favorite of his numerous acquaintances–his earthly happiness was of the purest kind. His mind richly stored with scientific theory and with correct moral and religious principles, he entered the school of experience and became emphatically a practical man. Possessed of an ample fortune he could devote his time to what he deemed most useful. Having early imbibed a love for rational liberty and having fully canvassed the conduct of the British ministry towards the American Colonies, Mr. Lee resolved to oppose the encroachments of the king upon the rights clearly guaranteed by the English constitution. He could not consent that the trappings of the crown, the pomp of the courts, the extravagance of the ministry and the expenses of the Parliament of Great Britain should be borne by the yoemanry of America who were eloigned from the protection and fraternal feeling of that power, deprived of participating in legislation, subject to the caprice of every new cabinet created by the King, dragged from their native homes to be tried by a foreign jury, oppressed by the insolence of hireling officers, driven from under the mantle of constitutional rights and treated as mere vassals of the mother country.

In 1765 he was elected to the house of Burgesses to represent Loudoun county where his estate was situated. He at once took a bold stand in favor of rational Liberty. Blessed with a strong and investigating mind, a deep and penetrating judgment, a clear and acute perception, a pure and patriotic heart, a bold and fearless disposition—he became one of the most efficient advisers in the legislative body. He continued to represent Loudoun county until 1772 when he married the estimable Rebecca–daughter of Col. Taylor of Richmond county where he located permanently. The same year he was elected from his new district and continued to do good service in the house of Burgesses until he repaired to the Continental Congress. Amidst the gathering storm of the Revolution and the trying scenes that accumulated thick and fast around him–he stood unmoved and undismayed. He advocated every measure calculated to promote the independence of his country and was prolific in plans for the accomplishment of that much desired object. As a member of committees he had no superior. He was familiar with every form of government and understood well the rights conferred by Magna Charta and the British constitution. He was prepared to act advisedly and was resolved to resist unto blood the illegal advances of the designing and avaricious ministry. He made no pretensions to oratory, seldom spoke in public but when so highly excited as to rise he poured upon his opponents a flood of keen and withering logic that often made them quail.

On the 15th of August 1775 Mr. Lee was elected to the Continental Congress. A more expansive field was then opened before him. To do or die–to live in chains or peril everything for Liberty had become the dilemma. Columbia's soil had been saturated with the blood and serum of Americans shed by the very men who had been cherished by their bounty and fed by their labor. The dim flickerings of hope for redress and conciliation were fast expiring in the socket of forbearance. The great seal of the compact had been broken by the British ministry–the last petitions, addresses and remonstrances were prepared–the final course for the Colonies to pursue was soon to be determined. Inglorious peace or honorable war were the two propositions. In favor of the last Mr. Lee put forth the strong energies of his mind. Eternal separation from England and Independence for America could only satisfy his views. Being upon numerous committees his influence was strongly felt. Liberty had become a *desideratum* with him. When the proposition of final separation from the mother country was submitted by his brother his soul was raised to the zenith of patriotic feeling. When the Declaration of Rights was adopted his mind was in an ecstacy of delight. His influence, vote and signature told how pure and strong were his desires in its favor.

He rendered essential aid in framing the Articles of Confederation that governed Congress and the Colonies during the Revolution. This was a subject of great delicacy and labor. Besides the work of the committee it passed through thirty-nine discussions in the House. He contended that the rights of contiguous fisheries and the free navigation of the Mississippi river should be incorporated in the claims of the United States in all propositions of peace. The wisdom and sagacity of his position are now fully demonstrated. It was then opposed by some and not duly appreciated but by few.

Mr. Lee was continued in Congress up to 1779 when he declined a re-election and retired from the public arena to scenes more congenial to him but less beneficial to the deliberations of the august body he had long graced with his wisdom. His enjoyment of domestic life was transient. Contrary to his wishes he was elected to the legislature of his native state and repaired to the post of duty. After aiding in removing the perplexing difficulties that embarrassed the government of the Old Dominion he again retired to the peaceful retreat of private life where he remained until April 1797 when he was summoned to appear forthwith at the Bar of the God he loved and had honored through life. Calm and resigned he bowed submissively to the messenger who bore the mandate—bid his friends an affectionate farewell and took his departure triumphing in faith with a full assurance of a joyful reception in a brighter and better world. He died of pleurisy and was followed in a few days by his wife. They had no children but their graves were moistened by the tears of numerous relatives and friends.

In public life Mr. Lee was eminently useful—his private worth shone with equal brilliancy. Always chaste, cheerful, amusing and instructive—he delighted every circle in which he moved. Wealthy, benevolent and liberal—he was the widow's solace, the orphan's father and the poor man's friend. Kind, affectionate and intelligent—he was a good husband, a faithful companion and safe counsellor. Polished, urbane and gentlemanly—his manners were calculated to refine all around him. Moral, discreet and pious—his precepts had a salutary influence upon the minds of all who heard them and were not callous to good advice. He spurned the slanderer, kindly reproved the vicious and by counsel and example disseminated the principles of morality and religion. He was a bright model of human excellence.

It has been erroneously stated that he was unfriendly to Washington. The mistake of the writer probably arose from incorrectly associating Gen. Charles Lee, who came from Wales in 1773, with the

Lees of Virginia and who was suspended from his command one year for disobedience to orders at the battle of Monmouth. He was a brave officer and only made a small mistake which he deeply regretted. The approval of the sentence was voted for in Congress by Francis. After the adoption of the Federal Constitution he was asked his opinion upon it. His answer shows his confidence in Washington. "I am old and do not pretend to judge these things now but one thing satisfies me it is all right—General Washington is in favor of it and John Warden is opposed to it." Warden was opposed to our Independence.

Let the shining examples of Mr. Lee be reflected forcibly on our minds and lead us to do all the good in our power whilst we live and prepare for a peaceful and happy exit from the abysm of time.

RICHARD HENRY LEE.

Rhetoric, as defined in the lexicons, as taught in the schools, as practised in times of peaceful leisure—is not the kind that graced the forum during the American Revolution. No studied or written speeches were then crowded upon the audience to kill time or gain popularity. Judge McKean remarked just before his death—"I do not recollect any formal speeches, such as are made in Parliament and our late Congresses. We had no time to hear such speeches—little for deliberation—action was the order of the day."

School eloquence is very different from native heart-thrilling soul-stirring rhetoric. The former is like the rose in wax without odor—the latter like the rose upon its native bush perfuming the atmosphere with the rich odors distilled from the dew of heaven. The former is the finely finished statue of a Cicero or Demosthenes, more perfect in its lineaments than the original—the latter is the living man animated by intellectual power—rousing the deepest feelings of every heart—electrifying every soul as with vivid lightning. The former is a picture of the passions all on fire—the latter is the real conflagration pouring out a stream of impassioned words that burn like liquid flames bursting from a volcano. The former brings the fancy of an audience into playful action—the latter sounds an alarum that vibrates through the tingling ears to the soul and drives back the rushing blood upon the aching heart. The former moves the cerebral foliage in waves of recumbent beauty like a gentle wind passing over a prairie of tall grass and flowers—the latter strikes a blow that resounds through the wilderness of mind like rolling thunder through a forest of oaks. The former fails when strong commotions and angry elements agitate the public peace—the latter can ride upon the whirlwind of faction, direct the tornado of party spirit and rule the storm of boiling passion. This was the only kind of eloquence practised by the Sages and Heroes who achieved our Independence. At such times school elocution is a mockery—a vain show that disgusts men when the fate of millions is suspended by a single hair. At such a crisis the deep fountains of the soul are broken up and gush out in living streams of natural overwhelming eloquence.

Among the powerful orators of '76 was Richard Henry Lee, son of Thomas Lee, born in Westmoreland County, Virginia, on the 20th of January 1732. His ancestors were among the early settlers of the Old Dominion and were prominent in directing the destiny of the Colony. They were men of liberal principles and at all times promptly resisted every encroachment upon their rights. The arbitrary power exercised by Charles I. over his European subjects which hurled him from his throne, was resisted by the Lees. When Cromwell assumed the crown he was never recognised by Virginia. The mandate that proclaimed the second Charles King—originated with Lee and Berkley of the Old Dominion. The plan of ultimate Independence was cherished by the elder Lees. Through the bright vista of the future they contemplated the millennium of Freedom in America. So strongly impressed was the father of Richard Henry with this idea that he fixed in his mind the location of the seat of government and purchased lands in the vicinity of Washington. By some historians this act is called a paradox that philosophy has been perplexed to explain. To my mind the solution has no perplexity. A man of deep reflection and large intelligence does not draw his conclusions alone from present appearances. He compares the past with the present and makes deductions for the future. The historic map of the world is covered with the rise, progress and extinction of nations, kingdoms and empires. From the causes and effects delineated upon the same map, it was the natural conclusion of a penetrating mind that the expansive territory of this country, with all the bounties of nature lavished upon it, must eventually become so densely populated that its physical force would be too powerful for any European country to hold dominion over it. The geographical centre was also plain as the settlements were then progressing. This prophecy, as it has been termed, was the result of deep thought arriving at conclusions drawn from the unerring laws of nature, showing that Mr. Lee possessed an analyzing mind that moved in an extensive orbit.

Richard Henry Lee commenced his education at Wakefield, Yorkshire, England and remained in that kingdom until he completed it. He returned a finished scholar, an accomplished gentleman with a reputation untarnished by vice or folly. From his childhood honesty and morality were his darling attributes—he delighted in reposing under the ethic mantle. During his absence his innate republicanism did not become tinctured with the farina of European courts or the etiquette of aristocracy. In classic history he found the true dignity of man portrayed—his inalienable rights delineated. In the philosophy of Locke he saw the rays of light reflected upon human nature—the avenues of the immortal mind opened to his enraptured vision. In the Elements of Euclid the laws of demonstration were presented to his delighted understanding and gave fresh vigor to his logical powers. Endowed with these qualifications he was prepared to enter upon the great theatre of public action and adorn the circle of private life.

His first public act was in raising a company of troops and tendering his services to Gen. Braddock. That proud Briton considered the Provincials puerile and declined the proffered aid. His fate is a matter of history. In 1757 Mr. Lee was appointed a Justice of the Peace and President of the Court. Shortly after he was elected to the House of Burgesses and made himself thoroughly acquainted with the laws of legislation and government—the true policy and various interests of the colony and with the rules of parliamentary proceedings. Retarded by an almost unconquerable diffidence, he took very little part in debate at first. It was not until he became excited by a subject in which he felt a deep interest that his Ciceronean powers were developed. A bill was before the House imposing a duty on the importation of slaves into Virginia—virtually amounting to a prohibition. It was strongly opposed by several influential members. Mr. Lee became roused and poured upon his astonished audience such a flood of burning eloquence against the importation of human beings to be made slaves, that his opponents trembled as they listened. In vivid colors he painted the cruelties of Cortes in South America, the Saracens in Spain and passed through the dark catalogue of monsters who had disgraced humanity with barbarism—then pointed his colleagues to the darker blot—the more barbarous practices that branded with infamy the unhallowed slave-trade then monopolized by mother Britain. He pointed to the bloody scenes of other times when the physical force of the slaves had enabled them to rise and crush their masters at one bold stroke. By stopping the traffic, the evil entailed upon them might be provided for and the certain and dreadful consequences of a constant influx from Africa be warded off. His eloquence was applauded but his philanthropic views were voted down by the friends of the crown. The trade was virtually originated and long continued by Great Britain, now so loud in complaints against us for not at once providing for an evil entailed by her. Had this bill passed, her revenue would have been less and thousands of Africans left at their peaceful homes. O! shame where is thy blush!

This powerful effort raised Mr. Lee to the rank of the Cicero of America. The exposure of the base corruptions practised by Mr. Robinson, then treasurer of the Colony, was the next important service rendered by him. As this was an attack upon the aristocracy, it required much skill, boldness and sagacity to introduce the probe successfully. This he did in a masterly manner and proved clearly that the treasurer had repeatedly re-issued reclaimed treasury bills to his favorite friends to support them in their extravagance by which the Colony was robbed of the amount by their payment a second time without a *quid pro quo* [equivalent.] For this bold act Mr. Lee was applauded by every honest man—hated and dreaded by public knaves.

When Charles Townshend laid before the British Parliament the odious and more extensive plan of taxing the American colonies which Mr. Grenville called *the philosopher's stone*, Mr. Lee was among the first to sound the alarm. Within one month after the passage of the preliminary Act in Parliament followed by a revolting catalogue of unconstitutional and oppressive laws, he furnished his London friends with a list of arguments against it sufficient to convince every reasonable man of the injustice and impolicy of the measure. When Patrick Henry proposed his bold resolutions against the Stamp Act in 1765 Mr. Lee gave them the powerful aid of his eloquent and unanswerable logic. He was very active in the formation of associations to resist the encroachments of the crown. He aided in compelling the collector of stamps to relinquish his office, deliver up his commission and the odious stamp paper. The people were advised not to touch or handle it. His pen was also ably used and produced many keen, withering, logical, patriotic, pungent essays that had a salutary influence upon the public mind. He corresponded with the patriots of New York and New England. According to the testimony of Col. Gadsden of S. C. and the public documents of that eventful era, Mr. Lee was the first man who proposed the Independence of the colonies. He had unquestionably imbibed the idea from his father whose ancestors had predicted it for the last hundred years and had probably handed it down from sire to son. In a letter from Richard Henry Lee to Mr. Dickinson dated July 25th 1768 he proposes upon all seasonable occasions to impress upon the minds of the people the necessity of a struggle with Great Britain "*for the ultimate establishment of independence—that private correspondence should be conducted by the lovers of liberty in every province.*" His early proposition in Congress to sever the maternal ties was considered premature by most of the friends of Liberty. He had long nursed this favorite project in his own bosom—he was anxious to transplant its vigorous scions into the congenial bosoms of his fellow patriots.

Soon after the House of Burgesses convened in 1769, as chairman of the judiciary committee, Mr. Lee introduced resolutions so highly charged with liberal principles calculated to demolish the Grenville superstructure and reduce to dust his talismanic *philosopher's stone*, that they caused a dissolution of the House and concentrated the wrath of the British ministry and its servile bipeds against him. The rich fruits of their persecution were the formation of non-importation associations, committees of safety and correspondence and the disaffection of the English merchants towards the mother country in consequence of the impolitic measures calculated to prostrate their importing and exporting trade. Lord North now assumed the management of the grand drama of oppression and laid more deeply the revenue plan. By causing a repeal of the more offensive Acts he hoped to lull the storm of opposition that was rapidly rising and prepare for more efficient action. Had the Boston Port Bill been omitted his dark designing treachery might have succeeded more triumphantly. This fanned the burning flame of resentment to a white heat. It spoke in language too plain to be mistaken—too strong to be endured.

In 1774 Mr. Lee was a delegate to the Congress convened at Philadelphia. At that memorable meeting he acted a conspicuous part. After Patrick Henry had broken the seal that rested on the lips of the members as they sat in deep and solemn silence, he was followed by Mr. Lee in a strain of *belles-lettres* eloquence and persuasive reasoning that took the hearts of his audience captive and restored to a calm the boiling agitation that shook their manly frames as the mountain torrent of Demosthenean eloquence was poured upon them by Henry. He was upon the committee that prepared an address to the king—the people of Great Britain and to the Colonies. Those documents were written by him and adopted with but few amendments. He was upon the committee that prepared the address to the people of Quebec and upon the committee of rights and grievances and non-intercourse with the mother country. In the warmth of his ardor he proposed several resolutions that were rejected because considered premature at that time—not that the purity of his motives were doubted. Many of the members still hoped that timely redress of grievances would restore peace. They had clearly and forcibly set forth their complaints and desires and could not yet be persuaded that ministers were madly bent on ruin. For solidity of reasoning, force of sagacity and wisdom of conclusion—the proceedings of that Congress stand without a parallel upon the historic page. So thought Lord Chatham, Burke and many of the wisest English statesmen at that time.

In 1775 Mr. Lee was unanimously elected to the Virginia Legislature where the same zeal for Liberty marked his bold career. He received a vote of thanks for his noble course in Congress and was made a delegate for the next session. A more congenial field now opened for this ardent patriot. Temporizing was no longer the order of the the day. Vigorous action had become necessary. His zeal and industry had ample scope. With all his might he entered into the good work. Upon committees—in the house, everywhere he was all activity. In 1776 he was a member of Congress. In obedience to the instructions of the Virginia Legislature and his long nursed desires, on the 7th of June he rose amidst the assembled patriots of the nation in the Hall of Liberty and offered the resolution for the adoption of a Declaration of Independence This resolution he enforced by one of the most brilliant and powerful displays of refined and forcible eloquence ever exhibited in our country. On the 10th of the same month he was called home by the illness of his family which prevented him from taking his place as chairman of the committee upon his resolution agreeably to parliamentary rules. Mr. Jefferson was put in his place. The wrath of British power against him was now at its zenith. During his short stay at home an armed force broke into his house at night and by threats and bribes endeavoured to induce his servants to inform them where he could be found. He was that night a few miles distant with a friend. They were told he had gone to Philadelphia.

In August he returned to Congress and most gladly affixed his name to that sacred instrument upon which his imagination had feasted for years. He continued at his post until June 1777 when he returned home to confute a base slander charging him with unfaithfulness to the American cause in consequence of having received rents in kind instead of Continental money. He was honorably acquitted by the Assembly and received a vote of thanks from that body for his fidelity and industry in the cause of freedom—rather a cooler to his semi-tory enemies. During the two ensuing years his bad health compelled him to leave

Congress several times, but his counsel was at the command of his colleagues at all times. Nothing but death could abate his zeal in the good cause.

The portals of military glory were now opened to Mr. Lee. He was appointed to the command of the militia of his native county and proved as competent to wield the sword and lead his men to action as he was to command an audience by his powerful eloquence. Defeated in the north the British made a rush upon the Southern States. Whenever they approached the neighbourhood under the charge of Mr. Lee they found his arrangements a little too precise for their convenience and abandoned their visits entirely. In 1780–1–2 he served in the Virginia legislature. The proposition of making paper bills a legal tender—of paying debts due to the mother country and of a general assessment to support the Christian religion—were then before the House and excited great interest. Mr. Lee advocated and Mr. Henry opposed them. From the necessity of the case he was in favor of the first. Upon the sacredness of contracts he based his arguments in favor of the second and from ethics he drew conclusions in favor of the last. He said refiners might weave reason into as fine a web as they pleased but the experience of all time had shown religion to be the guardian of morals. He contended that the declaration of rights was aimed at restrictions in the form and mode of worship and not against the legal compulsory support of it. In this Mr. Lee erred. He probably had forgotten that Christ declared his kingdom was not of this world and that the great Head of the Christian religion had for ever dissolved the bans of church and state by that declaration. In other respects the position is untenable in a republican government and can never promote genuine piety in any.

In 1784 he was again elected to Congress and chosen President of that body. At the close of the session he received a vote of thanks for the faithful and able performance of his duty and retired to the bosom of his family to rest from his long and arduous toils. He was a member of the Convention that framed the Federal Constitution and took a deep interest in the formation of that saving instrument. He was a U. S. Senator in the first Congress that convened under it and fully sustained his previous high reputation. Infirmity at length compelled him to bid a final farewell to the public arena. His last public services were rendered in the legislature of his own state. On his retirement a most flattering resolution of thanks for his numerous valuable services was passed by that body on the 22d of October 1792. He then retired to the peaceful shades of Chantilly in his native county crowned with a chaplet of amaranthine flowers emitting rich odors lasting as time. There he lived—esteemed, beloved, respected and admired until the 19th of June 1794 when the angel of death liberated his immortal spirit from its clay prison—seraphs conducted his soul to realms of bliss there to enjoy the reward of a life well spent.

Mr. Lee was a rare model of human excellence and refinement. He was a polished gentleman, scholar, orator and statesman. In exploring the vast fields of science he gathered the choicest flowers—the most substantial fruits. The classics, *Belles Lettres*—the elements of civil, common, national and municipal law—the principles of every kind of government were all familiar to his mind. He was ardently patriotic, pure and firm in his purposes, honest and sincere in his motives, liberal in his principles, frank in his designs, honorable in his actions. As an orator the modulation of his voice, manner of action and mode of reasoning were a *fac simile* of Cicero as described by Rollin. He richly merited the appellation—CICERO OF AMERICA.

His private character was above reproach. He possessed and exercised all those amiable qualities calculated to impart substantial happiness to all around him. To crown with enduring splendor all his rich and varied talents—he was a consistent Christian—an honest man. As his dust reposes in peace let his examples deeply impress our hearts and excite us to fulfil the duties of life to the honor of ourselves, our country and our God.

FRANCIS LEWIS.

THE patriotic sages and daring heroes of the American Revolution were from different countries and of various pursuits. One feeling pervaded the bosoms and influenced the actions of all—the love of LIBERTY. This main spring of action was confined to no business or profession. All classes who loved their country and hated chains flew to the rescue. Self interest lost its potent powers and thousands pledged their lives and fortunes to defend their bleeding country against the merciless oppression and exorbitant demands of an unyielding monarch. No class of men better understood the injustice of the mother country than those engaged in commerce. Many bold spirits rushed from the counting house to the forum and the field, resolved on victory or death.

Among them was Francis Lewis, born at Landaff, in the shire of Glamorgan, South Wales, March 1713. His father was an Episcopal clergyman, his mother was the daughter of the Rev. Dr. Pettingal of the same sect who officiated at Cærnarvonshire in North Wales.

Francis was an only child and lost both his parents when only fifteen. A maternal aunt, named Llawelling, became his guardian. She had him early instructed in the Cymraeg language which he never lost. He was subsequently sent to a relative in Scotland where he was taught the original Celtic language. From there he entered the Westminster school at London and became a good classical scholar. He then entered a counting house and became thoroughly acquainted with the entire routine of commercial transactions which prepared him to enter into business understandingly and with safety.

When arrived at his majority he inherited a small fortune which he laid out in merchandize and embarked for New York where he arrived in the spring of 1735. He found his stock too large for that city--entered into partnership with Edward Annesley, leaving with him a part of his goods, proceeding with the balance to Philadelphia. At the end of two years he settled permanently in New York and married Elizabeth Annesley, sister of his partner in trade. To these ancestors may be traced the numerous and respectable families of the same name now residing in and about New York.

Commercial transactions frequently called Mr. Lewis to the principal ports of Europe and to the Shetland and Orkney Islands. He was twice shipwrecked on the coast of Ireland. His great industry, spotless integrity and skill in business, gave him a high position in commercial circles, showing clearly the great advantage derived from a thorough apprenticeship in business before a young man sets up for himself.

At the commencement of the French war he was the agent for supplying the British army with clothing. At the sanguinary attack and reduction of Oswego by the French troops under Gen. Dieskau, Mr Lewis was standing by the side of Col. Mersey when he was killed. He was taken prisoner and held a long time by the Indians enduring the severest sufferings. As a small compensation the British government granted him five hundred acres of land.

Mr. Lewis was among the early and determined opposers to the unjust pretensions of the British ministers. He was a distinguished and active member of the Colonial Congress that assembled in New York in the autumn of 1765 to devise and mature measures to effectuate a redress of injuries. A petition was prepared to the King and House of Commons and a memorial to the House of Lords. The language was respectful but every line breathed a firm determination no longer to yield to injury and insult. The chrysalis of the Revolution was then and there formed. The eruptions of the volcano occasionally subsided but as the lava of insubordination would again burst out the crater was enlarged and the volume increased until the whole country became inundated by the terrific flood of war, red with the blood of thousands.

In 1771 Mr. Lewis visited England and became familiar with the feelings and designs of the British ministry. From that time he was fully convinced that the infant Colonies in America could never enjoy their inalienable rights until they severed the parental ties that bound them to the mother country. On all proper occasions he communicated his views to the friends of freedom and did much to awaken his fellow citizens to a just sense of impending dangers.

When it was determined to convene the Continental Congress Mr. Lewis was unanimously elected a member by the delegates convened for that purpose on the 22d day of April 1775. He immediately repaired to the Keystone city and entered upon the important duties assigned him. The following year he was continued in Congress and recorded his name upon the chart of Independence. His great experience in commercial and general business united with a clear head, a patriotic heart, a matured and reflecting mind richly stored with intelligence—rendered him a useful and influential member. As an active and judicious man on business committees he stood pre-eminent. As a warm and zealous advocate of his country's rights he had no rival.

He was continued a member of Congress to April 1779 when he obtained leave of absence. He had suffered much in loss of property which was wantonly destroyed by the British troops.

Time or angel's tears can never blot out the damning stigma that rests upon the escutcheon of Great Britain for personal abuse and the wanton destruction of private property during the Revolutionary War. Talk of savage barbarity. He is a Pagan and knows none but his own mode of warfare. England has professed to be the conservatory of Christianity for centuries. Compared with the brutality of her armies in America, looking at her in the light of even a *civilized* nation, savage barbarity is thrown in the distance so far that it could not be seen through a microscope of a million power.

Not content with destroying the property of Mr. Lewis, the British seized his unprotected wife and placed her in close confinement without a bed—a change of clothes—almost without food and exposed to the cowardly and gross insults of wretches who were degraded so far below the wild man of the wilderness, that could an Archimedian lever of common decency have been applied to them with Heaven for a fulcrum and

Gabriel to man it, they could not have been raised, in a thousand years, to the grade of common courtesy. No true American can trace the cruelties of the British troops during the times that verily tried men and women's souls, without having his blood rush back upon his aching heart—his indignation roused to a boiling heat.

Mrs. Lewis was retained in prison several months and finally exchanged, through the exertions of Gen. Washington, for a Mrs. Barrow, the wife of a British paymaster retained for the express purpose but treated in the most respectful manner and made perfectly comfortable with a respectable family. The base imprisonment of Mrs. Lewis caused her premature death.

At the close of the war Mr. Lewis was reduced from affluence to poverty. He had devoted his talents, his property to the cause of Liberty and what was infinitely more—the wife of his youth—the mother of his children had been brutally sacrificed by the hyenas of the crown. Notwithstanding these heart rending misfortunes the evening of his life was made comfortable by his enterprising children and on the 30th day of December 1803, calm and resigned, peaceful and happy, he closed his eventful and useful life.

He left a well earned fame that will survive, unimpaired, the revolutions of time. His private character was a fair unsullied sheet as pure and valued as his public life was useful and illustrious. As a man of business he stood in the front rank. He was the first merchant who made a shipment of wheat from America to Europe. He was the pioneer in the transporting trade. He was a full man in all that he undertook. His shining examples are worthy of our imitation in all the walks of a good and useful life.

PHILIP LIVINGSTON.

Men often originate designs and engage in transactions that produce results in direct opposition to their desires. Religious persecution scattered the primitive Christians to various parts of the world and instead of annihilating the doctrines of the Cross they were thus more widely spread over the earth. For the enjoyment of the liberty of conscience the emigrants to New England left their native homes. For the same reason the Huguenots of France fled before the blighting edict of Nantes in 1685, many of them settling in the city of New York. To the persecuted and oppressed—America was represented as a land of rest. Immigrants poured in upon our shores from France, Holland,

Germany, England, Ireland and Scotland—among whom were many eminent for piety, intelligence and liberal principles. They were also men of courage and fortitude, at that time considered necessary requisites in the perilous undertaking of leaving the old for the new world. Among those who came to our country were men of all the learned professions, the liberal arts and sciences, trades and occupations.

Robert Livingston was the son of an eminent Scotch divine who died in 1672. Robert then came to this country and obtained a grant for the manor along the Hudson River. He had three sons—Philip, father of the present subject—Robert, grandfather of Chancellor Livingston, and Gilbert, grandfather of the Rev. Dr. John H. Livingston.

Philip, the subject of this brief sketch, was born at Albany on the 15th of January 1716. He was one of the few who enjoyed a collegiate education at that period. After his preparatory studies he entered Yale College and graduated in 1737. He had strong native talent improved by the lights of a liberal education. Religion and moral rectitude prepared him for a career of usefulness. In those days of republican simplicity and common sense the graduates of an American college did not believe themselves licensed to ride rough shod over those whose literary advantages were less—nor did they believe themselves exonerated from the field, the shop and the counting house and destined only for the learned professions. They thought it no disparagement to apply themselves to agricultural, mechanical and commercial pursuits and wear apparel spun and wove by the hands of their noble mothers and hale sisters. An enervating change is visible.

Mr. Livingston engaged extensively and successfully in mercantile business in the city of New York and became noted for punctuality, honesty and fair dealing. Reposing full confidence in his integrity, *then* a necessary passport to public honors, his fellow citizens elected him an alderman in 1754, which office he filled for nine consecutive years, doing much to promote the peace and prosperity of the city. In 1759 he was elected to the colonial assembly which had important business on hand. Great Britain was at war with France which brought the northern Colonies in contact with the French and Indians. Twenty thousand men were to be raised by the colonists to guard the frontier settlements and carry the war into the Canadas. The province of New York raised 2680 men and 250,000 pounds to aid in the proposed object.

Mr. Livingston took an active and judicious part in these deliberations. He introduced laws for the advancement of commerce, agriculture and various other improvements—manifesting a sound judgment and liberal views. He was an active member on the Committee of Foreign Relations that wisely selected Edmund Burke to represent the interests of the Colony in the British Parliament. Through the lucid communications of Mr. Livingston that celebrated statesman and friend to America was made thoroughly acquainted with the situation, feelings and interests of the colonists.

After the dissolution of the Assembly by the death of George II. Mr. Livingston was elected to the one organized under the new dynasty. In 1764 he wrote an answer to the message of Lieutenant Governor Colden, pointing out, in bold but respectful language, the oppressions and infringements of the British ministry upon colonial rights. He at once became the nucleus around which a band of patriots gathered and formed a nut too hard to be cracked by the sledgehammer of monarchy. The governor uniformly dissolved the Assembly at the commencement of its session if he found a majority of the members were liberals.

In 1768 the Assembly consisted of the brightest luminaries of talent then in the Colony. Mr. Livingston was unanimously elected Speaker. Discovering that a majority of the members were not pliant enough for tools nor submissive slaves, Governor Moore dissolved them and ordered a new election. He succeeded in obtaining a majority of creeping things but patriots enough were elected to hold the minions of the crown in awe. Disgusted at the tyranny of the governor, Mr. Livingston declined a re-election in the city but was returned to the Assembly by the people upon his manor. On mature deliberation he took his seat but was objected to because not a resident of the district for which he was elected. The Argus eyes of the patriots quickly discovered that by this very plan the governor had succeeded in obtaining a majority in his favor—most of his creatures being in the same predicament. To save their own glass houses from a smash they withdrew their objection to Mr. Livingston. During the session he offered a resolution setting forth the grievances of his countrymen and the violation of chartered rights. This gave great umbrage to the adherents of the crown and they determined to expel him from his seat on the ground of his non-residence in the district he represented. This was done by a vote of 17 to 6, a very large majority of the members being in the same situation. This blind act was on par with the whole course of the infatuated ministry and their hirelings. It constituted a thread in the web that England wove to make a straight jacket for herself.

A wider field now opened for Mr. L. He was elected to the first

Congress at Philadelphia and became a brilliant star in the galaxy of national patriots. He was one of the committee that prepared the spirited address to the British nation and roused from their lethargy those whose attention had not been turned to the all important subjects then in agitation–involving a nation's rights and a nation's wrongs. He was continued a member of Congress and when the grand birthday of our nation arrived–aided in the thrilling duties of the occasion–invoked the smiles of Heaven upon the new swathed infant and gave the sanction of his name to the Magna Charta that secured to our nation a towering majesty–a sublime grandeur before unknown.

In 1777 he was a member of the convention that framed the constitution of New York. He was elected to the Senate and attended the first legislature of the empire state. The same year he was elected to Congress, then in session at York, Penn. having been compelled to flee before the conquering foe. Deeply afflicted with *hydro-thorax* [dropsy of the chest] he felt that his labors must speedily close. It was in the spring of 1778 when the dark mantle of gloom hung over the bleeding Colonies. Under these circumstances he was willing to devote his last hours to the interest of his beloved country. He had freely given her his best services and a large portion of his pecuniary means. His family had fled to Kingston on the approach of the enemy. He repaired there to arrange his private business in the best possible manner. He wrote a valedictory letter to his friends at Albany–urged them to remain firm in the cause of Liberty–trust in God for deliverance and bade them an affectionate–a final farewell. He then clasped his lovely wife and dear children to his bosom for the last time on earth–commended them to Heaven's guardian care–gave them a look of tenderness–a fervent kiss and was gone.

On the 5th of May he took his seat in Congress, exhausted and feeble, but determined to remain at his post until the lamp of life should burn out.

Although standing on the confines of eternity, his zeal in the cause of human rights shone brightly to the last. For himself he could not anticipate the enjoyment of the fruit of his numerous and protracted toils but for his family and his countrymen he felt deeply–hoped ardently. He had full confidence that Independence would be sustained and that a glorious Republic would rise upon the ruins of monarchy.

In June his health failed rapidly and on the 12th of that month, 1778 he yielded to the monarch Death to whom he owed a momentary allegiance–paid the debt–took a release and a passport to mansions in the skies. He was buried the same day with all the mournful honors due to his great worth–deeply lamented by all the friends of freedom. His amiable wife was not with him but he had a friend that sticketh closer than a brother–one that had been his stay and support in every hour of trial and smoothed the pillow of death–Religion. Angels waited for the transit of his immortal soul–opened wide the gates of Heaven to let the patriot in–the King of glory decked him with a robe of white, enrolled his name in the book of life and crowned him with that peaceful rest which is the reward of a pure heart and a virtuous life.

The private character of Mr. Livingston was a continued eulogy upon virtue, philanthropy, benevolence, urbanity, integrity, nobleness, honesty, patriotism, consistency and all the leading qualities that render man dignified on earth and fit for Heaven.

His public career was an exemplification of all the noble qualities that render a patriot complete and endear him to a nation of freemen. With such men to wield the destiny of our expanding nation–our country is safe–our UNION secure.

THOMAS LYNCH Jr.

The prudent man soars in peerless majesty above the trifling vanities and corrupting pleasures of this world and lives in constant readiness to enter the mansions of bliss beyond this vale of tears. He regards the past, present and future in the light of Revelation and meets the dispensations of Providence with calm resignation. He views mankind in the bright sunshine of charity–exemplifies the golden rule in his intercourse with the world. He investigates impartially, reasons logically–condemns reluctantly. Prudence is not the necessary result of shining talents, brilliant genius or great learning. A profound scholar may astonish the world with scientific discoveries–pour upon mankind a flood of light–enrapture the immortal mind with theological eloquence–point erring man to the path of rectitude and render himself powerless by imprudent conduct. One grain of prudence is of more value than a cranium crowded with unbridled genius or a flowing stream of vain wit. Dangers gather thick around the frail bark of man without it and hurry him to destruction. It is the real ballast of human life. So thought and so acted the Sages of the American Revolution, else their efforts would have been vain, their exertions powerless.

Among them stood the young patriot Thomas Lynch Jr. born on the plantation of his father on the bank of the North Santee river in the parish of Prince George S. C. on the 5th of August 1749. His paternal ancestors were of Austrian descent and highly respectable. The direct ancestor of young Thomas removed to Kent in England, from thence to Ireland, a son of whom, Jonack Lynch, removed from Connaught to South Carolina in the early time of its settlement. He was the great grandfather of the subject of this short sketch–a man of liberal views and pure morals.

In childhood Thomas Lynch Jr. was deprived of his mother by death. At the proper age he was placed at the Indigo Society School at Georgetown, S. C. where some of the most eminent sages of the south were educated. Warmed by the genial rays of science the mind of young Lynch soon burst from its embryo state and exhibited a pleasing and luxuriant growth. His progress was rapid and highly gratifying to his anxious father whose only child he was. At the age of thirteen he entered the far famed school at Eton, Buckinghamshire, England, founded by Henry VI. At that school he commenced his classical studies. After completing his course there he was entered as a gentleman commoner in the University of Cambridge where he became a finished scholar and polished gentleman, esteemed and respected by his acquaintances. He then entered the law temple and became well versed in legal knowledge and general science and was well prepared to enter upon the great theatre of action.

During his stay he cultivated an extensive acquaintance with the whigs of England and became familiar with the designs of British ministers upon the Colonies. He investigated closely the relative situation of the two countries and came home in 1772 prepared and determined to oppose the oppressions of the crown and strike for LIBERTY. As the dark clouds of the Revolution loomed up from the horizon and increased in fearful blackness the firmness of his purpose increased. These were fostered by his patriotic father and responded to by the people of the parish. Hand in hand, shoulder to shoulder did the sire and son march to the rescue resolved to put forth their noblest efforts to throw off the chains of tyranny.

The first attempt of this young patriot to speak in public after his return was at a large town meeeting in Charleston. His father had just addressed the assembled multitude on the subject of British oppression and sat down amidst the enthusiastic cheers of his fellow citizens. His youthful son then rose. A profound silence ensued. The eyes of the dense mass were fixed upon him. For a moment he paused. The blood rushed back upon his aching heart. It returned to its thousand channels–his bosom heaved–the struggle was over–an impassioned strain of eloquence burst from him that carried the insulating fluid of patriotism to the hearts of his astonished and delighted audience with irresistible force. Tears of joy ran down the furrowed cheeks of his father–bursts of applause from the enraptured multitude made the welkin ring. Such men could not remain slaves.

When the crisis arrived for physical action he was among the first to offer his services. In July 1775 he received a captaincy and repaired to Newbern, N. C. where he unfurled the star spangled banner and in a few weeks enlisted a full complement of men. His father objected to his acceptance of so low a grade to whom his affectionate son modestly replied–" My present command is fully equal to my experience" – a reply worthy the consideration of every young man who desires to build his fame upon a substantial basis. If a man is suddenly placed upon a towering eminence to which he is unaccustomed, the nerves of his brain must be unusually strong if he does not grow dizzy, tremble, totter–fall. If he ascends gradually–pauses at different points of altitude as he advances, he may reach the loftiest spire, preserve his equilibrium and stand in safety. Sudden elevations often prove disastrous.

On his way to Charleston with his company Capt. Lynch was prostrated by the bilious fever from which he never entirely recovered and was not able to join his regiment for several months. Soon after this he received intelligence of the dangerous illness of his father–then a member of Congress at Philadelphia. He applied to Col. Gadsden for permission to leave for that city which was refused on the ground that his services were paramount to all private considerations. His unexpected election to Congress to succeed his father, by a unanimous vote of the Assembly, enabled him to leave at once. With great diffidence he took his seat in the Congress of 1776 amidst veteran sages and statesmen whose combined talents and wisdom are without a rival on the pages of history.

On his arrival at Philadelphia he found his revered father partially relieved from a paralytic attack and in August started with him for home. They only reached Annapolis where the venerable sage died in the arms of his son.

On entering the national legislature Capt. Lynch became a bold and eloquent advocate for the Declaration of Independence and soon convinced his senior colleagues that he had a full share of wisdom to conceive, patriotism to impel and prudence to guide him in the glorious cause of freedom. He cheerfully and fearlessly affixed his name to the Magna Charta of our rights and did all in his power and more than his feeble health would warrant to advance the best interests of his excoriated—bleeding country. He was finally compelled to yield to increasing ill health and relinquish his honorable station.

Medical skill proved futile and as advised by his physicians, he and his accomplished wife embarked for Europe at the close of 1779 with Capt. Morgan, whose vessel was never heard from after she had been a few days at sea and then from a Frenchman who left her from some cause unexplained and went on board another vessel. Soon after he left her a violent gale came on and beyond all doubt the vessel went down with all on board. Previous to embarking he made a will bequeathing his large estate to three sisters in case of the death of himself and wife, having no children.

The private character of this worthy man was pure and in all respects amiable. Had his valuable life been spared his eminent talents and great zeal promised important services to his country and an elevated rank among the sages and patriots of the eventful era at which he commenced his brilliant but transient career. Short as was his public tenure he did enough to immortalize his name. Although his bright morning sun did not reach its meridian, its splendor contributed largely in illuminating the horizon of LIBERTY and shed a rich lustre over his name that will render his memory sacred through all future time.

The brief career of Thomas Lynch Jr. admonishes us that life is held by a slender cord and that exalted talents and splendid accomplishments, like some rich flowers, often bloom just long enough to be gazed at and admired—then close up their petals and hide their beauties for ever from our enraptured sight.

THOMAS McKEAN.

GREAT designs require the deep consideration of strong, vigorous and investigating minds. Imposing events open a wide field for fame and bring to view powers of intellect that would never unfold their beauties under ordinary circumstances. Hence the brilliancy of talent that illuminated the glorious era of the American Revolution. Many who became eminent statesmen and renowned heroes during that memorable struggle would have remained within the sphere of their particular occupation in time of peace. The public gaze would never have been fixed upon them—they would have passed away with a rich mine of undeveloped mental powers. Hence the erroneous expression

I have heard from men who do not analyze all they read, hear and see—that we have no men among us *now* with the exalted talents of the sages of '76. Just such an occasion would explode the error.

That many of the patriots of that eventful period were men of unusual ability and acquirements—I freely—proudly admit. That the momentous transactions that engaged their attention served to add an unequalled lustre to their names is emphatically true. The perils that encompassed them—the dangers that surrounded them—the mighty work they conceived, planned and consummated—all combine to shed a sacred halo around their well earned fame.

Prominent among them was Thomas McKean, a native of Chester County, Pennsylvania, born on the 19th of March 1734. He was the son of William McKean who immigrated from Ireland at an early age. He placed this son under the tuition of Rev. Francis Allison then principal of the most popular seminary of the province. He was a gentleman of profound erudition and science.

The intellect of Thomas budded and bloomed like the rose of spring. He was a close student—his rapid attainments gave an earnest of a bright future. He left the seminary a thorough linguist, a practical mathematician, a moral philosopher, a finished scholar, an accomplished gentleman—esteemed, respected and admired by his numerous friends.

He then commenced the study of Law under David Kinney, of Newcastle, Delaware. He explored the interminable field of this science with unusual success and was admitted to the bar under the most favorable auspices. He commenced his professional career at Newcastle—soon acquiring a lucrative practice and proud reputation. He extended his business into his native province and was admitted to the Supreme Court of Pennsylvania in 1757. His strict attention to business and superior legal acumen made him extensively and favorably known. He avoided the modern error of too many young lawyers who suppose an admission to the bar closes the toils of the student. Fatal mistake my young friends. You are at the very threshold of your reading. Relaxation is professional suicide. This is a rock on which many have been shipwrecked in all the learned professions. The laws of nature demand a constant supply of food in the intellectual as well as in the physical economy. The *man* requires more and stronger food than the *child*. The corroding rust of forgetfulness will mar the most brilliant acquirements of science if laid upon the shelf of neglect. Much study is required to keep up with the march of mind and the ever varying changes produced by the soaring intellect and reaching genius of man. It has been said that the basis of law is as unchangeable as a rock of adamant. Of elementary law this is true. It does not follow, *a priori*, that the superstructure is so. Precocious legislators have made *that* a labyrinthian maze. *They* use a political kaleidoscope in legislating and that not skilfully. It puzzles *competent* judges to arrive at a satisfactory construction of statute laws. The *incompetent* —not few and far between—use the instrument above named carelessly if not politically. Hence no lawyer can succeed without an endless round of reading.

In 1762 Mr. McKean was elected to the Delaware Assembly from Newcastle county and continued in that body for eleven consecutive years. He then removed to Philadelphia. So much attached were the Delawarians to him that they continued to elect him to their Assembly for six years after his removal although he could not serve them in that. Under the old regimen, he was claimed by both Delaware and Pensylvania and served them conjointly in the Continental Congress.

In 1765 he was a member from Delaware to the Congress in New York. He was upon the committee that drafted the memorable address to the House of Commons. His patriotism, love of liberty and firmness of purpose were fully demonstrated in that instrument and by his subsequent acts. He was republican to the core—despised the chains of political slavery—the baubles of monarchy and the trappings of kingly courts. He struck high for Liberty and scorned to be a slave.

On his return from New York he was appointed Judge of the Common Pleas, Quarter Sessions and Orphans' Court of Newcastle county. The Stamp Act was then in full *life* but not in full force in Delaware. Judge McKean was the first judicial officer who put a veto on stamped paper—directing the officers of the courts over which he presided not to use it, as had been ordered by the hirelings of the crown. He set them at defiance and was sustained by the people of the nation. That circumstance, trifling as it may *now* seem to superficial readers, was big with consequences. It was one of the entering wedges to the Revolution that made an awful opening in the monarchical mass that was ultimately split into atoms and annihilated by the wedges and malls of the hard-fisted sons of America. From that time Judge McKean was hailed as one of the boldest champions of Freedom—one of the ablest defenders of his country's Rights.

He was a prominent member of the Congress of 1774. He had talent to design—energy to execute and at once made himself useful.

He was the only man who served in the Continental Congress during the whole time of its duration. He was a strong advocate for the Declaration of Independence and promptly put his name to that revered instrument. When it came up for final action, so anxious was he that it should pass *unanimously*–that he sent an express for Mr. Rodney who arrived just in time to give an affirmative vote.

Notwithstanding the arduous duties that devolved on him as a member of Congress–of several important committees and Chief Justice of Pennsylvania–so ardent was his patriotism that he accepted a colonel's commission–took command of a Philadelphia regiment and marched to the aid of Gen. Washington, remaining with him until a new supply of recruits was raised. During his absence his Delaware constituents had elected him to a convention to form a constitution. On his return he proceeded to Newcastle, put up at a tavern and without consulting men or books, hastily penned the constitution that was adopted by the convention. Understanding the feelings and wants of the people–well versed in law and republicanism–a ready writer, he performed the labor in a few hours that has required a large number of men nearly a year to accomplish in more modern times. How changed are men and things since the glorious era of '76. How changed the motives that impel many politicians to action–how different the amount of useful labor performed in the same time and for the same money. *Then* all were anxious to listen–*now* nearly all are anxious to speak. *Then* legislators loved their country *more* and the loaves and fishes *less* than at the present day. I do not blame the politicians–it is their trade and living. Office seeking has become a card game in which the applicants are the pack–demagogues the players and the *dear* people and government the table played upon. The bone and sinew of our country can and should block this ruinous game at once. We have as good men as lived in '76 and a *few* of them on duty. There should be no others selected. They will not *seek* office but we should be careful to seek *them* and cleanse the temple of our Liberty from political peculation and venality. If our country is ruined it will be the fault of the mass.

On the 10th of July 1781, Judge McKean was elected President of Congress but declined serving in consequence of his duties as Chief Justice of Pennsylvania. He was then urged to occupy the chair until the court should commence the next term. To this he assented and made an able presiding officer. On the 7th of November he vacated the chair and was complimented by the following resolution :–" *Resolved*–That the thanks of Congress be given to the Honorable Thomas McKean, late President of Congress in testimony of their approbation of his conduct in the chair and in the execution of public business." His duties upon the Bench of the Supreme Court commenced in 1777 and were extremely onerous. He did not recognize the power of the crown and held himself amenable only to his country and his God. An able jurist–an unbending patriot–at the hazard of his life he punished all who were brought before him and convicted of violating the laws of the new government. No threats could intimidate–no influence reach him when designed to divert him from the independent discharge of his duty. His profound legal acquirements–ardent zeal–equal justice–vigorous energy and noble patriotism–enabled him to outride every storm and calm the raging billows that often threatened to overwhelm him. He marched on triumphantly to the goal of LIBERTY and hailed the star spangled banner as it waived in grandeur from the lofty spire of the temple of FREEDOM. He beheld, with the eye of a sage, philosopher and philanthropist, the rising glory of Columbia's new world. He viewed, with emotions of pleasing confidence, the American eagle descend from the ethereal regions beyond the altitude of a tyrant's breath and pounce upon the British lion. With increasing vigor and redoubled fury the mighty bird continued the awful conflict until the king of beasts retreated to his lair and proclaimed, in a roar of thunder–AMERICA IS FREE! Angels rejoiced–monarchs trembled–patriots shouted a loud–AMEN!!! The torch of England's power over the Colonies expired in its socket–the birth of a new nation was celebrated by happy millions basking beneath the genial rays of the refulgent glories of the sun of LIBERTY. The harvest was past–the summer ended–our country saved. The stupendous work of political regeneration was accomplished–the Independence of the United States acknowledged–an honorable peace consumated. Judge McKean then sat down under his own fig tree to enjoy the full fruition of the comforts resulting from his faithful labors in the cause of equal rights.

He continued to discharge the important duties of Chief Justice up to 1799 illuminating his judicial path with profound learning, sound discretion and impartial decisions. His Supreme Court opinions, based, as they generally are–upon equal justice, correct law and strict equity–delivered when the form of government was changed, the laws unsettled, the state constitution just formed, the Federal Government under its Constitution bursting from embryo–are monuments of legal fame enduring as social order–revered, respected–canonized.

He was a member of the convention that formed the constitution of Pennsylvania adopted in 1790 and exercised a salutary influence in that body. In 1799 he was elected Govornor of the Keystone state and contributed largely in adding new strength and beauty to the arch of our Union. For nine successive years he directed the destinies of the land of Penn–commencing at a period when the mountain waves of party spirit were rolling fearfully over the United States with a fury before not dreamed of. Amidst the foaming and conflicting elements, Governor McKean stood at the helm of his commonwealth calm as a summer morning–firm as a granite rock and guided his noble ship through the whirling storm–unscathed and unharmed. He proved himself a safe and skilful pilot.

For elegance and force of language–correct and liberal views of policy–a luminous exposition of law and the principles of government–his annual messages to the legislature stand unrivalled. The clamors of his political enemies he passed by as the idle wind. The suggestions of his friends he scanned with the most rigid scrutiny. Neither flattery or censure could drive him from the strong citadel of his own matured judgment.

The fawning sycophant–the designing demagogue he spurned with contempt. By honest means only he desired the advancement of the party that had elevated him to a post of honor. Open and avowed principles–fully proclaimed and strictly carried out were frankly and without prevarication or disguise submitted to the people by him. He was a politician of the old school when each party had plain and distinctive landmarks, significant names and fixed principles. Political chemists had not then opened shop and introduced the modern mode of amalgamation–producing a heterogeneous mass that defies the power of analysis, analyzation or scientific arrangement. No one of the yclepped classes is homogeneous.

Governor McKean respected those who honestly differed from him in politics and had among them many valued friends. He was free from that narrow minded policy based upon self, which is too prominent at the present day among those who assume the high responsibility of becoming the arbiters of the minds of their fellow men. His views were expanding, liberal–broad–charitable. He aimed at distributing equal justice to all–the rich and poor, the public officer and private citizen. He preferred future good to present aggrandizement. To lay the deep foundations of increasing and lasting prosperity in his own state and through our nation was the object of this pure patriot, enlightened statesman and able jurist. The vast resources of our country, her wide spread territory, majestic rivers, silvery lakes, mineral wealth, rich valleys, majestic mountains, rolling uplands, beautiful prairies, extensive sea board, enterprising sons and her virtuous daughters–were all arrayed before his grasping mind and passed in grand review. He was firmly convinced that our people have only to be wise and good to be great and happy. With this end in view he embraced every opportunity in public and private life to inculcate those great principles of moral rectitude, inflexible virtue, purity of motive and nobleness of action–that alone can preserve a nation. He cast a withering frown upon vice in all its deluding forms. He exerted his strongest powers to arrest the career of crime. He was a terror to evil doers and inspired confidence in those who did well.

In 1808 he retired from public life. He had devoted forty-six years to the faithful service of his country and had earned an imperishable fame. He stood approved at the bar of his country–his conscience and his God. He had acted well his part and contributed largely in raising our country to a proud elevation among the nations of the earth: He outlived all the animosities that a faithful discharge of duty too often creates. On the 24th of June 1817 he resigned his immortal spirit to Him who gave it and fell asleep in the arms of death as peacefully as a babe slumbers. He died at Philadelphia.

The private character of Judge McKean was unsullied as the virgin sheet. His person was tall and erect–his countenance intelligent, bold and commanding–his manners urbane, gentlemanly and affable–his feelings noble, generous and humane–his actions open, frank and republican. He was a refined philanthropist, a sterling patriot, an acute philosopher, an enlightened statesman, a profound lawyer, an impartial judge, an able magistrate and a truly good man. Legislators, statesmen, magistrates and judges–imitate the bright examples of this friend to his country–then our Republic is secure–our UNION safe.

FRANCIS MARION.

The patriots of '76 proved the purity of their motives in the pursuit of emancipation more by *acts* than *words*. They were a united band of brothers who aimed at the general good of their *whole* country- pledged to make her free or perish in the effort. No local interests–no sectional jealousies–no fire-brands of discord could *then* disorganize the phalanx of sages and heroes who struck for LIBERTY. Under the guidance of Heaven they were crowned with victory. They purchased FREEDOM with torrents of blood and millions of treasure. That sacred boon they transmitted to us in pristine purity. Do we *all* fully appreciate this priceless legacy? Far from it. For years it has been the foot-ball of reckless demagogues--the neglected nursling of our people.

Many *talk* loud and long of their patriotism–sing the pæans of our FREEDOM–laud the dear sovereign people to the skies–whose *acts* too plainly show that they look upon our UNION as a mere rope of sand and not as an invaluable treasure to be preserved at all hazards. They look upon the people as a mass of hood-winked worshippers at the shrine of party spirit–not as those who can, should and *must* banish them from our councils or be plunged into the vortex of fearful destruction. People of America! open your eyes to our true position! Look at the mighty struggles, the herculean labors, the gigantic efforts of the few pure patriots in our national council who have nobly warded off the lightning thunderbolts of the disorganizers. See the upheaving throes of the volcano that is rocking us in the consuming cradle of civil discord! Ponder well the danger of concentrating men in Congress whose boiling passions cannot be restrained by the safety-valve of reason–men who do not prize our UNION above all other considerations–whose burning zeal for local measures–party success and self interest would be their ruling passion amidst the smoking ruins of the temple of our LIBERTY. People of America! it is for you to perpetuate this expanding Republic. You *can* and *should* preserve it. Banish all questions that can place it in jeopardy–permit all agitators to remain at home–let the people of each state strictly observe the eleventh commandment–then we may fondly hope that our course may be onward and upward for centuries to come.

Among those who acted a noble part in the American Revolution and exemplified patriotism by his acts–was Francis Marion who was born in 1733 near Georgetown in South Carolina. His early inclination led him to embark on board a vessel bound for the West Indies at the age of sixteen. During the voyage the vessel was upset in a gale and nothing saved but the boat in which the crew and a dog took refuge. They had no provisions but the raw flesh of Carlo and were out a week during which time several of them died. The sufferings and perils then endured cured Marion of his partiality for Neptune. As soon as possible he planted himself on terra firma and devoted his time to agriculture until 1759 when he received the commission of a lieutenant under Capt. Moultrie who was engaged in the expedition against the Cherokee Indians conducted by Gov. Lyttleton. Two years subsequent Marion was raised to the post of captain and served under Col. Grant in a second attempt to chastise the Cherokees. At the commencement of the Revolution of Independence he was on hand and ready for action. He was soon raised to the rank of major and served under Col. Moultrie in his gallant defence of the fort named in honor of that officer. He was then promoted to the rank of lieutenant-colonel and commanded a regiment at the siege of Charleston. In the early part of the siege one of his legs was fractured which saved him a journey to the Spanish Castle in Florida where all the unwounded prisoners were sent.

On his recovery he proceeded to North Carolina and was commissioned a Brigadier General of the militia and became one of the severest scourges the enemy had to encounter. He was enthusiastic in the cause of freedom and imparted this enthusiasm to all who rallied under him. He was remarkably shrewd, bold, energetic and persevering. With a small chosen band around him he retired to the intricate retreats in the low grounds of the Pedee and Black rivers, from which he would suddenly emerge and strike a sanguinary blow into the ranks of the enemy at an unexpected moment and retreat so quickly that they knew not from what direction he came or where to follow him. Even his friends were often ignorant of his location for days. He became a terror to the British army and led detached parties into many a quagmire where they frequently surrendered at discretion—knowing him to be as humane and generous as he was brave and wary. Col. Horry relates the following pleasing incident of Marion.

" About this time we received a flag from the enemy in Georgetown S. C. the object of which was to make arrangements about the exchange of prisoners. The flag, after the usual ceremony of blindfolding, was conducted into Marion's encampment. Having heard great talk about Gen. Marion, his fancy had naturally enough sketched out for him some stout figure of a warrior, such as O'Hara or Cornwallis himself, of martial aspect and flaming regimentals. But what was his surprise when led into Marion's presence and the bandage taken from his eyes, he beheld in our hero, a swarthy, smoke-dried little man with scarcely enough of thread-bare homespun to cover his nakedness and instead of tall ranks of gay dressed soldiers, a handful of sun burnt, yellow legged militia-men—some roasting potatoes and some asleep, with their black firelocks and powder horns lying by them on the logs. Having recovered a little from his surprise, he presented his letter to Gen. Marion, who perused it and settled everything to his satisfaction.

" The officer took up his hat to retire. ' Oh no'—said Marion—' it is now about our time of dining and I hope, sir, you will give us the pleasure of your company at dinner.'

" At the mention of the word dinner, the British officer looked around him, but to his great mortification, could see no sign of a pot, pan, Dutch oven, or any other cooking utensil that could raise the spirits of a hungry man.

" 'Well Tom'—said the General to one of his men—'come give us our dinner.' The dinner he alluded to was no other than a heap of sweet potatoes that were snugly roasting under the embers and which Tom, with his pine stick poker soon liberated from their ashy confinement—pinching them every now and then with his fingers, especially the big ones, to see whether they were well done or not. Then, having cleansed them of the ashes, partly by blowing them with his breath and partly by brushing them with the sleeve of his old cotton shirt, he piled some of the best on a large piece of bark and placed them between the British officer and Marion on the trunk of the fallen pine on which they sat."

" 'I fear sir'—said the General—' our dinner will not prove as palatable to you as I could wish—but it is the best we have.'

" The officer, who was a well bred man, took up one of the potatoes and affected to feed, as if he had found a great dainty—but it was very plain he ate more from good manners than good appetite. Presently he broke out into a hearty laugh. Marion looked surprised. 'I beg pardon General'—said he—'but one cannot, you know, always command one's conceits. I was thinking how drolly some of my brother officers would look if our government were to give them such a bill of fare as this.'

" 'I suppose'—replied Marion—'it is not equal to their style of dining.'

" 'No, indeed'—quoth the officer—' and this I imagine is one of your accidental dinners—a sort of *ban yan*. In general, no doubt, you live a great deal better.'

" 'Rather worse'—answered the General—'for often we don't get enough of this.'

" 'Heaven!' rejoined the officer—'but probably what you lose in *meal* you make up in *malt*—though stinted in *provisions* you draw noble *pay.*'

" '*Not a cent*'—said Marion—'*not a cent.*'

" 'Heavens and earth! then you must be in a bad box. I don't see, General, how you can stand it?'

" 'Why, sir—replied Marion with a smile of self approbation—'these things depend on feeling.'

" The Englishman said—'he did not believe it would be an easy matter to reconcile *his feelings* to a soldier's life on Gen. Marion's terms—*all fighting, no pay and no provisions but potatoes.*'

" 'Why sir'—answered the General—' the *heart* is all and when that is much interested a man can do anything. Many a youth would think it hard to indent himself a slave for fourteen years. But let him be over head and ears in love and with such a beauteous sweetheart as Rachel and he will think no more of fourteen years servitude than young Jacob did. Well now this is exactly my case. I am in love and *my* sweetheart is LIBERTY. Be that heavenly nymph my champion and these woods shall have charms beyond London and Paris in slavery. To have no proud monarch driving over me with his gilt coaches—nor his host of excisemen and tax gatherers insulting and robbing—gloriously preserving my national dignity and pursuing my true happiness—planting my vineyards and eating their luscious fruit—sowing my fields and reaping the golden grain and seeing millions of brothers all around me equally free and happy as myself. This, sir, is what I long for.'

"The officer replied 'that both as a man and a Briton he must certainly subscribe to this as a happy state of things.'

"'*Happy*'—quoth Marion—'yes, happy indeed. I would rather fight for such blessings for my country and feed on roots, than keep aloof though wallowing in all the luxuries of Solomon. For now, sir, I walk the soil that gave me birth and exult in the thought that I am not unworthy of it. I look upon these venerable trees around me and feel that I do not dishonor them. I think of my own sacred rights and rejoice that I have not basely deserted them. And when I look forward to the long-long ages of posterity, I glory in the thought that I am fighting their battles. The children of distant generations may never hear my name but still it gladdens my heart to think that I am now contending for *their* freedom with all its countless blessings.'

"I looked at Marion as he uttered these sentiments and fancied I felt as when I heard the last words of the brave De Kalb. The Englishman hung his honest head and looked, I thought, as if he had seen the upbraiding ghosts of his illustrious countrymen—Sidney and Hamden. On his return to Georgetown he was asked by Col. Watson why he looked so serious?

"'I have cause, sir, to look serious.'

"'What! has Gen. Marion refused to treat?'

"'No, sir.'

"'Well then, has old Washington defeated Sir Henry Clinton and broke up our army?'

"'No sir, not that neither—but *worse*.'

"'Ah! what can be worse?'

"'Why sir, I have seen an American General and his officers *without pay* and almost *without clothes*, living on *roots* and drinking *water*–all for LIBERTY! What chance have we against such men?'

It is said Col. Watson was not much obliged to him for his speech. But the young officer was so struck with Marion's sentiments that he never rested until he threw up his commission and retired from the service."

It would be well if more of our own countrymen were as deeply impressed with the sentiments of Marion as was that honest Briton. It would be a new and glorious era in the later history of our Republic if the unadulterated patriotism of Marion could be revived in the bosoms of the increasing millions of our land. Then our national council would not be disgraced by wrangling, pugnacious, reckless demagogues. They would be left to blow off their explosive gas in retirement instead of exerting their thunder for nearly a year at a time at the capitol at an enormous expense and with less sense and benefit than boys exhibit with fire crackers in the streets.

Gen. Marion continued in active service until that Liberty was won with which he was so deeply in love. He then retired to private life, had the good sense to marry an amiable lady and continued to enjoy the fruits of his toils in the camp until February 1795 when an arrow from the quiver of death pierced the shining mark and consigned his mortal remains to the peaceful tomb. In life he was beloved by all who knew him--in death he was deeply mourned. His whole course had been marked by a stern integrity--an untarnished virtue--a lofty patriotism-- that ever command sincere respect and merited admiration. He was small in stature but large in soul. Strong common sense guided him in every action. He rarely said or did what was not absolutely necessary and for the best. Few men have lived who were as free from all surplusage. Let every reader ponder well the useful career of the noble Marion and profit by his examples. Then our UNION will be safe.

ARTHUR MIDDLETON.

A careful examination of the history of England–of her Magna Charta and Constitution–of the rights by them secured and of the gross violation of those rights at various periods will show the reader why so many men of high attainments and liberal minds came to America. Disgusted with oppression at home they sought Liberty abroad. They fled from religious and political persecution as from a pestilence. The same cause that induced them to leave their native land prompted them to vigorous action when imported tyranny invaded their well earned privileges. The mind of every man and woman who came to this asylum of the oppressed for the sake of freedom was as well prepared to meet the crisis of the Revolution as were our native citizens. The feelings created by remembered injuries which drove them from the mother country rendered them as formidable opponents to the unjust pretensions of the crown as those who had never breathed the atmosphere of Europe. In tracing our own history back to the early settlements we find frequent struggles between the people and the officers sent by the king to rule them—the former claiming their inherent rights—the latter often infringing them. The time finally arrived when forbearance was no longer a virtue.

Among those who espoused the cause of inalienable rights at an early period was Edward Middleton the great grandfather of the younger Arthur. He came from England to S. C. near the close of the 17th century. He left a son Arthur who imbibed the liberal views of his father. In 1719 he headed an opposition that boldly demanded and obtained the removal of the insolent crown officers then in power. He left a son Henry, one of the same sort who was the father of the subject of this sketch and took an active part at the commencement of the Revolution by rousing his fellow citizens to action.

His son Arthur was born at Middleton place on the bank of Ashley rivers S. C. in 1743. His mother was the daughter of Mr. Williams a wealthy planter and was faithful to her children. She lived until 1814, esteemed in life—lamented in death. Arthur was the eldest child and received the best advantages of an early education. At the age of twelve years he was placed in the celebrated seminary at Hackney near London and two years after entered the classic school of Westminster. His industry was unremitting—his conduct unexceptionable. At eighteen he became a student in the University of Cambridge and at the age of twenty-two graduated. He was a profound scholar and untarnished in his morals. Trivial amusements and dissipation had no charms for him. Although liberally supplied with money economy was a governing principle, wisdom his constant guide. Students of our country will do well to imitate his example. After the completion of his education he made the tour of Europe. Familiar with the Greek and Roman classics he enjoyed great pleasure in visiting the ancient seats of learning. He was well versed in all the technicalities of sculpture and architecture and had an exquisite taste for poetry, music and painting. He took notes of all he saw—improved by all he learned.

After travelling for two years he returned to his native home and bosom of his family and friends. His education completed he took the next wise step of a young man about to enter upon business and married a worthy daughter of Walter Izard. The next year the happy pair visited their relatives in England—spent some time in France and Spain—returned in 1773 and took possession of the old paternal mansion which his father had conveyed to him placing him in affluent circumstances.

Possessed of an observing mind his knowledge of English policy and of the principles of monarchy was of a superior order. The effects of this policy and of these principles were painfully visible throughout the American Colonies. Rocked in the cradle of patriotism by his father—tracing its fair lines in the history of his genealogy—LIBERTY was to him an heir-loom. Everything around him prompted his onward course towards the goal of freedom. He boldly espoused the cause of the people which is uniformly the cause of RIGHT. The Middletons were the nucleus of the opposition to tyranny in South Carolina. Their influence reached over the entire province. Although wealthy, aristocracy found no resting place with them. They were Republicans of the first water. They freely and promptly pledged life, fortune and honor in behalf of rational liberty.

Arthur Middleton was upon the various committees of the people to devise means of safety. He was one of the committee of five that decided a recourse to arms and led the people into the royal magazine who removed the deposits in defiance of the threats and growls of the British lion. This occurred on the 17th April 1775. On the 14th of June following the provincial Congress appointed a Committee of Safety composed of thirteen of which Arthur Middleton was one. This committee was fully authorized to organize a military force and adopt such measures as might seem most expedient to arrest the mad career of the royalists.

During the session of the first provincial Congress of South Carolina Lord William Campbell, the new governor, arrived fresh from the British office mint. He was to reduce the rebels at one bold stroke. At first he was all mildness and did not pretend to justify the oppressions of which the people complained. To prove the insincerity of which Mr. Middleton believed him guilty, Adam McDonald, a member of Council, was introduced to him as a Tory from the upper country who seemed anxious to have the rebels put down. The governor requested him to keep quiet a short time as troops would soon arrive to put a quietus upon the *new fangled* authorities. When this report was made known to the Council Mr. Middleton moved to have the governor arrested although nearly related to him by marriage. His colleagues were too timid *then* for such a measure, but so rapidly did their courage increase that his excellency soon retired on board a sloop of war to avoid the popular fury. In a few days Sir Henry Clinton and Sir Peter Parker arrived with an armed fleet and troops to enforce the authority of Lord Campbell and teach peace to the rebels. An immediate attack was made on Fort Moultrie which was a perfect failure. The governor was wounded and Sir Peter had the nether part of his silk unmentionables badly mutilated by an unpolished rebel cannon ball.

On the 11th February 1776 Mr. Middleton was one of the committee that drafted the first constitution of his native State. Soon after he was elected to the Continental Congress and became a conspicuous member. He boldly advocated and by his signature sanctioned the adoption of the Declaration of Independence. He used but few words in debate briefly presenting the strong points of the subject under discussion. He was always heard with attention and had great influence. He stood at the head of the delegation of his State. He exemplified strong common sense—attending to the business of his constituents and the good of his country. He was an intimate friend of John Hancock who held him in high estimation.

In 1778 he was elected governor of his native State without his knowledge, advice or consent. The mode of election was by the legislature and secret ballot. Caucuses, insulated with intrigue and corruption, were then unknown. Love of Liberty and country, exemplified by the acts of freemen, were all the "pledges" required. He declined accepting the office for the reason that a constitution was before the legislature not as republican as he desired and if adopted required the assent of the executive. Believing it would be sanctioned and could be amended at some future time he preferred not placing himself in the way. Rawlin Lowndes was then elected who approved of the constitution on the 19th March 1778.

Political honesty was a marked trait in the character of Arthur Middleton. No inducements could turn him from the path of rectitude and duty. He weighed measures, men and things in the unerring scales of justice. He went with no man unless he believed him clearly right. He was sound at the core. His mind was pure and free as mountain air—his purposes noble, bold and patriotic. In 1779, when the British troops were devastating S. Carolina, he took the field with Gov. Rutledge and cheerfully endured the privations of the camp. At the attack upon Charleston by Gen. Provost, he manifested great coolness and courage. His family was driven away by the destroying enemy and his property plundered. Several valuable paintings were mutilated in the most shameful manner. At the surrender of Charleston in 1780, he was among the prisoners sent to the Spanish Castle at St. Augustine, Florida and manfully endured the cowardly indignities there imposed upon the Americans. In July 1781 a general exchange of prisoners took place when he returned to Philadelphia. He was again elected to Congress and resumed the important duties of legislation. Soon after this the last important act of the revolutionary tragedy was closed at Yorktown, where the Heroes of the revolutionary stage took a closing benefit at the expense of British pride and kingly ambition. With the surrender of Lord Cornwallis the last hope of the crown in America expired in all the agonies of mortification.

In 1782 Mr. Middleton was again returned to Congress where he continued until November when he returned to his long neglected home. He declined remaining in Congress that he might serve his own state. He did much towards restoring order, harmony and stability in the new government of South Carolina. He was several times a member of her legislature and used his best efforts to advance her prosperity. At intervals he improved his desolated plantation and looked forward to years of domestic felicity. But alas! how uncertain are all sublunary things. In the autumn of 1786 he was attacked with the intermittent fever which terminated in serious disease and caused his death on the first day of January 1787, leaving a wife, two sons and six daughters to mourn their irreparable loss. He was deeply lamented by the nation at large. He was held in great veneration by every friend of freedom in the country. He had only to be known to be loved and admired. He was a consolation to his friends, a shining light in the cause of freedom, an ornament to society, a good and honest man. The examples of such a man are living epistles, worthy to be known and read by all who desire the happiness of our beloved country and the perpetuity of our glorious UNION.

LEWIS MORRIS.

A MILITARY despotism is a national curse, a blighting sirocco, a foe to liberty. Laws that require the bayonet to enforce them for an extended length of time are bad or the people for whom they are made are unworthy of freedom. Moments of excitement do occur in the best organized communities arising from a sudden local impulse that require a show of military power and even its force–but in a little time reason resumes her sway, the spirit of mobocracy subsides, the soldier again becomes the peaceful citizen and rests for security upon the strong arm of civil power.

Quartering the military upon the citizens of a community is full of danger. After having enjoyed the bounty and hospitality of the inhabitants let that military be directed to enforce laws that are obnoxious to the people–an indignation is roused that is increased tenfold from the circumstance of previous familiarity. The citizen conceives he has bestowed a special favor upon the soldier. He looks upon the attempt to force unjust laws upon him as base ingratitude–the blackest crime out of pandemonium. Favors forgotten and ingratitude displayed add desperation to revenge. Previous to the American Revolution the military were quartered upon or drew their support directly from the people. The Colonies had contributed largely in money and blood to aid the mother country in conquering her most inveterate foe in America–the French in Canada. No return was asked but the quiet enjoyment of chartered privileges guaranteed by the constitution. This was denied them. Petitions were treated with contumely–remonstrances were laughed to scorn. Then it was that a band of Sages and Heroes rose in all the majesty of man's native dignity and vindicated their inalienable rights.

Among the boldest of the bold was Lewis Morris, born at Morrisania in the vicinity of the city of New York in 1726. The preserved documents of this family trace their genealogy back to Rhice Fitzgerald. Rhys or Rhice Fitzgerald was a Cambrian chieftain who carried his military operations and conquests into Ireland during the reign of Henry II. By his valor and success he obtained the name of Maur [great] Rhice and the penultimate Fitzgerald being dropped gives us the name in plain English–Morris. In tracing genealogy we find names more changed than this. Genealogy and the origin of names is an amusing study–if you have leisure try it.

Lewis was the son of Judge Morris of the same Christian name who retained possession of the paternal estate formerly purchased by his grandfather, Richard Morris, who was a leader under Cromwell and came from Barbadoes in 1663 and purchased a tract of land near Harlaem on York Island. He left an only son, Lewis, who was Chief Justice of New York and subsequently governor of New Jersey.

After his preparatory studies Lewis entered Yale College at the age of sixteen. From the President, Dr. Clap, he imbibed a relish for moral and religious principles and became a good scholar. In 1746 he graduated—returned to his estate and became extensively engaged in agriculture. At that period the Colonies were free, prosperous and happy. The mother country had not discovered the philosopher's stone of taxing her distant children to support royalty. They were left to pursue their own course—enjoy the fruit of their labors and repose in peace. In this delightful retirement Mr. Morris continued to improve his farm and mind. By his suavity of manners, moral rectitude and honorable course he gained the confidence and esteem of all who made his acquaintance. He was the nucleus to a circle of friends of the highest attainments and respectability. He became a great favorite among the people and did all in his power to improve their condition and promote general good. He was a philanthropist and patriot.

The time rolled on rapidly when colonial repose was to be plucked up from the roots and perish under the burning heat of British oppression. The treasury of England had been drained by extravagance and war—her national debt had become frightfully large. The story of prosperity and wealth in America had been told to Mr. Grenville by an evil person in an evil hour. The plan of imperious taxation was devised. The Stamp Act was passed as a feeler. The descendants of the pilgrim fathers thought its feeling rather rough and recoiled from the touch with amazement. They loved their king but they loved their chartered privileges and country more. Legal remedies were resorted to. A Congress was convened at New York and several Colonies ably represented. Powerful addresses to the throne and people of Great Britain were prepared breathing the purest allegiance conditioned on the restoration of constitutional rights. The Stamp Act was repealed only to give place to a more voracious and obnoxious budget of Acts. The ministry bent all their force to accomplish their impolitic designs. They did more to prepare the people of America for Independence than the combined energies of the Sages could have effected without their co-operation. In devising a great evil they consummated a great good.

Mr. Morris took a deep interest in passing events—at first only as an adviser. Although Massachusetts took the lead in resisting oppression New York was not tardy in coming to the rescue. In 1767 an Act was passed by Parliament compelling the people of that Province to furnish the British soldiers that were quartered among them with provisions. By this order the burden fell upon certain portions of the inhabitants exclusively and not *pro rata* upon the whole. It was a direct invasion of personal rights and was most severely felt by the citizens of the city of New York and its vicinity. This measure brought Mr. Morris out. He publicly proclaimed it unconstitutional and tyrannical and contributed largely towards influencing the legislature to place a veto upon it. Might triumphed over right and enforced the contribution from the citizens. Spirits like that of Lewis Morris were not to be subdued. An unquenchable fire was only smothered to gather volcanic force under the brittle crust that covered it. It was constantly increased by supplies of fuel from Mr. Grenville and his more subtle successor Lord North. The statute of Henry VIII. was revived which doomed the disobedient to be sent to England for trial. Its eldest daughter–the Boston Port Bill was ushered into life and other screws of the rack tightened. The last petitions and remonstrances in the magazine of patience were finally exhausted. It was speedily replenished with materials more weighty than paper. Mr. Morris had become a prominent leader, a bold and substantial whig, rather too highly charged for the conciliatory Congress of 1774. The time came on apace when the people required just such a man and in April 1775 elected him to the Continental Congress. Even then most people attributed their sufferings to the venal ministry and hoped the king would cease to be an automaton and prove himself a man worthy of the high station he occupied. But hopes were vain– the olive branch withered beneath the scorching rays of corrupted power. The virtues of steel, powder and lead were then to be tried. Already had the purple current of Americans saturated the streets of Boston and heights of Lexington. Already had the groans of dying citizens, slain by the hands of those whom they had fed–pierced the ears of thousands. Already were widows weeping for husbands weltering in blood and orphans for fathers covered with gore. If imagination sickens–if language fails, if history is impotent in conveying but a faint idea of the consuming anguish, the bitter grief, the palsying terrors, the boiling revenge, the deep resolves of those dark hours– how heart breaking–how overwhelming must have been the dreadful reality to living witnesses.

Soon after he took his seat in Congress Mr. Morris was placed upon a committee of which the illustrious Washington was chairman to devise measures to obtain the munitions of war. This was a *desideratum* rather problematical. Comparatively a sling and a few smooth stones were all the patriots had with which to combat the British Goliah. But the battle of Bunker Hill convinced all parties that rusty guns in hands with nerves of steel guided by hearts of oak could do good service and that men resolved on liberty or death were not to be tamely yoked without a desperate effort to be free. Mr. Morris became an active member and advocated strong measures. The year previous he was considered rash—the time had arrived when all saw the necessity of pursuing the course he had marked out. He became early convinced that an honorable arrangement could not be had *under* Great Britain—nothing but a triumph *over* her would restore the equilibrium of justice. He was one of a committee to visit the Indian tribes to persuade them not to enlist under the blood stained banner of England. But British gold was stronger than the most eloquent reasoning. To the eternal disgrace of those who were then wielding the destinies of the mother country, a premium was given for *scalps* not for prisoners. So dark, so deep, so damning a blot rests not upon the escutcheon of any other nation upon earth. Why? Because that kingdom had been the proclaimed conservator of the peaceful, humane religion of the Cross for centuries—the crowning glory of which is love. The foul deed was committed in the full blaze of Gospel light and boasted civilization. There were noble souls in parliament at that time and millions of British subjects who looked upon the horrors of that demoniac policy with as much indignity as an American can. Mr. Morris also visited the New England States for the purpose of maturing plans to raise supplies and commence concentrated vigorous action.

In 1776 he again took his seat in Congress and was pleased to find the general pulse beating in unison with his own—a determination to sever the Gordian knot and proclaim an eternal separation from a nation that held power only to abuse it. He was on many important committees—was all activity in and out of the House. In his native neighborhood he had a herculean task in rousing the people to a sense of their true position. Gov. Tryon mingled the poison with the wisdom of the serpent—affected to be harmless as a dove and exercised a powerful influence over the people of the city of New York in favor of the crown. He pointed them to the certain destruction of the commercial interests by a war—the inequality of the two powers—the impossibility of Whig success and construed self interest into self preservation. To paralyze his influence required great exertion. Mr. Morris and his friends put forth their noblest energies in the mighty work. What they could not effect, British oppression and the powder and ball of Gen. Howe soon accomplished.

When the Declaration of Independence was proposed Mr. Morris became one of its ardent supporters. At that very time his large estate was within the power of the enemy. He well knew that his signature to the proposed instrument would be destructive to all his property within the reach of British hirelings. Most faithfully was the work executed. Even his extensive woodlands of a thousand acres were subjected to axe and fire—his family driven from home and every species of devastation resorted to that malice could invent, hatred design, revenge execute. But LIBERTY was dearer to this devoted patriot than earth and all its riches. He boldly sanctioned and fearlessly affixed his name to the great certificate of our national birth and rejoiced in freedom illumined by the conflagration of his own Elysian Morrisania. His family and himself suffered many privations during the remainder of the war. They endured every hardship with heroic fortitude without regret for the past and with buoyant hope for the bright future.

In 1777 he resigned his seat in Congress and rendered important services in the legislature of his native State. He also served in the tented field and rose to the rank of major-general of militia. He was a good disciplinarian and reduced the state troops to an excellent organization. In every situation he ably and zealously discharged all his duties and did not leave the service of his country until the American arms were triumphant and the Independence of our nation acknowledged by Great Britain. Then he retired to his desolated plantation—converted his sword into a pruning hook—his musket into a ploughshare and his farm into a delightful retreat where his friends from the city often visited him to enjoy his agreeable society—talk of times gone by and rejoice in the consolations of blood-bought Liberty. Peacefully and calmly he glided down the stream of time until January 1798 when his immortal spirit left its frail bark and launched upon the ocean of eternity in a more substantial vessel. He died serene and happy surrounded by an affectionate family and kind friends. His remains were deposited in the family vault upon his farm under the honors of an epic and civic procession.

The private virtues and public services of Mr. Morris rendered him dear to all who knew him. His appearance was in every way commanding. A noble and graceful figure, a fine and intelligent face, an amiable and agreeable disposition, a warm and ardent temperament, a benevolent and generous heart, an independent and patriotic soul—crowned with intelligence, refinement and goodness—he was in all respects worthy to be admired and beloved. His examples illustrate the patriotism that impelled to action during the Revolution. He had everything that could be destroyed to lose if successful—if not—death was his probable doom. Previous to the war he was a favorite of the king—his brother Staats was a member of Parliament and a general officer under the crown. But few made as great personal sacrifices and no one made them more cheerfully. Like Marion–he preferred a morsel of bread, a meal of roasted potatoes with Liberty–to all the trappings of royalty and all the honors that could be conferred by a king. So long as this kind of patriotism finds a resting place in the bosoms of a respectable majority of Columbia's sons–our UNION is safe. Let this be banished by the majority as it is by a fearful minority–the fair temple of our LIBERTY will perish in flames kindled by its professed guardians. Freemen of America! I warn you to preserve, in original purity, the FREEDOM purchased with the rich blood of our fathers.

ROBERT MORRIS.

SELF is the Sahara of the human heart where all the noble powers of the soul are buried in its scorching sands. We may pour upon it floods of human woe and streams of melting kindness without producing the least appearance of sympathy or gratitude. The blighting sirocco of cold indifference sweeps over this desert mind, increases the powers of absorption–annihilates all that is cheering and lovely. The keenest miseries of a fellow man cannot move it–the mournful obsequies of his death cannot shame it. It is one of the foul blots imprinted on human nature by Lucifer and should be hurled back to Pandemonium. It dwells only in little minds and pinches them as dandy boots do the feet –covering them with excrescences as painful as corns and chilblains. He who is a slave to self could calmly look on the "wreck of matter and the crash of worlds" if it would add one item to his sordid gains.

Man was created a social being–benevolent, sympathetic, kind, affectionate–quick to feel and prompt to alleviate the misfortunes of his fellow man. But for the soul-killing influence of self these noble germs of human nature, as originally cast in the mould of creative wisdom, would bud and blossom as the rose and crown the human family with millennial glory.

On the pages of history we find many bright spots of self sacrifice and blooming benevolence. Individuals have lived who banished self and devoted their lives, fortunes and sacred honors to promote the best interests of the human race–men whose motives, impelling them to action, were chastened by purity, who aimed to promote public good and personal happiness.

In the history of the American Revolution we find a cheering catalogue of such philanthropists whose memories we delight to honor.

No one among them did more to accomplish the great end in view than Robert Morris. He was born at Liverpool, Lancashire, England, on the 20th of January 1734. His father was a respectable merchant and settled at Oxford on the eastern shore of Maryland in 1746. He then sent for this son who arrived at Oxford at the age of thirteen. He received only a good commercial education. At the age of fifteen he lost his father by death. He was then in the counting house of Charles Willing one of the most thorough and enterprising merchants of Philadelphia. After having served a faithful apprenticeship Mr. Willing set him up in business and remained his fast friend and adviser. For several years he prospered *alone* but finding the cares of life pressing upon him he wisely resolved to take a partner to accompany him in his pilgrimage through this vale of tears. That partner was the meritorious Mary, daughter of Col. White and sister to the pious and learned Bishop White. She possessed every quality that adorns her sex and renders connubial felicity complete. What is *now* more than *then* considered by too many heartless bipeds a *sine qua non*—she brought with her—WEALTH. This *desideratum* is often a blighting substitute for genuine affection—too often the corroding mildew of matrimonial happiness. No man or woman with a good heart, clear head and sound discretion—ever married *riches* instead of the *person*. It is the quintessence of self.

Not so with Mr. Morris and his partner. Their richest treasure was mutual esteem flowing from the pure fountain of their kindred hearts anxious to promote the reciprocal happiness of each other and the felicity of all around them. Nothing occurred to mar their refined enjoyments until the revolutionary storm burst upon the Colonies.

Mr. Morris was a sterling patriot and did not look upon the commoving political elements with indifference. He had inhaled the atmosphere of inherent freedom—his soul was roused to god-like action—he resolved to hold his life and fortune subject to the drafts of LIBERTY. If self had held her withering sway he would have remained a loyal slave. His interests were entirely commercial—his wealth was exposed to the destructive power of the mother country. He amassed it only to do good. He was not fastidious as to the manner it was distributed so that his noble aim might be accomplished--the salvation of his country.

He was a member of the Congress of 1774 and took an unflinching stand against British oppression. Extensively and favorably known—his influence was of high importance to the friends of justice. Being an able financier he was hailed as the most efficient manager of the monetary department. To provide ways and means he was fully authorized.

Most nobly did he discharge his duty. Unfortunately no office of finance was then created to enable him to control the disbursements. The money he continued to provide–often from his private funds. When Congress fled before the conquering foe to Baltimore in 1776 Mr. Morris remained in Philadelphia some days after his colleagues left, for the purpose of raising government funds. In so doing he periled his life, as he had placed his name upon the Declaration of Independence–then sneeringly called the death warrant of the signers by the Tories and their coadjutors–the British. During his stay it became necessary for Congress to raise a specific sum. The treasury was empty. Notice of the wants of the army was communicated to him. Shortly after he met a member of the Society of Friends whose confidence he had. "What news friend Robert?" "The news is–I am in immediate want of of—— dollars hard money and you are the man to obtain it for me. Your security is to be my note of hand and my word of honor." "Robert thou shalt have it." The money was promptly forwarded to Washington which enabled him to meet the enemy at Trenton with signal success.

Mr. Morris made no parade or vain show in the performance of his duties and often furnished funds through agents under the injunction of secrecy who then had the credit of affording relief on their own account. When Gen. Greene took command of the troops in S. C. they were deplorably destitute of food, clothing and ammunition. To the agreeable astonishment of the army and people Mr. Hall of that state advanced the money to purchase supplies and enabled the General to commence vigorous operations. After the war had closed the accounts of disbursements showed that Mr. Hall had acted under Mr. Morris who furnished the needful from his private purse and saved the army from dissolution. On being made acquainted with the fact at the finance office, General Greene was at first displeased with the act but on analyzing it applauded the wisdom of this secrecy and said–" If I had known that I might have drawn on Robert Morris I should have demanded larger sums and effected no more than was accomplished with the means placed in my hands." His advances to the Southern army nearly produced his pecuniary ruin.

As a financier his genius was of the most prolific kind. When he found every government resource exhausted–the credit of the infant Republic paralyzed–the army writhing under the keenest privations–had his mind been of ordinary calibre he would have abandoned the ship of state amidst the breakers that were dashing over her and reported her to the underwriters as wrecked. But he had resolved never to desert her so long as a plank remained upon the hull or a beam retained its fastenings upon the keel. His own resources were large and his credit upon a firm basis. These were thrown in the breach and warded off the threatened destruction. To save himself and his country he proposed the plan of establishing the Bank of North America. This was sanctioned by Congress and a charter granted on the 7th of January 1782. This bank has ever stood firm amidst all the pecuniary panics and revolutions that have occurred to the present time.

As astounding as the fact may appear the office of Finance was not created until 1781. Up to that time there was no disbursing agent and large sums of money were placed in the hands of irresponsible agents and never reached their legitimate destination. When established it was placed under the control of Mr. Morris who reduced the expenditures of military operations three millions in a single year, showing that self can convert ostensible patriots into knaves no matter how sacred the cause engaged in or how binding the obligation to do justice. Avaunt! thou thing infernal! Had the office of Finance been established at the commencement of hostilities and Mr. Morris made the disbursing agent, the means of prosecuting the war would have been ample—our army would have been full and saved from the dreadful privations endured—our country would have been saved from a large portion of the devastations committed by the enemy—the struggle would probably have been terminated in half the time and the government been able to redeem every dollar of its paper issues. With so much concentrated talent and wisdom as were in the Continental Congress at all times, the problem of this disastrous omission cannot be solved by any approved rules of government or legislation. I have ever looked at it with deep regret and surprise.

Mr. Morris was the Roman Curtius of America, pledging his own fortune to save his country and deliver her from worse than Egyptian bondage. As a demonstration I will particularize one other instance of supplies furnished upon his private credit, which was the means of closing the unequal contest.

When the expedition against Cornwallis was planned by Washington the government treasury was empty and her credit shivering in the wind. The army was in a destitute situation and without the means of prosecuting a siege. Impressed deeply with the importance of the plan Mr. Morris undertook the herculean task of providing supplies for the expedition upon his private credit. Such confidence had Washington in this able financier that he at once took up the line of march. In the short space of four weeks he furnished near eighty pieces of battering cannon and one hundred pieces of field artillery with other necessary supplies not furnished by the South. Although aided by the patriotic Richard Peters he gave his own notes to the amount of one million four hundred thousand dollars which were all paid at maturity. This enabled the Americans to triumphantly close the long and bloody struggle of the Revolution and lay firmly the foundations of the prosperity and government we now enjoy. There was disinterested benevolence crowned with all the majesty of pure devotion to the interests of country and the human family–as free from self as angels are.

Under cover of the firm in which he was a partner–Willing, Morris & Co. many important and advantageous transactions were made for government although apparently for the firm, the large profits of which were placed to the credit of the public treasury. This was conclusively shown by an investigation instituted in Congress on motion of Mr. Laurens at the instance of Mr. Morris in order to repel base slanders put in circulation against this pure and honest patriot.

All the accusations that have been brought against Robert Morris before and since his death, charging him with peculation or speculation in government funds or of any improper conduct towards his country as a public agent are without foundation in fact and out of the record. From the numerous documents I have examined, I am fully convinced that Robert Morris was one of the most disinterested patriots of the Revolution and one of the most efficient instruments in consummating that glorious enterprise. He was so considered by the illustrious Washington–the Continental Congress and by all who were and are properly posted on the subject. General Greene was one of his most ardent admirers, whose biographer–long after the SAGE and the HERO had gone where none but slanderers dare rake up the sacred ashes of the dead, published a tirade of abuse against Mr. Morris that has impaired his dignity as an impartial writer so as to render his envy abortive–his malice powerless. His extracts from public documents are garbled–his conclusions are based on false premises–his inuendoes are ungenerous–his attack gratuitous and has justly recoiled upon the proud escutcheon of his literary fame.

The shafts of slander can never mar the fair reputation of this benefactor of our country although hurled like lightning thunderbolts from the whole artillery of malice and revenge. Upon the enduring records of our nation his acts are written. There they stand in bold relievo, bright as the moon, clear as the sun and as withering to his enemies as the burning sand of Sahara.

Congress elected Mr. Morris Superintendent of Finance on the 20th of February 1781. It was only from a deep sense of duty he could be urged to accept the office. It was at a dark and fearful period of the Revolution. His duties were onerous and multiform. He immediately instituted an examination of the public debts, revenue and expenditures—reduced to economical system the mode of regulating the finances and disbursing the public funds—executed the plans of Congress relative to monetary affairs—superintended the action of all persons employed in obtaining and distributing supplies for the army—attended to the collection of all monies due the United States—held a supervision over all the contractors for military supplies—provided for the civil list—corresponded with the Executive of each state and with ministers of our government in Europe and transacted business with all the public departments. Through the agency of the Bank of North America and with his own proverbial responsibility he improved the national credit so far that money was obtained from Europe on loan and a brighter prospect opened before the desponding patriots. He introduced rigid economy through all the avenues of public operations. He boldly entered the Ægean stable and was the Hercules to cleanse it. Corrupt agents and corrupting speculators fled before his searching scrutiny—hissing like serpents disturbed in their dens. Perfect system pervaded all his transactions reducing them all to writing so that he was able to produce a conclusive voucher for each and every public act during his term of service. He believed system to be the ballast, main-mast and helm of business.

At the time of his resignation he placed himself in the crucible of an examining committee of Congress before whom he exhibited a schedule of all his public transactions. The report of the committee placed him on a lofty eminence as an able and skilful financier—a patriotic and honest man. President Washington tendered him the office of Secretary of the Treasury, which he respectfully declined. He was a member of the convention that framed the Federal Constitution and a Senator in the first Congress that convened under it. He seldom spoke in debate but when he did he was eloquent, chaste and logical. He was heard with profound attention and had great influence with his colleagues. He possessed an inexhaustible store of useful information applicable to all the relations of public and private life. When the peace of 1783 was consummated Mr. Morris again entered largely into commercial business. He favored every kind of improvement and did all in his power to promote general good and individual happiness. He first introduced ice and hot-houses in our country. He was a rare specimen of industry, system, punctuality and honesty.

After spending a long life in skilfully wielding a capital of millions he at last foundered upon the rock of land speculation and closed his eventful career in poverty on the 8th of May 1806 at the city of Philadelphia sincerely mourned by his country and most deeply lamented by those who knew him best. He met the grim messenger of death with resignation and calmness—bid a cheerful farewell to friends, the toils of earth and all sublunary things.

Mr. Morris was a large man with an open countenance, pleasing in his manners and agreeable in all his associations. His private character was as pure as his public career was illustrious. Dying poor, no marble monument is reared to his memory but his name is deeply engraved upon the tablet of meritorious fame and will be revered by every true American and patriot until the historic page shall be blotted from the world—social order submerged by chaos.

JOHN MORTON.

Courage and perseverance, unaided by wisdom and sound discretion, often lead men into unforeseen and unanticipated difficulties. Combined—they are the fulcrum and lever of action. Guided by a wise discretion, with talent to conceive and boldness to execute, the weak become strong and effect wonders at which they look with astonishment after the mighty work is accomplished. To these combined qualities of the Sages and Heroes of the American Revolution we owe the blessings of liberty we now enjoy more than to the physical powers of our nation at that time. Compared with the fleets and armies of the mother country at the eventful era when the Declaration of our Independence was adopted, the available force of the Colonies dwindles to insignificance. The one a giant in the pride of his glory—the other an infant just bursting into life. The one a Goliah clad in bristling armor—the other a pioneer boy with a puerile sling. The one with a veteran army and navy armed in panoply complete, well clothed, fed and paid—the other with scattered fragments of raw recruits, a few light vessels—the men poorly equipped, sparingly fed, worse clothed and seldom paid. Without referring the successful termination of the revolutionary struggle to the wisdom and perseverance of the patriots, who, under God, conceived, planned and executed the noble work it would be an unsolved enigma.

John Morton was proverbial for his discreet, wise, courageous and persevering course of life. He was a posthumous child born in Ridley, Delaware county, Pennsylvania, in 1724. His ancestors came from Sweden at an early period and settled on the bank of the Delaware river near Philadelphia. John's father, of the same Christian name, married Mary Richards when he was very young and died before his majority. The widow subsequently married with John Sketchly an intelligent Englishman who proved a good husband and kind step-father. To him John was principally indebted for his substantial English education, having enjoyed the advantages of a school but three months. Being a good mathematician and skilful surveyor, his step-son became perfect master of this important branch of science, which, more than any other, is calculated to lead a man into precision of thought and action. Based on invariable truth and lucid demonstration, never resting on false premises, always arriving at incontrovertible conclusions, it gives a tone to the mental powers calculated to produce the most salutary results. Education is incomplete without mastering mathematics.

Young Morton continued with his faithful guardian until manhood dawned upon him, aiding in the business of agriculture and surveying, constantly storing his mind with useful knowledge—testing theory by practice. In 1764 he was commissioned a justice of the peace and shortly after was elected to the Assembly of his native state. He soon became conspicuous and was subsequently speaker of the House during several sessions. He took a deep interest in the welfare of his country and was a member of the Congress assembled at New York in 1765 to concert measures for the repeal of the odious Stamp Act. He concurred in the strong and bold appeals of that body which virtually kindled the fire of the Revolution. Although smothered for a time it was never extinguished until it consumed the last vestige of British power in America and expired for want of fuel. In 1767 he became the sheriff of his county which station he ably filled for three years. He was then appointed president judge of his district and gained the admiration and esteem of the entire community. About this time he performed a very sensible act by marrying Anne Justis of the State of Delaware who was worthy to be the wife of a patriot and contributed largely to his happiness through life.

When the dread clarion of war was sounded from the heights of Lexington the indignation of the people in his neighborhood was so roused that they at once raised a battalion of volunteers and elected Judge Morton colonel. He was compelled to decline the epic honor having been recently appointed a judge of the Supreme Court of Pennsylvania. In July 1774 he was made a member of the Congress that convened in Philadelphia the following September. The grand object of that Congress was to make a last and noble effort to effect a reconciliation between the two countries and heal instead of increasing the unfortunate breach. To this end men of cool deliberation, deep thought, matured judgment, profound wisdom and pure patriotism were selected for this important work on which depended the destiny of themselves and unborn millions. When the delegates assembled a deep and awful solemnity seemed to pervade every mind. No noise was heard but the still murmuring of the rushing blood, the beating of anxious hearts and the quick respiration of those who had congregated. The proceedings were opened by prayer. Every soul seemed to commune with the spirits of another world as by vesper orisons. After the address to the throne of grace the same awful silence reigned. Still nothing was heard but the rush of the purple stream and the throb of anxious hearts. Trembling tears and quivering lips told the emotions of many a bosom–too full to be expressed, too deep to be fathomed, too strong to be endured. At length the mighty spirit of Patrick Henry burst forth in all the sublimity of its native majesty and broke the mighty spell. In bold and glowing colors, shaded with dignified sincerity–painted upon the canvas of eternal justice with the pencil of unerring truth–he delineated American rights and British wrongs. When he closed every patriot responded a hearty–AMEN. Their mouths were opened, their burdens lightened–they breathed more freely.

In May 1775 Judge Morton took his seat in Congress and was re-elected in November. In July 1776 he closed his congressional career. Before leaving, he placed a brilliant star upon the bright escutcheon of his name by voting for and signing the chart of our Liberty–the manifesto of freemen against the usurpations of tyranny. During the time he was in Congress he was highly esteemed as a cool deliberate discreet man–purely patriotic and anxious to do all in his power to promote the righteous cause of his bleeding country. He weighed well the consequences of severing the bonds that bound the Colonies to the mother country. Unsustained, the Declaration of Independence was probable death to many–a more severe slavery for the survivors. To all human appearance the patriots must be crushed by the physical force of their enemies then pouring into the country by thousands and sweeping everything before them like a mighty torrent. There were five delegates from his colony. Two of them were bitterly opposed to the measure and two in favor, which gave him the casting vote. On him depended the enhanced misery or happy delivery of his country. When the final moment arrived he cast his vote in favor of the important instrument that should prove either the death warrant or the diploma of freedom. Some of his old friends censured him severely for the bold act and were so strongly tinctured with toryism that they would not be reconciled to him when he lay upon the bed of death. Such were the strong party feelings during the Revolution. His dying message to them was worthy the sage and Christian. "Tell them that they will live to see the hours when they shall acknowledge it to have been the most glorious service that I have ever rendered to my country." The truth of his prophecy has been most happily verified so far as his services were concerned—if the other part has not do not go in mourning for its failure.

When the Articles of Confederation were under discussion in Congress Judge Morton was frequently chairman of the committee of the whole and presided with great ability and dignity. In April 1777 he was attacked with a highly inflammatory fever which terminated his life in a few days in the midst of usefulness with fresh honors awaiting him as time rolled onward. His premature death was deeply mourned by his bereaved companion, eight children, a large concourse of bosom friends, the members of the bar, his associate judges, the State legislature, Congress and by every patriot of his country.

As a private citizen Judge Morton possessed an unusual share of esteem. He was endowed with all the amiable qualities that enrich the domestic circle and social intercourse. As the crowning glory of his fair fame he professed and adorned the religion of his Lord and Master and died triumphing in faith. His dust reposes in the cemetery of St. James' Church in Chester, Pa. His examples are worthy of the closest imitation—his brief career admonishes us of the uncertainty of human life—his happy death is an evidence of the truth of unvarnished piety.

THOMAS NELSON.

HONESTY is a virtue that commands universal respect. Like many others this term has lost much of its original force. When Pope pronounced an honest man the noblest work of God—he included purpose, word and action in all things, under all circumstances, at all times. He alluded to a man whose purity of heart placed him above every temptation to violate the original laws of integrity that emanated from the high Chancery of Heaven. He referred to a man whose every action through his whole life should pass the scrutiny of Omniscience unscathed and stand approved by the great Jehovah. Such a man is a noble work indeed worthy of the highest admiration and closest imitation. He would not take an umbrella or a newspaper from the owner without liberty. He is honest for the sake of this virtue—not from *policy*, the essential oil of dishonesty in disguise. Honesty that is based only on self interest is as unsafe as a keg of powder in the fire room of a steamboat. We have too much *policy* in morals and religion. It is cunning without wisdom, cowardice with hypocrisy, fear of man—not of God. The devil preaches religion from policy and the man who is honest only from *policy* is no better. Anecdote to the point. The Chinese philosopher Confucius met an insane woman with a pitcher of water and faggot of fire and asked her how she intended to use them. She replied—" With the fire I will burn up heaven—with the water I will put out hell—we shall then know who are good for the sake of goodness."

The Sages and Heroes of the American Revolution who persevered to the end were remarkable for integrity and freedom from self interest. None of them were more so than Thomas Nelson, born at Yorktown, Virginia, on the 26th of December 1738. He was the son of William Nelson whose father came from England at an early period and located at Yorktown. The father of Thomas was a wealthy merchant and planter. He filled many public stations with great ability. During the interval between the administration of Lord Bottetourt and Lord Dunmore, he presided over the Colony *ex officio*, being then President of the Executive Council.

At the age of fourteen Thomas was placed under the tuition of Mr. Newcomb whose school was near Hackney, England. He graduated at Trinity College under Dr. Beilby Porteus, the bright literary ornament of that time and afterwards Bishop of London. Guided by the master genius of this finished scholar, accomplished gentleman and pious divine, Mr. Nelson traced the fair lines of science and explored the avenues of literature. The principles of strict virtue and stern integrity were deeply impressed upon his mind and governed his actions through life. After spending eight years at the classic fountain in England he returned to his native home highly improved in mind and person. He entered upon the enjoyment of a large real estate and over one hundred and thirty thousand dollars in money. Not selfish at heart—unwilling to enjoy so much alone, as in duty bound he led to the hymenial altar Lucy—daughter of Philip Grimes of Brandon and settled happily and quietly at his native place. His house became the seat of domestic felicity and hospitality.

For a long time great intimacy existed between the leading men of

Virginia and England. This arose from consanguinity and the wealth that enabled the most prominent men of the Old Dominion to educate their sons in the mother country. For more than a century an interchange of good feelings and kind offices were kept up. The sons who were educated in Great Britain imbibed the same ideas of Independence as those which were the boast of the noblemen of that kingdom and very properly felt themselves entitled to as much confidence from the King as a native resident of Albion. For this reason, when the British ministry put the car of oppression in motion in Virginia, her wealthy and noblest sons were the most vigorous opposers of regal power. The very fact of former intimacy charged this opposition with stronger bitterness. The very chivalry that the proud Britons had taught the sons of the Old Dominion was brought to bear upon the hirelings of the crown with the force of an avalanche.

In 1774 Mr. Nelson was elected to the House of Burgesses and took a bold stand in favor of liberal principles. He was one of the eighty-nine members who assembled at a tavern the day after Lord Dunmore dissolved them and formed themselves into an association of non-intercourse with Great Britain. At the next election he was again returned. He was a member of the two conventions that appointed Congressional delegates in 1774–5. He supported the bold measures proposed by the daring Henry from which many of the patriots at first recoiled with terror and amazement. He had no ear for the siren song of peace when the shores of his country were darkened by foreign fleets and armies. At the convention in March 1775 the following resolutions were proposed by Patrick Henry and passed. The first germ of our militia system then burst from embryo.

" Resolved—That a well regulated militia, composed of gentlemen and yeomen, is the natural strength and only security of a free government—that such a militia in this colony would forever render it unnecessary for the mother country to keep among us, for the purpose of our defence, any standing army of mercenary soldiers, always subversive of the quiet and dangerous to the liberties of the people and would obviate the pretext of taxing for their support. That the establishment of such a militia is at this time peculiarly necessary by the state of our laws, some of which have already expired and will shortly be so and that the known remissness of government in calling us together in legislative capacity renders it too insecure in this time of danger and distress to rely that opportunity will be given of renewing them in general Assembly or making any provision to secure our inestimable rights and liberties from those further violations with which they are threatened.

Resolved—That this Colony be immediately put in a state of defence and that —— be a committee to prepare a plan for embodying, arming and disciplining such a number of men as may be sufficient for that purpose."

These resolutions were warmly supported by Mr. Nelson regardless of the certain destruction of a large portion of his property in case of an open rupture with mother Britain. The resolutions were carried and July fixed for the division of the Colony into military districts. From that time Virginia presented a bold front against the unwarranted pretensions and insolent assumptions of power on the part of the crown officers. In July the Convention again assembled and divided the Colony into sixteen military districts—the Eastern to immediately raise a regiment of six hundred and eighty men rank and file, the others to raise a battalion of five hundred men each—all to be at once armed and held in readiness to march at any moment. The Convention further directed the raising of two regiments of regulars of one thousand and twenty privates each—the first to be commanded by Patrick Henry, the other by Thomas Nelson. Virginia stands number one in the organization of a military system independent of mother Britain—a system that now pervades the United States.

On the 11th of August this Convention met again and elected Mr. Nelson and others to the Continental Congress in which he took his seat on the 13th of September following. He was an industrious and efficient member of many important committees but rarely took part in debate. By the following extract from his letter to Gov. Page dated 22d January 1776 it appears he was one of those who early agitated the question of Independence. "I wish I knew the sentiments of our people upon the grand points of Confederation and Foreign Alliance—or in other words—of Independence—for we cannot expect to form a connexion with any foreign power as long we have a womanish hankering after Great Britain and to be sure there is not in nature a greater absurdity than to suppose we can have any affection for a people who are carrying on the most savage war against us." On the 13th of February following he wrote to the same gentleman in the following strong language—"Independence, Confederation and foreign alliance are as formidable to some members of Congress—I fear a majority, as an apparition to a weak enervated woman. Would you think we have some among us who still expect honorable proposals from the administration! By heavens! I am an infidel in politics for I do not believe were you to bid a thousand pounds per scruple for honor at the court of Great Britain that you would get as many as would make an ounce. We are now carrying on a war and no war. They seize our property whenever they find it either by land or sea and we hesitate to retaliate because we have a few friends in England who have ships. Away with such squeamishness say I."

By this language we can judge of the ardent feelings that moved this friend of equal rights to noble and god-like action. It was the pure fire of patriotism fanned to a brilliant flame by a just indignation against a tyrannical and insolent foe. It was a fire that reflected a genial heat upon those around it and increased in volume as time rolled onward. Like separate particles of metal in a crucible, one member after another yielded to the power of the patriotic flame until all were united in one liquid mass and on the 4th of July 1776 the mould of LIBERTY was filled. When opened to the admiring view of a gazing world a new and purely original table of law and government was presented enriched with the embossments of equal rights and equal justice. On this fair tablet, more beautiful than mosaic work, Mr. Nelson engraved his name in bold relievo. Here we might leave him with glory enough for one man. But he had then just entered the vestibule of his useful career. His whole soul and body were enlisted in the glorious cause. He worked on, hoped on and hoped ever. He was again returned to Congress but was compelled to retire in May in consequence of a dangerous attack of brain fever that for a time threatened to impair his mental powers. Fortunately for the cause of Independence his health was restored.

During the ensuing August the British fleet entered the capes for the purpose of chastising the rebels of the Old Dominion. A general rally of the military was the immediate consequence. Mr. Nelson was made Brig. General and commander of all the Virginia forces. The appointment was popular—the incumbent competent. His appearance among the people inspired confidence. The troops rallied around him like affectionate children around a fond parent. Learning how the land lay the fleet went its way for that time and waited for a more convenient season. The soldiers again became citizens.

In October of that year Gen. Nelson took his seat in the legislature of his state and took an active part in the deliberations of that body. During the session a bill was brought before the House sequestering British property and authorizing those of the Colonists who were in favor of Liberty and owed subjects of Great Britain, to pay the amount into the public treasury. If the wives and children of such subjects remained in the state the Governor was authorized to pay them certain portions of this money for their support. With all his indignity against mother Britain, his sense of justice induced him to oppose the bill because it violated individual contracts. He became roused and made an able and eloquent speech against the measure and closed with the followiug emphatic language—"For these reasons I hope the bill will be rejected—but whatever be its fate—*so help me God* I will pay *my* debts like an honest man."

On the 2d of March 1778 Congress made an appeal to the patriotism of the wealthy young men of the several states urging them to raise a troop of light cavalry at their own expense. When this proposition was received in Virginia Gen. Nelson sent a circular to all the young gentlemen of fortune in the state recommending them to rush to the rescue in person and to open their purses to other high-minded young men who were poor in money but rich in patriotism. A company of seventy was promptly raised in that state and elected Gen. Nelson to command them. He proceeded with his charge to Baltimore and reported his youthful band to the brave Pulaski who received the young volunteers with admiration and delight. From that place the company proceeded to Philadelphia where the General and the young gentlemen soldiers received the applause and thanks of Congress. As their services were not needed at that time they returned home. Their expenses were principally paid by Gen. Nelson without any charge to government. For his services during the war he took no pay and expended a large portion of his fortune in the cause of freedom.

On the 18th of February 1779 he again took his seat in Congress and labored so intensely in the committee rooms that he brought on another attack similar to the former and was compelled to return home in April. Relaxation from business and domestic quiet soon restored his health. In May the British made a descent upon Virginia and marked their course with relentless cruelty and destruction. Gen. Nelson at once took the field and marshalled his troops near Yorktown. The enemy dared not approach him and filed off. During that short campaign he was a father to his soldiers and supplied them with food from his own funds. He distributed his laborers and servants among the poor families of the militia from his neighborhood to labor during the absence of the men. He was as benevolent as he was patriotic and brave. For the state he raised large sums upon his own credit for which he was remunerated but in part. This was done freely without any noise or boasting. He was good for the sake of goodness—honest for the sake of honesty—not from policy or to be seen of men.

In the spring of 1781 Virginia was the scene of murder, rapine and ruin. Judas Arnold and Lord Cornwallis were sweeping over the state like a tornado. Gen. Nelson was constantly in the field doing all in his power to arrest the savage career of the merciless foe. He became the hero of the Old Dominion. In June of that year he was elected governor of the state. He at once entered upon the duties of his office and bent his whole energies on raising troops to resist the enemy. About that time La Fayette arrived with a body of regulars. Gov. Nelson joined him in the field and placed himself and his troops under command of the Marquis. Everything in his power he grasped to aid his bleeding country. He placed his work horses and negroes in the public service. In the midst of these struggles a circumstance occurred that was exceedingly trying to his noble soul. By the constitution the governor could act only in concert with the Council. Two of that body had been taken prisoners by Tarleton—two had resigned when most needed. A quorum could not be raised. The crisis required prompt and decisive action. In this dilemma he proceeded to act as if a quorum of the Council was present. Long after he had retired to private life and at a time when he was sinking under disease, some wretches, who would be only scavengers in Pandemonium, made this a ground of complaint against him. A just legislature put the matter forever at rest by passing a special law sanctioning every act of the governor during his administration under the circumstances alluded to. Ingratitude is the prime minister of Satan—revenge its secretary.

By the vigilance of Governor Nelson and La Fayette Lord Cornwallis was snugly ensconced in Yorktown. A dark cloud hovered over his military fame. Awful forebodings haunted his blood-stained imagination. Retributive justice pierced his guilty conscience with a thousand viper stings. The cries of widows and orphans—the curling flames of hospitable mansions—the sweeping destruction of villages and towns—the dying groans of innocent victims—the damning fruits of his savage career, preyed upon his agonized soul like a promethean vulture. The die was cast. The siege was commenced. Washington was there. At the head of the Virginia troops was Governor Nelson—cool, brave, fearless, vigorous. His native town—his own mansion and property were now to be razed to the ground. At first he observed the American batteries carefully avoid his house. The principal British officers had made it their head quarters for this reason. Learning it was out of respect for him he directed the gunners to point their cannon at his mansion. The first discharge after this order sent several shot through it—killed two of the officers and frightened the rest from a table well spread with edibles and wines. They were at dinner and feared no danger. The result of the siege was glorious and closed the war of the Revolution.

The following extract from the general orders of the illustrious Washington of the 20th of October 1781 will best inform the reader of the estimate placed upon the services of Governor Nelson at that memorable siege.

" The General would be guilty of the highest ingratitude–a crime of which he hopes he shall never be accused, if he forgot to return his sincere acknowledgments to his excellency Governor Nelson, for the succors which he received from him and the militia under his command, to whose activity emulation and bravery the highest praises are due. The magnitude of the acquisition will be ample compensation for the difficulties and dangers they met with so much firmness and patriotism."

The fatigues of this campaign and his arduous gubernatorial duties proved too much for the physical powers of Governor Nelson. He again sunk under disease and resigned his office on the 20th November 1781 and retired from the public arena to private life. He spent the remainder of his days on a small estate he had gathered up from the wreck of his princely fortune, situated at Offly in the county of Hanover. His health continued to decline until the 4th of January 1789 when he was numbered with the dead. His obituary, written by his bosom friend Col. Innes, fully portrays the character of this devoted patriot and will best close this annal.

" The illustrious Nelson is no more! He paid the last debt of nature on Sunday the fourth day of the present month at his estate in Hanover. He who undertakes barely to recite the exalted virtues which adorned the life of this great and good man will unavoidably pronounce a panegyric upon human nature. As a man, a citizen, a legislator and a patriot, he exhibited a conduct untarnished and undebased by sordid and selfish interests and strongly marked with the genuine characteristics of true religion, sound benevolence and liberal policy. Entertaining the most ardent love for civil and religious Liberty, he was among the first of that glorious band of patriots whose exertions dashed and defeated the machinations of British tyranny and gave to united America freedom and independent empire. At a most important crisis during the late struggle for American Liberty, when this State appeared to be designated as the theatre of action for the contending armies, he was selected by the unanimous suffrage of the legislature to command the virtuous yeomanry of his country. In this honourable employment he remained until the end of the war. As a soldier he was indefatigably active and coolly intrepid. Resolute and undejected in misfortune, he towered above distress and struggled with the manifold difficulties to which his situation exposed him with constancy and courage. In the memorable year of 1781 when the whole force of the southern British army was directed to the subjugation of this State, he was called to the helm of government. This was a juncture which indeed 'tried men's souls.' He did not avail himself of this opportunity to retire in the rear of danger, but on the contrary took the field at the head of his countrymen and at the hazard of his life, his fame and individual fortune. By his decision and magnanimity he saved not only his country but all America from disgrace if not from total ruin. Of this truly patriotic and heroic conduct the renowned commander-in-chief, with all the gallant officers of the combined armies employed at the siege of York, will bear ample testimony. This part of his conduct even contemporary jealousy, envy and malignity were forced to approve and this, more impartial posterity, if it can believe, will almost adore. If, after contemplating the splendid and heroic parts of his character we shall inquire for the milder virtues of humanity and seek for the MAN, we shall find the refined, beneficent and social qualities of private life, through all its forms and combinations, so happily modified and united in him, that in the words of the darling poet of nature, it may be said,

> 'His life was gentle, and the elements
> So mixed in him, that nature might stand up
> And say to all the world—THIS IS A MAN.'"

JAMES OTIS.

DEATH is a source of terror to most persons. It should be a source of anticipated joy to every reasonable being. Death is viewed as the great enemy of man. He is our best friend. Many Christians tremble at the thought of being folded in the arms of this friend who performs for us the last–the greatest kind office that can be awarded this side of eternity. Why should we treat death as an enemy? Is he an enemy who delivers us from pain, disappointment, folly, error, misery and all the ills of our earthly pilgrimage? Is he an enemy who transfers us from the land of delusive dreams, the region of phantoms and corroding cares–to an Elysium of substantial joys and enduring bliss? It is a *libel* on DEATH to call him a foe–a king of terrors–an enemy.

Frail man comes into this world crying–cries on through life and is always seeking after some earthly object he intends to christen happiness when obtained. When he reaches the bubble it often bursts at the slightest touch–it never imparts unalloyed comfort. He is often mourning over the misfortunes that lie thickly along the road of life. He is forced to learn there is nothing pure but Heaven. Within the restless mortal body there is an immortal soul that requires more than earth can give to satisfy its lofty aspirations. This soul hails death as the welcome messenger to deliver it from its ever changing decaying prison of clay–called MAN–on which time wages an exterminating war until DEATH breaks the carnal fetters–sets the prisoner free–opening the door of immortality–returning the redeemed spirit to its original abode of refulgent glory to go no more out for ever. To be terrified at the thoughts of death is to endure unnecessary fear and add to the discomforts of life. We should be in constant readiness to give this friend a hearty welcome. All who are wise will do so.

It is evident the Sages and Heroes of the American Revolution did not quail at the thought of sacrificing their lives upon the altar of LIBERTY. By the British and Tories the Declaration of Independence was called the death warrant of the signers. Had the first open opposers of the crown fallen into the hands of the royalists their lives would have been terminated in a summary manner. Among these was James Otis who was born at Barnstable, Mass. in 1725. He graduated at Harvard College when but eighteen years of age. He read law with Mr. Gridley–settled in Plymouth and became one of the most brilliant lights of the profession. He was an uncompromising and fearless opposer of British wrongs–an able and unwavering advocate of American rights. In 1761 he appeared before the judges of the Supreme Court in defence of the people against the writs of assistance. His logic, eloquence and boldness astonished all who heard him. He insulated the people with patriotic fire that all the powers of mother Britain could never extinguish. Among others he was listened to by John Adams who often remarked–" Independence was then and there born." By the patriots of that day he was called the originator of the Revolution. He was the first man who placed his name to a bold and vigorous pamphlet which he wrote and published–exposing the innovations of the British ministry upon the chartered rights of the Colonies. He was threatened with arrest which only roused him to more vigilant action in defence of human rights. He was a member of the Congress that convened in New York in 1765. During that year he wrote his " Rights of the Colonies Vindicated"–which was a masterly production and published in London. He was of a warm temperament–impulsive –if hard pressed was sometimes harsh in his language. He was lashed severely by the ministerial organs which caused him to publish pungent strictures upon the conduct of several of the crown officers. Soon after these appeared he was attacked in a public room by a band of British ruffians led on by custom house commissioner Robinson, who nearly took his life. This occurred on the 5th of September 1769. So much was he injured that his reason soon fled for ever. He may appropriately be called the first mover and the first martyr of the American Revolution. He obtained a judgment of $20,000 against Robinson for the base assault and on receiving a written apology relinquished it.

His towering mental powers broke rapidly until he became a mental wreck. The repeated blows upon his head had permanently deranged his brain. Occasional lucid flashes would pass over his mind like brilliant meteors and pass as quickly away. He had often expressed a wish that he might be killed by lightning. That desire was granted on the 23d day of May 1783 while leaning on his cane at the door of Mr. Osgood. His body was taken to Boston and buried with every mark of respect attended by an unprecedented concourse of sympathizing freemen.

No patriot of the Revolution merits our reverence, admiration and gratitude more than James Otis. He commenced that opposition against tyranny which resulted in the emancipation of the new continent—prepared an asylum for the oppressed and set an example for patriots worthy of imitation through all future time and over the civilized world.

WILLIAM PACA.

CREATIVE wisdom has not designed every man for a Demosthenes or a Cicero but every man of common sense is designed to be good and useful. If all were alike gifted with splendid talents the monotony would become painful. Variety, the spice of life, would lose its original flavor. If all our legislators were eloquent orators and were affected by the mania of speech making as most of our public speakers are at the present day, we should be constantly as we are frequently, overwhelmed with talk and have but little work commenced and less completed. No one admires true eloquence more than the writer but not too much of this good thing at the expense of the dear people. Business is of higher importance. Like our bodies that end in a narrow cell—the long, elaborate and in some instances—sensible and eloquent speeches of our legislators receive their finale in the approving-*Aye*-or the emphatic-*No*. Although based upon the purest motives-dictated by the most enlightened understanding-strengthened by the soundest logic-embellished with the richest flowers of rhetoric-illumined by the most brilliant intelligence-*Aye* or *No* decides the most gigantic efforts of every speech maker. I indulge no desire to extinguish these intellectual lights or to snuff them too closely. Their wicks should be cut shorter and the volume of their flame diminished so as to emit less smoke. Brevity is the soul of wit-despatch the life of business. In the committee room every man can be useful. The responsibilities of a vote bear equally upon all. Let the importance of no man be undervalued by himself or compeers because he was not born with a trumpet tongue. If his head is clear and his heart right he can do good and be useful.

Among those who rendered essential service in the cause of the American Revolution in a retiring and unassuming manner, was William Paca born at Wye Hall on the eastern shore of Maryland October 31st 1740. His father was an estimable man. He gave this son a good education and planted deeply in his mind the principles of virtue and moral rectitude. He graduated at the college in Philadelphia and in 1758 commenced the study of law at Annapolis in his native state. He applied himself closely to the investigation of that branch of science that unfolds the nature and duty of man in all the relations of life-shows what he is and what he should be under all circumstances-unveils his passions, his propensities and his inclinations-carries the mind back through the abysm of lights, shadows and darkness to pristine happiness and illuminates the understanding more than any other course of reading. Law is a compound of all the sciences in theory and practice. An honest lawyer who is actuated by principles of strict justice, pure ethics, equal rights and stern integrity-can do more to sustain social order and promote human happiness than a man pursuing either of the other professions. A lawyer is not complete until he understands at least the theory of all the practical sciences, professions, trades and the whole routine of business and the nature of man. The acquisition of elementary law is only the vestibule to a full prepation for practice.

Upon the firm basis of an honest lawyer Mr. Paca commenced a successful business and built an enduring fame. He was esteemed for his clearness of perception, purity of purpose, decision of character, prudence of action and substantial usefulness-all exhibiting a clear light but not a dazzling blaze. Upon a mind like his the oppression of the mother country made a gradual impression that was deepened by the graver of continued violations of right until it became so firmly fixed that all the powers of earth could not efface, deface, erase or expunge it. As constitutional privileges were more openly infringed his soul became more strongly resolved on liberty or death. He was on intimate terms with Mr. Chase who possessed all the powers to command whilst Mr. Paca was endowed with the indispensable requisites of a safe and skilful helmsman. With qualities thus differing these two patriots simultaneously commenced their voyage upon the boisterous ocean of public life destined for the same port—the haven of LIBERTY.

Soon after he commenced practice at the bar Mr. Paca was elected to the Maryland legislature and became a very useful member. In 1771 he was one of the committee of three that prepared a letter of thanks to Charles Carroll for his able advocacy of the cause of freedom in a written controversy with the royal governor and his subordinates. In that letter the committee expressed a determination never to submit to taxation without representation or to the regulation of taxes by the executive authority—thus furnishing the crown with an index of the public mind in advance of the text. Mr. Paca was a member of the Congress of 1774 which was rendered illustrious by proceedings of propriety and wisdom emanating from minds like his. Upon such men we can always rely in times of peril. They view everything in the calm sunshine of reason and justice being never overwhelmed by sudden emotions or angry passions. Ever upon the *terra firma* of prudence ready for action they are prepared to render assistance to those whose loftier barks often run into the breakers and need a cable from on shore to haul them in.

Mr. Paca was continued in Congress until 1778 and rendered valuble service to his country. In 1775 he joined Mr. Chase in furnishing a new military corps with rifles to the amount of nearly a thousand dollars from their private funds. He devoted his time, talents and fortune to the cause of freedom. His examples had a powerful influence upon reflecting men. All had unlimited confidence in his opinions —always deliberately formed. When the Declaration of Independence was proposed his feelings and views were decidedly in its favor but his instructions were opposed to it. The Maryland members of Assembly considered the project wild—believing the power of the mother country would crush all opposition in embryo. Redress they fondly but vainly hoped for. The British authorities soon furnished arguments steeped in blood that removed all restrictions and left Mr. Paca and his colleagues to act freely. The first decided vote in favor of stringent measures was on the 28th of May 1776 at which time the Chaplain of the Maryland Assembly was directed not to pray for the King. As trifling as this may now appear it then had a favorable and potent influence upon the people. When the glorious day arrived to decide the fate of the Chart of Liberty Mr. Paca was at his post and enrolled his name with the apostles of FREEDOM whose fame will continue to rise in peerless majesty until the last trump of time shall sound its closing notes and assemble the world of mankind in one grand army for the final inspection of the great Jehovah.

In 1778 Mr. Paca retired from Congress and was appointed Chief Judge of the Superior Court of Maryland. In 1780 his duties were increased by his appointment to preside over the Prize and Admiralty Court. He stood approved as an able statesman–he was an ornament to the judiciary. The acumen of his mind and legal acquirements made him a *strong* judge–his honesty and impartiality made a *popular* one. In 1782 he was elected governor and discharged the duties of the office with great usefulness. He was a devoted friend to religion and education and did much to render them prosperous. He inculcated principles of economy and morals and held a parental supervision over every department of state that came within the pale of his executory or advisory jurisdiction. His wise and judicious administration rendered malice powerless, paralyzed slander and left no loop for jealousy to hang upon.

At the end of his term he retired to private life which he enjoyed until 1786 when he was again called to direct the destinies of his native state. In 1789 President Washington appointed him Judge of the U. S. District Court of Maryland which office he ably filled up to 1799 when he was summoned to appear at the Bar of God to render an account of his stewardship. He cheerfully obeyed the summons, launched his immortal spirit on the ocean of eternity and disappeared from earth. He had lived the life of the righteous–his last end was like his.

Mr. Paca was a man of polished manners, plain and dignified in his deportment with an intelligent and benignant countenance. His course in life demonstrated clearly that moderation and mildness joined with discretion and firmness govern more potently than authoritative dictation. His memory is revered–let his examples be imitated.

ROBERT TREAT PAINE

Virtue affords the only sure foundation of a peaceful and happy government. When the wicked rule corruption accumulates. Not that rulers must be members of some visible church—but they should venerate religion and be men of pure morals and political honesty. Disease affects the body politic and produces dissolution with the same fearful certainty that it destroys the physical powers of man. If the head is disordered the whole heart is sick. If the political fountain becomes polluted its dark and murky waters will rapidly impregnate every branch of the body politic with their contagious miasma. The history of all time proves the truth of this proposition. The passing events of the present exciting era are fruitful with demonstrations of the baneful effects of intrigue, peculation, political fanaticism and disunion.

Without virtue our UNION will become a mere rope of sand—a spoil for knaves and the sport of kings. Self-government will be an unsolved enigma, rational liberty a paradox, a republic the scoff of monarchs. With Argus eyes the crowned heads of Europe are watching our career and embracing every opportunity to weaken our government. Each year of our prosperous existence endangers their power. The Elysian story of our liberty is enrapturing their subjects and preparing them for freedom. The tenure by which they hold their thrones is becoming weaker as time rolls onward. If we are true to ourselves, if virtue predominates—if patriotism, discretion and an enlightened honest policy guide our rulers—the American Republic will increase in beauty, strength and grandeur and become the nucleus of Liberty for the world. Freemen! look to this matter in time and nobly perform your whole duty. Obey the precepts and imitate the examples of the Sages and Heroes who wisely conceived and boldly achieved the Independence we now enjoy. They were virtuous, many of them devotedly pious—all of them politically honest.

Holding a conspicuous place among them was Robert Treat Paine, born at Boston, Mass. in 1731. He was blessed with truly pious parents. His father performed the duties of a clergyman until his health compelled him to leave the sacred desk. He then commenced the mercantile business. The mother of Robert was the daughter of the Rev. Robert Treat, an eminent divine of Eastham. From these religious parents he imbibed those virtuous principles that guided his course through life. Were there no other blessings flowing from Christianity than its salutary influence upon social order and harmony of society, mankind would be richly paid for obeying its precepts. This consideration alone should close the *mouth* of every infidel let the conclusions of his *mind* be what they may with reference to its origin and reality. No other system has ever been devised that confers as much happiness upon the greatest number.

At an early age Robert Treat was placed in the classical school of Mr. Lowell in Boston where his embryo talents expanded into a rich and luxuriant growth. At the age of fourteen he entered Harvard College. When he graduated his parents had become so reduced in circumstances as to need pecuniary aid. To provide ways and means he at once commenced teaching a public school—an occupation of more importance and dignity than is generally awarded to it. When Greece and Rome flourished—teaching took the front rank in professions. For a single course in rhetoric, one hundred Athenean scholars paid Isocrates fourteen thousand eight hundred dollars. It is not surprising that the highest order of talent was employed to advance literature in Greece. The same liberality would effect wonders in our country.

From the avails of his school Mr. Paine supported his parents and a maiden sister in poor health and at the same time pursued his professional studies. He commenced theology but subsequently read and entered upon a successful practice of law. For a time he continued at the Boston Bar but ultimately settled at Taunton where he acquired a substantial reputation as an active, sound and discreet lawyer. He enjoyed the confidence and esteem of his numerous acquaintances and became celebrated as an advocate. He was among the first to oppose the innovations of the crown and promulge liberal principles. He was a member of the Convention called by the citizens of Boston in 1768 to devise measures for the preservation of their sacred rights and which Governor Bernard vainly attempted to disperse before the members had completed their deliberations. At the instance of Samuel Adams he was employed to conduct the prosecution against Capt. Preston for ordering his men to fire upon the people of Boston on the 5th of March 1770. Upon that trial he exhibited great zeal and ability. During the accumulation of the revolutionary storm he was uniformly in the conventions and upon the important committees of the people. Many of the boldest resolutions that were adopted came from his pen.

In 1773 he was elected to the Assembly of his Province and was one of the members who conducted the impeachment of Peter Oliver, then Chief Justice, who was accused of acting under the dictation of the king instead of the Assembly. In the prosecution of that trial Mr. Paine manifested strong talent and great professional skill. In 1774 he was again returned to the Assembly and boldly warned the people against the dangers to be apprehended from the appointment of Gov. Gage to succeed Gov. Hutchinson. It was plain to his mind that the nefarious designs of the British ministry were to be enforced by the bayonet unless the people tamely submitted to slavery. An awful crisis was approaching. A larger committee than at any previous time convened at Boston, which proposed and urged the plan of a General Congress to be convened at Philadelphia. Gov. Gage sent an order for them to disperse but his orderly was refused admittance. Five delegates were appointed to meet the General Congress of whom Mr. Paine was one. This measure was originated in Massachusetts in 1765 and was strongly urged in a circular in 1768. The set time to favor Liberty had now come. The galling yoke had become painful—most of the colonies approved the plan. By the originators of this proposition a separation from England was not contemplated—a restoration of chartered rights was all that was asked and this in the most loyal and respectful language. With this object in view the Congress convened. When the delegates compared notes they were astonished at the wide spread system of abuses that was on the flood tide of advancement throughout the Colonies. Each had supposed his own constituents most oppressed. Indignation increased but wisdom and deliberation stamped every transaction with a manly dignity. The proceedings were calm as a summer morning but firm as the rock of ages. The delegates appealed to the king, to Parliament, to the British nation, to the American people—to a gazing world for the justice of their claims—the equity of their demands. But appeals were vain, cries useless, remonstrances unheeded. They were answered by legions of hireling troops in all the panoply of war with the shrill bugle grating harshly upon the ear. They saw the glittering steel of the foe dazzling in the sun beams. Open resistance or servile submission were the alternatives.

Mr. Paine was a member of the Provincial Congress convened in Concord, Mass. in October 1774. He superintended the preparation of a spirited address to the people of England which put many in the mother country right and did much to rouse the Colonists to a just indignation towards the overbearing ministry. In 1775 he was a member of the Continental Congress and was placed upon many important committees. He was chairman of the committee on the manufacture of arms and for furnishing the army. He was indefatigable in his labors in the glorious cause of Liberty. He often said—" I fear we shall become slaves because we are not industrious enough to be free." Mr. Paine was one of the committee to prepare a constitution for his native state and had the credit of framing that instrument. In 1776 he was a member of the Continental Congress. He was on the committee with Messrs. Jefferson and Rutledge who prepared the rules that governed the action of that body. He was one of the committee to inquire into the causes of the disasters of the campaign in Canada. When the glorious 4th of July 1776 dawned upon Columbia's sons like smiling Heaven and the Eagle of LIBERTY soared in peerless majesty over their blood-stained soil–Mr. Paine was at his post. With a buoyant heart and firm hand he wrote his name upon that matchless instrument which is the consolation of freemen–the consternation of tyrants.

He did much to rouse his friends to action by his letters written in the most happy style. In his native State he stood high in the temple of fame–in Congress he was esteemed by all its members. He was continued in that body for several years and when he could be spared served in the legislature of his State. In 1777 he was speaker of the House of Representatives. The same year he was appointed attorney-general by the unanimous vote of both branches of the legislature. He was a prominent member of the committee that formed the Act reducing the price of labor and goods to a standard of equality. In 1779 he was elected to the Executive Council. The numerous duties imposed upon him he discharged to the satisfaction of his constituents. He was continued in the office of attorney-general until 1790. He then declined in order to pursue some more lucrative business to provide for the increasing wants of a large and destitute family. He had expended all his earnings in the cause of freedom but a scanty support. He was then appointed a judge of the Superior Court. He continued on the bench until 1804 when ill health compelled him to resign. He discharged his judicial duties with justice and ability and did much to advance the interests of religion, social order and a sound state of society. On his resignation he was appointed a counsellor of the commonwealth and continued to impart his salutary advice and shed around him a benign influence until the king of terrors closed his useful career on the 11th of May 1814. Calm and resigned he slept in death. He entered Jordan's flood with a full assurance of being hailed with the joyful sentence–" Well done good and faithful servant, enter thou into the joys of thy Lord." If the bright examples here presented fail to benefit the reader his virtue and patriotism are paralyzed.

In the life of Judge Paine we have a picture which the Christian, patriot, jurist and statesmen may contemplate with delightful pleasure.

Because he administered the laws strictly some called him harsh but no one dared accuse him of injustice. His integrity was beyond the reach of slander and the assaults of malice. From his solicitude to direct a wayward son in the paths of rectitude he was reported unkind to his family. The tale was as false as the heart was base that originated it. He was all kindness and affection. His anxiety for the welfare and usefulness of this very son is proof of the deepest paternal regard. He was a friend to common school education and the sciences. He was the founder of the American Academy of Massachusetts in 1780. The degree of LL.D. was conferred upon him by the Cambridge University.

Mr. Paine was a striking example of the happy results of perseverance and industry. He became greatly useful and acquired his fame without the aid of patrons in early life—rising by his own exertions and supplying the wants of his destitute and aged parents to the day of their death. His career in public and private life was marked with the purest integrity, the loftiest patriotism, the strictest morality, the most refined consistency and the most exemplary piety. His life was a continued round of usefulness—his labors a blessing to mankind—his death a loss that was keenly felt by his personal friends and the nation at large. A review of his bright examples affords the highest eulogy that can be pronounced upon his character. They will be held in veneration to the remotest period of truth-telling time by all who revere virtue and love Liberty.

JOHN PENN.

A FEDERAL republican government is an unlimited partnership of the noblest character. Based upon an equality of original representative stock, an equality of interest in the welfare of the firm devolves upon each individual of the compact. Unlike monopolizing corporations that often make the poor poorer and the rich richer—each stockholder has a right to speak, vote and act upon all questions in primary meetings irrespective of the number of shares held. The specie of the firm consists in equality of representation, natural rights, protection in person, property and freedom. These precious coins cannot be diminished in quantity or reduced in quality by alloy without courting danger. To aid in preserving them pure is the duty of *all* and should not be entrusted to the aspiring *few.* Separately and collectively each and the whole are solemnly bound to pursue all honourable means to advance the general good. Each one is bound to bring every talent into use—to leave none in the dark quarry of ignorance, the quagmire of negligence or to rust by inertness. The unfaithful steward that had but one talent was condemned because he did not put it to use. Who can tell what his talents are until he brings them to the light? Rich ores often lie deep. Many men have passed their majority without rising to mediocrity in point of developed intellect and have then suddenly risen, like a blazing meteor and illuminated the world. By several of the signers of the Declaration of Independence this was beautifully demonstrated.

Among these was John Penn, born in Caroline county, Virginia, the 17th of May 1741. He was the only child of Moses Penn who married Catharine, the daughter of John Taylor. The education of the son was confined to the commonest of common schools—the only kind then in his neighbourhood. A little learning has been called a dangerous thing but the amount taught in some common schools at the present era of light is too small to be dangerous—too limited to do much good. The most important branch of the education of that era his parents attended to themselves. By example and precept they taught him the principles of religion, social virtue and moral honesty. Upon a farm young Penn labored with his sire who had but few books and did not desire more. When John was but eighteen years of age his father died and left him a small fortune. He had an increasing thirst for knowledge but no library fountain at which he could drink and drink again until he should have within himself a living stream of mental light. He communicated his ardent desire to improve his education to his neighbor and relative, Edmund Pendleton who was a profound lawyer and an able statesman. Convinced that young Penn possessed strong native talent he made him welcome to his valuable library and became deeply interested in his improvement. After exploring the fields of general science this young philomath commenced the study of law with his relative and brought out mental ores from his long neglected intellectual quarry of a rare and rich variety. Mr. Pendleton was delighted with his pupil and the pupil delighted in pleasing him.

Mr. Penn surmounted the barriers that lay before him with an astonishing rapidity. Before some of his friends supposed he had mastered the elementary principles of Blackstone he presented himself at the court for examination—was admitted to the Bar and at once exhibited the bright plumage of a successful lawyer. But three years previous his now soaring talents were buried deep in their native quarry—unknown and unsuspected—a strong admonition to every reader under similar circumstances to examine closely the quarry of his own immortal mind. The professional eminence of Mr. Penn rose as rapidly as his appearance in the forum was surprising. He gained the confidence of the community, the respect of the courts and the esteem of his senior brethren. In 1763 he doubled his original stock in the firm of the social compact by leading to the hymenial altar the amiable and accomplished Susannah Lyme—thus avoiding the hyemal frost that creeps chillingly over lonely bachelors.

In 1774 Mr. Penn removed to North Carolina. Carrying with him a high legal reputation he soon obtained a lucrative practice. He had participated largely in the patriotic feelings that were spreading over the Colonies like an autumn fire on a prairie. He had fully imbibed the principles of his venerable preceptor who was one of the boldest of the bold Virginians in the vindication of chartered rights and was a member of the general Congress of 1774. The liberal views and splendid talents of Mr. Penn were soon appreciated by his new acquaintances. On the 8th of September 1775 he was appointed to the Continental Congress and repaired to the post of duty and honor the ensuing month. He became an active and prominent member of that venerated assembly of sages whose wisdom, sagacity and intelligence emblazoned the historic page with a new and more brilliant lustre. He served on numerous committees and acquitted himself with great credit in the discharge of every duty that devolved upon him. In the committee room, in the House, among the people—in every situation in which he moved he made the cause of liberty his primary business. So highly were his services appreciated by his constituents that they continued him in Congress until the accumulating dangers that were threatening his own state induced him to decline a re-election in 1779. He was an early and warm supporter of the Declaration of Independence. When the joyful day arrived to take the final question he most cheerfully and boldly sustained it by his vote and signature—enrolling his name with the brightest constellation of illustrious statesmen that ever illuminated a legislative chamber.

South Carolina had been devastated by Lord Cornwallis who was preparing to carry destruction to North Carolina. Emissaries from the British were already within its precincts to prepare the way for the triumphant entry of the cruel foe. Already had the friends of royal power received instructions to seize the most prominent whigs and the military stores with an assurance of immediate support. The cruelties that had been practised in South Carolina carried terror to all but hearts of oak. The sacrifice of Col. Hayne at Charleston in that state, will give the reader a faint idea of the spirit of demoniac revenge that characterized some of the refined and christianized British officers.

When that city fell into his hands, Lord Cornwallis issued a proclamation promising all who would desist from opposing the authority of the king the most sacred protection of person and property on condition that each should sign an instrument of neutrality which obligated the signers not to take up arms against the mother country and exonerated them from serving against their own. Being a prisoner and separated from his wife and six small children then residing in the country–his lady confined with the small pox–Col. Hayne finally signed the fatal instrument with great reluctance upon the solemn assurance of the highly civilized and professedly christianized English officers and James Simpson–intendant of British police, that he should never be required to bear arms in support of the crown. Like Bishop Cranmer, Col. Hayne subscribed to that which his soul detested that he might fly to the relief of his suffering family. As in the case of Bishop Cranmer his enemies pursued him with a relentless persecution that nothing but death could allay–a persecution that would have made the untutored Indian shudder at broken faith and weep tears of blood over violated vows. It was a total disregard of law, justice and humanity.

Soon after his return to his dying wife and little ones the British called at his house and ordered him into the army of the mother country and threatened him with close confinement if he refused. In vain he referred them to the conditions upon which he so reluctantly signed the article of neutrality. In vain he claimed protection under the provincial militia law that imposed a fine when a citizen chose not to render personal service. To his relentless oppressors all was a dead letter. He pointed them to the wife of his bosom–the mother of his children–sinking under the small pox and rapidly approaching another world. Their sympathy was sealed–their compassion frozen up. In a few short hours Mrs. Hayne closed her eyes in death. She rested in peace. A different fate was in reserve for the afflicted husband. The order to enter the British army must be obeyed or immediate imprisonment would follow. By the violation of the pledges made to him on their part he correctly considered himself absolved from all obligations to the officers of the crown. He at once entered the American army, preferring death to the ranks of the invaders. A brilliant but short career in the service of his country awaited him. He was soon made a prisoner and sent to Charleston where Lord Rawdon, a general of his most *Christian* majesty, loaded him with irons–submitted him to a mock trial—*ex parte* in its proceedings and conclusions—based on revenge and cruelty, resolved on the speedy and ignominious death of his victim. Col. Hayne was sentenced to be hung. Amazement and dismay, indignation and surprise were strongly manifested by all classes. A large proportion of the friends of the crown deemed the transaction a species of murder. A petition—headed by the royal governor and numerously signed by persons of high standing who still adhered to the mother country was presented to Lord Rawdon in behalf of the unfortunate prisoner but all in vain.

> "Still revenge sat brooding on his dark and sullen brow
> And the grim fiends of hell urged his soul on to murder."

The ladies of Charleston—wives and daughters of royalists and whigs, then united in a petition couched in the most moving language—praying that the life of Col. Hayne might be spared. This met with a cold reception and peremptory refusal. As a last effort to rescue their father from the gallows—his infant children, dressed in deep mourning and bathed in tears, were led before Lord Rawdon. Upon their knees, with their suffused eyes fixed upon him, they addressed the monster in a strain of heart-moving eloquence that none but infant innocents can express—none but fiends resist. " *Our mother is dead—spare! O! spare our dear father ! ! !*

> "But still he stood unmoved,
> Hard as the adamantine rock,
> Dark as a sullen cloud before the sun."

So melting was this scene that veteran soldiers wept aloud and all were astounded at the demoniac course of the blood thirsty and relentless Rawdon. A request was then made that Col. Hayne might be permitted to die as a military officer and not hung as a felon. This was also denied. As a devout Christian the martyr resigned himself to his cruel fate and prepared his mind for the approaching crisis. His little son was permitted to visit him in prison. When he saw his father loaded with irons he burst into tears. The parent remarked to him, " Why will you break my heart with unavailing sorrow? Have I not often told you that we came into this world to prepare for a better? For that better life, dear boy, your father is prepared. Instead of weeping, rejoice with me that my troubles are so near an end. To-morrow I set out for immortality. When I am dead bury me by the side of your mother." No imagination can fully conceive—no fancy can truly paint—no pen clearly portray, no language can half express the heart rending reality of that last sad interview between the father and his son. When upon the fatal drop with the accursed halter around his neck–Col. Hayne shook hands with his friends–bade them an affectionate farewell–urged them to persevere in the glorious cause of freedom–recommended his children to the protection of three gentlemen present and the next moment was struggling in death. The sight was too much for his son–his brain became disordered–his reason fled–he died insane. With his expiring breath he faintly whispered–"*My mother is dead!–Spare! O! spare my dear father!!!*"

Fortunately for North Carolina the efficient and sagacious Greene with his brave officers and half clad soldiers checked the triumphant and murderous career of the British army. The operations of this brave General were greatly accelerated by Mr. Penn. In 1780, when Lord Cornwallis penetrated the western part of the state to Charlottetown, the crisis became alarming and this bold patriot was placed at the helm of public affairs with almost unlimited power. He was authorized to seize supplies by force and do all things that he deemed necessary to repel the invading foe. He proved equal to the emergency. He knew his duty and performed it with such discretion and prudence that no complaints of injustice were heard. The state was saved from a merciless enemy–Tarleton was humbled–Ferguson killed and Cornwallis put on his back track at double quick time.

After discharging the duties imposed by his own state Mr. Penn retired to private life and the pursuit of his profession. In 1784 he was appointed Receiver of Taxes for North Carolina–a high encomium upon his reputation for integrity. Fatigued with public service he resigned this office in a few months. He then bid a final farewell to the perplexing duties of political life and took his exit from the public arena decked with a civic wreath of unfading honor. He again entered into the soul-cheering enjoyments of domestic felicity which were soon exchanged for those of another and brighter world. In September 1788 he was gathered to his fathers and laid in the silent tomb there to await the resurrection of the great day. He was cut down just as he began to enjoy the fruits of his labors–in the prime of life and left a vacuum in society not readily filled. His grave was moistened with tears–a nation mourned his loss.

In all the relations of private life and public action Mr. Penn was a model of rare perfection. As a counsellor and advocate he stood on a commanding eminence. His forensic eloquence was strongly pathetic. The court and jury were often suffused with tears when listening to his appeals. As a patriot and statesman he stood approved by his country.

His disposition was mild and benevolent–his purposes pure and firm. He was a good and honest man. Let the young men who are just stepping on the stage of action imitate John Penn in his successful efforts to be useful. Banish the doctrine that power shall be monopolized by a few. This principle should never gain credence in a republican government where every individual is equally interested in the cardinal points of freedom–*personal liberty equally secured–personal rights equally enjoyed*. So long as these points are fully exemplified our UNION is safe.

JOSIAH QUINCY.

The magic power of the press cannot be too highly appreciated nor its abuses too deeply deprecated. The newspapers of the day have become the controlling power of public opinion. No course of reading so fully presents the present aspect of society. Were all our editors governed by lofty patriotism, sound logic, strict justice, enlarged philanthropy, universal charity, moral courage, sterling integrity and undeviating courtesy–a harmonious tone would be given to community that would usher in the day-spring of transporting harmony. But few of the editorial corps seem to feel the high responsibility resting upon them. Too many are the automatons of political parties and issue sheets not calculated to improve the mind, correct the head or better the heart. The politics of the present day have become disgusting to genuine patriots who deem the good of their country paramount to party triumph. Demagogues discard the old landmarks of '76. Many of our laws are based upon party principles without reference to the good of our country– a very sandy foundation. Let editors banish all party control and venality from the press and send forth rays of living light that will purify our political and moral atmosphere–then our government will be healthful, vigorous and strong.

The silken cords of our Union have been strained to their utmost tension several times. We have an accumulating mass of combustible materials in our midst. Our bond of Union has been put at issue by the meddlesome and sensitive–the fanaticism of the one part and the boiling passions of the other are encouraged by demagogues–the virtue of the people can alone preserve it. A little more steam upon the locomotive of disunion–a little more fuel from the north and fire from the south may burst the boiler and destroy the beautiful engine of our Liberty. More than any other class–editors can insure the perpetuity of our UNION. Let conductors of the public press soar above all selfish and demagogue influences and become shining examples of purity in the broadest sense of the term. Then our tree of LIBERTY will continue to rise in majesty sublime and as it towers upward will send forth flashes of light upon the oppressed millions of the old world who will yet rise in all the might of their native dignity—demolish the thrones of monarchs—sing the requiem of tyrants and strike for FREEDOM—the crowning glory of man.

All the patriots of the American Revolution whose opinions we know, deprecated the venality of the press. Among the pioneer sages was Josiah Quincy who was born in Boston, Mass. in 1745. In childhood he manifested unusual talents which were highly cultivated in Harvard College where he graduated with high honors. He then read law and became an ornament to the Boston bar. His eloquence was of that commanding kind that at once rivets the attention of an audience. His logic was forcible, his demonstrations clear, his arguments convincing, his conclusions happy, his action captivating. A bright career was apparently before him which gave promise of extensive usefulness to his country and honor to himself.

He was among the first to espouse the cause of the oppressed Colonies. He was one of the boldest champions of the people. He had their confidence, esteem and admiration. Although surrounded and threatened by the myrmidons of the crown he fearlessly and publicly opposed the unrighteous pretensions of the British ministry. He lucidly pointed out the various innovations upon chartered rights that had become sacred by long enjoyment and repeatedly sanctioned by declaratory Acts of Parliament. Had the colonists tamely surrendered them they would have been unworthy of the rights of freemen. Thank God—they did not surrender them. Anxious to maintain them peaceably, they sent Mr. Quincy to England in 1774 for the purpose of reconciling existing difficulties. Among the people he found many who deprecated the course of ministers—a respectable minority of the eminent British statesmen considered the advisers of the king visionary in their plans—unreasonable in their demands. Finding that mother Britain was madly bent on ruin Mr. Quincy left for his native land. He reached Cape Ann Harbor on the 25th·of April 1775 and died the same day deeply mourned by a nation just bursting into life.

His course was brilliant but transient. Like some rich flowers that bloom at distant periods only for a short time—so bloomed this distinguished patriot—then disappeared for ever from the human gaze. He bloomed long enough to richly perfume the atmosphere of patriotism around him and rouse those to action who inhaled the rich perfumes of

LIBERTY emitted from his noble soul. With such men as Josiah Quincy our Press would be pure—our UNION safe.

GEORGE READ.

WHEN an individual is presented with both horns of the dilemma—Liberty or slavery—the one to be obtained with blood—the other a tame submission to chains—if he is worthy the name of MAN—his mental and physical powers are at once roused to action. He does not stop to explore the avenues of obtuse metaphysics, speculative dogmas or fastidious etiquette. He flies to first principles and strains his reason and genius to their utmost tension to aid him. He puts forth his mightiest efforts—boldest exertions—strongest energies to extricate himself from surrounding difficulties—impending dangers. He performs astonishing feats rather than become a serf and surmounts the cloud-capped summit of an Alpine barrier that he would have never reached under ordinary circumstances.

The same proposition may be extended to a nation. The history of the American Revolution demonstrates it most clearly. The colonists were placed upon the piercing horns of an awful dilemma—apparently doomed to slavery or death. By their unparalleled efforts, crowned with the blessing of God, they were ultimately delivered from their perilous situation and survived the gores and bruises received in the unequal conflict. This was effected by men of strong intellect, clear heads, good hearts and sound judgments—men of strong moral courage who could reason, plan, execute. The *flowers* of literature were not then culled to form a boquet for legislative halls. Plain common sense, sterling worth, useful knowledge, practical theorems, honesty of purpose, energy of action—all based upon pure patriotism and love of LIBERTY were the grand requisites to ensure popular favor.

All these were concentrated in George Read, who was the son of John Read a wealthy and respectable planter who came from Dublin, Iraland and located in Cecil County, Maryland, where George was born in 1734. The father subsequently removed to Newcastle County, Delaware and placed this son in a school at Chester, Pennsylvania, where he received his primary tuition. From there he was transferred to the seminary of Rev. Dr. Allison who was eminently qualified to mould the mind for usefulness by imparting correct and liberal principles, practical knowledge and general intelligence fit for every day use—combining the whole with refined classics and polite literature. Under this accomplished teacher Mr. Read completed his education and at the age of seventeen commenced the study of law under John Moland a distinguished member of the Philadelphia bar. So astonishing was his proficiency that he was admitted to the practice of his profession at the age of nineteen with a better knowledge of the elements of law than some practitioners obtain through life. He was also well prepared to enter upon the practice of his profession, having had the entire charge of Mr. Moland's business for several months. He was one of those rare geniuses that seemed endowed with intuition.

He commenced a successful practice at Newcastle in 1754 and at once grappled with old and experienced counsellors. His thorough knowledge of the primary principles of law, his acuteness in pleading, his urbanity of manners, his noble and courteous bearing in court, gained for him the esteem and confidence of the judges, his senior brethren and of the community. As a natural consequence his practice soon became lucrative. His forte did not consist in a flowery show but in a deep-toned and grave forensic eloquence that informs the understanding and carries conviction to the mind. He rarely appealed to the passions of court or jury–preferring to stand upon the legitimate basis of the law clearly expounded–the testimony honestly stated.

On the 13th of April 1763 he was appointed Attorney General for the three lower counties of Delaware and held the office until called to the duties of legislation. The same year he led to the hymeneal altar an amiable, pious and accomplished daughter of the Rev. George Ross of Newcastle–thus adding largely to the stake he held in the welfare of his country–enhancing his earthly joys and giving him an influence and rank in society unknown to lonely bachelors. She fully supplied the vacuum abhorred by nature and proved a consolation to him amidst the toils, perils, pains and pleasures of subsequent life.

Mr. Read was a republican to the core. From the commencement to the close of the Revolution he was a bold and unyielding advocate of equal rights and liberal principles. When the questions in dispute assumed the form of serious discussion between the two countries he at once resigned the office of Attorney General held under the crown. In 1765 he was elected a member of the Delaware Assembly and was instrumental in laying deep the foundations of the superstructure of LIBERTY. He was prudent, calm and discreet in all his actions–but firm, bold and resolute. He was a member of the committee of the Delaware Assembly that so ably addressed the king upon the subject of grievances and redress. He was in favor of exhausting the magazine of petition and remonstrance–if to no purpose then to replenish with powder and ball. He did not nor did any of the Signers of the Declaration originally contemplate a dissolution of the ties that bound the Colonies to the mother country. They could not believe until "the death" forced the truth upon them–that ministers would commit political suicide. This done, as Americans are proverbial for humanity and decency the compound *felo de se* was interred with a calm dignified solemnity.

Mr. Read and his coadjutors understood the rights secured by Magna Charta and the Constitution of England and knew that those rights were trampled upon by the hirelings of the crown. To vindicate them was his firm resolve. He knew and weighed well the superior physical powers of the oppressors but he believed the majesty of eternal justice and the kind aid of Heaven would be vouchsafed to sustain the patriots in their struggle to sustain their inalienable rights. He believed the project of taxation without representation to pamper royal corruption to be so heinous that the scheme would be crushed by the blighting curse of an offended Deity. Nor did he err in his reasonable conclusions. That curse came with the force of a sweeping avalanche–British power was annihilated in America.

On the 17th of August 1769 he published an appeal to his constituents, calling upon them to resist the encroachments of tyranny. Its language was bold and forcible, portraying in colors deep and strong their rights and wrongs, pointing out the path of duty so plain that a tory need not have erred therein. This talismanic production sealed the fate of British power in patriotic Delaware–small in size but a giant in action. The hirelings of the crown saw the writing upon many walls and were suddenly attacked with a Belshazzar tremor and found no balance in America to restore an equilibrium.

Mr. Read sanctioned the various non-importation resolutions passed by his own and other Colonies. This was the first measure adopted to negative the designs of ministers by refraining from the use of all taxable articles whether of luxuries or daily consumption. Had the colonists not presented so bold a front at the onset the non-importation resolutions would have probably been paralyzed by an Act of Parliament compelling them to use the taxable articles in quantities so large that the accruing revenue would have enabled the cabinet to revel in profligacy.

He was chairman of the committee of twelve appointed by the people of Newcastle on the 29th of June 1774 to obtain subscriptions for the Boston sufferers, then writhing under the lash of the infamous Port Bill passed by Parliament for the purpose of chastising the refractory " rebels" of that patriotic city. In February following he had the exquisite pleasure of remitting nine hundred dollars to them. The receipt was eloquently acknowledged by Samuel Adams who was one of his faithful correspondents.

Mr. Read was a member of the Congress of 1774 and continued a member during the Revolution. He was also President of the Convention that formed the first Constitution of Delaware in 1776. He was a member of the Delaware Assembly for twelve years in succession and a portion of that time Vice President of the state. In the autumn of 1777 President M'Kinley fell into the hands of the enemy which compelled Mr. Read to leave Congress for a season and perform the duties of Chief Magistrate of his state. On his way home with his family he was compelled to pass through Jersey. In crossing the Delaware from Salem his boat was discovered by those on board the British fleet then lying just below. An armed barge was sent in pursuit. Mr. Read's boat stuck in the mud and was soon overtaken. By effacing the marks upon his baggage before he was boarded and having with him his wife and children he convinced those from the fleet he was a country gentleman on his way to his farm and solicited their assistance to put him and his family on shore. They cheerfully complied with his request and landed him and his precious charge safely on the Delaware side of the river. The open frankness and calmness of himself and lady saved them from the horrors of a prison-ship and probably him from an exhibition upon the yard-arm of a man of war.

The duties of Chief Magistrate of his state were very imposing at that time. Internal dissensions were to be reconciled—an intercourse by many of the inhabitants with the British fleet to be broken up—ways and means for his own and the general government to be provided and some plan devised to procure the release of the President. A conquering foe was flushed with victory in all directions. In the midst of all these perils he stood firmly at the helm and outrode every storm. He proved equal to every emergency and added fresh lustre to his growing fame.

When the Declaration of Independence was under discussion he believed the measure premature but when adopted he cheerfully placed his name on this monument of fame. In 1779 ill health compelled him to retire from the public arena for a year when he again resumed his legislative duties. In 1782 he was appointed a judge of appeals in the Court of Admiralty. In 1785 he was one of the commissioners to settle the boundary line between New York and Massachusetts. The next year he was a delegate to the convention of states convened at

Annapolis to regulate the Commerce of the Union. In 1787 he was one of that talented convention that framed the Federal Constitution. He was a Senator in the first Congress convened under that Constitution and served six years. He was Chief Justice of Delaware from 1793 to the time of his death. Upon the Bench he had few equals and no superior. In all these responsible stations he acquitted himself nobly and did honor to his country and the cause of rational freedom.

The person of Mr. Read was above the middle size, well formed with a commanding and agreeable deportment. He was scrupulously honest, rigidly just. When he arrived at his majority he assigned his portion of the paternal estate to his brothers, deeming the expenses of his education equivalent to his share. He was systematic even in the smallest concerns of life. He abhorred vice of every kind. He enjoyed good health in his old age up to the autumn of 1798 when, after a sudden and short illness, he closed his eyes on terrestrial scenes and resigned his spirit into the hands of the wise Disposer of all events.

As a civilian, statesman, magistrate, patriot, philanthropist, gentleman, husband, father, citizen and public benefactor—George Read was a model worthy of all admiration and the exactest imitation. All who imitate his noble career will go for the UNION forever.

CÆSAR RODNEY.

GENEALOGY was once a kind of titular idol held in great veneration. The biographer made it his first stepping-stone—one of the main pillars of his superstructure. In countries where the iron sceptre of monarchy is still swayed—where titles of honor create lineal dignity without regard to merit—where blood is analyzed by political chemistry and all the precipitants are rejected but the carbonate of noble and royal pedigree—where the crown descends upon a *non compos mentis* incumbent with the same certainty that it reaches a man of good intellect—genealogy is still measurably the criterion by which to determine the importance and weight of character. As light and intelligence shed their benignant rays upon mankind the deference paid to this titular phantom will be diminished. Where rational liberty reigns triumphant merit alone creates dignity. The man is measured by his actions—not by the purple fluid in his veins or conduct of his relations. In our free country genealogy is a matter of curiosity—not of veneration. The son of a coal cracker or cobbler can rise to the highest station within the gift of the people by the force of talent and merit. I am aware that the aristocracy of wealth is a noxious weed that spreads its deleterious branches through our cities and large towns but not yet so widely and luxuriant as to prevent merit and genius from acquiring a rapid and healthful growth. In times of danger and peril its power will be lessened in the same ratio that these increase. In an atmosphere purely republican it withers and dies.

But few families in these United States can trace their ancestors so far back as the Rodneys of Delaware. They came into England with the Norman queen Maud [Matilda] in 1141 and were among the bravest military chieftains who led in the Norman conquest. At all subsequent periods they were prominent in directing the destinies of Britain. To those who are conversant with the history of the various periods of public commotion in that kingdom—the name of Sir Walter de Rodney is familiar, with many others of the same lineage. They were able in council and war. They were conspicuous in the civil, military and naval departments and received the highest honors that could be awarded to their rank by kings and queens. They were marked for magnanimity and liberal views.

Under the auspices of William Penn William Rodney came to Philadelphia who was a branch of this ancient family. He was the son of William Rodney of England and settled in Kent, Delaware. His mother, Alice, was the daughter of Sir Thomas Cæsar a wealthy English merchant. William Rodney left one son, Cæsar, who was the father of the subject of this biographette. This son was born at Dover, Kent county, Delaware in 1730. He received a good education and inherited a large real estate from his father. He possessed a strong and penetrating mind, firmness of purpose, decision of character, an abundant share of keen wit and good humor, a large stock of experimental intelligence and practical knowledge with discretion to know how, when and where to bring these important qualities into action. With endowments like these Mr. Rodney spread his canvas to the popular breeze and commenced his voyage of public life. His cabin stores were purely republican and liberal in quantity.

In 1758 he became high sheriff of his native county and discharged his duties in a manner that gained for him the confidence and esteem of the citizens generally. At the expiration of his term he was appointed a Justice of the Peace and a judge of the lower courts. In October 1762 he took his seat in the Legislature at Newcastle and became an active and influential member. He was one of the committee that prepared the answer to the message of the governor and was on other important committees. At the close of the session he was put in possession of the great seal to be affixed to the laws that had been passed at that term.

When the rights of the Colonies were infringed by assumptions of arrogated power on the part of mother Britain, Mr. Rodney was among the first who took a bold stand in favor of justice. He was a member of the Congress that convened at New York in 1765 to remonstrate against the Stamp Act and other threatened innovations upon the privileges of the Colonies that had been long enjoyed and were guaranteed by the social compact between the king of Great Britain and his " dutiful and most loyal subjects in America." After the Stamp Act was repealed Messrs. Rodney, M'Kean and Read were appointed a committee to prepare an address to the king expressive of the joy produced throughout the Colony by this event. It is substantially the same as those prepared by the other Colonies and shows clearly the feelings of loyalty that pervaded the people at that time. The following is the body of the address.

"We cannot help glorying in being the subjects of a king that has made the preservation of the civil and religious rights of his people and the established constitution the foundation and constant rule of government and the safety, ease and prosperity of his people his chiefest care—of a king whose mild and equal administration is sensibly felt and enjoyed in the remotest part of his dominions. The clouds which lately hung over America are dissipated. Our complaints have been heard and our grievances redressed–trade and commerce again flourish. Our hearts are animated with the warmest wishes for the prosperity of the mother country for which our affection is unbounded and your faithful subjects here are transported with joy and gratitude. Such are the blessings we may justly expect will ever attend the measures of your Majesty pursuing steadily the united and true interests of all your people throughout your wide extended empire assisted with the advice and support of a British Parliament and a virtuous and wise ministry. We most humbly beseech your Majesty graciously to accept the strongest assurances that having the justest sense of the many favors we have received from your royal benevolence during the course of your majesty's reign and how much of our present happiness is owing to your paternal love and care for your people. We will at all times most cheerfully contribute to your majesty's service to the utmost of our abilities when your royal requisitions, as heretofore, shall be made known–that your majesty will always find such returns of duty and gratitude from us as the best of kings may expect from the most loyal subjects and that we will demonstrate to all the world that the support of your majesty's government and the honor and interests of the British nation are our chief care and concern, desiring nothing more than the continuance of your wise and excellent constitution in the same happy, firm and envied situation in which it was delivered to us from our ancestors and your majesty's predecessors."

With the feelings expressed in this address the conclusion is irresistible that nothing but the most cruel oppressions could have driven the American people to a revolution. A similar expression of feeling was sent to the king from all the Colonies.

"Whom the gods would destroy they first make mad."

So with the British ministry—they were madly bent on reducing their American brethren to unconditional subjection and after a short interval commenced a system of oppression upon a broader, bolder scale. Again the people appealed to their king—but appealed in vain. Mr. Rodney was upon the committee that prepared a second address to his majesty just before the Revolution in the following language:

"The sense of our deplorable condition will, we hope, plead with your majesty in our behalf for the freedom we take in dutifully remonstrating against the proceedings of a British Parliament—confessedly the wisest and greatest assembly upon earth. But if our fellow subjects of Great Britain, who derive no authority from us, who cannot, in our humble opinion, represent us and to whom we will not yield in loyalty and affection to your majesty, can, at their will and pleasure, of right give and grant away our property—if they can enforce an implicit obedience to every order or act of theirs for that purpose and deprive all or any of the Assemblies on this continent of the power of legislation for differing with them in opinion in matters which intimately affect their rights and interests and everything that is dear and valuable to Englishmen—we cannot imagine a case more miserable—we cannot think we shall have the shadow of Liberty left. We conceive it to be an inherent right in your majesty's subjects, derived to them from God and nature—handed down by their ancestors—confirmed by your royal predecessors and the constitution, in person or by their representatives, to give and to grant to their sovereign those things which their own labor and their own cares have acquired and saved and in such proportions and at such times as the national honor and interest may require. Your majesty's faithful subjects of this government have enjoyed this inestimable privilege uninterrupted, from its first existence till of late. They have at all times cheerfully contributed to the utmost of their abilities for your majesty's service as often as your royal requisition was made known and they cannot, but with the greatest uneasiness and distress of mind, part with the power of demonstrating their loyalty and affection for their beloved king."

Addresses similar to this were laid before the king from all the Colonies and from the Congress of 1774. The struggle between loyal affection and a submission to wrongs was truly agonizing. This affection and the physical weakness of the Colonies are proof strong as holy writ that British oppression was raised to the zenith of cruelty. The history of the American Revolution should be a striking lesson in all future time to those in power not to draw the cords of authority too tightly. It affords a cheering example to all persons to resist every encroachment upon their liberty.

In 1769 Mr. Rodney was chosen speaker of the Assembly of Delaware and continued to fill the chair for several years with honor and dignity. Among other things he introduced an amendment to a bill relative to slaves, prohibiting their importation into the Colony. So ably did he advocate this humane proposition that it was lost only by two votes. The same philanthropic feeling was increasing through the slave states until England, by her emissary Dr. Thompson, sowed the seeds of abolition broadcast in our country for the express purpose of dissolving our Union and of destroying the only republic Europe fears. Digging around the roots of a decaying tree often revives it. Honest men may err.

As the specks of war began to concentrate Mr. Rodney became one of the most active opposers of British tyranny. Excepting a short interval he was a member of Congress from 1774 to 1777 and took a conspicuous part in the general business and discussions of that august body. In his own province he had much to do. The royal attachments were deeply rooted. It required greater exertions to thwart the intrigues of foes within than to repel the attacks of enemies without. In addition to his duties of speaker of the Delaware Assembly and member of Congress those of brigadier-general of militia devolved on him. His numerous messages to his legislature and letters to his officers urging them to decisive action manifested great industry, clearness of perception, firmness of purpose and patriotic zeal. He was in favor of the Declaration of Independence from its first inception. The day previous to the final decision upon this important measure he was in Delaware devising means to arrest the career of certain Tories in the lower end of the province. Mr. McKean informed him by express of the approaching crisis. He immediately mounted his horse and arrived at Philadelphia just in time to dismount and enter the hall of Congress and give his vote for LIBERTY and affix his name to that bold instrument that dissolved allegiance to England's king and created a compact of freemen.

In the autumn of 1776 the Tories defeated his election to Congress. With increasing zeal he entered the field of military operations. He repaired to Princeton soon after the brave Haslet and Mercer fell, fighting for the cause of justice and freedom. He remained with the army two months and received the approval of Washington expressed in the following letter written from Morristown, N. J. on the 18th of February 1777.

" The readiness with which you took the field at the period most critical to our affairs—the industry you used in bringing out the militia of Delaware State and the alertness observed by you in forwarding troops to Trenton—reflect the highest honor on your character and place your attachment to the cause in the most distinguished point of view. They claim my sincerest thanks and I am happy in this opportunity in giving them to you."

On his return he was appointed a judge of the Supreme Court organized under the new order of things. He declined serving believing he could be more useful in some other sphere. About that time an open insurrection broke out in Sussex County in his State. He immediately repaired to the scene of insubordination and quelled it with only the appearance of force. At the time the British were preparing to march from the Chesapeake to the Brandywine he was stationed south of the American army for the purpose of throwing his force between the enemy and their shipping. In the field and in the legislative hall he was alike active.

In December 1777 he was again elected to Congress. The legislature of his State being in session he concluded to remain until it rose. Before its adjournment he was elected President of Delaware which prevented him from serving in the national legislature. His services in his new station were of great importance. His exertions in raising supplies for the army were of the most vigorous character—especially during the winter and spring of 1779 when the troops were often on half allowance and the magazines so bare that it seemed impossible to sustain the army a single week. During the four years he directed the destinies of Delaware he had many refractory spirits to manage—many difficult questions to decide that brought into useful action his prudence, wisdom and firmness. Upon his own matured judgment he relied. So well did he balance the scales of justice that he gained the admiration of his friends and the approval of his enemies. The affairs of the State were never in better hands.

Mr. Rodney was remarkably fond of a good joke if inoffensive and chaste. He often exhibited brilliant displays of wit but was extremely careful of personal feelings. When in Congress Mr. Harrison had often called Virginia the Dominion of the Colonies. When threatened with invasion by the enemy he asked immediate aid to protect her from the approaching foe. When he sat down Mr. Rodney rose with assumed gravity and apparent sympathy and assured the gentleman that the *powerful Dominion* should be protected–" Let her be of good cheer–she has a friend in need–*Delaware* will take her under protection and insure her safety." The portly Harrison and the skeleton Rodney both enjoyed the hit which convulsed the other members with laughter.

In view of the great amount of business performed by Mr. Rodney and his proverbial cheerfulness and playful good humor the reader will be astonished to learn that he was afflicted with a cancer upon his nose from his youth which spread over one side of his face and compelled him to wear a bandage over it for many years before his death. It so reduced his flesh that he was a walking skeleton. It terminated his active and useful life in 1783. He met death with calm submission and Christian fortitude and died rejoicing in the bright prospects that were dawning upon the country he dearly loved and had faithfully served.

Mr. Rodney was naturally of a slender form with an animated countenance, easy and polished manners and very agreeable and gentlemanly in his intercourse. From his writings he appears to have held religion in high veneration and practised the purest morals–producing the fruits of righteousness in richer abundance than many who make loud pretensions to piety but do not prove their faith by their works. He was liberal, kind, benevolent and so strongly sympathetic that he was obliged to avoid scenes of physical suffering if possible. He could not endure to be in the room of a dying friend or relative. The poor, the widow, the orphan, his relatives and friends, his country–all deeply mourned the loss of CÆSAR RODNEY.

GEORGE ROSS.

IDLENESS is the tomb of a living man–the progenitor of want, the substratum of misery–the fountain of crime. It was scarcely known and never countenanced by the pilgrim fathers or revolutionary patriots. We now have many among us who had rather be pinched with hunger and shine in rags than labor. A more numerous and dangerous class is composed of gentlemen idlers who pass down the stream of time at the expense of those who constantly pull at the oar. They live upon the best, dress finely by borrowing and spunging and when these fail they take to swindling, stealing, gambling, robbing and often pass on for years before justice overtakes them. So long as they can keep up fashionable appearances and elude the kind hearted police whose good will they generally have, they are received into the company of the upper ten exquisites with marked complacency. By virtue of a fine coat, lily hand and graceful bow, which cover more sins than modern Christian charity, many an idle knave has been received into fashionable circles with eclat and walked rough-shod over a worthy young clerk, mechanic or farmer who had too much good sense to act the monkey flirtations of an itinerant dandy. When the counting-house, the mechanic shop, the plough and the kitchen fall into disrepute and are submerged by vain show, pomp and parade–the sun of our country's glory will set to rise no more. When the republican simplicity of Greece and Rome receded before imported fashions, luxuries and rules of etiquette–when they ceased to call men from the shop and the plough to the cabinet and the field–when the women exchanged the kitchen for the drawing-room and plainness for extravagance of dress–corruption supplanted virtue–the genius of LIBERTY veiled her face and fled–dissolution followed–RUIN closed the dreadful scene.

Industry and plainness were marked characteristics of the Sages and Heroes of the American Revolution. Among them George Ross stood conspicuous. He was born at Newcastle, Delaware, in 1730. He was the son of Rev. George Ross, pastor of the Episcopal church at that ancient town. Under the instruction of his father the strong native talents of George unfolded their richness. At the age of eighteen he was a good classical scholar. He then commenced the study of law in Philadelphia with an elder brother, John Ross, where he was admitted to the Bar in 1751. To have elbow room he located at Lancaster, Pennsylvania–then on the confines of civilization bordering on the far west. Noble in his disposition, plain and agreeable in his manners, learned and diligent in his profession, candid, honest and just in his course–he gained the confidence and love of the people and a lucrative practice. To plant himself more firmly in his new location and give additional proof of his good sense, he married Ann Lawler a highly esteemed lady who proved an affectionate and worthy companion.

He built his legal fame on the genuine basis–close application to his professional business unconnected with public politics. Unfortunately for themselves many young lawyers enter the political arena for the purpose of obtaining professional, notoriety and business. This error has prevented many talented young men from rising to legal eminence in modern times. The Revolution was a different matter. Liberty or death was then the issue. Now it is a feigned one. If a young attorney becomes pledged to a political party he has not a *client* but a *master* that exacts the most abject, humiliating services with a contingent promise to pay in bogus coin. Either his legitimate business or that of the party must be neglected. Reflecting men know this. Aware that it requires close application to become learned in the law they keep aloof from young political lawyers. A few high toned partisans, whose tools they are, may employ them in small cases but when *they* have an important one—the studious industrious counsellor who has not inhaled the corrupting atmosphere of modern politics is the one employed. A word to the wise should be sufficient.

It was not until long after his location at Lancaster that Mr. Ross entered upon his legislative course. The time had arrived when the people began to feel the smart of British oppression and became more particular in selecting men of known worth and talents to guard their interests against the machinations of an avaricious and designing ministry. He was elected to the Colonial Assembly in 1768. His reputation stood high as an able lawyer and a man of liberal views, sound judgment and decision of character. His influence was sensibly felt—his labors highly appreciated. At that time the legislative body replied to the message of the governor *in extenso*. At his first session Mr. Ross was appointed to reply to this document. In respectful but bold language he objected to every proposition that he considered impolitic or in opposition to the best interests of the people. He was a fearless sentinel, a powerful champion in the cause of Liberty. In every leading measure in favour of freedom he was a leading man. He was continued in the Assembly until he took his seat in Congress in 1774. He was upon the committee that reported in favor of sending delegates and the man who prepared the instructions of the Assembly to the congressional delegates. As these are substantially the same as those that were given to all instructed delegates I insert them that the reader may see that redress of grievances was all that was asked or then anticipated.

" The trust reposed in you is of such a nature and the modes of executing it may be so diversified in the course of your deliberations, that it is scarcely possible to give you particular instructions respecting it. We shall therefore only in general direct—that you are to meet in Congress the committees of the several British Colonies at such time and place as shall be generally agreed on, to consult together on the present critical and alarming situation and state of the Colonies and that you, with them, exert your utmost endeavors to form and adopt a plan which shall afford the best prospect of obtaining redress of American grievances, ascertaining American rights and establishing that union and harmony which is most essential to the welfare and happiness of both countries. And in doing this you are strictly charged to avoid everything indecent or disrespectful to the mother state."

Under instructions like these the first general Congress convened and acted. The Colonies used all honorable means to restore harmony—more than the British Constitution and common justice required. Nothing but an infatuation that makes men blind, deaf and dumb could have resisted the appeals and unanswerable arguments in favor of chartered rights, showing their violations—that were poured upon the king, Parliament and people of Great Britain from the deep translucent fountain of intelligence concentrated in the Congress of 1774. The members were determined to clear their own skirts of blood and not draw the bow of physical opposition until their arrows were barbed with divine wisdom and dipped in the refining fire of eternal justice.

Mr. Ross was continued in Congress until 1777 when ill health compelled him to retire. He had rendered great service on numerous committees and was listened to with marked attention when he spoke in debate. When he could be spared from his place he served in the legislature of his State where his salutary influence was strongly felt. For some time the royal governor and his friends presented a formidable opposition. Mr. Ross put his whole weight on the people's end of the political lever with his popularity for a fulcrum and greatly aided in hoisting the tree of monarchy from its deep bed of alluvial corruption. He was a member of the convention of his State that commenced the new government and on the committee that prepared the declaration of rights. He was chairman of the committee that organized the government and of the one that prepared the declaratory ordinance defining high treason and misprision of treason and the kind and measure of punishment to be inflicted. His high legal knowledge rendered him an important member upon such committees.

Immediately after he closed his legislative career the citizens of Lancaster County passed the two following resolutions with great unanimity.

" Resolved—That the sum of one hundred and fifty pounds out of the county stock be forthwith transmitted to George Ross [' *Honorable*' was not then republican] one of the members of the Assembly for this county and one of the delegates for this Colony in the Continental Congress and that he be requested to accept the same as a testimony from this county of their sense of his attendance on public business to his great private loss and of their approbation of his conduct.

" Resolved–That if it be more agreeable, Mr. Ross purchase with part of the said money a genteel piece of plate, ornamented as he thinks proper, to remain with him as a testimony of the esteem this county has for him by reason of his patriotic conduct in the great struggle for American Liberty."

Here is old fashioned republican simplicity in language and sentiment flowing from its native fountain–gratitude strongly felt and plainly expressed. It forms a rebuking contrast with the fulsome, hypocritical, heartless flattery of modern times showered upon our statesmen by fawning sycophants whose gratitude is based alone upon the loaves and fishes of favor and office. Mr. Ross declined accepting the gift, assuring the committee that waited upon him that he had performed no more than his duty and that at such a period all were bound to exert their noblest energies to secure that Liberty which would afford a reward more precious than gold–more valuable than diamonds.

On the 19th of July 1779 Mr. Ross was appointed Judge of the Court of Admiralty for Pennsylvania. He continued to discharge his duties ably until confined by a sudden and excruciating attack of the gout which terminated in death the same year he was appointed judge. In the full career of life and usefulness–rising on the wings of fame–flushed with hopes of Liberty for his country–pressing right onward toward the goal of freedom–an arrow from the quiver of death pierced his patriotic heart and consigned him to the insatiate tomb near the close of 1779. His dust reposes in peace whilst the lustre of his living examples will continue to shine and enlighten millions yet unborn.

In private as in public life Judge Ross stood approved, admired and beloved. No blemish rests upon the fair escutcheon of his name. He soared above the vanities of this world and dignified his bright career with purity of motive, firmness of purpose, wisdom in action and usefulness to his fellow men and beloved country. Could the lofty patriotism that impelled him to enter the thorny arena of politics be imparted to *all* the public men of the present day–the Federal Constitution would be venerated–our government safe–our UNION preserved.

BENJAMIN RUSH.

Benevolence is a celestial quality imparting consolation to its possessor and the recipient of benefits bestowed. It renders its favors valuable by the delicacy with which they are conveyed. Those who most merit the aid of the benevolent are usually possessed of fine feeling. The subjects of real misfortune—they are the keenly sensitive and dread the approach of those who carry a speaking trumpet or a public scroll to proclaim to the world the alms they have bestowed.

Pure benevolence falls upon its object like the dew on drooping flowers—not at the blaze of noon day but in the stillness of night. Its refreshing effects are felt, seen and admired—not the hand that distilled it. It flows from a good heart and looks beyond the skies for an approving smile. It never opens but seeks to heal the wounds of misfortune. It never ruffles but seeks to calm the troubled mind. Like their Lord and Master—the truly benevolent go about doing good. No parade—no trumpet to sound their charities—no press to chronicle their acts. The gratitude of the donee is a rich recompense to the donor—purity of motive refines the joys of each. Angels smile on such benevolence. It is the attribute of Deity—the moving cause of every blessing we enjoy.

So thought Benjamin Rush, a native of Bristol, Bucks County, Penn. born on the 24th of Dec. 1745. His ancestors came to this country under the auspices of William Penn in 1683. His father was a respectable farmer and died when this son was a child. At the age of nine years Benjamin was placed under the tuition of his maternal uncle, Rev. Dr. Samuel Finley. He continued under his instruction five years when he entered Princeton College, then under the direction of President Davis. Like an expanding flower courting the increasing warmth of spring the talents of this young freshman rapidly unfolded their rich and varied hues as they were brought into mellow life by the genial rays of the sun of science. At the end of the first year he received the degree of Bachelor of Arts. During his brief stay at Princeton he was highly esteemed and was considered one of the most eloquent speakers among the students. At the age of sixteen he closed his collegiate studies and commenced reading medicine with Dr. John Redman, then one of the most eminent practitioners in the city of Philadelphia. The same industry that had marked his previous course made him a favorite son of Æsculapius. The same urbanity and modesty that had made him a welcome guest in every circle in other places, gained for him good and influential friends in his new location.

After pursuing his studies with great industry for six years under Dr. Redman he entered the Medical University at Edinburgh, Scotland, where he reaped the full benefit of the lectures of the celebrated Munro, Cullen, Black and Gregory. In 1768 he received the degree of M.D. having toiled severely for *seven* years to prepare himself to take in charge human life. As in the study of law, theology and most of the professions and trades–how great the change in numerous instances. I have known so called doctors made in a month–lawyers in six months and preachers in a single night–sprouts of quackology to be sure–but they pass in these days of humbuggery and often distance the man of acquirements and real merit who is too modest to make a bragadocia dash. Self-assurance and brazen impudence are performing wonders in this enlightened age. As elementary and practical books increase terms of study decrease. When Cheselden's Anatomy and Cullen's Materia Medica stood almost alone in this country, students were longer at their studies. The lectures you may reply have shortened the term. True–but why so few Rushes, Physics, &c. among the flood of modern M.D.'s?

On receiving his diploma he went to London and was admitted to practise in the hospitals of that city where he remained nearly a year and became eminent as a bold and successful operator–a skilful and judicious physician. He then visited the hospitals of Paris and returned to Philadelphia in the spring of 1769, where he met the warm embrace of his connections and friends and commenced his useful career in that city.

His professional fame had preceded him and his superior acquirements were immediately had in requisition. In addition to a rapidly increasing practice he performed the labors of a Professor in the Medical School that had been recently organized by Drs. Bond, Kuhn, Morgan and Shippen. He was elected to that important station a few months after his return. Upon a substantial basis he continued to build an honest and enduring fame–participating in all the passing events that concerned the good and glory of his country and his fellow men.

Although a close student of medicine and surgery, it was soon discovered that he well understood the relative situation of the mother country and the American Colonies. He had closely examined the unwarranted pretensions of the former and the aggravated grievances of the latter. His benevolent soul was touched by the sufferings of oppressed humanity and warmed by the patriotic fire of FREEDOM. He at once became a bold and able advocate in the cause of LIBERTY–a firm and fearless opposer of British tyranny–a strong and energetic supporter of equal rights. Mingling with all classes through the medium of his profession, his influence was as extensive and multiform as it was useful and salutary. The Independence of his country was the *ultimatum* of his desires. To see her regenerated and free was the anxious wish of his heart. So conspicuous was he in the glorious cause, that he was elected a member of the Congress of 1776 and had the proud pleasure of placing his name upon the chart of FREEDOM.

The year following he was appointed Surgeon General of the Military Hospital for the middle department and rendered himself extensively useful during the entire period of the Revolution. He was ever ready to go where duty called and exerted his noblest powers in the glorious cause he had espoused until he saw the star spangled banner wave in triumph over the land of the brave and free and the incense of LIBERTY ascending to Heaven in cerulean clouds from the altar of FREEDOM.

The Independence of his country secured—he desired no occupation but that of his profession. For a time his services were diverted from this channel in the Convention of his state to take into consideration the adoption of the Federal Constitution. Having carefully read the published arguments as they progressed in the National Convention, he was fully prepared to enter warmly into the advocacy of the adoption of that instrument. When this was adopted by the states, the measure of his political ambition was filled and hermetically sealed. He retired from that arena of turmoil crowned with the evergreen laurels of fame that will bloom with living freshness until patriotism shall be lost in anarchy and the last vestige of LIBERTY be swept away by the tornado of faction. The only station he ever consented to fill under government subsequently was Cashier of the U. S. Mint.

During the remainder of his life his time and talents were devoted to his profession, the improvement of medical science and the amelioration of the ills of afflicted humanity. In 1789 he was elected Professor of the Theory and Practice of Physic. In 1791 he was appointed Professor of the Institutes of Medicine and Clinical Practice. In 1806 he was honored with the united Professorships of the Theory and Practice of Physic and Clinical Medicine, the duties of which he ably discharged until sickness and death closed his useful career.

Besides the multiform duties already enumerated he was an efficient member of various benevolent associations. He was President of the American Association for the Abolition of Slavery—Vice President of the Philadelphia Bible Society—President of the Philadelphia Medical Society—a Vice President of the American Philosophical Society and a member of several other philanthropic institutions in this country and in Europe. For many years he was a physician of the Pennsylvania Hospital and did much to promote its prosperity. He was ever anxious to be useful in counsel, influence and action. To soothe the troubled bosom heaving with anguish–to alleviate the suffering patient writhing under pain–to aid the poor and needy sinking under misfortunes–to visit the widow and the fatherless in their distress–afforded Dr. Rush a richer pleasure than to have reached the loftiest pinnacle of political fame–a holier joy than to have been the triumphant chieftain of a conquered world.

Although his duties were onerous and various he arranged his time with such system and order that a harmonious routine was produced. His professional duties, his books, his pen each had their specific time. He wrote numerous literary, moral and philosophical essays–several volumes on medical science among which were his "Medical Inquiries and Observations" and a "History of the Yellow Fever." He spent much time in the investigation of that alarming disease–endeavoring to arrive at the best mode of treatment. In this, as in many other cases of disease–the lancet was his anchor of hope. His theory and practice in this particular have fewer advocates now. The theory and practice of medicine have virtually turned a somerset within the last half century in the regular departments of the science–to say nothing of the locust swarms of quackologists who are making awful havoc on the foliage of human life.

During the prevalence of any disease his exertions to arrest its progress and alleviate distress were unremitting. He obeyed the calls of the poor as promptly as those of the rich. He was particularly attentive to those in adverse circumstances who had employed him when in affluence. He put a veto on sunshine friends by precept and example. A pious and consistent Christian–he often cheered the desponding heart where medicine failed to save the body from the grave. His counsels were full of wisdom and benevolence and saved many a frail bark from shipwreck. His enlivening presence and soul-cheering advice drove despair from many an agonized mind–imparting fresh vigor by administering the elixir of hope and the tonic of fortitude. This is an important talent in a physician–often more potent than any chemical.

Blessed with a vigorous constitution–Dr. Rush was active until a short time previous to the 19th of April 1813, when he rested from his labors and was numbered with the dead. As the news of his death spread, a universal sorrow pervaded all classes–funeral sermons were preached–eulogies pronounced and processions formed throughout the United States as a just tribute to the memory of the departed sage, patriot, scholar and philanthropist. His goodness had decked his name with the rich garniture of profound esteem.

When the sad tidings reached England and France, the same demonstrations of respect were manifested there. The tears of sympathy suffused many European eyes. In the halls of science on both sides of the Atlantic, Dr. Rush was well known and highly appreciated. By our own country his loss was most keenly felt–by the civilized world deeply lamented. The graves of but few men have been moistened by as many tears from the rich and poor–high and low–as that of Dr. Rush. His fame is based upon substantial merit. His name is engraved in deep and indelible traces on the hearts of our countrymen. His untarnished reputation is written on the monument of history in letters of gold by the pen of justice dipped in the font of gratitude and will endure, unimpaired, until the last trump shall proclaim to the astonished millions on this whirling planet–TIME SHALL BE NO LONGER!!!

The private character of this great and good man was as unsullied and pure as his career was brilliant and useful. His heart overflowed with the milk of human kindness–his benevolence often carried him beyond his professional income. He was temperate in his habits–neat in his person and dress–social and gentlemanly in his intercourse–urbane and courteous in his manners–interesting and instructive in his conversation–modest and unassuming in his deportment. He was a warm and affectionate companion–the widows' friend and the orphans' father.

He was a little above the middle height–rather slender but a good figure. His mouth and chin were well formed–his nose aqueline–his eyes blue and animated–his forehead high and prominent. The diameter of his head from back to front was unusually large. His combined features were commanding and prepossessing, his physiognomy indicating a gigantic intellect.

When attacked by the disease which terminated his life he was aware a rapid dissolution awaited him. He was fully prepared to enter upon the untried scenes of the other and brighter world. He could look back upon a life well spent. He had run a noble race–was ready to finish his course–resign his tabernacle of clay to its mother dust–his immortal soul to Him who gave it.

In the history of this great and good man we see nothing to censure but much to admire. To be useful and do all the good in his power was his constant aim. No blanks appear on the record for the apologist to fill up. But few men have performed as much–no one performed more in the same time. If such examples as his, spread out in bold *relievo* on the historic page, will not exercise a salutary influence on the reader–if his devotion to his country–benevolence and unsurpassed virtues do not mellow your heart–you cannot be a patriot or a philanthropist–you do not realize the priceless value of our UNION.

EDWARD RUTLEDGE.

The name of every patriot, sage and hero who aided in gaining the Liberty we now enjoy, is repeated with veneration and respect. But a few of those noble spirits who breasted the storm of the Revolution are lingering on earth. All who were prominent leaders have paid the debt of nature and gone to their permanent and final home. A particular veneration is felt for those whose names are enrolled on that bold and soul-stirring production–the Declaration of Independence. Their names, with many others, will glide down the stream of time on the peaceful waves of admiration and gratitude until merged in the consummation of this whirling planet–" the wreck of matter and the crush of worlds." Among the names of the signers of the Declaration of Independence, is that of Edward Rutledge, born in Charleston S. C. in November 1749. He was the son of Dr. Rutledge, a native of Ireland, who married Sarah West, a lady of refined accomplishments, piety and good sense.

Edward lost his father at an early age and like those of many great and good men, his mind was happily moulded by his accomplished mother. After passing through the usual routine of an education he commenced the study of law with an elder brother who stood high at the Charleston bar. As a relaxation from Coke and Bacon he occasionally entered the bowers of elocution. In 1769 he went to England, became a student at the temple–made himself familiar with the courts, rules of parliament, the policy, designs and feelings of the British ministry and cultivated an acquaintance with the celebrated orators and statesmen–Chatham, Mansfield and others. He returned in 1773, richly laden with stock for future use.

He commenced a successful practice–uniting an expressive countenance, a good voice, a rich imagination, elegance of action, an honorable mind and a good heart–with strong native talent improved by superior advantages and great industry. He soon acquired a well earned eminence as a bold, discreet and able advocate. He was ever ready–the spur of the moment made him shine most conspicuously. His lamp was always trimmed and burning. With true Irish zeal he was always ready to enter the arena where duty called—especially if it was to defend the weak—aid the oppressed or relieve the distressed.

It was self-evident that with a soul and talents like his, he could not remain an idle spectator of the elements of revolution that were in motion. He was the kind of man to rouse the popular fury when circumstances would justify and required it. Warm-hearted, zealous, bold and daring—he was a necessary part in the political machine of that time to put the more sluggish parts in motion. He was an admirable fireman, a safe engineer, a good pilot and a popular captain. Liberal in his views, republican in his principles, a stickler for equal rights—he was among the first to strike for Liberty.

He was elected a member of the first Congress in 1774. None but men of superior merit, known fortitude and pure patriotism were selected to represent their country's rights and repel the wrongs of monarchy. Such a man was Mr. Rutledge. His open frankness and bold exposure of the corruptions of the British ministry—preying upon the Colonies like canker worms, rendered him obnoxious to the adherents of the crown—the very thing to rouse such a man to determined action. Opposition seemed to kindle in his manly bosom a brighter flame of patriotic fire which he imparted to the friends of freedom without stint or measure.

With his ardor and zeal he united prudence and discretion—was a friend to order and cool deliberation. He acted from enlightened principles—aiming to build every superstructure on the firm basis of reason and justice. To this nobleness of design—conceived and adhered to by all the signers of the Declaration, may be attributed that lofty dignity which pervades that unique document.

Revolution is a tornado rarely chastened by prudence or discretion to neutralize its baneful effects. Up to the time of the American Revolution history claims no body of men to compare with those who constituted the Continental Congress—men who commanded the whirlwind of passion to stay its fury—who conducted the lightning of revenge by the silken thread of reason to the goal of deliberation.

Mr. Rutledge was made a member of several important committees. He was appointed, in conjunction with Benjamin Franklin and John Adams to meet Lord Howe when he came to offer terms of ministerial peace. They were received with marked attention and respect by the royal messenger. He only had power to pardon repenting rebels—these were not to be found. His insulting proposition was repelled with indignation. The committee disclaimed all allegiance to the crown—it had been sacrificed at the shrine of an ambitious and oppressive ministry. FREEDOM was their motto—LIBERTY their watchword—their terms—INDEPENDENCE OR DEATH. They had nobly resolved "to do or die."

As a sound, judicious and able statesman, Mr. Rutledge was highly appreciated. He had also earned laurels in the battle field. He had long commanded a company in the ancient battalion of artillery. When the British landed at Port Royal in 1779, he led his company to the attack with the skill and courage of a veteran. At no Revolutionary battle was more personal bravery displayed than at this—nor was the enemy at any time more chagrined at a total defeat by raw militia. It was a mystery to them to find in the same man the statesman and the hero. He was subsequenly elected colonel. During the investment of Charleston in 1780, he was again on military duty—taken prisoner—sent to St. Augustine and was not exchanged for nearly a year. Before his return the dark clouds began to recede before the rays of rising hope and the day star of Liberty.

He returned to his native state and aided in restoring the civil government to order and systematic arrangement He was a member of the enraged Assembly at Jacksonborough in 1782. With his recent personal injuries pressing upon him and those of his friends bleeding fresh before him, he was induced to sanction the bill of pains and penalties, which, under other circumstances he would have opposed. During the time it remained in force he smoothed its roughness as much as possible.

Among those who had been tortured by persecution was his venerable mother who had been taken from her quiet home in the country and confined in Charleston then occupied by the British—because she was the mother of one of the rebels who had signed that burning instrument—the Declaration of Independence—a high compliment to her talents and patriotism—placing her on the list of fame with the noble matrons of Greece and Rome.

During the entire period of the unequal struggle with Great Britain, Mr. Rutledge rendered all the aid in his power to his injured country. At the final termination of hostilities—in a free land and with a free heart he returned to the bosom of his friends and the labors of his profession. His private worth, urbanity of manners and persevering industry in business, gained for him the confidence and esteem of community.

In the organization of the government of the state he took a conspicuous and useful part. Many difficulties were to be surmounted—clashing local interests reconciled and laws adopted to restore to order and harmonious system the confusion consequent upon a change of government. A great commotion existed between debtors and creditors.

Specie was not to be had–the paper currency was nearly annihilated–many who had periled life for Liberty and shaken off the foreign yoke felt that they were again in cruel bondage. Many avaricious creditors were as destitute of mercy as the pirate is of compassion. Such bipeds still live, move and have a being–but thanks to the philanthropy and good sense of our legislatures, they are disarmed in many of the states from the most barbarous feature of their power–that of thrusting a poor debtor into prison for the crime of poverty. I am pained to own that there are instances on record in our country where veterans, who bled for our boasted freedom, have been incarcerated by the cold inquisitorial creditor for a sum so trifling that the miser would blush to name it.

As a panacea for this malady a law was passed making land a lawful tender for debts–a law purely republican but obnoxious to avarice and aristocracy. Mr. Rutledge did much to effect the adoption of this measure, imperiously demanded by the then existing circumstances of the community. He also advocated the instalment law and used his best exertions to ameliorate the condition of the poor and do justice to the rich by salutary and humane legislation. He took an active part in the public business generally. When the Federal Constitution was presented to his state for consideration he was in favor of its adoption although it contained some objectionable features in his mind. He was always opposed to slavery deeming it a national curse entailed by England.

If slavery did not exist in the South and the people knew its evils as *they* only can know and feel them, a very large majority would oppose its introduction. I have recently travelled in most of the southern states and speak from the record. Two-fifths of the white population of those states do not own a slave. The institution is one of a domestic nature to be governed and regulated by themselves. But for the unfortunate interference of our northern brethren, many, but not *all* of them prompted by philanthropic motives, gradual emancipation would have commenced years ago and left no food for demagogues and disorganizers to gorge themselves upon. Should the South interfere with any of the domestic concerns of the North, resistance would be instantaneous. I am no advocate of slavery–but understanding its origin, progress, present condition and practical operation and the feelings of the South–I repeat, that the interference of the North is a misfortune to the slave and the peace of our common country. But for this, four of the slave states would now be free. This Bohun Upas was dying a natural death–digging around it has renewed its age fifty years. The plan was conceived and put in operation by England through her emissary Dr. Thompson, as a *dernier* resort to destroy the only republic hated and feared by the crowned heads of Europe. Let the South alone to correct their own evils. Let the subject be consigned to the capulet tombs rather than it should for a moment disturb the harmony of our glorious UNION. To the slave–sudden emancipation would be an irreparable injury. The question is one of *fact* rather than *law*–of imperious expediency rather than abstract reasoning. The slaves of the South are better bred, fed and clothed and more intelligent than the great majority of free negroes in free states.

Although partial to the French, when difficulties arose between that nation and England, Mr. Rutledge strongly censured the conduct of M. Genét and the French Directory for the stringent measures adopted. He was a moderate–not an ultra party man and always acted from a sense of duty and a pure desire for the good of the whole. His was a stern unflinching moderation–calculated to awe a mob, paralyze a faction and preserve pure and undefiled that lofty patriotism which commands esteem and respect and leads to peace and safety.

In 1798 Mr. Rutledge was elected governor of his native state. Soon after he entered upon the imposing duties of his office, disease suddenly seized and handed him over to the King of Terrors in the bright career of his gubernatorial term. During the legislative session of 1800, his health failed so rapidly that he felt a full assurance that his dissolution was fast approaching. He was anxious to return to Charleston that he might yield up his breath where he first inhaled the atmosphere. The constitution required the presence of the governor during the session of that body and so scrupulous was he to fulfil its letter, that he determined to remain unless both branches passed a resolution sanctioning his absence. The subject was submitted and becoming a matter of debate he at once withdrew it and remained until the adjournment. He was barely able to reach home when he laid down upon the sick bed and yielded to the only power that could conquer him–Death–on the 23d of January 1800. The same fortitude that had characterized his whole life was fully exemplified during his illness and dying hour. His loss was keenly felt and deeply mourned by the entire community of the state and by the friends of freedom throughout the nation. South Carolina had lost one of her brightest ornaments–one of her noblest sons.

Governor Rutledge stood high as an orator. He was familiar with the machinery of human nature–knew when to address the judgment and when the passions. In exciting the sympathy of a jury he had no equal at the Charleston Bar. He knew how, when and where to be logical and what is all important in public and private life–he knew how, when and where to speak and what to say and stopped when done. His private worth and public services were an honor to himself, gratifying to his friends and beneficial to his country. His usefulness continued to the close of life–his fame is untarnished with error–his examples are worthy of imitation–his life had no blank. He married for his first wife, Harriet, daughter of Edward Middleton his colleague in the Continental Congress. By her he had a son and daughter–the latter settled in Charleston–the former, Maj. Henry M. Rutledge, was one of the pioneers of Tennessee. God grant that his descendants may imitate the virtues of their ancestor and fill the blank occasioned by the death of the wise, judicious, benevolent, patriotic and high-minded EDWARD RUTLEDGE.

ROGER SHERMAN.

THE man who has been rocked in the cradle of letters from his childhood–who has become familiar with general science, the classics and the philosophy of the schools–who has had a wealthy father to aid and doting mother to caress–who has enjoyed an uninterrupted course in some far-famed college and the most refined society–such a man is expected to mount the ladder of fame and become a shining light to those whose advantages have been limited to a primary school or no school. If, with all these advantages lavished upon him he sinks into obscurity, the fond anticipations of his doting parents and anxious friends set in gloom. Such has often been the case.

When we see a man whose opportunities of acquiring an education during childhood and youth carried him not far beyond the spelling-book–a man who had no father to aid him by wealth–warn him against the quicksands of error or point him to the temple of science–his intellect encased in the rude quarry of nature at the age of twenty–when we see such a man bursting the fetters that bind his mental powers–throwing off the dark mantle of ignorance–by a mighty effort unveiling his dormant talents and shining in all the beauty of intelligence and greatness, we are filled with admiration and delight.

Such a man was Roger Sherman, the great grandson of Capt. John Sherman, who came from England to Watertown, Mass. in 1635. Roger was the son of William Sherman, born in Newton, Mass. on the 19th of April 1721. His father was a respectable farmer with means too limited to educate his son and bound him an apprentice to a shoemaker. At the age of nineteen he left his master to seek his fortune. His genius had become restless in embryo and pressed for enlargement. No shop could confine—no obstacle deter, no impediment prevent its expansion. The course of his mind was onward and upward like a blazing star, illuminating the horizon of his intellect as it rose. Nature designed him to be great and good—he obeyed her kind commands.

He went to New Milford, Conn. where he followed his trade for three years, devoting every leisure moment to his books, often having one open before him when using his lap-stone. Every obstacle to the pursuit of knowledge was removed by his untiring industry—he ascended the hill of science with a steady pace. He lived within the strictest rules of economy, appropriating a part of his earnings to the support of a widowed mother with a family of small children. The education of these children also received his attention.

In June 1743 he removed his mother and children to New Milford and entered into the mercantile business, still improving every leisure hour in the acquisition of an education. He rapidly stored his mind with a fund of useful information that ultimately enabled him to commence a public career of usefulness. He also became a member of the church and adorned his profession through life. In 1745 he was appointed surveyor of Litchfield County, having mastered mathematics. Like his cotemporary and friend Benjamin Franklin, he made the calculation for an almanac for several years for a publisher in New York.

At the age of twenty-eight he married Elizabeth Hartwell of Staughton, Mass. who died in 1780 leaving seven children. He subsequently married Rebecca Prescott who had eight children. His fifteen children were carefully trained in the paths of wisdom and virtue. He also supported his mother and a maiden sister until death relieved them from the toils of life.

In the prosecution of his literary pursuits he turned his attention to the study of law in which he made astonishing proficiency. In 1754 he was admitted to the bar, better prepared to enter into this arduous profession and do justice to his clients than many who are ushered into notice with great *eclat* under the high floating banner of a collegiate diploma.

The following year he was elected a member of the colonial Assembly and remained in that body during the remainder of his residence at New Milford. He had the confidence and esteem of his fellow citizens which enabled him to exercise a salutary influence upon those around him. His reputation as a lawyer and statesman stood high. For industry, prudence, discretion and sound logic—he was unrivalled in the

Colony. Strong common sense, the safety valve of human action, marked his whole career. He was a philanthropist of the highest order—a patriot of the first water—rendering himself substantially useful to his fellow men and common country.

In 1759 he was appointed a judge of the county court of Litchfield, discharging his duties with great faithfulness and impartiality—correcting vice and promoting virtue.

In 1761 he removed to New Haven where he was appointed justice of the peace—elected to the Assembly and in 1765 was placed upon the judicial bench of the county court. He received the degree of Master of Arts from Yale College, of which he was treasurer for many years, fulfilling the trust with scrupulous honesty and fidelity.

In 1766 he was elected to the Executive Council which was hailed as an auspicious event by the friends of liberal principles. The mother country had manifested a disposition to impose unjust taxation upon the Colonies. It required discretion, experience, nerve and decision to comprehend and expose the corrupt plans of an avaricious and reckless ministry. The Colonies had borne the great burden of the French war in which they had sacrificed large sums of money and fountains of their richest blood. After years of incessant toil the foe had been conquered—an honorable peace obtained for England—the frontier settlements measurably relieved from danger and the soldier had again become the citizen. Whilst their rejoicings on that occasion were yet on the lips of echo, oppression from the crown threatened to blast their fond anticipations of happiness and repose and bind them in chains more to be dreaded than the tomahawk and scalping knife.

His Colony had furnished more money and men and lost more of her brave sons in the French war than any other with the same population. Mr. Sherman had been an active member of the Assembly during the period of its prosecution and remembered well the sacrifices that had been made to oblige the king. He understood well the rights of his own country and those of the crown. He was eminently prepared to discover approaching danger and sound a timely alarm. He was fully competent to probe the intrigues and venality of designing men although the broad Atlantic rolled between him and them.

Mr. Grenville was the master spirit of the British ministry. He determined to put in practice his long cherished theory of taxing the American Colonies. The alarm was soon spread from the north to the south. Appeals for redress, petitions and remonstrances, numerously signed, were forwarded to Parliament. These were passed by like the idle wind. Reason, justice, mercy—all were banished from the bosoms of the ruling power. The rack of oppression was put in motion–screw after screw was turned–the sinews of affection for the mother country began to snap–the purple current rushed from its fountain with increased velocity–indignation was roused in millions of bosoms. In humble imitation of the ancient inquisitors, the screws of the infernal machine were relaxed to give the subjects a confessing respite. The tax upon glass, paper, &c. was repealed. But the main screw was not turned back. The tax on tea was still enforced. This exception was death to the colonial power of England–to America–FREEDOM. The indignation of woman was roused. Her high toned chords were touched– the reverberation electrified the mass as with vivid lightning. Tea was banished by every female patriot and with it all British luxuries and taxed articles.

Mr. Sherman remained undaunted at his post calmly watching the moving elements. Although elevated to the bench of the Superior Court he remained in the Executive Council, a firm and consistent advocate of his country's rights–a bold expounder of Britain's wrongs. He viewed the gathering clouds as they rolled up from the horizon–he saw the streams of lurid fire with which they were charged and calmly waited the crash of thunder that should usher on the terrific storm. The British lion prowled in anger–the Albion Goliah buckled on his armor–the shining steel dazzled in the sun–American blood flowed–popular fury was roused–the sword of vengeance was drawn–allegiance was dissolved– the Colonies were FREE.

Judge Sherman was a member of the first Continental Congress and remained firm and unwavering at his post during the heart rending scenes of the Revolution, the formation of the new government and the adoption of the Federal Constitution. With a mind of iron strength enlarged and improved by close study–inured to the toils and intricacies of legislation–the history of his country and of nations stamped upon his memory–the ingratitude and insults of a foreign ministry preying upon his soul–all these combined to press him onward to deeds of noble daring. His capacity was equal to every emergency. He omitted no duty, moving, with the mathematical precision of a planet, within the orbit of sound discretion. He was familiar with all the avenues of men and things--scanned the deep recesses of human nature–traced causes and results to their source and probed to the bottom the springs of human action. The arcana of economies was open before him–solving problems, demonstrating principles and placing them in the full blaze of illustration– clear as light, intelligible as Euclid–irresistible as truth. Youth and young mechanics of our country such was the self-taught self-made

Roger Sherman. Read the history of his life closely. Ponder it well and firmly resolve to make him your model.

The Congressional session of 1775 was one of great labor, anxiety and embarrassment. It required veterans in patriotism to sustain the tremendous shock, the fearful onset. An army was to be raised and organized, military stores provided, fortifications erected, rules of government adopted, plans of operation matured, internal foes to be encountered and legions of hireling soldiers to be repelled. To meet these pressing emergencies the members of Congress had hearts full of courage but an empty treasury. A forlorn hope was before them—a merciless foe on their shores. The torch of hope shed but a dim light. In the name of high Heaven they resolved on *Liberty or Death*. Nor did they "split on the rock of resolves and re-resolves, where thousands live and die the same." They met the fury of the king with a firmness, wisdom and patriotism before unknown. Their course was onward towards the goal of FREEDOM. No threats of vengeance dismayed them—the shafts of terror fell harmless at their feet—the vials of ministerial wrath were poured out in vain.

In 1776, the Colonies bleeding, reverses rolling frightfully upon them, a conquering army sweeping over their land like a tornado, the streams red with the blood of their kinsmen—the cries of widows and orphans ringing in their ears, the sky illumined with the curling flames of their towns—this band of patriots conceived the bold and sublime plan of INDEPENDENCE—a plan that wreathed its projectors with laurels of unfading freshness.

Early in the summer Messrs. Sherman, John Adams, Franklin, Livingston and Jefferson were appointed a committee to draft a Declaration of Rights. It was prepared with much deliberation—reported and on the memorable 4th of July 1776 received the hearty sanction of the Continental Congress amidst the transporting joys of FREEMEN who hailed it as the bright morning star—to them a prelude to future bliss—to tyrants, a blazing meteor of devouring fire.

Illustrious in all their actions the signers of the Declaration of Independence were pre-eminently so—when, assuming their native dignity, they rose in all the majesty of greatness—bursting their servile chains—cutting asunder the cords of forfeited allegiance—sublimely passing the grand Rubicon and in the eyes of an approving God and an admiring world—declared their country FREE AND INDEPENDENT. The era was one of refulgent glory, sacred to the cause of human rights—enduring as genuine patriotism—cheering as the oasis of the desert.

No member of the Continental Congress had studied more closely and understood more clearly political economy and finance than Mr. Sherman. His mind was moulded in system. He was a practical man and conversant with every department of government. He was an efficient member of the board of war, ordnance and the treasury. He served on important committees during the whole time of the Revolution. His plans for replenishing the public funds, regulating expenditures and disbursing moneys, were based on rules of frugality and economy corresponding with the embarrassments of that trying period. Fraudulent contractors quailed before his scrutiny--speculations and peculations on government were often paralyzed by his torpedo touch. He guarded, with an Argus eye and parental care the interests of the young Republic.

In the estimation of his colleagues and of our nation, Roger Sherman was second to no one in that bright constellation of sages for sterling integrity and substantial usefulness. At that time honesty and modesty were attributes of merit. It required no stump speeches or bar-room harangues to gain popular favor. Foaming bragadocia--bullying gasconade--personal crimination and a violation of the sanctity of the domestic circle were not then current coin. No bogus politicians were found among the patriots of the Revolution. *Principles*--not *men* were the political landmarks--not the seven principles of five loaves and two fishes but the heaven-born principles of eternal justice, truth, honesty, equality, freedom, love of country, patriotism, humanity, universal charity and pure benevolence--all harmoniously growing in rich clusters upon the tree of LIBERTY.

That was also a time of labor. Inglorious ease was not known to legislators. Long written speeches were not read to the speaker and the walls to be printed for party effect among constituents. Turmoil and billingsgate slang were unknown in the halls of legislation. The business of the nation was performed promptly, faithfully and effectually. Posts of honor were then posts of duty--not of profit. No demagogue bipeds were permitted to fatten at the public crib--no droning sinecures were lounging under the mantle of government. How changed the scene--how fearful the contrast at the present writing! Awake! patriots of my beloved country to a sense of our true interests. Throw off the incubus of ultra party spirit--think, know and act for yourselves--avoid the paralyzing touch of reckless demagogues and purge our land from political corruption.

By his fellow citizens at home Mr. Sherman was held in high esteem. He was continued in the Council during the Revolution. When the city of New Haven was chartered in 1784 he was elected the first mayor–filling the office with great dignity to the close of his life.

When peace was restored Judges Sherman and Law were appointed to revise the judicial code of Connecticut which duty they performed with great ability and satisfaction to all concerned. Mr. Sherman was a member of the convention that framed the Federal Constitution. From a manuscript found among his papers it appears that this instrument received many of its bright features from him. To his conceptive mind and practical wisdom we are much indebted for the towering greatness and unparalleled prosperity we so eminently enjoy and which will increase and endure so long as the people protect their own interests and are true to themselves. Intimately acquainted with all the local conflicting interests of the Colonies, he was enabled to exercise a salutary influence among the members in reconciling differences between them, which, for a time, threatened to hurl back the elements of government into original chaos and prostrate the fair fabric of Liberty. By examining the earnest discussions, the variety of opinions, the multifarious interests, the intense anxiety, the agony of soul and sacrifice of private views that characterized the formation of the Federal Constitution—we discover wisdom, discretion, charity and patriotism of the loftiest kind shining in all the grandeur of self sacrifice. Based upon the Declaration of Rights–it forms a superstructure, towering in sublimity above all others–radiating its heart cheering influence over our increasing millions of freemen–revered by all patriots at home–respected abroad–unrivalled in the annals of legislation.

Judge Sherman did much to remove the objections made to this important document by the people of his own and adjoining States. He demonstrated to them clearly and convinced them fully–that to effect and perpetuate the Union, private feeling and interest must yield to public necessity to procure public good and that each State should strive to produce an equilibrium of the general government, forming a grand centre towards which it should ever tend with harmonious and fraternal gravitation–immovable as the perpetual hills.

Judge Sherman was elected a member of the first Congress under the new Constitution and resigned his judicial station which he had so long adorned with the ermine of impartiality and equal justice. His influence was beneficially felt in the national legislature. He used his noblest exertions to promote the wide spread interests of the new-fledged Republic. Traces of his magnanimous propositions and prophetic policy are upon the journals and many of them incorporated in the Acts of that period. When members differed and exhibited the least acrimony, they were sure to find the peaceful wand of Judge Sherman fanning their heated feelings into a healthful coolness.

At the expiration of his representative term he was elected to the United States Senate of which he was a member when he closed his useful career—bade a long adieu—a final farewell to earth and its toils. He died on the 23d of July 1793 in the full enjoyment of that religion he had honored and practised and which had been a consolation and support amidst the changing scenes of his eventful pilgrimage. He had lived the life of a good man—he died calm, serene and happy. Through faith he triumphed over death and the grave and pressed upward to receive the enduring prize of unfading glory. He could approach the dread tribunal of the great Jehovah—smiling and smiled upon and enter into all the realities of heavenly bliss—enduring as the rolling ages of eternity. Thus lived and thus died Roger Sherman.

He had been a faithful public servant nearly forty years. He had participated in all the trying scenes of the Revolution—he had seen his country burst the fetters of tyranny and become a nation of freemen. He had aided in the consolidation of the general government—she was prosperous and happy. In all the important measures of the state of his adoption and of the American nation, he had acted an important part from the commencement of the French war to the time of his departure to "that country from whose bourne no traveller returns."

As a Christian he was esteemed by all denominations for his consistent piety and expansive charity. With him sectarianism was not religion—for him it had no charms. His philanthropy was broad as the human family—it reached from earth to heaven. He was familiar with the abstruse branches of theology and corresponded with several eminent divines. The Bible was his creed—not the dogmas of men.

In the history of Roger Sherman we have one of nature's sheets of purest white covered with all the sublime delineations that dignify a man and assimilate him to his Creator. His life was crowned with unfading evergreen produced by the rich soil of genuine worth and substantial merit. No ephemeral roses decked his venerable brow. A chaplet of amaranthine flowers surmounts his well earned fame. The mementos of his examples are a rich boon to posterity through all time. Whilst patriotism, religion and social order survive—the virtues of this great and good man will shine in all the majesty of light. His private character was as pure as his public career was illustrious.

Roger Sherman clearly demonstrated that man is the architect of his own fortune. By industry and perseverance in the use of books—now accessible to all, apprentices and mechanics may surmount every barrier and reach the summit of science and take their stations, with superior advantage, by the side of those who have been enervated within the walls of a college. No one in our land of intelligence is excusable for remaining under the dark mantle of ignorance. The sun of science has risen—all who will can be warmed by its genial rays. The means of acquiring knowledge are far superior to those enjoyed by Sherman and Franklin. Let their brilliant examples be imitated by Columbia's sons—our far famed Republic will then be as enduring as time. Let ignorance, corruption, ultra party spirit and fanaticism predominate—then the fair fabric of our FREEDOM, reared by the valor and cemented by the blood of the Revolutionary patriots—will tremble, totter and fall. Chaos will mount the car of discord—sound the dread clarion of the dissolution of our UNION and LIBERTY will expire amidst the smoking ruins of her own citadel. Forbid it patriotism—forbid it philanthropy—forbid it Almighty God! O! my countrymen! remember that with us is deposited the rich behest of LIBERTY—let us guard it with god-like care and transmit it to our posterity in all the loveliness of native purity.

JAMES SMITH.

MEN sometimes forsake the path designed for them by their Creator in their manner of speaking, acting and writing. They vainly strive to imitate some noble personage of a higher order by nature and cultivation than themselves and become poor specimens of the Ape. Some young men of respectable talents and acquirements—when they mount the rostrum, endeavor to imitate some orator of notoriety instead of acting out free and unvarnished nature. Originality alone gives beauty and force to eloquence in all its varied forms. Like a piece of marble under the skill of the statuary—a more systematic form may be produced by art but the native material cannot be improved in beauty by the finest art—the brightest paint. Originality must form the base or the richness is lost. No ingenuity can remould the work of nature and retain the full strength of the grand original. We should profit by the wisdom and virtues of great and good men—improve by their precepts and examples—our *manner* in public speaking, our *language*, our *style* of writing—all *must* be original to render them forcible and interesting. Affectation in anything is disgusting to sensible men. It is a coin that cannot be palmed upon the discerning for genuine. Of all counterfeits this is the most readily detected. Away with this worthless trash.

If you have not gold, use silver—if neither, use copper—if you have only *brass* you need no urging to use that.

James Smith was a fine specimen of originality and pleasing eccentricity. He was born in Ireland in 1713. His father came to this country when James was a boy and settled on the west side of the Susquehanna river nearly opposite Columbia in Pennsylvania. James acquired a good classical education under Dr. Allison and retained a great partiality for authors of antiquity to the end of his life. He delighted in mathematics and became an expert surveyor. After finishing his course of study with Dr. Allison he read law in Lancaster, Pennsylvania, probably with an elder brother in that town and with Mr. Cookson. When admitted to the bar he located in the then far west near the present site of Shippensburg in Cumberland County of that state. He blended law and surveying in accordance with the desire and wants of the frontier settlers. Large tracts of valuable land were held under hasty and imperfect surveys and others were located by chamber surveys. Litigation was the natural consequence. No witness could tell more truth than the compass and protractor of Mr. Smith which were free from prejudice and partiality. Possessed of a penetrating mind he scanned future prospects and secured much valuable land. In his compound profession he had full employment. He was on the flood-tide of prosperity. Not willing to sail alone he took for his mate Eleanor Armor of Newcastle who superintended his freight and cabin stores with great skill and prudence.

Mr. Smith was original in everything. With a strong mind, an open and honest heart, a benevolent and manly disposition—he united great conviviality and amusing drollery—yet so discreet and chaste as not to offend the most modest ear. He delighted in seeing the contortions of the risible muscles which were uniformly on duty in all proper circles when James Smith was present. Whenever he came in contact with a pedant he would propound some ludicrous question to him with the utmost gravity—such as this—"Don't you remember that terrible bloody battle which Alexander fought with the Russians near the straits of Babelmandel? I think you will find the account in Thucydides or Herodotus." His memory was retentive and stored with numerous anecdotes which he sometimes related in court and often in company to amuse his friends. His manner was original beyond imitation. With all his wit and humor he held religion in great veneration and was a communicant of the church. No one that knew him dare utter one word against it in his presence, knowing that his cutting lash of keen ridicule would at once be applied. Such a mixture of qualities are rarely blended in one man. His mind ranged with the quickness of lightning from the deep-toned logic and the profoundest thought to the eccentric ludicrous—all balanced by the equilibrium of discretion, and each used at the appropriate time and place. His manner, language, style—everything which he said or did from the most trivial circumstance to the momentous concerns of the nation was purely original.

Of the affairs of his country James Smith was not an idle spectator. No man delights in liberty and independence more than an Irishman. Nor have the Irish people a warm affection for mother Britain. As oppressed as she is, no nation is more sensitive of her rights than "sweet Ireland." When British oppression showed its hydra head in the American Colonies Mr. Smith took a terrible dislike to the *baste* and declared he would make fight unless it withdrew its visible deformity at once. His heart beat high for his adopted country—he came promptly to the rescue. At that time he resided at York and was extensively engaged in iron works and pressed with professional business. He had never consented to fill public stations. Nothing but the importance of the crisis could have induced him to enter the public arena. He reasoned as did Josiah Quincy that—"We must be grossly ignorant of the importance and value of the prize for which we contend—we must be equally ignorant of the power of those who have combined against us—we must be blind to that malice, inveteracy and insatiable revenge which actuate our enemies, public and private, abroad and in our midst—to hope we shall end this controversy without the sharpest—sharpest conflicts—to flatter ourselves that popular resolves, popular harangues, popular acclamations and popular vapor will vanquish our foes. Let us consider the issue—let us look to the end."

Mr. Smith was a man who looked at the beginning and ending. He examined closely causes, effects and results. He understood human nature and knew well the pulsations of the colonists. He believed the bone and sinew of the land would never yield to the tyranny of mother Britain without a "sharp conflict." For that conflict he was prepared. He well knew that there was but little sinecure mushroom dandy stock on hand—that the great mass was bone and sinew of the first water. He was for prompt action. A convention of delegates from each county in the state was convened to consider the course proposed by the patriots of New England when the Revolutionary storm had commenced its precursory droppings. Of this convention Mr. Smith was a prominent member and one of the committee that prepared an address to the members of the general Assembly recommending them to appoint delegates to the proposed general Congress with the following instructions which specify the grievances complained of.

"We desire you therefore–that the deputies you appoint may be instructed by you strenuously to exert themselves at the ensuing Congress to obtain a renunciation on the part of Great Britain of all the powers under the statute of 35th Henry VIII. ch. 2d–of all the powers of internal legislation–of imposing duties or taxes internal or external and of regulating trade except with respect to any new articles of commerce which the Colonies may hereafter raise–as silk, wine, &c. reserving a right to carry them from one colony to another–a repeal of all statutes for quartering troops in the colonies or subjecting them to any expense on account of such troops–of all statutes imposing duties to be paid in the colonies that were passed at the accession of his present majesty or before this time, whichever period shall be judged most advisable–of the statutes giving the Courts of Admiralty in the Colonies greater power than the Courts of Admiralty in England–of the statutes of 5th George II. ch. 22d and of the 23d of George II. ch. 29th–of the statute for shutting up the Port of Boston and of every other statute particularly affecting the province of Massachusetts Bay passed in the last session of Parliament. If all the terms abovementioned cannot be obtained, it is our opinion that the measures adopted by the Congress for our relief should never be relinquished or intermitted until those relating to the troops–internal legislation–imposition of taxes or duties hereafter–the 35th of Henry VIII. ch. 2d–the extension of Admiralty Courts–the Port of Boston and the Province of Massachusetts Bay are obtained. Every modification or qualification of these points in our judgment should be inadmissible."

By these instructions, directly from the people, we can judge of the feeling that pervaded the great mass of the yeomanry at that time. By referring to the instructions given to the delegates to Congress by the general Assembly, it will be seen that royal influence pervaded that body as they contain scarcely a feature or point similar to those from the primary convention of the people. See them in the life of Ross. That the reader may more fully understand the points referred to in the instructions above copied I will explain the statutes alluded to in their order.

By the statute of 35th Henry VIII. ch. 2d a citizen of America was liable to be arrested and taken to England to be tried for high crimes. By the 5th of George II. ch. 23d the colonists were prohibited from exporting hats and hatters were limited to a specific number of apprentices–" that hatting may be better encouraged in Great Britain." The statute 23d George II. ch. 29th imposed similar but more numerous restrictions–the whole and the other particulars named in the instructions being in violation of the constitution of England and of the charters predicated upon it. Constitutional and charter privileges had grown sacred by long and acknowledged usage, by learned and legal construction and by numerous declaratory Acts of the British Parliament passed when sitting under the mantle of reason, justice and sound policy. So fully convinced was Mr. Smith of the true issue between the Colonies and mother Britain that on his return home he raised a company of volunteers and was elected captain by acclamation. This was the pioneer company of Pennsylvania raised for the purpose of confronting the ugly *baste*-tyranny. It was nine months before the bloody affair at Lexington, showing that Mr. Smith had arrived at a correct conclusion as to the true issue. He introduced thorough discipline in his new corps and imparted to every member the same patriotic fire that illuminated his own noble soul. Around this military nucleus the bone and sinew continued to rally until a regiment was raised. Mr. Smith accepted the honorary title of Colonel but imposed the active commanding duties upon a younger man. He had put the ball in motion and was gratified to see it rolling onward with increasing momentum towards the goal of Liberty. When the time arrived for action this regiment did honor to all concerned.

Mr. Smith was a member of the next people's convention which convened at Philadelphia in January 1775. He was one of the foremost to oppose force to force and peril life for freedom. He was called an *ultra* whig and accused of treating the government of his most Christian majesty indecorously. His patriotism had carried him six months in advance of most of the leading men. No one could outstrip him in zeal in the cause of equal rights. His course was onward–right onward to action. For this the time soon arrived. In the spring of 1776 he was on a committee with Dr. Rush and Col. Bayard to organize a camp of 4500 troops to be raised in Pennsylvania. No man was better calculated to render efficient service in this important branch of business. The committee immediately prepared an appeal to the yeoman military which was approved by Congress and widely circulated. It was written in bold and forcible language pointing to the Independence of the Colonies as the great incentive to action. It had a powerful and salutary effect and met with a response from the people that caused the hirelings of the crown to fly from the province like chaff before the wind. The complement of men was promptly raised.

Almost simultaneous with the promulgation of the Declaration of Independence by Congress a convention of delegates convened for the purpose of raising the arch of a republican constitution and government over the Keystone State. Of this convention Mr. Smith was a prominent member and one of the committee that prepared the Declaration of Rights. For this the committee had the guidance of a polar star that had been brought to light by the illustrious Jefferson and placed in the cerulean canopy of Liberty by the Sages of Congress a few days previous. The *ultraism* of Mr. Smith had become an admired quality and was surnamed *patriotism* by the very persons who had misconceived it a few months previous. His zeal and worth were then properly appreciated. On the 20th of July he was elected to the Continental Congress without an intimation to him of the intended honor until he was officially notified of the fact. Being at the State convention in Philadelphia he immediately took his seat enrolled his name with the apostles of Liberty upon the chart of freedom and then returned to the convention and essentially aided in completing the new government of the State.

Early in October he fully assumed his congressional duties. The instructions to the congressional delegates had become reversed in two short years. The first clause is worthy of special notice and should be printed in bold *relievo* and placed over both chairs in Congress—there to remain through all congressional time. Read and ponder it well ye public men who think more of your personal concerns than the business of your constituents.

"The immense and irreparable injury which a free country may sustain *by* and the great inconveniences which always arise *from* a delay of its councils, induce us in the first place strictly to enjoin and require you to give not only a *constant* but a *punctual* attendance in Congress."

At the commencement of our free government the will of the people was respected and obeyed. Their public servants were not then their political masters. Committee rooms were not then diverted from their legitimate use by partisan caucuses. The halls of legislation were not then the forum of chaos, personal crimination—recrimination and unparliamentary procedure. The mantle of infantile purity was then hanging from the shoulders of those in high stations in all the beauty of tasteful drapery. *Pro bono publico* was the order of the day—*pro libertate patriæ* was the motto of each freeman. Mr. Smith obeyed his instructions to the letter. He entered with all his might upon the work set before him. A dark gloom hung over the cause of Liberty at that time. Many of its warmest friends considered success quite problematical.

At such a time the sprightliness and proverbial drollery of Mr. Smith were a talismanic antidote against despondency. Always cheerful and elastic—spicing his conversations in private and his speeches in the forum with original wit and humor—he imparted convivial life to those around him. Amidst the waves of misfortune and the breakers of disappointment—like a buoy upon the ocean, he floated above them all and pointed the mariners of Liberty to the port of Freedom. The following extract of a letter written to his wife when Congress was on the point of retreating before Gen. Howe shows that no hyppish feelings cramped the elasticity of his mind.

"If Mr. Wilson comes through York give him a flogging—he should have been here a week ago. I expect to come home before election—my three months are nearly up. General left this on Thursday—I wrote to you by Col. Kennedy.

"This morning I put on the red jacket under my shirt. Yesterday I dined at Mr. Morris's and got wet coming home and my shoulder got troublesome, but by running a hot smoothing iron over it three times it got better. This is a new and cheap cure. My respects to all friends and neighbors—my love to the children.

"I am your loving husband whilst
"JAMES SMITH.
"Congress Chamber, 11 o'clock."

On the 23d of November 1776 Mr. Smith was placed on the committee to devise means for reinforcing the American army and for arresting the destructive career of Gen. Howe. The powers of this committee were very properly transferred to Washington soon after. He was on the committee that laid before Congress conclusive testimony of the inhuman treatment of the American prisoners at New York. The ensuing year he declined a re-election but his constituents informed him he was public property and must be used *nolens volens*. He obeyed their will and continued at his post with unabated zeal and industry. When Congress was compelled to retreat to York he closed his office against his clients and placed in it the Board of War. He sacrificed all private interests that would promote the glorious cause of Liberty. In November 1778 he resigned his seat in Congress and for a season enjoyed the comforts of domestic life. Being advanced in years and having full confidence in the ability of the United States, aided by the French, to maintain Independence—formed his excuse for leaving the field of his arduous labors. In 1780 he consented to serve in the State Legislature. He then retired finally from the public arena. He continued to pursue his professional business successfully and profitably up to 1800 having been a member of the bar for sixty years. His eccentricity, wit and humor retained all the freshness of originality to the end of his life. He was a great admirer of the illustrious Washington. A castigation from his ironical tongue was the certain consequence to any one who spoke against religion or Washington in his presence at any time or place. Upon these two points he was very sensitive. The former he adored–the latter he revered. He corresponded regularly with Franklin and several others of the patriarch sages of '76. He had preserved a rich cabinet of letters, all of which were burnt with his office about a year before his death.

Surrounded by an affectionate family and a large circle of ardent friends--this happy son of Erin glided smoothly down the stream of time until the 11th day of July 1806 when his frail bark was anchored in the bay of death--his immortal spirit in the haven of bliss. In life he was useful–in death happy. In life he was loved and honored–in death his loss was deeply mourned. His exit from earth left a blank not readily filled. His public and private character were unsullied by a spot or wrinkle. When living he was the life of every circle in which he moved–no one who knew him could forget him when dead. Ennui could not live in his presence. He was warm hearted, kind, affectionate and a friend to the poor. He never entertained malice. He used his opponents much as a playful kitten does a mouse–teasing without a desire to hurt them–a propensity that rendered him more formidable than a knight of the sword and pistols. Such pure originals as James Smith are like the inimitable paintings of the ancient artists–few in market and hard to be copied.

JOHN STARK.

INGRATITUDE is the extract of baseness, the essence of blackness, the ergot of meanness, a concentrated poison, the spawn of a demon–the fuel of Pandemonium. Its breath is pestilence, its touch is palsy. Of all the vile acts of man towards man none throw such a freezing chill over the whole body and drive back the rushing blood upon the aching heart like base and damning ingratitude. Indifference continued, coldness persevered in, favors forgotten, friendship unrequited and sometimes cruel abuse–from one who has been the willing recipient of our love, bounty and voluntary aid–brings a palsying horror over the soul that thickens the purple current in the veins making the head sick and the heart faint.

A nation may be ungrateful as well as an individual. Thus it was with England towards the American Colonies. In addition to contributing to the support of the home government of the mother country, much blood and treasure were expended by the Americans in conquering Canada for the special benefit of Great Britain. It was owned by the French who were long the common enemy of the English. Immediately after that conquest the most ungrateful and unjust oppression was commenced by the ministry of England upon her Colonies here. To cap the climax—the very Indians the Americans had conquered and made allegiant to the mother country—that cruel mother employed to murder and scalp those who had aided her. A premium was given for *scalps*—not for *prisoners*.

Among those who essentially aided in the conquest of the Canadas was John Stark, born in Londonderry, New Hampshire, on the 25th of August 1728 O. S. When John was but eight years of age his father removed to what is now called Manchester. Clearing land and an occasional hunting or fishing excursion with his father was the business of John in early life. In this manner the tide of time carried him along until the 28th of April 1752 when he was taken prisoner by the St. Francois Indians. He left home with two others to visit their beaver traps and at the time of his capture was separated from them. The savages ordered him to lead them to his companions which he pretended to do but led them two miles in the opposite direction. Their position was discovered by the discharge of their guns to call Stark to them. The Indians proceeded below where their boat was moored and ordered Stark to hail them when they approached. He did so and told them to escape to the opposite shore. They attempted to do so—one of them was immediately shot and killed—the other Stark saved by snatching the gun from the Indian who aimed at him for which he was most cruelly treated. His companion was then taken prisoner. In about six weeks they were ransomed and restored to their anxious friends. Thus ended his first lesson in the school of peril.

In the winter of 1753 the Court of New Hampshire sent an exploring expedition into Coos County and employed young Stark as pilot to the company. He performed his undertaking to the entire satisfaction of all concerned. In 1754 a party was sent to the upper part of this county to learn if the French were erecting a fortification—if so, the reason why. Stark was again employed as conductor and led the expedition upon the track he travelled when a prisoner. On the commencement of hostilities with the French and Indians in 1755 he was commissioned a Lieutenant under Captain Rodgers whose boldness and enterprise were in unison with those of Stark. They speedily raised a company of brave hardy men and were ordered to join the regiment at Fort Edward. They arrived shortly after Sir William Johnson was attacked by the French and Indians near Bloody Pond. In the fall the troops returned to their homes. In the winter of 1756 a corps of rangers was raised to protect the frontier settlements. Rodgers and Stark were put in command and repaired to Fort Edward in April with their company. Nothing worthy of note occurred until the winter of 1757 when this company and two others were ordered to seize the supplies on the way from Crown Point to Ticonderoga. The Colonial troops had taken a few sleighs and were on their way to Fort George when they were furiously attacked by the combined force of the French and Indians. A desperate and bloody battle was fought—Captain Spickman was killed and Captain Rodgers severely wounded. The entire command then devolved upon Lieut. Stark. Being overpowered by numbers he ordered a retreat. With the coolness and skill of an experienced veteran he drew off his men keeping the enemy at a respectful distance by a well directed fire when too closely pressed. He brought away all his wounded men and had them conveyed in sleighs to Fort George. He was at once elected to fill the place of Captain Spickman. The next spring he was ordered to New York where he suffered severely from the small pox and was unfit for duty until the next autumn when he returned and wintered at Fort Edward.

In 1758 Gen. Abercrombie planned an attack upon Ticonderoga. The rangers under Major Rodgers were sent forward to reconnoitre the enemy and make way for the main body of troops. The evening previous to that fatal attack the Major received orders to carry the bridge between Lake George and the plains of Tie early the next morning. On the approach of the rangers the French and Indians were assembled in force to dispute their passage. A halt was made— Capt. Stark advised the Major to advance rapidly by which means the bridge was cleared instantly. During the whole of that sanguinary action no officer manifested more cool and determined bravery than Capt. Stark. The Colonial troops were defeated which ended that campaign. It was an unfortunate affair inspiring the Indians with boldness in their career of predatory warfare.

Early in 1759 Capt. Stark obtained leave of absence and hastened to his fond parents and friends. Above all he consummated his plighted vows to Elizabeth Page who he promptly led to the hymeneal altar in the good old fashioned way. The tables were covered with spare-ribs, baked pork and beans, pumpkin pies, short cake, gingerbread and dough-nuts. Smiling faces, hearty kisses and good wishes had free course and were not cramped into nonentity by modern etiquette. Imported refinement has been frittering away the richest enjoyments of American life for the last fifty years.

The ensuing spring he repaired to his post in the army and added to his military fame in the reduction of Crown Point and Tie. He served to the end of the French war and saw the English standard wave triumphantly over the Canadas. His bravery forced unqualified applause from his superiors who were subsequently compelled to witness a new edition of his military tactics fresh from the font of liberty.

At the consummation of the conquest of the Canadas he retired to the bosom of his family where he drank deeply of the untold joys of domestic felicity until British tyranny roused him to action in a nobler cause. He had fought in the army of the mother country until her most hated enemy had been conquered on the heights of Abraham. He had been her faithful subject but was not willing to become her slave. He boldly opposed the usurpations of the crown and kindled the fire of patriotism in all around him who had courage to be free. He was prudent but firm as the granite rock. He hoped for the best—prepared for the worst. He delighted in the sunshine of peace but held himself ready to meet the fury of the impending storm should it burst upon his beloved country. He pointed his neighbors to the dark clouds as they rose higher and blacker and urged them to prepare for the approaching crisis. Soon American blood stained the heights of Lexington—the cry—*to arms! to arms!*—rent the air and was carried, as on wings of mighty wind, to the remotest bounds of the down-trodden colonies.

On the reception of this heart-rending news Capt. Stark mounted his horse and hastened to the scene of action. On his way he imparted patriotic fire to those he met urging them to rally at Medford where he would meet them on his return. Large numbers assembled there with their rusty muskets, powder-horns and slugs. By acclamation he was made their leader with the rank of Colonel aided by Lieut. Col. Wyman and Maj. McClary. Ten large companies promptly rallied around him with hearts beating high for their injured bleeding country. The necessary discipline was introduced—all were anxious to learn military tactics. Shortly after the organization of his regiment Col. Stark was ordered by Gen. Ward to examine Noodle's Island for the purpose of locating a battery. With two other officers he repaired to the place designated and returned under a brisk but harmless fire from a British boat in close pursuit. At the battle of Bunker's Hill his regiment seemed invincible. Unbroken and undismayed—his brave soldiers repelled the repeated attacks of the enemy with dreadful slaughter. When ordered to retreat his men reluctantly obeyed the command.

In the service of enlisting troops and obtaining supplies for the army Col. Stark had no superior. His influence was broad and commanding. When Boston was evacuated he marched his regiment to New York to aid in erecting fortifications. The ensuing May he was ordered to Canada. In June he met his troops at St. Johns and proceeded to the mouth of the Sorrel. The unfortunate expedition to Three Rivers was undertaken contrary to his advice. At Chamblee he and his men rendered essential service to the troops at that place then suffering under the small-pox. From there he crossed over to Chimney Point and encamped. When ordered to Ticonderoga by Gen. Schuyler he drew up a formal remonstrance assigning his specific objections and correctly pointed out the disasters that must and did render the expedition abortive. On presenting his views to the General he obeyed the order. When Gen. Gates took command of the northern army he placed Col. Stark over a brigade. Towards the close of that campaign Congress was led into the error of raising several younger Colonels to Brigadiers—a violation of common justice—a source of discord in the army. About the same time Col. Stark marched into Pennsylvania and joined Washington a few days before the battle of Trenton. So poorly shod and disheartened were the soldiers that then composed the mere nucleus of the American army, that they melted the snow with gushing blood from their feet and scalding tears from their eyes. At the battle of Trenton Col. Stark led the vanguard and contributed largely towards obtaining the most important victory of the Revolution. At Princeton he was equally efficient. On retiring to winter quarters at Morristown Washington despatched him to his native state to raise recruits and supplies. In April he was surprised to learn that a new roll of promotions had been made out and his name omitted. He was too patriotic to complain—too high-minded to submit to such ingratitude. He surrendered his commission and retired to his farm—still urging every man to action in the cause of Liberty.

When New Hampshire was called upon to furnish men to oppose the onward march of Burgoyne Gen. Stark was urged to take command of her troops. He informed the Council he was willing to lead the troops where duty called but would not place himself under any power but that of his own state. His terms were promptly accepted. The brave Stark was immediately under way with an independent corps of dauntless soldiers who were ready to follow *him* through storms of iron hail and British thunder. He encamped at Bennington, Vermont, where he was waited upon by Maj. Gen. Lincoln who had orders to conduct the New Hampshire troops to head-quarters. The Maj. Gen. found himself in the wrong box and returned to Gen. Gates who complained to Congress and Washington that Gen. Stark was bent on fighting upon his own hook which he was permitted to do with great effect. Apprised of this apparent discord Burgoyne despatched Col. Baum to cut off the Americans by detail. Gen. Stark determined to give the illustrious visitor a warm reception. On the 13th of August 1777 Baum encamped on an eminence near the town and erected a breastwork of logs–his ardor for a sudden attack having abated. Early the next morning Gen. Stark formed his troops into two divisions of attack and a reserve. The two divisions advanced upon the front and rear of the enemy at the same time and drove them so rapidly upon the reserve that many were killed and most of the balance taken prisoners. In a short time a formidable reinforcement approached from the British army ready to snatch the laurels of victory from the Americans. At that critical moment Col. Warner advanced with his bold Green Mountain boys and kept a far superior number at bay until Gen. Stark could bring all his men into action that could be spared from guarding the prisoners. The red coats were routed and were so generous as to leave their artillery for the use of the patriots. A considerable number of prisoners were taken in the second engagement–the mantle of night saved many more from the same fate. As Gen. Burgoyne advanced, Gen. Stark retired to the vicinity of the American army to take part in a general engagement which he saw must soon occur.

On the 15th September his term of service expired when he returned home with his troops. He immediately reported himself to the council and urged the necessity of sending new recruits at once to aid in capturing the British army. In a few days he joined Gen. Gates with a stronger force than before. He was in favor of a bold movement and placed his troops in the rear to cut off all communication with Lake George. The surrender of Gen. Burgoyne took place soon after when Gen. Stark returned home with his troops. Shortly after his return Congress commissioned him to prepare an expedition against Canada making his head quarters at Albany, New York. He performed the duties assigned him with promptness and fidelity. The project was abandoned and he permitted to return to his family. Early in 1778 he was put in command of the northern department which was in a chaotic condition–with but few troops to protect an extensive frontier–a combination of tories, peculators, defaulters and reckless speculators around him–all tending to render his situation unpleasant and embarrassing. He commenced a rigid reform and continued in the vigorous discharge of his duty until October when he joined Gen. Gates in Rhode Island where he continued until the close of that campaign. During the ensuing winter he was engaged in raising recruits and supplies for the army. The next spring he was stationed in Rhode Island to attend to any calls that might be made by the enemy and received all their visiting parties with such marked promptitude and attention that they took final leave in November. About this time he was ordered to join Gen. Washington in New Jersey with such troops as could be spared from the garrison. The campaign closed without the anticipated battle and Gen. Stark was put upon his usual winter service of obtaining recruits and supplies for the army. Early in the ensuing May he joined Washington at Morristown and was in the battle of the Short Hills. Gen. Washington found it necessary to send him back to New England to obtain more recruits and supplies and concentrate them at West Point. This duty he performed nobly and successfully. He then repaired to his troops at the Liberty Pole in New Jersey. In September he joined Gen. St. Clair. Shortly after that he was ordered to advance near York Island with 2500 men and a large train of wagons and secure all the grain and forage possible and remain their for further orders. He was completely successful, returning to West Point with a large supply of necessaries for the army. On his return he was reduced very low by sickness which rendered him unfit for duty until the next spring when he was put in command of the northern department. He found it in a worse condition than when he took charge of it previously. Tories, spies, traitors and robbers were acting in concert with the army in Canada. Energetic measures were required and adopted. A military post was established at Saratoga. A leader of the plunderers was arrested and his company secured. A British Lieutenant's commission was found upon his person–he was tried by a court martial–condemned as a spy and hung the next day. His friends were threatening and noisy–a copy of the proceedings was sent to Washington–received his unqualified approbation and placed Gen. Stark in a position to restore the department to a healthy tone. He continued at that station until after the surrender of Cornwallis when he returned to his native state for the winter to raise recruits and supplies. It is believed Gen. Stark did more in this service than any one individual during the Revolution.

Deservedly popular, a patriot of the first water, an officer of cool undaunted bravery and great skill–he exerted a large and salutary influence. He was very successful during the winter and reported himself to Gen. Washington early in April–receiving the hearty thanks of the commander-in-chief for his faithful services during the struggle for freedom. At West Point he closed his long and useful military career–took an affectionate leave of his companions in arms–urged upon his troops the propriety of returning to their homes in peaceful and dignified order and of preserving pure and untarnished the rich laurels that decked their manly brows. He was greeted with enthusiastic applause and tears of affection unknown to the present era. He returned to the warm embrace of his dear family and bid a last farewell to public life. His advice was often asked and wisely imparted in public affairs. Quietly and happily he passed down the current of time until the 8th day of May 1822 when his frail bark of earth was moored in the port of death–his immortal spirit in the haven of eternal rest.

In all the private relations of life Gen. Stark was pure beyond all suspicion. He was worthy, virtuous, amiable and honest in the fullest sense of these terms. In reviewing his life we are carried back to that eventful era when the pilgrim fathers held their lives by a slender tenure amidst the red men of the wilderness that they might enjoy that liberty of conscience which is the inalienable gift of God. If all could but faintly realize the value of the blood and treasure that our Liberty cost–the reckless party spirit that is now stripping that Liberty of its richest foliage, would be banished from the heart of every reflecting man–patriotism would revive like drooping plants after a summer shower–demagogues would find their proper level and disorganizers have permission to stay at home or make an excursion up salt river. Then we might more fondly hope for the perpetuity of our glorious UNION–the preservation of that FREEDOM which has been sacredly transmitted to our care.

RICHARD STOCKTON.

DISCRETION is wisdom put in practice. It is the development of a sound judgment and good heart. It seeks a happy equilibrium in all things–aims at pure happiness in time and futurity–seeks to accomplish noble ends by honorable means–shuns every appearance of evil–meets the ills flesh is heir to with Christian fortitude and resignation

It applies the touch stone of plain common sense and Revelation to everything. The discreet man discerns what is clearly right and has moral courage and energy to pursue it. He is cool, deliberate, resolute, strong, efficient. He practices economy without parsimony, benevolence without ostentation, sincerity without dissimulation, goodness without affectation, religion without hypocrisy, power without abuse.

Parents should teach this sterling virtue to their children by precept and example. Teachers should enforce it upon their pupils as the helm of human action. It should be the bright morning star in the political arena–legislative halls–cabinet–executive chamber–international intercourse–courts of justice–seminaries of learning–pulpit–social meetings–domestic circle–family government–juvenile nursery–in short–discretion should regulate all our conduct for time and eternity.

So thought and so acted Richard Stockton, born near Princeton, New Jersey, in October 1730. His great grandfather of the same name came from England in 1670–purchased some 7000 acres of land near Princeton and in 1682 effected the first European settlement made in that part of the Province. On this estate the Stockton family continued to reside happily until driven off by the army of Lord Howe.

Under the instruction of the celebrated Rev. Dr. Samuel Finley, Principal of West Nottingham Academy in Maryland, the talents of Richard were rapidly and strongly developed in early youth. From that seminary he went to the college at Princeton and graduated at the first annual commencement of Nassau Hall in 1748. At the age of eighteen he commenced the study of law under David Ogden then at the head of the New Jersey bar. He studied closely for six years when he was admitted fully prepared for the practice of law. How different the course of law students now. Two years of superficial study is deemed a hardship by some young men. A mere smattering of the elementary principles is imprinted on their *memories* not on their *understandings*. A collegiate diploma and influential friends are thrown into the dangerous breach, a slight examination is made–the young *men* not the young *lawyers*, are admitted to the bar, fully prepared to create litigation and lead their clients into the vortex of error and trouble–perhaps ruin them.

Not so with Mr. Stockton. Years of toil had prepared him to become a safe and judicious adviser. He could clearly discern the right and wrong between litigants–then kindly enforced the one and correct the other by sound reasoning and a lucid exposition of the principles of law and equity applicable to the case. Such lawyers are peace makers–a blessing in community. The reverse are cancers upon society—an annoyance to courts the sepulchres of their clients' money—living nuisances in the commoving mass.

Mr. Stockton opened an office at his paternal mansion and rose rapidly to the zenith of professional eminence. His fame expanded so widely that he was frequently employed to try important suits in other colonies. In 1763 he was honored with the degree of Sergeant at Law. In 1766, he closed his professional career richly rewarded for his faithful and arduous labors. He committed the settlement of his business and his practice to Elias Boudinot who had married his sister and who was well qualified to follow in the steps of his illustrious predecessor.

Anxious to further enrich his mind, in June of that year he embarked for Europe and arrived safely at London. His legal fame had been spread in that country—his visit was anticipated and he was received by the dignitaries of England with marked attention. He was presented at the Court of St. James by one of the Cabinet members and delivered to the King an address from the College of New Jersey, expressive of their joy at the repeal of the peace disturbing Stamp Act.

During his stay in Europe he rendered lasting service to this college by inducing Dr. Witherspoon to become its President pursuant to his recent election to that station—adding another brilliant star to the list of high minded talented patriots who nobly conceived, boldly prosecuted and gloriously consummated the emancipation of the colonies. During his visit he communicated freely with the statesmen of England who were friendly to the cause of constitutional rights and confirmed them more strongly in favor of the Americans.

In February following he visited Edinburgh where he received the kindest attention from those in commission who gave him the freedom of the city and a magnificent public dinner at which he delivered an eloquent and thrilling speech—fully sustaining his reported forensic fame—more than realizing their most sanguine anticipations. His company was courted by the most scientific of that ancient seat of learning. He was made the honored and welcome guest of every nobleman on whom he could call

He also visited Dublin and received the hearty Irish welcome so characteristic of that warm hearted nation. The oppressed situation of that down trodden people convinced him more strongly of the fate that awaited his native country if she yielded to the imperious and humiliating demands of the British ministry. His noble resolves were then and there made—he was prepared for future action.

Mr. Stockton was surprised to find so few in England who understood the situation and character of the Americans–the English were astonished to find so great a man from the western wilderness. Misapprehension often produces disastrous consequences to individuals and nations. The comprehensive mind of this philanthropist readily saw the result of this ignorance of the people of the mother country relative to the colonists and embraced every opportunity to dispel this dark mist that hung over the land of his ancestors like the mantle of night. With many he succeeded–but when those who wield the destiny of a nation are wading in corruption–breathing the atmosphere of tyranny–influenced by sordid avarice–thirsting for a stretch of power–delighting in cruelty and oppression–they dethrone reason–would dethrone Jehovah if they could–defy justice–trample on constitutions and laws–stop at nothing to accomplish their demoniac purposes. Thus acted the British ministers when they turned a deaf ear to the petitions and remonstrances of the Americans and the wise counsels and warning voices of the ablest statesmen in their Parliament. With untiring industry and determined perseverance they wove the web of our Independence and gave it an enduring and beautiful texture before unknown.

The mind of Mr. Stockton was enriched and embellished by his varied intercourse with the great men of the United Kingdom. He had listened to the forensic eloquence and powerful arguments of Blackstone and the other celebrated pleaders in Westminster Hall. He had treasured his mind with the clear and erudite decisions of the learned judges who then graced the English bench. He had witnessed the enrapturing rhetoric of Chatham–the logical genius of Burke–the fascinating manners of Chesterfield and saw Garrick on the flood tide of his glory.

After an absence of a little over a year he embarked for home and arrived in September 1767. He was received with demonstrations of the liveliest joy by his fellow citizens and with great kindness and affection by his relatives.

In consequence of the high opinion of his talents entertained by the king he appointed him to a seat in the Supreme Judiciary and Executive Council in 1769. In 1774 he was appointed an associate judge of the Supreme Court with David Ogden his law preceptor. Two better judges could not have been selected for the people–but to the king they ultimately became as obnoxious as a crown of thorns and plume of thistles.

The revolutionary storm was gathering. Dark clouds were rolling into a conglomerated mass. An awful crisis had arrived. The flames of revenge were spreading like fire on a prairie in autumn. Mr. Stockton was a favorite of the crown. It became necessary for him to choose whom he would serve. The immense influence he wielded made his decision of great importance to the king and Colonies. Now came the test of patriotism. Sordid self and inflated aristocracy could have had no difficulty in deciding. Nor had he, but came to a very different conclusion from most of the crown officers. He knew much of the mother country–he knew and loved his own better. The pomp of kings and pageantry of courts had no charms for him. He was a republican, a patriot, a friend of LIBERTY. In her cause he promptly enlisted–under her banner he took his stand willing to sacrifice kingly favor, property and life in defence of the sacred rights of his bleeding injured country. He carried with him his friend, Rev. Dr. Witherspoon, both of whom were elected to the Continental Congress in June 1776, just in time to immortalize their names by recording them on the Magna Charta of our rights. Mr. Stockton was among its boldest advocates, brandishing the amputating knife fearlessly in public and private circles. Nor did he stand alone. The members of that body soon acquired the art of cutting *five* and *six*. They forged and finished a blade, pure as Damascus steel and placed it in the hands of their proscribed President. At one bold stroke the cords of parental authority were cut asunder. America was redeemed, regenerated and free. LIBERTY dipped her golden pen in the cerulean font of JUSTICE and recorded the names of the FIFTY-SEVEN upon the shining tablet of enduring fame. Heaven smiled its approbation–angels shouted for joy–nations gazed with admiring wonder–every patriot responded a loud–AMEN!!!

The rich store of information, matured experience, soaring talent and enrapturing eloquence of Mr. Stockton–rendered him one of the most useful members of that Congress. His acute knowledge of law, political economy, human nature, chartered rights and of men and things–commanded the respect and esteem of all his colleagues. He performed every duty with zeal, industry and integrity. In the autumn of 1776 he was sent with George Clymer to inspect the northern army, with power to supply its wants and correct any existing abuses. In the able discharge of this duty they had the approbation of Congress and the army.

Soon after his return Mr. Stockton was called to remove his family to save his wife and children from the proverbial brutality of the approaching enemy. In the effort to do this he was taken prisoner and in the most inhuman manner taken to New York and consigned to the common prison. He was deprived of every comfort–kept twenty-four hours without any provision and then received a coarse and scanty supply–the British violating the laws of humanity–of nations and all rules of civilized warfare. This base treatment impaired his health and laid the foundation of disease that hastened his death. His capture was effected by the information of a Tory who was subsequently indicted and punished for his perfidy.

This abuse of one of its members roused the indignation of Congress. Gen. Washington was directed to send a flag of truce to Gen. Howe and through great exertions finally obtained the release of Mr. Stockton. Simultaneous with his capture the demoniac enemy committed to the flames his extensive library, papers and everything combustible–leaving his highly ornamented plantation a blackened waste.

Oppressed by want and disease he was unable again to take his seat in Congress but continued to be a consulted counsellor in public affairs at his residence near Princeton. His opinions had great weight and proved a national blessing. Among his complicated diseases he had a painful cancer upon his neck. He endured his severe affliction with Christian fortitude up to the 28th of February 1781 when death relieved him from pain and consigned him to the peaceful kingdom of the dead. At his exit to the world of spirits many warm hearts were sad–thousands dropped the sympathetic tear–our nation mourned the loss of a valued son.

Thus prematurely closed the brilliant career of one of the bright luminaries of that eventful period. His science and knowledge were unusually extensive. He was the first Chief Justice of his state under the new constitution. He acquitted himself nobly in all the relations of life– lawyer, judge, statesman, patriot, gentleman, citizen, friend, husband, father, Christian and man. He was an ornament to society–an honor to his country and a blessing to mankind.

THOMAS STONE.

The man who has a just sense of the responsibilities of a high public office is the last to seek it. The more clearly a sensible unassuming man perceives the magnitude of a public trust the more he mistrusts his capacity to discharge its duties–yet such a man is the very one to be trusted. It was with great diffidence that Washington assumed the command of the American armies. No one can be pointed out who possessed as fully all the requisites to meet the times that tried the souls and bodies of men. John Hancock quailed under his appointment to the

Presidential Chair of Congress. No one manifested more firmness in the cause of freedom—no one could have filled that chair with more dignity.

It is only in times of danger that men of the greatest worth become most conspicuous. They are then sought for by the virtuous portion of community. In times of peace and prosperity the same men may be called to the councils of a nation without exciting great applause whilst the names of noisy demagogue politicians are carried over the world on the wings of venal partisan prints and held up as the conservators of the body politic. It is at such times that our best men shrink from the public gaze. It is at such times that the canker worm of political intrigue carries on the work of death. It is at such times that peculation stalks abroad at noon day with hideous form and unblushing impudence. It is at such times that the conclave caucusers consume the midnight oil to concoct plans to dupe the dozing people and secure to themselves the loaves and fishes. It is only in times of strong commotion and certain peril that men of sterling merit become most prominent and are duly appreciated. This fact was fully demonstrated during the American Revolution. Many were then called to deliberate in the solemn assemblies who had not been previously known as public men and who retired when the mighty work of Independence was completed. They were selected for their discretion, honesty, wisdom, firmness and patriotism.

Of this class was Thomas Stone, a descendant of William Stone who was governor of Maryland during the reign of Cromwell. He was born at Pointon Manor, Charles County, Maryland in 1743. He was well educated under the instruction of a Scotch clergyman and read law with Thomas Johnson of Annapolis. He commenced a successful practice at that place and was held in high estimation by the community in which he lived. Modest, unassuming, industrious, a close student, a judicious counsellor and an honest man—he was admired and beloved for his substantial worth and sterling merit. He possessed a clear head, sound judgment and good heart. His mind was vigorous, analyzing, investigating and philosophical. He was a friend to equal rights and delighted in seeing every one happy. He detested oppression in all its various shades from the abuse of a worm up to the capstone of the climax of creation—Man. He was patriotic, kind, noble, benevolent, generous.

With such feelings he could not carelessly look upon the oppressions of the Grenville administration. When the Stamp Act was passed he was a youth in politics but the discussions upon its odiousness deeply interested him. He was an attentive listener and a thorough investigator. His opposition to such encroachments became firm. A holy indignation was awakened in his manly bosom and prepared him for future action. Still he avoided the public gaze. In private circles he conversed freely, lucidly and understandingly upon the subject of American rights and British wrongs. But just previous to his being called by his country to deliberate in her councils could he be induced to mount the rostrum in the forum and display his very respectable forensic powers. When the Boston Port Bill was proclaimed Mr. Stone surmounted the barriers of diffidence and came out boldly against abused power. His example had a salutary influence upon those around him. All knew there must be something radically wrong–that some portentous cloud hung over the Colonies if Thomas Stone was roused to public action. In times of peril the influence of such men is of the highest value. The declaimer who is always on hand at public meetings charged with a Niagara cataract of words must be a Demosthenes or Cicero to long keep a strong hold upon the hearts of the people. And if he does so his influence is only popular–not of that deep-toned kind that moves the living mass only from a deliberate conviction of imperative duty. The cool, the reflecting, the calculating, the timid and the wavering are operated upon magically when they see such a man as Thomas Stone go boldly forward and advocate a cause that they at first believed problematical.

On the 8th of December 1774 he was elected to the Continental Congress and took his seat on the 15th of the ensuing May. The meeting had been deeply solemn and imposing the year before but at that time increased responsibilities rested upon the members. The cry of blood was ringing in their ears–the fury of the revolutionary storm was increasing–the clash of arms and mortal combat had commenced–the vials of British wrath were unsealed–civil government was at an end. To meet such a crisis required the wisdom of Solon, the patriotism of Cincinnatus, the acuteness of Locke, the eloquence of Demosthenes and Cicero, the caution of Tacitus, the learning of Atticus, the energy of Virginius, the honesty of Socrates, the justice of Aristides, the boldness of Cæsar, the perseverance of Hannibal, the concentrated and harmonious action of all the colonies. These qualities were all represented by the members of the Continental Congress to a degree that has no parallel in history. Mr. Stone commenced his legislative duties with vigor and prosecuted them with zeal. He was at first trammelled by instructions from the Maryland Assembly the members of which hoped for peace without recourse to arms. Increasing oppressions soon removed this injunction and enabled him to join in all measures calculated to promote the cause of Independence. When the millennial sun of LIBERTY rose upon the new world on the 4th of July 1776 Mr. Stone was at his post and became a subscribing witness to the dissolution of that unequal partnership where the labor had been performed by one party and the profits consumed by the other.

Mr. Stone retired from Congress in 1777. He had been a faithful laborer in the committee rooms—an influential member in the House. He had bestowed much time and thought upon the Articles of Confederation and felt bound to remain until they were perfected and adopted. That important work completed he left the national Council carrying with him the esteem of his co-workers in the cause of freedom, the approbation of a good conscience and the gratitude of his constituents. In 1778 he was elected to the Maryland legislature and became an important and influential member. During that session the Articles of Confederation that he had aided in framing at the preceding Congress were submitted for consideration. At first they met with strong opposition. Better understanding them Mr. Stone was able to meet every objection and was largely instrumental in their adoption. In 1783 he again took his seat in Congress and fully sustained his high reputation for usefulness. Devoted to the best interests of his country, free from political ambition, sincere in his profession of republican principles, frank in his intercourse, honest in his purposes—he was safely entrusted with every station he was called to fill. He was present when Washington resigned his commission and retired from the field of epic glory to the peaceful shades of Mount Vernon amidst the loud plaudits of admiring millions and the mingled tears of joy and gratitude that stood like pearly dew-drops in the eyes of his countrymen and compatriots in arms.

The ensuing year Mr. Stone closed his labors in Congress and retired from the public arena. During the last session of his services he frequently presided and was esteemed highly as President *pro tempore* by all the members for his ability, dignity and impartiality. As a further mark of esteem he was elected to the convention in 1787 that framed the Federal Constitution but declined any further public service and did not attend. On the 5th of October the same year he was suddenly called from the judicial Bar of Port Tobacco, Maryland, to the Bar of the Judge of quick and dead to render an account of his stewardship. His decease was deeply lamented by his numerous friends, a grateful nation and millions of freemen.

Mr. Stone was cut off in the prime of life, in the midst of a brilliant career of usefulness with the prospect of future honors opening brightly before him. He lived long enough to be extensively useful and earned a rich fame—imperishable as the pages of history—lasting as human intelligence. From the moment he first took his place in society to the present—the tongue of slander or the breath of detraction have never attempted to cast a slur upon his reputation as a public man or private citizen. He was a rare model of discretion, propriety and usefulness—a true specimen of the Simon pure salt of the body politic, rendering efficient services to his country without noise or parade and without the towering talents of a Henry. Such men are above all price and can be relied upon in the hour of danger as safe sentinels to guard the best interests of our nation. We have more of the same sort who are living in retirement. Let the people break them in and bring them out that our UNION may be preserved.

GEORGE TAYLOR.

A PURELY republican government is enrapturing in theory. To reduce this beautiful theory to successful operation the body politic must be sound and healthful in all its parts. It must be wielded by enlightened rulers whose hearts are free from guile, whose judgments are strong and matured, whose characters are without reproach, whose conduct is always consistent, whose patriotism extinguishes all self, whose virtue lifts them above all temptation to digress from the most exalted honesty and rigid morality, whose minds are stored with useful knowledge—large experience and whose souls are imbued with wisdom from above.

In such a condition and in such hands this kind of government is calculated to bring out and elevate the intellectual powers of man, unfold to the mind correct and liberal principles, promote social order and general happiness by diffusing its radiant light, its refulgent rays, its benign influence to the remotest bounds of the human family. In such a condition and in such hands it would become the solar fountain of mental improvement, the polar star of soaring genius, the brilliant galaxy of expanding science, the prolific field of religious enterprise, a shining light to benighted man. Its sunbeams of living light would warm into mellow life the ignorant, the oppressed, the forlorn. Its harmonious links would form a golden chain that would encircle earth and reach to heaven. It would be a messenger of peace inviting the weary pilgrims of bondage in every clime to a reposing asylum of peaceful, quiescent rest. This is the kind of government the Sages and Heroes of the American Revolution aimed to form and have perpetuated by posterity.

Among those who laid the foundation and commenced the superstructure of our growing Republic was George Taylor, born in Ireland in 1716. His father was a clergyman and gave him a good education. He then placed him with a physician under whose direction he commenced the study of medicine. Not fancying the idea of becoming a son of Æsculapius he flew the course and without money or the knowledge of his friends entered as a redemptioner on board a vessel bound for Philadelphia. Soon after his arrival his passage was paid by Mr. Savage of Durham, Bucks County, Pennsylvania, for which George bound himself as a common laborer for a term of years. This gentleman carried on iron works and appointed his new servant to the office of *filler*–his work being to throw coal into the furnace when in blast. His hands became cruelly blistered but being ambitious to gain the approbation of all around him he persevered without a complaint. Learning his situation his humane master entered into a conversation with him and was surprised to find him possessed of a good education and superior talents. He immediately promoted him to a clerkship in the counting house. He filled his station admirably and gained the esteem and friendship of all his new acquaintances. He endeavored to improve by everything he saw, heard and read. His reflecting and reasoning powers became rapidly developed. He made himself acquainted with the formula of business, the customs and laws of his adopted country and reduced to practice the theories he had acquired at school. To add to his importance in society Mr. Savage was removed by death and after the usual season of mourning had passed, the widow Savage became Mrs. Taylor and Mr. Taylor came in possession of a large property and a valuable and influential wife. By persevering industry and good management he continued to add to the estate and in a few years purchased a tract of land on the bank of the Lehigh River in Northampton County upon which he built a splendid mansion and iron works, making it his place of residence. Not being prospered there he removed back to Durham. During his residence in Northampton County he became extensively and favorably known.

In 1764 he was elected to the provincial Assembly and took a prominent part in its deliberations. He was endowed with a strong mind, clear perception and sound judgment. He had not been an idle spectator or careless observer of passing events or of subjects discussed. He had examined the principles upon which various governments were predicated and became enraptured with the republican system. He had closely observed the increasing advances of British oppression. He had not imported a large share of love for the mother country. He was too patriotic to tamely submit to the English yoke. So fully had he gained the confidence of his fellow citizens that he was placed upon the important committee of grievances. He took a bold stand against the corruptions of the proprietary government and strongly advocated an alteration of the charter that peculation might be diminished and abuses corrected.

The ensuing year he was again elected to the Assembly and was one of the committee that prepared instructions for the delegates to Congress that convened in New York in 1765 to adopt measures for the restoration and preservation of colonial rights. This document combined caution and respect with firmness of purpose and deliberation of action. It instructed the delegates to move within the orbit of constitutional and chartered rights and to respectfully but clearly admonish the mother country and her advisers not to travel out of the same circle. Shortly after that the Stamp Act was repealed. Mr. Taylor was on the committee to prepare a congratulatory address to the king on the happy event. So ably did he discharge his public duties that he was uniformly placed upon several of the standing committees of great importance, assigning to him an onerous portion of legislative duties. Upon the committee of grievances, assessment of taxes, judiciary, loans on bills of credit, navigation, to choose a printer of public laws, the name of George Taylor was generally found and often the first. He was a member of the Assembly for six consecutive years. In 1768 he was upon a committee to prepare an address to the governor censuring him for a remissness of duty in not bringing to condign punishment certain offenders who had openly and barbarously murdered several Indians thereby provoking retaliation. It was respectful and manly but keen and cutting as a Damascus blade. It was a lucid exposition of political policy, sound law, equal justice and public duty. In 1775 Mr. Taylor was one of the committee of safety for Pennsylvania, then virtually the organ of government. The awful crisis had arrived when American blood was crying for vengeance. The revolutionary storm had commenced–the mountain waves of British wrath were rolling over the Colonies. Firmness, sound discretion and boldness of action were required. Mr. Taylor possessed and endeavoured to inspire these requisites in others. He was a faithful sentinel in the cause of freedom–not a blazing luminary but a reliable light. Although cautious he was not affected by the temporizing spirit that paralyzed many who desired Liberty but preferred that others should fight for it. He continued to exercise a salutary influence in the Assembly until the summer of 1776 when he became a member of the Continental Congress and sanctioned the principles of freedom he had boldly advocated by his vote for and signature upon the Magna Charta of our Liberty. Although he did not tempt the giddy height of declamation Mr. Taylor knew where and when to speak, what to say and how to vote—the highest qualifications of a legislator.

In the spring of 1777 he retired from public life crowned with the honors of a devoted and ardent patriot, an industrious and useful legislator, an enlightened and valuable citizen, a worthy and honest man. On the 23d of February 1781 he closed his eyes upon terrestrial things, bid a last farewell to earth and its toils and bowed submissively to the king of terrors. He died at Easton, Pennsylvania, where he had but recently removed.

From this brief sketch of Mr. Taylor the reader may learn that without the luminous talents of a Lee, the towering intellect of a Jefferson or the profound researches of a Franklin, a man can be substantially useful and render important services to his country and the world. In the grand machinery of human society there is a place for every individual to occupy. Let all fulfil the design of their creation and exert their best energies to preserve our blood-bought LIBERTY and perpetuate our glorious UNION until TIME shall be merged in ETERNITY.

MATTHEW THORNTON.

THE study of human nature is one of the highest importance but criminally neglected. Many who do undertake it begin at the wrong place. They commence upon their neighbors instead of first exploring the avenues of their own nature and there learning the thousand springs that put their own machinery in motion. In no other school can we successfully acquire this branch of knowledge. Self examination is deplorably neglected. But few men know themselves and are sadly mistaken when they suppose they fully understand those around them. To a large portion of the human family man is a sealed book. But few parents study or understand the nature and disposition of their children. If asked to define them they would succeed no better than the unlettered red man would in expounding geology and botany. Both live in the midst of the subjects of investigation but only know them by sight. Upon the closest application we can only arrive at general rules by which to try others. I deny the hackneyed doctrine that the minutiæ of human nature is the same in every individual. It cannot be deduced from an examination of man mentally or physically. It cannot be shown from analogy in the laws of nature. It cannot be proved by revelation but the reverse. Hence so few become masters of this intricate study. The error lies in looking at human nature as a mass. The man who does not understand geology may be shown every variety of rock selected and placed in layers before him and he can give you but one name for the whole–*rock*. The same with reference to the other departments in the kingdom of nature. So in the great machinery of society. Every observing person knows that what will impel *one* man to do certain acts would not move *another* one inch. Apply a great principle that operates upon every man–say the law of self-preservation–its operation is not alike on different persons. On the field of battle I have noticed a striking difference in the effect upon different men. This was exemplified at the commencement and during the American Revolution. The machinery that was put in motion was composed of wheels from the smallest to the largest and springs of every elasticity. To rouse the people to a becoming sense of their injured rights and induce them to rise in the majesty of their might and vindicate them, was the first business of the illustrious patriots who boldly achieved our Independence. To effect this all the varied forms of eloquence were necessary–the rushing torrent of logic that overwhelms–the keen sarcasm that withers and the mild and winning persuasion that leads.

The latter talent was the forte of Matthew Thornton born in Ireland in 1714 and came to this country with his father in 1717 who settled at Wiscasset in Maine. This son received a good academical education and was greatly admired for industry, correct deportment and blandness of manners. After completing his course at school he commenced the study of medicine with Dr. Grant of Leicester, Mass. He made rapid progress in the acquisition of that important department of science and gave great promise of future usefulness. When he finished his course he commenced practice in Londonderry, N. H. which was principally settled by people from his native country. He soon acquired a lucrative business and the confidence of his numerous patrons. In the expedition against Cape Breton, then belonging to the French, he was appointed surgeon to the New Hampshire division of the army and performed his duty with great skill and credit.

He was an early and prominent advocate of American rights–a bold and uniform opposer of British usurpations. He had a great opportunity to disseminate liberal principles among the people and most effectually improved it. When the revolutionary storm burst upon the Colonies he had command of a regiment. He had filled various important offices which had made him widely and favorably known. His urbanity of manners, sincerity of purpose and uncommon powers of persuasion gave him great influence in private intercourse and public assemblies.

He was President of the first convention of New Hampshire after the expulsion of kingly government. At the commencement of the Revolution the people of that province did not form into line with the patriots but Dr. Thornton and other kindred spirits soon brought them into the rank and file of opposition to the invading foe and banished from them all fugitive fear. In 1774 they sent delegates to Congress and came nobly up to the work. In December of that year several members of the committee of safety in the town of Portsmouth entered the fort and carried off one hundred barrels of gun powder before the governor could rally crownites to prevent them. Great Britain had prohibited the exportation of this article to the Colonies.

Soon after the flight of Gov. Wentworth upon being apprised of the battle of Lexington, an address was prepared and published by a provincial committee over the signature of Matthew Thornton President. To the young reader this may seem not important unless informed that it was evidence to convict him of high treason and consign him to the gallows had he fallen into the hands of the British. The address was written in strong and bold language. Sample—" You must all be sensible that the affairs of America have come to an affecting crisis. The horrors and distresses of a civil war which of late we only had in contemplation, we now find ourselves obliged to realize. Painful, beyond expression, have been those scenes of blood and devastation which the barbarous cruelties of British troops have placed before our eyes. Duty to God, to ourselves, to posterity—enforced by the cries of slaughtered innocents, have urged us to take up arms in our own defence. Such a day as this was never before known either to us or our fathers. We would therefore recommend to the Colony at large to cultivate that Christian union, harmony and tender affection which constitute the only foundation upon which our invaluable privileges can rest with any security or our public measures be pursued with the least prospect of success."

On the 10th of January 1776, Dr. Thornton was appointed a judge of the Superior Court of New Hampshire. On the 12th of September of the same year he was elected to the Continental Congress and when he took his seat, affixed his name to the Declaration of Independence. It may be supposed by many that those who signed this instrument, so often referred to, were all present on the memorable 4th of July when it was adopted. This was not the case. Messrs. Franklin, Rush, Clymer, Wilson, Ross, Carroll, Taylor and others, as in the case of Dr. Thornton, were not members on that day. Finding the measure would probably be sanctioned by a majority, fear seized several members who resigned their seats and run for dear life. Let their names rest in oblivion. The name of Thomas McKean is not upon the printed records although he was present and signed the Declaration at the time of its adoption. Henry Wisner a member from Orange County, New York, was present and signed the original manuscript whose name has never been properly recognized. He was a highly respectable member and a fearless patriot. How these errors occurred cannot now be told.

Dr. Thornton ably discharged the important duties of his station until his services were required upon the Bench. On the 24th of December of the same year he was re-elected to Congress and served until the 22d of January following, when he took his final leave of the National Legislature highly esteemed by his colleagues, enjoying the approval of his constituents and the proud consciousness of having performed his duty toward his country and his God.

For six years he served on the Bench of the Superior Court and on that of Chief Justice of the Common Pleas, the combined duties rendering his services arduous. He filled these stations with dignity and impartiality. In 1779 he removed to Exeter and soon after purchased a farm upon the bank of the Merrimack river that he might enjoy that repose his advanced age required. But in this he was disappointed. He became a member of the General Court and served in the State Senate from that time up to 1785. On the 25th of January 1784 he was appointed a justice of the peace and quorum throughout the state, an important office under the original constitution but abridged in jurisdiction by amendments in 1792. In 1785 he retired from the political arena but continued to afford salutary counsel on all important matters involving the public good. During the controversy between his state and Vermont relative to disputed territory, he wrote several letters to those in power urging conciliatory measures and unconditional submission to the decision of Congress. They were highly creditable to him as a writer and a discreet man. In public or private matters he was a peace maker.

Dr. Thornton was a large portly man over six feet in height, well proportioned with an expressive countenance lighted up with keen piercing black eyes. He was one of the most fascinating men of his time. He was seldom known to smile but was cheerful, entertaining and instructive—in many respects similar to Dr. Franklin. His mind was stored with a rich variety of useful knowledge which rendered him an interesting companion. He sustained an unblemished private character and discharged all the social relations of life with faithfulness and fidelity. He was wisely opposed to sectarianism—belonged to no church but was devoutly pious, exemplifying primitive Christianity in all the beauty of practical development and apostolic simplicity. He was a regular attendant of public worship.

He was a kind husband, an affectionate father and a good neighbor. He was exact in collecting his dues and as exact in paying his creditors. The poor he never pressed. If he found they were unable to pay he cancelled their account. He was kind, charitable and liberal.

He died at Newburyport, Mass. on the 24th of June 1803, whilst on a visit with his daughter. His remains were conveyed to New Hampshire and deposited near Thornton's Ferry on the bank of the Merrimack river where a neat marble slab rests over his dust with the following laconic and significant epitaph.

MATTHEW THORNTON,
AN HONEST MAN.

JOSEPH B. VARNUM.

The man who despises labor and treats the working man as an inferior being—except on the eve of an election or time of war—should never be elevated to an office of honor or profit. Such men seem to forget that every article used is the result of labor. They do not realize that the working classes are the original producers of the physical comforts they enjoy. I refer particularly to those who dig the soil, work our minerals, shape our timber—manufacture our fabrics and conduct our commerce—the bone and sinew of our country who have raised it to a scale of grandeur unparalleled in point of greatness in so short a time. By the force of labor our lands, wilderness, minerals, rivers, lakes—all have been made the means of rapidly advancing the prosperity of our expanding nation. Labor is a dignity conferred on man by his Creator—a dignity that is highly appreciated by all sensible men. Aristocracy depreciates it to make serfs and reduce its value. Monopolists often undervalue it to increase their sordid gains by short allowance and poor pay. Demagogues look down upon it and aim to impress the working man with their assumed fictitious superiority that they may obtain his vote by a little condescending familiarity just before election. Away with all this trash and much more that might be named. Let the laborer assume his proper dignity—know and feel that without him our country would become a barren waste—our improvements moulder in ruins—our nation rush back to original chaos. All should be employed in some laudable manner. Idleness is not sanctioned by nature, ethics, theology—Pagan or Christian philosophy—by experience or common sense. Man was made for action—noble and god-like action. Working men of America! on you depends the onward and upward course of these United States. On you rests the high responsibility of perpetuating our glorious UNION. You have the votes—if you think, judge and act with intelligence and independence—all will be right. If you are made the abject tools of dishonest politicians—LIBERTY is lost—FREEDOM is gone.

The Sages and Heroes of the American Revolution were actively laborious. Most of them were from the classes above enumerated. Washington and Jefferson thought it a respectable healthful exercise to work on their plantations. Among those who did not despise labor and highly appreciated the working man—was Joseph B. Varnum, born in Dracut, Massachusetts, in 1750. He was raised upon a farm and left his plough to do battle for his bleeding country. He had acquired a good English education—had studied men and things thoroughly—understood the rights of the Colonies and strongly felt the wrongs imposed upon them by mother Britain. He promptly rendered his best services to advance the cause of human rights. He became an active military man and filled various posts—up to Major General of militia. He was long conspicuous in the political field. He warmly approved of the Declaration of Independence and every measure calculated to advance the cause of Liberty and drive from our shores the last vestige of British power. He was also a zealous advocate for the adoption of the Federal Constitution and a member of the Massachusetts Convention that sanctioned it. "Federalist" was first applied to those who were warmly in favor of this sacred instrument—"Democrat" to the opposite party. Those who understand the doctrines of the various governments can comprehend the terms.

Gen. Varnum was repeatedly elected to the legislature of Massachusetts. He was long a member of the House of Representatives and Senate of the United States and speaker of the lower house at a time when the storm of party spirit increased to a tornado and threatened to dash the ship of state upon the rocks of dissolution. Under all circumstances he was calm, collected, impartial, just and independent. Nothing could induce him to swerve from the stern path of strict integrity. Party spirit had no charms or terrors for him. The good of his whole country he aimed to promote regardless of personal consequences. Beyond or short of that he had no favors to ask or grant. Would to God that all our public men were of the same stamp at the present day.

After filling the measure of his country's glory, Gen. Varnum retired from public life to his paternal mansion in Dracut to enjoy the refreshing comforts of domestic life. There he glided peacefully down the stream of time until the 11th of September 1821 when he was taken suddenly ill and became fully sensible he must enter upon the untried scenes of eternity in a few hours. He called his family around him—arranged his earthly concerns—directed that no military display should be made at his funeral—that it should be conducted without vain pomp—appointed his pall-bearers and slumbered in death. Not a stain rests on the fair escutcheon of his public or private character.

GEORGE WALTON.

In this enlightened age and in our free country, ignorance is a voluntary misfortune arising from idleness—the parent of want, vice and shame. Under the benevolent arrangements of the present day every child, youth, woman and man can have access to books and generally to schools. At no former age of the world has the mantle of education been so widely spread. All who will may drink at the pure fountain of intelligence and walk in the light. They may obtain that knowledge which will lead them to the green pastures of virtue—the parent of earthly happiness and heavenly joys. By a proper improvement of time the plough boys of the field—the mill boys of the slashes and the apprentice boys of the shops may lay in a stock of useful information that will enable them to take a respectable stand by the side of those who know more of colleges but less of men and things. Instances of this kind have occurred and I trust will be rapidly increased. Youth and young men of America—in your own hands are the materials of future fame and usefulness. Neglect to properly improve them, oblivial obscurity or withering infamy will be your fate. You are the architects of your own fortunes. You will rise in the scale of respectability and importance just in proportion to the correct culture of your mental powers. Your immortal minds cannot be dormant. If you do not sow the seeds of wisdom noxious weeds will grow spontaneously and leave you to reap the whirlwind of keen regret and consuming anguish. Youth and young men of America—if you desire the perpetuity of that Liberty purchased by the blood and treasure of your ancestors—store your minds with useful knowledge. If you love a Republic more than monarchy, freedom more than slavery, religious liberty more than hierarchy—store your minds with useful knowledge. Imitate the bright examples of those whose history is spread upon the pages of this book who raised themselves to usefulness, fame and glory by the force of their own exertions.

In the history of George Walton another striking instance of this kind is beautifully illustrated. He was born in Frederic County, Virginia, in 1740. Without any school education he was apprenticed to a morose carpenter at an early age, who was too penurious to allow George a candle to read by although an unusually active and faithful boy. Fortunately pine knots were plenty and free. By the light of these he prosecuted his studies during his boyhood and youth. He fulfilled his indentures to the letter. When manhood dawned upon him he was free in person and mind. He had accumulated a rich stock of useful knowledge to what purpose the sequel will show. This he had acquired alone by untiring industry during those hours of night when a large proportion of boys and youth are either reposing in the embrace of Morpheus or hastening on their ruin by associating with corrupt and vicious companions—demonstrating most clearly that ignorance is a voluntary misfortune—that man is the architect of his own character.

At the age of twenty-one Mr. Walton went to Georgia and read law under Henry Young and became a safe counsellor and able advocate. During his investigation of the principles laid down by Blackstone and other elementary writers, he was forcibly impressed with the gross violations of the charter and constitutional rights of the Colonies. The more closely he investigated the more his indignation was roused. He freely expressed his views and feelings and was among the first to oppose the high-handed policy of the British cabinet. He found a few kindred spirits—but by a large majority the crown was sustained in Georgia longer than in any other colony. Many desired freedom but believed its attainment a visionary idea. They preferred present sufferings rather than make an abortive attempt to disenthrall themselves lest heavier burthens should be placed upon them. They felt their own weakness—they dreaded the power of England. Not so with George Walton and a few others who had clustered around him. No display of chains or bayonets could intimidate them. To die in the cause of Liberty was more glorious in their view than to wear the shackles of a tyrant. They were determined never to bend a knee to kings or sacrifice at the altar of monarchy. Freedom or death was their motto.

In order to test the public mind Messrs. Walton, Noble, Bullock and Houston published a notice over their proper signatures, calling a public meeting to be held at the Liberty Pole, Tondee's tavern, Savannah, on the 27th of July 1774 for the purpose of considering the constitutional rights and privileges of the American Colonies. This was the first Liberty pole planted in that state—the first meeting that was held on that subject. A large concourse of citizens assembled—an intense anxiety was manifest—hearts beat more quickly—the heaving bosom, the deep sigh, the quivering lip—all told that the meeting was one big with importance. Soon George Walton rose with a dignity peculiar to a man who knows he is right. With the profoundness of an able lawyer—the wisdom of a sage and the eloquence of a Henry—he portrayed American rights and British wrongs in such glowing colors that a stream of patriotic fire ran through the hearts of his audience that concentrated into a broad and unextinguishable flame. A committee was appointed to rouse the people to a sense of impending danger. Governor Wright, with his hireling phalanx, used great exertions to obtain a written pledge from the inhabitants of each parish to sustain the mother country and submit more implicitly to the yoke of bondage. Promises of redress were made only to be broken. But the fire of patriotism had commenced its insulating course. From Mr. Walton and his companions the burning flame spread from heart to heart, from sire to son, from parish to parish and rushing to a common centre rose in one broad sheet of light—illuminating the horizon of Liberty with cheering refulgence. Many of the more timid patriots of Georgia were long perched on the pivot of indecision. Self-interest and self-preservation caused many to remain inactive for a time—but what persuasion could not do the increasing insults from the crown officers soon effected and roused them to action. Mr. Walton did much to remove the incipient paralysis and produce a healthy tone in the body politic. All the other colonies had united in the glorious cause of freedom—that his state should form a doubtful rear-guard was irksome to his noble spirit. But he stood firm at his post. His exertions became equal to the herculean task he had undertaken. His powers of mind rose with the magnitude of the occasion—his eloquence and logic bore down every opponent who dared confront him.

When the cry of blood—of *murder*—was raised on the heights of Lexington and reverberated from hill to dale, it came upon the Georgians like a clap of thunder without a cloud. The people started from their reverie—burst the cords that bound them—rose in the majesty of their power—buckled on their armor and bid defiance to the British lion. In

May 1775 the Parish of St. Johns sent Lyman Hall to the Continental Congress and in July four colleagues took their seats with him. The Council of Safety was reorganized and vigorous measures adopted to resist the encroachments of imported dictators. In January 1776 the legislature appointed Mr. Bullock President of the Executive Council. He was a bold and active patriot and very obnoxious to the crown officers. Gov. Wright threatened the members with bayonets—the next hour he was their prisoner and permitted the liberty of his own house only upon his parol of honor. This he violated—fled on board the armed fleet in the harbor—commenced an attack upon the town—was badly whipped and glad to flee from the vengeance of an insulted and enraged people. British authority was at an end in that Province.

In February 1776 Mr. Walton was elected to the Continental Congress and entered upon the high duties of legislation. He was a bold and efficient advocate of every measure calculated to advance the cause of Independence. He warmly supported the Declaration of Rights and proved his sincerity by his vote and signature. Excepting 1779 when he was Governor of Georgia, he was a member of Congress until 1781. He was raised to work and being placed on many committees showed that he could still endure a vast amount of labor. When Congress was compelled to retire to Baltimore on the 13th of December 1776, Messrs. Morris, Clymer and Walton were left as superintendents to aid the army with $200,000 in funds. Mr. Walton was also a member of the Treasury Board and Marine Committee. In every station he ably discharged his duty. In 1777 he performed a very important act in the drama of life by marrying the accomplished daughter of Mr. Chamber.

In 1778 he became Col. Walton and behaved with great gallantry in the battle at Savannah between the American troops and the British. The regiment under his command made a desperate fight until their Colonel was severely wounded, fell from his horse and was taken prisoner. After his wound would permit he was sent to Sunbury and confined with the other prisoners. He was soon after exchanged and returned to Congress. In January 1783 he was appointed Chief Justice of Georgia. He also filled the gubernatorial chair a second time. He was one of the commissioners that effected a treaty with the Cherokee Indians. He discharged all the onerous duties imposed upon him with credit to himself and usefulness to his country. At one time he was involved in an apparent difficulty which was as singular as it proved harmless and lost none of its romance in the end. During the war a jealousy existed between the civil and military authority in

Georgia. Judge Walton was at the head of the former–Gen. McIntosh at the head of the latter. In 1779, when Judge Walton was first Governor of the state, a forged letter, purporting to be from the legislature, was forwarded to Congress requesting the removal of the General. The governor was charged with a knowledge of the transaction–positively denied it–but few if any believed it. It became a party matter–a vote of censure was passed upon him by the same legislature that had appointed him Chief Justice the day previous–the Attorney General was directed to institute proceedings against him in the Court over which he presided–the only one that had jurisdiction over the offence charged. That was the finale of the great bubble. It was more like a modern political demagogue compromise than any farce found in the history of that eventful period. It inflicted no injury on the fair fame of Judge Walton.

During his latter years Judge Walton confined his public duties to the Bench of the Superior Court. Though the intervals between terms he enjoyed the rich comforts of domestic life with his faithful wife and an only son. He was not wealthy–was free from avarice and was contented with the competence afforded by his public emoluments and the produce of a small plantation. He indulged in good living. Previous to his last illness he suffered much from the gout and other complicated derangements of his system. His useful career was closed on the 2d of February 1803.

Judge Walton was a close student during his whole life. He added to his large experience a general knowledge of the sciences and became an ornament to the judiciary of his state. He was a ready writer and very satirical upon vice and folly. He was of a warm temperament, resenting every indignity but honorable and just, moving within the orbit of consistency under all circumstances showing clearly that the wildest passions may be controlled by wise discretion. He was a stranger to disguise, ardent in his attachments, firm in his purposes, stern and reserved in his manners in general intercourse but free and familiar in the private circle with his friends. He was an open and manly opponent. He was fond of brevity in all things, systematic in his public and private arrangements and remarkable for punctuality.

Taken as a whole Judge Walton was one of the most useful men of his day and generation. His examples are worthy the imitation of the apprentice, the student, lawyer, judge and statesman. By the force of industry he rose from the humblest walks of life to the most dignified stations within the gift of his constituents. Youth and young men of America–ponder well the history of George Walton. Let it stimulate you to embrace every opportunity for improvement–drink often and freely at the crystal fountain of useful knowledge now open to all. Remember, O! remember that you are the architects of your own fortunes. Soon the affairs of a mighty nation, the destiny of increasing millions will devolve upon you. Prepare yourselves to assume the high stations you must fill–for weal or for wo will depend upon the fitness you acquire. Enter upon the great theatre of action free from every vice–armed with every virtue. Then and then only will you be prepared to guard the dearest interest of our expanding republic and counteract the fearful evils that are put in motion by wild ambition, sordid selfishness and base intrigue. Upon you will soon depend the happiness of moving millions and of millions yet unborn. Nothing but death can relieve you from this high responsibility–when death calls you, be found at the post of duty.

JOSEPH WARREN.

The popularity of a measure depends much upon the character of those who engage in it. Its justice is inferred from its ardent and unwavering advocacy by men of high moral and religious worth. For righteous cause and consistency in its prosecution–the American Revolution has no parallel on the pages of history. It commanded the noblest exertions of the best and most talented men of that eventful era. Their conduct elicited the admiration of a gazing world. Pure patriotism pervaded their bosoms–self was banished to its original Pandora box. Truckling politicians were despised–demagogues frowned down–disorganizers silenced–the general good of the whole country was the prime object of deep solicitude. On that bright picture the patriot and philanthropist can feast their eyes with increasing delight. The artists have passed away and left to us the priceless gem of republican FREEDOM. In lines of living light they traced the path of duty in which we must tread to insure safety and preserve our priceless UNION. In language solemn as eternity they said to us–WALK YE THEREIN. People of America! is this injunction of the venerated dead implicitly obeyed by all? A fearful negative must be responded by every thinking, observing, intelligent, honest man. The alluvion of political corruption has submerged this path of duty and safety. Reckless party spirit has broken down its land-marks. Disorganizers trample under foot the precious blood that cemented its pavement–the blood of the covenant of LIBERTY. They treat it as an unholy thing and put our country and themselves to open shame. People of America! will you, *can* you hear the portentous thunders of disorganization—disunion and stand motionless—speechless—until the crash of our LIBERTY—the wreck of our FREEDOM shall unveil to you the wild horrors of chaotic ruin? *You* are the conservators of our Republic—nobly perform your duty.

Among the lofty patriots who were sacrificed at the shrine of American Liberty was Joseph Warren, born in Roxbury, Mass. in 1740. He entered Harvard college at the age of fifteen with a maturity of mind and a manly bearing seldom equalled by one of his years. On the completion of his classical education he studied medicine and acquired a high reputation and a lucrative practice in the city of Boston. He took an early and decided stand in favor of emancipation from mother Britain. He was an able writer and an eloquent public speaker. His pen and voice were warmly enlisted in the cause of equal rights. He was in favor of resisting every species of taxation for the support of England. He believed the people were prepared for self-government and could best manage their own affairs free from foreign interference. He was one of the first members of the secret committee in Boston that put the revolutionary ball in motion. He had a large and happy influence on those around him. He was bold and energetic but prudent and discreet. It was him who sent an express late at night to Lexington to advise Messrs. Hancock and Adams of their contemplated capture. At the battle of Lexington he took an active part and had a portion of his ear lock shot off. In consequence of his high standing and zeal he received the commission of Major General on the 13th of June 1775. Over the army at Cambridge he had a salutary influence. He aided greatly in its first organization—bringing order out of confusion. On the 17th of June he engaged in the battle at Bunker's Hill as a volunteer where he received a ball in his head and died in the entrenchment. Thus prematurely fell one of the brightest ornaments of his day and generation. He was the first American General whose life was sacrificed in the cause of Liberty. He was favorably known as an efficient correspondent to the friends of freedom throughout the colonies and as widely mourned by every patriot. The nation deeply deplored his fall.

The battle of Bunker's Hill was of vast importance. It convinced the British that they had widely mistaken Yankee prowess and our own people that the enemy was not invincible. A defence of only a few hours' labor was thrown up—the whole force of the Americans was but 1200. This was furiously attacked by a superior number of veteran troops. So closely were they permitted to advance that they supposed the idea of resistance was abandoned. At the dread moment when they were on the point of entering the works a stream of liquid fire sent into their ranks a storm of lead and iron hail that caused the survivors to retreat with terror and confusion. Again and again were they repulsed with dreadful slaughter until the ammunition of the Americans failed and compelled them to retreat. The returns of Gen. Gage show 1054 of the British killed   The patriots had 139 killed. In prisoners, wounded and missing 314. They also lost five pieces of artillery.

Eulogy cannot add to the lustre of the name of Warren. Nature had lavished upon him all the noble qualities that adorn a man. In the spring of 1776 his remains were removed to Boston. Having been Grand Master of the Masonic institution of the State, he was buried under the forms of that time-honored order in presence of a large concourse of mourning friends. His memory is perpetuated by a monument erected by his fellow citizens

GEORGE WASHINGTON.

When God resolved to set his people free from Egyptian bondage he raised up able and mighty men to effect his glorious purposes. These he endowed with wisdom to conceive, genius to plan and energy to execute his noble designs. Their oppressive and heartless task-masters had been increasing their burdens with a relentless severity for years. To mercy they were blind, to reason they turned a deaf ear, complaints they treated with contumely, the judgments from heaven they heeded not.

There is a striking resemblance between the history of the Israelites bursting the chains of slavery riveted upon them by the short-sighted Pharaoh and that of the American Colonies throwing off the yoke of bondage imposed by the British king. Like Moses, Washington led his countrymen through the dreary wilderness of the Revolution and when the journey terminated he planted them upon the promised land of Freedom and Independence. Like Moses he placed his trust in the God of Hosts and relied upon his special aid and direction under all circumstances. Like Moses he was nobly sustained by a band of Sages and Heroes unrivalled in the history of the world.

The pedigree of Gen. Washington, as traced and illustrated by Mr Mapleson, carries back his descent to William de Hertburn, Lord of the Manor of Washington, in the county of Durham, England. From him descended John Washington of Whitfield in the time of Richard III. and ninth in descent from the said John was George, first President of the United States. The mother of the John Washington who emigrated to Virginia in 1657 and who was great-grandfather to the General, was Eleanor Hastings, daughter and heiress of John Hastings, grandson to Francis, second Earl of Huntingdon. She was the descendant, through Lady Huntingdon of George, Duke of Clarence, brother to King Edward IV. and King Richard III. by Isabel Nevil, daughter and heiress of Richard, Earl of Warwick, the King-maker. Washington, therefore, as well as all the descendants of that marriage, are entitled to quarter the arms of Hastings, Pole, Earl of Salisbury, Plantagenet, Scotland, Mortimer, Earl of March, Nevil, Montagu, Beauchamp and Devereaux.

George Washington was born in Westmoreland County, Virginia, the 22d of February 1732. He lost his father at an early age and leaned on the wisdom of a fond and judicious mother for the exquisite moulding of his youthful mind. He attributed his success in after life to the early training and faithful pruning of his revered mother. Mothers of America! imitate the example of the mother of the illustrious Washington. The prosperity and perpetuity of our UNION depends much upon the training of your sons. Teach them wisdom, virtue, patriotism, love of country, Liberty. Teach them to prize, dearer than life, the sacred boon of FREEDOM that was nobly won and sacredly transmitted to us by the Sages and Heroes of '76.

During his childhood and youth Washington exhibited a strong and inquiring mind. Industry, stability, perseverance, modesty and honesty were early developed in his character and marked his brilliant career through life. He was frank, generous and humane from his childhood. Nothing could induce him to utter a falsehood, practise deceit or disobey his fond mother. He soared above the trifling amusements that so often lead boys and youth astray and prepare them for a useless, often an ignominious existence. He was designed by his great Creator to be a star of the first magnitude on the great theatre of action–the Moses of America. He studied his part thoroughly before he entered upon the stage of public life. When the curtain rose he was prepared for his audience, acquitted himself nobly and retired amidst the grateful plaudits of admiring–reverent millions.

At the age of twenty-one Washington was selected by Gov. Dinwiddie to visit the hostile French and Indians and endeavor to induce them to withdraw from the frontiers and smoke the pipe of peace. The mission was one of great peril. His path lay through a dense wilderness for four hundred miles infested by wild savages and beasts more wild than them. He arrived at Fort Du Quesne in safety. Whilst the French commandant was writing an answer to the governor, Washington took the dimensions of the fortress unobserved by any one. He then returned home unmolested and unharmed by any accident. Peace was not desired by the red men. It was necessary to raise a regiment of troops to repel the murderous invaders. Washington was invested with the commission of Colonel and took the command. He marched, in April 1754, upon the track he had pursued when he visited the fort previously. On his way he surprised and captured a number of the enemy. When he arrived at the Great Meadows he erected a small stockade fort and appropriately named it Fort Necessity. Here he was reinforced swelling his little army to four hundred men. He then contemplated an attack upon Fort Du Quesne, situated at the junction of the Alleghany and Monongahela rivers forming the Ohio and the present site of the iron city of Pittsburgh. He now learned that the French and Indians, to the number of fifteen hundred, were advancing upon him. The attack was commenced with great fury and continued for several hours when the French commander offered liberal terms of capitulation and gladly permitted the young champion and his brave Virginians to march away unmolested. This brilliant achievement placed Washington high on the scale of eminence as a bold, skilful and prudent military officer. It occurred on the 4th of July–a happy prelude to the glorious 4th of July 1776.

The ensuing year another expedition was sent against Fort Du Quesne of about two thousand troops under command of the unfortunate Braddock who had more courage than prudence–more self-conceit than wisdom. He spurned the advice of the " beardless boy" and rushed into an ambush where he and near one-half of his men met the cold embrace of the king of terrors. The enemy consisted of only five hundred French and Indians secreted in three ravines forming a tringle. In this triangle of death Braddock formed his men and remained until he had five horses killed under him and was mortally wounded. During all this time not one of the enemy could be seen. One hundred native Virginians with fixed bayonets and led by Washington would have routed them in ten minutes. I speak from the record as I have examined every rod of the ground. After the fall of Braddock Washington saved the survivors under Col. Dunbar by a judicious retreat. He had warned the British General of his danger who spurned the " beardless boy." At a subsequent period he negotiated a peace with the Indians on the frontiers and was voted the thanks of mother Britain.

Unwilling to again witness such a waste of human life Washington resigned his military command and retired to his peaceful home. Shortly after this he was elected to the legislature and was highly esteemed as a wise, discriminating legislator–exhibiting a mind imbued with philanthropy and liberal principles guided by a sound discretion and cultivated intellect adorned with a retiring modesty too rare in men of talent at the present day. From this field of labor he entered one of greater magnitude, of vaster importance–one big with events involving consequences of the most thrilling interest to his country and himself. He was elected to the Congress of 1774. The solemnity that pervaded the opening ceremony of that august assembly has been before portrayed. During the opening prayer, Washington only was upon his knees, imitating the attitude of his pious mother in her earnest appeals to the throne of Grace. On all occasions his mind seems to have reached from earth to Heaven. He seemed to dwell in the bosom of his God. Devoted, unsophisticated, humble, relying piety marked his whole course of life– a piety sincere in its motives, consistent in its exhibitions and illumined by the refulgent sunbeams of living charity. He was returned to the next Congress and took his seat little anticipating the mighty work in reserve for him. On the memorable 19th of April 1775, American blood was again made to leap from its fountain by order of Major Pitcairn on the heights of Lexington. Justice looked at the purple current as it flowed and sighed. Mercy carried the tragic news to the ethereal skies– the eagle of LIBERTY heard the mournful story–descended in a stream of liquid fire–planted the torch of freedom in the serum of the murdered patriots and bid eternal defiance to the British lion. The alarm spread with lightning rapidity. It was sounded from church bells and signal guns–echo carried it from hills to dales, from sire to son. Vengeance was roused from its lair–the hardy yoemanry left their ploughs in the furrow–the merchant rushed from his counting house, the professional man from his office, the minister from his glebe, shouldered their rusty muskets and with powder horn and slug hastened to the scene of action determined to avenge the blood of slaughtered brethren, maintain their chartered rights or perish in the attempt.

In June following Washington was appointed commander-in-chief of the American armies by the unanimous voice of Congress. He accepted the high command with great reluctance and diffidence–knowing that it involved responsibilities, consequences and results too mighty for him hastily to assume, too vast for him confidently to encounter. He did not view the camp as the field of glory, ambition, conquest or fame. He did not thirst for human blood or exult in the profession of arms. Love of country, liberty, human rights, liberal principles—the duty to resist the oppressions of tyranny, prompted him to action. For these reasons he consented to serve his country at the perilous post assigned him.

As soon as practicable he hastened to Cambridge Mass. and entered upon the duties of his office in July. Before his arrival there, Crown Point and Ticonderoga had been surrendered to the patriots—the sanguinary battle of Bunker's Hill had been fought and the British convinced that men contending for their just rights, their dearest interests—their bosoms charged with fiery indignation and burning patriotism—could not be made to yield to the glittering arms of a haughty monarch without a bold and desperate effort to maintain that Liberty which they inherited from their Creator and which was guarantied by the British constitution.

The horrors of war were accumulating like electrified clouds preparing a tornado. The bloody toils of the Revolution had commenced. England poured in her legions by thousands. To cap the climax of barbarity she called to her aid the blood thirsty Indian with his tomahawk and scalping knife and bid a premium for scalps. The welkin rang with the savage war-whoop The terrific screams, the expiring groans of mothers and babes were enough to draw tears from rocks and dress all nature in deep mourning. The contest was that of an infant with a giant—a lamb with a wolf. The dark clouds blackened as they rose and were surcharged with the lightning of revenge and thunder of malice. Washington viewed their fiery aspect with calm serenity, heard their portentous roar without a tremor. With his soul reaching to Heaven he met the awful crisis with firmness and prudence before unknown. His gigantic genius soared above the loftiest barriers his enemies could rear. His course was onward—right onward towards the goal of LIBERTY. Beneath his conquering arm monarchy trembled, tottered, fell. His whole energy was at once directed to the complete organization and perfect discipline of the army. By the aid of the king's troops some of the royal governors still maintained a show of authority in several of the colonies. As opposition assumed a systematic form and military arrangements increased, they retired on board the British armed vessels from whence they issued their proclamations with about the same effect as the puffing of a porpoise would have upon old Boreas.

Early in March 1776, Washington planted his army before Boston where Lord Howe had concentrated his forces. On the 17th this caused his lordship very modestly to evacuate the town. On the 2d of July Gen. Howe landed nine miles below the city of New York with 24,000 men. He sent an insulting communication to Washington which he very properly refused to receive. On the 27th of August that part of the army stationed at Brooklyn under Gen. Sullivan was attacked and defeated with great loss and Generals Sullivan, Sterling and Woodhull taken prisoners. Two days after, Gen. Washington effected a retreat and landed his troops safely in New York without the movement being discovered by the enemy until completed. Chagrined and mortified at the loss of their prey the British prepared to attack the city which induced the Americans to evacuate it and retire to White Plains. Here they were attacked on the 28th of September—the British were repulsed, a considerable loss was sustained on both sides and no victory to either. The disasters of the patriots multiplied—Fort Washington and Lee fell into the hands of the English—the American army was flying before a relentless foe. Washington crossed the Hudson and retreated through Jersey into Pennsylvania with Lord Cornwallis pressing on his rear. His army was now reduced to 3000 men who were destitute of almost every comfort of life. They could be tracked by blood from their naked feet upon the frozen ground. Think of this ye who are now enjoying the rich behest of Liberty so dearly purchased and but by few properly appreciated. Reverses had chilled the zeal of many leading men who at first espoused the cause of freedom but whose hearts were not yet sufficiently harrowed by oppression to have the good seed take root. A fiery cloud of indignation, ready to devour them, hung over the bleeding colonies. Washington was still confident of ultimate success. He believed that in the archives of eternal justice their FREEDOM was written. Guardian angels listened to the vesper orisons of those who were true to themselves, their country and their God who directed their destiny. The bold career of the roaring lion was arrested. This Spartan band was crowned with victory. On the night of the 25th of December Washington crossed the Delaware to Trenton amidst floating ice—surprised and took one thousand prisoners—pushed on to Princeton, killed sixty and took three hundred prisoners, spreading consternation in the ranks of the enemy. This success re-animated many of the cold hearts that could be warmed only by prosperity—sunshine patriots whose love of freedom was very similar to self-righteousness. Washington retired to Morristown N. J. for the winter—the English occupied Brunswick.

In the spring of 1777 the army of Washington amounted to about 7000 men. No action occurred between the main armies until August when the British landed in Maryland with the intention of capturing

Philadelphia. On the 11th of September the two armies met at Brandywine—a desperate battle ensued and a partial dearly purchased victory was gained by the English. On the approach of the enemy the City of Penn was abandoned. On the 4th of October another severe battle was fought at Germantown which proved disastrous to the American troops in consequence of their becoming separated and confused by a thick fog. These keen misfortunes were more than balanced by the capture of the entire British army in the north under Burgoyne by Gen. Gates on the 17th of October. On the reception of this news France recognised the Independence of the United States, entered into a treaty of alliance and furnished important aid by sending many of her brave sons to the rescue. The English retreated to New York in the spring of 1778 from which place they made frequent descents upon various places, destroying private property, murdering the inhabitants and spreading desolation wherever they went. They sent an expedition to Georgia and were crowned with victory. During this year no decisive battle was fought. The same during 1779. The British seemed to be best pleased with a predatory warfare than pitched battles which they carried on in a manner that put savage barbarity in the shade and made the inquisitor general of Madrid mourn for lost humanity. Alas for the Christian majesty of mother Britain.

Again the exertions of Washington were almost paralyzed for the want of men and money. The French Admiral D'Estaing was unfortunate in all his movements. The British lion was prowling through the land in all the majesty of cruelty. The anchor of hope could scarcely keep the shattered bark of Liberty to its moorings—the cable of exertion lost thread after thread until but a small band of *genuine* patriots and heroes were left as a nucleus to breast the fury of the storm that rolled its dashing surges over them. But they clung to the creaking craft with a death grip and weathered the terrific gale. The campaign of 1780 terminated more favorably to the American arms. The south had become the main theatre of action. The cruelties of the enemy had prepared more hearts to do service in the cause of Liberty. The people were brought to see their true interests and rallied under the banner of freedom determined on victory or death. Gates, the hero of Saratoga, was put in command of the southern army—fresh aid arrived from France—the conflict was one of desperation. On the 18th of August a severe battle was fought near Camden, S. C. The British were the victors. Defeat now only served to rally the bone and sinew of the land. The hardy sons of Columbia rose like a phœnix from ashes and hurled the thunderbolts of vengeance among their savage foes with the fury of Mars. Every battle weakened and disheartened the enemy when a victory was gained. A few more conquests like those at Camden and Guilford Court House would seal their doom. The energetic Greene succeeded Gates. The campaign of 1781 opened. Washington moved to the south. Wayne, Lee, Greene, La Fayette, Nelson and other brave officers were there. Count de Grasse was co-operating with his fleet. In their turn the British lords, admirals and generals found themselves surrounded with impending dangers. An awful crisis was pressing upon them. Retribution stared them in the face. Their deeds of blood haunted their guilty souls—consternation seized their troubled minds. Lord Cornwallis concentrated his forces at Yorktown which he fortified in the best possible manner.

On the 6th of October the combined forces of Washington and Rochambeau commenced a siege upon this place which surrendered on the 19th of the same month. The grand Rubicon was passed—the work was done—the Colonies were free. That was the dying struggle of British monarchy in America. Hope of conquering her indomitable sons expired like the death flickering of a glow-worm. Heaven had decreed they should be free—that decree was consummated. Like Jordan's dove, the Eagle of Liberty descended to cheer the conquering heroes—snatched the laurels from Britain's brow and placed them triumphantly upon the CHAMPIONS OF AMERICAN INDEPENDENCE. To the friends of FREEDOM the scene was joyful, sublime—to its enemies—painful, humiliating. This victory was hailed with enthusiastic gratitude. It placed Washington on the loftiest summit of immortal fame—secured Liberty to his beloved country, stopped the effusion of human blood, sealed the foundations of our Republic—prepared an asylum for the oppressed—planted deep the long nursed TREE OF LIBERTY.

On the 30th of September 1783 a definitive treaty was signed at Paris by Messrs. Fitzherbert and Oswald on the part of Great Britain and Messrs. John Adams, Franklin, Jay and Laurens on the part of the United States. On the 2d of November Washington issued his farewell orders to his army in terms of affectionate eloquence and parental solicitude. On the 3d the troops were disbanded by Congress. With mingling tears of joy and gratitude they parted and repaired finally to their homes to meet the warm embrace, the fervent grasp of their families and friends—there to reap the rich fruit of their perilous toils free from the iron scourge of despotism. On the 23d of December Washington appeared in the hall of Congress and resigned his commission. This act was one of sublimity and thrilling interest. The past, present and future—all rushed upon the mind of this great and good man as he invoked the blessings of Heaven to descend and guard the Liberty of his beloved emancipated country. Every eye was fixed upon him—every heart beat quicker—emotion rose to its zenith—he laid the commission on the table—a burst of applause rent the air—a flood of tears closed the scene.

No longer under the maternal care of their old mother, the people of the United States were left to try the yet problematical experiment of self government. Difficulties arose from local jealousies and conflicting interests—a debt of forty millions of dollars had been contracted—government paper became greatly depreciated—the public credit was shivering in the wind—the Liberty that had been so dearly purchased seemed doomed to a premature dissolution. To avoid this threatened disaster delegates convened at Philadelphia from all the States except Rhode Island for the purpose of devising a plan to preserve and perfect that freedom which had cost millions of treasure and fountains of noble blood. Washington was unanimously elected President of this august body. After long and patient deliberation the labors of these patriots resulted in the production of the Federal Constitution, one of the brightest specimens of a republican form of government on record. It is the grand palladium of our LIBERTY, the golden chain of our UNION, the broad banner of FREEMEN, a terror to tyrants, a shining light to patriots, the illustrated chart of our rights and duties, a safeguard against disorganizing factions and stamped its illustrious authors with a meritorious fame that succeeding generations will delight to perpetuate.

On the 17th of September this was reported to Congress and was promptly approved. It was immediately sent to the several states for consideration all of which sanctioned it at that time except North Carolina and Rhode Island. The former acceded to it in 1789, the latter in 1790. Confidence was then restored and Independence made secure. From that time to the present our nation has advanced on the flood tide of successful experiment and been blessed with an increasing prosperity that has no parallel in the annals of history. The star spangled banner waves proudly on every sea and is respected by all the nations of the earth. Our improvements at home have marched in advance of the boldest conceptions of the most visionary projectors—the fondest anticipations of their most ardent friends. They have often outstripped the most adventurous speculators.

By the unanimous voice of a free and grateful people Washington was elected the first President of the new Republic. With the same proverbial diffidence and modesty that had marked his whole career he took the oath of office on the 30th of April 1789. This imposing ceremony was performed in presence of the first Congress under the Federal Constitution assembled in the city of New York and in presence of a crowded audience who deeply felt and strongly expressed their filial affection for the father of their country. He at once entered upon the important duties that devolved upon him which were neither few or small. A cabinet was to be created, a revenue raised, the judiciary organized, its officers appointed and every department of government to be established on a firm, impartial, just and humane basis. In all these arrangements he exhibited great wisdom, exercised a sound discretion and proved as able a statesman as he had been a general. Deliberation and prudence guided him at all times. He acted up to but never transcended the bounds of equal justice and delegated authority. An angel could do no more.

During his administration of eight years he brought into full force his noblest energies to advance the best interests of his country–meliorate the condition of those who were suffering from the effects of a protracted war–improve the state of society, arts, science, agriculture, manufactures–commerce–disseminate general intelligence–allay local difficulties and render the infant Republic as happy and glorious as it was free and independent. His patriotic exertions were crowned with success–his fondest anticipations were realized–he finished the work assigned him with a skill before unknown–the government foundations were laid deep and strong–the superstructure was rising in grandeur– Washington wrote his farewell address and on the 4th of March 1797 retired from public life honored and loved by a nation of freemen, respected and admired by a gazing world–crowned with an unsullied fame that will grow brighter and more brilliant through all time. He then repaired to Mount Vernon to repose in the bosom of his family and enjoy that domestic peace by his own fireside that he had long desired. He had served his country long, ably, impartially, justly. He could look back upon a life well spent in the cause of human rights, liberal principles and an enlarged philanthropy.

For his arduous services during the revolutionary war Washington took no compensation. More than this, owing to the depreciation of continental money he paid three-fourths of his own expenses. He kept a correct book entry of every business transaction and produced a written voucher for every disbursement he had made of public funds. During his presidential terms his expenses exceeded his salary over five thousand dollars a year which he paid from his private funds and refused a proffered remuneration. With the exception of his appointment as commander-in-chief of the American army in 1798 when France threatened invasion, Washington was relieved from any farther participation in public affairs. He continued to live 'at Vernon's sacred Mount until the 14th of December 1799 when his immortal spirit left its noble tenement of clay–soared aloft on angel wings to realms of enduring bliss there to receive a crown of unfading glory–the reward of a spotless life spent in the service of his country and his God. His body was deposited in the family tomb where it slumbered amidst the peaceful groves of his loved retreat until 1837, when it was deposited in a splendid marble sarcophagus designed by Mr. Strickland and manufactured and presented by John Struthers, marble mason, both of the city of Philadelphia. Upon the top of this masterpiece of workmanship is most exquisitely and boldly carved the star spangled banner surmounted by the American Eagle. Under these the name WASHINGTON is carved in bold relievo. The design and finely finished work do great credit to Mr. Strickland as an architect and to Mr. Struthers as an artist. The gift and the delicate manner it was presented by the latter worthy gentleman do honor to his head and heart. The body was in a state of preservation as remarkable as the history of the man in life. The face retained its full form and fleshy appearance and was but slightly changed in color. The ceremony of removal was sublimely interesting and witnessed by a large concourse of tearful spectators. This hallowed spot is visited yearly by large numbers who approach it with profound veneration and awe. All nations revere the memory of the father of our country–unborn millions will chant his praise. Foreigners are proud to say they have visited the tomb of Washington at Mount Vernon. This estate was left to George Washington by his brother Lawrence in 1754. This brother served under Admiral Vernon in his memorable attack upon Carthagena in 1741. Having been treated with marked attention by the Admiral he named his estate in commemoration of him.

The name of George Washington is associated with every amiable and noble quality that can adorn a man. It is encircled by a sacred halo that renders it dear to every philanthropist–respected by all civilized nations. His fame is too bright to be burnished by eulogy–too pure to be tarnished by detraction. His praises have been proclaimed by talents of the highest order, hearts of the warmest devotion, imaginations of the happiest conception–eloquence of the loftiest tone. It would require an angel's pen dipped in ethereal fire and an angel's hand to guide it to fully delineate the noble frame work and perfect finish of this great and good man. Like the sun at high meridian, the lustre of his virtues can be seen and felt but not clearly described. His picture is one on which we may gaze with increased delight and discover new beauties to the last. Like that of our nation–his history is without a parallel. Unblemished rectitude marked his whole career, philanthropy his entire course, justice his every action. Under the most trying circumstances and afflictive dispensations a calm holy resignation to the will of God added a brighter lustre to his exalted qualities. Like a blazing luminary–his refulgence dims the surrounding stars and illuminates the horizon of biography with a light ineffable. His brilliant achievements were not stained with that reckless effusion of blood that marked the ambitious Cæsar, the conquering Alexander and the disappointed Bonaparte. He was consistent to the last.

In private life he was graced with all the native dignity of man, reducing all things around him to a perfect system of harmony, order, economy, frugality and peace. In every thing he was chastened by sterling merit, actuated by magnanimity, mellowed by benevolence, purified by charity. He was a living epistle of all that was great and good. He was the kind husband, the widow's solace, the orphan's father, the faithful friend, the bountiful benefactor, the true patriot, the devoted Christian the worthy citizen, the honest man. He has left examples worthy the contemplation and imitation of all who figure on the stage of public action or in the walks of retired life. His private worth was crowned with amaranthine flowers, richer and sweeter than the epic and civic wreaths that decked his brow in the public view of an admiring world. His virtues were enlivened by the richest colors of godliness–his mind was finished by the finest touches of creative power. His sacred memory will live through the rolling ages of time–will be revered until, the wreck of worlds and the dissolution of nature shall close the drama of human action–Gabriel's dread clarion rend the vaulted tombs–awake the sleeping dead and proclaim to astonished millions– TIME SHALL BE NO LONGER.

ANTHONY WAYNE.

The history of the Sages and Heroes of the American Revolution cannot be too often examined by the present and coming generations. To learn their disinterested patriotism, bold conceptions, daring exploits, unparalleled sufferings, indomitable perseverance, noble fortitude, enduring patience and their exalted virtues–is to know something of the high price our freedom cost. To properly appreciate the liberty we enjoy is one of the best safe guards of its perpetuity. In the peaceful enjoyment of inestimable blessings we are too apt to forget their origin and their value. Could the torrents of blood shed to obtain the high privileges we now inherit be placed in one mighty reservoir upon which all our people could look for a single moment, millions would blush at their own apathy in the preservation of our dearest interests. We have many reckless demagogues and bold disorganizers in our midst who should be baptized in this fountain of blood for the remission of their political sins—some who set the Federal Constitution at naught and would glory in the dissolution of our blood bought UNION. When our love of country grows cold and respect for the chart of our Liberty is lost—the sooner we emigrate the better for all concerned—not up salt river but to Chinese Tartary or Chimborazo.

Among those who freely contributed to the revolutionary fountain of blood was Anthony Wayne, born in Waynesborough, Chester County, Pennsylvania on the 1st of January 1745. His grandfather held a commission in the army of William III. and fought at the battle of the Boyne on the 1st of July 1690 and at Aughrine on the 12th of July 1691 at both of which the Irish under James II. were defeated. At the last battle their struggle for Independence ended and has never been renewed. His father was a respectable farmer and placed this son at school in Philadelphia where he received a good English education. He was delighted with the study of mathematics and became familiar with surveying and engineering at an early age. His taste for military tactics was developed during his boyhood. His father and grandfather were both men of military prowess. As young Anthony listened to the story of their exploits he contemplated the field of battle, the clash of arms and the shouts of victory with burning enthusiasm. This grew with his growth and ripened with his manhood.

In 1773 he succeeded his father in the Colonial Assembly where he became an active member and took a bold stand in favor of liberal principles and equal rights. He did much to rouse the people to a just sense of impending danger. His boldness inspired confidence—his energy prepared for action. He preferred digging a grave with his sword rather than tamely submit to foreign dictation based upon tyranny and enforced by the insolent task masters of the crown. In 1775 he received a Colonel's commission and speedily raised a fine regiment in his native county. He was soon called into active service under Gen. Thompson in his unfortunate expedition against Canada. When that officer was defeated and taken prisoner with a part of his little army, Col. Wayne manifested great presence of mind, skill and bravery in effecting a retreat although writhing under a severe wound. From that time his military fame rose and expanded until it reached the maximum of his patriotic ambition—the pinnacle of his fondest desires. In 1776 his services were very useful on the northern frontier in conducting the engineer department in addition to the duties of his command. He had the confidence of his superiors and the friendship of all around him. His course was onward and upward. As a merited reward for his active services and in consequence of his superior talents he was commissioned Brigadier General at the close of that campaign.

At the battle of Brandywine he kept a superior British force from passing Chad's Ford for a long time. After the partial defeat of the American army Gen. Wayne was detached with his division to keep the enemy at bay in view of another attack. The invading army was stationed at what was then called Fredyffrin. Gen. Wayne encamped three miles in the rear of the left wing near the Paoli Tavern and gave special orders to guard against surprise. On the night of the 20th of September his troops were suddenly attacked by a division under Gen. Gray who rushed upon the Americans with fixed bayonets killing and wounding about 150 men. Overwhelmed by a superior force Gen. Wayne retreated a short distance—rallied and formed his men and was no farther molested. At his own request his conduct on that unfortunate occasion was investigated by a court martial. Not the slightest fault was found against him. At the battle of Germantown he led his men on to action with a boldness and impetuosity that carried terror into the ranks of the imported veterans. He had two horses shot, one under him and one as he was mounting and was wounded in the left foot and hand. When a retreat was ordered his military skill shone conspicuously in protecting his men.

He was uniformly selected by Washington to conduct hazardous and daring enterprises, reconnoitre the enemy and collect supplies. His energy was of the most vigorous tone whether on the field or in a council of war. Previous to the battle of Monmouth he and Gen. Cadwallader were the only officers who at first united with Washington in favor of attacking the British army. So bravely did he act on the day of that brilliant victory that the commander-in-chief made special mention of him in his report to Congress. In July 1779 Gen. Wayne was selected to attempt a bold and daring exploit. Stony Point was in possession of the enemy, strongly fortified and filled with heavy ordnance. One side was washed by the Hudson River, on the other was a morass passable only in one place. This fort was on an eminence of considerable height. In front were formidable breastworks at every accessible point. In advance of these was a double row of abattis. Col. Johnson was in command of the garrison with 600 men principally Highlanders, the bravest and most brawny troops that were imported. A number of vessels of war were moored in the Hudson in front. All things combined to render a successful attack more than problematical with a much superior force. It was the very kind of adventure for Gen. Wayne. To please our young military gentlemen I will describe the arrangements for attack.

On the evening of the 15th of July, at 8 o'clock, he arrived within a mile and a half of the fort and immediately communicated his plan of operation to his officers. The hour of low twelve was fixed for the desperate assault. Every officer and non-commissioned officer was held responsible for each man in his platoon. No soldier was permitted to leave the ranks until the general halt near the fort and then only with an officer. When the troops arrived in rear of the hill on which the fort stood Col. Febiger formed his regiment in solid column of a half platoon in front. Col. Meigs formed in his rear–Maj. Hull in his rear, the three forming the right column. The left was formed in the same manner by Col. Butler and Maj. Murphy. Every officer and soldier placed a piece of white paper in front of his hat or cap that they might recognise each other if mixed with the enemy. Col. Fleury was put in command of 150 picked men and stationed about twenty paces in front of the right column with fixed bayonets and unloaded muskets. A little in front of these an officer and twenty of the boldest men were placed whose duty was to secure the sentinels and remove the abattis that the main column might pass freely. The same with the left column. The main columns were to follow the advance with shouldered unloaded muskets relying entirely on the bayonet–according to the tactics of Gen. Gray at Paoli. Any soldier who departed in the minutest particular from orders was to be instantly killed by his officer. A reward of $500 was offered to the first man who entered the fortification–$400–$300–$200–$100 to each in succession of the other four who first followed. The whole being formed, "*March!*" thundered from Wayne who led the right column with Col. Febiger–the left was led by Col. Butler followed by Maj. Murphy. Never were men more determined on victory or death–never were orders more strictly obeyed. So simultaneous was the attack by each division and so equally rapid their movements that they met in the centre of the fort. The victory was as complete and triumphant as the assault was bold and overwhelming. All was accomplished without the discharge of a gun by the Americans who advanced facing a tremendous shower of musket, grape and canister shot. On the surrender of the fort Gen. Wayne ordered a salute of iron hail for the benefit of the armed ships in the river which caused them to slip their cables and move off with all possible despatch. Fifty-seven of the enemy were killed and five hundred and forty-three taken prisoners. As the columns were advancing Gen. Wayne was severely wounded in the head with a musket ball–as he believed mortally–which felled him to the ground. He rose on one knee–" *Onward my brave fellows–onward!*" burst from him in stentorian accents. He requested his aids to carry him into the fort that he might die amidst the music shouts of victory. The garrison made a determined resistance at every point of attack. Of the forlorn hope of the twenty led by Lieut. Gibbons seventeen were killed. The wounded and killed of the Americans amounted in all to ninety-eight. After entering the fort had the Americans opened a fire the slaughter would have been dreadful. Gen. Wayne preferred setting an example of humane treatment towards his conquered foes, proving himself as magnanimous as he was brave and victorious. He scorned retaliation although the dying groans at the Paoli massacre were still ringing in his ears. Within an hour after the surrender, writhing under his severe wound, Gen. Wayne addressed the following laconic letter to Gen. Washington.

"Stony Point, July 16, 1779, 2 o'clock A. M.

"Dear General–The fort and garrison with Col. Johnson are ours. Our officers and men behaved like men determined to be free.
"Yours most sincerely,
"Anthony Wayne.
"Gen. Washington."

Here is a model letter worthy the imitation of the elaborate epistle manufacturers of the present prolific era of verbosity, ambiguity and repetition. It should serve as a modest hint to our speech-makers and induce them to say less and do more. Millions would then be saved to the States and our nation.

So highly did Congress appreciate the capture of Stony Point that on the 26th of the same month the House passed a series of resolutions highly complimentary to Gen. Washington for conceiving and to Gen. Wayne and his brave companions in arms for planning and accomplishing the capture of that important post. The amount of the military stores was divided amongst the officers and men and the rewards offered promptly paid. The letter of Mr. Jay, the President of the Continental Congress to Gen. Wayne enclosing a copy of these resolutions, shows the concise and systematic mode of doing business at that time.

"Philadelphia July 27, 1779.

"Sir—Your late glorious achievements have merited and now receive the approbation and thanks of your country. They are contained in the enclosed act of Congress which I have the honor to transmit. This brilliant action adds luster to our arms and will teach the enemy to respect our power if not to imitate our humanity. You have nobly reaped laurels in the cause of your country and in the fields of danger and death. May these prove the earnest of more and may victory ever bear your standard and Providence be your shield.
"I have the honor to be &c.
"John Jay, President."

Here is another *multum in parvo* worthy of imitation. Plain common sense plainly and briefly told—every line gemmed with the purest patriotism.

Gen. Wayne was blessed with great presence of mind in sudden emergencies. When in the vicinity of James river, Virginia, he was incorrectly told that the main body of the British army had passed to the opposite side. He advanced with only 800 men for the purpose of capturing the rear guard but found the whole force of Lord Cornwallis formed in line of battle. He immediately commenced a vigorous attack and then retreated in good order. Believing this to be an ambuscade stratagem the British dared not pursue him. In 1781 he was put in command of the forces in Georgia. After several sanguinary engagements he expelled the enemy from the state and planted the standard of freedom upon the ruins of tyranny—upon the firm basis of eternal justice. As a reward for his services that state presented him with a valuable plantation reversing the adage—republics are ungrateful. He continued in active service up to the close of the siege of Yorktown, a bold, prudent, skilful and reliable patriotic officer. He remained in the army until the Independence for which he had fought and bled was fully recognised by mother Britain when he retired to the bosom of his family crowned with the highest military honors he desired and with the rank of Major General of the American army. But few of the Heroes of the Revolution did as much hard service as Gen. Wayne and no one did it up more brown.

In 1789 he was a member of the Pennsylvania convention to which was submitted the Federal Constitution. He warmly advocated its adoption. In 1792 he succeeded Gen. St. Clair in command of the army operating against the predatory Indian tribes in the far west. Gen. Wayne formed an encampment at Pittsburgh and thoroughly disciplined his troops preparatory to future action. So determined were the red men to maintain the rights that God and nature had bestowed upon them that many of the powerful tribes combined their war forces to resist their common enemy–the Christian white man. To meet them on their own ground and adopt their mode of warfare was the only way to insure success. For such a service it required time to prepare and energy to execute. In the autumn of 1793 Gen. Wayne had led his army to Greenville six miles from fort Jefferson where he established his winter quarters. He fortified his camp and built fort Recovery on the ground where the whites had been defeated on the 4th of November 1791. He collected the bones of those who then fell and had them buried under the honors of war. The presence of the army kept the Indians quiet during the winter. For the want of supplies the army did not reach the junction of the rivers Au Glaiz and Miami until the 8th of August where a fort was erected for the protection of military stores. Thirty miles from that place the English had erected a fort near which the Indians were in full force. On the 18th the army reached the Miami rapids. There a fortification was erected for the protection of baggage and the position of the red men examined. They were found in a dense forest five miles distant advantageously posted. On the 20th the attack was arranged and the troops advanced. When reached the fire from behind trees was so effective that the front, led by Major Price, was compelled to fall back. At that moment–*trail arms–advance*–ran through the ranks with electric velocity and effect as it thundered from the strong lungs of Wayne. In a few brief moments the conquered red men were flying in every direction closely pursued by the victorious troops for two miles. So rapid was their retreat that Scott, who was ordered to turn their left flank, found naught but trees like men standing but not like men running for dear life. Gen. Wayne had 33 men killed and 100 wounded. From this defeat the injured red men never recovered. They fled before fire and sword–their corn fields and villages were destroyed, their power paralyzed and a chain of forts established which kept them in constant awe and compelled them to relinquish their rightful domain after having struggled nobly to maintain their inalienable rights. True they were savages. Newton, Shakespeare, Washington, Henry–

savages born–savages would have died. The Indians have their fixed customs–we have ours. They had their rights–the white men took them forcibly away. Justice, money, time, or angels' tears can never expunge the wrong. This is my opinion–others have the same right to theirs–if different it will be easier to *plead* justification than to *prove* it.

The result of the vigorous operations of Gen. Wayne was a general and definitive treaty with many of the different tribes of Aborigines who were compelled to bury the tomahawk and smoke the pipe of peace. This treaty was ratified on the 3d of August 1795. Tranquillity then spread her cheering mantle over our country from the shores of the Atlantic to the inland seas of the west. General Wayne continued in the field of operations for the purpose of completing the extended chain of forts proposed and planned by him. No one was better calculated for that arduous service. He continued to prosecute the work until December 1796, when he was cut down by disease in the flood-tide of his eventful career, deeply mourned and widely lamented. He died far from his family in a hut on Presque Isle, a peninsula in Erie county, Pa. that extends into Lake Erie, where he was buried and remained until 1809 when his son Isaac removed his remains to his native county and deposited them in the cemetery of St. David's church. The Pennsylvania State Cincinnati Society has erected a beautiful white marble monument over his grave with the following inscription on the south front.

In honor of the distinguished
Military services of
Major General
ANTHONY WAYNE,
And as an affectionate tribute
of respect to his memory
This stone was erected by his
companions in arms
THE PENNSYLVANIA STATE SOCIETY OF
CINCINNATI,
July 4th, A. D. 1809,
Thirty-fourth anniversary of
The Independence of
THE UNITED STATES OF AMERICA,
An event which constitutes
the most
Appropriate eulogium of an American
SOLDIER AND PATRIOT.

On the north front is the following inscription.

>Major General
>ANTHONY WAYNE
>Was born at Waynesborough
>in Chester County
>State of Pennsylvania
>A. D. 1745.
>After a life of honor and usefulness
>He died in December, 1796,
>at a military post
>On the shores of Lake Erie,
>Commander-in-chief of the army of
>THE UNITED STATES.
>His military achievements
>are consecrated
>In the history of his country,
>and in
>The hearts of his countrymen.
>His remains
>Are here deposited.

Although stricken down at the age of fifty-one years Gen. Wayne lived long enough to fill his measure of glory and see the star spangled banner wave triumphantly over his native land. Far from his family as he was and in a rough cabin, he died peacefully. His spirit ascended to reap the rich reward of his labors in the cause of rational freedom and equal justice.

He was a large, portly man of commanding military mien, with an open bold countenance. All the relations of private life he honored with the most rigid fidelity. In the legislative hall as in the field he was active and decisive. As a citizen he was esteemed in life and regretted in death.

WILLIAM WHIPPLE JR.

THAT knowledge is of most importance that leads us in the shortest path to truth. A thorough common education, like common sense, is most useful. By a close observation of the laws of nature in full operation around us, of things as presented to our understandings, of men as they move and act before us—we obtain a treasure of knowledge not always taught in the high schools and seldom hinted at–much less expounded in modern books. Without this the classic scholar is afloat without a rudder. This is the kind that best answers the definition of the adage–*Knowledge is power.* In the great store-house of literature the quantity of fancy goods has, for some time past, far exceeded the coarser kind fit for everyday use. Whether this is an advantage to the intellect of man calculated to increase its strength and volume–or like luxurious diet, enervate and weaken, is a problem worthy the solution of every reader. Certain it is our hardy ancestors were not mentally or physically pampered with knick-knacks that now supplant much solid matter. Certain it is that many of the patriots of the Revolution were self-made practical men and shone as conspicuously in the galaxy of sages as those whose early literary advantages were greater–conclusive evidence that there is a shorter path to truth.

Among them William Whipple Jr. was conspicuous. He was the eldest son of William Whipple–born at Kittery, Maine, in 1730. At a common English school he was taught reading, writing, arithmetic and navigation. These he mastered at an early age and was then entered a cabin boy on board a merchant vessel in accordance with his father's wishes and his own inclination. Before he reached his majority he became captain of a vessel and made several successful voyages to Europe. Some ignoramuses have vainly attempted to stigmatize his fair reputation at that era in his life because he participated in the inhuman slave-trade. If they will learn the true state of feeling at that time upon this subject their anathemas will evaporate in thin air. The trade was then sanctioned by Great Britain under whose government Capt. Whipple acted and according to her laws–*The King can do no wrong.* The correctness of the trade was not then doubted but by a few philanthropists and its first cousin, the *Apprentice System,* is still a favorite project with England. Time and reflection caused Captain Whipple to see the impropriety of the traffic and entirely abandon it at an early day. He also manumitted the only slave he owned who would not leave him during the war and fought bravely for the liberty of our country. If every man is to be condemned for the licensed or unlicensed errors of youth whose riper years are crowned with virtue, the list of fame will require many bold erasures and would be robbed of some of its proudest names. He who would do it must belong to the big crowd ignorant of human nature.

In 1759 Capt. Whipple relinquished his oceanic pursuits and commenced the mercantile business in Portsmouth, New Hampshire. He also added the swivel link to his chain of earthly happiness by marrying

Catharine Moffat. Every farmer, sailor and blacksmith knows the importance of this link in the common chain. The wise Creator designed it in the chain of life and no man should be without it. If of the right metal, it will save him from many a dangerous twist and often from a break. A word to the wise should be sufficient.

During his numerous voyages Capt. Whipple had treasured up a large fund of useful knowledge. He was a close observer of men and things—an analyzing reader and mingled with the best and most intelligent men when in port. In England he had listened to the unwarranted pretensions of ministers—in America—to the increasing complaints of the Colonists. He was familiar with the chartered rights of his own country and with the tyranny of the infatuated step-mother. He was prepared for action and took a bold stand in favor of freedom. He took a conspicuous part in public meetings and became one of the Committee of Safety. He rose rapidly in public esteem—the former cabin boy became a leading patriot.

In January 1775 he represented Portsmouth in the Provincial Congress at Exeter convened for the purpose of choosing delegates to the Continental Congress. On the 6th of the next January he was made a member of the Provincial Council of New Hampshire. On the 23d of the same month he was elected a member of Congress then in session at Philadelphia and continued actively and usefully engaged in that important station until the middle of September 1779. He was present at the adoption of the Declaration of Independence and affixed his name to that bold instrument with the same fearless nonchalance as if signing a bill of lading. He was emphatically a working man and rendered himself extremely useful on committees. As a member of marine and commercial boards, his practical knowledge gave him an advantage over his colleagues. He was one of the superintendents of the commissary and quarter masters' department and did much towards correcting abuses and checking peculation. He was untiring in industry, ardent in zeal, philosophic in views, pure in purposes and strong in patriotism. When he retired from Congress to serve his country in a more perilous sphere, he had the esteem and approbation of his co-workers in the glorious cause of LIBERTY.

In 1777 he became Brigadier General Whipple and took command of the first brigade of the Provincial troops of New Hampshire acting in concert with Gen. Stark who commanded the other. Gen. Burgoyne was on the flood tide of military glory—rushing down upon the north like a herd of wild buffaloes over a prairie—spreading consternation far and wide. He was first checked in his triumphant career by Gen. Stark at

Bennington, Vermont. Gen. Whipple joined Gen. Gates about the same time and was in the bloody battles of Saratoga and Stillwater where the palm of victory was measurably attributed to the troops under his command. To the consummation of the brilliant victory over the British army Gen. Whipple contributed largely. Col. Wilkinson and himself were the officers who arranged and signed the articles of capitulation between the two commanders. He was one of the officers who conducted the conquered foe to Winter Hill near Boston. His faithful negro participated in all the perils of his old *massa* and could not have been more elated with the victory had he been the commanding general.

In 1778 Gen. Whipple was with Gen. Sullivan at the siege of New Port which was abandoned for want of the aid of Count D'Estaing whose fleet was injured by a gale. A safe retreat was effected in the night. In 1780 Gen. Whipple was appointed a Commissioner of the Board of Admiralty which he declined, preferring to serve in the legislature of his own state in which he continued for years. In 1782 he was appointed Financial Receiver for New Hampshire by Robert Morris. The office was arduous, unpopular and irksome but in his hands lost much of its odiousness. At the end of two years he resigned. On the 20th of June 1782 he was appointed a judge of the Superior Court. On the 25th Dec. 1784 he was appointed a Justice of the Peace and Quorum throughout the state which latter office he held to the day of his death. He was one of the commissioners on the part of Connecticut to settle the controversy between that state and the Commonwealth of Pennsylvania relative to lands in Wyoming valley. In all the multiform duties that devolved upon him in the various public stations he filled he acquitted himself nobly. He possessed a strong analyzing mind, deep penetration of thought, a clear head and good heart.

During the latter part of his life he suffered much from disease in his chest which terminated his useful career on the 28th of Nov. 1785. At his request before death, his body underwent a *post mortum* examination. His heart was found ossified. The valves were united to the aorta and an aperture not larger than a common knitting kneedle was all that remained for the passage of the blood. This explained the reason of his faintness under sudden emotion.

In all the relations of private and public life–from the cabin boy up to the lofty pinnacle of a well earned fame, Gen. Whipple was a model of consistency and virtue. He left a reputation pure as the virgin sheet. His career demonstrated clearly that in our country fame is confined to no grade in life and that practical knowledge, crowned with strong common sense, enables a man to be substantially useful to his country and fellow men. Citizens of America of only a common education—you are and should be useful. Look at this bright example and govern yourselves accordingly.

WILLIAM WILLIAMS.

INFIDELITY, in all its multiform aspects, is a legitimate child of inconsistency. The man who has impartially read the Bible—who understands physiology, the philosophy of mind—the minutiæ of anatomy, the unerring laws of nature, the powers of reason—the revolving circuit of his own immortal soul and denies the existence of Him who spake and it was done—who commanded and it stood fast—disrobes himself of the noblest power bestowed by creative Wisdom and forfeits the high dignity of a man. All things, from the leaf that vibrates in the gentle breeze to the etherial sky spangled with stars, proclaim the existence of a God. Most assuredly there is a Supreme Being who rules, with unerring wisdom, in the kingdoms of Nature, Providence and Grace. Beyond all cavil this position is most conducive to the happiness of the human family in this life. The superstructure of the Infidel is clustered with present misery. If its foundation should prove sandy he curses himself in this world to be more wretched in the next. Aside from the question of its divinity—Religion is the substratum of social order and human felicity. Infidelity is the destruction of both. History is crowded with demonstrations of this position. Banish the Bible and religion from our Republic—remove this firm foundation upon which the Sages of the Revolution based it—anarchy would ensue and we should rush into the same vortex of ruin which engulphed the French Republic.

By many of our Revolutionary patriots religion was exemplified—by all it was venerated. Among those of them who enjoyed its full fruition through life was William Williams born at Lebanon, Windham County, Connecticut, on the 8th of April 1731. He was the son of Rev. Solomon Williams whose paternal ancestor came from Wales in 1630. Solomon was pastor of the Congregational church at Lebanon for fifty-six years. He was a man of consistent and uniform piety—of liberal and expansive views and believed religion to be the foundation of rational liberty. His own soul enraptured with the substantial joys of practical piety—he strongly desired his children might inherit the same blessing. His prayers were answered. Of a large family of sons and daughters—all consecrated themselves to the Lord of glory and became exemplary members of the church over which their father presided.

After completing his preparatory studies William entered Harvard College and graduated in 1751. He sustained a high reputation for correct deportment untiring industry and scholastic lore. His father then directed his theological course preparatory for the sacred desk. But his talents were too diversified for a clerical life. He had a taste for classics, architecture, mechanics, mathematics and general science.

He was also inclined to travel. In 1755 he accepted a commission in the staff of Col. Ephraim Williams a kinsman of his and founder of Williams College at Williamstown, Mass. Sir William Johnson, who commanded the English troops, detached Col. Williams with 1100 men to reconnoitre the army of Baron Dieskau composed of a large force of French and Indians. After proceeding some four miles the detachment was attacked by a superior force lying in ambush. Col. Williams fell in the early part of the engagement bravely fighting for the mother country. His troops then retreated in good order until the main body came up and repulsed the enemy

The French war cost the Americans much blood and treasure. It was a matter of allegiance–not of interest. The Canadas were won by the Colonies for Great Britain. The pilgrim fathers were long treated and used as vassals of the English crown. Blended with the unparalleled cruelties of the hired minions of the mother country was damning ingratitude–the concentrated essential oil of Pandora that drives back the rushing blood upon the aching heart.

During the campaign Mr. Williams became disgusted with the hauteur of the British officers towards native Americans who were by far the most efficient troops against the Indians and French, whose mode of warfare they better understood. Released from the army, he resolved never again to submit to such indignities. He returned home and commenced the mercantile business. Soon after, he was elected town clerk, a member of the assembly and appointed a justice of the peace. These were unsought favors–purely a tribute to merit. For a long time he was either speaker or clerk of the House of Representatives in which he served nearly one hundred sessions. For fifty years he faithfully served in a public capacity.

When the Revolutionary storm began to darken the horizon of public tranquillity he boldly met its raging fury. Extensively and favorably known–his salutary influence had a wide range. When the tocsin of war was sounded he closed his commercial concerns and devoted his whole time to the glorious cause of equal rights and rational

Liberty. His learning, piety, honesty of purpose, energy of action and large experience—combined to give great weight to his character. He was an active member of the council of safety and on the second Thursday of October 1775, was appointed a delegate to the Continental Congress. He entered zealously into the deliberations of that revered body and made himself truly useful. He was ever ready to go as far as any one to obtain the liberation of his suffering country from the serpentine coils of tyranny. He was in favor of bold and vigorous measures and advocated the Declaration of Rights from its incipient conception to its final adoption. He was greatly instrumental in dispelling the doubts of many whose motives and desires were as pure but whose moral courage was less than his. He was well versed in the different forms of government, international law and the routine of legislation. When he spoke in public he was listened to with profound attention. He was a member of Congress in 1776–7 and when the final vote was taken upon the Magna Charta of our Liberty William Williams responded a thundering—AYE—that told his boldness and his zeal. That vote stands confirmed by his signature—a proud memento of his unalloyed patriotism—a conclusive proof of his moral firmness.

He was free from that aspiring ambition that is based on self and nurtured by intrigue. His motives emanated from the pure fountain of an honest heart. To promote the glory of his country was the ultimatum of his earthly desires. Upon the altar of Liberty he was willing to sacrifice his property and life. To vindicate the cause of Freedom he was willing to spend his latest breath. He used every honorable exertion to rouse his fellow citizens to a sense of danger and induce them to enlist in the common cause against the common enemy. At the time Congress was compelled to flee from Philadelphia he risked his life to rescue Colonel Dyer from the fangs of the British who had planned his arrest. They both made a hair-breadth escape. When the government treasury was drained of its last dollar, Mr. Williams threw in what he termed a mite of hard money, being over two thousand dollars for which he took continental money only to die in his hands. How emphatically things are changed. Now the public treasury distributes mint drops profusely upon many whose pretended services are as worthless as continental rags—in some instances absolutely injurious.

He was remarkably active and fortunate in obtaining private donations and necessaries for the army. He went from house to house, receiving small parcels of any and every article that would alleviate the wants of the destitute soldiers. At different times he forwarded to them more than a thousand blankets. During the winter of 1781 he gave up his own house for the accommodation of the officers of the legion of Col. Laurens and did all in his power to render officers and soldiers comfortable. His industry was equal to his patriotism seldom retiring until after twelve and up again by the dawn of day.

Mr. Williams was a member of the convention of his state when the Federal Constitution was adopted and gave it his hearty sanction. He was never permitted to retire from the public arena until prostrated by disease which terminated his useful career on the 2d of August 1811. He had lived the life of a good man—his end was peaceful, calm and happy.

He was a fine figure of the middle size, dark complexion and hair, piercing black eyes, an aquiline nose, an open and ingenuous countenance, a stentorian voice and strong physical powers. He was blessed with a clear head, a noble heart, a sound judgment, an acute perception and a logical mind. Not a blot could be found upon the fair fame of his public or private character. During the latter part of his life he was troubled with an increasing deafness and spent much of his time in Christian devotion. But few men have served their country as much and no one more faithfully than did WILLIAM WILLIAMS.

JAMES WILSON.

THE history of party spirit is red with blood. Its career has been marked with desolation and ruin. It often rides on the whirlwind of faction or on the more dreadful tornado of fanaticism. It has blotted kingdoms and empires from existence, consumed nations, blighted the fairest portions of creation and sacrificed millions upon its sanguinary altar. Confined to no time or place—it has taken deep root in our own country. Its poison has contaminated our political and religious atmosphere most fearfully. It has had its victims of blood in this land of republican and Christian professions. Its miasma has reached our ballot boxes, violated the peaceful fireside, traduced private character, invaded patriotism, induced perjury, countenanced forgery, corrupted our elective franchise and produced mobocracy in its most direful aspect. Great and good men have been victimized by reckless partisans who stop at nothing and stoop to everything to accomplish their purposes—right or wrong. They look at the end regardless of means.

In recurring to the eventful period of the American Revolution those who are not familiar with the history of the local politics of that day may naturally conclude that party spirit found no place in the bosoms of those who were engaged in a common cause against a common enemy. Far different was the fact. Many of the best men of that trying period were scourged, lacerated and for a time paralyzed by reckless party spirit.

Among its victims was James Wilson, born of respectable parents near St. Andrews, Scotland, in 1742. His father was a farmer in moderate circumstances which he moderated still more by rushing into the whirlpool of speculation—an unfortunate propensity that adhered to this son. He graduated at St. Andrews, Edinburgh. This done he took lessons in rhetoric under Dr. Blair and in logic under Dr. Watts. He then came to Philadelphia and obtained the situation of usher in the college of that city. His moral worth, strong talents and high literary attainments gained for him the esteem and marked respect of Dr. Richard Peters, Bishop White and many others whose friendship and influence were most desirable. Those who knew him best admired him most.

He subsequently studied law under John Dickinson and settled at Carlisle, Pennsylvania, where he rose rapidly to the head of the Bar. A powerful exhibition of Ciceronian eloquence and legal acumen at the trial of an important land case between the Proprietaries and Samuel Wallace gained for him an early professional celebrity. The Attorney General, Mr. Chew, fixed his eyes upon him soon after he commenced his argument and gazed at him with admiring astonishment until he closed his lucid speech. He was immediately retained in another important land cause and was considered equal to any member of the Pennsylvania Bar. He removed ultimately to Annapolis, Maryland and at the end of a year to Philadelphia where he was liberally patronised but rushing occasionally into the whirlpool of speculation his circumstances were uniformly embarrassed. As an evidence of his goodness of heart, amidst the most keen reverses he remitted money regularly to his poor widowed mother in Scotland to the day of her death using every means in his power to smooth her path to the tomb.

With the intolerant commencement of British oppression the political career of Mr. Wilson began. He boldly spoke and ably wrote in favor of equal rights and liberal principles. He was an early and zealous advocate of the American cause. Of a consistent and reflecting mind he sometimes censured the rashness of others which brought upon him malicious slanders which enabled his enemies several times to envelope him so completely in the dark fog of party spirit as to partially paralyze his exertions until the sun of truth would rise and dispel the vapors of calumny.

He was a member of the Provincial Convention of 1774, convened for the purpose of devising plans for the redress of grievances imposed by England. During the session he was nominated to the Congress soon to meet. He was bitterly opposed by Mr. Galloway but was elected by a handsome majority. He was continued a member of Congress until 1777 when his enemies succeeded in their long nursed machinations against him. At the commencement of hostilities he was commissioned colonel and appointed a commissioner to treat with the Indians. On the 4th of July 1776 he proved his sincerity in the cause of Liberty by a fearless vote and a bold signature in favor of the Declaration of Independence. In the minds of all who were not blinded by party spirit his action on that day refuted the base slanders that had been promulged against him. At the shrine of this dread monster the brightest subjects of purity have often been sacrificed. No goodness of heart–no brilliancy of talent–no exalted worth–no sanctity of character can shield a public man from the base assaults of party spirit–be he benefactor, philanthropist, saint, sage or hero. Even Washington writhed under the ostracism of this withering scourge. Some men are born *demi-gogs* and live under the influence of Gog and Magog during their deleterious existence.

Mr. Wilson was an esteemed and active member of the Continental Congress. Born a Scot he would not have exemplified the marked trait of his nation had he not been cool and cautious in everything. He, with many others, opposed the immediate adoption of the Declaration of Independence–not because they doubted its justice but because they believed the Colonies were not in a physical condition to sustain it. His patriotism and republicanism both stood forth in bold *relievo* when the question was finally put. He venerated the instrument and was bound by principle to submit to the will of the majority in what he believed to be clearly right although he believed it premature. His opposition was based upon the single fact of the physical weakness of the Colonies clearly expressed, yet his partisan enemies branded him with a want of patriotism. The people were not long deceived and esteemed him the more for his candor.

In 1782 he was again elected to Congress and was hailed as one of its most efficient members. The same year he was appointed one of the counsellors and agents of Pennsylvania to meet the commissioners who convened at Trenton, New Jersey, for the final settlement of the protracted controversy between Connecticut and that commonwealth relative to certain lands in the Wyoming Valley. The luminous and unanswerable arguments of Mr. Wilson had a controlling influence over the commissioners who decided in favor of Pennsylvania and closed an unpleasant litigation of years.

During the *interim* when he was not in Congress he held the office of advocate-general for the French which led him to a close investigation of national and maritime law. For this service the French king gave him 10,000 livres. He was at the same time a director in the Bank of North America and had the full confidence of Robert Morris as a safe and able financial adviser. As an active and discreet member of important committees he stood in the front rank. He traced the lines of every subject with the compass of wisdom and closed its bearings and measurement with mathematical precision. He arrived at the desired goal with less show but with more certainty than some whose zeal was more impetuous but not more pure than his. He sought more to bestow lasting benefits on his country than to elicit the huzzas of the multitude. He well knew that effervescent popularity was not an index of that substantial usefulness which lives long after that transient vapor consigns its ephemeral subjects to the mellow repose of peaceful oblivion. Balloon politicians may become inflated by the hydrogen of party spirit and rise in the political atmosphere followed by the eyes and elated by the shouts of thousands. A single spark of fire from the furnace that created the gas will show most of them to be treacherous and unsafe gasometers. Modest worth avoids ethereal excursions. It stands like a rock of granite on the *terra firma* of deep thought, calm reflection and sound discretion. Nothing but a sense of imperious duty can induce the very men who should be there to enter the whirling vortex and thorny arena of politics. How many such men are now in public stations guarding the rights and directing the proper destiny of our nation is a subject worthy of careful and anxious inquiry. If the people in mass are not true to themselves demagogues will not be true to them.

Mr. Wilson was one of the most useful members of the Convention that formed the Federal Constitution. He strongly opposed the popular project of the appointment of members of Congress by the legislatures of the States and was mainly instrumental in placing their election in the hands of the people. This principle should have been applied to every office named in that instrument not subject to the control and supervision of the President and Senate. Mr. Wilson was one of the committee that put the Constitution in form and reported it to the Convention. When completed by amendments and presented to his own

State he was its most powerful advocate and bore down upon the opposition with a sweeping torrent of eloquence and logic that was irresistible. He was also a member of the Convention of Pennsylvania to amend its Constitution, in which he took a decided stand in favor of placing the elective franchise in the hands of the people. The last vestige of aristocracy trembled before him and the last whisper of slander against the purity of his republicanism died upon the lips of echo. The boldest features of liberal principles in the old revised Constitution of that State were penned by James Wilson. Had his views been fully incorporated in that instrument I presume a second revision would not have been made.

When the Supreme Court of the United States was organized Washington selected Mr. Wilson for one of its judges. This high office he filled with great ability up to the time of his death. In 1790 he was appointed the first professor of the Law College in Philadelphia. When that and the University of Pennsylvania were united he filled the chair. As a learned and eloquent lawyer he had no superior at the Philadelphia bar. He was honored with the degree of LL.D. and during the first year of his professorship delivered an admirable course of lectures to the law students. Like most of the Scotch literati, towards them he was distant and reserved. His writings were vigorous and logical. In 1774 he wrote a spirited essay on the assumptions of the British Parliament not warranted by Magna Charta and portrayed the blessings arising from a republican form of government in such fascinating colors that it exercised a wide and salutary influence. To the uninitiated in party politics it may seem strange that any one accused James Wilson of aristocracy or a want of patriotism. A purer friend of his country or a more ardent advocate of the cause of freedom could not be found among the sages of '76. He passed through the ordeal of party persecution several times but truth-telling time forced his enemies to retrace their steps disgraced and shamed.

On the 28th of August 1798 this venerable sage, eminent lawyer, able statesman, profound jurist and impartial judge took a final leave of earth and closed his eyes in death. He died of strangury whilst absent on his circuit. Fortunately he was with his friend Judge Iredell in Edenton North Carolina where his ashes repose in peace. During his last illness he realized the proverbial hospitality of the south and was cared for in the kindest manner.

The private character of Judge Wilson was beyond reproach. He was a warm friend, an affectionate husband, a faithful father, a consolation to the widow and the fatherless, an upright and honest man.

In reviewing the history of this worthy man no one can doubt his patriotism and purity. No room is left to question his devotion to the American cause and his firm opposition to British oppression. Influenced by noble motives, guided by liberal principles–it is painful to reflect that he was often wounded in the house of his professed friends by those who had sworn to support the same cause he so ardently and ably espoused. The solution of this paradoxical problem may be found in the present state of things without travelling back to that time of times, when party spirit should have withdrawn its hydra head into its legitimate Pandora box. We have those among us who live under the protective mantle of the Federal Constitution and the laws based upon it, who denounce that Constitution and refuse obedience to statutes according with it unless those statutes advance their interests and chime with their revolutionary views. They are cancers on the body politic loathsome to the sight of every friend of our country–to every advocate of our UNION. It would promote our safety and their happiness to colonize them beyond fifty-four forty.

JOHN WITHERSPOON.

THE man who makes the Bible his counsellor–the polar star of his actions, will not go far astray. Divine in its origin, the sublimity of its language caps the climax of composition. As a history of the grand epoch when God said–" Let there be light–and there was light"–it stands alone clothed in all the majesty of Divinity. As a chronicle of the creation of man after the moral image of Deity–of his ruinous fall–of the glorious plan of his redemption–it must remain unrivalled. As a chart of human nature–human rights and wrongs and of the attributes of the great Jehovah–in precision, fullness and force of description it far exceeds the boldest strokes, the finest touches of the master spirits of elocution in every age. As a system of morals and religion–the efforts of men to add to its transcendent beauty–its omnipotent strength–are as vain as an attempt to bind the wind or imprison the ocean. As a book of poetry and eloquence–it rises in grandeur above the proudest production of the most brilliant talents that have illuminated and enraptured the classic world. As a book of Revelation–it cast a flood of light upon the wilderness of mind that shed fresh lustre upon reason, science and philosophy. As a book of counsel–its wisdom is profound, boundless, infinite. It meets every case in time and is a golden chain reaching from earth to Heaven. It teaches our native dignity–the duties we owe to our God, families, parents, children and our fellow men. It teaches us how to live and how to die—arms the Christian in panoply complete—snatches from death its painful sting—from the grave its boasted victory and points the pious soul to its crowning glory—a blissful immortality beyond the skies. The man who is led by this sacred book to lean upon the Supreme Ruler of revolving worlds, has a sure support that earth cannot give or take away. When we can rightfully appeal to Heaven for aid in our undertakings, faith bids us onward and fear no danger.

A large portion of the most prominent patriots of the American Revolution were pious men. I am not aware of one who did not believe in an overruling Providence. Several of them were devoted ministers of the gospel. Among these was John Witherspoon, born in the parish of Yester near Edinburgh, Scotland, on the 5th of February 1722. He was a lineal descendant of John Knox the celebrated reformer. The father of John was minister of Yester parish and moulded the mind of this son in the ways of wisdom, virtue and science. At an early age he placed him in the Haddington school where the rare beauties of his young mind unfolded like the flowers of spring. He soared above the trifling allurements that too often lead childhood and youth astray. His studies were his chief delight. He exhibited a maturity of judgment, clearness of perception and depth of thought—seldom maifested in juvenile life. He entered the Edinburgh University at the age of fourteen and fully realized the anticipations of his friends in his educational advancement. Especially did he excel in theology. He passed the ordeal of his final examination at the age of twenty-one and was licensed to proclaim to his fellow men the glad tidings of the Gospel of Peace. He immediately became the assistant of his revered father—a favorite among their parishioners—an eloquent preacher of plain practical Christianity.

On the 17th of January 1746, he was a "looker on in Vienna" at the battle of Falkirk and with many others whose curiosity had led them to the scene of action, was seized by the victorious rebels and imprisoned in the castle of Doune. After his release he resided a few years at Beith, subsequently at Paisly—rendering himself very useful as an exemplary and faithful minister. During his residence at the latter place he received urgent calls from Dublin, Rotterdam and Dundee. He also had an invitation to fill the presidential chair of the College of New Jersey in America to which he had been elected on the 19th of November 1766. This was done at the suggestion of Richard Stockton. A general demurrer by his friends and a special demurrer by his relatives were entered against his acceptance. Ingenious arguments were used to sustain the pleas put in. The delights of his native home—the horrors of the western wilderness were placed before him in fearful contrast. A very wealthy bachelor relative offered to will him his large estate if he would remain. For a year he declined the proffered chair. During that time his lady caught "the missionary fever" and became anxious to embark for the new world–removing every obstacle with the ingenuity and perseverance peculiar to woman when bent upon the accomplishment of a noble object. On the 9th of December 1767 Mr. Stockton had the pleasure of communicating his acceptance to the trustees of the college which was most joyfully received.

Early in the ensuing August he arrived with his family and was inaugurated at Princeton on the 17th of that month. His literary fame had been spread through the Colonies and caused an immediate accession of students–a new impetus to the institution–a renovation of the empty treasury of the college. He introduced a thorough and harmonious system in all its departments and fully answered the most sanguine anticipations of his warmest friends.

His mode of instruction was calculated to expand the ideas of his students and launch them upon the sea of investigation. He expelled the dogmatical and bewildering clouds of metaphysical fatality and mystic physiology that rendered darkness visible in the old schools. He illuminated the minds of his students with the mellow rays of scientific truth based upon enlightened philosophy, sound reason, plain common sense and liberal principles. He taught them to explore the labyrinthian avenues of human nature–the vast circuit of their own immortal minds. He raised before them the curtain of the material, moral, physical and intellectual panorama–lucidly demonstrated their harmonious unity of action–perfected by the great Architect of this mighty machinery made for man. He pointed them to the duties they owed to themselves, their fellow men, their country and their God. He awakened in their souls the living energies of charity that assimilates man to Deity and prompts him to noble god-like action. He taught them how to live and be useful–how to throw their mortal coil when the journey of life should end. His instructions were luminous and enriching–his precepts fertilizing as the dew of Hermon.

On the flood tide of a high literary and theological fame he floated peacefully along until the revolutionary storm drove him from the college and the pulpit of his church to a different sphere of action. Before coming to America he understood well the relations between the mother country and the colonies. He was master of civilian philosophy, international law, monarchical policy and the principles of rational freedom. The enrapturing beauties of Liberty and the hideous deformity of tyranny passed in review before his gigantic mind. In the designs of creative Wisdom he saw the equal rights of man and resolved to vindicate them. He at once took a bold stand in favor of his adopted country. With an eagle's flight he mounted the pinnacle of political fame—with a statesman's eye he surveyed the mighty work before him. The plan of political regeneration stood approved by Heaven—he determined to give his aid to the glorious cause. Most nobly did he discharge every duty assigned him.

From the commencement of revolutionary agitation he was a member of various committees and conventions formed for the purpose of seeking redress from the king—*peaceably* if possible—*forcibly* if necessary. He was a member of the Convention of New Jersey that framed the new Constitution in 1776. On the 20th of June the same year he was elected to the Continental Congress and most ably and eloquently advocated the Declaration of Independence to which he affixed his name, appealing to his God for approval—to the world for the justice of the cause he espoused. He was continued a member of Congress up to 1782 with the exception of one year and contributed largely in shedding lustre over its deliberations. With a mind and intelligence able to grasp, comprehend and expound the whole minutiæ of government and legislation, he combined a patriotic zeal and holy devotion for his country—unsurpassed by any of his colleagues. His labors were incessant, his industry untiring, his perseverance unyielding—his patriotism as clear as the crystal fountain—pure as the pellucid stream.

During the time he served in the legislative halls he did not neglect the higher honors of the vineyard of his Lord and Master. He was often at the family altar, in the closet and the pulpit. He was one of the most able, eloquent and profound preachers of that eventful period. He was one of the brightest ornaments of the religion of the Cross—one of the strongest advocates in the cause of Liberty. As a speaker he was listened to with deep interest—as a systematic and logical debater he had few equals. His arguments were *a posteriori, a priori* and *a fortiori*—leading the mind from effect to cause, from cause to effect and deducing the stronger reason. His corollaries were often of the most thrilling character. He sometimes resorted to syllogism with great effect. His speeches would be a syllabus to many of modern times upon the same subjects. His memory was remarkably retentive, his perceptions clear, his judgment acute.

He was a member of the secret committee of Congress the duties of which were delicate and arduous. He was a member of the committee to co-operate with Gen. Washington in replenishing and regulating the army–of the committee of finance and upon several other working committees. The eloquent appeals to the people from Congress, recommending days for fasting and prayer were from his nervous pen. The burning and melting manifesto, protesting against the inhuman treatment of the American prisoners confined on board the filthy prison-ships at New York, was supposed to emanate from him.

Dr. Witherspoon was prophetic in his mode of reasoning when pointing out the results of propositions laid before Congress and opposed all those he believed would terminate unfavorably. He strongly remonstrated against the issue of continental money. His predictions of sudden depreciation were too fully realized. It took a rapid downward course and soon reached the ruinous discount of one hundred and fifty dollars of paper for one of silver and then took a fatal leap and plunged into the abysm of worthlessness. So deeply did he probe every subject that he investigated, that his powers of penetration became proverbial. Most of the measures he proposed when he entered the legislative arena that were adopted proved successful and those he opposed and were adopted uniformly proved disastrous.

In the halls of classic literature, the ecclesiastic courts or on the floor of Congress, he was a shining light to those around him. His literary, theological and political writings were numerous, of a high order and are justly celebrated here and in Europe. They exhibit a pleasing and rich variety of thought–a strong and chaste imagination–a luminous and flowing fancy–a keen and sarcastic wit–a brilliant and fascinating style–broad and liberal views–philosophic and logical propositions–clear and convincing conclusions–all mellowed with the rich freshness of living charity and universal philanthropy.

In 1779 he resigned his seat in Congress in consequence of ill health. His son-in-law, Rev. Dr. Smith was Vice President of the college and relieved him from the most arduous duties of President. The next year he was again elected to Congress and resigned finally in 1782. The trustees of the college then persuaded him to embark for Europe for the purpose of raising funds for the institution. As he predicted before he left, his efforts were unsuccessful. He returned in 1784 and retired to his country seat a mile from Princeton, there to enjoy the blessings of peace and the golden fruits that had been richly earned by years of peril and toil. Surrounded by relatives and friends, enjoying the praise and gratitude of a nation of freemen–his name immortalized as a scholar, divine, civilian, statesman and patriot–he sat down under the bright canopy of a clear conscience–an approving Heaven–anticipating a crown of unfading glory beyond the skies.

In this manner he glided down the stream of time peaceful and happy until the 15th of November 1794, when he fell asleep in the arms of his Lord and Master, calm as a summer morning, serene as a cerulean sky—welcoming the messenger of death with a seraphic smile. He was buried at Princeton.

A review of the life of this great and good man affords an instructive lesson for every considerate reader. He was endowed with all the qualities calculated to ennoble and dignify man and assimilate him to his Creator. His superior virtues and endowments eclipsed his frailties and placed him on a lofty eminence beyond the reach of envy, malice or slander. His fame is clustered with refulgent beauty that will spread a lustre over his name that will brighten and shine until the death knell of LIBERTY shall be sounded and social order rush back to original anarchy.

In all the relations of public and private life, Dr. Witherspoon stood approved, admired, revered. Let all strive to imitate his examples that our lives may be useful in time—our final exit tranquil and happy—ever remembering that virtue is the crowning glory of talent.

OLIVER WOLCOTT.

THE unrestrained oppressions of imperial and kingly power, long exercised with impunity, have been receding before the light of intelligence with an ominous but rather unsteady pace for the last few centuries. As the genial rays of Liberty illuminate the crowding millions of the human family the tenure of thrones will become more slender—monarchies more limited if not annihilated. In Europe kingly power has been vibrating for years in the cradle of a political earthquake. The love of freedom has never been extinguished in the old world. The same motive power that prompted the pilgrims to court the dangers and privations of this western hemisphere, still pervades the bosoms of those held in bondage by military force. Volcanic eruptions occasionally occur—new craters open—the time is rolling on rapidly when these craters will rush together and deluge kingly and imperial power with one broad sheet of liquid fire. In thunder tones of retribution the people will proclaim their FREEDOM.

When our ancestors planted themselves on the granite shores of America they had clear conception of a republican form of government as organized by Greece and Rome. Many of them had read the thrilling history of the rise, progress and fall of those republics in the original languages where none of the beauties or force are lost by translation. They were prepared to improve upon those governments by avoiding their errors and preserving all that was valuable. With these lights the pilgrim fathers appear to have been illuminated when rearing the incipient superstructure of a more pure republic than any before known. At first, articles of association were entered into by the people of a single or contiguous settlements, based upon the broad platform of equal rights and universal Liberty circumscribed only by eternal justice and sterling honesty. Among the earliest of these miniature republics was that consolidating Windsor, Hartford and Weathersfield in Connecticut. The articles of association adopted by this infant Colony were penned by Roger Ludlow. The revised constitution of that state is either substantially copied from the instrument drawn by Ludlow or the ideas of republicans must run in a channel that has no change.

Among those who directed the destiny of the pioneers of the new world the name of Wolcott stands conspicuous. Henry Wolcott, the patriarch ancestor, removed from England to Dorchester, Mass. in 1630. In 1636 he founded the town of Windsor, Connecticut. During the perils of the Indian wars—the difficulties with the Canadian French and through all the various vicissitudes that have pervaded New England down to the present time, the descendants of Henry Wolcott have acted a conspicuous part. They were ready to go where duty called—to the field or legislative hall.

Oliver Wolcott, the subject of this brief sketch, was the son of Roger Wolcott who was appointed Governor of Connecticut in 1751. This son was born on the 26th of November 1726 and graduated at Yale College in 1747. The same year he was commissioned to raise and command a company which he marched to the defence of the northern frontiers where he remained until the peace of Aix la Chapelle. He then returned and applied himself to the study of medicine until he was appointed the first sheriff of Litchfield County formed in 1751. In 1755 he married Laura Collins a discreet woman of great merit. In 1774 he was appointed counsellor which station he filled for twelve consecutive years. He was also chief judge of the Common Pleas Court and for a long time a judge of the Probate Court. In the military field he rose from the grade of captain to that of major-general. In the summer of 1776 he commanded the fourteen regiments raised by Gov. Trumbull to act with the army in New York. He headed his division at the memorable battle that resulted in the capture of Burgoyne and revived the drooping spirits of those who were engaged in the glorious cause of equal rights. He was uniformly consulted on important military movements and listened to with great confidence. From its commencement he was a zealous and efficient advocate of the cause of freedom and stood firm amidst the revolutionary storm undaunted by the roaring of the British lion.

In 1775 Congress made him commissioner of Indian affairs for the Northern Department then an important trust. During the same year he effected much towards reconciling disputes between Colonies relative to their boundaries. Amiable and persuasive in his manners—imbued with a clear sense of justice, he was an admirable mediator. He merited the blessing pronounced on peace-makers.

In 1776 he took his seat in Congress and remained until he affixed his signature to that Declaration of Rights which burst the chains of maternal bondage—gave birth to our nation in a day—astonished gazing millions—shook the British throne to its centre and gave us a Republic that surpasses all Greek—all Roman fame.

He then returned to the field and on all occasions proved a brave, skilful and prudent officer. When he deemed his services more useful in Congress than in the army he would take his seat in that body, which he did at intervals up to 1783. In 1785 he was associated with Arthur Lee and Richard Butler to conclude a treaty of peace with the Six Nations of Indians. The year following he was elected lieutenant-governor and performed the duties of that office with great ability and dignity up to the time of his death which occurred on the 1st day of December 1797. He died regretted by the nation at large, but most by those who knew him best.

His numerous public services were highly appreciated. They were promptly and judiciously performed without any parade, pomp or vain show. His private character was adorned by all the richness of purity—purpose and action, that render a man an ornament among the virtuous. He possessed all the sterling virtues—was a devout and consistent Christian—a useful and honest man. In the hands of such men our government is secure—our UNION safe.

GEORGE WYTHE.

To be born rich is oftener a misfortune than a blessing. Action is designed by the great Creator—noble and god-like action. Riches are prone to produce inertness. With the young, who are left to the bent of their own inclinations either by the erroneous indulgence of parents or for the want of parents or an efficient and kind guardian, an abundance of riches often proves their ruin. A thousand emissaries are abroad to lead them into the purlieus of vice and hurry on their sure destruction. Money attracts attention in all circles. Although the love of it is the root of all evil–still it commands undue attention. Thousands live who will not earn, but must have it. These sharks are ever on the lookout for young men of fortune and too often succeed in plucking every feather from their newly fledged wings. The poor young man is in less danger. He has no attractions for fashionable blacklegs–the vilest things that creep on earth. Necessity impels him to action. He labors industriously–studies economy–saves his earnings and eventually becomes rich. Many of the most wealthy men of our country commenced without a dollar. Few who are left large fortunes retain them and but few who have lost them in profligacy have moral courage to break the fetters of vice, spurn the demons who have robbed them, return to the paths of rectitude, redeem a lost fortune–a shattered reputation and again stand up like men. We wonder and admire to behold such instances–rare to be sure–but they have occurred.

This was fully exemplified by George Wythe born in Elizabeth City, Virginia, in 1728. His father was a wealthy planter–his mother a woman of unusual talents, learning and worth. To her this son was indebted for his education and early impressions of the correct and noble principles that actuated him after he assumed the dignity of a man. From her he acquired the Greek and Latin languages and general science. Unfortunately for him both his parents were snatched away by death nearly at the same time, leaving him a buoyant youth without a hand to guide or a voice to warn him against the allurements of vain pleasure or the seductions of ruinous vice.

His father left him a fortune which was sufficient to have made a prudent man in easy circumstances for life. Like too many *only* sons, he had been put to no business. He was a stranger to labor and had no inclination to make its acquaintance. He was soon led away by idle company, became dissipated and pursued the road to ruin until he was thirty years of age, neglecting study and business and spending all his substance.

Like the prodigal he then came to himself–returned to the paths of virtue, studied the profession of law, was admitted to the Bar and became one of its brightest ornaments. During the remainder of his life he walked in the ways of wisdom most scrupulously and proved to his friends and the world that a young man may be led astray by the prowling wolves of vice–be torn and lacerated by the demon robbers that are permitted to prey upon the community by the official guardians of our cities and towns and yet recover from his wounds, redeem his character and become a virtuous and useful member of society. God grant that this example may influence thousands to go and do likewise.

No man ever dignified his profession more than Mr. Wythe. He was rigidly honest and would not proceed in a cause until convinced justice required his services. If drawn into a cause by misrepresentation that was tinctured with wrong, he would abandon it the moment he discovered that fact and return the fee. His virtuous habits, extreme fidelity, legal acquirements and untiring industry, gained for him the esteem and confidence of his friends and the people at large. He was a member of the House of Burgesses for a long time and under the new government was appointed Chancellor of the State, which office he filled with great ability to the time of his death. He was highly esteemed as a legislator for integrity, talent and independence. In politics he was guided by his own matured judgment irrespective of party. On the 14th of November 1764 he was appointed on a committee to prepare a petition to the king, a memorial to the House of Lords and a remonstrance to the House of Commons on the impropriety and injustice of the proposed Stamp Act.

The remonstrance was from the able pen of Mr. Wythe and was drawn in language so bold and strong that it alarmed many of his colleagues and underwent a modification to divest it of what they deemed a tincture of treason. He understood and properly appreciated the true dignity of man and did not live to quail at the tyranny of a haughty monarch or corrupt ministry. He was a prominent member of the House of Burgesses in 1768, when Virginia blood and Virginia patriotism were roused and passed the memorable resolutions asserting their exclusive right to levy their own taxes—accused ministers and Parliament of violating the British Constitution and denied the right of the crown to transport and try persons in England for crimes committed in America. In passing these resolutions parliamentary rules were dispensed with, the members anticipating the proroguing power of the governor, who, on learning their tenor, immediately dissolved the House. He was half an hour too late—they had passed their final reading—were entered upon the records and beyond his power to veto or expunge. This action of the governor was unfavorable to the interests of the crown—the people took the helm as they should do now and returned all the old patriotic members to the next session with several new ones of the " same sort."

Among the new members was Thomas Jefferson who had been a law student under Mr. Wythe—was charged with the same *rebel* principles and was a bold and fearless champion of Liberty and equal rights. The atmosphere was becoming rather too highly charged with patriotic fire to be comfortably inhaled by the governor and the bipeds of the crown. It was rather too caloric for the free respiration of monarchical lungs. The people, awakened to their true position—saw the path of duty and pursued it. With an enlightened mass there is safety.

From that time Mr. Wythe continued to oppose parliamentary and ministerial oppression and boldly vindicated the rights of his injured country. At the commencement of the revolutionary movements he joined a volunteer corps, determined to vindicate in the field the principles he had advocated in the legislative hall. He lived up to the motto—" we do what we say."

In August 1775 he was elected a member of Congress and took a high rank in that body—then the observed of all observers. When the proposition of Independence was made it met his warm approbation. He was to the hilt in this measure. When the day arrived for final action he put his name to that bold instrument that he knew must prove the Chart of Liberty or the death warrant of the signers. In all the majesty of conscious dignity these master spirits of freedom shook off the corroding rust of kingly power, planted deep the tree of Liberty and proved to a gazing world that a nation can be born in a day and live. Language can never portray nor imagination fully conceive the enthusiastic joy that marked the promulgation of the Declaration of Independence among the people. The bells sounded a requiem and tolled the funeral knell of monarchy—illuminations and roaring artillery conveyed the glad news from the central arch of the Union to its remotest bounds—the replenished torch of Liberty rose, a pillar of fire to guide the patriots in their onward march—on the wings of thanksgiving and praise the happy tidings were carried to the throne of Heaven, received the sanction of Jehovah's high authority and were recorded in the book of everlasting fame by the hand of justice with an angel's pen.

In November 1776 Messrs. Wythe, Pendleton and Jefferson were appointed to revise the laws of Virginia. Although much other business devolved upon them they prepared and reported one hundred and twenty-six bills by the 18th of the ensuing June. The new code commenced the revision at the time of the revolution in England and brought it down to and in accordance with the new government.

In 1777 Mr. Wythe was chosen Speaker of the House of Delegates—

the same year a Judge of the High Court of Chancery and subsequently Chancellor. A more impartial judge never graced the Bench. Nothing could induce him to swerve from strict justice. He was a profound jurist and a lucid expounder of the law. He graced the law professorship in the College of William and Mary until other duties compelled him to resign. He was a member of the legislature when Virginia sanctioned the Federal Constitution.

He put in full practice his principles of Liberty by the emancipation of his slaves and providing them with the means of support. He tried the experiment of education upon one so far as to teach him Latin and Greek when he suddenly died. He was extremely anxious to see a development of African intellect that its calibre might be more clearly known.

Chancellor Wythe died suddenly on the 8th of June 1806, believed to be from the effects of poison administered by George Wythe Sweny, a grandson of his sister, for the purpose of arriving immediately at the enjoyment of a part of his estate which was fortunately prevented by a codicil made just before his decease. Although there was not proof to convict the ungrateful demon, circumstances were so strong against him that the public verdict stamped upon him the damning stigma—*murderer*.

In his private character Chancellor Wythe was amiable, modest, charitable and humane. He sought to improve the society in which he moved and used great exertions to guard young men against the purlieus of vice. He was industrious, temperate, frugal but liberal and proverbial for charity and a practical Christian.

Jefferson, in delineating the character of his law instructor—remarks—" No man ever left behind him a character more venerated than George Wythe. His virtue was of the purest kind—his integrity inflexible and his justice exact. Of warm patriotism and devoted as he was to Liberty and the natural and equal rights of men he might be truly called the Cato of this country without the avarice of a Roman, for a more disinterested person never lived. ·Such was George Wythe—the honor of his own and a model for future times."

ROBERT YATES.

Time is wasted by many persons as if it had no limit and they were to live for ever. But few place a proper value upon it—but a small portion of *these* reduce it to an advantageous system. If every person realized that "time is money" and ends in eternity–it would be used very differently by many–not by all. The instances are very rare where a man of fifty can look back upon his career and not see that he has squandered a large portion of his time in senseless vacuity or improper appropriation. If he then realizes its full worth he will gaze upon the past with keen regret and vainly wish he could live his life over again–a wish that the illustrious Washington said he did not indulge. If no one of the human family wasted or improperly used time, earth would be a Paradise–Pandemonium a fable. If all would assign a due portion of time for each class of incumbent duties–rigidly adhere to the one and promptly perform the others–a harmony in action and an amount of labor would be produced that would effect a change in the social, religious and business departments that would astonish the most visionary theorist of system and order. Profligacy of time too often commences in childhood–increases in youth and is made bankrupt in manhood. Let all feel more deeply the importance of a judicious arrangement and wise improvement of precious TIME. Its whirling wheels are rolling us on rapidly to " that country from whose bourne no traveller returns." It is a boon from our Creator–to Him we must render an account of every hour from the moment our reason assumed and presided over its empire. Let all be prepared to render that account with a joy that shall increase in ecstacy through the ceaseless ages of ETERNITY.

In perusing this history of the Sages and Heroes of the American Revolution the reader has learned that all of them were industrious–several of them bright models of perfect system in the distribution of their time. No one was more diligent in the performance of his duties than Robert Yates who was born in the city of Schenectady, N. Y. on the 27th day of January 1738. The early developments of his mind were of unusual solidity and free from that frivolity that too often retards the course of boys in their preparation for manhood. Let my young readers remember this and become men in conduct during your minority. You will then be prepared to appear upon the stage of action with credit to yourselves and usefulness to our common country. Improve your minds by storing them with useful knowledge. If the tree has no blossoms in spring we gather no fruit in autumn. If your youth is barren of healthful culture–if the vain allurements–the trifling amusements of this deceiving world exclude from your immortal minds salutary improvement–your mental powers may darken with age and rush you into the murky waters of lasting disgrace–perhaps ruin you for ever. Soon the mighty concerns of our country will devolve on you.

In your hands will be placed the destiny of our nation. Some of you must fill up the swelling ranks of the professions–the arena of politics and posts of honor and profit. Let these reflections raise you above the trifles that amuse without benefitting you. Learn to be men when you are boys–you may then be intellectual giants when you reach manhood. Remember your Creator–study the Bible and let it be deeply impressed upon your minds that to become eminently great you must be truly good.

Robert Yates commenced his classical education in the city of New York and completed it at an early age. He then read law with William Livingston of that city and became an ornament to the profession. He located at the city of Albany–obtained a lucrative practice–the high esteem of his numerous acquaintances and a title of honor too rare and priceless–" THE HONEST LAWYER." An additional proof of his good sense was exhibited by his leading to the hymeneal altar the amiable Miss Jane Van Ness who proved worthy of the noble man of her judicious choice. They sailed buoyantly, prosperously and joyfully on the flood tide of domestic felicity until the angry elements of an oppressed people were concentrated by British oppression and raised the rough storm of the Revolution. Mr. Yates was a whig of the first water–bold, fearless, calm, prudent and firm as the iron mountain of Missouri. No one better understood the relative condition of the two countries–the powers and rights of each and the law of nations. He was conversant with the liberal principles of Magna Charta as granted by King John and as improved and confirmed by King Henry III. in the ninth year of his reign. He was familiar with the provisions of the British Constitution–the Charters of the Colonies and the various declaratory Acts of Parliament defining the rights of the American people which had grown sacred by long and peaceful enjoyment. To see them now rudely trampled upon by a venal ministry roused the patriotism and indignation of Mr. Yates. He wrote and published several pungent essays exposing the usurpations of the British Cabinet. He took an active part in the public meetings of the people that prepared them to strike for LIBERTY. At that time he was a member of the corporation of Albany and attorney for that board. He was a leading member of the Committee of Safety when it was virtually the supreme government of the empire state. The *tories* greatly feared and most sincerely hated this bold champion of equal rights. His ardent zeal was tempered with a discreet moderation and equal justice to all. He never passed the orbit of legitimate power nor hesitated in performing his whole duty regardless of consequences. He was an active member of the first Provincial Congress of New York–

chairman of the committee to organize the military and did much towards producing a concert of action against the invading enemy. In 1777 he was an efficient member of the Convention that framed the first constitution of his native state. Under that constitution he was appointed a judge of the Supreme Court. His acceptance raised him to the zenith of rebellion in view of the creatures of the crown. He was menaced by them and threatened by the tories. He promptly assumed the duties of his responsible station and boldly performed them. Stern justice, tempered with charity, directed his course. Officially he favored no friend—persecuted no enemy. His courts were held in the midst of bitter foes. No dangers could intimidate—no threats deter him from the faithful discharge of all the duties devolving upon him. When tories were arraigned before the court the overcharged zeal of jurors sometimes paralyzed their sense of right. On one occasion he sent out a jury of this kind four times with a direction to change their verdict of "guilty" which was not warranted by the testimony. The legislature talked loudly of calling him to an account for this act but on a sober second thought wisely determined to permit the old Roman to pursue the even tenor of his ways. His salary was far below the income of his practice at the Bar. To advance the interests of his country was above all pecuniary considerations. His salary for one year was paid in paper apology for money which depreciated so much in a few days that it took the whole to buy a pound of tea. This did not disturb his equanimity or abate his zeal in the glorious cause of Independence.

After the close of the Revolution Messrs. Robert Yates, Alexander Hamilton and Chancellor Livingston were chosen to represent the state of New York in the Convention that framed the Federal Constitution. His services on that important occasion were highly appreciated. He was opposed to some features of that sacred instrument but voted for its adoption when it came before the Convention of his own state. When it became the supreme law of the land he was one of its firmest supporters. In his first charge to the grand jury after it had been legally sanctioned he used the following language which I implore the reader to ponder well and let it come home with all the force of living truth proclaimed from the tomb of a departed patriot.

"The proposed form of government for the Union has at length received the sanction of so many of the States as to make it the supreme law of the land. It is not therefore any longer a question whether or not its provisions are such as they ought to be in all their different branches. We, as good citizens, are bound *implicitly to obey them*. The united wisdom of America has sanctioned and confirmed the act and it would be but little short of treason against the Republic to hesitate in our obedience and respect to the Constitution of the United States of America. Let me, therefore, exhort you gentlemen—not only in your capacity as grand jurors but in your more durable and equally respectable character as citizens—to preserve inviolate this Charter of our national Rights and safety—a Charter second only in dignity and importance to the Declaration of our Independence. We have escaped, it is true, by the blessing of divine Providence, from the tyranny of a foreign foe—but let us now be equally watchful in guarding against *worse and far more dangerous enemies*—DOMESTIC BROILS AND INTESTINE DIVISIONS."

Would to God this patriotic language of Judge Yates could be written in flaming capitals of living fire raised in bold relievo on plates of burnished gold and suspended in every court room, legislative hall, church, school-house and public place in our land. It should be circulated by every press in our country and committed to memory by every child.

Judge Yates was one of the Commissioners to settle the boundary question between New York and the States of Massachusetts and Connecticut. He was subsequently employed to prosecute claims of his native State against Vermont. In 1790 he was appointed Chief Justice of the Empire State and presided with great dignity until the 27th of January 1798 when his age reached the constitutional limit and closed his long, useful, arduous and brilliant judicial career. He had been an ornament to the Bench for twenty-one years. Not a stain had soiled his official ermine. He then resumed the practice of law and was appointed by the legislature of his state to settle disputed titles in the military tract which office he held until the Act creating it expired.

In comparative poverty and peace he glided down the stream of time until the 9th day of September 1801 when an arrow from the quiver of death pierced the shining mark—released his noble soul from its earthly prison and returned it to its original home of enduring bliss. He had exemplified primitive Christianity—his last hours were bright with hope, strong in faith, calm, peaceful and happy. He was greatly beloved in life—deeply mourned in death. In the performance of all the multiform duties of public and private life he stood approved by his friends, his country, his conscience and his God. He was an admired model of system in all the concerns of life—arranged his time judiciously, improved it wisely and earned a lofty fame that will endure while virtue is esteemed and patriotism lives. In the hands of such men our Republic will continue to rise in majesty sublime until its burning light shall illuminate the world and become too brilliant for the vision of all those who do not love and support our UNION.

PART II.

ALLEN ETHAN was a native of Salisbury, Connecticut and removed to Vermont when a boy. He was a man of strong mental powers which were improved by a close observation of men and things–not by a school education. He took an active part in public affairs from an early age to the time of his death. He was emphatically a " Rough and Ready." When the revolutionary storm commenced he was the kind of man to brave its fury. He was then a militia colonel and at once rallied a brave band of Green Mountain boys around him. Soon after the battle of Lexington he received orders from the general Assembly of Connecticut to make a descent on Ticonderoga and Crown Point. About that time Arnold had been charged by the Massachusetts Committee to raise 400 men for the same purpose. On his arrival he found Col. Allen prepared to march with 300 men and became his aid in the expedition. On the 9th of May 1775 they arrived at the lake opposite Ticonderoga and with great difficulty landed 83 men near the garrison during the night. As day was approaching the Colonel determined on an immediate attack. He led his Spartan band to the wicket gate where a sentinel snapped his gun at the bold intruders and fled into the fort closely followed by the Green Mountain boys who rushed in and formed on the parade ground facing the two barracks and made the welkin ring with three loud huzzas. One of the guard who begged for quarter pointed out the apartment of the officers. Col. Allen entered with his sword drawn and demanded the surrender of the fort from the astonished Capt. De la Place who was in command. He jumped out of bed, rubbed his eyes and asked by whose authority the demand was made. The Colonel quickly replied–" *I demand it in the name of the great Jehovah and the Continental Congress.*" The summons was promptly obeyed. Crown Point surrendered the same day and shortly after, the only British sloop of war, which gave Col. Allen the mastery of Lake Champlain. In the fall of that year Col. Brown pledged himself to act in concert in an attack upon Montreal but failing to meet him Col. Allen was overwhelmed by numbers and taken prisoner, loaded with irons and treated with proverbial British cruelty–a mistaken policy on the part of the crown officers that did much towards rousing the Americans to resistance. He was sent to England with a strong promise of a halter on his arrival. In 1776 he was returned to N. York and was not exchanged until the 6th of May 1778. Bad treatment had ruined his iron constitution. A base attempt was made to bribe him which he resented with the dignity of an honest freeman. He wrote a history of the cruelties uniformly practised upon the American prisoners. During his confinement in N. York he estimated that over 2000 perished by hunger, cold and disease produced by the impurity of the prisons and prison ships. Col. Allen was highly esteemed as a stern patriot, a good citizen–an honest man. He died suddenly at his home in Colchester, Vermont, on the 13th of February 1789.

ALLEN EBENEZER a brave subaltern officer who was with Col. Allen at the capture of Ticonderoga. At the head of only 40 of his Spartan comrades he took the fortress on the hill Defiance without the loss of a man. At the brilliant affair near Bennington he headed the small division that was stationed behind a ledge of rocks and kept the enemy at bay until Gen. Stark could form his men to drive back the reinforcement that came up before he could properly dispose of the large number of prisoners he had taken. Mr. Allen closed his mortal career in 1805.

ALLEN MOSES was born in Northampton, Mass. on the 14th of September 1748. He graduated at Princeton college–prepared for the ministry–became pastor of the Presbyterian church at Medway, Georgia–advocated the cause of equal rights in the pulpit and when mingling with the people. In 1778 the British under Gen. Provost made a descent upon Medway–laid in ashes the meeting house and most of the private dwellings. Mr. Allen was made chaplain of the Georgia brigade–repaired to Savannah–was there taken prisoner–sent on board a ship of war–was treated with great cruelty–attempted an escape by swimming to the shore and was drowned on the 8th of February 1779.

ALEXANDER WILLIAM was born in the city of New York in 1726. He was a Major General in the Continental army–fought bravely at the battle of Long Island on the 27th of August 1776 where he was taken prisoner. At the battle of Germantown his brigade was a part of the reserve. At the battle of Monmouth he commanded the left wing of the American troops and did himself great credit as a brave, discreet and accomplished officer. This noble veteran died at Albany, New York on the 15th of January 1783.

ARMSTRONG JOHN was early enrolled with the list of heroes that periled life for Liberty. He was one of the brave officers who so nobly defended fort Moultrie against the desperate attack of Sir Peter Parker when he visited Charleston harbor on a belligerent pleasure excursion. He was raised to the rank of Brigadier General and distinguished himself at the battle of Germantown and other places. After the Revolution he located in Pennsylvania and was elected to Congress from that state. He was in all respects a worthy man and took his final leave of his friends in 1795.

BARRY JOHN was born in the county of Wexford, Ireland in 1745 and came to Philadelphia, Pa. when he was but 15 years of age. Previous to the American Revolution he became a skilful mariner and rose to the rank of captain of a large merchant vessel. In February 1776 Congress put him in command of the brig Lexington with 16 guns with which he made several successful cruises. In 1777 the British attacked the little American Navy in the Delaware, then under the command of Commodore Barry and destroyed it at White Hall. He subsequently took charge of the Raleigh of 32 guns and was run on shore in Penobscot Bay by the enemy and lost his ship. He was then transferred to a ship commissioned with letters of marque and reprisal and cruised among the West India Islands with success. On his return he was put in command of the Alliance frigate and left Boston in February 1781 for France with John Laurens, American minister to that kingdom. When returning he came in contact with the British ship Atlanta and brig Treposa on the 29th of May and captured them both after a severe engagement. In February 1782 he had what the British captain called a drawn battle with an English frigate of equal metal with his own but could out sail her. The enemy had 37 killed and 50 wounded–Com. Barry but 3 killed and 11 wounded. Lord Howe offered him 20,000 guineas and command of the best frigate in the British navy if he would turn traitor. This base proposition was repelled with contempt. When war seemed inevitable with France he was put in command of the frigate United States and cruised on the West India Station. He was noble in spirit, humane in discipline, discreet and fearless in battle, urbane in his manners, a splendid officer, a good citizen, a devoted Christian and true patriot. He died in Philadelphia on the 30th of September 1803.

BEATTY WILLIAM born in Frederick county Maryland on the 19th of June 1758. In 1776 he was commissioned an Ensign under Col. Griffith and served under Gen. Washington at New York. The next year he was commissioned Lieutenant and in a few months was raised to the rank of Captain and ultimately transferred to the renowned 1st Maryland regiment of regulars under Col. Gunby which was ordered south and performed astonishing feats of noble daring at the battle of Cowpens and at Guilford court house on the 15th of March 1781. He there engaged in single combat when the battle was raging with the fury of desperation and pierced his antagonist through the heart. That battle was emphatically fought hand to hand like those of Chippewa, Lundy's lane and Bridgewater during our last war with mother Britain. At the battle near Camden South Carolina on the 25th of the next April, Captain Beatty fell mortally wounded as he was gallantly leading on his company to the charge. His loss was keenly felt. He was in all respects a noble man and an officer of great promise. In his report Gen. Greene remarked–" Among the killed is Capt. Beatty of the Maryland-line one of the best of officers and an ornament to his profession."

BIDDLE NICHOLAS was born in the city of Philadelphia, Pennsylvania in 1750. He became a seaman when but 14 years of age and gave great promise of becoming one of the noblest sons of the main. He and his shipmates were cast away on a barren island on the 2d day of January 1766 two remaining there with him for nearly two months in a state of extreme suffering. In 1773 he and Horatio–afterwards Lord Nelson, doffed their uniforms and shipped before the mast on board the Carcase bound on a voyage to the north pole and penetrated to 81° 39′ north latitude. At the commencement of the American Revolution Capt. Biddle was put in command of the Camden galley on the Delaware. He was subsequently transferred to the Andrew Dorin of 14 guns with 130 men and attached to the infant fleet of Commodore Hopkins, destined for the Island of New Providence. On arriving at the capes the small pox became general among the other crews–disease obliged the fleet to run into New London. After replenishing his numbers Capt. Biddle was ordered to cruise off the banks of Newfoundland where he was so successful in capturing British ships that when he arrived in the Delaware he had but five of his original crew, the others having been put on board the prizes.

On his return he was placed in command of the frigate Randolph of 32 guns and sailed from Philadelphia in February 1777 with a crew partly made up of English seamen. Shortly after he got to sea he was overtaken by a gale which carried away nearly all the masts of his frigate. He then steered for Charleston to repair. On the way mother Britain's children formed a plan to dispatch the Americans and take the ship although they were shipped upon their own urgent solicitation professing to sustain the cause of Independence. They were promptly put down and sullenly returned to duty. When thoroughly repaired he again put out to sea. On the third day he fell in with four English vessels, one the True Briton with 20 guns, all of which he captured. He took several other prizes and returned to Charleston. So highly did the citizens of that city esteem Capt. Biddle as an officer and gentleman that they fitted out the ship General Moultrie–the brigs Fair American, Polly, and Notre Dame and placed on board the Randolph fifty men from the first regiment of the South Carolina infantry to act as marines– the whole of which were placed under command of Capt. Biddle. His little fleet continued cruising and capturing prizes until the night of the 7th of March 1778 when it came in contact with the English two decker ship Yarmouth of 64 guns, Capt. Vincent. At 8 P. M. a severe action commenced. Capt. Biddle was severely wounded in the thigh but continued on deck encouraging his brave tars. His fire was incessant–at least three broad sides to that of one from the enemy. In 20 minutes after the commencement of the fight the Randolph blew up–the brave, accomplished, intrepid and gallant Biddle was launched into eternity. The Yarmouth was so badly crippled that she permitted the other vessels to depart unmolested.

BLAND THEODORIC was born in Virginia in 1742. He was one of the early patriots and left a lucrative medical practice and took command of a regiment of dragoons. In several actions he proved himself a brave and efficient officer. In 1779 he was put in command of the convention troops at Albemarle barracks. The next year he was elected to Congress. He was a member of the Virginia Legislature when the Federal Constitution was adopted and voted with the minority for the same reasons that induced Patrick Henry to oppose it. When adopted he was its firm adherent and was a member of the first Congress that convened under its broad mantle. He died on the 1st of June 1790 while a member of the House of Representatives. He was a good, discreet and honest man.

BLOUNT THOMAS was born in North Carolina in 1760. He entered the Continental army at the age of 16 and served faithfully to the close of the war. He was subsequently made a major-general of the militia of his native state. He was a valued member of Congress for many years. He was a man in the full sense of the word. He died on the 8th of February 1812 while at his post in the national legislature.

BOUDINOT ELIAS was ushered into life on the 2d day of May 1740 in the city of Philadelphia. He read law with Richard Stockton, a signer of the Declaration of Independence. In 1776 Congress appointed him Commissary General of prisoners. The next year he was elected to the Continental Congress and proved an able and efficient member. In 1782 he was elevated to the presidential chair of that bright galaxy of sages and had the high honor–the untold pleasure of signing the treaty of peace forced from mother Britain. In 1789 he was elected a member of Congress under the new constitution. In 1795 President Washington placed him at the head of the Mint at Philadelphia which office he filled for 12 years. He then retired from the public arena and settled at Bordentown, N. J. where he died on the 24th of October 1821. He was a noble, generous, talented and good man. He was the first President of the American Bible Society and made liberal donations to that and several other benevolent institutions.

BOWDOIN JAMES first breathed the vital air in Boston, Mass. in 1727. He became a prominent public man at an early age–was a bold and sterling whig–opposed the usurpations of the crown–was one of the trio of the committee that bearded Gen. Gage, who ostracised him, Dexter and Winthrop from the General Assembly. Mr. Bowdoin was elected to the first General Congress in 1774 but was prevented from attending by ill health. He was President of the Convention that framed the first constitution of Massachusetts under the new order of things. In 1785-6 he was Governor of his native state. He was an able statesman, a firm patriot, a devoted Christian–an honest man. He died at Boston on the 6th of November 1790.

BRADFORD WILLIAM was born in the city of Philadelphia, Pa. on the 14th of September 1755. In the spring of 1776 he was made brigade-major under Gen. Roberdeau who commanded the flying camp. He subsequently commanded a company of regulars under Col. Hampton for a short time and was then appointed Deputy Paymaster General and served two years when he left the military service–resumed the study of law–was admitted to the Bar in 1779 and in 1780 was made Attorney-General of the Keystone state. On the 22d of August 1791 Gov. Mifflin raised him to the Bench of the Supreme Court of Pennsylvania which office he filled with great dignity until the 28th of January 1794 when he was appointed Attorney-General of the United States, which office he held up to the time of his death. He performed all the duties of public and private life with great ability and strict fidelity. He stood approved by his country, his conscience and his God. He died at Philadelphia on the 23d of August 1795 in full hope of an unfading crown of glory.

BROAD HEZEKIAH was born in Massachusetts in 1748. He was a man of strong common sense, great moral courage, stern integrity–discreet and consistent in all things. He early and firmly opposed British oppression. He was a member of the Provincial Congress in 1774 and a delegate of the Massachusetts Convention that framed the state constitution in 1779. He filled various public offices with honor to himself and usefulness to his constituents. He died at Nantick, Mass. on the 17th of March 1824.

BROOKS ELEAZER was first introduced to his friends in Concord, Mass. in 1726. He was a man of bright intellect and untiring perseverance. Without the advantages of a school he became a man of extensive information by studying books, men and things. In 1774 he was elected to the General Court and remained a distinguished member of the different branches of the Legislature for 27 years. He was an uncompromising enemy to all tyranny. At the battle of White Plains in 1776 he commanded a regiment with the skill of a veteran soldier. At the battle of Still Water on the 7th of October 1777 his cool and determined courage was the subject of general remark. He lived esteemed and died lamented at Lincoln, Mass. on the 9th of November 1806.

BROOKS JOHN was first presented to the human family in Medford, Mass. in 1752. He was well educated—became a physician and commenced a successful practice in the town of Reading near his native place. When the revolutionary storm commenced its fury he exchanged his amputating knife for a sword. His noble bearing and skill in military tactics attracted the attention of Washington. He was soon promoted to the grade of lieutenant-colonel and rendered important service in the capture of Burgoyne. At the close of the war he resumed the practice of medicine at Medford. He became major-general of militia and commanded the military that put down the insurrection in Massachusetts in 1786. During the last war with mother Britain he was the adjutant-general of Gov. Strong and succeeded him as chief magistrate of the State. He performed all the duties of public and private life with a well tempered zeal and unquestioned integrity. He died in Medford, Mass. in 1825.

BROWN ANDREW was one of those brave spirits who seized their rusty muskets, powder horns and slugs and met the enemy on the heights of Lexington. At the noted battle of Bunker's and Breed's Hill he was among the last who left the entrenchments for want of " a little more grape." He removed to Philadelphia when his war-toils were over and conducted the Federal Gazette in Chestnut Street. On the 27th of January 1797 his office and dwelling house were consumed by fire. His wife and three children perished in the flames. In an attempt to rescue them he was so severely injured that he expired on the 4th of February following.

BROWN JOHN was born in Providence, Rhode Island in 1736. He led the party that dared to resist the crown task-masters and destroyed the British sloop of war Gasper in Narraganset Bay in 1772. That was the second kick the Rhode Islanders gave the revolutionary ball. He was an enterprising merchant—at one time member of Congress—a friend to education and public improvements, a good citizen and worthy man. He died at Providence, R. I. in 1803.

BROWN MOSES was welcomed to earth in 1741 at some place in New England—of the precise location we have no record. He was a bold mariner—never liked old England—became an active patriot—commanded several privateers with great success and did good service for his country until he saw her free and independent with the white, red and blue floating in the breeze of LIBERTY. He lived respected and died regretted in 1803.

BROWN ROBERT was born in Northampton County, Pa. in 1745.

He was among the first officers who entered the field against the invading foe and was taken prisoner at the unfortunate affair on Long Island. Being a man of fine sense, pleasing manners and good address, he was not closely confined and was permitted to work at his trade of blacksmith and distributed his earnings among the destitute prisoners. He was subsequently raised to the rank of brigadier-general of militia in his native State–filled many civil stations–was member of Congress for sixteen years–voted for the war in 1812–lived to see mother Britain flogged a second time–spent his last years in the full sunshine of quiescent peace–died at Allentown, Pa. in 1823 most deeply mourned by those who knew him best.

BRYAN GEORGE was a native of Ireland–when he came into the world and made his final exit the record saith not. He came to Philadelphia soon after he reached his majority and became a wholesale merchant and highly respected citizen. He had imbibed no love for England during his youth–in manhood he sternly opposed her innovations upon the chartered rights of his adopted country. He was a member of the Continental Congress in 1775. He was subsequently made Vice President of Pennsylvania and in 1778 filled the presidential chair of that State. He adorned every station he occupied with becoming dignity and usefulness. He was a Christian, gentleman and scholar.

BURD BENJAMIN was born at Fort Littleton, Bedford County, Pa. in 1755 and was made a lieutenant in Col. Thompson's regiment of riflemen at the age of twenty. He was in several fights near Boston in 1775. He was at the disastrous battle of Long Island and behaved with great gallantry. In 1777 he was commissioned captain in the 4th Pennsylvania Regiment–was at the battles of Trenton, Princeton, Brandywine, Germantown and Monmouth and in every instance stood highly approved by his superior officers. At Germantown he acted as major. In 1779 he was with the detachment that dispersed the Indians up the Hudson and burnt their towns. After the war he located at Fort Littleton–subsequently removed to Bedford where he lived highly esteemed for his past noble services, uniform virtue and correctness in the discharge of all the duties of a life well spent. He died at Bedford on the 5th of October, 1823.

BURR AARON commenced his remarkable life in Newark, N.J. in 1756. As manhood dawned upon him his genius rose in all the brightness of the sun on a cloudless morning. He was hailed as a brilliant luminary to light up the pathway to the goal of LIBERTY. He was a powerful advocate in the cause of FREEDOM and exemplified his precepts by feats of noble daring in the battle field. He was aid to the brave Putnam and rose to the rank of lieutenant-colonel. At the close of the Revolution he stood on a lofty eminence and commanded the admiration of the populace. His towering genius was fast ascending to high meridian in refulgent glory. He was elected to the United States Senate where his giant intellect became more conspicuous–his thirst for power more prominent. He was next elected Vice President and made a desperate attempt to supplant Thomas Jefferson as President. He made an unsuccessful Cataline grasp at the presidential chair which blotted out his political sun for ever. Alexander Hamilton made some prophetic remarks upon the prospective danger shadowed by his reaching demonstrations and ulterior designs. He planned and consummated the death of that illustrious statesman. The commingled clouds of wild ambition, consuming malice and fell revenge eclipsed the sunbeams of his genius. A blacker cloud spread its ebony mantle over these. The charge of TREASON veiled the bright morning of AARON BURR in darkness impenetrable and paralyzed his day-spring of usefulness. His great legal acumen and consummate shrewdness saved him from its technicality—not from the burning curse of a nation of freemen. To render his darkness more visible he was the Promethean vulture that devoured blooming innocence—the blighting sirocco that withered the bowers of domestic felicity. Like an isolated majestic oak with its green foliage seared by lightning fire—he stood alone for nearly half a century exposed to the scorching heat of bitter scorn—the chilling blasts of cold neglect—a fearful warning to those who wander from the path of wisdom—the only path of safety. He died on Staten I. 14th. Sept. 1836.

BUTLER RICHARD is first introduced by the record as a brave lieutenant-colonel in Morgan's rifle corps. For his correct deportment at all times and noble daring on various occasions at the south under La Fayette, he was raised to the rank of colonel. He was next in command under Gen. St. Clair in his unfortunate expedition against the western Indians in 1791. At the sanguinary and disastrous battle of the 4th of November of that year Col. Butler commanded the right wing of the army with the rank of general and repeatedly led his men to the charge and for a time seemed certain of victory. Bleeding from several wounds he retired for surgical aid and in a few moments was rushed upon by an Indian warrior who gave him a mortal wound with his tomahawk. He immediately killed the savage with his pistol—they slumbered in death together.

BUTLER THOMAS was introduced into the great family of man in 1754. He was brother to Col. Richard Butler just mentioned. There were five brothers engaged in the Continental army. They appear to have been natives of Pennsylvania. Thomas was a law student under James Wilson of Philadelphia at the commencement of the Revolution. In 1776 he exchanged the law office for the camp and proved a brave and efficient officer. He had command of a company to the close of the Revolution and was in nearly every severe battle in the middle States. At Brandywine he received the thanks of Gen. Washington on the field of battle through his aid Gen. Hamilton, for rallying a detachment of flying troops and giving the enemy a severe check. At the battle of Monmouth he received the thanks of Gen. Wayne for defending a defile while Col. Richard Butler removed his regiment from a perilous position. He had command of a battalion under Gen. St. Clair on the memorable 4th of Nov. 1791 and behaved with great coolness and intrepidity. Mounted on his horse he led his men to the charge after his leg was broken by a ball. His surviving brother—Capt. Edward Butler, had great difficulty in bringing him from the field. In 1794 he was promoted to the rank of lieutenant-colonel and put in command of the 4th sub legion. He commanded at Pittsburgh and by his undaunted courage more than by the numerical force of his troops he prevented the whisky insurgents from taking possession of the garrison. He was continued on the peace establishment—made several treaties with the Indians—was persecuted by jealous enemies—charged with misconduct—tried by a court martial—honorably acquitted and died the 7th of September 1805.

CADWALADER THOMAS was ushered into this world in 1743 in the city of Philadelphia, Pa. At the commencement of the struggle for Liberty he was in the front rank of the brave revolutionary generals and enjoyed the unlimited confidence of the illustrious Washington. At the beginning of the war he commanded a corps called the " Silk Stocking Company"—rather a problematical name for patriot soldiers as they were—for so perfect was this corps in military tactics that nearly all of its members were made commissioned officers. He was soon made a brigadier-general and put in command of the Pennsylvania troops. During 1776–7 he was constantly on duty—participated in the battles of Princeton, Brandywine, Germantown and Monmouth—displaying great courage, skill and prudence on each occasion. He loved Washington better than his own life. When Gen. Conway slandered the commander-in-chief he was at once challenged by Gen. Cadwalader and was dangerously wounded. Supposing he might not survive, he wrote to Washington acknowledging he had done him great injustice. Gen. Cadwalader was an ornament to the age in which he lived. In him the soldier, statesman, gentleman and scholar were all harmoniously blended. In public and private life he filled up the measure of a good man and crowned the design of his creation with an imperishable fame. His career was a continued round of usefulness.

CASWELL RICHARD is first introduced by the record in the capacity of Governor of North Carolina previous to the Revolution. He was an esteemed member of the Bar and remarkable for his kindness to the poor. He was a staunch whig and member of the first general Congress in 1774. In 1776 he commanded a regiment and proved himself a brave and skilful officer. With 1000 minute men he engaged Gen. McDonald with a force of 1500—killed and wounded 70 of his men—took him prisoner with 1500 rifles. This victory gave a fresh impetus to the glorious cause of Independence in North Carolina. This bold patriot ultimately reached the rank of major-general of militia. He was President of the Convention that framed the first Constitution of his State and governor for four years under that Constitution. He was President of the Senate at the time of his death. His life was nobly spent, his usefulness extensive, his reputation unsullied, his death deeply lamented. He died at Fayetteville, N. C. on the 20th of November 1789.

CHAMPE JOHN was introduced on this whirling planet in Loudoun county, Virginia, in 1752. He was naturally a soldier. In 1776 he was appointed sergeant-major of Lee's legion of cavalry and gained a high reputation for bravery and noble daring. He was engaged in the hazardous enterprise of apparently deserting to the enemy at N. York for the purpose of capturing and returning Arnold to the American camp that the life of Andre might be saved. Arnold changed his quarters on the very evening fixed for his abduction and thus saved himself and sacrificed one of the brightest ornaments of the British army. Had Sir Henry Clinton complied with the request of Washington and exchanged Arnold for Andre, justice would have been vindicated–humanity honored and England relieved from supporting a base traitor and his present descendents. Champe went south with the enemy–returned to his corps the first opportunity and met with a warm reception from his old companions. Washington rewarded him liberally and discharged him from the service for fear he might fall into the hands of the British and be treated with a halter. He removed to Kentucky where he died in 1797.

CHRYSTIE JAMES was born near Edinburgh, Scotland, 1750. At the age of 15 he came to Philadelphia and the next year received the commission of Lieutenant in the Continental army. He was soon put in command of a company and held the commission of Captain to the end of the war. He was one of Washington's favorites. No one better deserved his esteem. He was a brave soldier, a firm patriot, a good citizen, an honest man and a consistent Christian. The time of his death is not on the record. Lieutenant Colonel James Chrystie of the 15th regiment of U. S. Infantry, who fought so desperately at Queenston and other places during the last war with England, was his son and worthy of his noble sire.

CLARK GEORGE ROGERS is first introduced to us as a colonel in the service of the state of Virginia and the pioneer warrior of the then far west. No man ever understood better the Indian character and mode of warfare and no man did as much hard service on the frontier as Col. Clark. He was the protecting father of all the early settlements in Kentucky, Illinois, Indiana, Ohio and south western Pennsylvania. He became a terror to the red men. During the whole time of the Revolution he had command of the small forces on the western frontier and was commissioned a Brigadier General of the Continental army in 1781. In all respects Gen. Clark was well qualified to perform the hazardous duties that devolved upon him and did more than the acutest human sagacity dared anticipate. After a general peace took place with mother Britain and ultimately with her savage ally–the red men–Gen. Clark settled near Louisville, Kentucky to enjoy the fruits of his long and arduous toils. He was looked upon as the father of that broad section of country. Respected, beloved and honored–he glided down the stream of time until 1817 when his noble spirit went to its final rest.

CLINTON CHARLES father of James and George, was born in Longford, Ireland in 1690. On the 20th of May 1729 he embarked for America and after a tedious passage with a ruffian captain who compelled the passengers to give him a large sum of money above the price of their passage, he landed at Cape Cod instead of Philadelphia according to agreement. Mr. Clinton ultimately located in Ulster County New York, then a dense wilderness filled with wild beasts and savages more wild than them. He became a prominent public man and opposed the first indications of British oppression. He diffused liberal principles among his neighbors and planted them deep in the minds of his sons who did honor to their noble sire. He lived long enough to see the lurid clouds that portended the Revolutionary storm–just long enough to prepare his brave sons and neighbors for the approaching crisis. He was an honest man and a Christian. He died at his original residence in Ulster County on the 19th day of November 1773.

CLINTON GEORGE, a brother of James, born in Ulster county, New York, on the 26th of July 1739. They were sons of Col. Charles Clinton who was a native of Ireland. George was liberally educated, possessed a strong mind, great decision of character and highly charged with original–not modern demagogue patriotism. He was a member of the Congress of 1775-6. He was present and voted for the Declaration of Independence but being a Brigadier General of the Continental army he was compelled to leave before that sacred instrument was prepared for signatures–the reason why his name is not enrolled with the other sages. In April 1777 he was elected the first Governor of the State of New York under the new order of things and filled that office 18 consecutive years when ill health compelled him to decline. He commanded at Forts Clinton and Montgomery on the Hudson when they were taken by an overwhelming force after a most desperate resistance of several hours. The British force amounted to 4000–the American to only 500 within a very imperfect fortification. The works were stormed in the night which enabled the governor and many of his officers and men to escape through the defiles in the mountains. In 1801 he was again elected Governor of New York and in 1805 Vice President of the United States in which office he continued until the time of his decease which occurred at the city of Washington on the 20th of April 1812 when Congress was in session. A nation mourned the loss of one of her noblest sons, his friends one of their best companions, his kinsmen one of their dearest relatives. The closing sentence on his monument at Washington speaks volumes. "While he lived, his virtue, wisdom and valor were the pride, the ornament and security of his country and when he died he left an illustrious example of a well spent life worthy of all imitation."

CLINTON JAMES was first announced to his friends on a bright Thursday–the 9th of August 1736 in Ulster County, New York. He was by nature a military genius–by heritage a stern patriot. With an iron constitution and great physical powers he united an accomplished education, great military experience acquired in the French war of 1756 and the subsequent border wars up to the time the American Revolution commenced. In 1775 he was appointed colonel by the Continental Congress and fought by the side of the brave Montgomery when he fell at Quebec. On the 9th of August 1776 Congress raised him to the rank of Brigadier General. He was at the desperate defence of Fort Clinton in October 1777 and was severely wounded and escaped after the enemy had stormed the imperfect works with 4000 regulars against 500 soldiers mostly raw militia. He commanded a division under Gen. Sullivan in his expedition down the Susquehanna against the Indians and was one of his most reliable officers. He was raised to the rank of Major General and closed his brilliant military career at the siege of Yorktown. He subsequently filled several civil stations. In all the duties of public and private life he acquitted himself nobly and with great usefulness to his country. He died on the 22d of December 1822 near his native place.

COMSTOCK ADAM was first introduced to his relatives in 1743.

He was a soldier by nature–powerful in body, of undaunted courage, an enthusiastic patriot and good disciplinarian. He had the confidence of Washington who raised him to the rank of Colonel in the Continental line. At the brilliant victory at Red Bank he was the officer of the day. Alternately with Gen. Smith of Maryland he commanded at the successful defence of Mud Fort. After the war he filled various civil stations and was many years a member of the New York Legislature. His long and arduous services are a matter of history–no higher Eulogy need be pronounced. He died at his home in Saratoga County, New York on the 10th of April 1819.

COWARD JOSEPH was a native of Monmouth County, New Jersey. In view of this cognomen we may well exclaim–"What's in a name my lord?" He was a Coward and yet one of the bravest of the Revolutionary captains. He was a great terror to the refugees *alias* tories. At the battle of Monmouth and several other places his undaunted courage was conspicuous. When the British fleet lay off Sandy Hook, one of the supply ships ran too near the shore and stuck fast. With a few men Capt. Coward captured her in defiance of two barges manned with superiors numbers that were sent to the rescue. At the close of the war he returned to his farm–became the esteemed citizen and fully exemplified the noble attributes of an honest man.

CROGHAN WILLIAM was born in Ireland in 1752 and came to America at an early age. He had imbibed no love for mother England in his native country–he detested her tyranny in America. At the commencement of the Revolution he pledged his life in favor of equal rights. In 1776 he received the commission of Captain in the Continental army and took command of a company of Infantry in the Virginia line. He was in the battles of Brandywine, Germantown and Monmouth and received the high approbation of his superior officers. When the enemy invaded the south he was ordered to that field and raised to the rank of Major. At Charleston he was among the prisoners surrendered by Gen. Lincoln and was not exchanged during the war. He returned on parole and was a looker on at the siege of Yorktown but could not participate in that glorious victory. In the spring of 1784 he located at Locust Grove, Jefferson County, Kentucky, where he lived respected until September 1822 when he departed to the spirit world deeply mourned by his numerous friends.

CROPPER JOHN was born in Virginia in 1746. He was a captain in the 9th Virginia Regiment at the age of 19 which joined the northern army in December 1776. He was soon raised to the rank of major in the 5th Virginia Regiment which was literally cut to pieces at the battle of Brandywine. He retreated with those who could march and lay concealed in a thicket until after midnight and then proceeded to Chester with a red handkerchief upon a ramrod for a flag. His friends were no less astonished than rejoiced to see him and his brave remnant of soldiers, supposing they had fallen or were prisoners. He was subsequently raised to the rank of colonel and commanded the 11th Virginia Regiment until the 30th November 1782 when he returned to his long neglected home. When Commodore Whaley was attacked in the Chesapeake Bay by five British barges and was deserted by the three that were with him at the commencement of the fight, Col. Cropper was in the barge with him. The Commodore and half of his men being killed the Colonel continued the action and for some minutes defended himself against two white men and a negro of his own who was the means of saving his life. The moment he discovered it was his young master he cried out—"*Save my young master!*"—for which Col. Cropper gave him his freedom and settled him comfortably in Baltimore. The Colonel was ultimately promoted to the rank of general—lived highly esteemed at Bowman's Folly until the 15th of January 1812 when he departed in peace to the upper world leaving an untarnished reputation and a well-earned fame on the records of history.

CUSHING THOMAS was ushered into life at Boston, Mass. in 1725. He received a good education and commenced a useful public career soon after reaching his majority. In 1763 he was chosen speaker of the General Court of Massachusetts and was continued for several years. He was with Adams, Hancock and the other bold Whigs in all the measures of that eventful period. He was a member of the Continental Congress in 1774–5 and continued active and unwavering in the cause of freedom until it was consummated. He filled various legislative and judicial stations after the Revolution and performed all the duties of public and private life with ability and fidelity. He adorned the Christian character. He was lieutenant-governor when he died on the 28th of February 1788.

DALE RICHARD was born in Virginia in 1756. In 1776 he was made a midshipman on board the Lexington. The next year he was taken by the enemy and sent to the celebrated Mill Prison in England. At the end of a year he escaped to France and joined Paul Jones on board the American armed ship Bon Homme Richard and was made first lieutenant. He was in the desperate action with the British frigate Serapis. In 1794 he became a captain in the United States navy. In 1801 he was put in command of the American squadron that sailed to the Mediterranean and humbled the insolent Bashaw of Tripoli by battering down his castle. On his return in 1802 he located in Philadelphia where he lived in peace and plenty until 1826 when he made his final bow to the king of terrors and launched upon the ocean of eternity. He earned an enduring reputation for bravery, skill and humane discipline as a naval officer. As a citizen he sustained an unblemished character.

DARKE WILLIAM made his first appearance on earth in the county of Philadelphia, Pa. in 1736. His parents removed to Virginia when he was a child. He was with Braddock at his memorable defeat in 1755. At the commencement of the Revolution he entered the Continental army with the commission of captain and served faithfully to the close of the war when he had reached the rank of major. In 1791 he was put in command of a regiment under Gen. St. Clair—lost a son in the disastrous battle of the 4th of November of that year and had several hair-breadth escapes himself. His latter years were peaceful and happy. He died at his seat in Jefferson County, Virginia, on the 26th of Nov. 1801. He left an unsullied reputation.

DAVIE RICHARDSON WILLIAM came into the world under the auspices of the crown of Britain at Egremont, England, on the 20th of June 1756. In 1763 his father brought him to North Carolina and left him with the Rev. William Richardson a maternal uncle, who adopted him as a son and gave him a liberal education. At the commencement of the Revolution he resolved to join the patriots in the defence of equal rights. He was soon put in command of a company of dragoons and annexed to the legion under Count Pulaski. In a few months Capt. Davie was promoted to brigade major of cavalry. When Gen. Lincoln attempted to dislodge Lieut. Col. Maitland at Stono, Maj. Davie was severely wounded and disabled for five months. After his recovery he raised a corps of one company of dragoons and two of mounted infantry and spent the last shilling of a large estate in furnishing equipments and supplies for the service. He participated in the trying scenes of the southern campaigns under Generals Gates, Greene and others, until the foe was conquered and Independence secured. No officer of his grade did more to promote the cause of Liberty. After the war he became an eminent lawyer. He was a member of the Convention that framed the Federal Constitution. Every station he occupied in public and private life he filled with dignity and integrity. He was major-general of militia—governor of his State and minister to France in 1799. On his return his amiable wife was ill and soon died. He then removed to South Carolina and died at Chester in 1820. In life he exemplified all those high qualities that adorn the man and the Christian. He never united with any church because he considered manufactured creeds too dogmatical and sectarian lines drawn too closely for the growth of charity which he considered as broad as the human family—as diffusive as mountain air.

DAVIDSON WILLIAM was first presented to his fond parents in Lancaster County, Pa. in 1746 and when but four years of age removed with his father to Rowan County, N. C. At an early age he enlisted under the star spangled banner and was presented with the commision of major in one of the first regiments raised in North Carolina. Under Gen. Nash he repaired to the main army then in New Jersey. In 1779 he returned south, colonel of his regiment. By calling a few days at his home he escaped being made prisoner at the surrender of Charleston. He was very efficient in raising troops and supplies in his own state. In an engagement at Colson's Mills he was severely wounded and disabled for five weeks. On the last day of January 1780 Gen. Greene detached him with 300 men to prevent the enemy from passing the Catawba river. His corps was too small to repel the overwhelming force of Lord Cornwallis. He made a desperate defence and was instantly killed at his post. Col. Hall and several more of the British fell at the same time. In life Col. Davidson was greatly beloved and was an officer of great promise. His loss was keenly regretted and sincerely mourned.

DICKINSON PHILEMON was ushered into blooming life at Dover, Del. on the 5th of April 1739. Previous to the Revolution he located on a farm near Trenton, N. J. where he soon became prominent in public affairs. As in duty bound he boldly opposed the arrogant assumptions of mother Britain. He was a member of the Convention that formed the first constitution of his adopted state. He was made Commander-in-chief of the militia of N. J. and was very active in promoting the glorious cause of Independence. When stationed at Somerset Court House in January 1777 with only 300 plough boys of the true blue, Lord Cornwallis sent a foraging party of 400 regulars to a mill on the opposite side of Millstone river. Gen. Dickinson and his men forded the cold river which was up to their hips and rushed upon the enemy with such impetuosity that the red coats ran for dear life leaving their field pieces, nearly 50 wagons and over 100 English draft horses with a considerable number of cattle and sheep. So rapid was the flight that but 10 prisoners were taken. A number of killed and wounded were carried away in light wagons. Gen. Washington reported the brave act to Congress. Gen. Dickinson possessed great energy of character. When Red Bank was in jeopardy the Governor refused to order out the militia because his time had just expired and the election had passed through his own default. The General assumed the responsibility and brought them into the field in good time. He rendered essential service at the battle of Monmouth. He performed all the duties of life with promptness and fidelity. He was a member of the Senate of the U. S. He died at his residence in February 1809.

DRAYTON WILLIAM HENRY commenced his infantile career at some place in South Carolina in 1742–at what point the record saith not. He was educated in England but did not fall in love with the principles of monarchy. He was among the first, boldest, ablest and most energetic patriots of his native state. He did much with his pen to open the minds of the people to a sense of their true condition politically. In 1774 he addressed a pamphlet to the Continental Congress under the title of "FREEMEN" which raised him to a prominent position among the patriots. It contained a bill of American Rights which was substantially adopted by that Congress. In 1775 he was President of the Provincial Congress and issued the first official order to oppose the enemy by force of arms. It was addressed to Col. William Moultrie directing him to "oppose the passage of any British naval armament that may attempt to pass Fort Johnson." This marked his boldness and his zeal. He passed through several judicial offices up to Chief Justice of the state. In April 1776 he used this remarkable language in his charge to the grand jury–remarkable in point of time and the then existing circumstances of the Colonies. "The Almighty created America to be independent of Britain. Let us beware of the impiety of being backward to act as instruments in the Almighty hand now extended to accomplish his purpose." So long as South Carolina can produce such men she will not secede from the UNION but leave the fanatics of the north to blow off their harmless gas in their political deploys at home. In 1778–9 Mr. Drayton was a member of the Continental Congress and died at his post in Philadelphia in September 1779. He was cut down in the prime of life and in the midst of a bright career of usefulness. He had earned an imperishable fame and stood approved by his country–his conscience and his God.

DYER ELIPHALET commenced his first stage of human life at Windham, Conn. on the 28th of September 1721. He was liberally educated and became a sound lawyer. He took command of a Connecticut regiment in 1755 and served ungrateful mother Britain faithfully during most of the French war. In 1763 he went to England on business and there became thoroughly acquainted with the base designs of the ministry upon the American Colonies. On his return he was prepared to warn the people of approaching danger. He was an ardent whig–a fearless opposer of tyranny. He was a member of the Congress of 1766-74. He was Chief Justice of his state for many years and retired from public life in 1793. He adorned the prominent virtues that dignify a man and make him useful in life-happy in death. He closed his earthly pilgrimage in 1807.

ELLSWORTH OLIVER was born at Windsor, Conn. on the 29th of April 1745. He graduated at Princeton College, N. J. and became an eminent member of the Bar. He was a firm advocate of chartered rights-a stern opposer of British wrongs. He used his noblest exertions to induce the people to strike for LIBERTY. In 1777 he was elected to the Continental Congress. His commanding talents, stern integrity, powerful eloquence, keen perception, conclusive logic, lucid demonstrations-all combined to render him an efficient and highly appreciated member. He was a useful delegate of the Convention that framed the Federal Constitution. In 1789 he was elected to the U. S. Senate-in 1796 appointed Chief Justice of the Supreme Court of the United States-in 1799 Envoy Extraordinary to France and dignified each of these high stations. Owing to ill health he resigned his seat at the head of the Supreme Bench in 1800. Several high offices were subsequently tendered to him which he respectfully declined. His whole life was chastened with a republican simplicity and primitive purity seldom found among those in high life at the present ominous era. All admire his brilliant examples-too few will imitate them. Judge Ellsworth slumbered in death on the 26th Nov. 1807.

FORREST URIAH was ushered into life in the county of St. Mary, Md. in 1756. In his youth he was commissioned a lieutenant in one of the Maryland regiments and soon gained the reputation of a brave and skilful officer. He rose rapidly to the rank of lieutenant-colonel. He acted a brilliant part in the battle of Germantown where he lost a leg which closed his active military career. A man of strong intellect improved by a good store of useful knowledge-he had a bright career before him. He was a man of unbounded popularity and influence-filled various public stations in his native State-was a member of the Continental Congress-of the Legislature of Maryland and a member of Congress under the Federal Constitution. He was for many years major-general of the Maryland militia. In all his public stations he acquitted himself nobly-in private life he had the esteem of a large concourse of friends. The time of his final exit is not upon the record.

GADSDEN CHRISTOPHER was born in South Carolina in 1724. He was the originator of the LIBERTY TREE in America. To cut loose from mother Britain was a cherished project in his penetrating mind long before the Revolution. He did not join in the general joy caused by the repeal of the Stamp Act. He looked upon it like the transient calm in a storm that often precedes the increased fury of the elements. As early as 1762 he frequently said that nothing but open resistance would ever obtain justice from Great Britain. Upon these matured conclusions he continued to act until his long nursed vision became a happy reality and was eclipsed by the more refulgent glories of the Declaration of Independence. He was a member of the Congress convened at New York in 1765 and of the one at Philadelphia in 1774. He was also a general of militia. He was of great service in rousing the people to action. He was among the prisoners at the city of Charleston and then lieutenant-governor. Being ill he was paroled. On the 27th of August 1780 he was dragged from his sick bed–put on board a prison ship and taken to the castle at St. Augustine in violation of the rights of prisoners on parole. He was there treated with great cruelty. A parole for the town was offered him at St. Augustine which he indignantly refused, saying he could place no dependence on any promise from a British officer. When Maj. Andre was executed Gen. Gadsden was tauntingly admonished to prepare for death as he would be made the retaliatory sacrifice. He firmly replied–" I am always prepared to die for my country." A more inflexible patriot, a more noble spirit, a more ardent friend of Liberty never came from the clean hands of the Creator. Gen. Gadsden had the love, sympathy, confidence and admiration of every friend of the American cause. He died in 1805.

GANSEVORT PETER entered upon the first stage of human life at Albany, N. Y. on the 16th of July 1749. His taste for military tactics was manifested in his boyhood. When he arrived at manhood he raised a company of grenadiers that elicited the admiration of every beholder. Not one of its members was under six feet–Capt. Gansevort was six feet three. In point of discipline and martial appearance, this company had no superior. Being a firm Whig Capt. G. was ready to do good service for his country at the commencement of the Revolution. He was appointed a major by Congress on the 19th of July 1795. On the 19th of the next month he took command of the second battalion of the New York forces and shared the perilous campaign with Gen. Montgomery which terminated the life of the latter. Congress made him lieutenant-colonel on the 19th of March 1776 and on the 21st of November of that year appointed him colonel of the 3d Regiment in the Continental army. His defence of Fort Stanwix in August 1777 was one of the most brilliant achievements of the American Revolution. It was besieged by a large body of British, Tories and Indians, commanded by Col. St. Leger, who threatened summary vengeance unless an unconditional surrender was made. He soon found he had waked up the wrong passenger. He was promptly informed that Col. Gansevort never surrendered. The fort was defended until aid was sent when Col. St. Leger was compelled to leave suddenly. For this brave act Congress recorded him a vote of thanks on the 4th of October of that year. In 1778 he was ordered to Albany–the next year accompanied Gen. Sullivan in his expedition against the Indians and with a chosen band of kindred spirits surprised and took the lower Mohawk castle and a large number of prisoners. In 1781 an arrangement was smuggled through Congress by improper influences that legislated this officer and several other gallant men out of the army to the great mortification of Washington. His native State made him a major-general of militia. After the war he held the office of sheriff in Albany County– was commissioner to fortify the frontier posts–make treaties with the Indians–military agent of the Northern Department and in 1802 was commissioned a brigadier-general in the army of the United States which he held until the 2d of July 1812 when he was suddenly called from time to eternity at the moment our country needed just such men to conduct the second war of Independence. Gen. Gansevoort was endowed with an unusual share of the noble qualities that dignify a man in public and private life all of which were purified by a life of practical piety.

GIBSON JOHN was born in Lancaster, Pennsylvania on the 23d of May 1740. At the age of 18 he was an excellent classical scholar. He was in service under Gen. Forbes when Fort Du Quesne [now Pittsburgh] was taken from the French and Indians. He settled there in 1763 for the purpose of trade. In a short time he was taken prisoner by the Indians and had his life saved by an old squaw who adopted him in the room of a lost son. He was detained several years—became familiar with the language of several tribes—with the general habits of red men which prepared him for future duties. On gaining his liberty he returned to Pittsburgh and served under Lord Dunmore in his expedition against the Shawnee Towns which resulted in a treaty with the children of the forest. Gen. Gibson was the mediator and interpreter. To him alone was the celebrated speech of the noble hearted Logan delivered in a copse a short distance from the council ground. By him it was communicated to the other Chiefs and to Lord Dunmore. At the commencement of the Revolution Gen Gibson commanded a regiment in the regular army—served a short time in New York and New Jersey—was then transferred to his more appropriate place upon the frontiers to keep in check the Indians. After the war he filled various civil stations and was appointed Secretary of Indiana in 1800 and filled the office until the state was formed. He then took up his residence with George Wallace, near Braddock's Field, who had married his daughter with whom he lived until the 10th of April 1822, when his immortal spirit returned to Him who gave it.

GIBSON GEORGE first made his appearance among his friends at Lancaster, Pennsylvania in 1747. He was well educated—became a clerk to a merchant in Philadelphia—sailed to the West Indies several times as supercargo and finally went to his brother John at Pittsburgh. There he was employed in a trading voyage down the Ohio and was unfortunate. He changed his location and business several times up to the period of the Revolution when he raised a company of the border men who were not of polished manners but would fight like tigers. With them he joined the Virginia troops at Williamsburgh, Virginia. They were all sharp-shooters of which Lord Dunmore became convinced on the 25th of October 1775 when he attacked Hampton with a naval force and was driven back by this company with considerable loss. Capt. Gibson performed a perilous journey to New Orleans for the purpose of obtaining powder for the army from the Spanish which was a very delicate mission and was performed with skill and success. He returned through the wilderness and Indian tribes and travelled 1800 miles on foot. Wonder how many public functionaries we have now who would perform a similar journey for the sake of their country—even if they should get their mileage, hot toddy, roast beef and $8 per day. On his return he was put in command of a Virginia regiment and joined Lee's division of the Continental army at New York. This division covered the retreat of the main army and formed a junction with it on the west bank of the Delaware. At the battle of Trenton Col. Gibson served under the direct command of Washington.

He continued with him and participated in the battles, privations and sufferings of that forlorn hope of American Freedom up to 1779 when the term of his regiment expired. He was then put in command of the prison station near York, Pennsylvania, where he continued to the close of the war. In 1791 he commanded a regiment under Gen. St. Clair and acted a most gallant part in the unsuccessful sanguinary battle of the 4th of November of that year where his regiment was nearly annihilated and himself mortally wounded. He lingered in great pain at Fort Jefferson until the 11th of December following when death relieved him from his sufferings. While living he was the delight of every circle in which he moved—noble, generous, warm hearted, persevering, brave, prudent, just and honest. His well earned fame is enduring as history.

GREENE CHRISTOPHER commenced his earthly career at Warwick, Rhode Island in 1737. He received a good English education—became familiar with mathematics—was partial to military tactics and became a member of the "Kentish Guards" at an early age and was made their Lieutenant. In May 1775 he was commissioned a Major in the brigade under his kinsman Gen. Nathaniel Greene. At the attack on Quebec he commanded a company in the division of Gen. Montgomery and headed the party that entered the town and was taken prisoner. Soon after he was exchanged he was put in command of the regiment previously commanded by Gen. Varnum. In 1777 Washington placed Fort Mercer, at Red Bank on the Delaware, in his charge with only 500 men. This was attacked soon after the battle of Brandywine by Col. Donop on the Jersey side with 1200 men. The enemy were repulsed with great slaughter—Col. Donop, Lieut. Col. Mingerode and several other officers were killed and 400 of their soldiers killed and wounded. At the same time the British fleet and a battery on the Pennsylvania side opened a heavy fire on the contiguous Fort Mifflin, then called Mud Fort, and succeeded in having their favorite ship Augusta, of 64 guns, blown up with a part of her crew and the armed ship Merlin burned—glory enough for one day. Col. Greene received the thanks of Congress and was voted a splendid sword which was presented to his son Job in 1786. In 1781 Col. Greene was posted in advance of the army near Croton river above New York and had quartered his men in several farm houses. On the night of the 13th of May of that year he was suddenly attacked by a superior force of refugees *alias* tories. They broke into the room of the Colonel who despatched a number of them with his sword but was eventually overpowered and cut up in the most horrid manner. Maj. Flagg was also murdered with every soldier they could find. No officer fell during the Revolution more deeply lamented—no one of his grade better deserved the gratitude and esteem of his country.

GRAEFF GEORGE was born in Lancaster, Pa. in 1755. He was a brave captain in the Continental army and did good service in the cause of Independence. He acted a gallant part at the battle on Long Island in 1776. Subsequent to the war he filled several civil offices with credit and usefulness. He was emphatically an honest man. He died at his native town on the 13th of November 1823.

GRIFFIN CYRUS was one of the bold Virginians who early

advocated the glorious cause of Independence. He used every energy to rouse the people to a sense of impending danger. He ably filled every public station—was a member of the Continental Congress and one of the Presidents of that august assemblage of Sages. He lived in the esteem of his country and associates until 1810 when he made his exit to the spirit world.

GURNEY FRANCIS was first introduced on this whirling planet in Bucks County, Pa. in 1738. His military genius became early developed. He entered the service of mother Britain at the age of 18 and braved the perils and hardships of the French war from its commencement to its close. His reputation for bold enterprise and noble daring he carved high on the temple of epic fame. At the capture of Cape Breton he acted a conspicuous part. At the taking of Guadaloupe his bravery was a subject of general remark. At the close of these arduous services he commenced a successful career in the mercantile business in the city of Philadelphia. There he was when the revolutionary storm loomed up. He looked upon the conduct of mother England as basely ungrateful. He snuffed the breeze of Liberty and struck for Freedom. His noblest energies were roused to action. His large military experience and keen perception enabled him to point out those who were best calculated to make efficient officers. Mifflin, Cadwalader and others were first recommended by him. His zeal and activity in the cause of suffering humanity were above all praise. Believing he could render more service out of the army than in it—he declined a commission until the 25th of May 1775 when he took command of an infantry company of volunteers. The next year he entered the regular service with the commission of lieutenant-colonel in the 11th regiment of the Pennsylvania Line. He was in the battle of Iron Hill, Brandywine and Germantown where he fully sustained his reputation for daring bravery. The wire-working system of promotions that was early introduced and injuriously pursued did not comport with his fine sense of military usage which caused him to resign. This did not abate his zeal in the cause—he continued to advance the best interests of the patriots until he saw his country free from bondage. After the Revolution he resumed his business at Philadelphia—filled many municipal and legislative stations—commanded a regiment in the army of 1794 which put down the whiskey insurgents—became brigadier-general of militia—performed every duty that devolved upon him in public and private life with ability and fidelity—was in all respects a man who commanded the confidence and esteem of all who made his acquaintance—adorned the Christian character and slumbered in death at his country seat near Philadelphia on the 25th of May 1815.

GWINN WILLIAM was born in Ireland in 1748. In 1772 he came to Pennsylvania and from that time to the close of his life manifested a deep interest for the welfare of his adopted country. During the Revolution he served in the staff of Gen. Mifflin and was highly esteemed for his faithful performance of every duty and his uniform zeal in the cause of Independence. After the war he removed to Monkton Mills, Baltimore County, Md. where he lived highly respected until the 1st of October 1819 when he died deeply mourned by his numerous friends.

HALE NATHAN entered upon his eventful career of life at Coventry, Conn. at what time we have no word. He was liberally educated—a young man of great promise and entered the army at the commencement of the Revolution in command of a company under Col. Knowlton. He was at the battle of Long Island on the 27th of August 1776 and one of the 9000 who effected a retreat during the night to the great chagrin of the British who were encamped not over 600 yards from the Americans. Shortly after that disastrous affair Washington employed Capt. Hale to enter the English camp as a spy. Unfortunately he was detected and executed the next morning by order of Sir William Howe under circumstances of fiendish barbarity that left a black spot upon the escutcheon of that proud officer that time or angel's tears can never expunge. He was denied a clergyman and a bible and the letters that he wrote to his widowed mother and relatives were destroyed. He died a brave and willing martyr to the cause of Liberty and lamented with his last breath that he had but one life to sacrifice for his country. How great the contrast between the course our country has pursued in memory of this young hero and that of England towards Andre. In point of talent and exalted character, Hale was equal to him. The one was engaged as a simple spy—the other was in league with a base traitor on a grand scale. The one has no extended notice in our history—the other has been lauded to the skies by the historians of both nations. Not a stone marks the resting place of Capt. Hale—a splendid monument has been erected by England sacred to the memory of Andre. The family of the one was neglected by our government—that of the other pensioned in a princely manner. The fact that our nation was then just bursting into life is the only apology to be offered.

HAMILTON ALEXANDER was born on the Island of Nevis in 1757. His father was an Englishman, his mother an American and brought him to New York in 1773 and placed him in Columbia college. His towering genius burst upon the world like a blazing meteor in the darkness of night. At the age of 17 he grasped the mighty concerns that were then rocking England and America in the cradle of fearful commotion. He then wrote several essays upon the rights and wrongs of the two nations that were attributed to Mr. Jay. College walls could not keep him from the field of glory. At the age of 19 he commanded a company of artillery and was ever ready for a little more grape when it could be used to advantage. He soon attracted the attention of the penetrating Washington who appointed him one of his aids in 1777 with the rank of lieutenant-colonel. A selection was never more judiciously made—no commander could be better served. From that period to the close of the war our country was benefited by the combined wisdom and noblest efforts of two of the brightest constellations of genuius that have ever illuminated our world. In every battle where Washington commanded Col. Hamilton was at his post regardless of danger. When the two destructive redoubts were carried at the siege of Yorktown facing a storm of iron hail he led the advanced corps under La Fayette. Not a gun was fired—the charge was like a rushing avalanche. The surrender of that garrison closed his Revolutionary services. His manly brow was decked with epic laurels that can never lose their amaranthine freshness whilst patriotic fire glows or history endures.

In 1782 he was elected to Congress and shed fresh lustre on that august body of sages. He grasped every subject with a gigantic mental power that filled the more experienced members with astonishment and admiration. He originated measures with a surprising facility and wisdom that were truly beneficial. He was a member of the Convention that framed the Federal Constitution. He was in favor of what he considered a stronger government than the one formed—one that some would call *ultra* federal. At the final organization under the new Constitution he was placed at the head of the Treasury Department. To the surprise and joy of all concerned he raised the credit of the nation rapidly from the lowest depths of depreciation to a lofty eminence of credit. At the end of six years he resigned and resumed the practice of law in the city of New York. When the provisional army was raised in 1798 in anticipation of a war with France, he was placed next in command to Washington and proved one of the most efficient disciplinarians that ever graced the profession of arms. On the disbanding of this army he again resumed his profession at the bar. In 1804 he was challenged by Col. Burr and sacrificed his life on the barbarous field of false honor contrary to his better judgment and finer feelings. He was mortally wounded on the 11th of July 1804 and died the next day. So opposed was he in principle to duelling that he fired his pistol in the air. He died deeply regretting the sad error, with full faith in the merits of his Saviour to wash every stain from his noble soul and present him with a crown of unfading glory. His sudden death and the manner his bright career was terminated spread a mantle of gloom over our country and the civilized world. His transcendent talents had attracted the admiring gaze of Europe and America. He was in all respects a remarkable man. His flashes of genius were like vivid lightning that startles—their force like crashing thunderbolts that shiver every obstacle in their way. He mastered everything in the course of his business by talismanic intuition. He filled the orbit of every station he occupied—he illuminated his pathway with a brilliancy that dazzled. He left a pillar of living light on the bright pages of history that will reflect its mellow rays on the horizon of LIBERTY through all time.

HAMILTON PAUL was one of the unflinching native patriots of South Carolina who resolved on Liberty or death. He filled a large space in the public mind and performed many public duties with ability and fidelity. He was governor of his State—Secretary of the Navy under President Madison and dignified every station he occupied. He bid farewell to his friends, earth and its toils in 1816.

HATHAWAY BENONI was born in New Jersey in 1754. He was among the first who boldly struck for Liberty. He did not wait until the iron was hot before he raised his hammer but heated it by continuous and heavy blows. He commanded a company of citizen rangers that became a terror to the scouting and foraging parties of the enemy and frequently captured them and the sentinels of their main camp in the darkness of night. When Gen. Kniphausen was encamped at Elizabethtown with his Hessians his most bewitching hours were often interrupted by this sleepless company. At one of these attacks Capt. Hathaway was wounded in the head by a musket ball and was unconscious for several hours but recovered and continued his guerrilla warfare until the last loyal Briton made good his retreat across the great heron pond. He was highly esteemed through life and met death with Christian fortitude at Newark, N. J. on the 19th of April 1823.

HAWKINS NATHAN was first introduced to the human family in Rhode Island in 1749. His patriotism grew with his growth and strengthened with his strength. When a mere youth he was the delegate of South Kingston to carry assistance to the citizens of Boston when reduced to distress by the infamous Port Bill. The war-cry from the heights of Lexington broke his slumbers at the hour of midnight–in less than twelve hours he was leading a brave volunteer corps to the rescue. He served faithfully during the whole period of the Revolution–acted a gallant part in several battles and is fully entitled to a place upon the records of enduring fame. When the war closed he located and closed his life at Charlestown, Mass.–filled several civil offices –was highly esteemed by his fellow citizens–sustained the noble reputation of an honest man–died October 3d 1817.

HAWLEY JOSEPH entered upon his earthly pilgrimage in Northampton, Mass. in 1724. He was one of the first who opposed the usurpations of the crown officers and the patriot who wrote to John Adams just as the Congress of 1774 closed and used the truly prophetic language–" AFTER ALL WE MUST FIGHT." He was a man of strong intellect, great penetration of mind, a close observer of men and things, an inflexible friend to the cause of equal rights. In public meetings, in the legislature, in his social intercourse–at all proper times and places–he sowed the seeds of Liberty broadcast. When told the Colonies were too weak for resistance he replied–" We must put to sea–Providence will bring us into port." He was a lawyer of eminence and strongly opposed to accepting public office although he served his State in the Legislature several times. He exemplified the Christian religion by a life of primitive piety but was an uncompromising foe to fanaticism, bigotry, sectarianism and the dogmatical creeds of men. His charity spread its broad mantle over the whole family of man. He held the commission of major of militia but owing to his frequent and sudden attacks of illness he did not serve in the tented field. He enjoyed the esteem and confidence of every friend of freedom and passed peacefully from earth on the 10th of March 1786.

HAYNE ISAAC–[see the Biography of John Penn in Part I.] I can find no record of his birth.

HEATH WILLIAM was born in Roxbury, Mass. in 1737. He left his plough in the furrow the moment the war-cry reached him and hastened to the field of epic glory. He was constitutionally a military man. Congress conferred upon him the commission of brigadier-general in 1775. The next year Congress raised him to the rank of major-general. He commanded a division at the battle of King's Bridge in 1776 and next year was placed over the Eastern Department with his headquarters at Boston and filled that arduous station until November 1778. Burgoyne and his army were under his charge as prisoners of war and at first gave him much trouble. The haughty British general and his officers supposed General Heath a novice in the rules of military etiquette and put on airs that induced insubordination among the English soldiers. In this they were mistaken. Gen. Heath had been a close military student from his boyhood. He had nothing new to learn from these high dignitaries but an insolent assumption of importance that he soon cured and reduced them to their proper level. With the humanity of a philanthropist and the polish of an old school gentleman he united the firmness of a Roman, the courage of a hero and the dignity of a nobleman.

In the summer of 1780 he was master of ceremonies at Rhode Island on the reception of the French fleet under the command of Admiral de Ternay with the troops that were sent to aid in sustaining our Independence. A mutual pleasure was experienced on that occasion which matured into lasting friendship. In 1781 Gen. H. was successfully employed at the east in raising supplies for the army. When Gen. Washington repaired to Yorktown Gen. Heath was left in command of the northern and eastern branches of the army that remained to sustain the garrisons upon the Hudson and Atlantic. At all times and under all circumstances he acquitted himself nobly and received a letter of sincere thanks from Washington at the close of the war for his zeal and promptness in the performance of the long and arduous services that had devolved upon him. After the war closed he filled various legislative and judicial stations with dignity and ability. He was elected lieutenant-governor in 1806 but refused to serve. He had earned a lasting fame—was beloved by his countrymen at large and glided down the stream of time peacefully until the 24th of January 1814 when his spirit returned to its original happy home.

HESTON EDWARD was ushered into Hestonville, county of Philadelphia, Pennsylvania in 1745. He was one of the brave farmers who exchanged the plough for the sword. He entered the army as Captain and rose to the rank of Lieut. Colonel. By his vigilance in watching Lord Cornwallis when in Philadelphia he saved the brigade of Gen. Potter from being captured. The day previous to the battle of Germantown, with a few bold spirits he faced a heavy fire and succeeded in cutting the rope at the middle ferry to prevent the communication of the enemy with Philadelphia. In a skirmish with a party of British he received a severe sword cut on the back of his head, was taken prisoner and sent to Long Island where he was detained for seven months. After the Revolution closed he was an active member of the legislature of his native state and was esteemed through life for benevolence, charity, patriotism and rigid honesty. He died at his residence in Hestonville on the 14th day of March 1824.

HOLDEN LEVI was born in New Jersey in 1754. He entered the Continental army as Captain in 1776 and served faithfully until mother Britain relinquished her maternal care over the Colonies and left her froward child to act its own will and pleasure—a prudent course for the old lady and a fair business transaction. For three years Capt. Holden was attached to Washington's life guard and was highly esteemed by him. After the war he located at Newark, New Jersey where he enjoyed the esteem of the community for 30 years and descended to the tomb on the 19th day of April 1823, ripe in years and rich with honors.

HOUSTON JOHN was one of the nucleus of patriots who put the Revolutionary ball in motion at the Liberty Pole meeting in Georgia. Himself and Mr. Bullock were among the few who dare express their opinions at that meeting. Before it adjourned the fire of patriotism was kindled in so many bosoms that royal power trembled at the probable result. Mr. Houston was a member of the Continental Congress in 1775 and performed his duty nobly. He was subsequently a judge of the Supreme Court and governor of his state. He was a man of fine talents, great energy, sterling integrity and devoted patriotism. He enjoyed the full fruition of the love of his country and friends until 1796 when he passed peacefully from time to eternity.

HOWARD JOHN EAGER commenced infancy in Baltimore Md. in 1752. He resolved on Liberty or death at the commencement of that long and doubtful struggle that resulted in FREEDOM to America. He was among those who dared snatch the laurels from the proud sons of mother Britain and place them upon their own manly brows. He entered the army with the commission of Captain and was raised to the rank of Lieut. Colonel in 1779. He was one of the bravest of the brave. At the victory of Cowpens he held the swords of seven British officers at one time who had surrendered personally to him. His skill and bravery were exhibited at the battles of Germantown, White Plains, Monmouth, Camden and Hobbick's Hill. So highly were his services appreciated by Gen. Greene that he used this strong language— " As a patriot and soldier Col. Howard deserves a statue of gold no less than the Roman and Grecian Heroes." This short sentence is the crowning capital of the climax of eulogy. At the close of the Revolution Col. Howard returned to his large real estate in the city of Baltimore. Subsequent to the formation of the Federal government he was a member of the United States Senate and Governor of Maryland. No man was more beloved by his fellow citizens—no one better deserved their esteem. He died at his residence in 1827.

HUMPHREY DAVID commenced his career of life in Derby, Conn. on the — of July 1752. He was a graduate of Yale college and frequently danced attendance to the muses. He was a staunch friend of his country and entered the army a Captain. In 1773 he was aid to Gen. Putnam and in turn aid to Parsons, Greene and in 1780 became an aid to Gen. Washington with the rank of Lieut. Colonel with whom he remained until Lord Cornwallis fired his last gun at Yorktown. On all occasions Col. Humphrey acted a brave and noble part. His chivalrous conduct at the siege of Yorktown induced Congress to vote him an elegant sword. In 1784 he was the secretary of Mr. Jefferson then minister to France. In 1786 he retired to his native place and was elected to the legislature. In 1788 he was placed in command of a regiment raised for the western service. In 1790 he was appointed ambassador to the Court of Portugal and in 1797 minister plenipotentiary to the Court of Madrid. On his return from Spain he introduced the Merino sheep into the United States and deserves great credit for his successful exertions in the improvement of wool and its manufacture. In all the multiform duties of his active life Col. Humphrey had the full approbation of his country. In private life he exemplified the virtues that make a good citizen. He closed his useful career at New Haven Connecticut on the 21st of February 1818.

HUNTINGTON JEDEDIAH was born in Norwich, Connecticut in 1743. He was a graduate of Harvard College, an enterprising merchant and a whig of the first water. He led his regiment to the head quarters of the army at Cambridge early in 1775. His activity, zeal, courage and efficiency in the field gained the admiration of Washington who procured his advancement to the rank of Brigadier General. He rendered his best services to promote the glorious cause of Independence and remained in the field during the whole period of the war. He subsequently filled various civil offices. He was appointed Collector of the Port of New London by Washington and performed his duties faithfully during four consecutive administrations. He enjoyed the profound respect of the very intelligent citizens of New London until the 25th of September 1818 when he took his departure to the spirit world.

IRVINE ANDREW was a native of Ireland, brother to Gen. William Irvine spoken of more at length in Part I. Dr. Matthew Irvine of Charleston, South Carolina was a third brother and served in the Continental army. Andrew entered the regiment of his brother William as Lieutenant and was engaged in the Canada service under Gen. Wayne. He was in every action with that General up to the massacre of Paoli where he received seventeen bayonet wounds and miraculous as it was, recovered and was actively engaged in the northern and southern campaigns. No officer of his rank did more service—no one could do it in a more heroic manner. After the war he lived in the esteem of the citizens of Carlisle, Pa. where he died on the 4th of May 1789.

IRWIN JARED was born in Mecklinburg, North Carolina in 1751. At the age of seven years he became a resident of Georgia. At the commencement of the Revolution he was a pioneer in one of the frontier settlements adjacent to the Indian tribes where he became the leader of his neighbors in keeping the red men at bay and teaching the tories salutary lessons. In that department he rendered himself eminently useful during the war. He was a member of the first legislature of Georgia under the new government which convened at Savannah in 1784. From that time forward he became emphatically a leading public man. He was long a member of the Georgia Senate and for many years its president. He was repeatedly Governor of the state. He filled every station in a manner that gained the unqualified approbation of his constituents. His public life was adorned by those private virtues that are indispensable to render a man truly great. He died at Union, Washington County, Georgia, on the 1st of March 1818.

JACKSON ANDREW commenced his brilliant life in the Waxhaw settlement, S. C. in 1767. He was constitutionally a patriot, soldier and statesman. He enlisted in the Continental army at the age of 14 and performed feats of noble courage that would have honored manhood. When fighting bravely for his country he was wounded and taken prisoner. After much suffering he was exchanged and at the close of the war prosecuted his studies and became a respectable member of the Bar. He commanded a successful expedition against the southern Indians—in 1820 was the commissioner to receive the Floridas from Spain—was made governor of that territory and performed many public duties with great energy. He was a major-general during the last war with mother Britain. His defence of New Orleans against the veteran army of Gen. Packenham has no parallel in modern warfare. In 1828 Gen. Jackson was elected President of the United States and served two terms. He was emphatically a man of the people. In point of physical and moral courage he had no superior. He was stern in his integrity, honest in his purposes, unbending in his resolves–determined in his course of action. When time shall absorb the bitterness of party spirit that his bold administration created–the historian will trace the fair lines of the career of Andrew Jackson and present a picture to after generations that will command their profound admiration. He lived a patriot–he died a Christian in 1845.

JACKSON JAMES first inhaled the atmosphere at Moreton Homstead in the County of Devon, England, on the 21st of September 1757. His father was a strong whig and brought him to Georgia in 1772 and left him with his friend John Wereat, Esquire. James Jackson did not fancy hereditary monarchy or purse-proud aristocracy. His very nature was republican. At the dawn of the Revolution he was ready to peril his life in the cause of equal rights. The war cry that came rushing on mighty wind from the blood stained heights of Lexington he hailed as the day-spring of FREEDOM–the morning star of LIBERTY. At the age of 18 he was a volunteer in the party of bold spirits that made a descent on Savannah. At the attack on Tybee his dauntless courage attracted the attention of Archibald Bullock who was the acting head of the patriots. In a short time Jackson was in command of a volunteer company of light infantry. In 1778 he rose to the rank of brigade-major of the Georgia militia. At the storming of Savannah his gallantry could not be excelled. He was in the battle of Blackstocks on the 20th of August 1780. After Tarleton had retreated Major Jackson was put on his track and brought back 30 horses. At the battle of Cowpens the Major received the thanks of Gen. Morgan on the battle field. When in service under Gen. Pickens his noble daring was particularly noticed in the reports of that officer. About this time he was made a Colonel with the privilege of raising his own regiment, which he quickly accomplished. He commanded at the capture of the British fort at Ogechee, the post at Butler's White house and seemed to court danger whenever an opportunity presented. In his victory over Col. Brown on the 21st of May 1782, Gen. Wayne awarded great praise to Col. Jackson. On the 12th of July of that year the British surrendered Savannah and by arrangement delivered the keys to this brave Colonel who continued to command it until the close of the war. He then commenced a successful practice of law and stood on a lofty eminence of merit. He was hailed as one who had contributed largely towards achieving the Liberty all then enjoyed. He was raised to the office of major-general of militta–was a member of the legislature–quorum of the state and a member of the U. S. Senate. He was found equal to every station he was called to fill. He died at Washington city while at his post in the Senate on the 19th of January 1806.

JAMES JOHN was born in Ireland in 1732. His father and several of his neighbors came to Virginia in 1733 and settled at Williamsburg which name they gave to the place in honor of King William. They had all imbibed an unconquerable dislike towards England. At the commencement of the Revolution all their descendants were prepared to oppose her unjust pretensions. No one amongst them was a more determined opponent than John James. Familiar with border warfare he was prepared to act efficiently. He had long been a captain of militia under the crown and at once resigned his commission. His company all declared for Liberty and retained him in command. In 1776 he left his plough and marched his men to the defence of Charleston where he remained for some time. He was soon promoted to the rank of major and became one of the most active officers in service. He was with Gen. Moultrie when he was closely pressed by Gen. Provost. At the skirmish at Tulifinny he commanded the rifle corps. He acted a brave part at the battle of Eutaw. His riflemen expended 24 rounds of cartridges on the enemy and rarely wasted any ammunition. He was the original nucleus of Marion's brigade. He performed many bold exploits—had numerous hair-breadth escapes. At one time he was alone and attacked by two British dragoons who were in advance of their comrades. As they drew their sabres to cut him down he brought them to a sudden halt by drawing an empty pistol and then leaped over a chasm a little too broad for Tarleton's sportsmen. Just previous to the close of the war he returned to his rusty plough and lived in the high esteem of a grateful country and his numerous acquaintances until 1791 when he closed his useful career in death. He was a member of the Virginia legislature and filled several civil offices with credit and fidelity.

JASPER WILLIAM was a brave sergeant in the division of Gen. Moultrie. For personal bravery and shrewdness he had few equals. In the heat of the attack upon Fort Moultrie the flag staff was shot off by a cannon ball. The banner fell outside of the works. Amidst a storm of iron hail Jasper leaped from one of the embrasures, recovered the flag, mounted it on his spontoon staff and unfurled it to the breeze. He was promoted to the highest rank he would accept—a roving commission and the privilege of selecting his companions to aid him in his bold and romantic enterprises. He often brought in prisoners before Gen. Moultrie was aware of his absence. On one occasion several prisoners were ironed and put under a guard of eight soldiers with a corporal and sergeant and started for Savannah with a fair prospect of the hemp. One was a Mr. Jones whose young wife was in great agony on his account and followed him with their only child—a lovely boy five years of age. Jasper and his kindred spirit Sergeant Newton, resolved on their rescue. Within two miles of Savannah in a copse of wood is a spring of excellent water about six rods from the road. There Jasper and Newton lay in ambush. When the party arrived eight of them laid down their guns in the road and went to the fountain to drink, leaving two to guard their prisoners. The next moment the two on guard slumbered in death—the rest of the British party were all made prisoners—the Americans released and the whole arrived at the American camp the next morning at Perrysburg. The distressed wife had no intimation of the heroic adventure until the crack of the two guns from Jasper and Newton. The next moment she clasped her fond husband to her convulsed bosom. Her joy may be faintly imagined—not described. Gov. Rutledge presented Jasper with an elegant sword for his noble daring at Fort Moultrie. Soon after the brave defence of Fort Moultrie Mrs. Elliott presented a splendid stand of colors to Col. Moultrie's regiment that composed the force in that action. At the storming of Savannah two officers fell in an attempt to plant these colors upon a redoubt of the enemy. When a retreat was ordered Jasper was mortally wounded while in the act of rescuing this standard from the enemy. After the retreat Maj. Horry called to see him and was made the bearer of the following message. " I have got my furlough. That sword was presented to me by Governor Rutledge for my services in defence of Fort Moultrie. Give it to my father and tell him I wore it in honor. If the old man should weep tell him his son died in hope of a better life. Tell Mrs. Elliott I lost my life in supporting the colors she presented to our regiment. Should you ever see Jones, wife and son—tell them Jasper is gone but the remembrance of that battle which he fought for them brought a secret joy in my heart when it was about to stop its motion for ever." In a few moments after he closed this message his noble soul soared to heaven.

JAY JOHN was born in the city of New York in 1745. He was one of the noble sages who dared to be free. He took an early and decided stand in favor of Liberty. He was of great service in rousing the people to a sense of their true interests. He was elected to Congress and took his seat in that body the latter part of 1776 and presided in the presidential chair for some time. In 1778 he was minister to Spain—in 1782 he was one of the commissioners to negotiate a treaty with Great Britain. In 1795 he was elected governor of the Empire State. He was an able public officer—a valuable private citizen. His soul joined its kindred in the spirit world in 1829.

JOHNSON FRANCIS was born in Pennsylvania in 1749. At the commencement of the conflict with mother Britain he was enjoying a lucrative practice at the bar. He well understood the merits of the high contending parties and enlisted under the banner of FREEDOM. He commenced his military career with Gen. Wayne with the commission of lieutenant-colonel in the first regiment raised by that brave officer. He shared with him all the fatigues and glory of the numerous expeditions and battles in which he was engaged up to the time Gen. Wayne went south. He succeeded him in the command of the 5th Pennsylvania regiment. His services were ably and zealously rendered and highly appreciated. He ventured his life and spent his fortune for Liberty. After the close of the Revolution he was elected sheriff of the city and county of Philadelphia as a tribute of merit awarded by both political parties. No man could be more generally beloved—no one better deserved it. He died in Philadelphia on the 22d of February 1815.

JOHNSON SAMUEL was one of the most talented and ardent patriots of the chivalric south. From the dawn of the Revolution he boldly espoused the cause of equal rights. He was a member of Congress and after the adoption of the Federal Constitution he was made a United States Senator. He was a judge of the Supreme Court of North Carolina and governor of that State. He discharged the duties of public and private life with energy, ability and scrupulous fidelity. His career of life was closed in 1806.

JOHNSON WILLIAM SAMUEL was a native of Connecticut and a zealous friend of the cause of Independence. He was a man of strong native talents improved by a sound education. He exercised a salutary influence over his constituents and served them faithfully in various public capacities. He was a member of the old Congress–a delegate to the Convention that framed the Federal Constitution and the first United States Senator from his native State. He lived in the esteem of his numerous friends until 1819 when his lamp of life went out.

JONES JOHN PAUL commenced his remarkable life in the district of Galloway, Scotland, in 1747. His original name was John Paul and Jones was added when he came to America in 1775. He had been a mariner from the age of 15 and was master of his profession. He left England in disgust in consequence of improper treatment by the authorities relative to his quelling a mutiny on board his ship, in doing which he was compelled to kill the ringleader, for which he was tried and acquitted and was threatened with a second trial. In the expedition of Com. Hopkins against New Providence he was a lieutenant and exhibited a dauntless spirit that at once placed him on the list of the brave. On his return he was placed in command of a sloop with 12 guns. In a short time he captured a British vessel with 18 guns. He then cruised boldly along the coast of Scotland–made several landings and a few contributions and proceeded to the Irish coast where he found the English armed vessel Drake in the harbor of Waterford–gave her a challenge she entered the list of combat–was quickly flogged and hastened back to her old moorings crippled and her commander mortified. In the summer of 1779 he was put in command of the Bon Homme Richard of 40 guns and 415 men with some small craft. After visiting France he sailed from there on the 14th of August of that year–took several vessels of war and merchantmen and proceeded in search of the Baltic fleet which he discovered on the 22d of September at 2 P. M. off Flamborough Head under convoy of a frigate and sloop of war. He at once prepared for action. Just as the moon was rising, at quarter before 8 P. M. one of the most desperate naval actions commenced that can be found recorded on the pages of history. When the two larger ships came within pistol shot the British frigate opened the ball with a brisk fire from her upper and quarter deck. Jones returned the compliment with the grace of a naval hero. At the onset three of his six 18 pound guns burst and killed those around them. He ordered the other three not to be used. This accident induced him to grapple with the frigate and come to close quarters which he accomplished so completely that the muzzles of the guns of each were in contact. The rage of battle then commenced with all the desperation of gladiators. The Englishman had nailed his flag to the mast–Jones never surrendered. His ship was the most crippled–more of his guns silenced than on the frigate. This preponderance of metal was soon changed by a brave tar advancing over the frigate on the main yard of the American ship with a basket of hand grenades and lighted match. He dropped these messengers of death among the enemy and through the scuttles–killing many and setting the cartridges on fire in every direction. The fight raged on–the frigate was several times on fire–the Bon Homme Richard was leaking from shots between wind and water–all her guns silenced but four and not until both ships took fire was the fury of the conflict relinquished for a moment. When the flames were extinguished the carnage was renewed. Jones had taken over 100 prisoners and put them to the pumps under the direction of Lieut. Dale who was severely

wounded. The English flag was at last torn down by the captain of
the frigate which proved to be the Serapis mounting 50 carriage guns
commanded by Capt. Pearson. All hands were removed on board the
prize and at 10 the next morning the Bon Homme Richard went to the
bottom. Capt. Pearson had 137 men killed and 76 wounded. Capt.
Jones had 165 killed, 137 wounded. It is supposed many of his men
were killed and wounded by one of his own vessels that fired into him
some time by mistake at pistol shot. At the commencement of the
action he received the fire of both British vessels until he closed with
the frigate. The next morning the Pallas, Capt. Cotineau, attacked the
British sloop of war and after a severe battle of over two hours compelled her to surrender. She was the Countess of Scarborough. Capt.
Jones then proceeded home with his prizes and prisoners and was hailed
with an enthusiasm that none but freemen so ardently feel and so
strongly express. On the 14th of April 1781 Congress passed a strong
resolution expressive of their high appreciation of his valuable services.
A more skilful, daring and resolute man never commanded a ship.

After the termination of the Revolution he visited Russia and held
a naval commission for a time under the Empress Catharine. From
there he went to Paris in France where he died in 1792.*

KENNARD NATHANIEL was born in Massachusetts in 1755.
He was a volunteer in one of the first regiments raised in Massachusetts. In that he served one year and then entered on board a private
armed vessel—was taken prisoner—taken to England and confined in
Mill Prison for 27 months with a standing threat he should be hanged.
He was finally sent to France and shipped on the Bon Homme
Richard and was in the action described in the preceding article. He
was put on board one of the prizes and ordered for France—was again
taken prisoner—put on board the British frigate Unicorn and compelled
to do duty until he found an opportunity to escape on the Island of
Jamaica and reached home just before the close of the Revolution.
During the war of 1812 he commanded a Revenue Cutter. From
that period he was Inspector of Customs at Portsmouth N. H. up to
the time of his death which occurred on the 24th of June 1823.

KING RUFUS commenced his life career in New York in 1755.
In his youth he was an ardent friend to the cause of FREEDOM and
a patriot in action. He was a member of Congress when convened at
Trenton New Jersey in 1784. He was a very efficient member of the
Convention in 1787 that formed the Federal Constitution and was soon
after elected to the United States Senate. From 1796 to 1803 he was
minister at the Court of St. James. In 1813 he was elected a United
States Senator and was minister to England during the administration
of John Quincy Adams. All his public and private duties were performed with a single eye to the glory of his country, the good of the
human family and the preservation of our glorious UNION. He bid
farewell to earth, its toys, toils, griefs and joys in April 1827.

KIRKWOOD ROBERT was a native of Newcastle county, Dela
ware. When the oppression of mother Britain became so intolerable
that forbearance was no longer a virtue, Robert Kirkwood exchanged
the implements of agriculture for the sword and entered the Delaware
regiment under Col. Hazlet with the commission of Lieutenant. He

* Com. Jones's remains are expected here shortly on board the Frigate St. Lawrence.

was in thirty-two battles during the war and received the highest praise from every general officer under whom he served. At the battle of Camden fought by Gen. Gates, the Delaware regiment was reduced to 195 men who were formed into a company under the command of Capt. Kirkwood. A particular history of his bold exploits would fill a respectable volume. At the close of the war he was brevet Major. He was a universal favorite and richly deserved to be so. He fell fighting under Gen. St. Clair on the 4th of November 1791.

KNOWLTON THOMAS was a native of Ashford Connecticut and one of the first brave spirits that entered the field and among the first martyrs in the cause of FREEDOM. He commanded a regiment at the battle of Long Island in August 1776 which formed the van of the American army. In September following he came in contact with Gen. Leslie with a superior force and fell while gallantly leading his men to the charge. The command then devolved on Major Leitch of Virginia who was severely wounded but drove the enemy from the field. Col. Knowlton was an officer of great promise, an esteemed citizen—an honest man.

KNOX HENRY was born in Boston, Mass. on the 25th of July 1750. He was created a freeman and nobly fulfilled the design of his creation. In early life he became familiar with the engineer department of military tactics. He was among the first Major Generals appointed by Congress and directed the ordnance operations during the whole period of the Revolution. The practised veterans of mother Britain were often compelled to admit that he had no superior in the management of artillery. His skill was effectually illustrated on every battle field where he was present. The victory at Monmouth over superior numbers was attributed by the enemy to the artillery of Gen. Knox. Washington referred to the fact in his report to Congress. From the commencement of his useful military career at Cambridge to its brilliant close at Yorktown, this brave and accomplished General stood on a lofty eminence of fame, admired and beloved by the commander-in-chief, by the whole army, by Congress and by our nation. He succeeded Gen. Lincoln in the War Department after the close of the Revolution and was the first Secretary of War under the Federal Constitution. On retiring from public life he settled at Thomastown, Maine, where his death was occasioned by a chicken bone lodging in his throat on the 25th of October 1806. In the private walks of life he exemplified those virtues most prominently that best adorn the man and assimilate him to his Creator.

KOSCIUSZCO THADDEUS commenced his noble existence in 1746 in the palatinate of Brescia, Lithunia, once an independent grand duchy containing 60,000 square miles which was united to Poland in 1569 and now forms the Russian provinces of Wilna, Grodno and Minsk. When reading the classics in his youth this noble patriot became enraptured with the vision of a Republic. He completed his education by a military course that he might be better prepared to battle for Liberty. When the story of the American Revolution reached him he at once resolved to enroll his name with those who dared to make an effort to be free. On his arrival, Washington appointed him a Colonel of engineers and one of his aids. His undaunted bravery on all occasions, his patriotic zeal, his amiable disposition, his purity of life, his noble bearing—all combined to endear him to the army and to every friend of freedom. He returned to his native land at the close of the Revolution and left his name carved high on the temple of our Liberty. Having aided in achieving the Independence we now enjoy, he saw his long nursed vision of a Republic reduced to a happy reality. His own countrymen were groaning under a bondage more servile than that which had oppressed the Americans. He longed to see them free. A few noble spirits were prepared to strike for Liberty. The time arrived for action. Kosciuszco was made commander-in-chief in 1789. Five years passed in preparation. In 1794 his army was attacked at Raslavice by the Russian General Denisoff who was defeated with great slaughter. For six months he kept at bay the combined forces of Russia and Prussia. On the 4th of October of that year, the officer who commanded the advance position of the Polish army proved a traitor and permitted the enemy to occupy it without opposition. This effected the ruin of the liberating army—Kosciuszco fell covered with wounds and was incarcerated in a dungeon at St. Petersburg until Alexander was crowned who at once restored him to freedom. He then visited the United States and landed at Philadelphia where he was made a welcome guest. He subsequently spent some time in France. From thence he went to Solence in Switzerland where he died on the 16th of October 1817.

LACY JOHN was born in Bucks County, Pa. on the 4th of February 1755. His paternal ancestor came from the Isle of Wight under the auspices of William Penn. John's ancestor and all his descendants belonged to the Society of Friends. The love of Freedom predominated over the anti-war creed of John and he made up his mind to obtain it, peaceably if he could—forcibly if he must. He took the commission of captain from Congress on the 6th of January 1776 and was at once thrown over the fence by his Quaker brethren. He left his home, his society and his mill to do battle for his country. He served under Gen. Wayne in Canada and performed the hazardous duty of carrying an express from Gen. Sullivan to Arnold when before Quebec. On his return the next year he resigned in consequence of a difficulty with Gen. Wayne. He was then appointed by the legislature of Pennsylvania to organize the militia in Bucks County. He was soon elected colonel. He was now in the midst of tories and Quakers who were acting in concert with the enemy and threatened him with personal vengeance. These threats he disregarded as the idle wind. He brought his regiment into the field and performed feats of valor that at once raised him to a high standard on the list of heroes. His conduct was particularly noticed by Washington and he was honored with the commission of brigadier-general on the 9th of January 1778 and ordered to relieve Gen. Potter. He was then but 22 years of age. Probably influenced by his refugee neighbors—the British in Philadelphia determined on taking him dead or alive. His duties were onerous, his watchfulness untiring. On the 1st of the ensuing May he was stationed at what is now Hatborough with less than 500 men, mostly raw militia. Owing to the negligence of the officer of his picket guard his little camp was surrounded just at the dawn of morning by about 800 British infantry, rangers and cavalry. He formed his men quickly and cut his way through with such impetuosity that he threw the enemy into confusion and escaped with the loss of only 26 killed with a few wounded and prisoners who were treated with a barbarity that casts savage warfare so far in the shade that their most cruel tortures would appear as refulgent sun light in comparison. This bold manœuvre of Gen. Lacy and his brave Spartans was a matter of applause throughout the country. He was constantly employed by Gen. Washington on hazardous enterprizes and in every instance received his unqualified approbation. After the evacuation of Philadelphia Gen. Lacy was made a member of the legislature and served three consecutive sessions. In 1781 he closed his military career and like a good citizen, married an amiable daughter of Col. Reynolds of New Jersey and commenced a successful career of domestic felicity. He filled various civil offices, lived in the esteem of every patriot (not of all his Quaker relatives) and died at the village of New Mills, Burlington County, N. J. on the 17th of February 1814.

LAURENS HENRY was ushered into the world at Charleston, S. C. in 1724. He was one of the first in his state to put the revolutionary ball in motion. He was President of the Provincial Congress of South Carolina that convened in June 1775. He prepared articles of association that demonstrated how clearly he perceived—how strongly he felt the oppressions of mother Britain. In November 1777 he succeeded John Hancock in the Presidential chair of the Continental Congress. In 1780 he was comissioned to proceed to Holland to negotiate a loan and form a treaty with the United Netherlands. On his passage he was captured by a British war vessel and on the 6th of October was committed to the tower in London under the charge of high treason. He was there confined for 14 months and treated with the proverbial cruelty that has left a dark stain upon the names of the British ministers then in power, that if they were linen the concentrated powers of a thousand suns could not efface it in a million of years. Many stratagems were devised to obtain from him concessions and promises that would lessen his sufferings and apparent danger but which did not honor his country. They were spurned with an indignity that none but FREEMEN can so burningly exhibit. When his son was sent to the court of France the father was requested to write and request him to desist from his mission or the life of his parent would be taken. He promptly refused and replied—"My son is of age and has a will of his own. I know him to be a man of honor. He loves me dearly and would lay down his life to save mine but I am sure he would not sacrifice his honor to save my life and I applaud him for it." The indignation of the Americans and many in the mother country was roused against those who held Mr. Laurens in bondage. The authorities found themselves in a tight place. They dare not try and condemn him as a rebel. For this a swift retribution awaited them. Burgoyne and many other high functionaries were prisoners of war. The old patriot could not be moved from the position of a freemen. He correctly considered himself only a prisoner of war—his own countrymen and other nations were of the same opinion. After much ado about a plain simple matter the king's counsellors had him bound, with Messrs. Oswald and Anderson as sureties, to appear at the Easter term for trial after being compelled to strike from the recognizance the words " our sovereign lord the king." Before leaving he was entirely released and requested by Lord Shelburne to hasten home to assist in consummating a peace. Before leaving he received a commission from Congress to repair to Paris and act in conjunction with Messrs. Franklin, Adams and Jay and had the proud satisfaction of signing the preliminaries of peace on the 30th of November 1782. His cruel deprivations during his imprisonment laid the foundation of disease which terminated his life near Charleston, S. C. on the 8th of December 1792. His name is enrolled with the patriotic, the virtuous and the good.

LAURENS JOHN was the noble son of Henry before alluded to. He was one of the bravest of the brave. He entered the army in 1777 with the rank of lieutenant-colonel and was a member of the military family of Washington. At Germantown he was severely wounded in an attempt to dislodge the enemy from Chew's house. He gained laurels at Rhode Island, Monmouth, Savannah, Charleston and at several other points of desperate conflict. He was among the first to enter the lines at Yorktown. He courted danger ardently—his courage was impetuous—he knew no fear. Dr. Ramsay said of him—"A dauntless bravery was the least of his virtues and an excess of it his greatest foible." His love for Washington knew no bounds. He challenged Gen. Charles Lee for speaking disrespectfully of the father of our country and marked him for life. He was asked how young Laurens behaved and replied—"I could have hugged the noble boy he pleased me so." His mission to France in 1781 to effect a loan was successful. His private virtues were as bright as his public career was brilliant. He was a high-minded, honorable, accomplished gentleman. At a trifling skirmish after the war was virtually closed this noble young man was killed in 1782.

LEDYARD WILLIAM was born in Connecticut in 1738. He was a murdered martyr in the glorious cause of Liberty. After bravely defending Fort Griswold at New London against an overwhelming force under the traitor Arnold he was compelled to surrender [see the Life of Arnold]. A British officer entered and asked who commanded the fort. Col. Ledyard replied—"I *did* but *you* do now" and handed him his sword which he immediately plunged through the body of his defenceless prisoner. Nearly 70 were slaughtered after the surrender. The fort was manned by 157 militia hastily collected and poorly armed. But 6 were killed in the regular attack. The British had two commissioned officers and 40 privates killed—135 non-commissioned officers and privates wounded—conclusive proof of the bravery of Col. Ledyard and his men in an action of only forty minutes. The following extract from the inscription on the tomb-stone of Col. Ledyard shows the high estimation in which he was held.

" By a judicious and faithful discharge of the various duties of his station he rendered most essential services to his country and stood confessed the unshaken patriot and intrepid hero. He lived the pattern of magnanimity, courtesy and humanity—he died the victim of ungenerous rage and cruelty."

LEE ARTHUR commenced his mortal career in Virginia in 1740. He was highly educated in England—took the degree of M. D. at the medical university of Edinburgh–returned to Williamsburg in his native State and commenced the successful practice of his profession. In a few years he returned to England–read law in the Temple and became a political writer over the signature of Junius Americanus which gave him an acquaintance with the popular party and gained him a membership in the famed society of the supporters of the Bill of Rights. His numerous political essays in favor of the cause of Liberty gained for him a high reputation at home. He was associated with Messrs. Franklin and Deane in negotiating a treaty of alliance with France in 1776. Upon learning that false accusations had been circulated by Mr. Deane alleging improper political conduct he resigned and returned home. He was elected to the Virginia Legislature in 1781 and then to Congress where he remained until 1785. The previous year he had effected a treaty with the Six Nations of Indians. He went from Congress into the Treasury Department where he continued up to 1789 when he left the public arena and died in 1792. He was a man of parts and a zealous patriot.

LEE CHARLES was a native of North Wales and held a military commission at the age of eleven. His was emphatically the life of a soldier. He served at an early age in Canada–under Burgoyne in Portugal–in the Polish army–travelled the tour of Europe–killed an Italian officer in a duel–came to America in 1773–declared for Liberty and was made a major-general by Congress in 1775. He commanded for a time in New York–then in the south–was soon transferred to New Jersey where he was made prisoner in 1776 and treated in the most brutal manner and not exchanged until the close of the next year. In 1778 he was arraigned before a court martial for disobeying orders at the battle of Monmouth and suspended for one year. He lived in seclusion in Virginia until 1782 when he repaired to Philadelphia and died in October of that year–poor and friendless–friendless because he was poor. He was a man of energy–a brave officer–rather morose and not calculated to captivate or gain popular applause.

LEE HENRY was born in Virginia in 1756 and entered the military arena in 1776 with the rank of captain of cavalry. At the battle of Germantown his company was the body guard of Washington. In 1780 he was commissioned lieutenant-colonel and put in command of the celebrated "Lee's Legion" so often referred to and which was a terror to the enemy during the war. At Eutaw Springs and in numerous battles he gained imperishable laurels. From 1786 to the time of the adoption of the Federal Constitution he was a member of Congress and a member of the Convention that framed that sacred instrument. In 1799 he was elected to Congress and selected to pronounce the funeral oration of President Washington. In 1792 he was governor of Virginia. For military courage, skill and prudence Col. Lee stood in the front rank. His capture of the garrison of Paulus Hook opposite New York in open day without the loss of a man and in sight of the main British army and navy, was a feat scarcely equalled during the Revolution. So perfect were his plans–so rapid were his movements that he eluded pursuit and took every man found in the garrison to the American camp. He commanded the army that put a quietus on the Whisky boys in Pennsylvania. With all his honors fresh upon him he was incarcerated in prison for the crime of debt. He there wrote his "Memoirs of the Southern Campaign." He was severely wounded at the riot in Baltimore in 1814. He died at Cumberland Island in Georgia at the house of a friend in 1814. His remains repose near those of Gen. Greene who was his warm friend and companion in arms. His relentless creditors could rob him of his personal liberty but could not chain his noble mind nor rob him of a well earned fame or of the glorious title of an HONEST MAN.

LEE EZRA was born in Connecticut in 1749. He left his plough in the furrow to avenge the wrongs that were heaped upon his country by the hirelings of the crown. With the commission of a Captain he entered the service under Gen. Parsons. He had the marked esteem of Gen. Washington and performed many secret missions for him. He fought with him at Trenton, Monmouth and Brandywine. When the British fleet lay in New York bay he sent every war vessel to Sandy Hook as fast as wind could take them–the men sweeping the bottoms of the ships with chains for fear some live Yankee might still be there. An ingenious apparatus for blowing up ships was invented by David Bushnel of Saybrook, Conn. Washington employed Capt. Lee to put it in operation. For the want of a resisting power to work the attaching screw he was not able to penetrate the copper on the bottom of the vessel. He finally detached the apparatus containing the magazine of powder and left it under one of the large war ships. In due time it exploded–put the water in earthquake agitation and shook the very earth. The brave Britons were as badly frightened as when they had the dreadful battle with the kegs on the Delaware opposite Philadelphia. They were missing in a short time. After the Independence of his country was secured Capt. Lee returned to his farm where he lived in the esteem of his fellow citizens and pursued the even tenor of his ways at Lyme Connecticut until the 29th of October 1821 when his noble soul returned to its original happy home.

LEE THOMAS SIM was a citizen of Maryland and early espoused his country's rights and sternly opposed British wrongs. He served his country in various public capacities–was a member of the Continental Congress–a delegate to the Convention that framed the Federal Constitution and governor of his state. He lived in the full enjoyment of the esteem of his numerous friends until 1819 when his lamp of life was snuffed out by death.

LINCOLN BENJAMIN was introduced on our rolling planet at Hingham, Mass. on the 23d of January 1733. Like Cincinnatus he left his plough and hastened to repel the invading foe. As Colonel of militia he had taken the entered apprentice degree in military tactics and rose rapidly in rank. In 1776 the Council of Massachusetts made him a Major General and in February of the ensuing year Congress conferred on him a similar commission at the suggestion of Washington. He was with him at New York and in Jersey and rendered efficient aid during that trying period. In July 1777 he joined the northern army and did much toward preparing the way for the capture of Burgoyne. He made his head quarters at Manchester, Vermont. On the 13th of September he sent Col. Brown to lake George with 500 men who surprised the enemy–seized 200 batteaux–took 293 prisoners and liberated 100 Americans with a loss of only three killed and five wounded. He soon united his force with that of Gen. Gates and was second in command. During the bloody battle of the 7th of October he commanded within the lines. On the 8th of October he was severely wounded in the leg and disabled for a long time. He suffered several surgical operations and lost a considerable portion of the bone which lamed him for life. In 1778 he was put in command of the southern division of the army then in a miserable condition. Near the last of December Gen. Provost arrived with several armed vessels and 3000 fresh troops and occupied Savannah. In September 1779 Gen. Lincoln and Count D'Estaing made a bold but unsuccessful attack upon the enemy. A column under Count Dillion missed their way and were not in the action, to which accident may be attributed the failure of success. In leading on a corps of cavalry Count Pulaski was mortally wounded. Gen Lincoln then repaired to Charleston and used his best exertions to place it in a state of defence. In February 1780 Sir Henry Clinton arrived and on the 30th of March planted himself in front of that city. After wasting considerable powder he demanded a surrender on the 10th of April which was promptly refused. A vigorous siege was prosecuted until the 11th of May when terms of capitulation were arranged. Gen. Lincoln had kept the enemy at bay much longer than was anticipated by friend or foe. His conduct stood approved by all whose good opinion he valued. At Yorktown he commanded the central division. His conduct elicited the high approbation of Washington who mentioned him particularly in his report to Congress. In 1781 he was placed at the head of the War Department. At the end of two years he resigned and was complimented by Congress with a resolution of strong commendation. In 1784 he was one of the commissioners who made a treaty with the Penobscot Indians. In 1787 he commanded the troops who quelled the rebellion of Shay and Day. The same year he was elected Lieut. Governor. In 1789 he was one of the commissioners who effected a treaty with the Creek Indians and in 1793 with the Western Indians. He was appointed Collector of the Port of Boston in 1789 which office he held until two years before his death which occurred on the 9th of May 1810. In all respects he was a worthy citizen and exemplified every virtue that renders a man truly useful.

LIPPITT CHRISTOPHER was born in Rhode Island in 1744. From early life he took a deep interest in the welfare of his country and filled many public stations. When the war cry was sounded he was Colonel of a regiment and marched his yeoman troops to the battle field. He subsequently entered the Continental army—was raised to the rank of Brigadier—fought bravely at Harlaem Heights, White Plains, Trenton and Princeton and received the high commendation of Washington for his zeal, courage and uniform consistent course. He was elected governor of his native state before the close of the war and was several times called out to repel the invading foe. He was always at the post of duty and knew no fugitive fear. He acted a noble part in the drama of life—when the curtain of death closed upon him he was ready. He died at Cranston, Rhode Island in 1824.

LIVINGSTON ROBERT R. was a native of the Empire State and

one of the early and bold patriots who bearded the British lion and drove him from his lair of illegitimate power. He was an acute lawyer, a profound jurist, an able statesman. He was a member of Congress in 1776 and on the committee appointed to prepare the Declaration of Independence. He was Secretary of Foreign Affairs–minister to France and for a long time chancellor of the State of New York. He dignified every station he occupied, graced the walks of private life and made a peaceful exit from earth in 1813.

LIVINGSTON WILLIAM was born in New York in 1723. He was a ripe scholar, a firm patriot and was among the first to expose the usurpations of mother Britain and rouse the people to a vindication of their chartered rights. He was an able writer and was most sincerely hated by the creatures of the crown. He removed to New Jersey just previous to the war storm. He was an able member of Congress in 1774. He was the first governor of his adopted State under the new order of things and ably filled that dignified office for fourteen consecutive years when he was called " to that country from whose bourne no traveller returns." He died near Elizabethtown, N. J. on the 25th of July 1790 full of years and crowned with honors enduring as history.

McCLINTOCK NATHANIEL commenced his earthly career in New Hampshire on the 21st of March 1757. He received a finished education and was a favorite in every circle where he moved. He was courted by the hirelings of the crown with the promise of high honors. He was affianced to Liberty and could not entertain their propositions. Soon after the war-cry was raised on the heights of Lexington he entered the army with the commission of lieutenant. He rose quickly to the rank of major over older captains which created dissatisfaction among them although they fully agreed that his talents and services made him worthy of the promotion. He proved the noble magnanimity of his soul by at once resigning that perfect harmony might be restored. He had fought bravely at Trenton–at Ticonderoga and in all the battles with the troops of Burgoyne up to the time of his surrender. On leaving the army he entered on board the private armed ship General Sullivan of 20 guns, Capt. Manning, as second lieutenant. In 1780 this ship was captured by two British cruisers of much superior force after a severe engagement in which Maj. McClintock was killed. Thus prematurely fell one of the brightest and most promising sons of New Hampshire.

McKINSTRY JOHN is first ushered into historic notice at the battle of Bunker's Hill where he acted a brave part in repelling the overwhelming force of the enemy. From that time to the surrender of Yorktown he was constantly in the field with a commission of captain often commanding a partisan corps in bold and daring enterprises. In Canada he had become a terror to the enemy. At Cedar Keys, 30 miles above Montreal on the St. Lawrence, he was taken prisoner and soon bound to a tree by the savages and surrounded with faggots. All hope of escape had fled–a torturing death seemed inevitable–the torch was ready to be applied–the war dance was arranged–the Captain uttered what he supposed was his last prayer. At that awful moment Heaven reminded him that he was a Mason and had heard that the ruling chief,

Brandt, belonged to the same time honored fraternity. He gained his eye—gave him the proper sign—was instantly released—treated with great kindness and exchanged in a short time. Many instances are on record of a similar character and others of a different nature where a brother has been rescued from the jaws of death. Gen. Freegift Patchin, of my native place was rescued by Brandt when a prisoner in Canada under exactly similar circumstances. I have often heard it from his own lips. If all mankind were true Masons and no black sheep in the flock—a harmony would succeed before unknown. The instances above cited should silence every objector to an institution pure in principle but sometimes dishonored by the unworthy.

Capt. McKinstry resumed the business of agriculture when the army was disbanded and lived in the esteem of his countrymen in the town of Livingston, N. Y. until 1822 when his mourning neighbors performed the last solemn duty of placing him in his grave.

McPHERSON WILLIAM was born at Philadelphia, Pa. in 1756. He was made a cadet in the British army when but 13 years of age. At the commencement of the American Revolution he was adjutant of the 16th Regiment of the king's troops. This did not make him a loyalist. His innate love of freedom induced him to at once tender his resignation which was not accepted till 1779 when he repaired to the American camp. Having been stationed at Pensacola up to this time he had never drawn his sword against his country. He had been long personally and favorably known to Gen. Washington who at once made him a brevet major. He was an aid under Gen. La Fayette for some time and subsequently placed over a corps of cavalry in Virginia. On all occasions he acquitted himself nobly. On the 19th of September 1789 he was made surveyor of the port of Philadelphia—in 1792 inspector of revenue—in 1793 naval officer, which station he held until 1813 when he was called from time to eternity.

MADISON JAMES was born in Orange County, Virginia, on the 16th of March, 1751. Although young at the commencement of the Revolution he took a deep interest in its success. After the close of the struggle for Independence he was among those who clearly saw that the old Articles of Confederation could not preserve the priceless Liberty obtained. He has the imperishable honor of proposing the Convention that framed the inestimable Federal Constitution that has thus far held our ship of state to its moorings amidst the dashing waves of party spirit—the roaring breakers of political fanaticism—the angry surges of impolitic ultraism. His fame as a far-seeing statesman stands on a lofty eminence. His voluminous writings bear the impress of giant intellect—unalloyed patriotism—sterling integrity and untiring industry. He succeeded Thomas Jefferson in the Presidential chair and served two terms. He steered the ship of state through the second war of Independence and run her close to the wind. His life was a continued course of usefulness—his demise left a vacuum in our nation not readily filled. The curtain of death closed upon him in 1836.

MANLY JOHN commenced his earthly pilgrimage in Massachusetts in 1734. He was one of the first who met the enemy on her favorite element. He was put in command of the armed schooner Lee on the 24th of October 1775 and cruised in and around Massachusetts

Bay. His success was beyond all anticipation. He made numerous captures of great value to the American army and embryo navy. His noble daring and consummate skill were hailed as germs of future greatness. He was transferred to the privateer Hancock and launched out upon a more extensive cruise and captured the British sloop of war Fox and several other prizes. On his return he was received with great enthusiasm and transferred to the privateer Jason. Soon after he sailed he was attacked by two English privateers of 18 and 10 guns. He ran the Jason between them before he fired a gun and in a few brief moments they both surrendered. On his return passage with these prizes he was captured by the Rainbow of 40 guns on the 8th of July 1777 and was confined in Mill Prison and at Halifax until near the close of the war and treated with the proverbial cruelty so often before noticed. In 1782 he was put in command of the frigate Hague. During his cruise he was run on a sand bank near Guadaloupe by a 74 gun ship which was joined by three other ships of the line. They opened a tremendous fire upon the frigate which was continued for three days. On the morning of the fourth day the Hague swung clear, hoisted the Continental colors–fired a farewell salute of 13 guns and returned to Boston. Charges were there brought against this gallant captain by one of his officers. These were partially sustained before a court martial but appear not to have been placed upon the public records nor well understood by the community. His unsurpassed bravery may have operated in his favor. He died at Boston on the 12th of February 1793.

MARSHALL JOHN was born in Virginia in 1756. He was one of the noble sons of the Old Dominion who threw themselves in the breach made upon our country by the corrupt British ministry. He was a long time in the tented field under Washington and acted a bold and glorious part in the achievement of our Independence. He was a man of superior talents–sound education and strong mind. In 1797 he was envoy to France–Secretary of State under Thomas Jefferson and soon after was made Chief Justice of the United States Supreme Court which station he dignified to the close of his life. He wrote an elaborate Life of Washington. He was universally esteemed as an ornament to the bench, his country and to every circle in which he moved.

MATHEWS THOMAS is first spoken of as a citizen of Norfolk, Virginia and a brave officer of the Revolution. It is painful to the historian in search of facts relative to the Sages and Heroes of the American Revolution to be unable to ascertain even the birth-place of many who did good service in the glorious cause of Independence. So in this case. Mr. Mathews was a prominent man–rose to the rank of general–was speaker of the House of Delegates in Virginia and nobly performed the public and private duties of life that devolved upon him. He died at Norfolk, Va. on the 20th of April 1812.

MERCER HUGH was born and educated at Aberdeen, Scotland. He became a physician and was surgeon's mate at the battle of Culloden Moor, Scotland, where the young Pretender was defeated by the Duke of Cumberland in 1745. He came to Pennsylvania in 1746 and was actively engaged in the border wars. He was with Gen. Braddock in 1755 and witnessed the awful slaughter on the day that general was mortally wounded. He formed an intimacy with Washington during that campaign. The next year he served under Gen. Armstrong and greatly distinguished himself at the battle with the Indians at Kittanning above Pittsburgh. He there narrowly escaped being captured–had his right arm broken with a ball–became separated from his companions and was alone in the wilderness two weeks before reaching Cumberland without any food but water and the flesh of a rattlesnake that he fortunately killed. The city of Philadelphia presented him with a splendid medal for his bravery on that occasion. In 1763 he removed to Fredericksburg, Va. where he enhanced his importance in society by leading Isabella Gordon to the hymeneal altar. He soon gained a good practice in his profession and the esteem of a large circle of acquaintances. He was an ardent Whig and was among the first to repel the enemy by force of arms. He was at once made a brigadier-general. His brigade was a part of the left wing of the American army at the battle of Trenton in December 1776. On the 3d of January following he commenced the attack at Princeton with 350 men. Before the main force could be brought to his support he was charged by the whole regiment commanded by Col. Mawhood. His line was broken–he was surrounded in person and compelled to surrender after which he was mortally wounded. At that moment Washington came up and quickly routed the enemy and rescued the brave Mercer. He lived but one week and was buried at Princeton. His death was not only deeply deplored by his friends, the army and Congress but was a most serious loss to the country at large. His age, experience, talents, high character–all combined to render him one of the most important men of our nation at that eventful era. In the memoirs of Gen. Wilkinson he is placed next in rank to Washington in point of prospective usefulness. His whole soul was enlisted in the glorious cause of Liberty.

MEIGS RETURN JONATHAN was a native of Middletown, Conn. At the commencement of the struggle for FREEDOM he had his military lamp trimmed and burning brightly with the fire of patriotism. He was in command of a splendid company of infantry volunteers in beautiful uniform, well armed and eager for service. He marched to Cambridge immediately on receiving intelligence of the battle of Lexington. He was soon raised to the rank of major and endured the fatigues of the expedition to Quebec under Arnold. In the desperate attack on that fortress he commanded a battalion and was among the first who scaled the walls and entered the city where he was taken prisoner and was not exchanged until near the close of 1776. In 1777 he was made a colonel and performed many astonishing feats of valor. On the 23d of May of that year he proceeded to Sag Harbor, Long Island, with 170 men–destroyed 12 British vessels fully laden with supplies for the army then in New York–killed six of the enemy–took 90 prisoners and returned to New Haven without the loss of a man. For this bold and successful enterprise Congress voted him an elegant sword. In 1779 he commanded one of the regiments under Gen. Wayne at the storming of Stony Point. He was a reliable man on all occasions and under the most trying circumstances. In 1787 he was one of the pioneer colony that located at the mouth of the Muskingum river on the Ohio. He was their esteemed governor until the officers of the territory arrived. He formed a code of regulations which were subscribed and placed upon a venerable oak where they were as frequently and more usefully consulted than the oracle Apollo at Delphi. He was a man of great philanthropy–a warm friend of the injured red men and accepted the agency of the Cherokee station. He gained the confidence and love of that noble nation who named him "*the white path.*" With them he lived usefully and died peacefully on the 28th of January 1823 strong in hope, rich in faith with a full assurance of a glorious immortality.

MIFFLIN THOMAS commenced his earthly career in Pennsylvania in 1744. He was an influential Quaker until he was read out of meeting in 1775 because he dared strike for Liberty. He was an early, warm and able advocate of equal rights. He was an efficient member of the Congress of 1774. He was commissioned Quarter-Master-General in August 1775. He was one of the most successful stump-orators of that time. No one could more effectually excite the populace–when incited to action it needed a cooler head to direct the tornado and rule the storm of passion. He was very useful in rousing the militia to rush to the rescue. In 1787 he was a member of the Convention that framed the Federal Constitution. In October 1788 he succeeded Franklin in the chair of the Executive Council of the state. He aided in forming the first republican Constitution of Pennsylvania and was the first Governor under it. He was eminently useful in terminating the whisky rebellion. In all that he undertook he executed with great zeal and energy. His life was devoted to the good of his country–he filled his measure of usefulness and left the theatre of life at Lancaster, Pa. on the 20th of January 1800.

MILLER HENRY is first introduced as one of the bravest officers of the Continental army. He rose to the rank of colonel and was a thorny customer of the enemy when retreating through New Jersey. At numerous battles he was distinguished for cool and undaunted courage. At the battle of Monmouth he had two horses killed under him while leading his men to the charge. He commanded a brigade of militia at Baltimore the last time mother Britain attempted to chastise her truant child. He filled several civil offices and dignified them with old school civility–an article rather on the decline in these modern days of new fangled notions. He died at Carlisle, Pa. on the 5th of April 1824.

MONROE JAMES commenced his busy life in Virginian in 1759. He entered the Continental army at the age of 17 and proved a noble and brave boy. He distinguished himself in the battles of Harlaem Heights, White Plains, Trenton, Brandywine, Germantown and Monmouth. At the latter he was aid to Gen. Sterling. At the close of the war he held the commission of Captain. He then read law with Thomas Jefferson–became a member of the Virginia legislature–was elected to Congress in 1783–in 1790 was a member of the United States Senate–in 1794 was minister to France–in 1799 governor of Virginia–in 1803 minister to France, the same year minister to England–in 1804 minister to Spain–in 1806 minister to England–in 1811 Secretary of State under Madison–then Secretary of War–in 1817 President of the United States and served two terms–labor and glory enough for the life of one man. James Monroe came from the searching crucible of all these responsible stations like gold seven times tried–free from dross and full in weight–a fact that renders the eulogy of words on his fame imbecile. He made his last bow upon the stage of life on the glorious 4th of July 1831 when the curtain of death dropped and hid him from the admiring view of a gazing world.

MONTGOMERY RICHARD commenced his journey in this world of fickle spirits in the north of Ireland in 1737. He was one of the noblest sons of the Emerald Isle. His genius was brilliant–his education finished, his manners accomplished, his soul patriotic–the whole man was worthy of admiration. He fought for Great Britain under Wolfe and fell on the very ground where he had joined in shouts of victory in 1759. He came to America to remain permanently in 1772–purchased an estate near 100 miles above New York City–married a daughter of Judge Livingston and become a prominent citizen and a warm friend to the cause of Liberty. In 1775 he was appointed Major General and in conjunction with Gen. Schuyler placed over the northern forces. In October the illness of his colleague left him in sole command. He captured Fort Chamblee, St. Johns and Montreal by the 12th of November. He then proceeded to Quebec and formed a junction with Arnold at Point Aux Trembles. On the 1st of December a siege was commenced on Quebec and continued until the 31st of that month. On the memorable last day of 1775 the gallant little band under these two ardent soldiers was led to the storming attack of the town in four divisions with strong fortifications to overcome and double their force within the walls. The first gun that was fired upon the division led by the gallant Montgomery killed him and his two aids. His death spread a general gloom over our land and was deeply lamented in the mother country. Congress caused a monument to be erected to his memory in front of St. Paul's church in the city of New York with a suitable inscription. By direction of the legislature of the empire state his remains were brought from Quebec and deposited near this monument on the 8th of July 1818. His widow lived to see the last vestiges of the husband of her youth,–our nation rejoiced to have this noble hero repose in the bosom of our own soil. The fame of Gen. Montgomery is above eulogy. It will grow richer with age–time cannot corrode it.

MORGAN DANIEL was a native of Durham, Bucks county, Pa. From there he removed to New Jersey and then to Virginia where he was a common laborer for some time and by his industry and economy saved money sufficient to ultimately purchase a farm in the county of Frederic. When a common laborer his company was not of the highest order–his habits not rigidly moral but in that company he was the ruling spirit. He was with Braddock when defeated by the French and Indians and received a wound that marked him in the face for life. Like many more with a rough exterior, he had a noble heart within him–a heart full of daring courage, patriotism and philanthropy. He was among the first who rushed to the standard of Washington at Cambridge with the commission of Captain. He was with Arnold in his memorable expedition to Quebec and was taken prisoner during the attack on that city. On being exchanged he returned and took command of the celebrated rifle corps that so often carried death into the ranks of the enemy. At the capture of Burgoyne the carnage produced by this corps was terrific–especially among the bravest of the

British officers—contributing very largely in achieving that splendid victory that first rolled back the tide of war upon the conquering foe. Of this all seemed sensible but Gen. Gates who did not award to him his just share of credit in his report to Washington and Congress. For a time he left the service. When Gates was ordered to the command of the southern army he personally solicited Col. Morgan to accompany him. He was plainly referred to past improper treatment but the Colonel ultimately repaired to that field with the commission of Brigadier General. He became the hero of the Cowpens for which Congress voted him a gold medal. That brilliant affair has been previously described. About that time Gen. Greene succeeded Gates. A disagreement occurred between him and Morgan as to the route to be taken in the retreat. Morgan took his own way—joined Greene at Guilford court house and then left the service. He subsequently commanded the Virginia troops in the campaign against the whisky boys in Pennsylvania. He was elected a member of Congress and filled the station with dignity. He ultimately located at Winchester, Va. where he lived in the high esteem of his fellow citizens—became a consistent member of the Presbyterian church and died in 1799. He was possessed of strong common sense—a brave but sensitive soldier—a good citizen—a worthy and honest man.

MORGAN JOHN was born in Philadelphia in 1735 and became an eminent physician and sterling whig. In 1765 he was elected Professor of the Theory and Practice of Medicine in the Medical College of Philadelphia. In October 1775 he was appointed chief physician of the hospitals of the American army. Jealousy and envy put the tongue of slander in motion and induced false accusations against him and succeeded in effecting his removal in a few months. He did not again enter the thorny course of public life and died at Philadelphia in 1789.

MORRIS GOVERNEUR commenced his earthly pilgrimage near the city of New York in 1752. He was liberally educated and became an eloquent and sound lawyer. He was a member of the Provincial Congress of N. Y. in 1775 and on the committee that drafted the first constitution of that state. In 1777 he was a member of the Continental Congress—in 1781 was associated with Robert Morris as assistant superintendent of Finance—in 1787 a member of the Convention that framed the Federal Constitution—in 1792 minister plenipotentiary to France and in 1800 was elected to the U. S. Senate where his extensive acquirements and Ciceronean eloquence shed fresh lustre on that body—on his country and his own high reputation. Mr. Sparks has published his speeches and writings with an interesting biographical sketch of his life. He was an ornament to every circle in which he moved—an honor to every station he filled—a particular star in the galaxy of the Sages of his day and generation.

MOULTRIE WILLIAM was ushered upon this mundane sphere in England in 1730 and came to Charleston, South Carolina to enjoy Freedom. When mother Britain violated that inherent privilege he was among the first to resist the invading foe. He was a prominent member of the public meetings and conventions that prepared the people to vindicate their rights. He was appointed colonel of one of the three regiments raised in his adopted state in 1775. He superintended the erection of the Fort on Sullivan's Island that bears his name. So hastily was it constructed and so slender was its formation that he was advised to abandon it on the approach of the British fleet. On the 28th of June 1776 Sir Peter Parker came up with eight ships of war and opened a tremendous fire upon this fragile fortress and the presumptuous rebels. To his utter astonishment streams of flashing fire gleamed from the American battery–a storm of iron hail came crashing among his ships. Splinters flew–rigging dropped–blood flowed–men fell. For ten hours Sir Peter raved and foamed with anger and urged his men to renewed exertions. At length a rebel cannon ball kissed off the nether part of his silk breeches which he considered a personal reflection upon his dignity and sullenly retired with his fleet after having been badly cut up. This brave defence by a few raw militia against an overwhelming veteran force was a theme of enthusiastic praise throughout America and Europe. Col. Moultrie was raised to the rank of brigadier-general and in 1779 was made a major-general in the Continental army. He participated in the most trying scenes of the south up to the surrender of Charleston on the 12th of May 1780 when he became a prisoner and was not exchanged until near the close of hostilities. He then returned to his home and aided in perfecting measures to preserve that Independence for which he had so nobly fought and conquered. He was elected governor of Virginia and filled several minor offices with usefulness and dignity. He died at Charleston S. C. on the 27th of September 1805.

MUHLENBURG PETER was born in Pennsylvania in 1746. His father was the Patriarch of the German Lutheran church in the Keystone state. This son was liberally educated and became the Rector of an Episcopal church. He loved his flock well but loved his country and her freedom more. At the commencement of the struggle for Liberty he exchanged his gown for regimentals, his pen for the sword, his pulpit for the tented field. In 1776 he received the commission of colonel–raised a regiment and marched it to head-quarters. The next year he was raised to the rank of brigadier and near the close of the war to the rank of major-general. He was a prudent, deliberate, brave and reliable officer. He had the unlimited confidence of Washington and performed his duty nobly on all occasions. At the siege of Yorktown he acted a bold and conspicuous part. After the war closed he was Vice-President of the Executive Council, member of the legislature, a U. S. Senator, Supervisor of excise and Collector of the Port of Philadelphia at the time of his death which occurred on the 1st of October 1807 at his country seat in Montgomery Co. Pa. As a Christian, minister, soldier, general, civil officer, citizen, husband, father, relative and friend–he acted a noble part and fulfilled the design of his creation.

NICHOLSON JAMES was born at Chestertown, Md. in 1737. He was a hardy son of Neptune from his youth and an uncompromising opponent of tyranny. When the revolutionary storm commenced he dared to brave its fury and tempt the bosses of its foaming surges. He was put in command of the armed ship Defence at the commencement of the war of Liberty and for a long time was a successful cruiser. Just before the close of the Revolution he was captured and put on board a prison ship at New York. He was a skilful, daring, noble and vigilant officer. His name is worthy of a place with the Sages and Heroes of our Independence. He died in 1806.

OGDEN MATTHIAS was a brave colonel in the Continental army and among the first in the field of military glory. He passed through the wilderness to Quebec with Arnold and was carried from the walls of that city severely wounded on the day of the unfortunate attack by the Americans. He served to the close of the war with credit to himself and usefulness to his country. Near the termination of the Revolution he was raised to the rank of brigadier-general. He was a man highly honorable in all things and under all circumstances–liberal, charitable and honest. He died at Elizabethtown N. J. on the 31st of March 1791.

OLNEY JEREMIAH commenced his exemplary life in Rhode Island in 1750. He was remarkable for mildness and an abundant share of the milk of human kindness and just as remarkable for his undaunted bravery in the field of battle and unshaken firmness in the cause of Freedom. He was much admired by Washington and frequently led the Rhode Island line to victory. He participated in the dangers and glory of the battles of Springfield, Monmouth, Red Bank and Yorktown. Subsequent to the war he was Collector of the Port of Providence and President of the Society of Cincinnati of his native state. No man enjoyed more fully the affection of all who knew him–no one more richly merited it. He died at his residence on the 10th of Nov. 1812.

ORR JOHN was born in New Hampshire in 1748. He was an officer under the brave and independent Stark and so severely wounded in one of his legs at the battle of Bennington that he was crippled for life. He was a man of strong intellect and filled several judicial and legislative offices with ability and strict fidelity He had the respect and confidence of his fellow citizens through life and was sincerely mourned at his death which occurred at Bedford, N. H. in 1823.

PAINE THOMAS commenced his eventful life in England in 1737. He pursued the business of stay maker for some time in London–then went to sea in a British privateer–was subsequently an excise man and a grocer. On learning the situation of the American Colonies from Franklin he became deeply interested in their behalf and came to this country in 1775 when his intellectual powers suddenly burst into a blaze of light. His vigorous essays and eloquent speeches in favor of American Independence did much towards consummating that glorious event. Had he published or said nothing against that religion which is held sacred by the great mass of our nation he would have remained as he was at first–one of the most popular political men of that time. If professing Christians all honored the religion of the cross infidelity would be robbed of its richest aliment. Hypocrites, degenerate and lukewarm church members, bigoted sectarians, dogmatical dictators, deluded fanatics–are all caterers for infidelity. The editor of the Cottage Bible remarks in commenting on the 19th chap. of Judges–" More inhumanity and villany may be found among degenerate professors of Christianity than among infidels and in general where we expect the most kindness we meet with the greatest injuries." This remark is painfully true but is not an argument against primitive Christianity. If we had no pure coin or solvent banks, counterfeit notes and bogus money could not be circulated. If Christianity was not essentially good, hypocrites would be left without a motive to profess it. Aside from the question of its divine origin, as a system of social order—as the foundation of rational liberty and moral rectitude—as a system imparting the greatest amount of happiness to the greatest number—it rises sublimely above all others. This is conceded by the ablest infidel writers. I refer to primitive Christianity as taught and practised by the immaculate Redeemer and his disciples. As this *is* not—*cannot* be denied, common sense dictates that all should practice at least its moral precepts if only upon the ground of self-preservation and interest which are ever dependent upon social order and good government. Thomas Paine took an active part in the French Revolution—was a member of the National Assembly—incurred the displeasure of Robespierre—fled to escape the guillotine—returned to America and died in the city of New York in 1809 not in a quiescent state of mind.

PARSONS SAMUEL HOLDEN was a citizen of Connecticut and an eminent lawyer. When the Revolution commenced he left his office for the tented field resolved on Liberty or death. His zeal and daring courage gained for him the commission of major-general. He had the unlimited confidence of Washington—the esteem of his fellow officers—the love of his brave soldiers—the admiration of his numerous acquaintances—the gratitude of his bleeding country. His useful career was cut short by his being drowned near Pittsburgh, Pa. in 1789.

PAULDING JOHN was born in the State of New York in 1732. He was a brave soldier and rose from the ranks to the grade of major after he aided in the capture of Major Andre. For that noble act the names of Paulding, Williams and Van Wert are embalmed in the affections of every patriot whilst the name of the traitor Arnold rouses a manly indignation in the bosom of every man who loves his country. His portrait will darken as time rolls on. For this important capture Congress passed a highly complimentary resolution on the 3d of November 1780 and made the following order which was placed upon the records. " That each of them receive annually, out of the public treasury, two hundred dollars in specie or an equivalent in the current money of these States, during life and that the Board of War procure for each of them a silver medal, on one side of which shall be a shield with this inscription—' FIDELITY' and on the other the following motto—'*Vincit amor patriæ*' [the love of our country prevails] and forward them to the commander-in-chief, who is requested to present the same, with a copy of this resolution and the thanks of Congress for their fidelity and the eminent service they have rendered their country." Maj. Paulding died at Staatsburgh, Duchess County, N. Y. on the 30th of December 1819.

PETERS NATHAN was a native of Connecticut and a bold defender of his country's rights. On the morning after the cry—" *To arms! to arms!*" sounded in his ears and ran through his soul like vivid lightning he was on his way to the field of battle. He rose rapidly from the grade of lieutenant to that of major and became one of the boldest of the bold. He fought bravely at Long Island, Frog's Point, Trenton, Princeton and in every place where he met the enemy in mortal combat. On the 6th of September 1781, before Arnold left Fort Griswold, he caused a slow train of powder to be set on fire communicating with the magazine. Just before it reached the volcanic mass Major Peters rushed into the fort and prevented a destructive explosion. No dangers prevented him from the prompt performance of every duty. At the close of the successful struggle for freedom he resumed the practice of law at New London where he lived in the high esteem of his friends and his country to a ripe old age. He was a sound lawyer, a safe counsellor, a brave soldier, a good citizen—AN HONEST MAN.

PETERS RICHARD was born in the balmy month of June in 1744. He was educated at Philadelphia and became an eminent member of the bar of that city. Understanding the rights of his country and the advantages of freedom he determined to maintain them at all hazards. In 1776 he was made secretary to the Board of War and faithfully performed the arduous duties of that important station until 1781 when he was elected a member of Congress and continued in that august body to the close of hostilities. He was appointed the first United States District Judge for Pennsylvania and highly honored that dignified station for thirty-six consecutive years. His decisions in the Court of Admiralty form the foundation on which our superstructure of that branch of jurisprudence is raised. This platform was adopted by the celebrated maritime judge Lord Stowell of England—a high compliment to the judicial acumen of Judge Peters. He was deservedly popular because scrupulously impartial, rigidly just and proverbial for humanity and kindness. In his performance of all the public and private duties of life he was a luminous example of human excellence worthy of admiration and imitation. He was a liberal patron of public improvements and did much to improve agriculture. He died at his residence in August 1828.

PETTIT CHARLES was born in New Jersey in 1737. He was a sensible lawyer and opposed to the usurpations of the hirelings of mother Britain although himself secretary of his native province when the revolutionary storm commenced its pitiless peltings. Congress made him a deputy quartermaster under Gen. Greene in conjunction with Col. Coxe. They performed the perplexing and arduous duties of that responsible office whilst Gen. Greene was in the field to the entire satisfaction of Washington, the army and Congress—a high encomium upon their perseverance and activity when we reflect upon their limited means to perform a mighty work. At the close of the Revolution he removed to Philadelphia and became a successful merchant. He was a member of Congress from Pennsylvania under the old Confederation—a member of the State Convention that sanctioned the Federal Constitution and in every public station which he was called to fill he performed his duty with the strictest integrity and great industry. His private virtues rendered him dear to every good man. He was president of the first insurance company incorporated in Philadelphia. He died at his residence on the 6th of September 1806.

PICKERING TIMOTHY commenced his infancy at Salem, Mass. in 1746. He was favored with a classical education and superior talents. He took an early and active part in the cause of equal rights and rendered efficient service in organizing the new government of his native State. He was made a judge of the Common Pleas and Maritime courts—adjutant-general of the United States army and a member of the Board of War. From 1790 to '98 he negotiated several treaties with sundry tribes of Indians. Under President Washington he was in succession Postmaster General, Secretary of War and Secretary of State. From 1803 to 1811 he was a member of the United States Senate–from 1814 to '17 was a representative in Congress. Few men of his time performed more public work–no one acted with more fidelity and faithfulness. He was an able judge, a firm patriot, a judicious legislator, an efficient officer–a credit to his State–an honor to our nation and in all respects a worthy man. He died in Salem, Mass. in 1829.

PICKENS ANDREW commenced his earthly existence in Bucks County, Pa. on the 13th of September 1739. When Andrew was a child his father removed to Augusta County, Va. and then to Waxhaw, in South Carolina. Andrew commenced a brilliant military career in the French war–served with Marion and Moultrie in 1761 in the sanguinary expedition against the Cherokees under Lieut. Col. Grant and became a hardy frontier warrior. When mother Britain became insolent and oppressive he was as ready to fight as he had been to serve her. He became a terror to the refugees *alias* Tories. At Kettle Creek he pounced upon an army of them under Col. Boyd of double his force and flogged them so severely that they were quiet until the British army afterwards spread over the south. At the Cowpens he commanded the militia and inspired them with the courage of veteran regulars. Congress voted him a sword for his gallantry on that occasion. At Eutaw he commanded the Carolina militia in conjunction with Marion. He was severely wounded in the breast by a musket ball early in the action and but for the buckle of his sword belt would have been shot through. When Charleston surrendered he was obliged to flee before the enemy to North Carolina and was among the first to rally under the indomitable Greene. In 1781 he commanded the last expedition against the Cherokees and laid the foundations of the peace that has never since been broken. Through the entire course of his military career he stood approved by his superiors and beloved by those under his command. He rose to the rank of brigadier-general in the regular army and was made major-general of militia in 1794. At the close of the war he filled several civil offices and aided essentially in consummating the treaty of Hopewell with the Cherokees to which place he removed soon after. He was a member of the convention that formed the Constitution of his State–a member of the legislature and in 1794 was elected to Congress. In 1797 he was returned to the legislature of his State where he remained fourteen consecutive years. He was a commissioner in all the treaties with the southern Indians. In this department Washington considered him the most useful man of that time. He took a deep interest in the war of 1812 and was that year governor of his State. He then retired to private life full of honors and years with a fame that will grow richer as it shall be rehearsed by each succeeding generation. His private character was as spotless as his public life was brilliant. He died at his residence on the 11th of October 1817.

PORTER ANDREW was born in Worcester, Montgomery County, Pa. on the 24th of September 1743. Without the advantages of a school education he became an eminent mathematician by the force of his own genius and industry. When the Revolution commenced he was at the head of a large mathematical school in the city of Philadelphia. Deeming the cause of Liberty paramount to all other interests he tendered his services to Congress and on the 19th of June 1776 he was made a captain of marines and placed on board the frigate Effingham. He was shortly after transferred to the artillery corps where he made himself extremely useful during the whole period of the war. He was ultimately raised to the rank of Colonel and commanded the 4th Pennsylvania regiment of artillery. He distributed iron hail effectually at the battles of Trenton, Princeton, Germantown and Brandywine. At Germantown he received the thanks of Gen. Washington on the field for his skill and undaunted courage. He was with Gen. Sullivan in his expedition against the Indians on the Susquehanna. It was Col. Porter who suggested to Gen. Clinton the plan of raising the water of Otsego Lake by a dam at its narrow outlet which produced a flood sufficient to float his troops on rafts to Tioga Point where they formed a junction with Sullivan. When the siege of Yorktown was planned Gen. Washington placed Col. Porter in charge of the military laboratory in Philadelphia to prepare the shells, cartridges, &c. for that important occasion. Although deprived the pleasure of being at the siege he had the high honor of preparing the thunder and hail that terminated the sanguinary conflict. Subsequent to the war he was one of the commissioners to run a line by astronomical observations between Pennsylvania and the adjoining States. He succeeded Gen. Muhlenberg as major-general of militia. Governor Snyder appointed him surveyor-general of the State of Pennsylvania in 1809 which office he ably filled until the 16th of November 1813 when he left earth for a fairer, brighter world on high. He was buried in the Presbyterian church-yard at Harrisburg with military honors.

PREBLE EDWARD commenced his earthly career at Portland, Maine, on the 15th of August 1761. From his youth he gloried in hazardous enterprises. At the age of eighteen he became a midshipman on board the Protector of 26 guns commanded by the brave Capt. John Forster Williams. On his first cruise young Preble had the proud satisfaction of contributing to the capture of the Admiral Duff of 36 guns after a brief but sanguinary action which so injured the British vessel that she sunk in a few moments with 40 of her crew. In the second cruise the Protector was captured and most of the officers taken to England. Preble was permitted to return and was made first lieutenant on board the sloop of war Winthrop. Shortly after that he took a party of brave tars in the night and captured a British armed brig lying in Penobscot Bay and of superior force to the Winthrop. This was accomplished with fourteen men dressed in white frocks. The brig lay near the shore and a large number of the enemy jumped overboard as the shrouded tars gained the deck and made for land where lay a considerable British force with artillery. Amidst a brisk fire Preble towed out his prize and moored her safely along side of the Winthrop. He continued on this ship till the close of the war. In 1801 he commanded the frigate Essex—in 1804 was made a commodore and placed in charge of the Mediterranean fleet of seven sail which prepared the way for placing the Bashaw of Tripoli upon his proper level and induced him to enter upon an honorable peace and relinquish all claims to a tribute. This act placed Com. Preble high on the list of naval heroes. He died on the 25th of August 1807.

PRESCOTT WILLIAM was born at Goshen, Massachusetts in 1726. He early engaged in the service of mother Britain and acted a distinguished part at the capture of Cape Breton in 1758. He was a Colonel of militia when the war commenced and one of the first in the field. He commanded at the sanguinary battle at Bunker's and Breed's Hill on the 17th of June 1775. With 1200 men hastily collected and with a temporary breast-work—made principally by excavating a shallow ditch and placing two rail fences parallel near each other and filling the interval with fresh mowed grass—he continued to repulse 5000 veteran troops, with a slaughter equalled only at the battle of New Orleans, until his ammunition was expended when he retreated with a loss of 453 men—killing 1054 of the enemy. Col. Prescott then entered the regular service and continued in the army until 1777 and then resigned. He was a volunteer at the capture of Burgoyne and rendered essential service. After the Revolution he served in the legislature and filled various civil offices with fidelity. He was brave, noble, generous and humane. In his "Memoirs" Gen. Lee beautifully remarks—"When future generations shall inquire where are the men who gained the brightest prize of glory in the arduous contest which ushered in our nation's birth? Upon Prescott and his companions in arms will the eye of history beam. The military annals of the world rarely furnish an achievement which equals the firmness and courage displayed on that proud day by the gallant band of Americans and it certainly stands first in the brilliant events of the war." Col. Prescott died in 1795 sincerely mourned.

PRIOLEAU SAMUEL was a native of Charleston, South Carolina, born in 1743 and among the first of that noble band of patriots who resolved on Liberty or death. He was in active service until taken prisoner at the surrender of his native city. He was then taken to the castle at St. Augustine and treated with great cruelty. His wife with five children fled to Philadelphia. He possessed great firmness and was emphatically a true patriot—a good citizen—an honest man. He died at Charleston on the 23d of March 1813.

PULASKI COUNT was a native of Poland and put forth his noblest efforts to redeem her from thraldom. In 1771 he called around him a few brave spirits—penetrated the capitol and carried away King Stanislaus in the face of his petrified guards. He soon made his escape and proclaimed Pulaski an outlaw. He then came to America and was created a Brigadier General. Being unacquainted with our language he could not command to advantage but no one could better lead a column of cavalry in a charge. He served some time at the north and was then transferred to the south and fell at Savannah boldly charging the enemy with his daring dragoons. His noble bearing, polished urbanity, open frankness and amiable disposition had gained the admiration of all who knew him—his patriotism, bravery and unwavering love of Liberty placed his name upon the records of unfading glory.

PUTNAM ISRAEL commenced his eventful life at Salem, Mass.

on the 7th of January 1718. He was a man of iron constitution and herculean powers. He served mother Britain faithfully in the French war and had many hair breadth escapes. He was taken prisoner and nearly burned to death by the savages. He was rescued by a French officer. His great feat with a wolf is familiar to every school boy. His manner of capturing an armed vessel when under Gen. Amherst was as novel as it was simple and successful. With four others he proceeded under her stern in the night–drove several wedges between the rudder and hull which placed her at the mercy of the wind–she drifted on shore and was easily captured the next morning.

When the war cry from Lexington reached his ears he left his plough in the furrow–mounted his horse–rode 100 miles in a single day to reach the scene of action–was soon created a Major General and carried more original thunder than any other man in the army. His voice could be heard above the roar of battle. He was in the sanguinary affair at Bunker's Hill and had charge of erecting the temporary fortifications. He was at the battle of Long Island–superintended the fortifications at Philadelphia and in all his duties manifested an energy and skill that placed him high in the estimation of every patriot. In the spring of 1777 he was placed in command of the troops at the High Lands. A refugee Lieutenant was detected in his camp as a spy. Governor Tryon wrote him to at once liberate the officer or he would give him particular thunder. Old Put replied thus laconically.

"SIR–Nathan Palmer, a Lieutenant in your king's service, was taken in my camp as a spy–he was tried as a spy–he was condemned as a spy and he shall be hanged as a spy.

"P. S. Afternoon. He is hanged.

"ISRAEL PUTNAM."

Gen Putnan was the founder of West Point. Whilst superintending the fortifications at that place he was disabled from further duty by an attack of paralysis. This did not impair his mental powers or disturb the equanimity and cheerfulness of his mind or prevent him from being a pleasant, amusing and interesting companion. He lived at Brookline Conn. in the enjoyment of the gratitude of a nation of freemen until the 29th of May 1790 when his soul left its tenement of clay and returned to its Creator. He was truly an honest man. On the 16th of June 1776 he spurned a princely bribe that was tendered to him by Sir William Howe.

PUTNAM RUFUS was born in Sutton, Mass. in 1738. At the age of 16 he commenced serving mother Britain in the French war and proved a gallant soldier. In the Continental army he was the principal engineer with the rank of Brigadier General. He was at the head of the Ohio Company for the purpose of settling the North West Territory. On the 7th of April 1788 he planted about forty emigrants at Marietta on the Ohio river. In 1789 he was appointed a judge of the Supreme Court of that territory–in 1791 a Brig. General in the army of the United States under Gen. Wayne and in 1795 Surveyor General of the United States which office he held until towards the close of Jefferson's administration. He adorned all the virtues that dignify the man and crowned his life with a consistent course of primitive piety. He continued to reside at Marietta until the 4th of May 1824 when his happy spirit soared to realms of unending bliss beyond the skies.

RAMSAY DAVID was ushered into life at Lancaster, Pa. in 1749. He was thoroughly educated and became an eminent physician. After a brief residence in Cecil County, Md. he removed to Charleston, S. C. in 1773. He was an ardent patriot and was commissioned a surgeon in the Continental army. At the surrender of his adopted city he was among the prisoners who were sent to St. Augustine. In 1782 he was elected a member of Congress and continued there up to 1786 except one year. A part of that time he was President of that body. He became an able historian and has enriched our libraries with a history of the Revolution–of South Carolina–of America and a biography of Washington and several other interesting publications. He stood at the head of his profession in Charleston. In 1815 he was called into court to give evidence relative to an insane man who followed him in a rage and killed him on the street.

RANDOLPH EDMUND was a native of Virginia and an eminent member of the Bar. He aided largely in giving an impetus to the revolutionary ball and was among the boldest patriots who early resolved to cut the maternal cords that bound the American Colonies to mother Britain. He was a member of Congress in 1779–subsequently Governor of Virginia–Attorney-General of the United States and for a time Secretary under Washington whose confidence he lost in 1795 for reasons not on the record. He lived in the esteem of his friends until 1813 when he quietly retired to the spirit world.

RANDOLPH PEYTON was a native of Virginia and early engaged in the border wars. He was a good lawyer and Attorney-General under the crown as early as 1748. He became a prominent legislator and was among the first and boldest to expose and oppose British oppression. He was prudent but firm. He threw his whole soul into the cause of Liberty. In all the preliminary meetings of the Old Dominion he was a leading member and a perfect regulator among those whose zeal sometimes led them beyond the orbit of sound discretion. He was President of the important Congress of 1774 and added to the dignity of the proceedings of that august assemblage of Sages. He was returned to Congress the next year but was detained as speaker in the legislature of his state until late in the session. On the 21st of October 1775 he attended a dinner party at the house of a friend and while there fell from his seat in a fit of apoplexy and expired in a few moments. His body was taken to Virginia and interred. Thus prematurely was extinguished one of the bright luminaries that illuminated the horizon and dawn of the Revolution. His loss was deeply deplored.

REED JOSEPH was born in New Jersey on the 27th of August 1741. He became a distinguished member of the Philadelphia Bar where he was pursuing a lucrative practice when he was called to aid in the emancipation of his country. He was a member of the committee of correspondence, President of the Provincial Convention and member of Congress. In 1775 he repaired to Cambridge where he was made an

Aid and Secretary of Washington. In 1776 he was adjutant-general of the army and acted a brave and useful part at Trenton, Princeton and in every battle under Washington. During the campaign of 1777 he was constantly in the field. He had a horse killed under him at Monmouth, Brandywine and White Marsh but was preserved from a wound in the numerous hard fought battles at which he was present. The following answer to a proposition of bribery from the British Governor Johnstone is attributed to him and has been claimed for another. "I am not worth purchasing but such as I am the king of Great Britain is not rich enough to buy me." Nor was she rich enough to buy the humble soldiers who captured Andre. In 1778 Gen. Reed was elected President of the Supreme Executive Council of Pennsylvania which station he held for three consecutive years and was very efficient in the work of infusing a proper spirit in the militia of his state. He filled every place he occupied with great zeal and ability. He was the man to be substantially useful wherever duty called him. He wore himself out in the service of his country and died in Philadelphia on the 5th of March 1785 in the very prime of life and when on the flood tide of an enduring fame.

REVERE PAUL was born in Massachussetts in 1735. It was he who carried the express from Gen. Warren to Messrs. Adams and Hancock the evening previous to the battle of Lexington. He was a colonel of militia and a devoted patriot. He was in the unfortunate Penobscot expedition in the summer of 1779. His was a life of purity and stern integrity. He died in Boston in 1818.

SARGENT WINTHROP was a native of Massachusetts and graduated at Harvard College in 1771. With all the circumstances of his life before him, the historian could present him to the admiring reader in a blaze of glory. Thousands of the noble actors on the stage of the Revolution have passed away without a place on the historic page. From the commencement to the close of the long and sanguinary struggle for Independence he was actively and honorably engaged in the military field. In 1786 he was appointed Surveyor of the North Western Territory and in 1787 Secretary of that government. He was adjutant-general of the army of Gen. St. Clair in his disastrous expedition against the Indians and of the army of Gen. Wayne when he conquered the same red men who had defeated St. Clair. He was subsequently Governor of Mississippi. In all the duties of public and private life he acquitted himself nobly and fulfilled the design of his creation. He died in 1820.

SCAMMEL ALEXANDER commenced his infancy in Mendon, Mass. about 1748. He was liberally educated and excelled in mathematics—strong evidence of an analyzing mind. He was among the first and the last in the war field of the Revolution. In 1775 he was made a brigade-major and the next year a colonel in the line of Continental troops raised by New Hampshire. At the battle of Saratoga in 1777 he commanded the 3d regiment and was severely wounded. He was subsequently appointed adjutant-general of the American army and was generally beloved. As this did not lead him into the din of battle and clash of arms he resigned and took command of a regiment of infantry. On the 30th of September 1781 he was examining the position of the enemy at Yorktown—was suddenly sprang upon and captured. After he had surrendered the barbarous foe gave him a mortal wound which terminated his brilliant career at Williamsburg, Va. on the 6th of October 1781. The death of no officer was more deeply lamented—no one of his grade deserved better of his country and his friends.

ST. CLAIR ARTHUR was a native of Edinburgh, Scotland. He was a Lieutenant under Wolfe and served through the French war. He subsequently located in Pennsylvania, became naturalized and took a deep interest in the prosperity of his adopted country. He was President of the Cincinnati Society of his state. At the commencement of the Revolution he espoused the cause of Freedom and in 1777 was commissioned a Major General. His military laurels increased and rested gracefully upon him during the war with mother Britain. In 1785 he was elected a member of Congress and in 1787 was President of that body. He was the first governor of the North West Territory. In 1790 he was put in command of the memorable expedition against the Miami Indians. On the 4th of November 1791 he met them in mortal combat and was defeated with the loss of many brave officers and soldiers who had braved the fury of the Revolutionary storm unscathed. By many he was censured—how justly is not a subject to be discussed in this place. That he was a brave and skilful officer when opposed to regular troops he had fully proved. Braddock had done the same. To fight the red man on his own ground is a very different affair. It is reasonable to presume that his disastrous defeat arose from an ignorance of Indian warfare—not from any want of courage or an ignorance of regular military tactics. On his return he resigned his military commission. He was severely pierced by the keen arrows of poverty during his latter years. He died in 1818.

SCHAICK GOSEN VAN commenced his mortal career at Albany, New York in 1737. He entered the British army in 1756 with the commission of Lieutenant and served mother Britain faithfully to the end of the French war at which time he had reached the rank of Lieut. Colonel. Had he not been a superior officer he could not have attained that rank among Englishmen. At the first sound of the war cry in 1775 he was on hand ready for action and spent his life and fortune in the cause of FREEDOM. He was placed in command of the first regiment of the New York line and ultimately rose to the rank of Brig. General of the regular army. He fought bravely at Monmouth and other places and had the high esteem of Washington. In 1779 he commanded the successful expedition against the Onondaga Indians for which Congress passed a resolution of most hearty thanks. Gen. Schaick did honor to his country and to every station in which he moved. He was an able officer, a good citizen—an honest man and repaired to his final rest in 1784.

SCHUYLER PHILIP was born in New England in 1732. He was commissioned a Major General and had no superior in energy, vigilance and courage. For some time previous to the approach of Burgoyne he ably discharged the multifarious duties of the northern command. When that proud General advanced he found traces of Schuyler's industry at every point and his scouts in all directions. Bridges were demolished—the roads blocked with trees—the navigation of Wood creek deranged—supplies removed and his army kept in constant alarm by the light troops of Schuyler who laid the foundation of the victory that virtually saved our Independence. This opinion was often expressed by a revered uncle of mine who was with Schuyler during all his services in the north. At the very time this General was prepared to snatch the laurels of victory from Burgoyne's brow and place them on his own—Gates superseded him. He loved his country too well to be governed by the strict rules of military etiquette at that momentous point of time. He surrendered the command to him with all the papers and information he had acquired, with these burning remarks—" I have done all that could be done, as far as the means were in my power, to injure the enemy and to inspire confidence in the soldiers of our army and I flatter myself with some success—but the palm of victory is denied me and it is left to you, General, to reap the fruits of my labor. I will not fail to second your views and my devotion to my country will cause me, with alacrity, to obey your orders." This language would have been more terrible to me than a thousand crashing thunder bolts. It would have taken more than the laurels of Saratoga to heal the deep gashes my mind would have received from this keen sarcasm of the injured but patriotic and magnanimous Schuyler. A sarcastic remark from Schuyler to Gen. Burgoyne when dining with Gates soon after the surrender is worthy of record. The British General had caused Schuyler's house to be reduced to ashes and attempted an apology which was interrupted by the other—" Make no excuses General. I feel myself more than compensated by the pleasure of meeting you at this table." Gen. Schuyler was in all respects a first rate man. Jealously had put slander in motion against him which was the reason he was superseded. Investigation cleared away the fog from the minds of those in power but did not heal the wounds in his. He was subsequently a member of the Continental Congress and served 12 years in the United States Senate under the Federal Constitution. He died in 1804.

SEDGEWICK THEODORE began his earthly career at Hartford Conn. in 1746. He became a strong lawyer and firm supporter of the cause of Liberty. He was frequently in the legistature of Massachusetts and a member of the Continental Congress. He was a member of the convention of his adopted state that sanctioned the Federal Constitution and was subsequently a member of the United States Senate. At the end of his term he was placed upon the Supreme Bench of Massachusetts and dignified his station until 1813 when he was summoned from earth and its toils to the dread tribunal of the great Jehovah.

SERGEANT JONATHAN DICKINSON was born at Princeton, New Jersey in 1746. He became an eminent lawyer and a strong advocate for American rights. He was elected a member of Congress in February 1776 and continued in that body until July 1777 when he was made Attorney General of Pennsylvania. Why he did not sign the Declaration of Independence is a problem I should like to see solved. In the Connecticut controversy he was employed by his adopted state to advocate her interests. When the yellow fever raged at Philadelphia in 1793 he was a very efficient member in the Board of Health and fell a victim to that fearful disease in October. His private virtues shone conspicuously through his whole life—his country, the poor, the widow and the orphan deeply mourned his premature death.

SMALLWOOD WILLIAM was a citizen of Maryland and a brave Brigadier General in the Continental army—a member of the old Congress and governor of his state. In every station and in all the departments of life he performed his whole duty and enjoyed the love and confidence of his friends and country until 1792 when he cancelled the debt of nature and descended peacefully to the tomb.

STEUBEN FRANCIS WILLIAM AUGUSTUS BARON DE commenced his noble life in Prussia in 1733. He became perfect master of military tactics at an early age in the Prussian army—was an Aid to Frederic the great with the rank of Lieutenant General and was in constant service in his native land until he embarked for America. He landed in New Hampshire in 1777 and was soon after appointed Inspector General of the American army with the rank of Major General. With untiring industry and great energy he rapidly introduced an effective system of discipline, tactics and evolutions, that essentially improved the whole army and rendered it much more efficient in the field. He participated in the battle of Monmouth and had charge of the entrenchments at the siege of Yorktown. At the conclusion of peace his valuable services were partially rewarded in the grant of a farm by the state of New Jersey and 16000 acres of land in Oneida county New York granted by that state. He died on his farm near New York city November 28th 1794.

STRONG CALEB was born at Northampton, Mass. in 1744. He was a profound counsellor at the bar of his native town—an able advocate in the cause of Independence. He was a prominent member of the Committee of Safety that was virtually the government of the State for some time. He was a member of the legislature and fearlessly espoused the cause of Liberty. He was a member of the convention that framed the Constitution of Massachusetts and of the one that formed that of the United States. He was elected to the United States Senate and was governor of his native State eleven years. He was an efficient public officer, a devoted patriot, an esteemed citizen—an honest man. He died in 1820 sincerely mourned by his country and most deeply regretted by those who knew him best.

SULLIVAN JOHN entered on his earthly career in Maine in 1741. His father came from that country called by Aristotle and Strabo *Irene*—by Cæsar, Tacitus and Pliny, *Hibernia*—by Mela and others *Juverna*—all of which names may be traced to the original—*Ir*, *Eri*, *Erin*—now called Ireland. Gen. Sullivan left a lucrative practice at the bar and was commissioned a brigadier-general in 1775 and the next year was raised to the rank of major-general. On the 4th of June 1776 he superseded Arnold in Canada and on the death of Gen. Thomas he was left in command of all the American troops then there. Owing to the illness of Gen. Greene Sullivan was put in command of his division on Long Island and was taken prisoner at the battle on the 27th of August. On the 22d of August 1777 he planned a successful expedition against Staten Island. He acted a brave part at the battles of Brandywine, Germantown and in every place where he was engaged. In 1778 he was placed in command of the troops at Rhode Island and commenced a siege on Newport in August of that year in anticipation of the co-operating aid of the French fleet which was prevented by a storm. This compelled him to raise the siege at once and retreat from a superior force which he effected with consummate skill and success after repulsing the pursuing enemy on the 29th of that month. The next year he commanded the successful but cruel expedition against the Six Nations of Indians. He penetrated the very heart of their country, killed and captured considerable numbers, burnt eighteen of their towns, many of their isolated wigwams–destroyed 160,000 bushels of their corn, all their vegetables, fruits and everything that could be found to sustain life. The expedition was suggested in consequence of the Wyoming massacre. It can be sanctioned by the law of retaliation–no other. Gen. Sullivan was subsequently a member of the Continental Congress for three years–president of New Hampshire and in 1789 was appointed a judge of the District Court which office he dignified until the 23d of January 1795 when he cancelled the debt of nature and slumbered in death. He was very efficient in quelling Shay's insurrection. In every sphere of life he exhibited talents of a high order and left a public fame and private reputation untarnished by corruption.

SULLIVAN JAMES was born at Berwick, Me. in 1744. He became a bright ornament of the bar and an able advocate of the cause of freedom. He was an active member of the legislature–of the Provincial Congress and of the Continental Congress. He was a judge of Probate and in 1790 was appointed attorney-general of his State. In 1807–8 he was elected governor of Massachusetts and died in December 1808. He was an admirable model of human excellence, adorned those qualities that dignify a man and crowned his life with the lucid exemplification of primitive Christianity.

STEVENS EDWARD commenced his earthly career in Culpepper County, Va. and his bold military achievements at the battle of the Great Bridge near Norfolk, Va. where he commanded the rifle battalion with a bravery and skill that elicited general commendation. Soon after that he was placed in command of the 10th Virginia regiment and repaired to the headquarters of Washington. At the battle of Brandywine his skill and courage in covering the retreat of the Americans astonished friends and foes and saved the army from capture. At the action of Germantown his gallantry was publicly applauded by Washington upon the field of glory. He was subsequently placed in command of the Virginia Brigade and fought with great bravery at Camden under Gates, at Guilford Court House under Greene and at the siege of Yorktown under Washington. From the formation of the republican Constitution of Virginia to 1790 he was constantly a member of her legislature. He was a man of untarnished reputation, substantial talent and usefulness. His patriotism soared above all party considerations– he could not be swayed by demagogues. He went for his whole country–the Constitution and our UNION for ever. He looked upon the Federal Constitution as the Jews did upon their ark–the repository of the safeguards and glory of our Republic. He closed his useful life at his residence in Culpepper, Va. on the 17th day of August 1820–ripe in years and full of honors.

THOMAS JOHN was reared in Kingston, Mass. He was a brave

officer in the service of England during the French war. He was one of the first who rushed to the battle field in 1775. At the siege of Boston—on the heights of Dorchester—in every place where duty called him he acted a bold and noble part. He was soon raised to the rank of brigadier-general and ordered to Canada to take command of the troops who had survived the fatigues of the campaign under Arnold and Montgomery where he fell a victim to the small pox. His great experience, ardent patriotism, known courage, untarnished character—all combined to render his loss a great misfortune to his country and his friends.

THOMAS THOMAS was born in the State of New York in 1745. He was among the first and most devoted patriots. He was a brigadier-general and commanded a body of troops in 1776 at the battle of Harlaem Heights and White Plains. In the autumn of that year the British burnt his house and carried his aged father to New York where their proverbial inhumanity soon produced his death. Gen. Thomas was a severe scourge to the enemy—ever on the alert—energetic, bold and shrewd. He was subsequently taken prisoner, stripped of his regimentals and hat and marched through the streets of New York in the most disgraceful manner. He was at length placed on parole and permitted the limits of Brooklyn. After he was exchanged he sought every opportunity to make up lost time until the foe was driven beyond the great heron pond. He then removed to the town of Harrison, Westchester County, New York where he lived respected and died deeply regretted in July 1824. He was several times a member of the legislature of his State.

TRUXTON THOMAS took his station on this rolling planet at Rhode Island in 1755. He was delighted with old Ocean from his boyhood and became an expert mariner at an early age. He loved Liberty and was willing to pay its price without discount. He was placed in command of an armed vessel in 1775 and continued capturing prizes during the whole period of the Revolution without a single reverse of fortune. He made constant inroads on the commerce of Great Britain and was too wary a fox to be trapped, cornered or run down by the celebrated British sportsman of the seas. In 1794 he was put in command of the frigate Constitution. In 1799 the French government became ripe for naval exercise and quite belligerent in its manners. The frigate L'Insurgent made battle with Commodore Truxton and after a brief action surrendered. The French ship of war La Vengeance then met the Constitution and after passing the very significant salutes usual at hostile meetings surrendered at discretion to Com. Truxton. On his return to the United States he retired to Philadelphia where he lived in the esteem of our nation and his friends until 1822 when his cable of life was cut and his soul launched on the ocean of eternity.

WADSWORTH JEREMIAH was a native of Connecticut and early in the field to do battle for his loved—his injured country. He rose to the rank of general and was remarkable for great energy, undaunted courage, ardent patriotism and untiring industry. He was a member of Congress for some time. In public and private life he adorned the virtues that ever dignify the man and passed from the stage of life peacefully in 1804.

WARD ARTEMUS was born in New England in 1727. He was a man of fine parts, strong common sense, thorough education, a zealous patriot. He was the first major-general commissioned by the Continental Congress, his commission bearing date the 7th of June 1775. At the siege of Boston he commanded the right wing of the army resting on Roxbury. His feeble constitution induced him to resign the ensuing April. In a legislative capacity he continued to serve his country faithfully. He was repeatedly a member of the old and new Congress. A more incorruptible man never came from the clean hands of the Creator. He patiently endured a lingering illness for years and was relieved from the toils and pains of earth on the 28th of October 1800.

WARD HENRY was a valued citizen of Rhode Island and stood in the front rank of her noble and daring patriots. He did good service in the tented field–was Secretary of his state–filled up his measure of usefulness and called his friends to mourn over his final exit and perform the last rites of sepulture in 1797.

WASHINGTON WILLIAM was a native of Stafford County, Va. He was a distant relative of George Washington and among the first of the chivalric sons of the Old Dominion to respond to the thrilling war cry– *Liberty or death.* He commenced his military career in command of a company of infantry in the 3d regiment of the Virginia line commanded by Col. Mercer. Captain Washington first distinguished himself for undaunted courage at York Island and in New Jersey. When Gen. Washington attacked Col. Ralle in command of the Hessians at Trenton, Capt. Washington led the advance of one of the columns. He received a musket ball through one of his hands which was not mentioned by him until after the enemy had surrendered. Soon after the brilliant affair at Trenton and Princeton he was transferred to Col. Baylor's regiment of cavalry with the rank of major and proceeded to Virginia with the regiment to increase its strength with fresh recruits. In 1775 this regiment was surprised by a superior force under Maj. Gen. Grey and nearly annihilated. Major Washington escaped and was then put in command of the consolidated remnants of the cavalry regiments of Cols. Baylor, Bland and Maylan and ordered to report himself to Gen. Lincoln in South Carolina. He was in constant service from the time of his arrival. His corps suffered at the battle of Monk's Corner and at Leneau's Ferry. He then proceeded with Col. White to North Carolina for the purpose of raising recruits. This laudable object was not approved by Gen. Gates for reasons not explained which formed a link in his chain of disasters. Col. Washington proceeded to replenish his regiment and resumed field service under Gen. Morgan. At Cowpens, Hobbick's Hill, Eutaw, Guilford Court House–Col. Washington gained increasing epic laurels for himself and Spartan corps. At the battle of Eutaw he was unfortunately taken prisoner and not exchanged until after the surrender of Yorktown. In 1782 he led the amiable and accomplished Miss Elliott to the hymeneal altar and located at the ancestral seat of his wife at Sandy Hill in South Carolina. He there enjoyed life with his family and friends in the happy way that Virginians well understand and fully exemplify. A braver soldier, a more noble and generous man than Col. Washington did not exist in the human family. He made his final exit in 1810.

WINDER LEWIS was a resident of Maryland and a brave soldier of the Revolution. In the struggle for Independence the best men were not office seekers but sought the good and glory of their country. Many soldiers in the ranks were men of strong intellect and substantial education. So with this veteran. After the close of the war toils he filled various public stations and became governor of his state. He enjoyed the esteem of his country and friends until 1819 when he slumbered in death.

JOHN WHEELOCK was a favorite son of Massachusetts and one of the noble patriots who left the halls of literature and periled their lives in defence of chartered rights. He was an active officer in the army and had the esteem of his countrymen. He was subsequently a popular President of Dartmouth College. He made himself extensively useful until 1817 when he took his journey to " that country from whose bourne no traveller returns."

WILLIAMS OTHO HOLLAND was ushered into life at the county of Prince George, Md. in 1748. At the commencement of the Revolution he resigned a lucrative office under the crown to teach the man who dishonored that crown that Americans dared to assert their rights at the cannon's mouth as well as in paper essays. He was lieutenant in a rifle corps under Capt. Price and marched to head quarters at Cambridge in 1775. In 1776 he was raised to the rank of major in the rifle regiment under Col. Stephenson. He was in the garrison of Fort Washington when attacked by the overwhelming force of Sir William Howe and was taken prisoner. When exchanged he was placed in command of the 6th regiment of the Maryland line and ordered to South Carolina with Baron de Kalb. He was raised to the grade of adjutant-general under Gen. Gates and shared the keen reverses of that general. Under Gen. Greene he was retained in the same office which he bravely filled to the close of the struggle for Liberty. At Guilford, Hobbick's and Eutaw his efficient services were warmly acknowledged by the judicious Greene, whose bosom friend and constant adviser he was. At all times and under all circumstances he nobly performed his duty in public and private life. At the close of the war he was commissioned a brigadier-general as a compliment to his high merit. Subsequent to the Revolution he was appointed Collector of the Port of Baltimore where he died in July 1794.

WOLCOTT ERASTUS was a favorite son of Connecticut of commanding talents—a strong lawyer—an ardent patriot—a good citizen—a brave officer—an honest man. He rose to the rank of brigadier-general and subsequent to the Revolution was elevated to the Bench of the Superior Court of his state. His measure of usefulness became full in 1798 when the hermetical seal of death closed his bright career.

WOOSTER DAVID was born in Stafford, Conn. in 1711. Although frosted with near 70 winters when the Revolution commenced, he was eager to share in the glory of repelling an insolent foe from his native land and in making that land the happy abode of the brave and the free. In 1775 he was made a brigadier-general by Congress and put in command of the Connecticut troops. This commission he resigned and became a major-general of the militia of his state. On the 27th of April 1777 he was mortally wounded in leading on his troops against a British force at Ridgefield and died on the 2d of May. His fall was deeply lamented by Congress and our nation. He had all the ardor of youth united with the experience of age. Such men were greatly needed in such a contest as the American Revolution–uniting the sage, hero, citizen and honest man in a harmonious whole.

WYLLIS SAMUEL was a citizen of Connecticut–a major-general of great promise–a man of sterling merit–a patriot of great zeal–a citizen of great worth and was killed by a party of British in 1777 on a predatory "beauty and booty" excursion.

Thus closes a condensed view of the most prominent Sages and Heroes of the American Revolution. I have aimed at an object of greater importance than the relation of historical incidents–an illustration of the heaven-born principles–the god-like actions of the patriots of '76. If these are not cherished and practised by the present and coming generations of our expanding Republic–the LIBERTY–the *priceless* FREEDOM we now enjoy will be buried in the smoking ruins of the Elysian temple of our INDEPENDENCE–now towering in majestic grandeur. I have honestly and frankly expressed what I strongly feel relative to the vital interests of our beloved country. My conclusions are based upon laborious investigation, close observation and large experience. In common with every true friend to our government I feel a deep interest in the portentous question of slavery which has so recently rocked our nation in the volcanic cradle of civil discord. I have taken full notes of its whole course from its embryo inception to the present time. I have listened to the arguments of the ablest men in each of the high contending parties. I have read all I could find upon the subject of West India emancipation. So far as the British politicians were concerned I am satisfied that act was a bold stroke of ulterior policy–not of philanthropy. I have made myself familiar with the practical operations of the slave system in our own country by leisurely visiting all the cities, large towns, most of the small ones and numerous plantations in all the slave States except Florida and Texas. Without such a tour no man can well form a correct conclusion upon this momentous subject. He can only make an imaginary chamber survey–not the best evidence to present in court. I am not an advocate for the *principle* of bondage–but few can be found in the slave States who are. I look at slavery as it is–not as represented on the high colored charts of ultra abolitionists. It was *forced* upon the American Colonies by mother Britain. It is here by entail–not from original choice [see the Preamble of the Virginia Constitution.] This charges George the Third with "prompting *our negroes* to rise in arms among us–those very negroes, whom, by an inhuman use of his negative he hath refused us permission to exclude by law." Its present form in the south is infinitely more humane than the cunningly devised apprentice system of England. Instead of rescued Africans being returned to their native land by that arrangement they are put to hard labor on the British Islands for a season and may then be sent adrift at the pleasure of the employer. A provision for life is insured to all the subjects of bondage in the slave States. There the free man may be stripped of the means of support by process of law–the slaves never. They are practically the most potent freeholders in those States. A large majority of the slaves there are better cared for than the same proportion of the colored population in the free States, both mentally and physically. Larger numbers of them enjoy religious instruction and become church members.

Immediate emancipation would involve these slaves in the keenest misery unless they were provided with means of support far beyond the resources of their owners and the abolitionists combined. Humanity would recoil with horror at the practical workings of the proposed abolition system. It was originated in Europe for the express purpose of destroying our UNION. Its paternity is illegitimate—its object our ruin—its tendency chaotic. Its tare seeds were first sown broadcast in our country by Thompson—*a hired emissary* from Great Britain who is now in our midst a second time on the same demoniac mission. His breath is pestilence—his pathway is marked with the fomenting scum of a meddlesome demagogue. In addition to his salary paid by England he is filling his pockets from the hard earnings of our people whom he blinds to destroy. The Syracuse Journal states that after the meeting this member of the British Parliament addressed at that place a short time since "*had passed resolutions against the Union* the remainder of the time was consumed in receiving subscriptions to support Mr. Thompson in his anti-slavery itineracy. Thus the anti-slavery agitators are obliged to call in paid British assistance to help them break up the Union." At the same meeting this vile emissary made this startling assertion in substance—You have not famine and pestilence but what is worse you are cursed with 30,000 recreant priests. No American would be permitted to pursue this course in Europe a moment. If we tolerate such foreign interference we are unworthy of FREEDOM. When I speak of abolition I refer to ultra political abolition—that which tramples upon our Constitution as an unholy thing and would rejoice at the dissolution of our UNION and urge the slaves on to murder. I have no sympathy for ultraism in any section or in any cause.

We must look at slavery as it exists in our country. Time has planted it too deeply to be eradicated by the caustic of abolition. Fine spun arguments upon the Declaration of Rights—the Federal Constitution—the Missouri Compromise—free soil and philanthropy cannot remove it. The question is local and belongs exclusively to the slave States. As well may the south interfere with the internal policy of the north as for us to dictate to the high minded slave owners who might have been gained by the talismanic power of love—never by threats or coercion. As a whole, a more humane, noble, generous people never came from the clean hands of the Creator. They can be led by a single hair of kindness—fanatical power may crush but can never drive them. But for the unfortunate issue of abolition raised by the foreign emissary alluded to—gradual emancipation would long before this have been on the flood tide of progress in several of the slave States. I write from the record. A violation of the eleventh commandment has added greatly to the perpetuity of slavery in our country.

For these reasons and others I would name if space permitted, I verily believe the abolition issue fraught with more danger to our Independence than any that has yet been conceived and promulged by the enemies of our Liberty. It is like cutting off the head of a man to cure a cancer on his face. The preservation of our glorious UNION is paramount to all other considerations which have yet engaged the attention of our nation. Could the following advice from the Farewell Address of the illustrious Washington be carefully read and implicitly obeyed by all in our land–then our FREEDOM would be safe–our UNION preserved.

" In contemplating the causes which may disturb our Union, it occurs, as a matter of serious concern, that any ground should have been furnished for characterizing parties by geographical discriminations–northern and southern–atlantic and western–whence designing men may endeavor to excite a belief that there is a real difference of local interests and views. One of the expedients of party to acquire influence within particular districts, is to misrepresent the opinions and aims of other districts. You cannot shield yourselves too much against the jealousies and heart burnings which spring from these misrepresentations. They tend to render alien to each other those who ought to be bound together by fraternal affection.

" To the efficacy and permanency of your Union a Government for the whole is indispensible. No alliances, however strict, between the parts can be an adequate substitute. They must inevitably experience the infractions and interruptions which all alliances in all times have experienced. Sensible of this momentous truth, you have improved upon your first essay by the adoption of a Constitution of Government better calculated than your former for an intimate union and for the efficacious management of your common concerns. This government, the offspring of our own choice, uninfluenced and unawed, adopted upon full investigation and mature deliberation, completely free in its principles, in the distribution of its powers, uniting security with energy and containing within itself a provision for its own amendment, has a just claim to your confidence and your support. Respect for its authority, compliance with its laws, acquiescence in its measures, are duties enjoined by the fundamental maxims of true liberty. The basis of our political systems is the right of the people to make and alter their constitutions of government. But the constitution which at any time exists, till changed by an explicit and authentic act of the whole people, is sacredly obligatory upon all. The very idea of the power and the right of the people to establish government presupposes the duty of every individual to obey the established government.

" All obstructions to the execution of the laws, all combinations and associations, under whatever plausible character, with a real design to direct, control, counteract or awe the regular deliberation and action of the constituted authorities, are destructive of this fundamental principle and of fatal tendency. They serve to organize faction–to give it an artificial and extraordinary force–to put in the place of the delegated will of the nation the will of a party, often a small but artful and enterprising minority of the community and according to the alternate triumphs of different parties to make the public administration the mirror of the ill-concerted and incongruous projects of faction rather than the organ of consistent and wholesome plans digested by common counsels and modified by mutual interests.

"However combinations or associations of the above description may now and then answer popular ends, they are likely, in the course of time and things, to become potent engines by which cunning, ambitious and unprincipled men will be enabled to subvert the power of the people and to usurp for themselves the reins of government destroying afterwards the very engines which have lifted them to unjust dominion.

" Towards the preservation of your government and the permanency of your present happy state, it is requisite, not only that you steadily discountenance irregular oppositions to its acknowledged authority but also that you resist with care the spirit of innovation upon its principles however specious the pretexts. One method of assault may be to effect in the forms of the constitution, alterations which will impair the energy of the system and thus to undermine what cannot be directly overthrown. In all the changes to which you may be invited, remember that time and habit are at least as necessary to fix the true character of governments, as of other human institutions, that experience is the surest standard by which to test the real tendency of the existing constitution of a country–that facility in change upon the credit of mere hypothesis and opinion exposes to perpetual change from the endless variety of hypothesis and opinion and remember, especially that for the efficient management of your common interest in a country so extensive as ours, a government of as much vigor as is consistent with the perfect security of liberty is indispensable. Liberty itself will find in such a government, with powers properly distributed and adjusted, its surest guardian. It is, indeed, little else than a name where the government is too feeble to withstand the enterprises of faction, to confine each member of the society within the limits prescribed by the laws and to maintain all in the secure and tranquil enjoyment of the rights of person and property.

" Against the insidious wiles of foreign influence (I conjure you to believe me fellow citizens) the jealousy of a free people ought to be *constantly* awake since history and experience prove that foreign influence is one of the most baneful foes of republican government.

" In offering to you, my countrymen, these counsels of an old and affectionate friend, I dare not hope they will make the strong and lasting impression I could wish–that they will control the usual current of the passions or prevent our nation from running the course which has hitherto marked the destiny of nations! but if I may even flatter myself that they may be productive of some partial benefit, some occasional good–that they may now and then recur to moderate the fury of party spirit–to warn against the mischiefs of foreign intrigue–to guard against the impostures of pretended patriotism–this hope will be a full recompense for the solicitude for your welfare by which they have been dictated."

NOTE—In a recent speech the emissary Thompson used this most specific language:—"I do not believe there is one minister in the United States who believes what he says. I know enough of ministers in that country to believe that they preach wilfully and designedly what they know to be false! These men deliberately go to their closets, and, for purely political and pro-slavery purposes, write sermons for the Sabbath-day, which they all the while know to be palpably and damnably untrue!"